MACMILLAN

1957 - 1986

Volume II of the Official Biography

Also by Alistair Horne

Back Into Power
The Land is Bright
Canada and the Canadians
The Price of Glory: Verdun 1916
The Fall of Paris: The Siege and the Commune 1870–71
To Lose a Battle: France 1940
The Terrible Year: The Paris Commune 1871
Death of a Generation
Small Earthquake in Chile
Napoleon: Master of Europe 1805–1807
The French Army and Politics 1870–1970
A Savage War of Peace: Algeria 1954–1962
Macmillan 1894–1956: Volume I of the Official
    Biography

MACMILLAN
1957 - 1986
Volume II of the Official Biography
Alistair Horne

**MACMILLAN
LONDON**

First published 1989 by
MACMILLAN LONDON LIMITED
4 Little Essex Street, London WC2R 3LF
and Basingstoke

Associated companies in Auckland, Delhi, Dublin, Gaborone,
Hamburg, Harare, Hong Kong, Johannesburg, Kuala Lumpur,
Lagos, Manzini, Melbourne, Mexico City, Nairobi, New York,
Singapore and Tokyo

British Library Cataloguing in Publication Data

Horne, Alistair, *1925–*
    Macmillan: 1957–1986
    Vol. 2
    1. Great Britain. Macmillan, Harold,
    1894–1986
    I. Title
    941.085′092′4

    ISBN 0-333-49621-3

Photoset in Great Britain by
Rowland Phototypesetting Limited
Bury St Edmunds, Suffolk

Printed by Butler and Tanner Limited
Frome, Somerset

For Sheelin

Contents

List of Illustrations

Macmillan

Preface

For a week and more after his death in December 1986, the British media overflowed with tributes to Harold Macmillan, first Earl of Stockton – obituaries, recollections, anecdotes about the man. No Briton had received such top billing on his death since Winston Churchill; and, with rare exceptions, almost all of it was favourable, kindly and nostalgic. It even spilled over into the US and Europe. In the effusiveness of its eulogies, it was almost as if Fleet Street were endeavouring to atone for all the harsh (and largely forgotten) judgements it had made about the man during his premiership, now so many years past. The word 'giant' proliferated: 'Giant of post-war politics', proclaimed the *Independent*'s headline of the day Macmillan's death was announced; 'Many would regard him as Britain's most successful postwar Prime Minister. . . .'[1] '"Supermac", one of the giants of 20th century British politics', the *Daily Mail* called him, declaring in one of its headlines that he had 'BROUGHT GREAT BRITAIN YEARS OF PROSPERITY, PEACE AND PROGRESS', and rating him 'Supermac . . . the Super Statesman'.[2]

Few British newspapers during Macmillan's term of office would have dared even to use the word 'statesman' – let alone 'giant'.

Among his successors, Mrs Thatcher, though often fiercely criticised by him in his later years, declared in a long and generous tribute – with a magnanimity that was manifestly not contrived – that his death 'leaves a place which no one else can fill'; he was 'an idealist, a shrewd politician', and a man of outstanding bravery, fortitude, wit, erudition and compassion. In America, John F. Kennedy's former Secretary of State, Dean Rusk, praised him for the almost paternal influence that he had had upon the young

President, as 'one of the greatest Prime Ministers in my judgement'; he and Kennedy both looked on him 'as a sort of uncle and advisor'. Ex-President Nixon, whom Macmillan himself had never highly rated, wrote his own special tribute in *The Times*, lauding him as a 'consummate realist' in his dealings with the Russians and expressed enduring gratitude and 'affection' for the 'message of sympathy and good will' Macmillan had sent at the time of Watergate.[3]

Out of all the tributes, there emerged agreement on two scores; first, that Harold Macmillan was a greater and more considerable figure than had been the view at the end of his premiership; secondly, it might still be too early to assess his precise place in British, and world, history.

Perhaps the most outstanding attribute of Harold Macmillan as a statesman and political thinker was his remarkable capacity to think forwards, and to relate issues to the lessons of the past, of which he was such an adept student. If he could not furnish all the answers, he certainly saw – and comprehended – most of the questions. As his colleague, Lord Carrington, saw it, on 'the big views he was always consistent, and never seemed to deviate at all . . .'. He was generally right about the things that really mattered.[4]

Whatever the considered verdict of future historians about his exact location in the constellation of British Prime Ministers, there could be no disputing that, as a personality, Harold Macmillan had star quality. He remains one of the most intriguing figures in British political history, her best-read and perhaps most intelligent Prime Minister, certainly of this century – and one of the most complex ever. It is this very complexity that makes him so difficult to evaluate, on almost every single issue in which he was involved. Some of Harold Macmillan's chief characteristics were unambiguous, and uncompromising; his religious faith and patriotism, his humanity and sense of humour, his intelligence and mental toughness, the courage which he so much admired in others and which in him, on occasions, amounted to recklessness. But few men could have been more composed of paradoxes than he; it was what gave him his charm (and mischief) as a conversationalist, and made him a fascinating (but elusive) subject for a biographer. There were things that did not fit. Every element in him seemed to have its counterpoise; every uttered view its antithesis. Friend and foe alike dubbed him the 'actor–manager' (his own wife, Dorothy, once remarked, 'Perhaps my husband should have been an actor!'),[5] and they often wondered which was the actor, and which was the manager; which was the mask, and which was the real man. Harold Wilson, with some small performing experience himself, possibly put his finger on it when he observed that his 'role as a poseur was itself a pose'.[6] Perhaps even Macmillan himself was not always quite clear about his own identity; perhaps it was all a game to tease and baffle the pedestrian mind – if not future biographers. Proteus incarnate, he was by turns crofter and duke *manqué*, scholar and swordsman; he was compassionate and ruthless, pessimist and optimist, fatalist and devout Christian. He never missed the absurdities of life; though deeply sceptical, and given to cynical remarks, he was never at heart a cynic. And there were strains of Celtic romanticism.

Though he showed it to few, he was a man haunted by ghosts and buffeted by tragedy. Family and friends, he had either seen them die in the trenches, or had outlived them all. The scars of the 1930s were indelible, and perhaps made him what he was – a great human being. If he did not achieve true historical greatness, then it eluded him by a few hairsbreadths.

Back in September 1979, when he was eighty-seven, in what he called his 'Declaration', he spoke about 'the strongest element in my life':

> ... I don't think a nation can live without religion. I don't find a man who could ... if you don't pray every night, and if you don't believe in God, and if you don't think you can serve God eventually, you can't solve these problems and you can't even then survive them, I don't think. And so that's my philosophy of life – there are neither successes or failures, you do your best, and that's my life. ...[7]

Typically, Faith, Hope and Charity was the note on which he ended his emotive maiden speech in the House of Lords, and it was faith that brought him through it all, and through all the adversities of old age, the pain of ancient wounds, the loss of a wife, of family and colleagues, and loneliness. When in New York in 1980, he remarked on television to William F. Buckley Jr: 'If you don't believe in God, all you have to believe in is decency ... decency is very good.

Better decent than indecent. But I don't think it's enough.'[8] He
fundamentally believed both in God and decency.

Volume I of *Macmillan* took the subject through the first sixty-two
years of his life, culminating with the Suez débâcle of 1956, and the
beginning of the 'Macmillan era', which was to comprise seven of
the most eventful years in contemporary British history. From the
diffident, unhappy young man plagued by self-doubts and bouts of
the Black Dog, and the pre-Second World War idealist, battered
by a broken marriage that brought much misery and years in the
political wilderness, to the 'Supermac' of the late 1950s shows an
extraordinary progression by any yardstick. But when an individual
ascends to the role of Prime Minister, or President, his private
existence virtually ceases and he becomes public property. Thus
here, in a biography, a change of gear inevitably takes place. The
functions of office, and epic events associated with it, at home
and abroad, take precedence over personal thoughts and feelings.
Nevertheless, his personality remains at the heart of all his judgements, successes and failures. In the case of Harold Macmillan, his
public life as Prime Minister (and the three out of the six volumes
of his memoirs that he wrote about it) was also illuminated by
hundreds of pages of diary that he wrote, night after night, in a
spidery longhand (made arduous by a German bullet through his
hand in 1915) in the small hours after work.

I have already drawn attention to this valuable source of archive
material in Volume I; but for the premiership years these hitherto
unpublished diaries – unrestrained, outspoken, acrid and occasionally savage – provide a treasure trove for any biographer. His
comments there on *bêtes noires* like Diefenbaker of Canada, or Chancellor Adenauer of West Germany – sometimes even of John F.
Kennedy (for whom he had great esteem and personal affection) –
are forthright, sometimes blistering.

Macmillan himself always warned that his diaries should be
treated with caution; that, written in the heat of the moment, they
were not always factually accurate, nor fair, in that they gave vent
to passing piques, which he would often modify or expunge the
following day. But they did represent both the mood and the colour
of the times, and what Macmillan himself was then thinking,
without the influence of self-justifying hindsight. To me, they were
also revealing of the man in a way which he perhaps may never

have intended. Certainly they provide an invaluable chronicle of his era, and (though heretofore made available exclusively to his biographer) doubtless will be published *in extenso* in the fullness of time.

In addition to this material, and all the rich archives collected at Birch Grove, as explained in the Preface to Volume I I had the unique good fortune to have access to the (quite outstanding) memory of my subject during his lifetime. After one particularly arduous session (I think it was over Suez, 1956), he jokingly introduced me to neighbours as 'a cross between Boswell and Torquemada!' The result of all this was many tapes of interviews, and notes of less formal conversations (at which, in old age, Macmillan came to excel above all contemporaries). I have also benefited greatly from recourse to information available in the USA, under the Freedom of Information Act, and to British government documents released by the Public Record Office at regular intervals under the thirty-year rule, each 1 January. At the time of writing, these have just taken in the year of 1958.

There was, furthermore, no shortage of writings by others about Macmillan and his times, or of autobiographies by his eminent contemporaries. Many of these I used; but of greater value still was the ability to have direct recourse to the memories of many then still alive. I was particularly fortunate in being granted lengthy interviews with four out of five of the Prime Ministers who succeeded Macmillan; Edward Heath alone remained inaccessible. Innumerable people, both in Britain and America alike, gave most freely of their time, recollections and advice. I may have overlooked many to whom I am beholden; if so, I beg their forgiveness but (in addition to those already acknowledged in Volume I) I must particularly mention the following: Miss Rosemary Aimetti; Rupert Allason MP; Joseph Alsop; Mrs Susan Mary Alsop; Lady Catherine Amery; the Rt Hon. Julian Amery MP; Lord Amory; George Ball; Lord Barber; Lord Blake; Henry Brandon; Mrs David Bruce; W. F. Buckley Jr; Lord Bullock; McGeorge Bundy; Lord Butler; Lord Callaghan; Lord Carrington; Lord Charteris; Lord Cranborne; Lord Dacre of Glanton; H.E. Baron Geoffroy de Courcel; Professor David Dilks; Lord Duncan-Sandys; Viscount Eccles; Pamela, Lady Egremont; Sir Harold Evans; Oliver Everett; Lord Fanshawe; the Rt Hon. Michael Foot MP; Lord Fraser of Kilmorack; Professor J. K. Galbraith; Anne Glyn-Jones; General A. Goodpaster; Lord

Hailsham; Lord Harlech; W. Averell Harriman; the Rt Hon. Denis Healey MP; Sir Nicholas Henderson; the Rt Hon. Michael Heseltine MP; Sir William Heseltine; Lord Home of the Hirsel; Lady Lorna Howard; Sir Charles Johnston; Dr Henry Kissinger; Joseph Kraft; Robert McNamara; Sir Peter Marshall; Drew Middleton; Miss Sheila Minto; Professor Richard Neustadt; John Newhouse; Mrs Eileen O'Casey; Mrs Aristotle Onassis; Mme Pandit; Miss Jane Parsons; Chapman Pincher; M. Edgar Pisani; the Rt Hon. Enoch Powell MP; Lord Redmayne; Sir William Rees-Mogg; Lord Reigate; Sir Patrick and Lady Reilly; Lord Rhyl; Lord Richardson; Archie Roosevelt; Anthony Sampson; Professor Arthur Schlesinger Jr; Lord Shinwell; Lord Soames; Theodore Sorensen; the Rt Hon. Mrs Margaret Thatcher MP; Lord Thorneycroft; D. R. Thorpe; William Tyler; Alan Watkins; Dame Rebecca West; Lady Wheeler-Bennett; Sir Dick White; Frank Whitehead; Lord Wigg; Lord Wilson of Rievaulx; Sir Denis Wright; Lord Zuckerman; Sir Philip de Zulueta.

No biographer of a living subject could have received greater help, and understanding, and friendship, from the immediate family, and I am – once again – especially grateful to Alexander Stockton, both as publisher and as grandson of Harold Macmillan.

I am particularly indebted to Macmillan Publishers for permission to quote from the Macmillan memoirs, war diaries, etc., and to the Macmillan Trustees for the privileged access, given to me solely, to the Harold Macmillan Archives, including his unpublished diaries of 1950–63.

In the United States, I owe a vast debt of gratitude to the Woodrow Wilson Center of Washington DC, which, by generously granting me a fellowship in 1980–1, enabled me to carry out valuable research on the Eisenhower (and, later, Kennedy) years. In this I was most ably assisted by Neil M. Robinson, appointed as my researcher by the Center. I am additionally beholden to the Dwight D. Eisenhower Library in Abilene, Kansas, the John Foster Dulles (Mudd) Library of Princeton, New Jersey, and the John F. Kennedy Center of Boston, Massachusetts, whose archives were readily made available to me.

I wish, once again, to record my unbounded gratitude to two brilliant women, and close personal friends, whose invaluable assistance and encouragement was tragically terminated by untimely deaths – Serena Booker and Venetia Pollock. In the ten long years that this book took to complete, the editorial work begun by Venetia Pollock was continued by several, to all of whom I owe much gratitude for their patience as well as their professionalism: Ann Wilson, Tom Weldon, Hazel Orme and Peter James. While working on Macmillan's *War Diaries*, Peter James developed an intuitive knowledge into the way of thinking of the author, which was of great additional assistance to this author. My grateful thanks are due also to Nicky Byam Shaw, my longest-surviving friend at court at Macmillan Publishers, for his enthusiasm and good sense at the worst moments; to Philippa Harrison of Macmillan and to Christine Pevitt and Dan Frank of Viking Penguin for invaluable support in the latter stages; to Michael Sissons of A. D. Peters, always a constant tower of support and encouragement; and, lastly but emphatically, to Helen Whitten, who over the past five years assumed the work of researcher and most of the seemingly endless task of retyping two long volumes.

Sir Philip Goodhart, Conservative Member of Parliament for Beckenham, to which he was elected shortly after Harold Macmillan came to power in 1957, and which had once been part of Harold Macmillan's own constituency of Bromley, read the manuscript with a penetrating eye for the solecisms that a political innocent might perpetrate; to him I am eminently grateful, and also for his sustaining enthusiasm. He came up with many suggestions; I rashly did not accept all of them, and therefore any remaining errors of fact or judgement are peculiarly my own.

Finally, I owe a further, unquantifiable debt of a different kind to my wife, Sheelin, who knows what it all cost, but whose encouragement never flagged.

Alistair Horne
Turville, February 1989

Chapter One

'It's Macmillan'
January–March 1957

IT'S MACMILLAN: *The Queen names him the new Premier. Butler:*
'I wish him the greatest success.'

> (Evening Standard, *10 January 1957*)

Mr Macmillan is essentially a man of good will and he has a
capacity to engender it. He is a man of warm emotions and generous
humanity . . . he is a man of energy.

> (The Times, *11 January 1957*)

By January 1957, Britain had barely recovered from the devastating shock of Suez. Nothing quite like it had ever happened before in British history. Viewed from the vantage point of the 1980s, those monochrome cinema newsreels of Suez seem to belong not to our age, but to the Crimean War. The equipment of the troops, the speechifying, the postures struck, the very voices of the commentators – plummy and talking of 'our men' and 'giving Nasser a lesson' – in one sense it is all a light year away. Yet, because of the vividness of the memories they left, and because the consequences remain so ever-present in the world we inhabit today, those phrenetic days of the second half of 1956 are still extraordinarily close, constantly being relived by all who played a part or took a position. Suez remains, on a par with Vietnam, a crucial turning point of the post-1945 era – and not just for the Western world.

But especially was this true in terms of the impact it had on the inhabitants of Britain, perhaps even more than for their French allies. When Nasser nationalised the Suez Canal Company on 26 July 1956 they went to bed one night, as it were, regarding themselves as belonging to a power of the first rank, and woke up to the reality of relegation to the second division, no longer with a capacity for manipulating their global destinies in the imperial manner of the past. Across the board, immediate emotions were at least as violent as, the atmosphere possibly more febrile than, when Argentina invaded the Falklands in 1982; at times it looked as if the nation too had become infected by Eden's disordered bile duct. Political parties were split, friends broke with friends, journalists with fellow journalists. In college common rooms across the country, one half refused to speak to the other. Families divided angrily within themselves. In the bitterness, there were rifts that sometimes never healed. Never before, even at the time of Munich in 1938, had passions risen so high.

The Suez crisis dramatically backlit the essential fragilities of Britain that had remained to some extent concealed in backstage shadows. The country had not fully recovered from the exhaustions of six years of war, followed by the austerity of five years of Attlee socialism. The British economy remained shaky, while her new competitors – the old enemy Germany, and even the old friend France (though still enmeshed in the crippling Algerian War) – were quietly catching up, and even about to overtake. Above all Suez had focused a spotlight on the inherent Achilles heel of Britain's perennial problems of her currency reserves, where Macmillan as Chancellor of the Exchequer (not helped or set right by the Treasury) had miscalculated. After American pressures and the flight from the pound had forced the Anglo-French operation to cease in November 1956, and that failure had been followed by the physical collapse of Prime Minister Anthony Eden, the country at large had never felt flatter, more discouraged, more bewildered or more uncertain of the future. The picture was of a Britain thoroughly menaced, at odds with America, all her alliances shaken after Suez.

Out of this débris, quite unexpectedly, there had suddenly emerged the Chancellor of the Exchequer, Harold Macmillan, who had hitherto regarded the Foreign Secretaryship as the summit of his political achievement. 'First in, first out,' in the biting words of Harold Wilson, his role during the Suez crisis had been far more considerable, and controversial, than has hitherto been accepted. Yet, for him, Suez provided the essential catalyst, without which the great-grandson of the poor Scottish crofter would have been most unlikely ever to have ascended to the supreme political office; though its baneful impact would cast a heavy shadow over much of the first two years of his new administration, in almost all its endeavours from diplomacy to the economy, jeopardising policy in the Middle East as it affected every exchange with Washington. This much was fairly clear already on 10 January 1957, the day when the Tory Cabinet had selected him as successor to the sick and defeated Prime Minister.

'So it was settled,' he wrote laconically in his memoirs of that date.

Nellie Macmillan's Ambition Fulfilled

'We'd been out for the day,' recalled Alexander Macmillan, then a fourteen-year-old on holiday from Eton, 'and, coming back, there was a nursemaid waiting in the bushes to warn us: "The Press has arrived. Your grandfather is Prime Minister." Before then, there was absolutely no Press at the gates of Birch Grove. They were all hovering around Butler, the favourite. . . .'[1]

Young Alexander was not the only one to be taken by surprise. The London press had been almost unanimous in handing the laurels to Rab Butler. Randolph Churchill, reporting for the *Evening Standard* from the distant reaches of Suffolk, got it right; but, in retirement in Sussex, John Wyndham expected his old boss from Mediterranean days to be defeated. Even Dorothy Macmillan did not quite realise what was happening until her husband appeared for lunch in a tailcoat, ready to go to the Palace, and then – distracted by the illness of a grandchild – she is said to have exclaimed: 'What do *they* want?'[2] At his first audience as Prime Minister, the Queen (so Macmillan noted in his diary) was 'gracious but brief';[3] but it was also the beginning of a new and important relationship. Macmillan warned her, 'half in joke, half in earnest, that I could not answer for the new government lasting more than six weeks. She smilingly reminded me of this at an audience six years later. . . .'

As of 10 January 1957, some Tories were doubting whether the new government could survive three weeks, let alone the six weeks Macmillan promised to the Queen. Under Britain's unwritten constitution, on the resignation of a prime minister or of a government the monarch can either invite a statesman to attempt to form a government, and report back, or give him the position of prime minister immediately. With Macmillan – given the circumstances – the latter course was adopted, and he 'kissed hands' forthwith. His sense of history reminded Macmillan of Lord Melbourne, who had been reluctant to accept the post, but had been encouraged by his friend, Tom Young: 'Why, damn it all . . . such a position was never held by any Greek or Roman: and if it only lasts three months, it will be worth while to have been Prime Minister of England.'[4]

As he drove back from the Palace, Macmillan noted revealingly, 'I thought chiefly of my poor mother.'[5] He had come a long way from when the ambitious Nellie Macmillan, in the 1930s, had reproved a visitor to Birch Grove for kicking a door that would belong to a future prime minister. The diffident young man of the 1920s and 1930s, battered by his war wounds and plagued by self-doubts and bouts of the 'Black Dog', the MP of those seventeen dispiriting years in the political wilderness in anguish at the infidelity of his wife with fellow MP Bob Boothby, had marked out an astonishing career for himself which no one in those years would have credited possible – except perhaps Nellie. It seemed almost as if those accumulated deceptions and reverses of his early life had prepared him for this supreme moment. But, much as one might search, there is no mention in the diaries of Dorothy or of the family (apart from the reference to his mother), least of all of his own emotions, at such a time of personal triumph. He was about to celebrate his sixty-third birthday, with eleven grandchildren, an age when many men retire, burned out.

The following evening a jubilant Macmillan called out for Edward Heath – 'Where is the Chief Whip? We're off to the Turf to celebrate!' – and swept him off to a supper of champagne and oysters. The gossip columnists immediately noted with delight the choice of food and venue; to which Macmillan remarked sardonically, 'In Smith Square – the Butler home – there would have been plain living and high thinking.' So began the new reign.

The Times in a leader acclaimed the news: 'Mr Macmillan is essentially a man of good will and he has a capacity to engender it. He is a man of warm emotions and generous humanity . . . he is a man of energy.'[6] Among many congratulatory messages was one from his first wartime chief, Lord Beaverbrook, reminding him that he had always hoped for and prophesied Macmillan's becoming prime minister. Given the acid exchanges between Beaverbrook and his cronies on the subject of Macmillan over recent years, and the fact that within the month the Beaverbrook press would already be clamouring for a general election, this seemed somewhat hypocritical. It would all be grist to the mill of Macmillan's growing cynicism about the British media. More forthright was the reaction of his political adversary, Aneurin Bevan; when Michael Foot, Bevan's subsequent biographer, brought him the news, he could only gasp in astonishment, 'Good God!': 'it was Butler whom he regarded as the most formidable adversary and he did not like to see merit spurned.'[7]

In America, Secretary of State John Foster Dulles, telephoning the White House with the news, observed that it was 'alright but not as good as Butler. The Sec. [Humphrey] would have liked Butler as PM and Macmillan as FM [i.e. Foreign Secretary]. He hopes they change [Selwyn] Lloyd. . . .'[8] To the Secretary of the Treasury, Humphrey, Dulles – revealing a certain ignorance about

British political and constitutional practices – said he would like the new Foreign Secretary to be Roger Makins, the former Ambassador to Washington. President Eisenhower was much more positive; in addition to a formal message, he sent his old wartime friend a warm personal letter, starting 'Dear Harold', and welcoming him to 'new headaches'.

> I assure you that the new ones will be to the old like a broken leg is to a scratched finger. The only real fun you will have is to see just how far you can keep on going with everybody chopping at you with every conceivable kind of weapon.
> . . . remember the old adage, 'Now abideth faith, hope and charity – and greater than these is a sense of humour.'
> With warm regard,
> As ever,
> D.E.[9]

Macmillan was highly gratified; though he made 'a suitable but not effusive reply' in return – feeling that, so soon after the bruising experiences of Suez, it was better to be pursued than pursuing.

Picking a Team

Macmillan's most immediate task was to choose his team. In the wake of all the stresses imposed by Suez, this required every ounce of the skill he had shown at picking people in the past; while the retiring of ministers to make way for new blood demanded a sensitive touch, as well as ruthlessness. Macmillan showed plenty of both. Taking ten days in the process of distillation, the result was an inspired concoction of balances and blends measured out with the finesse of an apothecary.

The most crucial interview was with his defeated rival, and long-time colleague, Rab Butler. 'I could imagine only too well his feelings,' Macmillan wrote; equally, everything depended on the two working closely together. Butler wanted the Foreign Office, but Macmillan had other ideas. Butler claimed that Macmillan's memory 'plays him false in averring that I "chose the post of Home Secretary"'.[10] Macmillan, in his diary, expressed the view that being Foreign Secretary was an onus 'from which I think he really shrank in today's circumstances';[11] nevertheless, it was a relief to him that Rab accepted the second-best post of Home Secretary. It was an office where many urgent reforms (which only marginally interested Macmillan) were long overdue and his successes were indeed to prove that no one could have filled it better than Rab over the ensuing five years. Without the disappointed Rab's unstinting support, the new government could scarcely have survived.

To the surprise of many, Macmillan had decided instantly that he had to keep Selwyn Lloyd on at the Foreign Office, although, as the most obvious scapegoat for Suez, his return to those august premises was greeted (in the words of *The Economist*) by 'a long, cold arch of raised eyebrows'.[12] Macmillan's explicit motive was that he felt, after Eden's resignation on genuine health grounds, that 'one head on a charger should be enough. Two was more than England's honour could support. . . .' In private, he spelled it out that he kept Lloyd (who had himself seemed surprised) because otherwise:

> we could never have defended Suez. . . . If I had let him go, it was admitting that certain statements made about Suez were not absolutely correct – which they weren't. It was vital to me to keep *either* the Minister of Defence, or the Foreign Secretary, or both . . . because in order to defend and rebuild the situation we had to say that we were right over Suez. . . .[13]

As he remarked years later on television: 'You don't give in to the world and get rid of the man who was most responsible for the thing which you yourself have supported. It would have been the most miserable, cringing thing to do. . . .'[14]

There was also just a touch of personal kindness involved. Recalling his own misery of three decades previously, he could understand the anguish of a broken marriage better than most, and Lloyd's wife had abandoned him for a more exciting younger man; so Macmillan arranged that 'he lived at Chequers most of my time. I gave him Chequers – Dorothy didn't like it much. His wife left him with this little child – Dorothy was very kind to him; he was very friendly. . . .'[15] (Rab, in a malicious aside, said that Lloyd had lost his wife 'because he got into bed with his sweater on! . . . You shouldn't be too sorry for him . . . he had a terrible chip – a feeling of being from the North Country – far from first class, and was lucky to get where he did. . . .'[16]) Macmillan recognised that

Lloyd was 'Addington, not Pitt. . . . he ended up as Speaker, like Addington – a very nice position,' and that he had 'no ideas of his own'.[17] But those who worked with him at the Foreign Office liked and respected him for his readiness to tackle the 'dirty jobs' with courage and total loyalty to Macmillan.[18] The truth, though he would not admit it, was that Macmillan – the frustrated Foreign Secretary (and just like Eden) – wanted to continue to run British foreign policy himself.

He also intended to keep Defence closely under his control, and this involved the painful sacking of a man whom he both liked and trusted. But he felt that Anthony Head, the former Household Cavalry Brigadier who had succeeded Monckton during Suez after five years in charge of the War Office, was too much in fee to the military chiefs to wield the axe as fiercely as Macmillan intended. Given a peerage and later sent as Britain's first High Commissioner to independent Nigeria, then to the newly independent Federation of Malaysia, Head was to prove an outstanding success in both. Instead, the services got Duncan Sandys – whom they disliked from the first moment, and with whom Cabinet Secretary Norman Brook had warned Macmillan 'the rows would be too great'.[19]

To fill his old post as Chancellor of the Exchequer, Macmillan promoted Peter Thorneycroft, a robust and outspoken figure with a background in the world of industry and finance. To replace him at the Board of Trade, Macmillan moved David Eccles – one of his fellow 'Europeans' from Strasbourg days – from the Ministry of Education. Into his slot was popped the ebullient Quintin Hogg, Lord Hailsham. Hailsham was also designated Party Chairman, an appointment which, said Hailsham with customary modesty, 'was definitely justified in the event'.[20] Macmillan's own view of Hailsham as 'one of the cleverest, if not always the wisest, men in the country'[21] would remain as relevant to the succession of 1963 as to that of 1957.

At the more junior levels of government, as Hailsham's deputy at Education Macmillan took the opportunity to bring back 'dear Edward Boyle', the young intellectual who had resigned over Suez. The inclusion from the left of the party of Boyle, who came to be regarded as the epitome of Tory progressive thought, and – at the same time – making the equally progressive Iain Macleod Minister of Labour, enabled Macmillan to perform a delicate balancing act to bring in his son-in-law, Julian Amery – the right-wing maverick and leading light of the Suez Group – as junior Minister at the War Office. Though criticised as an act of nepotism, Macmillan's motive lay more in the calculation that this would keep the Suez 'rebels' quiet.

Thus, too, he could boast that he had pursued the Middle Way in his appointments; while, to allay charges of nepotism, Macmillan had been aided by the early self-sacrifice of his brother-in-law, James Stuart. For many years (1941–8) Churchill's Chief Whip, respected for his acute ear and even feared for his sharpness of tongue, Stuart was currently Secretary for Scotland, but – as the kinsman who had teased the outwardly diffident 'publisher' back in the Chatsworth days of the 1920s and 1930s – he must have reckoned that Macmillan would not long cherish him near the throne, and he wrote offering his head on the day of the accession. From then on, with no claims on office, he became Macmillan's 'antenna' – a valued and trusted confidant rare in the loneliness of power. One further 'job for the family' went to Macmillan's nephew by marriage, David Ormsby-Gore (later Lord Harlech), whom he rated 'young but very able'.[22] In fact, in moments of supreme crisis in the Special Relationship that lay ahead, Ormsby-Gore was to prove one of Macmillan's most inspired choices. There was also 'Bobbety' Salisbury, who had played king-maker for Macmillan; the watchdog of Conservatism; he now continued as Lord President.

With a long memory, and always attached to old associations that had worked, Macmillan also promoted several figures out of his past. One was Ernest Marples, the bouncy self-made ex-Sergeant-Major, who had been such a success working under Macmillan at Housing. Marples was made Postmaster-General. This was not a post that sounded exciting but it was one that would hold him in reserve for greater things – such as building Britain's badly needed first motorway system. More unorthodox was the creation by Macmillan of a Minister of Power with full Cabinet rank. The man he chose was Sir Percy Mills, the industrialist who had so impressed him both at the wartime Ministry of Supply and later when he had brought him too into Housing. It was an appointment more in the American than the British style; Mills was not, and had never been, an MP, but to get over this Macmillan promptly set him up in the House of Lords, with a peerage. To answer for Mills in the Commons, Macmillan gave the up-and-coming young Reginald Maudling the job of being his deputy. Macmillan described Maudling as 'very clever, a little lazy; and a trifle vain'.[23] For Maudling, this was something of a demotion; but, as with Marples, it was made plain that he would soon be given other tasks. Another figure with an anomalous title was Dr Charles Hill, formerly the famous 'Radio Doctor', given the archaic post of Chancellor of the Duchy of Lancaster, but whose function would chiefly embrace government propaganda – an area vital to an administration promised a wretched lifespan of no more than three to six weeks.

In the course of building his administration, Macmillan reckoned that he saw nearly a hundred people. His character sketches made as a result were shrewd – though his private assessments often tough: 'Patrick Buchan-Hepburn [the sole figure, evidently, to opt for Butler against Macmillan] (whom I particularly wanted *out* of the H. of C.) seemed satisfied with the Barony. . . . I was sorry to lose Fitzroy Maclean;* but he really is so hopeless in the House that he is a passenger in an office . . . a great pity, since he is so able. . . .'[24]

In all these difficult decisions, Macmillan paid due tribute in his memoirs to the indispensable support given him by the Chief Whip he had inherited from Eden, Edward Heath. 'Chippy' and abrasive even in those days, a wartime gunner colonel and grammar-school product when so many of the inner Tories still came from Eton or other major public schools, Heath chivvied backbenchers with something of the manner of a sergeant-major; but even his successor, Martin Redmayne (who disliked him), admitted that he was a good Chief Whip. Macmillan, reckoning Heath 'excellent' in the job (but not possessing prime ministerial qualities), kept him, later promoting him to handle the hyper-delicate negotiations over the Common Market.[25]

In his audience with the Queen, Macmillan found her encouraging about his changes: 'She is astonishingly well informed on every detail. She particularly liked the decision about the F.O. . . .'[26] Early on in the process of Cabinet-making, on Saturday, 12 January, Macmillan had paid a courtesy visit, to 'seek the guidance' of his old chief, Winston Churchill. He was, wrote Macmillan, 'almost

---

* Churchill's envoy to Tito during the war; he stood for Parliament originally so as to be able to leave the Foreign Office for active service. Under Eden he had been junior Minister in the War Office.

paternal in his welcome. He grieved for Anthony; but he gave me a sort of blessing which was indeed heartening. . . .' Apart from the nostalgic affection, and gratitude, involved, the visit was also a political stroke of consummate skill; Churchill was the one public figure who had emerged unspotted by Suez – and, if anything, several feet taller – so that his 'blessing' counted for much. Macmillan noted, possibly with tongue in cheek, that photographers were on the doorstep, as his 'evening call somehow leaked out'.

The Private Office

Macmillan's first Cabinet totalled the compact number of eighteen. His last selections comprised his own personal entourage. Chief among them were three seconded civil service secretaries, who sat together guarding his ante-chamber at No. 10: Freddie Bishop, his Principal Private Secretary; Philip de Zulueta – inherited from Eden, and still on the Foreign Office payroll – his Foreign Affairs Private Secretary; and Neil Cairncross, for Home Affairs. Another key appointment made by Macmillan at this time (and who, like de Zulueta, stayed through to the end) was his Press Officer, Harold Evans. By coincidence, Evans, a journalist by profession, had been one of two hundred British volunteers in Finland in 1940, at the time of Macmillan's trip there, although the two had not met. In January 1957 he was in New York, as Information Officer at the Colonial Office, temporarily seconded to the British UN Delegation. When Macmillan asked the 'Radio Doctor' to provide 'the best Information Officer the Civil Service chiefs could find', Evans was the answer, and he was speedily summoned back from New York – with considerable misgivings. In the event, however, and given Macmillan's increasingly sulphurous views about the media, Evans – polished, charming and self-confident – was to prove an impeccable choice.

Last of all, in May Macmillan – having survived double the six weeks he had promised the Queen – wrote to John Wyndham asking him to 'rejoin the old firm'. Despite his earlier doubts about his government surviving, he admitted, in race-track metaphors: 'we do seem to have got over quite a number of jumps in this Grand National course, and having just managed to pull the old mare through the brook and somehow got to the other side with the same jockey up . . . I am plucking up my courage. . . .'[27] As before in wartime Algiers, superannuary, unofficial and unpaid, Wyndham was to provide a key ingredient of the Macmillan team – as well as a source of constant light entertainment.

A New Style

Perhaps the two most hard-worked words in Macmillan's extensive vocabulary of jocularity were 'fun' and a 'bore'. Being Prime Minister was, whatever the pressures and problems, always 'fun' – and he determined from the very first day that working for him should be, too. The atmosphere of No. 10 adjusted itself accordingly.

In one of the very rare passages of his lengthy memoirs where Macmillan, briefly, lets drop the mask to reveal the man inside, he tells how – after the rush of the first week in No. 10 had passed – he found 'a short opportunity for reflection'. Was he really Prime Minister? *What* was he? 'There was certainly attached to the whole affair a certain atmosphere of unreality and even absurdity. . . .' He reflected that one side of his personality was, by instinct and training:

> what has been called 'a gown man'; a product of a system which was intended to supply in the Middle Ages 'clerks' as priests and administrators, and in later times men to serve the Empire in its vast responsibilities . . . and, in addition, to provide instructors of the next generation. Even my family business had close connections with this quiet world of literature and art.

But 'The First World War turned me unexpectedly into a "swords man". Action – harsh, brutal, compelling, ousted learning. The gown was exchanged for a tunic.'

Macmillan admitted that he had 'ever since been conscious of this duality'. On the whole it had been an advantage; it had enabled him to escape from the worst moments of anxiety into the world of books. With considerable effort at self-mastery over the agony of nervous apprehension within, he had contrived to acquire externally 'a certain calm'. Though on a humbler scale, he liked to bracket himself with his two great heroes, Disraeli and Churchill, who 'both had this combination of the thinker and the doer – the artist and the man of action'.

His admiration for the wartime *style* of Field-Marshal Alexander showed just how important 'artistry' was to Macmillan. Deliberately, he set about achieving it at No. 10. He started by replacing the atmosphere of frenzy and 'flap' that had permeated the place under Eden with one of studied calm. Unashamedly he let it be known that he read Trollope. He silenced the klaxon on the prime ministerial car, which Eden had used liberally, while on the green-baize door of the Private Secretaries' room he pinned a quotation – in his own handwriting – from *The Gondoliers*: 'Quiet calm deliberation disentangles every knot.' (To it Wyndham, the ineffable Wodehousian humorist, once appended: 'And if it doesn't, you'll probably be shot!'[28]) The self-assured, ebullient Macmillan of the war years, 1939–45, the triumphant 'Viceroy of the Mediterranean', began to take command.

Unlike Eden, constantly interfering in departmental management, in Cabinet Macmillan would right away agree to basics, then leave the responsible minister to get on with the task on his own, and back him to the hilt. 'This had a very good effect in Cabinet,' observed one of his senior ministers, Derick Heathcoat Amory: 'It was exactly what ministers liked, it gave you a feeling of greater confidence. . . .'[29] For all the light-hearted informality he encouraged in Cabinet, a firm check was nevertheless kept on any levity that might threaten his authority. David Eccles, for four years his Secretary of the Board of Trade, recalled how, in Eden's day, letter-racks stood on the Cabinet table and Macmillan would amuse himself (and others) by detaching paper from them and scribbling ribald notes to his neighbours during dull moments – often (and perhaps deliberately) to the irritation of Eden. 'The day Harold Macmillan took over, the racks all disappeared.'[30]

For her part, Dorothy Macmillan, even though her first reaction, according to John Wyndham, had been one of horror – 'I married a publisher; now look at what I've got!'[31] – with the same uncontrived natural charm that had won the hearts of the voters at Stockton, immediately gained the affections of all, down to the humblest 'garden-room girl' typists. Her success here was unrivalled by any subsequent Prime Minister's wife. Although her attachment to Boothby evidently still continued, modified by middle age, the responsibilities of office now eclipsed the errant love affair of the

1930s. No one spoke of it any more. In contrast to the childless Edens, there was a constant presence of family, with 'bicycles, tricycles, scooters, as well as an occasional perambulator' making itself felt in the august hall of No. 10. Standing orders were issued to grandchildren that, if they wished to play draughts with the policemen, 'they should do so in a way which would never obstruct the arrival of ambassadors or Cabinet ministers'. Nevertheless Dorothy herself would often burst into the house unannounced with a vanload of vegetables and flowers from Birch Grove, as the cosy Queen Anne town-house possessed no back door. Always the passionate gardener, she was soon at work with a trowel in the garden. No. 10, Macmillan glowed, was 'very comfortable. I have a good room as a study, next to Dorothy's "boudoir". (She has arranged a working sitting room upstairs.) The house is rather large, but has great character and charm. It is very liveable. . . .'[32]

Chequers, despite the great mound in the grounds, reputed to have been the fortress of King Cymbeline, was less appealing to the Macmillans: 'It is certainly a fine house, but it has been rather spoilt . . . there seems to be too much of everything. . . .'[33] Dorothy felt like a temporary leaseholder there; there was no point working seriously on the garden when it would go to someone else – probably Mrs Gaitskell; so it seemed logical to let the unhappy Selwyn Lloyd have it. Consequently, the Macmillans spent most of their time at Birch Grove, or at No. 10.

Macmillan was not exaggerating when he claimed that all these factors had combined to provide 'a certain warmth and geniality to the new regime' in a very short time. Despite the loneliness at the top and the vast volume of work, his 'job-fulfilment' was manifest – and infectious. He enjoyed vastly his Tuesday evening audiences with the Queen, whom he found 'not only very charming, but incredibly well-informed'.[34] (Less 'fun' were visits from the Archbishop of Canterbury, then Fisher: '. . . I try to talk to him about religion. But he seems quite uninterested and reverts all the time to politics. . . .')

It was symptomatic of his 'job-fulfilment' that, amid all the pressures imposed by the take-over, Macmillan somehow found time to resume the private diaries which he had abandoned just four months previously in the heat of Suez. It had been impossible for him to find the time to resume them promptly in January on taking over the premiership, but on 3 February he began to write again, starting with a précis of all that had happened since Eden's collapse. It was remarkable that he was able to keep a diary at all – not even the closest members of his entourage were aware of it – but virtually every day for almost the seven years of his premiership, Macmillan would write (usually late at night, as he was by nature a committed 'owl') two, three, four or sometimes even six handwritten pages, totalling an average of several hundred ledger pages a year (although, with the wound suffered at Loos, handwriting pained him as indeed it did subsequent readers).

Rallying the Party and Nation

It was fortunate that Macmillan so soon felt – as the French say – 'well in his skin' at No. 10. The problems he had to face were mountainous. On coming to power, he listed them under six main headings. First was the impelling need 'to restore the confidence of the people in their Government and themselves'. Secondly, there was the messy aftermath of Suez to be cleared up in the Middle East. Thirdly, the alliance with the United States had to be restored. Fourthly, there was the perennial headache of balancing Britain's economy, which was – despite the help now at last coming in from the US – said Macmillan, 'like bicycling along a tightrope'. Fifthly, there was defence, where serious new reappraisals and cuts had to be faced with redoubled urgency after Suez. Finally, there was the future of the Commonwealth (which, immediately, meant the problem of Cyprus). Macmillan speculated whether he was 'destined to be the remodeller or the liquidator of Empire'.

By the end of his second month in office, he was identifying in detail a few more worries. Overseas, there was Syria's closing of the oil pipelines; India–Pakistan disputes over Kashmir; India's threats to leave the Commonwealth; a settlement in Malta about to founder on Dom Mintoff's intransigence; and Germany trying to 'wriggle out' of £50 million support costs to the British Army in Germany. At home, civil expenditure was too high; doctors were claiming an extra £20 million; there was the problem of Old Age Pensions. And, inevitably, there was the threat of 'devastating strikes' – and comfortless by-elections. By the end of his first two weeks in office, Macmillan reckoned there were 'more "balls" in the air than I remember . . . some of them are very hard to catch and throw up again. . . .'[35] It was a metaphor that would reappear with regularity in his diaries.

Struck by the volume of encouraging letters he had received, and 'how well everyone, i.e. the politicians, has behaved', putting 'the public interest and the desire to help me above all other considerations', Macmillan noted that in the early days of his accession 'there has been a kind of 1940 spirit abroad.'[36] If this was so, it was timely, for the state of the Tory Party was also probably as bad as at any time since 1940; few doubted that the calling of a general election would herald a Labour landslide.

But there was, mingled with a kind of expectant hopelessness and confusion, a great deal of intrinsic goodwill. The Party was longing to acclaim a new leader – and to ensure that he succeeded. Any display of confidence would be better than the dithering of Eden. Beyond the Party, after the stresses and divisions that Suez had caused, the British electorate – perhaps not explicitly at first – wanted a period of calm, peace and consensus politics, and – for the second time since 1945 – a certain removal from world worries and responsibilities. Even the right-wing Suez Group and its supporters had prepared themselves to write off Suez – provided retreat could be made to look like a victory, and here again Macmillan would pull the rabbit out of the hat. On 17 January, he made his first address on television, full of optimism, freshness and vigour, calling for an end to defeatist talk about Britain being a second-class power: 'What nonsense! This is a great country and do not let us be ashamed to say so. . . . there is no reason to quiver before temporary difficulties.'[37] Tackling the issue that perhaps worried most people after Suez, he said of restoring amity with the United States:

The life of the free world depends upon the partnership between us. Any partners are bound to have their differences now and then. I've always found it so. . . . But true partnership is based on respect. We don't intend to part from the Americans, and we don't intend to be satellites. . . .

On 22 January, Macmillan – accompanied by Dorothy – was confirmed as leader by the Party Meeting. At this ritual, he began a brief speech with generous praise of Eden, followed by a tribute to his wife, 'without whose help I could have achieved nothing' and who 'serves to remind me of the realities of life'. He went on to stress the vital importance of party cohesion in such difficult times, throwing out a clue to exactly where in terms of party philosophy he might now be expected to stand, through a quotation from Disraeli: 'we must be conservative to conserve all that is good and radical to uproot all that is bad. So it is that we have never been, and I trust that while I am your leader, we never will be, a Party of any class or sectional interest.' He differentiated his Conservative perception of the welfare state from the socialist: 'We believe that unless we give opportunity to the strong and able, we shall never have the means to provide real protection for the weak and old. . . .' This was an important personal credo, and indicated to what extent – while still marching under its banner – Macmillan had modified 'The Middle Way' over the past two decades.

That same day he made his first appearance as Prime Minister in the reassembled House of Commons, receiving what one newspaper described as only 'a dutiful rather than an enthusiastic cheer'. The day also that the Edens sailed for New Zealand and off the centre stage forever, it was a muted time all round: 'Everybody feels such a load of depression,' wrote MP Nigel Nicolson to his parents:

> It is partly because an ill man was led by illness into folly; and partly because his successors have had to pretend that it wasn't folly at all. Everyone as a result is confused. Nobody is acknowledged to have emerged well out of this business. There are no heroes. Only different sorts of traitors. . . .[38]

On 30 January, the Party Chairman, Oliver Poole, called to see Macmillan, warning him that there was 'a considerable sense of confusion and uncertainty in the ranks of the Party . . .'. Supporters said that they 'were prepared to support the Government all through, but they do not understand what is happening now'.[39] The press continued defeatist; by the end of March, Macmillan noted that it still predicted the early collapse of the government. The two-faced Beaverbrook's *Sunday Express* was 'particularly virulent. I always felt that these would be the critical weeks. If we last the summer, we shall stay the course. . . .'[40]

Meanwhile, Macmillan, with his many years of parliamentary experience coupled with that sensitivity of touch, was busy burrowing and entrenching himself in the true keeps of Tory power. It was certainly not for purely social reasons that he had selected the Chief Whip, Ted Heath (never renowned as convivial company), for that first celebratory supper of oysters and champagne at the Turf Club. Macmillan knew precisely where the roots of power resided. Whatever the pressures of office, he made a point of spending time, chatting to backbenchers, in the Smoking Room. The long-time Secretary (1960–79) of the 1922 Committee, Philip Goodhart, recalls that he went into the Smoking Room a few days after his own by-election victory in March 1957:

> Macmillan was sitting with Selwyn Lloyd. He clearly didn't recognise me and I could see that he was asking the Foreign Secretary who I was. I had a drink and left. A few moments later, as I was walking down the corridor, Macmillan overtook me. 'I'm Harold Macmillan,' he said. 'I do believe in youth.' I was enormously impressed by the fact that he had taken the trouble to talk to his most junior back-bench supporter.[41]

Nigel Nicolson reported to his parents, then voyaging in Singapore, an address Macmillan had made to the 1922:

> It was superb. His whole speech turned upon the distinction between pride and vanity in the conduct of international relations, and there was not much doubt what he had in mind. . . . He said that the greatest moments in our history have not been those when we have conquered, but when we have led. You see the subtle change? I was delighted. I said to the Chief Whip as we were going out 'What a pity it is that now we have the most intelligent Prime Minister of the century, he has to conceal his intelligence from the public for fear that they will suspect it, and that only we, on such occasions as this can be given the full quality of his mind.' 'Yes,' said the Chief Whip. 'Yes.'[42]

By the final Suez debate of 15–16 May, Prime Minister Macmillan had got fully into his stride. 'We are a great world power,' he told the Commons, hitting just the right note of confidence, 'and we intend to remain so.'[43] It was after that debate that he got a first feeling that 'we had turned the corner. We should now be able, with ordinary luck, to run till the normal end of the Parliament. . . .'

Overcoming Post-Suez Bitterness

There was, however, no mistaking the bitterness at Westminster that followed Suez. That stormy petrel of the Labour Party, Aneurin Bevan, called it 'the squalid Parliament', and thought it 'the most wretched' he had ever sat in – primarily because of 'the lingering stench of Suez about the place'. Angered by Macmillan's resistance to holding any official enquiry, he would repeatedly hit at him personally, totally ignoring Selwyn Lloyd – on the dismissive principle that 'there is no reason to attack the monkey when the organ grinder is present'. Equally he deplored what seemed to him a lack of vigour on the part of the Opposition in pursuing the Treasury bench.[44]

The first row in the Commons came at the end of February, when the Opposition leaders leaped on to what they claimed was a 'budget leak' by Macmillan's new President of the Board of Trade, David Eccles. During his speech opening the second reading of the debate on the Cinematographic Films Bill, Eccles had been tempted by a question from a Labour backbencher to suggest that the entertainment duty was bound to be reduced in the next Budget – then only a few weeks away. This slip seemed to set off a brief rally on the Stock Exchange in cinema shares – which had been depressed by the growing popularity of television. The press and the Opposition claimed that this was an improper budget leak, but constitutional purists noted that a remark in Parliament could hardly be described as a leak. The issue was technical and trivial; his slip obviously indiscreet rather than indecorous. Eccles was not a popular personality either in the House or with the press, where his elegantly dandy figure and a certain cold intellectual arrogance had earned him the unkind nickname of 'Smarty Boots'. Thus, recalling how the unpopular Hugh Dalton's famous 'leak' in 1947 had caused his resignation as Chancellor, and might have brought the government down, the Opposition thought it was on to a good thing. 'I had a rough time,' Macmillan noted on 28 February: '. . . Gaitskell, Bevan, Wilson – all joining in the "hue and cry". I felt sure that they were going to use this as an extra piece of pressure against a Government which is going through a bad patch. The by-elections all show a swing away from us. . . .'[45]

Macmillan was irked at the trouble caused by the 'small and venial' slip of Eccles ('a curious man – at once *very* intelligent and very foolish'), but was 'determined to protect him by drawing all the fire on to myself'. A debate, in which Gaitskell spoke 'very weakly', and Dalton made a fool of himself, degenerated 'into *opera bouffe*. It was brought back by Harold Wilson in an able, witty and effective speech. But there was really nothing in it all, and I had no difficulty demolishing the Opposition case in winding up.'[46]

The 'Eccles Affair' was a five-day storm in a teacup, but it was an avoidable irritant at a difficult moment and Macmillan saw it as a serious attempt 'to discredit a Government already in grave trouble'. But it ended as a clear triumph for Macmillan, and even one of his harshest critics, the Labour MP Emrys Hughes, was forced to admit that Macmillan, in his endeavour to command respect, 'did this with such success that in a couple of months he had confounded his Parliamentary critics and had become a dominant personality to whom the House of Commons responded . . . '.[47]

The importance of excelling in the House was always paramount to him. As long as he could dominate it:

> . . . I didn't worry. . . . I didn't mind even losing a by-election or bother too much with the outside world, if you can once impress upon the House of Commons that the Government is strong and the Prime Minister is in control . . . then gradually . . . it begins to go out into the country as the Members go back to their constituencies. Then gradually the Press begin to show a certain surprise at the success of the Government in overcoming one obstacle after another. . . .[48]

Meanwhile, there were several by-elections to be endured, mainly caused by the reconstruction of the government. First, on 14 February, North Lewisham was lost by 1100, with many Tory votes taken by the right-wing Empire Loyalist candidate; then came the inevitable loss of Wednesbury. Macmillan took heart in the fact that the swing against the government was only 4 to 5 per cent, compared with 7 per cent *before* Suez. More worrying was the result from the seat where Eden had resigned, Warwick and Leamington; there an 11,000 slump in the vote was registered, leaving this safe Tory seat with only a 2200 majority. On 8 March, Macmillan recorded:

The Socialists are very cock-a-hoop today and the press generally regards the by-election results as a great blow to the Government. The Opposition will demand a General Election. But we must be quite resolute and press on with our policies. . . . I am not dismayed. . . .'[49]

But, with a new election due in two years at most, and the dire memories of 1945 just twelve years behind the Conservatives, the omens all through 1957 were not promising – to say the least.

Repairing the Fences with Eisenhower

If consolidating his position at home was Macmillan's top priority, no less important was the task of repairing the fences between Britain and America that Suez had broken down; and it was clear that picking up the pieces in the Middle East would head the foreign agenda throughout most of 1957. As a result of Suez, relations within the Special Relationship had seldom been worse; in Britain, anti-American feelings – as Ambassador Aldrich warned Washington – were at a post-war high.[50] In January, Duncan Sandys, as Macmillan's new Minister of Defence, and the first Cabinet member to visit the US since Suez, had brought this forcibly home to Dulles, with his characteristically plain speaking. Reporting back to Macmillan, Sandys said he had told Dulles that what Britain most complained of in America's past behaviour over Suez was the way in which she had been misled by Dulles's scheme for a Suez Canal Users' Association as a method of bringing joint pressure to bear on Egypt: 'I said that, frankly, we felt that we had been "led up the garden path" and that from that moment onwards the British Government had lost all confidence in the friendly intentions of the American Government. Dulles seemed momentarily embarrassed by this. . . .'[51]

From the moment of his accession, Macmillan decided that he had to go to see Eisenhower in person at the earliest possible opportunity, but he was equally determined not to appear in the role of suitor even to his old friend. He would not go grovelling to Washington, on 'a pilgrimage to Canossa' as he put it. He, too, had minced no words to Eisenhower about his sense of hurt at having been 'let down' over Suez.[52] On 22 January there came an overture, in the shape of a private, highly secret and most friendly message from the White House. How about Bermuda, in March? Macmillan was delighted, and by 8 February – after some suitable show of hesitation – the meeting was set up. With a shade more optimism than had existed a few weeks previously, Macmillan wrote to Eden (with whom he maintained an amiable correspondence): 'Sooner or later the Americans will come round. If they don't, Europe is finished, for I am certain that the Russians are determined to get hold of the Middle East. . . .'[53] With the Americans, Macmillan now felt able to 'revert to our old friendly relations'. Bermuda, being British soil, 'makes all the difference to us. But I was afraid that the French would be hurt; or, worse still, want to make it a Tripartite meeting. However, they too have behaved very well, and agreed to go on their own to Washington. . . .'[54]

Yet, although the French premier, Mollet, with whom – though socialist – Macmillan always had excellent relations, had 'behaved well', Macmillan's diary also reveals a fundamental parting of the ways in Franco-British relations. Britain henceforth would pursue the road of the Special Relationship; France would go separately, and – implicitly – on a lower level, to Washington. Macmillan clearly and consciously gave the London–Washington entente priority over relations with Europe. Axiomatic with this, on the one hand, was that Britain should never again permit a basic policy conflict with the US; on the other hand, that it should at the same time go all out for the independent nuclear deterrent.

Gratified by Eisenhower's new warmth, Macmillan nevertheless revealed in his diaries how American policy over Suez continued to rankle. With the United Nations threatening sanctions to get Israel out of the Gaza Strip and Sinai occupied during Suez, Britain found herself caught between the two fires of inflaming Arab opinion or reneging on her former partner: on 9 February Macmillan was writing that 'The Americans are behaving very weakly over this, with legalism and pedantry . . .'; and, on the 18th, how they were 'now "up against" realities' and were 'angry and puzzled . . .'. The next day, he reported that 'President Eisenhower, who has been on holiday for the last month or two, golfing and quail-shooting, has returned to Washington. The situation regarding the Israel–Egypt dispute over Gaza and Gulf of Aqaba is getting more and more confusing and dangerous . . . poor Foster Dulles is floundering more and more. . . .' By 27 February, there was a 'very bad telegram both from Washington and New York [i.e. the British UN Delegation]. The administration have ratted again . . . more telegrams from Washington and New York. The Americans have re-ratted. . . .'[55]

At the beginning of March one of the biggest hurdles in the Middle East was got over when the Israelis – under heavy pressure from Washington – decided, 'as an act of faith', to withdraw their forces from Gaza and the Gulf of Aqaba, and to let the UN peacekeeping force move in. Macmillan commented: 'This follows a most complicated negotiation, in which it looks as if the American passion for being liked by everybody has got them into the position of being trusted by nobody. . . .'[56] The Israeli withdrawal, however, was a great relief to Macmillan as this meant that the work of clearing the Canal, which was Britain's major interest, could now proceed.

The Bermuda Meeting

Macmillan arrived at Bermuda's Mid-Ocean Club on 20 March, in advance of Eisenhower and his entourage, and was thus able to welcome the President to British territory: 'The whole population, white and black, of the island seemed to join in the welcome. The President seemed very well – bronzed and alert. He had rather a tiresome cough; but as I have caught a shattering cold myself, we are evenly matched in this respect. . . .' Dulles, despite his major cancer operation, appeared 'very little changed'. During a twenty-minute car drive, Macmillan had Eisenhower to himself, who:

> talked very freely to me – just exactly as in the old days. There were no reproaches – on either side; but (what was more important) no note of any change in our friendship or the confidence he had in me. Indeed he seemed delighted to have somebody to talk to! In America, he is half King, half Prime Minister. This means that he is rather a lonely figure, with few confidants. He told me very frankly that he knew how unpopular Foster Dulles was with our people and with a lot of his people. But he must keep him. He couldn't do without him. . . .[57]

After dinner that evening, the talk moved on to the general situation in the world. 'Nothing very startling was said and nothing settled; but the atmosphere was very good – I thought, in view of all the circumstances, surprisingly so. . . .' Macmillan made it at once clear to the Americans 'that we are not going to be the "supplicants" or "in the dock" at this conference. It is rather the other way round.'[58]

The next day the Conference proper began. As host, Macmillan made a welcoming speech, which concluded, with pointed observations on what, he explained, the British still regarded as the most 'urgent issue' – Nasser and the Suez Canal. He stated 'with that frankness which true partnership and comradeship' required:

> your Government and many of your people think we acted foolishly and precipitately and illegally. Our Government and many of our people think that you were too hard on us – and rather let us down. Well, that's over – spilt milk. Don't let's cry over it – still less wallow in it. But the Canal remains.

He went on with equal directness:

> *I hope you will do everything you possibly can* . . . to get a Canal settlement, short and long – especially regarding dues – which we can claim as reasonable, if not quite what we would like! But if we can't get it – if Nasser is absolutely obdurate . . . if we all have, in the *short* run, to eat dirt and accept a bad and unjust settlement, I hope you won't say in public or in private that it's a good settlement. I hope you will denounce Nasser and all his works in the strongest terms. Bring every pressure – political and economic – upon him. . . .

He closed with a forceful warning that a bad solution for Britain 'would I fear cause such a rift between our countries and people as would take much longer to repair than the urgent needs of the world allow'.[59]

Macmillan noted that Eisenhower in his reply took up 'rather sharply' the point about the British feeling 'let down', but was 'very gracious and fair'. The President admitted that he was taken aback by the strength of British feelings about Nasser; the fact that he should have been seems proof in itself of just how bad communications between the two countries had become. In his memoirs, Eisenhower recorded:

Foster and I at first found it difficult to talk constructively with our British colleagues about Suez because of the blinding bitterness they felt towards Nasser. Prime Minister Harold Macmillan and Foreign Minister Selwyn Lloyd were so obsessed with the possibilities of getting rid of Nasser that they were handicapped in searching, objectively, for any realistic method of operating the Canal.[60]

By the following day, Macmillan's cold had gone to his chest and – always something of a hypochondriac over lesser complaints – he felt frightful, until the President's personal doctor, General Howard Snyder, administered some 'potent drugs'. Over the next two days, between formal meetings, the two statesmen popped in and out of each other's rooms in the Mid-Ocean Club, sometimes in pyjamas, chatting like old school chums. Macmillan realised how much Eisenhower, weighed down with all the formality and loneliness of office, enjoyed these convivial 'bull sessions'. (Eisenhower, on his side, wrote: 'Any conference with the British requires the most detailed discussion. They do not like to sign any generalizations in a hurry, no matter how plausible or attractive they may be, but once their signature is affixed to a document, complete confidence can be placed in their performance. French negotiators sometimes seem to prefer to sign first and then to begin discussion.')[61] Macmillan's belief, handed down from war days, that he could 'handle the Americans' had led him into grave error in 1956, but now, tempered by his quick sensitivity, coupled with Eisenhower's cordial generosity of spirit, it enabled what remained of the ice to be swiftly broken.

On 22 March, Macmillan was reporting to his deputy, Rab:

as far as the President is concerned, there is a genuine desire to forget our differences and to restore our old relationship and cooperation in full measure. He could not be more friendly or more frank. We went over most of our problems and he wants to be helpful. But of course he leaves so much to Dulles, and neither the Foreign Secretary nor I feel so happy about his attitude. Even if he is willing to forgive and forget, I doubt whether he can do so as fully and as generously as the President. So he acts as a brake on the process of rebuilding confidence and help.[62]

By the 25th, Macmillan was able to write in a rather more optimistic vein, reporting two important achievements:

> First, we have not been in the dock. On the contrary, the Americans have been rather apologetic about their position. Secondly, the personal relations between myself and the President have been established upon a level of confidence which is very gratifying. . . . the test, of course, will be how far this spirit will in fact permeate the complicated machinery of Washington departments. . . .[63]

The following day he was writing to Prime Minister Menzies in Australia that, with Eisenhower, 'things are back on the old footing. Dulles, who by temperament and conviction is a sort of Gladstonian Liberal, who dislikes the nakedness of facts, has also come a long way. . . .'[64]

Eisenhower, too, was expressing himself with the same kind of positive enthusiasm in a letter to his old friend and confidant, Captain 'Swede' Hazlett: '. . . Macmillan is, of course, one of my intimate wartime friends and so it is very easy to talk to him on a very frank, even blunt, basis. . . .'[65] Later Eisenhower was to count Bermuda 'the most successful international conference that I had attended since the close of World War II'.[66]

What, in practical terms, was achieved at Bermuda? First, as a preliminary jump towards the British 'deterrent', sixty Thor intermediate missiles were given to Britain under the limitations of the 'two-key' system. Secondly, although no final conclusions had been reached over the crucial issue of Suez, Macmillan had succeeded in getting the Americans to face up to issues without any repudiation of British policy. The sudden realisation of the speed with which the Soviets might move into vacuums left by the British and French had begun to cause a major rethinking in the White House. With it, the foundations were laid for the historic 'Eisenhower Doctrine' which, for the first time, would involve the US directly in the Middle East, with the ultimate aim of safeguarding oil supplies and countering Soviet penetration – as well as the even more ambitious goal of ensuring 'peace and stability' in the area. Macmillan had also secured American help, now, to obtain a fair financial settlement over the Canal with the Egyptians; 'a gallant effort', as he described it with heavy irony in his memoirs, 'to shut the stable door'.

Clearly, however, by far and away the greatest success of the six days at Bermuda lay in the intangibles. Although in one of those famous characteristic throwaways, picked up by Joe Alsop, Macmillan depicted meeting Eisenhower in Bermuda as being 'not at all like an experience in the modern world. More like meeting George III at Brighton . . .',[67] he was thoroughly pleased by the way things had gone between the two of them. The Special Relationship had been restored, on a highly personal basis, to something almost approximating the old wartime intimacy of Algiers – or, at least, the first steps had been taken in that direction.

Chapter Two

Mending the Fences
March–December 1957

Among the most serious consequences of the Suez débâcle was that it nearly destroyed the Anglo-American alliance. It was one of Mr Harold Macmillan's greatest acts of statesmanship that he was able to heal the breach so very soon after he became Prime Minister. . . .

(Randolph Churchill, The Rise and Fall of Anthony Eden)

. . . I felt not altogether dissatisfied with the diplomatic efforts of this year. At the beginning of January, I had found our friendship with the United States destroyed, the European alliance almost shattered, and dismay and uncertainty in many parts of the Commonwealth.

(HM, Riding the Storm)

Macmillan was frequently to repeat his remark about the excessive quantity of 'balls in the air' which he had to keep aloft all at the same time, especially during this first critical year at No. 10. It was difficult enough to keep his eye on all the balls at once; but one ball was soon dropped, the significance of which seems not to have been immediately apparent at the time. On 25 March, while Macmillan was still with Eisenhower at Bermuda, the European 'Six' finally signed the Treaty of Rome; on 1 January 1958, nine months later, the European Economic Community of France, Germany, Italy, Holland, Belgium and Luxemburg formally came into being. The historic signature appears to have passed almost unnoticed by Macmillan. He made no mention of it in his diaries and only on the following day was there a passing reference to the fact that the Canadians had been 'very interested in the European Free Trade Area. I was able to reassure them about our plans . . .'.[1] (The Canadian Prime Minister, St Laurent, and his Foreign Secretary, Lester Pearson, had flown to Bermuda for separate talks with the British, chiefly with the aim of repairing fences which had also been holed by Suez.)

It was during Macmillan's period as Chancellor that, in July 1956, 'Plan G' had been evolved. This was the forerunner of the European Free Trade Association (or EFTA, or the 'Seven' – UK, Denmark, Norway, Austria, Switzerland, Portugal and Sweden) and would provide a link with the EEC or the Six. Few in Whitehall at the time reckoned that the EEC would become a fact or, if it did, that Britain could join it. 'Plan G' was limited in its ambitions: it would provide a free-trade area for all goods other than foodstuffs – which remained, perpetually, the single most controversial item. The area would embrace Britain, the Six, and all other European countries that wished to participate. It implied no political commitments. Or so Macmillan hoped.

The timing for the launch of 'Plan G' could, however, hardly have been less auspicious; it was almost immediately eclipsed by the Suez crisis, which was reaching its climax when the plan was put to the Party Conference in October 1956. The meeting of

Commonwealth Finance Ministers in Washington the previous month had also faced similar preoccupations. When 'Plan G' came before the Commons in November, with MPs in the throes of post-mortems over Suez, Macmillan noted 'a certain unreality about the discussions', because parliamentarians found it 'difficult to deal with more than one great issue at a time . . .'. He recalled that 'Plan G' was accepted without great enthusiasm by the Party and that anything further at the time would have been 'entering doubtful and dangerous ground'. There was no question then of joining the Six, who after all had still not signed any definite treaty.

Such were the delays of British decision-making that the Government's White Paper on the European Free Trade Area had only come out in January 1957. By 25 March, when the Six – after much hard bargaining and also undoubtedly animated by the consequences of Suez – finally signed the historic Treaty of Rome, Macmillan was giving top priority to repairing the breaches in the Anglo-American alliance. Yet this did not mean that Macmillan intended to turn his back on British involvement in Europe, or continue with Eden's apathy. Moreover, the structure of his own Cabinet had greatly strengthened the pro-European lobby; Thorneycroft was a convinced European, as were Eccles, Heathcoat Amory, Sandys, Home, Kilmuir and Watkinson. Butler and Hailsham were sceptical, but the most formidable anti-European, Lord Salisbury, was soon to find himself outside the Cabinet. None, however, was prepared to go as far as the federalism of Europeans like Spaak, or Macmillan's old friend from Algiers days, Jean Monnet; although Macmillan's own philosophy towards a united Europe always contained a strong streak of idealism that transcended such commercial considerations as 'fixing a price for prunes and a suitable method of marketing bananas'.[2]

What was not yet clear in early 1957 was the full extent of the havoc which Suez, and particularly the British decision to call a halt to the military operation, had wreaked upon Franco-British relations. The débâcle at Suez had dealt a hard knock to the regime of the veteran socialist premier, Guy Mollet; the war in Algeria (which Mollet had hoped Suez might resolve) was going from bad to worse, and the French Army was increasingly restive. Ostensibly as a matter of diplomatic tact, Macmillan had decided to go to Paris to see Mollet before the Bermuda Conference (though it was not lost on the French that their premier rated only a day-trip,

31

compared with the six days dedicated to the US head of state). This day-trip was bound to increase rather than to reduce latent tensions; for – at the top of Macmillan's agenda – the French were to be told about Britain's need to cut her defence contribution in Europe. Given the undertaking made by Eden three years earlier as the price of getting France to agree to West German rearmament, coupled with the denuding of the French contribution which the demands of Algeria had dictated, this was bound to be unpalatable.

According to Macmillan, his and Selwyn Lloyd's talks with Mollet and Pineau on 9 March began agreeably enough; but after lunch, 'a very long, and rather unpleasant argument' ensued about Macmillan's proposed force reductions. This was, Macmillan reckoned, partly due to an imminent debate in the Assembly where – like most leaders of the Fourth Republic – Mollet's future was in constant jeopardy; and once more there were implicit recriminations of *perfide Albion*:

> . . . I took a very tough line and made it clear to them that we would have to make these reductions. We had no alternative. The discussions on the Common Market and the European Free Trade Area were on a calmer plane. The French have got what they want, but they have put *us* in a great difficulty. If it had not been for the question of our forces in Europe, I would have attacked the French for the way in which they managed the last stages of the negotiations for the Common Market, especially the inclusion of the French Colonial Empire. This was got through at the last minute, and makes great difficulties for us.[3]

The following week, Macmillan noted at the end of a round of Western European Union talks that 'the French were very difficult and unhelpful throughout. The Germans got more reasonable. I think that Adenauer is only worrying about his election. . . .'[4] (Later he reflected that it might be a good idea if all general elections could be synchronised in the Western world.)

In May Macmillan paid his first visit to Bonn, to see Dr Konrad Adenauer, the 'sly old fox' of the Rhineland, at eighty-one Europe's senior statesman, who had already been at the helm of West Germany for nearly eight years. There began a relationship that was never to be easy, or relaxed. The Germans were apprehensive about France's continued distrust of them and about French intentions, but were at the same time 'alarmed' and suspicious at Macmillan's projected defence cuts in Europe. Macmillan decided not to beat about the bush, 'especially as I was told that the Chancellor is so old and powerful that no one really tells him the truth'.[5] He delivered two carefully prepared speeches, pulling out the stops about the human suffering caused by the partition of Germany and Russian oppression, and ending with a review of European history over the past century – 'our failures and follies, and now our opportunities'. Macmillan thought that his words left the old Chancellor much moved.

The next day, 8 May (no tactless references were made to the fact that it was also the twelfth anniversary of VE-Day), there was 'quite a gay party' on a Rhine pleasure boat, and in talks later about the EEC Macmillan was relieved to find that the Germans 'were, or professed to be, entirely on our side. They would regard the union of the 6 Messina powers as a disaster if it were *not* followed by the Free Trade area. . . .'[6] It was a German view that proved to be ephemeral. After a dinner at the British Embassy, Macmillan and Adenauer had a long conversation in private, of the kind incorporating a mix of philosophy and history that always particularly appealed to Macmillan:

> He said that no one who had lived through the years of Hitler could fail to believe in the Devil. He said 'I tell you, what I could not say to any German, no one realises the harm that Nazism has done to the German soul. It is by no means cured yet. We have got rich again too quickly. I don't want us to get strong again too quickly. I hate uniforms, the curse of Germany. You will see that our Generals in conference are like yours, in civil clothes. I see great dangers ahead. That is why I yearn so for European unity and (in view of France's weakness) for British participation.'[7]

It was a remarkable and rare baring of the soul of the 'sly old fox'.

Macmillan, however, was incensed by remarks relayed by Adenauer to Selwyn Lloyd, to the effect that Dulles had told him that Bermuda was a failure, and that 'the British had no foreign policy and were finished'. Momentarily, Macmillan considered talking to the American Ambassador, or even writing to Eisenhower, about this apparent lapse by Dulles: 'it may be that people are right

33

in dubbing him "double-crosser"'.[8] But, equally, it may have been Adenauer being mischievous.

On 21 May, shortly after Macmillan's return from Germany, Mollet fell from power, leaving France without government for twenty-two days, and bringing an eloquent valedictory letter from Macmillan which expressed warm appreciation at the way in which France had stood with Britain 'in the sombre days of last November, when other friends seemed to forget those things for which our two countries jointly stood . . .'. Referring, *en passant*, to the Common Market negotiations, he repeated the cautious line of the past about Britain being 'in a rather different situation' to her European allies, but ended on a note of hope: 'if one thing has come out of Suez it is certainly a greater willingness on the part of the British to cooperate closely with these allies. . . .'[9] It would take de Gaulle to show that France viewed matters differently.

Mollet's fall began a year-long period for France in which fresh governments succeeded each other with great rapidity, or simply did not exist at all – what de Gaulle termed scathingly 'this absurd ballet'. Over this whole period of instability the unwinnable Algerian war brooded in the background.

Maudling's Appointment

Meanwhile, in August, Macmillan appointed Reginald Maudling, with the title of Paymaster-General, to concentrate government efforts to reshape trade with Europe under the terms of 'Plan G'. Macmillan regarded Maudling's role as 'apostolic'; he would have to 'hold firm the Eleven' (all the European countries who were interested in a free-trade area), while trying 'to break into the Six'. 'He should therefore be something of a St Paul; not merely the Jews but the Gentiles should be his care. . . .' One of Macmillan's first instructions to Maudling was to go all out to 'get the Germans on our side. When the [West German] election is over, they will be prepared to take a stronger line. The Germans really agree with us and are against the French ideas of a high protective tariff wall round the Common Market. . . .'[10] Meanwhile, he had written to Sir Harold Caccia, the British Ambassador in Washington, instructing him to marshal Eisenhower's active support over EFTA:

while the Americans want nothing out of the French and can afford to lecture to them, we want a great deal from them. The French have it in their power to wreck the European Free Trade Movement, and that in the long run must mean a further division of Europe, the probable end of NATO and most serious reorientation of British policy. . . .[11]

In November, Macmillan was recording perceptively: 'The French seem in a dazed condition – until Algeria is conquered, evacuated or conciliated, they are immobilised.'[12] Relations were particularly strained at the time, following a small British shipment of arms to Tunisia, which France considered to be hand in glove with the Algerian Front de Libération Nationale. There were once again the familiar angry accusations in the French press about perfidious Albion. Macmillan later admitted that this was a 'serious error'. Britain did not then 'fully realise the true situation in France'; the French were 'back in a self-critical and hopeless mood, which expressed itself (as I had known so well in de Gaulle's time) by being as tiresome as possible to everyone else. . . .'[13] The 'tiresomeness' was one with which Macmillan would very soon be reacquainted.

Meanwhile, pressure groups began to form within Britain over British association with Europe. The Labour Party under Gaitskell progressively distanced itself from Europe; much of the press, led by *The Economist* and supported even by the pro-Labour *Daily Mirror*, was strongly pro-European. The most potent exception was the Beaverbrook newspapers, which would remain virulently hostile to any policy move that might threaten notional Commonwealth ties. The Treasury and the main spokesmen for industry began to back any European policy that promised to open up a bigger market. For a long time the Foreign Office remained entrenched in its scepticism, and its influence on Macmillan was considerable. Philip de Zulueta, the young and forceful Private Secretary who represented the Foreign Office line in Macmillan's Inner Office, voiced the view typical of the time: 'We really don't think the French and the Germans will ever bury the hatchet to the extent of getting together to make the Common Market work.'[14] For this reason, the Foreign Office continued to doubt for some time further whether the EEC would last. The Conservative Party was deeply divided; Macmillan sensed that it could not be pushed too fast into anything that smacked of supra-nationalism. Macmillan's own feelings were expressed in the memorandum he wrote to Edward Heath at the end of 1957, voicing disquiet at the growing isolationism within the Tory Party, the second form of which (after anti-Americanism) was 'directed against Europe, and of course inspires Beaverbrook and his followers. So we are reaching a position in which the English people of 50 million, who in material terms are quite unequal to the new giants, will move neither towards Europe nor towards America. It is a stultifying policy. . . .'[15]

Trouble at Home – Salisbury

On returning from his visit to Mollet in March, Macmillan had found a sea of troubles awaiting him at home: 'The shipbuilding strike, to be followed by a strike throughout the engineering industry, seems almost certain. Then the railways!'[16] The following week the situation looked even darker, with the threat of a general strike in the wind; Macmillan seriously contemplated whether he might not have to cancel Bermuda. On returning from Bermuda, worries over strikes continued but they were now superseded by a storm coming from a totally different direction. Earlier the EOKA terrorists of Cyprus had made an offer to call off killings if Archbishop Makarios were released from internment in the Seychelles, to which he had been deported in March 1956 because of terrorist connections. The situation in Cyprus had worsened over the past year, while failure at Suez had greatly reduced the strategic value of the isle of Aphrodite. On 15 March Macmillan wrote that he was 'as anxious as anyone to get clear of Cyprus',[17] and settlement there was in effect to constitute one of the first zephyrs of the 'wind of change'. But, on tactical grounds, he was at first against releasing the troublesome prelate.

The Cabinet was bitterly divided; 'no one seemed to know what to do about the Archbishop.'[18] Salisbury and Lennox-Boyd, the Colonial Secretary, 'took diametrically opposing views. At one time both had offered – or threatened – to resign. . . .'[19] While in Bermuda, perhaps pushed gently by Eisenhower and perhaps recalling the personal success he had had with that other Greek cleric, Damaskinos, during the war, Macmillan finally decided to take the plunge and release Makarios. Eisenhower afterwards wrote a comforting letter, reckoning that while Makarios could still cause mischief:

> . . . I think that Britain, as a great country, is in a better position in the matter than she was with him as a prisoner. Certainly you have taken away from demagogues one of their chief arguments against you. I have heard that one of our ambitious Governors has invited the Archbishop to come to this country. One is frequently tempted to ask 'How stupid can you get?' . . .[20]

On the day he returned from Bermuda, 27 March, Lord Salisbury came to see Macmillan: 'He was very charming, but seemed determined to resign about something. He is in one of his resigning moods.'[21] Makarios was, in fact, but the tip of the iceberg. During the Churchill administration Macmillan and Salisbury had already clashed over bigger issues. Salisbury's 'resigning moods' were a recognised feature; prior to the Khrushchev–Bulganin visit of 1956, Macmillan had noted in his diaries how Salisbury had been 'worried': 'and when he is worried, always wants to resign (this is a great Cecil tradition). . . .'[22] On 10 January, the very day of Macmillan's assumption of power, Salisbury in a somewhat theatrical letter had already threatened resignation if he failed to get his way over House of Lords reform, and over being appointed Leader of the Upper House.

Patrician and slightly overbearing, a figure wielding the kind of influence associated with the great Cecil clan since Elizabethan days, Salisbury represented the right-wing conscience of the Party. He was related, by marriage, to Macmillan with triple family bonds, and although Macmillan claimed 'Bobbety' as a 'very old friend', socially he always seemed to suffer a certain uneasiness in his shadow. He was conscious that his grand kinsman had played 'king-maker' for him in January 1957, but – as he said many years later:

> . . . I had a feeling that he was not in sympathy with the way I intended to run the Government. . . . I intended to run it . . . as a *centre* party. I was not prepared to run it on an extreme right-wing basis . . . and I expect his feelings towards me were those of his great-grandfather towards Disraeli. . . . he, the great Salisbury, thought Disraeli was not a good Tory. And I'm afraid

he was right. Nor am I, if you mean by that a very orthodox Tory! . . . but I couldn't quite see why he made such a fuss at this particular point. . . .[23]

On 29 March, Salisbury resigned. A relatively new figure to the inner circles of Tory power took his place as Lord President – Lord Home. Courteous letters of regret were exchanged, but there was a note of edge in Macmillan's: '. . . I have taken on a very difficult job, in circumstances almost unparalleled in political history. I wish you could have been with me to see it through. . . .' Far less restrained was the bitterness in the privacy of his diaries: 'All through history the Cecils, when any friend or colleague has been in real trouble, have stabbed him in the back – attributing the crime to qualms of conscience. . . .'[24]

It was, however, as Macmillan freely admitted, 'a terrible day'; some newspapers were liberally predicting the early collapse of the Government. But Macmillan's timing showed political skill. The news was announced just before the weekend, and the following week Macmillan contrived that it was eclipsed by a lengthy statement on the Bermuda talks. It was, as he recognised at the time, better to have lost 'Bobbety' over Cyprus than over what he called the 'water-jump' – the forthcoming debate over Suez, where it was anticipated that Salisbury could cause great trouble. Four days later Macmillan was able to note, with a sigh of relief – and a touch of brutality: '. . . Lord Salisbury's resignation has left scarcely a ripple on the surface. The Cabinet, much as they all like him personally, feel like a man who has got rid of an inflamed tooth. . . .'[25] Macmillan was now – almost – undisputed master in his own Cabinet.

John Wyndham (also a relation by marriage to Salisbury) considered that, in all his years at Downing Street, 'there was nothing to equal the astonishment' when Macmillan accepted Salisbury's resignation:

Why did the Prime Minister do it? He did it because he thought that he was not going to be in office much longer and, while he was there, he was determined to show who was the boss. He was not prepared, as Chairman of the Board, so to speak, to go back at the behest of another director and try to make the Board change its mind. . . .[26]

To Macmillan personally, the liquidation of Salisbury signified – in the words Salisbury himself had used when tendering his resignation – the removal of 'a very tiresome and inconvenient colleague'.[27] But it was more than just that; it also represented a triumph over all the slights and humiliations at the hands of Cecil and Cavendish grandees that Macmillan had suffered in the 1920s and 1930s – a kind of break with the past.

Within a few months of the Salisbury crisis, another break with the past occurred that was infinitely more painful for Macmillan. Since the issue of conversion to Catholicism had divided them back in 1915, when Macmillan had backed away at the eleventh hour, Macmillan and Ronald Knox had gone their different ways, and over the intervening years they had seen little of each other. Then, in 1957, came the news that Knox – now Monsignor – was dying of cancer of the liver. Macmillan was much moved. In June he arranged for Knox to have a second opinion from Eden's doctor, Sir Horace Evans, and housed him at No. 10 during the tests – which offered no hope. According to Knox's niece and biographer, Penelope Fitzgerald, the Prime Minister 'made him feel marvellous', and then accompanied the condemned man in person to Paddington. 'Harold Macmillan', recalled Knox, 'saw me off at the station himself, and the station-master took off his hat to me twice before the train left.' Macmillan wished him a comfortable journey. Knox replied: 'It will be a very long one.' Macmillan said, 'But, Ronnie, you are very well prepared for it.' Penelope Fitzgerald recognised that this generous gesture meant a great deal to her uncle. On 24 August Knox died.[28]

Suez Liquidated . . . Storm Clouds Again in Syria

The critical two-day debate on Suez, the 'water-jump' Macmillan dreaded, took place on 15 May. As he had confided to Eden, 'The Suez problem is now reaching a new crisis and we are in great difficulty. . . .'[29] Macmillan was forced to sell a compromise, worked out with the Americans, that he, and the majority of the Tory Party, would have found totally unacceptable nine months earlier. In April Macmillan was still indulging in wishful thinking, hoping 'for enough pressure on Nasser to bring him down'. At the same time, privately he was saying that on the 'water-jump' he and his government would themselves 'very likely fall'.[30] Predictably Salisbury joined the Suez Rebels, but that sting had been drawn by his resignation over Makarios. Right-wing critics were partially mollified by the coincidental testing in the Pacific of Britain's first H-Bomb. Macmillan was also helped by being able to announce the final abolition of unpopular petrol rationing, to take place in November, and the clearing of the Suez Canal – as well as by the inept fumbling of the Opposition's attack. Even the redoubtable Bevan proved ineffectual.

When the vote was taken, the government had a clear majority of 49, with only fourteen Tories abstaining. Macmillan rated it 'a great triumph for Ted Heath'; however, after the vote was taken, it was the Prime Minister for whom the Tory benches stood up and cheered: 'At the Speaker's chair, I turned and bowed. It was an extraordinary and spontaneous act of loyalty, which touched me very much. How odd the English are! They rather like a gallant failure. Suez has become a sort of Mons retreat. . . .'[31] In fact Macmillan's power in debate had become one of the government's major assets. In the Commons at the time, Emrys Hughes for the Opposition designated it the 'most spectacular retreat from Suez since the time of Moses'.[32]

Macmillan was exhausted. The next day he stayed in bed all morning, 'reading an indifferent novel – well written but not worth writing – by L. Kaufman, *Six Weeks in March*'. Thus, with a sigh of relief on Macmillan's part, ended the not very 'gallant failure' of Suez. Despite all the heat and fever generated in 1956, it was plain to him that Suez would no longer play any serious role in the next General Election.

Barely had the Suez debate ended, however, than a fresh storm burst in the Middle East – precipitated by Soviet penetration of Syria. In conformity with its tradition of exploiting, and moving in to fill, any vacuum wherever it might occur, the Russians appeared to have taken advantage of Suez to infiltrate Syria. At the same time, in Syria's small and weak but prosperous Lebanese neighbour, there were the first signs of widening splits between Moslem and Christian communities, and between pro-Western and pan-Arab factions; they were to prove tragically lethal in distant years to come, but more immediately looked enticing to a Soviet-backed intervention from Syria. The familiarity of the pattern was to return with multiplied force in the 1980s.

In August 1957, with Lebanon emitting strong distress signals, alarm seized Dulles and from then until the Washington Conference two months later a highly secret correspondence evolved between Macmillan and the US administration, in which Macmillan expounded to the (now by no means unreceptive) Americans some of the 'hawkish' views about the Middle East that he had held in the previous year. It began with his statesmanlike and prescient letter to Dulles of 28 August, in which he wrote that he felt sure 'that this Syrian venture is only one step in the Russian game, and that their aim is to extend Communist control bit by bit throughout the Middle East . . .'. In his opinion Khrushchev would prove:

> a more dangerous man even than Stalin. Under his direction we must expect continual Russian pressure but always by subversive tactics; by blackmail, not military operations. We have found an answer to the threat of war with all our mechanisms, inventions and military organisations. But we seem to be unable to deal with this method of infiltration, which brings about Communism by an internal coup.
>
> The next stage, then, may be an attempt to subvert Lebanon and Jordan by the same methods. If we do nothing, both of these countries might easily fall. Then I suppose the pressure will turn against Iraq, a country outwardly firm but inwardly subject to great tensions. . . .

Revolution there would prove Macmillan right the following year. He then stressed how 'When we built up NATO together, there was no great economic injury which the Russians or their satellites could inflict on us. But the Syrian pipelines are at present most important to the economy of Britain and of Europe. . . .'

Macmillan ended by talking about a possible 'operation' to drive Communist influence out of Syria. If such were successful, 'It would be an open defeat for Communist expansion,' and encourage all the friends of the West in the Middle East. On the other hand, if it were unsuccessful, 'it would be the greatest possible disaster. The neighbouring countries who are wavering would go over to the Russians, and Iraq would collapse. . . .' Such an operation, for which there must be no possibility of failure, 'ought to be undertaken by Syria's Arab neighbours, led if possible by Iraq . . .'. But how could a 'reasonable *casus belli*' be found; or could the 'neighbours' be invited in by internal anti-Communist forces?[33]

On the following day, the able new British Ambassador in Washington, Sir Harold Caccia, replied, giving Dulles's views. He agreed with Macmillan that any such operation 'once started must succeed'; and that 'if such an operation started in circumstances which the U.S. approved, the U.S. would feel committed to make sure that it did not fail.'[34] It was altogether a most propitious moment for Macmillan to visit Eisenhower on his home ground. Caccia told him that the atmosphere was such that 'almost anything might be decided, however revolutionary'.

In another personal telegram for the Prime Minister from Caccia that same day, Dulles committed himself another notch, while his British interlocutor – still nursing burned fingers from the previous year – expressed cautious scepticism:

> he would understand it if we preferred to stay out and leave this to the Americans. For what we might think it worth, his answer to any British accusation would be that we did not last year give the United States Government a chance of working out a plan together in which they could take a part or at least acquiesce.
>
> . . . On this occasion he did not think that the situation in Syria could be righted without the use of force. . . .
>
> . . . My impression is that Mr Dulles is trying to screw up his courage to act. As is his custom, he has allowed himself a great number of escape routes. . . .
>
> . . . If anything goes wrong, you may be sure that Mr Dulles will place the blame elsewhere. . . .[35]

It was indicative of how, despite the new 'spirit of Bermuda' and the forthcoming 'Washington honeymoon', suspicions about Dulles and untrustworthy intentions lurking in Foggy Bottom were still rooted in British minds.

On 6 September, Caccia was reporting (again direct to Macmillan, *not* through the normal channel of the Foreign Secretary, Selwyn Lloyd) that Dulles had told him that the '. . . C.I.A. had been asked to reexamine the possibilities of internal action in Syria. He was not hopeful that they would come up with anything, but this was a final measure to establish that a point had been reached at which military action was the only resort. . . .'[36] In the midst of these highly secret exchanges, Macmillan confided to his diary: 'the responsibility cannot really be shared with the Cabinet.'[37]

The next day, 7 September, a memorandum arrived, via Caccia, from Macmillan's Private Secretary, Freddie Bishop, who had been sent off to liaise in Washington:

> The United States judges that Syria has become, or is about to become, a base for military and subversive activities in the Near East designed to destroy the independence of those countries and to subject them to Soviet Communist domination. . . . This same view is taken by the governments of all the five nations bordering on Syria, as well as by the United Kingdom. . . .

It continued: 'If any of Syria's Arab neighbours were physically attacked by the Sino-Soviet *bloc*, the United States, upon request, would be prepared to use its own armed forces to assist any such nation or nations against such armed aggression. . . .'[38]

Here, in effect, was traced out the cornerstone of the new Eisenhower Doctrine that would bring US marines into the Lebanon the following year – representing both a dramatic shift in US policies as well as a turning point in Middle East history.

Continuing Problems in the Middle East

Meanwhile, in the small Gulf emirate of Muscat and Oman, Macmillan was fighting a minor war to head off a Nasser-supported revolt – without active US assistance. Aided by his son-in-law, Julian Amery, currently a junior minister at the War Office with special expertise stemming from his wartime experience with SOE (Special Operations Executive), and deploying its peacetime successor, the SAS (Special Air Service), in some highly secret actions, over the next two years Macmillan succeeded in pacifying the Oman rebels. It was an operation which he regarded with considerable personal pride to the end of his days.

But the Middle East continued to simmer over Syria through the autumn of 1957, and on 22 September, Macmillan noted in his diary:

> The fact is that the friendly Arab States (Iraq; Jordan; Lebanon) are weak internally and uncertain what to do. . . . King Hussein

[of Jordan] is anxious to start real pressure on Syria, by whose subversive and brigand forces he is all the time threatened. Even King Saud is said to be alarmed at the spread of Communism. All the same, nothing is done. . . .[39]

Macmillan decided to try to play down the crisis, and not hold a special Cabinet – because 'People will think it's about the Financial and Economic crisis. Moreover, I think the Cabinet took the vital decisions on Syria some weeks ago when they agreed to work hand-in-hand with the United States.'[40] Two days later, however, he was sending a note to Duncan Sandys at the Ministry of Defence – 'Personal', 'Top Secret' and 'not to be shown to the Chiefs of Staff'. He wanted the latter to provide an answer to the specific, but obliquely put, question: 'In the event of Iraq finding itself at war with Syria and Egypt attacking Iraq, if Iraq calls upon us under the Treaty to come to her aid, what military measures should we be able to take and what military consequences might be entailed?' He continued: 'It would be assumed for this purpose that the United States would also be bringing help to Iraq and would be taking military measures against Egypt. . . .'[41]

Macmillan's anxieties over the reliability of the Americans in the Middle East, despite the joint agreements recently reached, were revealed in a further letter to Eden, of 2 October: '. . . I confess to being very troubled. The Americans may be learning but they are playing their hand abominably and allowing the Russians to take trick after trick. . . .'[42] By mid-October Dulles was making fresh brinkmanlike noises warning the Soviet Union that, if Turkey were attacked, the US would not restrict herself to a 'purely defensive operation', and Russia would not be left in the position of a 'privileged sanctuary'. Then, on 29 October, Khrushchev at a party given by the Turkish Ambassador in Moscow jovially declared that there was no threat in the Middle East at all, and that the whole matter had been misconstrued. By the end of the year, in Macmillan's words, 'the bubble burst,' and – though only for the next few months – the crisis came to an end. Thoughts about a joint 'destabilizing' operation against Syria were pigeonholed; Dulles, said Macmillan, 'appeared satisfied with his experiment in brinkmanship'. In the light of the exchanges quoted above, and not least Macmillan's own hawkish contingency planning, the remark was perhaps rather less than fair.

In his memoirs published in 1971, Macmillan summed up the Middle East balance sheet:

It seems difficult today, when the Western world has been forced to accept not merely increasing Russian influence in Syria and Iraq, but the almost complete control of Egypt supported by a considerable fleet, to realise the concern which was felt in Washington and London at the first serious manifestations of Russian penetration into the Eastern Mediterranean. With all our efforts, we achieved at this period no conspicuous success. But this change in American policy from the autumn of 1956 to the summer of 1957, if belated, was at least dramatic.

Defence Reform and Sandys

Meanwhile, defence issues continued to occupy much of Macmillan's attention. On the first day of the May debate on Suez, the London papers were full of news of the explosion of the first British H-Bomb on Christmas Island in the Pacific. The previous month, the government had published the 'Sandys White Paper'. It was the most drastic of any White Paper on Defence since the end of the war. On 24 November 1956, only a short time after the last shots had been fired at Suez, and while he was still Chancellor of the Exchequer, Macmillan had addressed a long 'Top Secret' memorandum to the then Minister of Defence, Anthony Head. It encapsulated the whole philosophy that was not only to dominate Macmillan's Prime Ministership, but also to lay down the basis of British defence policy for many successor governments. Beginning with the statement that 'we face the most difficult economic situation in our history', with further heavy drains expected on Britain's already weak gold and dollar reserves, and industry threatened with dislocation by the shortage of oil, Macmillan argued the pressing need for economies in government expenditure, and looked to the defence budget for 'substantial' savings. From earlier soundings about defence cuts, he understood that 'the service departments felt that more was being asked of them than was reasonable' – but now he needed even *greater* savings'. Given this, he continued to Head,

45

'should we not now re-examine the bases on which our present defence policy rests?'

Macmillan then proceeded to list the 'order of priorities' for defence that had been outlined in October 1955, which he thought would be difficult now to keep unaltered, particularly in the light of the Suez experiences. The first – 'to prevent global war' – meant in fact the deterrent: the V-bombers and the nuclear weapons for them, and a ballistic missile and its warhead.

> The true Deterrent (that is, to the outbreak of war with Russia) is the Americans' possession, actual or potential, of these weapons on a far greater scale than anything that we could manage. Fortunately, until they possess an inter-continental ballistic missile, it would seem greatly to the Americans' advantage to be able to station their offensive weapon over here. As long as this is the position, however, there can scarcely be any question of our using Deterrent weapons unless the United States does so too.

From this, Macmillan suggested, the conclusion was that Britain's deterrent force required to be no stronger 'than the minimum necessary to convince the Americans, once they have been made fully aware of our economic difficulties, of our sincerity as allies . . .'. He conceded that:

> we should prepare against a time when the Americans may no longer need to use the U.K. as a base. But we ought to use every possible effort to get the Americans to share as much as possible of the knowledge they have acquired, or may acquire, about ground-to-ground ballistic missiles, as indeed about defence R & D generally. The relief which this would afford to our overstrained scientific resources would yield double or treble dividends.

In succeeding talks with Eisenhower, and later with Kennedy, this last paragraph was to contain the essence of what Macmillan most wanted from the Americans.

On the second and third 'priorities' – 'to maintain, and improve our position in the cold war' and 'to win any limited war, should it break out' – Macmillan thought 'a pretty drastic overhaul' was needed, which he hoped would be accomplished partly through

NATO. He suggested ceasing 'altogether to think in terms of local wars other than those fought under the auspices of U.N.O. – or, let us say, in conjunction with our American allies'.

The result from this rethinking, Macmillan hoped, was that 'we should soon be able substantially to reduce the Forces' manpower requirements.' In particular, he suggested major reductions in the forces in the Middle East and Far East:

We may have to run some risks regarding our lines of communications; but if, as appears, we cannot be at all certain of using our present bases in time of war, is there any real object in paying out large sums for garrisons or as 'key money' to the local landlords? There may in any case be other, cheaper, ways of attaining our ends (especially if the Americans would help).

Finally, he turned to the last 'priority' – 'to survive global war' – for which 'we must still be paying out huge sums . . . – in Europe, on Fighter Command, and on the Navy.' He acknowledged that this was partly seen as a 'secondary deterrent':

but in our present position we cannot afford to carry too many insurance policies. We cannot hope to emerge from a global war except in ruins. Surely, therefore, it is best to cut out of the defence programme all preparations for global war that we can without losing our power to influence world affairs or alienating our essential allies – whom we should, of course, try to carry with us.

Macmillan signed off by asking Head for an early discussion of these proposals for a new defence policy, stressing the 'urgent need to make real economies'.[43]

Head was appalled. Because of his commitment to the armed services, combined with his feeling that in the memorandum too much reliance was being placed on the nuclear deterrent, he knew at once that he would not be the man to implement the cuts required. On the day that Macmillan took over the premiership, Head recalled being summoned by him and asked if he 'could keep manpower down to "X" and costs to "Y"'. Macmillan told him to:

. . . 'Come back and tell me at 4pm.' I said, that afternoon, that I couldn't do it, that it would be a betrayal of the forces . . . so

> I had to resign. Perhaps it was just a neat way of getting rid of
> me, knowing that I couldn't accept the cuts. . . . I thought the
> forces would be pleased that I stood up for them, but they weren't;
> they got Sandys instead, whom they couldn't bear! . . .[44]

Head, according to his Labour successor, Denis Healey, was
'shattered' to learn that his job was going to be given to Duncan
Sandys.[45]

There was, however, no doubting that, from Macmillan's point
of view, Sandys was the ideal choice for the bloody work that
lay ahead. A tireless worker, ruthless and extremely tough, often
showing a certain brutal disregard for the sensibilities of others,
Sandys had justifiably earned the reputation of being the 'hatchet-
man' in successive governments. What Macmillan frequently used
to describe as Sandys's *cassant* manner' was perhaps in part attributable to the fact that a wartime leg injury left him in pain much of
the time. In personality he was probably the only man who could
be a match for Earl Mountbatten, First Sea Lord and the services'
most articulate spokesman, and the service chief who would play
the longest and closest role in the 'Sandys Reforms'. According to
Mountbatten's official biographer, Philip Ziegler, the First Sea Lord
came to feel a 'grudging admiration and even affection for his
termagant Minister. He found him obstinate and truculent in
defence of his views, but ready to listen to counter-arguments and,
once convinced, stalwart in his support.'[46] The two men shared the
somewhat *recherché* bond of being members of the conjuror's Magic
Circle. For Macmillan, much as he disliked his often downright
rudeness, Sandys was 'a very tough man – he wouldn't have any
nonsense . . . and was – quite simply – good at any job you gave
him to do. . . .'[47]

Sandys's first battle began with the navy, which had had him in
its sights as an enemy from the moment of his appointment in
January 1957. The former First Sea Lord and fiery war hero, 'wee'
Rhoderick McGrigor, wrote warning Mountbatten that, in the eyes
of Sandys, the navy 'is a luxury the country cannot afford'. In
February, Mountbatten was reporting to a fellow admiral 'a pretty
good tussle with Duncan Sandys just now. . . . Her Majesty's
Government intends to reduce defence expenditure ruthlessly. . . .'[48] Mountbatten, being Mountbatten, was prepared to
resort to any weapon to fight his case. He prepared a draft letter to

send to all admirals, in the event of the Navy Vote being cut to £290 million, proposing his own resignation and asking that no one else should agree to step into his shoes. He even went so far as to prepare to canvass support of the US admirals.

By July Macmillan had detected the hand of Mountbatten behind various intrigues that were afoot, and newspaper gossip of Cabinet 'splits' on defence: 'The First Sea Lord is a strange character and tries to combine being a professional sailor, a politician, and a royalty. The result is that nobody trusts him. . . .'[49] Nevertheless, over the course of the ensuing years, the Macmillan–Sandys–Mountbatten triumvirate was to prove a remarkable team in re-shaping Britain's defence structure.

As often happens in the course of horse-trading over defence cuts, things did not turn out quite as badly as predicted. Under heavy pressure Sandys retreated conspicuously on the issue of phasing out Britain's aircraft-carriers, although he had come to office believing them to be 'expensive, vulnerable and largely irrelevant to national needs'.[50] By the end of the year, a kind of compromise would be reached. But when the Defence White Paper was published on 4 April, the country gasped. It represented the most radical change ever made in peacetime. The most startling proposal was the abolition of National Service, so that by the end of 1962 the armed forces would consist only of volunteer regulars. The resulting reduction in numbers would cut the armed forces from 690,000 to 375,000 over a period of five years. The forces in Germany (to the accompaniment of loud wails from France and Germany) would be reduced from 77,000 to 64,000, while the tactical air force there would be roughly halved. But a major expansion of RAF Transport Command would enable Britain to fly reinforcements swiftly to trouble spots – a policy decision of lasting importance. The navy's last four battleships would disappear, though it was Macmillan's intention not to run down strength east of Suez. Home defence was slashed to the bone – on the pessimistic, or realistic, assumption that there could be no effective protection for the civil population against the dreadful new power of the H-Bomb. The financial saving in the current year would not be enormous: only £78 million. But the effect would be cumulative.

The overall aim was a strike force that – as Macmillan explained it – would be smaller, more streamlined, more mobile, better trained and better equipped, more efficient and more cost-effective.[51] With the first British H-Bomb about to be detonated, Macmillan's emphasis, then and always, lay very much in dependence on the nuclear deterrent – the policy of 'big bangs and small forces', the pros and cons of which have been vigorously debated ever since. As Macmillan declared: 'we must rely on the power of the nuclear deterrent or we must throw up the sponge.'[52] There was no 'Middle Way' here, and Macmillan stuck rigorously to his conclusions about the deterrent for the rest of his career.

Three main strands made up Macmillan's defence philosophy. The British armed forces badly needed to be modernised, to be brought out of the Second World War era into the nuclear and post-colonial world; although this had been on Macmillan's mind since his frustrating days at the Ministry of Defence, the message had been brought home with particular force by Suez. Secondly, at the back of Macmillan's reasoning, as always, there lay memories of the horrors and wastage of the First World War, the destruction of his generation, followed by the material and moral exhaustion wreaked by the Second World War upon his country. The danger of repetition had to be avoided at all costs, and to achieve this Macmillan was convinced that the only solution lay in a nuclear deterrent. Thirdly, and more immediately pressing, was the question of financial savings. The urgency of this Macmillan expressed in a letter to Salisbury just the week after he had entered No. 10, following a session with that all-powerful figure, the Governor of the Bank of England, who had 'stressed very strongly that unless some reduction can be made in the total burden [of the defence budget], it will be very difficult to hold the pound in the Autumn. If we lose the pound, we lose everything. We have put our last reserves into the Government line. We cannot borrow any more dollars. . . .'[53]

Financial strictures do not always prove the way to obtain the most effective military force, though they are usually found in the backdrop to most such reforms, certainly in modern times.

Among Macmillan's critics, Denis Healey – then Labour's leading expert on defence – considered, in retrospect, that he was right to abolish National Service; but wrong to cut the services without also cutting their tasks.[54] Anthony Head always regretted that conscription was not kept on the statute books – 'just in case a volunteer force couldn't produce the necessary manpower numbers'.[55] Many years later Macmillan himself expressed some regret that the principle of National Service had been abandoned: 'I think we made a mistake; we should have kept it for six months, something like the Swiss, just to teach soldiers the simple things. . . .'[56] However, in 1957, at a time without unemployment problems, the electoral support for ending National Service was quite unmistakable. And that was an imposing enough argument in itself.

Such was the controversy aroused by the Sandys White Paper that it ran into thirteen 'final' drafts before at last passing through Parliament, and in late December Macmillan was noting in his diary a persisting conflict: 'A tremendous discussion on the future of Fighter Command. The S. of S. Air and the CAS are in a very excited, resigning mood. . . .'[57] The battle spilled over into 1958, and beyond, with Macmillan frequently expressing doubts about the personality of Sandys and its effects on the service chiefs. In June 1958, he noted: 'The row about Defence Reorganization gets worse and worse. . . . the real truth is that Duncan Sandys, although an able and efficient minister, is disagreeable and *cassant* in relations with other ministers or officials. . . . I think he must have German blood.'[58]

In irritation, Macmillan found that the arguments with the Chiefs of Staff had become 'almost theological'.[59] At this point, he found a robust ally in the retired Field-Marshal Montgomery – who had spoken up strongly to Macmillan while Macmillan was himself Minister of Defence for the need of tri-service integration. Part of the 'theological' argument also involved a certain amount of self-interest; top-ranking generals did not want to see their ranks – as well as their authority – devalued, as seemed threatened by such reorganisation. In the medium term, some of the Macmillan–Sandys reforms were to be thwarted; nevertheless, under Sandys's drive and aggressiveness, the foundations for an integrated Ministry of Defence were laid. As Macmillan later remarked: 'We failed, yes. The services were too strong . . . but Duncan had prepared the ground.'[60]

The Nuclear Bomb, Sputniks and Windscale

The explosion of Britain's H-Bomb, the keystone of Macmillan's deterrence strategy, in April 1957, brought with it a new set of political headaches, including the burgeoning of the Campaign for Nuclear Disarmament. This was, at various times, to split the Labour Opposition almost as effectively as Rutherford had split the atom. At the beginning of April, Macmillan recorded how Gaitskell had 'made a shameful surrender' to the left wing of his Party, by switching his position to call for a postponement of nuclear testing. Two months later, he noted that Aneurin Bevan 'had really declared himself' on the H-Bomb: 'he thinks the H-Bomb can be an electoral winner of the Socialists and worked up into a sort of Peace Ballot Campaign. I fear he is right.' Then, at the Labour Party Conference in October, Bevan reversed his position 'with a passionate defence of the H-Bomb!' The trades union leaders also 'voted solidly *for* the Bomb! Of course, all this is very satisfactory from a National point of view. From a narrow political point of view, it makes them more dangerous. . . .'[61] Macmillan was swift to spot the political mileage that might be made out of Labour divisions over the H-Bomb, as well as the latent dangers. At the same time he was sensitive to the seriousness of the public debate on the Bomb. After a row in the Commons headed by Bevan on 4 June, Macmillan directed a reflective memo to the minister responsible for the government's public relations, Charles Hill: 'I wonder', he cogitated, '. . . whether all this propaganda about the bomb has really gone deeper than we are apt to think. . . .'[62] In his memoirs he recalled vividly the Aldermaston CND marches, when 'the genuine anxiety about nuclear arms, amounting almost to hysteria', reached a crescendo in England. But there was almost a note of flippancy as he remarked on the 'embarrassing moments' when young protesters began to lie down in front of his car: 'my wife had a robust contempt for such antics, and when she was driving me accidents were with difficulty avoided. However in the contest of wills she was generally successful. . . .' This often meant, in practice, the recourse to blistering language from the wheel. In December, he recorded the anti-Bomb campaign shifting to an attack on its being in the hands of the US Air Force based in Britain: 'All the pro-Russians and all the pacifists and all the sentimentalists (inspired by the clever politicians) have tried to work this up into a sort of "finger on the trigger" campaign. The only thing is to remain quite calm and see it through. . . .'[63]

There was, however, nothing basically flippant in Macmillan's awareness of the depth of real concern about nuclear holocaust.

The mounting danger of mutual annihilation was shortly to provide the impetus for a new initiative to the Russians.

Meanwhile, on 4 October, a unique 'bleep-bleep' reached the world's ears from outer space. The Russians had successfully launched into orbit mankind's first satellite, *Sputnik I*. The implications were that the Russians now must have a rocket capable of delivering the H-Bomb in an inter-continental missile, thereby putting themselves ahead of America for the first time in the nuclear arms race. The news sent unprecedented shock-waves through Western capitals. But, to Macmillan, it also provided a tactical advantage of considerable importance in the next round of his talks with Eisenhower, scheduled to start in Washington in less than three weeks' time.

He prepared the ground in a letter to the President: 'Dear Friend,' it began, '. . . what are we going to do about these Russians? . . . This artificial satellite has brought it home to us what formidable people they are, and what a menace they present to the free world.' Macmillan went on to question whether the free world was really equipped to meet the new Soviet challenge. It had tremendous resources to do so, if it acted together, said Macmillan, coming to the point: 'Has not the time come when we could go further towards pooling our efforts and decide how best to use them for our common good. . .?'[64] What specifically Macmillan was after was the repeal of the much resented McMahon Act of 1946, which forbade the American government to share nuclear know-how with Britain (or any other ally). A relaxing of the American restrictions, and a return to wartime co-operation, could reduce the heavy costs of Britain's future defence, even though she had now successfully produced her own (albeit crude) H-Bomb.

On the night of 10 October, the very day that Macmillan wrote his letter to Eisenhower, a completely unexpected event occurred which – had its full implications been known to the Americans – might well have struck a mortal blow at Macmillan's endeavours to have the McMahon Act repealed; or at least he feared it might at the time. A major fire broke out at Britain's infant nuclear reactor at Windscale, Cumbria; it has subsequently become apparent that the cloud of radioactive contamination thereby released, though small in comparison with that sent up by the explosion at Chernobyl in April 1986, was much more menacing to life than the fall-out caused by the melt-down at Three Mile Island in the United States which so shook world opinion in 1979. Contamination was spread across England, Wales and northern Europe, and milk banned from 200 square miles around the plant, with an evacuation of local people also considered. The affected pile was sealed off like a tomb, and never subsequently re-entered. Because both public and press were less instructed in the significance of nuclear disasters, the episode passed away with little furore. But there was another factor.

A thorough-going report was called for from Sir William Penney, the scientific genius behind Britain's nuclear weapons programme; it was available on 29 October, just after Macmillan's return from his successful visit to the States. When Macmillan read its conclusions – they raised grave charges that the accident (like Chernobyl many years later) had been caused by the faulty judge-ment of the staff and faulty instruments – his immediate reaction was that it could seriously jeopardise attempts to co-operate with the United States in developing Britain's nuclear weapons, by shaking confidence in British technical ability. He made only the briefest references to Windscale in his diaries, and those did not find their way into the memoirs. On 30 October, he recorded no more than:

> the problem remains, how are we to deal with Sir W. Penney's report? It has, of course, been prepared with scrupulous honesty and even ruthlessness. It is just such a report as the Board of a Company might expect to get. But to publish to the world (especially to the Americans) is another thing. The publication of the report, as it stands, might put in jeopardy our chance of getting Congress to agree to the President's proposal. . . .[65]

Eight days later, he noted simply that he had 'published a long White Paper (the substance of Penney's report) and this seemed to satisfy the House. At least, no-one asked about publication in full. . . .'[66] (The Opposition was at the time, conveniently, dis-tracted by another kind of leak: over the bank rate.) In fact, Macmillan had instructed the Atomic Energy Authority not to permit any leakage of the Penney report, to the extent that all prints of it obtained from the Stationery Office were to be destroyed; so even was the type used by the printers.

When interviewed thirty years later, Lord Plowden, Chairman of the Atomic Energy Authority at the time of the Windscale accident, defended Macmillan's decision to hush it up – on the grounds of what it might have done to endanger moves in America to share her nuclear secrets with Britain.[67] Thus the world's worst nuclear accident to date went largely unnoticed. Macmillan did, however, secretly warn President de Gaulle in a personal letter about the Windscale accident, to alert him to the dangers which could arise in French installations of the same type. In retrospect, it seemed a rare piece of Anglo-French co-operation, for that time.

To Washington . . . McMahon Repudiated

On arriving in America on 23 October, Macmillan found that the impact of *Sputnik I* 'has been something equivalent to Pearl Harbor. The American cocksure-ness is shaken. . . .'[68] Exceptionally, President Eisenhower and his policies were under severe attack, while Dulles was even more unpopular. Things now looked so sombre in the Middle East that American public opinion had come increasingly round to the view that Britain had been right over Suez, Eisenhower and Dulles wrong. Eisenhower was sorely in need of the support of a friend at that particular moment; his staff advised him that the meeting with Macmillan could go a long way towards recapturing America's lost international prestige. Meanwhile, since Bermuda, the personal liking and respect of the two men for each other had blossomed, to the point where relations between them were already as warm as those between Eden and Eisenhower had been cool. The President was prepared to listen to the Prime Minister. On top of all this, only the week before Macmillan's arrival, the Queen had made an immensely successful visit to Virginia to take part in its 350th Anniversary celebrations. 'She has buried George III for good and all,' commented Macmillan.[69] There could hardly have been a time when the British were more welcome in the States.

Macmillan was at once impressed by just how dramatic had been the reversal in relations since the previous October. Meeting the British entourage, Dulles immediately launched into a speech about how America now realised that she could no longer stand alone, 'still less "go it alone"'. Macmillan responded appropriately, 'with quite a romantic picture of what US and UK could do together . . .'. Eisenhower, he felt, seemed 'much better than at Bermuda. He was brisk, confident, and seemed more sure of himself. He complained a good deal about "politicians" and the attacks upon himself. (This is a new experience for him. Up to now, he has been immune.). . . .' The preliminary talks, however, were a trifle disappointing: Macmillan thought that the only point that got home was when he warned Eisenhower that if, together, they could not get things done over the next two or three years, 'with all the advantage of our close friendship, it was unlikely that our successors would be able to do the job.' Macmillan returned to the British Embassy 'tired – and a little depressed. Foreign Secretary was more hopeful. . . .' That night he hardly slept at all.[70]

The next day was more encouraging, with a plenary meeting of both teams held in the confines of the Cabinet Room of the White House. This meeting in the White House made Macmillan, once again, think of his American mother: 'how pleased my mother would have been to see me, as British P.M. in the American Cabinet Room, addressing a meeting presided over by the American President. . . .' Allen Dulles, head of CIA, then gave a sombre appreciation (endorsed by his British counterpart) of Soviet military potential, reckoning that the West could now reckon on no more than three to five years of nuclear superiority. At the end of the meeting, the President astonished the British by producing out of his pocket a directive setting up two joint Anglo-American committees, one dealing with collaboration on weapons, the second with nuclear co-operation. In effect, it spelled out 'the end of the McMahon Act – the great prize!' The directive was released to the press that night.

Macmillan recorded that he 'could hardly believe my ears' that such rapid progress had been made. As part of the deal, he agreed that the British would not press for admission of the Communist Chinese to the UN – long a source of concern in Washington – without the agreement of the US. In return, the US agreed to regard Hong Kong as a joint defence problem.* The meeting had gone on to draw up a Declaration of Common Purpose, a solemn and imposing undertaking which exactly conformed to the second of

* This particular part of the Washington agreement was kept secret for a long time. In 1970, when Macmillan presented the draft of Volume IV of his memoirs for security vetting by the Secretary to the Cabinet, Burke Trend, he had his knuckles mildly rapped (this was not the only time) over his inclusion of this information, and was requested to remove the offending passage.

Macmillan's objectives in Washington – to achieve a joint policy on ways of countering Soviet aggression or infiltration, notably in the Middle East. There were, evidently, attempts by US atomic experts to water down the agreement dealing with the McMahon Act, but – noted Macmillan – 'the President stood by his words.' Eisenhower even went so far, shocking some of his entourage, as to describe the restrictive act as 'one of the most deplorable incidents in American history, of which he personally felt ashamed'.[71]

On 25 October, as the Washington Conference ended, Dulles came to see Macmillan off at the airport. 'The job is done,' Macmillan recorded with moderate understatement, 'and I must frankly say better done than I expected.'[72] By good fortune, the Secretary-General of NATO, that staunch Atlanticist the Belgian Paul-Henri Spaak, also happened to be in Washington and was able to lend his warm endorsement to the Eisenhower–Macmillan Declaration. Macmillan then flew on to Ottawa, in high delight, to report on the Washington talks to the new, Conservative, Canadian Prime Minister, John G. Diefenbaker, whom he praised (at least initially) as 'a man of courage and high principle'; who 'resisted any expressions of "jealousy" and who seemed to appreciate the high plane' to which Macmillan had tried to raise the level of the talks.[73] While in Ottawa, Macmillan stayed in the Governor-General's residence of Rideau Hall, where he had courted young Dorothy Cavendish in 1920. It awoke mixed emotions in him: 'It was very thrilling – but rather sad too. . . . I sent her a telegram (it is sad that she is not with me) before leaving.'[74]

There were two postscripts to the 'Washington honeymoon'. On 3 November, the Soviets launched a second, larger satellite; this time with 'Little Lemon', the unfortunate dog that was to become world famous, inside it. Macmillan noted that this second satellite:

has created much alarm and despondency in U.S. The English people, with characteristic frivolity, are much more exercised about the 'little dawg' than about the terrifying nature of these new developments in 'rocketry'. Letters and telegrams were pouring in tonight to No. 10 protesting about the cruelty to the dog. . . .[75]

The impact on the Americans – though possibly less fanatic dog-lovers than the tender-hearted British – was, if anything, even more considerable than that of the news of the first Sputnik in October, and went far to underline all the elements of technical collaboration which had been agreed between the British and Americans in Washington.

Finally, the Washington visit was followed by a more sombre personal note: on 25 November Eisenhower suffered another slight stroke. Once again, he made a rapid recovery but he admitted to Macmillan in a private letter that he had suffered 'a marked "word confusion" with also some loss of memory of words alone'.[76] For Macmillan, the apparent debility of both American leaders, Eisenhower and Dulles, was a considerable worry.

At the beginning of December Macmillan was still voicing concern in his diaries about whether in fact Britain was going to get the nuclear know-how she needed from America. But, by 3 July of the following year, the McMahon Act – which the British had felt, long and bitterly, had reneged on the agreements of atomic collaboration made during the war when they had been an equal partner in the 'Manhattan Project' – was finally buried. In its place was signed the Agreement for Co-operation on Uses of Atomic Energy for Mutual Defence Purposes – one of the most mutually beneficial accords ever achieved in peacetime between Britain and the USA. Under it Britain was able to receive technical information on production of nuclear warheads, as well as fissile material. She was also the *only* nation to be so privileged – to the great chagrin subsequently of President de Gaulle. It meant, in practice, that Britain would be able to produce smaller and more sophisticated warheads for her own deterrent missiles, and be able to purchase atomic-propulsion plants for her first nuclear submarines. (On the other hand, it was not only a one-way traffic; US technicians were 'amazed' to discover the level of nuclear know-how the British had already achieved on their own.) On the broader plane, the 1958 Agreement, by 'the very act of nuclear-sharing', in the view of one expert, Andrew Pierre, 'created an environment in which American trust in the British government deepened so that American officials discussed a wider range of military and political topics more frankly with their British counterparts than with officials of other friendly nations.'[77] It lay at the heart of a new and lasting relationship, without which British victory in the Falkland Islands twenty-five years later would have been unthinkable.

The spectre of Suez had been effectively buried at Washington in October 1957. As Macmillan noted in his diary at the end of the year: 'The Americans, of course, are now completely converted – too late – and wish devoutly that they had let us go on and finish Nasser. . . .'[78]

On what Macmillan had achieved with the Americans by the end of his first year in office, the encomium written by Randolph Churchill was hardly excessive:

Among the most serious consequences of the Suez débâcle was that it nearly destroyed the Anglo-American alliance. It was one of Mr Harold Macmillan's greatest acts of statesmanship that he was able to heal the breach so very soon after he became Prime Minister. . . .[79]

Nor was it an excessive hyperbole for Macmillan to entitle the chapter in his memoirs that recounted 1957's last round of talks with Eisenhower, 'Honeymoon at Washington'.

Chapter Three

'Little Local Difficulties'
1957–1958

Let's be frank about it; most of our people have never had it so good. Go around the country, go to the industrial towns, go to the farms, and you will see a state of prosperity such as we have never had in my lifetime – nor indeed ever in the history of this country. What is beginning to worry some of us is 'Is it too good to be true?' or perhaps I should say 'Is it too good to last?'

(HM, Riding the Storm*)*

. . . I thought the best thing to do was to settle up these little local difficulties and then to turn to the wider vision of the Commonwealth. . . .

(Statement to press, 7 January 1958)

On 17 October 1957, Macmillan wrote to Michael Fraser, the head of the Conservative Research Department, 'Dear Michael: I am always hearing about the Middle Classes. What is it they really want? Can you put it down on a sheet of notepaper, and I will see whether we can give it to them.' The answer swiftly came back that the 'middle classes' wanted something that, because of the economic facts of life, no government would be able to give them – a return to the comfortable standards of life of pre-war days, which had fallen drastically '. . . both absolutely and/or in relation to the rapidly rising standards of the manual workers. They also feel,' added Fraser, without mincing words, 'that Conservative Governments, who should understand their problem, have not shown them much sympathy . . .'. Fraser's suggestion was that the only way the higher income brackets could be helped was by a reduction in direct taxation; but, '. . . Our tax reductions so far have been virtually nullified by the rise in the cost of living. . . .' However, for the bulk of the 'middle class', those with incomes below £1000 a year in 1958, the problem was much more difficult. Their desires were 'largely negative', wanting the government to ' "bash the other fellow" '; a reduction in direct taxation would help but little – most important was 'to maintain a stable price level'. Fraser continued with a recommendation that would not have been out of place in a Thatcher manifesto of thirty years later: '. . . to encourage "aspiration" by gradual adjustment of the Welfare State so as to make it more and more a matter of helping people to help themselves. . . .'[1]

Fraser called to see Macmillan at Downing Street on 22 February to discuss his paper, noting in his diary incidentally that the Prime Minister '. . . looks ten years younger than he did as Chancellor'.[2] As a result, he followed up with a second paper on 25 February,[3] further drawing attention to one sector of the middle classes that was in particularly desperate plight; those who were living on fixed incomes and pensions, and they particularly needed tax reliefs and exemptions. In the Thorneycroft Budget of six weeks later, Macmillan showed that he had heeded Fraser's recommendations,[4] but the solution was to prove as elusive to Macmillan as it was to most of his successors.

In all the remarkable turnaround in Tory fortunes the one persistent dark area remained the British economy. When one stands back and looks at the whole post-1945 course of British history, from Attlee to Thatcher, there hangs the same glum backdrop, with a bleak consistency not to be found in any other of the developed countries. The bankruptcy left by the war was one ineluctable fact. Then there were the union leaders demanding always just that much more than in other countries, their demands seldom related to productivity; and management that was often complacent and inefficient, comparing poorly with its opposite numbers in France and West Germany. The British *malaise* was deep-rooted: the young men of the 'entrepreneurial classes', who in Germany might have gone into BMW or Mercedes, did not seek their future at Cowley, but instead left Oxbridge with degrees in History, English and Estate Management, to enter the civil service or 'go into the City' or to farm. Meanwhile, successive Chancellors of the Exchequer had to juggle constantly with narrow margins of balance-of-payments, with inflation versus the incentive to expand, with taxation versus saving – and the ever present menace of devastating strike action. The only factor not present in the Macmillan years was massive unemployment; although there were times (as when in 1962 it reached the alarming peak of 800,000) when the threat seemed real enough.

The financial inheritance of Suez was also a forbidding one. In the Cabinet at the beginning of February 1957, the warning was made that the economic situation 'remained serious, for nearly all the available support for sterling had been mobilised. If the budget showed the £500 m. deficit forecast, it might be necessary to devalue sterling. . . .'[5] With accelerated American financial support, however, the picture had begun to look brighter by the time of the Budget in April. At this, his first (and last) budget, Peter Thorneycroft was even able to make some £100 million worth of tax cuts. Pressed hard by Macmillan, these included important concessions for companies operating abroad and surtax reductions on higher incomes – a measure vigorously attacked by the Opposition. Macmillan was pleased by the reception of the Thorneycroft Budget: 'It was an admirable speech. . . . The Opposition seemed rather dazed; our chaps were very pleased.'[6] Press comment was on the whole favourable. But the skies were soon clouding over again, with a fresh – and unexpected – run on Britain's gold reserves, which developed as a result of the weakness of the French franc with its root causes in the Algerian War, coupled with a new surge of strength by the rumbustious Deutschmark. At the end of May, Thorneycroft sent Macmillan a minute expressing alarm at the Treasury having liabilities of £4000 million and assets of £830 million. Macmillan attempted to soothe his Chancellor's fears, but ended his reply: 'Of course we are spending too much and we must go on with the credit squeeze. But I think we must also be selective.'

Talking two decades later, shortly after her own accession to the premiership, Mrs Thatcher (though hardly a supporter of Macmillan economics) remarked on how, 'somewhere towards the end of that second half of the 1950s, people got the idea that things were going to go on steadily improving, and they were. . . . [But] people somehow got the idea this steady increase would go on forever. . . .'[7] Macmillan was very aware of this problem; as he confided to Nigel Nicolson: 'The masses now took prosperity for granted. . . . The country simply did not realize that we were living beyond our income, and would have to pay for it sooner or later. . . .'[8] It was because of these worries that Macmillan uttered his famous *obiter dicta* often quoted and even more often misquoted, on 20 July 1957, to a large crowd in a Bedford football ground:

Let's be frank about it; most of our people have never had it so good. Go around the country, go to the industrial towns, go to the farms, and you will see a state of prosperity such as we have never had in my lifetime – nor indeed ever in the history of this country. What is beginning to worry some of us is 'Is it too good to be true?' or perhaps I should say 'Is it too good to last?' For, amidst all this prosperity, there is one problem that has troubled us – in one way or another – ever since the war. It's the problem of rising prices. Our constant concern today is – can prices be steadied while at the same time we maintain full employment in an expanding economy? Can we control inflation? This is the problem of our time.

He continued with this warning:

The great mass of the country has for the time being, at any rate, been able to contract out of the effects of rising prices. But they will not be able to contract out for ever, if inflation prices us out of world markets. For, if that happens, we will be back in the old nightmare of unemployment. The older ones among you will know what this meant. I hope the younger ones will never have to learn it. . . .

The haunting ghosts of Stockton in the 1930s were never to leave Macmillan, and undoubtedly if ever there were to have been a choice between *modest* inflation and the threat of a return to chronic unemployment, he would not have hesitated for many seconds. He wrote in his memoirs, on acceding to power,

> as I knew from my year in the Treasury and was to learn from the rest of my active life in politics, to maintain the British economy at the right level, between inflation and deflation, balancing correctly between too much and too little growth, was a delicate exercise. . . . It was not a subject to be solved by mathematical formulae, or exact calculation. It was like bicycling along a tightrope. . . .

But, during the Macmillan years, the alternatives were never so black-and-white. As a modern economist, Peter Oppenheim, points out, over the years 1952–64 in Britain retail prices rose by only about 3 to 4 per cent per annum, which was almost entirely due to 'the "normal" functioning of the UK economy', while – compared with later times – 'In the fifties and sixties price inflation as such was a nuisance rather than a menace, and its main impact was on the balance of payments.'[9]

Trouble with the Unions

More worrying even than inflation throughout 1957 was the constantly lowering menace of trades union discontent and major strike actions. So grave had this become that Macmillan had actually contemplated having to cancel the all-important March meeting with Eisenhower in Bermuda. All that the government's repeated warnings about 'Mr Rising Price'[10] seemed to do (he noted) was 'to *scare* the city and the foreign bankers without producing much effect on the T. Unions'.[11] The government's recently announced scheme for an independent Council on Prices, Productivity and Incomes had made little appeal to the trade union leaders. Macmillan's diary over the period tells a depressing but not unfamiliar tale:

> *15 March:* . . . the industrial position is very gloomy. Nothing can stop the shipbuilding strike. . . . Engineering; railways; coal-mines; power stations – this is the dreary sequence threatened over the next few days, threatening a General Strike. Yet I feel sure the men, apart from their Communist leaders, don't want anything of the kind.[12]

On 19 March, on the eve of departing for Bermuda, Macmillan and Macleod took part in a highly secret meeting with industrial leaders in an attempt to break the strike impasse, at which General Sir Brian Roberts (Chairman of the British Transport Commission) was persuaded to 'settle the railways at any reasonable figure – say 4% – as soon as possible. He would *not* be regarded as having sold the pass by private industry if he did this. On the contrary it was essential to get this out of the way as soon as possible. . . .'[13] Macmillan noted that the strike threats were already having a very damaging effect on the pound. On 2 April, there was a patch of blue sky; the shipbuilding and engineering strikes were called off: 'This is very good. Another hurdle surmounted – and no concessions.'[14] This last claim was, in fact, only true in part; the railwaymen had been bought off at 5 per cent, 2 per cent more than recommended by Sir John Forster's independent report. In July a thoroughly unhappy Cabinet agreed to accept 'altogether another £42 m. a year raised from the public, to pay *wages* . . .'.[15] On 2 August, Macmillan had recorded that after talks about the economy, 'Everyone is so exhausted at the end of a really terrible year that the Cabinet began to wrangle and almost to quarrel. So I sent them away. . . .'

Six weeks later, because of inflation and the falling pound, and under extreme pressure from the Bank of England and Thorneycroft combined, Macmillan yielded to allowing – against his better judgement – the Bank Rate (currently at 5 per cent) to rise 'by 2% – a thing practically without precedent . . .'.[16] Prices on the London

Stock Exchange slumped dramatically; the press, Macmillan noted, 'seemed dazed'.[17] But, by the time it recovered, a further slide of 7 per cent away from the Tories was registered. Gaitskell demanded an emergency debate on the financial crisis, but Macmillan was able to reject this with a skilful dig: '. . . I reminded him gently that this was, of course, necessary in 1947, when the £ was devalued!'[18] There was going to be no devaluation from the fixed rates of 1957.

The week after Thorneycroft had raised the bank rate to 7 per cent, his 'Shadow', Harold Wilson, wrote alleging a 'leak' which had led to some substantial private gains being made on the Stock Exchange. On the eve of the Tory Party Conference it looked like an opportunity not to be missed, and with his usual tenacity Wilson refused to be put off the scent by any government denials. On 7 October he called to see Macmillan and demanded that an independent judge should make an enquiry and not the Lord Chancellor as Macmillan had proposed. After discussing it with the Lord Chancellor, Kilmuir, Macmillan 'decided to reject Wilson's rather impudent demand and ask him to produce his evidence to the Lord Chancellor . . .'.[19]

By November Wilson was pointing a finger at Oliver Poole, the Deputy Chairman of the Conservative Party. Poole immediately asked for his name to be cleared by a formal enquiry, and Macmillan was compelled to set up a full-scale tribunal under Lord Justice Parker. After elaborate, and costly, investigations and much pother, the report published finally on 21 January proved all the charges to be 'wholly false and altogether unsubstantiated'. Wilson's allegations were tracked down to indiscretions between two minor civil servants picked up by a journalist, and to gossip in a railway carriage by a nineteen-year-old secretary, with the suitable name of Miss Chataway,[20] who had been employed for just one week in Conservative Central Office. The findings of the Parker Tribunal resulted in considerable humiliation for Wilson, and even for Gaitskell himself. Although in Australia at the time, Macmillan with some brutality ('Harold Wilson should be shown up for the mean little creature he is,'[21] he told Peter Carrington, then UK High Commissioner in Canberra) cabled Butler to ensure that the maximum political punishment be inflicted in the Commons.

Nevertheless, the rise in the bank rate represented the first exchange of shots in the battle shortly to explode between the Prime Minister and his Chancellor. Macmillan states that he had argued that the 'spectacular rise in the Bank Rate' was not the best way to deal with the run on reserves, and that 'this situation was already better and was not really the main issue'. He adds '. . . I deeply regret that I did not stick to my point. . . . Nevertheless, I stored up this incident in my mind and was determined not to yield indefinitely to pressure.'

The industrial clouds were not to disappear. In November, Macmillan was recording in his diaries: 'the Transport claims are gathering – buses, railway clerks, and the NUR etc. The timing is as bad as possible for me – with my proposed visit to Australia in January.'[22] After a visit to Paris the following month, Macmillan found himself reflecting with envy on the comparative good fortune of France, for all her political instability and in the ever mounting anguish of the Algerian War:

> The mass of peasants and bourgeois classes have (under their beds) more gold than the gold and dollar reserves of the Bank of England and H.M.G. The French Government and Bank have nothing. The French 'rich' classes have two or three times this wealth in Switzerland, and are continuing to export capital. Here, it is the opposite. Such wealth as we have, the Bank and the Government get hold of – and dissipate! Which country, France or England, is intrinsically the stronger?[23]

On the 8th, Macmillan had written a firm statement of principle on wage claims to the Cabinet:

> The most important of the general principles is simple, namely that, while we have no intention of interfering with the established processes of collective bargaining and will continue to accept the awards of arbitration tribunals, we shall refuse to create more money to finance wage awards which are not matched by increased output. This is the cardinal proposition; and on this proposition we should rest. . . .[24]

Despite his determination to seek consensus, however, rather than confrontation with the unions, Macmillan found himself under pressure to slide from this rigorous declaration of fundamentals, while at the same time increasingly drawn into direct arbitration with them. It was here that the precedent of the union bosses trooping in for beer and sandwiches at No. 10 – accepted as the reasoned voice of consensus politics under Macmillan, but carried on to excess under Harold Wilson – began to establish itself.

Immediately on coming to office, Macmillan found himself confronted by a formidable adversary in the shape of Frank Cousins, General Secretary of the powerful Transport and General Workers Union from 1956 to 1969. As with those other British trades union dinosaurs of the 1960s and 1970s, the name of Cousins has largely disappeared into the limbo of history; nevertheless at the time it sent regular shivers down the backs of government leaders. Cousins represented a kind of geological fault in the British trades union system, which had hitherto been dominated by moderate right-wingers such as Citrine, Deakin and Tewson, and with Cousins was now to experience a major shift to the left. By comparison with those before him, Cousins was the Arthur Scargill of his day; though not nominally a Marxist, this fact was barely noticeable from his policies during the Macmillan era. During the TUC Conference of September 1957, Macmillan noted in his diaries: '. . . Mr. Cousins has declared war on everyone and everything. This does not necessarily make things more difficult. . . .'[25] Events of the succeeding year were to make this last sentence sound perhaps unduly optimistic. Under the influence of Cousins, the delegates to the TUC Conference had carried by acclamation his motion rejecting wage-restraint in any form. In his memoirs,[26] Macmillan commented that the General Council 'gave no advice on this matter and offered no collective opinion. *Plus ça change.* . . .' He went on to record that it was useless having 'a head-on confrontation with the unions if an inflationary situation was at the same time creating an ever-increasing demand for labour . . .'. The key question was whether the Macmillan government was going to prove capable of controlling inflation. With Frank Cousins calling the shots, however, avoiding confrontation was going to be no easy matter in any event. After the railway dispute had been settled at the upper limit of 5 per cent the previous April, provoking accusations of the selling of passes, Macmillan had noted with just concern that 'Although the men have gone back to work pretty well, there is an ugly feeling in the industrial world. This is political, and inflamed by the Communists and left-wingers. . . .'[27]

'Little Local Difficulties'

In the clamour of their demands, the trades unions were undoubtedly aided by the fact that, at the end of 1957, it was still the threat of a world recession – and not inflation – that most preoccupied Macmillan, with his ever vivid memories of pre-war Stockton. He was equally influenced by a determination not to devalue the pound. The mantle of Maynard Keynes rested heavily on him, reinforced by the readily available advice of Keynes's champion, biographer and intellectual heir, Roy Harrod.[28] A copious correspondence was maintained between the Oxford economist and the Prime Minister, and as he states in his memoirs, 'encouraged by my old friend, Roy Harrod, I still resisted the idea of deflation as a permanent or even prolonged policy. . . .' He also noted that, during the late 1950s and early 1960s,

> Inflation ran at the rate of about 2½% a year, which is what Keynes always said to me was about right. If you had *deflation* of 2½% a year, ultimately the claims of the creditors become too great (after all, the creditor doesn't create wealth – it's the entrepreneur). If you have permanent *deflation*, the entrepreneur is destroyed, and the creditor makes too much money. If, on the other hand, you have a permanent *inflation* that's too high, it's not fair to the savers, the creditor, who is normally in the saving classes. . . . So Keynes always said, between 2½% to 3%, then nobody would notice. . . . And this we achieved. . . .[29]

This was the argument central to the dispute between the Prime Minister and the Chancellor of the Exchequer, Thorneycroft, and his team at the Treasury, and it was the argument that Macmillan, rightly or wrongly, would still be waging against the Thatcherite monetarists three decades later.

On 22 December 1957, a Sunday, Macmillan entered in his diary:

> . . . I went to London after tea and had a long talk with the Chancellor of the Exchequer. He is very worried about the Civil Estimates, which show a great rise for 1958–9. . . . Most of this is due to inescapable causes – the old (being pensioned), the young (at school) and the agricultural subsidies which rise automatically as world prices fall. (This, of course, is a gain to the

balance of payments but a loss to the Exchequer.) The Chancellor wants some swingeing cuts in the Welfare State expenditure – more, I fear, than is feasible politically.[30]

The following day, his last entry for 1957, Macmillan noted, after a long and heated discussion with a small group of ministers,

The Chancellor is feeling in a very determined (also resigning) mood. The rest are bitterly opposed to his main proposal, which is to abolish the Children's Allowances and thus save £65m. (2nd child only.) I summed up impartially, but laying most stress on the need to win the battle on the wages front. We must not be deflected from this.[31]

Thorneycroft was demanding that a cut of £153 million be made. Macmillan sent his ministers back to their drawing boards over Christmas. By the first week in January, economies amounting to £100 million were agreed, and Duncan Sandys pledged to find another £5 million. This still left a gap of £50 million, equal to approximately £400 million by values of the late 1980s, and not a great sum even in 1958 terms. But, says Macmillan in his memoirs, 'The Chancellor of the Exchequer held to his view with almost fanatical rigidity.'

This rather bland statement in fact papered over some extremely rough passages. Macmillan recapitulates in his diaries:

6 January (Monday): Since Christmas, a crisis has been developing, slowly but inexorably, in the Cabinet – as far as I can see, carefully planned by the Chancellor of the Exchequer and the Treasury Ministers. As far as I can judge, the Treasury officials have had no hand in it and have disapproved of it. It came to a head this morning, when a formal letter was sent to me by the Chancellor of the Exchequer, offering his resignation.

Thorneycroft's letter (which was clearly written some days ago (the date of the month was typewritten – the day filled in by hand!) was accompanied by letters from Birch (Economic Secretary) and Enoch Powell (F.S.T. [First Secretary to the Treasury]). . . .

On the Friday Cabinet (which lasted 4 hours) Thorneycroft behaved in such a rude and *cassant* way that I had difficulty

in preventing some of the Cabinet bursting out in their indignation. . . .[32]

Thorneycroft, a highly successful and energetic businessman, had
a manner which had already drawn Macmillan's disfavour two
years previously, with a diary entry that 'He shouts at one (with
a cockney accent) as if we were a public meeting';[33] while in later
life – affecting an amnesia with which he was certainly never afflicted
– Macmillan would refer dismissively to him as 'that man who looked
like an English butler, with the nice Italian wife – I forget his
name. . . .'[34] Birch he regarded as a 'natural intriguer';[35] while to
Macmillan, distrustful of the classical logic that spellbound others,
Enoch Powell always remained the 'fanatic'. (After Powell returned
to the fold as Minister of Health in 1960, Macmillan instructed the
Secretary to the Cabinet to have Powell transferred from his prescribed seat at the Cabinet table, on the grounds that 'I can't bear
those mad eyes staring at me a moment longer!'[36]

Macmillan's diary entry for 5 January 1958 (a Sunday) continues:

I saw the Chancellor at 10.30 am. and made an appeal to him –
on personal and public grounds – not to threaten us any more
but to tell the Cabinet that he would work along with his
colleagues and accept the collective view. . . . He looked uncomfortable; said he had not finally made up his mind; but I got
the impression that he had made up his mind to resign, unless
he got his full demand. (It struck me that he was in an excited
mood, and he has obviously been pushed on by the Treasury
Ministers.)

On Monday the 6th, the discussions continued:

This Cabinet – though less painful – was no more fruitful than
Friday's. Defence Minister stated his position very clearly. He
would do all he could to help further, but must warn us that to
abandon the pay and allowances proposals for the services would
mean the loss of any hope of all-regular forces; the resignation of
S of S War and of CIGS. . . . Chancellor re-stated his position
very firmly, but less offensively than at earlier Cabinets. He left
the door open, but made it clear that he would not accept much
less than the full £150 m. . . . Lord Home (who had not been at

Friday's Cabinet, where Chancellor had behaved really disgrace-fully) could scarcely conceal his rage – and contempt. . . .[37]

The Cabinet reassembled at 10.30 that night for about forty minutes, while Macmillan summed up, and then 'quietly dispersed'. Mac-millan notes that it was clear to him by dinner:

> that the greater danger was the complete disintegration of the Cabi-net – Treasury Ministers; Defence Ministers; Labour and Social Ministers – all might resign (for different reasons) and there would be no alternative to the resignation of the Government; a Labour administration; a dissolution; an election in which the Conserva-tive party would be in a hopeless and even ridiculous position, without policy or honour. This must at all costs be avoided.[38]

The prospects looked grim.

On the following morning (Monday, 6 January) – 'an extraordi-nary day' – Macmillan received Thorneycroft's bombshell:

> at 10.30 I received (without any covering note of personal regret) a formal – and very contentious – letter of resignation[39] from the Chancellor of the Exchequer, together with 2 letters from EST and FST. Thorneycroft's letter was in brutal terms, calculated, if unanswered, to do the maximum injury to sterling. It sought to give the impression that he alone in the Cabinet stood against inflation.
>
> Cabinet met at 11. I read out the letter, which was received with a good deal of indignation. We proceeded to other business – of which the new plan for Cyprus was the most important. . . . After Cabinet, I offered post of Chancellor of the Exchequer to Heathcoat Amory, now Minister of Agriculture. He was rather hesitant, but accepted. . . . Butler has been excellent throughout. The Chief Whip superb. . . . the Queen was very sympathetic. She was chiefly anxious about my (forthcoming) Commonwealth tour.[40]

Macmillan's overt sang-froid and detachment with which he cloaked a critically explosive situation was truly remarkable. He let it be broadcast that he had spent the Saturday before the resignation shooting at Birch Grove – while inwardly seething with worry, and not a little anger. On the morning of Tuesday, the 7th, he and Dorothy set off on his five-week-long Commonwealth tour. It was at the airport (where, as a gesture of solidarity, almost the whole Cabinet came to see him off) that he made his famous put-down remark to the press about the Treasury resignations: '. . . I thought the best thing to do was to settle up with these little local difficulties and then to turn to the wider vision of the Commonwealth.' When interviewed on the BBC thirteen years later,[41] Macmillan stuck to the line that he had 'just thought of it', thus maintaining the appearance of a throwaway remark made with the utmost casualness ('More panache than accuracy',[42] was Hailsham's assessment). But, in fact, he had thought it out most carefully, worrying about it throughout most of the previous night. A spontaneous utterance on a matter of such vital importance was simply not in Macmillan's character, and he calculated that it would 'annoy a lot of people, but I think it will give them a sense of proportion. I cannot believe that, if and when the truth is known, Thorneycroft will get much support.'[43]

Although in his memoirs Macmillan claims he was encouraged by the conviction that the economy had nearly turned the corner, nevertheless throughout the Commonwealth tour he was beset with anxiety about the impact of the 'little local difficulties' comment, and the true gravity of the problems it masked. In the event, however, it turned out to be gamesmanship of the highest order – not least for the mood it set in the Commonwealth, to which Macmillan, on the day of his departure, was according a higher priority than a major domestic crisis. Equally, the sang-froid it showed did much to assure the vital issue of foreign confidence in sterling. On the 6th, President Eisenhower had received a call from Dulles, reporting that 'Macmillan had had a bad weekend. Lloyd had appealed for our help to try to underplay the situation. . . .'[44] His new friends in Washington reaffirmed simultaneously the 'greatest admiration' they shared for Macmillan, and undertook to give all the support they could.

Angered by the brusque manner in which Thorneycroft had presented his case, the Cabinet itself was ranged massively on Macmillan's side; so, too, it appears was Sir Roger Makins,[45] Macmillan's old colleague from wartime days in the Mediterranean, whom, while Chancellor, he had requested to be brought home from being Ambassador in Washington to take over as Permanent

Under-Secretary in the Treasury – as it happened, at the height of the Suez crisis. Thirty years later, Makins (who retained an extremely sharp memory of those events) remarked that he still regarded the action of his political chief, Thorneycroft, as incomprehensible: 'It is hardly a point in any Permanent Under-Secretary's favour when he loses all of his ministers overnight.' He found his main responsibility to his chief, and old friend, Macmillan, was (unavailingly) 'to try to prevent my ministers from throwing themselves and the Government overboard'. He thought it absurd to resign over less than 1 per cent of total government spending; while Macmillan's handling of the affair had been 'masterly'.[46]

Once again, as with the Salisbury resignation the previous year (only this time the danger was that much greater), Macmillan displayed superb political acumen, and timing. He was able to leave England, with Butler in charge, and his ascendancy unchallenged. Although Macmillan did not take this ascendancy for granted, it was, nevertheless, a factor of perhaps wider significance than the issue of the £50 million.

A Matter of Principle? A Turning Point?

Who was right? Macmillan or the three Treasury ministers? An assessment seems essential to any evaluation of Macmillan's overall economic policy.

To begin with, although Powell always denied it, Macmillan seems to have been entirely correct in his guess that Thorneycroft had been 'pushed on' by his two juniors, notably Enoch Powell. Shortly before he died, Thorneycroft's successor, Derick Heathcoat Amory, gave the opinion – which was supported by another subsequent Tory Chancellor, Anthony Barber – that he 'would not have resigned but for the terrific pressure put on him'.[47] Years later Powell, never one to admit error, still stuck assiduously to the issue of 'principle'; reviewing the Macmillan memoirs in the *Spectator* of 24 April 1971, Powell stressed that – although it was neither the first nor the last time that 'the weary path of argument was trodden forth and back' – the year 1957–8 possessed:

some of the qualities of a turning-point which the other episodes lack. The year 1957 marked the end of seven years of decline in government expenditure as a proportion of national income. Through the subsequent six years of Conservative and six years of Socialist administration it rose steadily and rapidly. . . . More subjectively, 1958 appears in retrospect the point where the bogey of inter-war deflation was at last de-throned in the British mind in favour of 'growth'.[48]

Returning to the matter of 'principle' in a later interview, Powell insisted that 'it wasn't just £50 million . . . it was the government's own conviction that was at stake. . . .'[49] Why did Thorneycroft resign three months before the Budget?

Because he believed the way to proceed was to reduce government expenditure, not increase taxation . . . therefore he had to fight his battle on the *estimates*, pre-Budget. . . . also, as you recall, the PM was off for several weeks, so the move had to be taken before. . . .[50]

'If I had to criticise any mistake made by Thorneycroft now,' continued Powell, 'I would criticise the increase to the 7 per cent bank rate, because this distracted vision from the rate of government expenditure. . . .'[51] The £50 million had been the 'turning-point', because 'we were trying to reverse a philosophy . . . and were prepared to become monetarists fifteen or twenty years earlier – pre-Friedman.' But, concluded Powell, Macmillan's:

love of the winning trick predisposed him to a theory which hallowed this winning trick – e.g. buying votes for 1959 . . . but I am an unsympathetic witness; I consider that he allowed prejudice to cloud reason and thought – the trickster element in Macmillan was always very repugnant to me. He saw politics as essentially a game, just as Macleod saw it as a game of bridge . . . pure Whiggery. . . .[52]

The third Treasury Minister, Nigel Birch, an ill man who later became virtually blind, and who was increasingly embittered against Macmillan personally, also stressed the matter of 'principle', adding, 'It was the principle of will – you'll never conquer inflation unless you damn well mean to – and Harold hadn't the will. . . . Harold cheated on the figures, to show that it was only a small matter; at the time it did not seem a small matter. . . .'[53]

Curiously enough, of the three it was the most senior, Thorney-croft, who – over the passage of time – seemed the most moderate, almost apologetic, in his views. In the Commons debate on the resignations Thorneycroft defended his decision eloquently:

> for twelve years we have been attempting to do more than our resources could manage and in the process we have been gravely weakening ourselves. . . . over twelve years we have slithered from one crisis to another . . . a pound sterling which has shrunk from twenty shillings to twelve shillings. That is not a picture of the nation we would wish to see. . . . That is not the path to greatness. It is the road to ruin. . . .[54]

When interviewed in 1980, however, at a time when – as Chairman of the Tory Party – he was most deeply committed to Thatcherist monetarism, Lord Thorneycroft was pre-eminently honest in re-examining the wisdom of the 1958 resignations, in retrospect. Although he too underlined the 'principle' factor, by claiming that the dispute '. . . was really more fundamental than a matter of £50 million; (he loved to spend – that was the aristocratic Whig in him – always an element of the rake, rather than the more brutal view of the downhill descent of the country, which was my view. . . .)'. But 'whether we were right to resign I think was questionable. . . .[55] my ideas were very out of fashion in those days, before Milton Friedman – the prevailing idea was to spend your way out of a crisis. . . . I feel that we could have held it, but we probably made our stand too early. . . .'[56]

If Thorneycroft had remained at No. 11, his energy and drive might have made all the difference in galvanising British enterprise particularly at the time of maximum competition from West Germany. None of this, however, diminished the respect Thorneycroft (who two years later came back as Macmillan's Minister of Defence) continued to hold for Macmillan:

> The most educated of all PMs. . . . you tend to carry forward into government your earlier thinking, in his case Keynes; whereas a modern Chancellor might not worry about cutting milk subsidies, he would think back to an era where every glass of milk really mattered. . . .[57]

77

This aspect of the humane element in the political balance of 1958 is reinforced in a letter written on the day of the Thorneycroft resignations by Macmillan to David Eccles, Secretary of the Board of Trade, then on a trade mission in Mexico. Remarking on his 'great grief' that Thorneycroft had 'decided to play the hand in this way', he estimated that it might be 'a very Pyrrhic victory' if the deficient £50 million had been found: 'We might win a few millions for the Exchequer, and lose immensely on the wage front by appearing to take the offensive against the working class. . . .'[58]

Lingering Self-doubts

One of the interesting sidelights of the 'little local difficulties' affair is what it reveals of the true Macmillan – the still lingering self-doubts and insecurity, though becoming increasingly well concealed behind the mask of 'unflappability'.

On his Commonwealth tour Macmillan recorded with palpable relief on 24 January that the Economic Debate in the Commons was followed by an 'excellent majority – 62'. But the following week he was expressing rather more concern:

> Although we did very well in the division last week, it is clear that Thorneycroft made a very good speech and is playing his hand very well. I am beginning to suspect – behind his rough and uncultured manner, rude and *cassant* to an extreme – a deep plot. He may be calculating on another 'sterling crisis' this autumn and the breakup of the Government in conditions which would allow him to seize the leadership of the party from me and Rab. The immediate election, of course, would be lost. But he is young, and could afford to wait for the next. . . .
>
> I am beginning to feel the disadvantage of my absence from London, for it's very hard to keep track of all that is going on.[59]

In the knowledge, with hindsight, of the truly remarkable extent to which Macmillan had consolidated his power base as a result of the Thorneycroft resignations, together with Thorneycroft's own lack of any pretensions to the throne, Macmillan's renaissance suspicions seem groundless almost to the point of absurdity. What is important in this context, however, is what Macmillan *felt* at the time. His apprehensions about Thorneycroft's ambitions even persisted well after his return to England. By 6 May a national bus strike had started, and the railways threatened to follow suit. 'The Chief Whip is very anxious . . . Peter Thorneycroft (with Birch and Enoch Powell) are ready to pounce. . . .'[60] The following week, after much heart-searching, the Cabinet agreed – in order to defuse the railwaymen's menace – to offer a 3 per cent increase, with all its inflationary dangers: 'The Chief Whip is very unhappy about this and obviously thinks it will break the party and allow Thorneycroft to do on me "tit for tat" (like Palmerston on Johnny Russell). . . .'[61] (Reckoning that public sympathy lay with the railwaymen, although other ministers wanted a 'showdown', Macmillan in fact decided to let the 3 per cent increase go ahead.) 'Chief Whip at 10. He says that the Party is being stirred up against our Railway offer by Thorneycroft, Enoch Powell etc. . . .'[62] This was, however, the first time that Macmillan was able to add in his diaries: 'But I am not unduly alarmed. . . .' In fact Macmillan's position could not have been more secure. Now and on many future occasions, Macmillan could turn his back on Westminster with full confidence that he would not get a dagger in it, and this was entirely due to his unique and enigmatic deputy, Rab Butler, who – on a far more considerable scale – played the role that Willie Whitelaw played for Margaret Thatcher.

Rab and Domestic Reforms

With his oriental features making him seem even more inscrutable and devious than he really was, Rab Butler remains one of the most interesting, and baffling, figures of post-war British politics. Among many 'Rabbisms', it was said that he could serve six guests from a single partridge; equally, among Lobby correspondents (by whom he was much loved for his 'leaks') there was an unwritten golden rule: '(1) Never believe anything Rab Butler tells you. (2) Never ignore anything Rab Butler tells you.'[63]

Amazingly indiscreet, conspiratorial by instinct, and with every just grievance against the man but for whom he himself would now have been triumphantly touring the Commonwealth, Rab paradoxically was to remain creditably, and incredibly, loyal.

When one contemplates how, in the Thatcher era, the ink was

hardly dry on the resignation letter of a sacked cabinet minister before he was publishing a bitter book of self-justification, one appreciates to what a different age of Torydom the Rabs and Selwyn Lloyds belonged. In personal terms, Rab never had any love for his chief ('Like him?' he once chuckled to John Mortimer. 'I'd rather you said I admired him'),[64] and his second wife, Mollie, could not bear to be in the same room as Macmillan. Yet, as he remarked to the author in words that seemed to come straight from the heart, '. . . I couldn't deal with Eden, but I could deal with Mac. . . .'[65] Indeed, together they did provide a remarkably complementary team, the like of which has not been seen since in British politics. With a touch of that typical Rab irony, when reviewing the Macmillan memoirs (Volume IV) for the *Spectator*, Butler described his role with a clear eye: '. . . I was left, as so often in these pages for shorter or longer periods, holding what remained of the baby. . . .' He concluded with a reference to Alexander the Great, being informed when in Asia that a battle had taken place between Sparta and Argos: '. . . Alexander had dismissed this by saying that it was a battle between mice and frogs. Fortunately on Harold Macmillan's absences abroad I was able to keep the home front free of such conflict. . . .'[66]

This was hardly an excessive claim. Perhaps one of the fundamental factors underlying this unusual partnership, and which seems worth elaborating, is that – representing divergent strains of Conservatism, as well as interest – there was no competition between the two men from an operational point of view. This divergence was, in fact, probably a source of strength. Parrying criticisms of his indecisiveness, Rab had been heard to protest 'but I'm tough. I'm much tougher than I look. . . .'[67] His listeners remained not entirely convinced, but when it came to dealing with matters of domestic reform that profoundly interested him, he showed himself capable of both toughness and decision, as well as being outstandingly humane. Shortly before Rab died, Enoch Powell (who regarded Butler as 'one of the principal reforming Home Secretaries since the Second World War') recalled how, if he was ever absent for a week or two from his function as Chairman of the Cabinet's Home Affairs Committee, and someone else took the chair, 'It was as if government itself came to a standstill!'[68]

Rab's new empire at the Home Office was one in which, as noted earlier, Macmillan was never more than marginally interested, to put it mildly. Therefore there was no possible area of conflict here. Rab could say, with little fear of contradiction, that over the nearly ten years during which he presided over the Home Affairs Committee '. . . I am glad to say I never needed to call in the Prime Minister to help.'[69] This also presupposed, as far as Macmillan's premiership was concerned, no interference from above. Throughout the copious Macmillan diaries, with all their multifold interests, there is so conspicuously little reference to social reforms – urgently as many were needed – that one is entitled to reckon that they assumed a relatively low position in Macmillan's list of priorities. He could say, with equanimity, 'I left that side all to Rab and Henry Brooke.'[70]

While Rab constantly agonised over capital punishment,[71] in the confines of his home as well as in the Home Office, Macmillan admitted that he was against abolition and 'I don't remember Dorothy ever expressing views . . . it was not her kind of interest.'[72] He had a favourite tease of Rab and his reformist conscience, which ran as follows: '. . . I understand what it is you want to do. You want to popularise abortion, legalise homosexuality and start a betting shop in every street. All I can say is if you can't win the Liberal nonconformist vote on these cries you never will!'[73]

In fact, during Rab's five years of office, moves were made towards liberalising laws on homosexuality; legislation cleared the streets of London of prostitutes; traffic wardens and betting shops made their first appearance; licensing laws were made more flexible; procedures for child adoption were improved. Perhaps most important were Butler's moves towards penal reform and humanisation of Britain's antique prison system. In contrast to criticisms that Macmillan failed to give Rab Butler enough to do, he may have been given too much. Martin Redmayne, Heath's successor as Chief Whip, thought that this had the adverse effect that 'the one who was most capable of constructive thinking at home, in the two years when it was most urgently needed, had no time to devote himself to it.'[74] Rab's most controversial measure – then and now – was to be the Commonwealth Immigrants Act of 1962, and inevitably his liberal reforms brought a backlash from the Tory's 'hanging and flogging' lobby – with a result that, when his post was finally taken over by Henry Brooke in 1962, there was something of a swinging back of the pendulum.

During the first two years of the new government, 1957 and

81

1958, a considerable burden of domestic legislation was also carried out by the Macmillan Cabinet; there were reforms dealing with local government reorganisation, compensation for property compulsorily acquired, loans for small farmers, the future management of the New Towns and opportunities for house ownership which went some way towards the radical reforms promulgated later by the Thatcher government. Macmillan risked a further storm of unpopularity in the country by pushing through the Rent Act, which by providing for the decontrol of many houses and thereby permitting substantial increases in controlled rent appeared to favour the well-to-do landlord. Yet reform here was essential to improving the rundown state of much of Britain's accommodation; even so, public outcry against sections of the Bill dealing with eviction of tenants caused it to be amended, 'with some hesitation and reluctance',[75] by the Cabinet.

Macmillan and Life Peerages

Ever since 1945, the House of Lords and its hereditary privileges had been under attack from various directions. On the left of the Labour Party there were consistent calls for its abolition, and all through the 1950s voices had been raised throughout the spectrum of the Tory Party itself for some reform, or renovation. Although on the right there were equally strong feelings that Britain's unique system whereby hereditary peers were automatically granted a vote in the country's legislation should not be tampered with, by the time of Macmillan's accession there was wide agreement that in this particular field something needed to be done to bring Britain into the twentieth century. Macmillan, the pre-war radical, the crofter's scion married into a ducal family, was clearly the right man to do it – but *what*? The debate raged throughout 1957, until, in February 1958, Macmillan introduced his controversial Life Peers Bill. It was a compromise. The hereditary principle was safeguarded, but it was to be progressively watered down over the passage of time by the extension of the House of Lords to include nominated life peers, with no hereditary rights. Both governing and opposition parties were granted the right to nominate their own candidates, men and women; the latter qualification particularly was to transform dramatically the existing structure of the Upper House.

Putting his proposals to Gaitskell in April, Macmillan found him 'a little embarrassed – his party is again divided about all this. . . .'[76] Nevertheless, the Bill went through, with Labour producing its own half-dozen nominations for the first list of creations published on 24 July; and, for the next three decades at least, the Macmillan life peerage innovation has worked more successfully and harmoniously than most would have predicted at the time. At the top of that first list of ten men and four women in 1958 stood the name of Robert Boothby, who chose the grand title of Baron Boothby of Buchan and Rattray Head; it was an honour that astonished those 'in the know'. When Boothby had written asking for a peerage for his services to politics (with similar insensitivity, he had also evidently expected a Cabinet post), Macmillan's protective Private Secretary, John Wyndham, had pocketed the letter for several days out of concern for the Prime Minister's feelings. But Macmillan's reaction was, 'Of course he must have it.'[77] It seemed a remarkable act of magnanimity towards the man who had inflicted so much personal suffering those many years ago (though, inevitably, there were cynics who whispered that it only reflected Macmillan's disesteem for the House of Lords).

'When in Doubt, Go Away!'

Macmillan was later to recall that when on 7 January he and Dorothy set off on their six-week-long Commonwealth tour, the first (and last) of its kind ever made by a British Prime Minister in office, '. . . I was not sorry to sink my cares, like other holidaymakers, in the pleasures of travel.' Travelling with a substantial retinue (which included the indispensable John Wyndham and his new public-relations adviser, Harold Evans, as well as the Cabinet Secretary, Sir Norman Brook) and covering 35,000 miles and thirty-four different overnight stopovers, it was hardly to be a pleasure cruise.

Reaching back to the 1930s when he had opposed Churchill over India, Macmillan could by no stretch of the imagination be described as an 'imperialist' of the Churchill or Salisbury stamp; nor could he really be described as a Commonwealth-man – though he was abundantly aware of the emotional spark that the Commonwealth concept could still kindle when suitably invoked in domestic politics.

The 1958 tour began stickily, with Macmillan not seeming to be, as Anthony Sampson, an accompanying journalist, described it,

the man best equipped to inspire the Commonwealth. He arrived in India looking old, stiff, and uncompromisingly English. He stepped down from the plane at Delhi airport, straight from the English midwinter into the tropical sun, wearing a dark blue suit, the usual Old Etonian tie, and an expression of nervous confusion; he looked shy as the customary garland was hung round his neck, and anxiously aloof from the hubbub around him. He walked with his slow stiff shuffle as if half in a daze; and he spoke in each country with the same rehearsed phrases: 'My wife and I are indeed delighted . . .' 'This is the first time that a British prime minister . . .' 'This is a unique occasion . . .', with the same lack of expression. He was often nervous, clutching at the bottom of his coat or tapping with his fingers. In the active, hospitable atmosphere of India, he seemed an apparition from the imperial past. . . .[78]

But as the tour progressed, Macmillan's self-conscious nervousness eased. His first port-of-call was New Delhi. He was delighted at constantly meeting Indians who greeted him (he would imitate the accent engagingly) with 'I Balliol man too . . . ', and was gratified to discover how liked and trusted British businessmen seemed to be. Prime Minister Nehru treated him with great courtesy and warmth. In their shared sense of history, they found a bond that was to bring them progressively closer.

At a banquet in Delhi, Nehru endeared himself to Macmillan by speculating, 'I wonder if the Romans ever went back to visit Britain?'[79] Together they also participated in some unvoiced mockery at the expense of Nehru's other house guest at the time, President Sukarno of Indonesia:

this somewhat flamboyant phoenix, who had risen from the ashes of the Dutch Empire. His curious costume, a uniform of blue velvet, with silver stars – apparently a cross between those worn by little Lord Fauntleroy and Liberace – was in strange contrast to his host's simple dress. Moreover his habit of carrying about a sort of Field Marshal's baton (putting it on the sideboard during meals) was, I could see, not altogether appreciated. . . .

The net assessment Macmillan took away of Nehru as a politician was that 'His speeches (or monologues) are 5 or 6 well-tried records – the rise of Asian nationalism; the new Communism in Russia, and its renunciation of war; etc. Nevertheless, he is able, full of charm, cultivated, and ruthless – all great qualities in a leader. . . .' But the highlight of the visit was a 'civic reception' at the Red Fort, where the Macmillans had a 'moving and enthusiastic reception' from tens of thousands of Indians cramming every inch of the Fort. Their spontaneity persuaded Macmillan to tear up his prepared speech, and make an impromptu delivery – 'which "went" well'.[80] Macmillan was beginning to find his feet, with a new confidence.

On to Pakistan, which – after New Delhi – Macmillan found was:

> like going from Hampstead or North Oxford to the Border Country or the Highlands. Iskander Mirza, the robust President of Pakistan and his wife (a Persian lady) are 'grand seigneurs' – very charming hosts, not too intellectual, and good food and wine. (Nehru's food was uneatable. It was European but like a bad boarding house.)[81]

Macmillan was shocked by the poverty, political instability, corruption (Mirza told Macmillan that his last PM had 'scooped' £4 million!), and religious turmoil he saw in Pakistan, with the army its one stable element. Harking back to his 1947 visit, he conjectured sadly how, if the austere Jinnah had lived, he might have held Pakistan together with something of the authority exercised by Nehru; while, if Liaquat Ali in his turn had not been assassinated, he might at least have preserved a constitutional government with some integrity. To him, the bitterness which leading Pakistanis felt towards India was equally sad; 'Partition had indeed dealt a terrible blow to the sub-continent.' He left Pakistan with 'some foreboding'. (A few months later Mirza was deposed by Field-Marshal Ayub Khan and martial law replaced democracy, the first time that the inherited parliamentary system had been breached in a Commonwealth country.)

Ceylon (16 January) was a different story: 'Scarcely ever have I seen such merry faces.' Sinhalese enthusiasm was unmistakable, and the Macmillans 'had royal progresses wherever we went'. The political scene he found 'more like that of Whig politics in the eighteenth century than one would suppose'.[82]

Two days later (and in those days a seven-hour flight), Macmillan was in Singapore for just a one-day stopover. Here a mass of work, worry about Thorneycroft, but on the other hand reassurance in the shape of some 'excellent messages from Butler', caught up with him. Unfortunately, sleeping in an air-conditioned room gave him a bad cold; nevertheless, the stamina he showed was extraordinary. As Sampson noted,

> he was able to spend day after day travelling, speechmaking, talking and listening; he had the politician's ability to switch on to an overdrive, to listen without fully listening. In the evenings he would work at business from London with his private secretaries and the Cabinet secretary, Sir Norman Brook, often till the small hours; the entourage made up a new kind of airborne government.[83]

On the 19th he flew on to Auckland, a gruelling twenty-five-hour flight. Filled with drugs, he slept most of the way – which helped shake off the fever; nevertheless, he still managed to keep a dozen or more painfully handwritten pages of his diary. Both the Macmillans enjoyed and liked New Zealand. For all the immense distance, they felt it resembled home more than any other country and it made him think what:

> Britain must have been like before the sprawling growth of towns and disfiguring tentacles of industry had clawed away so much of our beautiful land. . . . If I were young, nineteen, I'd go to Australia – rather tiresome people, I'd have rows, but I'd get on; but if I were retired, I'd go to New Zealand . . . Boring? You mean you'd be unable to go to Whites?[84]

For both the Macmillans, New Zealand probably represented the high point of the tour.

On 28 January they left Christchurch for Canberra, with much regret and some apprehension. Macmillan began unpromisingly; photos appeared in the Australian press of him looking most uncomfortable with the national emblem, a koala, holding it with nervous uncertainty as if it were a leaking baby. Lord Carrington, the breezy and popular High Commissioner who did much to ease things for Macmillan, recalls how, on arrival he was:

a very unpublic figure . . . he was immensely taken aback by people cheering him in the streets – he had never experienced it before – he used to say at airfields 'I bring you greetings from the Old Country, hello, hello, hello!' It was all very stiff. Then he gradually expanded and loosened up. . . .[85]

By the end of Australia, a marked sea-change had taken place in Macmillan's style. The extroversion and all the noise, noted Anthony Sampson, seemed to break down his reserve, and he became 'suddenly almost jolly'.[86] Driving around in a jeep on a meet-the-people campaign, he would rush up to startled Australians with exclamations like 'How *are* you?', 'Very nice of you to come!'

Already an old-established friend of Prime Minister Robert Menzies, dating back to war days, he made tactful speeches about the importance of a multi-racial Commonwealth, and told his audiences that – as regards the challenge of Communism: 'though we may be able to reduce tensions here and there from time to time, the great struggle and conflict of ideas will continue. We must "lean up against them" – steadily and firmly. . . .'[87]

Macmillan celebrated his sixty-fourth birthday – 10 February – in Tasmania, but by now he was 'beginning to feel the disadvantages of so long an absence', and was anxious to return. Two days later he was winging his way homewards, via Singapore, after a truly tremendous send-off from Australia. There was absolutely no doubt that, by its end, the Commonwealth tour had been an unmitigated success. In one of those egregiously rare personal references to Dorothy that appear in his memoirs, he paid her a glowing and well-deserved tribute:

Our success was largely due to the wonderful support which my wife gave to me throughout. . . . she had at once conquered the hearts of the people by her own special gifts. Naturally reserved, and even shy except among those whom she knew well, the unexpectedly enthusiastic welcome which she was given seemed to have affected her deeply. This was her first experience of an almost royal progress, and it seemed to bring to the surface some of the hidden qualities of her deeply sympathetic character.

Those of his entourage who had observed his progress throughout the nearly six-week-long tour were almost unanimous on the end result. He became, said Harold Evans, his public-relations adviser, 'superbly good with the "Touring Press"'.[88] When he got back to England, the transformation was immediately detected by the press. In the *Spectator* of 28 February, Angus Maude – one of the Suez Rebels and therefore no friend of Macmillan – wrote that he now 'spoke with the attractive diffidence of a schoolboy who had been abroad for the first time, desperately eager to communicate something of the vision he had seen'. In his memoirs Macmillan himself quoted with gratification what one newspaper 'not unkindly said': '"Whatever Macmillan may have done for the Commonwealth, the Commonwealth has certainly done something for Macmillan."'[89] He admitted that he did come back 'inspired with a new ardour and a new faith' – but, perhaps above all, the success of the tour had assured him of the impact he could make in the world outside parish-pump politics. And it had done something for the Macmillan marriage.

'When in doubt, go away,' was the nonchalant motto that Macmillan coined in the aftermath of the Commonwealth tour; in fact, however, the moment he returned he was greeted with the bad news of the by-election at Rochdale. This volatile seat in Lancashire had been held by the Conservatives with a small majority at the 1951 and 1955 general elections. In the by-election, Labour won the seat with a majority of 7000. The Conservatives' gloom was deepened by the fact that the Liberals, who had not bothered to contest the seat at the 1955 General Election, pushed the Conservative candidate into third place. In 1955 the Conservative Member had received 26,518 votes. In February 1958 the Conservative candidate received a paltry 9827, while the Liberal vote was 17,603 and the victorious Labour candidate got 24,928. As Macmillan noted, it was a 'tremendous shock'.

Spring brought Macmillan a fresh challenge from Cousins and the trades unions. On 3 April, he was recording 'the almost certainty of a railway, bus, dock and general road transport strike'.[90] He decided upon tactics of divide and conquer: meet the railwaymen's demands, but confront Cousins's London bus-workers. They had, he reckoned, not got such a good case, in that they had agreed to arbitration and had been offered at least some increase; also, 'while they inflict inconvenience on the public . . . no vital interests were at stake. . . .' On 5 May, the London bus strike began: '. . . I fear we are in for a rough time. . . .'[91] On 10 May, Iain Macleod

(Minister of Labour) called both sides of the railway dispute together; Macmillan commiserated with the difficulty of his position, observing that it was 'a slight farce, when one of the parties is a Nationalised Industry, of which the Government is both equity holder and banker . . .'.[92] Two days later, after considerable nervousness that the Thorneycroft faction might split the government and in the teeth of considerable backbench grumbling, Macmillan persuaded the Cabinet to countenance a 3 per cent increase offer to the rail unions – despite the impact on inflation. It was with 'immense relief' that Macmillan heard that all three unions concerned had agreed to accept the offer, and he reckoned that MPs would find in their constituencies 'a good deal of sympathy for the railwaymen'.[93]

Next, having failed with the railways, Cousins threatened to withdraw 6000 men who drove the oil-delivery trucks, and thus paralyse all road transport, coupled with a threat to stop the electric power stations. Macmillan saw this as 'pure blackmail'.[94] Two days later a six-man TUC delegation called to see Macmillan at their own request. They included the two union secretaries, Vincent Tewson ('nice but ineffective') and George Woodcock ('left wing; intellectualist and therefore tricky, though agreeable'). Macmillan in his diaries described the talks as 'very friendly, but rather ineffective'.[95] However, it was plain to him that the TUC wanted to avoid any spreading of the strike, let alone a general strike, but that 'they have been and still are frightened of Cousins – partly because of his size (one and a quarter million members) and partly because of his character. . . .' They were also desperately anxious that Cousins should be helped out of the position into which he had got himself, if the government or Transport Board could do so: 'All the same,' concluded Macmillan, 'each one of these men individually *hates* Cousins just as much as he is frightened by Cousins. . . .' Meticulously, Macmillan that same day took the Cabinet 'all through the way I had personally handled the Railway problem', and then through the bus dispute. He received evidence that the TUC leaders had been 'pretty firm with Cousins'. Nevertheless, the strike continued, and looked like spreading to the docks. On 4 June, which Macmillan reckoned to be the vital date, he saw the TUC delegates again and 'urged them strongly *not* to widen the strike and give no support to Cousins . . .'. He made it plain, with some force, that the government would make no more concessions. 'It was now clearly a contest of will,' Macmillan wrote in his memoirs. 'Although I had treated the T.U.C. delegates with courtesy and understanding in private, in public we had taken firm action. . . .' The cancelling of weekend leave for selected troops was clear indication of intent.

Cousins continued to bluster, but by 20 June the bus strike had faded out. Macmillan always took great pride in his handling of the two strikes, reckoning that it had been a kind of turning point in the government's fortunes. By the beginning of July, he wrote, 'it was clear to me that the political as well as the economic tide had turned.' His tactically divisive handling of the two strikes appeared to have been vindicated; Cousins had been beaten, and by the next Labour Party Conference his star seemed to have waned; bank rate was further reduced to 5 per cent – and Thorneycroft was quiet. But had victory been purchased at the expense of the pound? It was a question that other British governments would long have to ponder.

Chapter Four

1958: The Year of
International Crisis

*His boredom with issues not concerned with foreign affairs [is]
evident on almost every page, a sharp change from the Tory reformer
of the 1930s and 40s.*

(Baltimore Sun, *21 November 1971*, Dr Donald Gordon's
review of Macmillan's memoirs)

*I may be cynical, but I fear it's true – if Hitler had danced in
London we'd have had no trouble with de Gaulle. . . .*

(HM, *September 1979*)

In 1958 Macmillan estimated that he spent more than half of his working time on foreign problems. These came thick and fast. In May 1958, President Chamoun of Lebanon asked the British and American governments if they would be prepared to provide military assistance within twenty-four hours of his appealing for help. Nasser, noted Macmillan,

> is organising an internal campaign there against President Chamoun and his regime. This is partly Communist and partly Arab Nationalist. Russian arms are being introduced from Syria, and the object is to force Lebanon to join the Egyptian–Syrian combination. . . .[1]

The Cabinet agreed that Britain would join the US in promising President Chamoun the help he might call for. Temporarily these assurances bolstered up the Lebanese. Macmillan continued his diary entry of 13 May with a sombre analogy from the pre-war world of what would succeed the swallowing up of Lebanon: 'after Austria – the Sudeten Germans. Poland (in this case Iraq) will be the next to go. . . .'[2]

Iraq's veteran Prime Minister, Nuri-es-Said, was now the lynch-pin of Western influence in the Middle East – specifically orientated towards Britain which, having created Iraq out of the carve-up of the Turkish Empire in the first place, had always played the role of its patron and protector. As far as the enemy, Nasser, was concerned, Nuri remained even more of a hawk than Macmillan himself, and during a visit he paid to London in February Macmillan had registered alarm at the 'impossible or dangerous schemes' Nuri had voiced for 'detaching Syria from Egypt'.[3] But Nuri's position at home was also far weaker than it looked; as Dulles had warned Eisenhower exactly one year previously, in the aftermath of Suez, Iraq of all the Middle East countries was 'suffering most, since they are the most pro-Western . . .'.[4]

The British Embassy in Iraq appears to have been about as ignorant of what was about to burst from below as were the

Americans in Teheran in 1979. Early on the morning of Monday, 14 July, Macmillan was telephoned by Selwyn Lloyd with the news that there had been a violent revolutionary coup by dissident army units in Baghdad. The twenty-three-year-old King, Feisal – only recently educated in Britain, together with his cousin and neighbour, Hussein of Jordan – had been murdered, so had his uncle, the Regent, Prince Abdulillah. Nuri-es-Said escaped in disguise, but was caught by the mob the following day, barbarously lynched and his naked body paraded through the streets. The British Embassy was invaded and the poorly informed Ambassador forced to seek refuge in a nearby hotel. Iraq had left the ranks of the Western Alliance. The Baghdad Pact was no more. It was, wrote Macmillan, 'devastating news, destroying at a blow a whole system of security which successive British Governments had built up, greatly to the interests of the Iraqi people and supported with generous aid in money, skill and experience'.[5]

The ripple effect on Lebanon and Jordan was instantaneous. President Chamoun appealed to the US and Britain to honour their commitments to send help. The President recorded that he found Macmillan 'completely in accord with my decision, almost eager . . .'. Within a matter of hours the US Sixth Fleet – the same that looked as if it might have interfered with the Franco-British Suez landings eighteen months previously – was approaching Beirut. Despite the dialogue that had started the previous August, it looked as if the Americans were prepared to 'go it alone' – in which case it was a *volte face* that, to Macmillan, represented 'a recantation – an act of penitence – unparalleled in history'. In a long telephone call, over another unscrambled line, that evening Macmillan chaffed Eisenhower: '. . . "You are doing a Suez on me," at which the President laughed . . .'. In fact, the clear difference was that, called in by the ruling government of Lebanon, the US was on good legal grounds under both the UN Charter and ordinary international law. Thus, although there was some heart-searching among the Opposition in Parliament, the Cabinet was unanimous in giving full 'moral support' to the Americans – though nothing more (in fact, nothing more had been asked).[6]

Macmillan in his memoirs claims that he was surprised by Eisenhower's decision for 'drastic intervention', and there remain gaps in one's understanding of the process by which, despite the dialogue of the previous August/September, the two allies ended up acting independently, though in close association, in the Middle East in 1958. As Harold Caccia had put it to Macmillan two months before the Lebanon landings:

> . . . Foster [Dulles] and others here are going through a bout of that chronic American phobia: the fear of being seen alone with the British. They badly want an assignation and a secret liaison. But they are scared stiff that we are going to ask for marriage bells. . . .[7]

The second stage of the crisis began two days later, however, as Macmillan was leaving the Commons at the end of the day's debate. Two telegrams were handed him by his Private Secretary, Bishop, both of them from the King of Jordan and appealing for British help against the Syrian threat in successively more urgent terms. Macmillan summoned the Cabinet and the Chiefs of Staff and by 11 p.m. 'There followed a very remarkable – and perhaps historic – Cabinet meeting in my room in the House of Commons. I don't think I have ever been through anything of the kind. . . .'[8] What the military could offer immediately was 'precious little': 'Two battalions of paratroops to be flown in from Cyprus to Amman, to hold the airfield and give succour to the King.'[9] The discussions lasted three hours, during which time Macmillan telephoned Dulles twice. Dulles – and, judging from the tenor of conversations recorded, some element of strain had crept back into the relations between the two – commented that he thought British action to help Jordan was 'rash but praiseworthy. He could not promise troops, but would give *moral* and *logistical* support. . . .'[10] This although both allies were in fact committed to the same objective. At the end of the discussions, Macmillan called up each minister in turn to express his view, 'without any lead from me. (I was determined not to repeat Anthony's mistake and let them say – if this venture were attempted and proved a disaster – that they had not been properly informed.)' For Macmillan the responsibility was so great that:

> Finally, I asked for ten minutes by myself. I went with Rab and Norman Brook into another room, and tried to make my decision. We all thought the Cabinet were determined to do this rather 'quixotic' act and that we would not forgive ourselves if the

King were murdered tomorrow, like the Royal Family of Iraq. Moreover, the Arab world (on the Gulf, etc.) might be more moved by our inaction than by some reaction to the loss of all our friends in Iraq.

When he returned and asked the Cabinet for their final views, 'All were "for". So I said "So be it." The Cabinet dispersed at about 3 a.m.'[11]

The airborne operation now went forward with extraordinary alacrity compared with all the shilly-shallying that so dogged Suez. Macmillan got to bed at 3.30 a.m., 'having been assured that everything would be done that needed to be done'.[12] But at 8 a.m. he was woken with the appalling news that an unforeseen disaster was confronting the airborne expedition. Through what, in retrospect, seems like an inconceivable, almost *opera bouffe* omission, sanction had been neither sought – nor obtained – from the Israelis for the force to overfly their territory. According to the Macmillan diaries, the previous night Sir Ivone Kirkpatrick's successor as Permanent Secretary at the Foreign Office, Sir Frederick Hoyer Millar – a bluff, relaxed and much loved figure as contented on a grouse-moor[13] as his predecessor, Kirkpatrick, had been burrowing about in the corridors of power – had 'seemed quite sure that the Israeli consent would be forthcoming. Sir F.H.M. had seen the Ambassador. It would be almost a matter of form. (This proved to be a disastrous judgement.)'[14]

In fact, through some extraordinary breakdown in communication (which Macmillan felt would never have happened had not the Foreign Secretary himself been absent in America) nobody had obtained Israeli consent. The next few hours, hideous for Macmillan, seemed to threaten 'a terrible disaster, which would (I think) have resulted in the collapse of all our policies and the fall of the Government . . .'.[15] Years afterwards his Private Secretary, Freddie Bishop, recalled that it was 'I think the only time I saw Harold rattled; it could have caused a real disaster, if the Israelis had shot a plane down.'[16]

Flights from Cyprus, over Israel, had already started during the night, and if the Israelis, in the nervous tension of the time, were conceivably to have intercepted or shot down any of the British planes, the disaster would certainly have been no less than that predicted by Macmillan. The next hours he spent trying to unscramble what had gone wrong, while all the time keeping up a façade that nothing was amiss. His diaries are eloquent on the crisis of the moment:

> Some machines (with about 200 men) had gone into Amman. Then the order was given to stop and other machines had to go back. At 10 a.m. Gaitskell was coming – fortunately he put this off himself till 1. We had tried telephoning (poor Norman Brook spent 3 hours trying to get through). We had tried telegrams. But nothing seemed to get through and certainly nothing came back.
>
> Cabinet at 11. I told them only a little of the difficulties, and then left Rab to carry on the routine business. In addition, all our telegrams to Commonwealth countries, and to NATO countries had gone (when we thought – as F.O. said – that it was a mere form). All had to be stopped, or withdrawn, or halted, or explained away.
>
> What was I to say in the House? I must announce the facts at least, at 3.30. But what were the facts? No one seemed to know. I waited throughout the morning in my study – trying to deal with other work and hide my sickening anxiety. All we knew, was that the Israeli Government was still sitting. Brook (who thought it was his fault) was almost in tears. F. Bishop and the other P.S.s were very kind and sympathetic.
>
> Gaitskell came at 1 p.m. – alone. I was just beginning to tell him about the political situation in Amman; the 'intercepts' and other secret service information which we had got about the Cairo plots in Jordan, when a small bit of paper was brought to me. 'The Israeli Government has agreed . . .'[17]

Macmillan heaved a sigh of considerable relief. There was an 'encouraging call from Anthony Eden', and 'More by good luck than good management, it all turned out pretty well – from the Parliamentary angle. . . .'[18] In fact the government received a comfortable majority of 62. It was no exaggeration, however, when he told the House that 'It had been the most difficult decision that I personally remember having to make.'[19] Typical of Macmillan's principle of never passing the blame to subordinates, the heads of neither Brook nor Hoyer Millar rolled.

A more bombastic telegram from Khrushchev arrived two days

later. It began: 'At the present historical moment the world is on the verge of a military catastrophe and the slightest careless step may entail irremediable consequences. . . .'[20]

And for a few days the West quaked. Meanwhile, the Jordan operation continued to give Macmillan some sleepless moments. Although Eisenhower subsequently claimed that 'During all this time we were in fingertip communication with Prime Minister Macmillan,'[21] the decision had been taken to leave Jordan exclusively to the British, and only support them if they got into trouble. While this showed how much trust had been restored between the two countries since Suez, it also – in the event – left the British considerably at risk. In an urgent communication to Eisenhower on 18 July, Macmillan gave full vent to his anxieties about Britain being committed in a country:

> where our troops will have no port, no heavy arms, and no real mobility. Without your help, our logistic support, passing over a country at least nominally neutral, would be tenuous. If the gamble with the Jordanian Army does not come off our troops will indeed be in a difficult position. . . .[22]

As it was, without American 'support', it was extremely doubtful whether Israel would have agreed to any British airlift. On the 21st, there was a further anxiety for Macmillan with Israel's Ben Gurion complaining that the Israeli permission to overfly was being abused. Macmillan noted in his diary (rather prophetically, as it was to turn out less than a decade later): 'The truth is that an extreme party in Israel thinks Jordan had better "collapse" and that they can then seize all territory up to the West Bank. . . .'[23]

On the 22nd Macmillan was requesting Eisenhower outright to send US troops to help:

> . . . I think we have reached a turning point in Jordan. If we are to hold the position the forces on the ground should be fortified by the visible presence of your troops. We must also ensure the safety of their supplies, and both for political and logistic reasons I am sure that you are in a much better position to do this than we are. . . . It would be disastrous for both you and us if we were forced to withdraw before some settlement has been ensured which will preserve the independence of Jordan. . . .[24]

Eisenhower pacified the Israelis, temporarily, and the sea route via Aqaba was opened for supplies, but a few days later there were fresh worries that King Hussein might be overthrown by a Nasser-sponsored army coup, *à la* Iraq; in which case 'we should have difficulty in extricating our troops. So it is – and will be – a continual worry, until we can get a U.N. force in their place. . . .'[25]

By 21 August, however, this Middle East crisis was defused by an unexpected Arab resolution in the UN which called upon the Secretary-General to make 'such practical arrangements as would adequately help in upholding the principles and purposes of the Charter in relation to Lebanon and Jordan'. With generous gratitude, Macmillan claimed this as 'a great triumph for Selwyn Lloyd'. By the beginning of November, the Anglo-American forces were withdrawn. Iraq had been lost; Lebanon 'saved', for at least the time being – while, in the view of the then British Ambassador in Jordan, Macmillan had been 'entirely responsible'[26] for saving the courageous young King Hussein and his government, at a time when Washington was wobbling badly. 'Defeatism' was the word Selwyn Lloyd used to describe the State Department's attitude of mind at that time.[27] In the short term, Macmillan himself reckoned the results of the operations 'were not unsatisfactory' though at the time it had certainly seemed like a much more close-run affair. He and Eisenhower exchanged warm letters of mutual thanks, Macmillan declaring, 'so long as your country and mine continue to act together in spirit and in deed, as we have over the last months, I am sure we can deal successfully with any eventuality.'

The record of the Anglo-American dealings over the 1957–8 Middle East crisis – as outlined above – do however suggest that when the crunch came, co-operation had perhaps been more in 'spirit' than in 'deed'. Privately Macmillan fretted that US policy in the Middle East 'seemed to be becoming all the time more fitful and uncertain . . .'.

To the Middle East crisis of 1958 there was appended one sad personal footnote. During the Commons debate of July on the murder of King Feisal of Iraq, the ageing Churchill had come to his former subordinate Minister Resident, gallantly offering to help by intervening in the debate. But on the day he had found that he was simply incapable of speaking; it was his last attempt in the Commons.[28]

Cyprus Resolved

As Macmillan had already become painfully aware while Foreign Secretary, in world affairs especially events seldom occur in isolation, but have a knock-on effect. One of the consequences of the Middle East crisis of 1958 had been to create an apparent threat to Turkey by allowing Russia to establish herself on Turkey's southern flank. This in turn succeeded in creating alarm in Ankara, and therewith a new readiness for a settlement over Cyprus. It was almost *pari passu* with the Anglo-American intervention in Lebanon and Jordan that there opened the last stage in resolving what Macmillan aptly entitled the 'Cyprus Tangle'.

During his short period as Foreign Secretary, Macmillan in 1955 had devoted 'much fruitless endeavour' to unravelling this tangle. Then he had taken a fairly classical line; as he had told the Tory Party Conference in 1955: 'Our strategic position in Cyprus is absolutely vital to the protection of the Middle East and to Great Britain's strategic and economic interests in time of peace. . . .'[29] Since then Macmillan's stance had shifted considerably. The year 1955 had ended in impasse, with riots in both Greece and Turkey and relations deteriorating sharply. The Greeks, feeling that EOKA terrorism was paying off, were increasingly intransigent, and the Turks ever more hostile towards their traditional enemy, Greece, and dubious about British intentions; while the US was making unhelpful noises about 'colonialism' on the sidelines. Britain's only success was to keep the issue off the UN agenda. In 1956, Archbishop Makarios was deported to the Seychelles. It was also the year in which, paradoxically, Cyprus reached the apogee of importance in British eyes, and yet, in doing so, was to lose much of it. Suez proved that Cyprus was simply no valid substitute for the Egyptian bases, and – like Egypt – was especially invalid when the surrounding populace was hostile. In December 1956, the Radcliffe Report had first mentioned the possibility of partition, setting off the inevitable hubbub in Athens and enthusiasm in Ankara. With his customary recourse to historical perspectives, Macmillan had come to realise that Curzon's post-1918 annexation had been a grave error without which the island could have been handed back to the Turks, in fulfilment of the lease given Disraeli. But, with Atatürk's mass expulsion of the Anatolian Greeks, many had settled in Cyprus – thereby upsetting the population balance and introducing an insoluble human problem. On 15 March 1957 Macmillan had set down with some clarity in his diary what was to be his settled policy on Cyprus:

> . . . I am as anxious as anyone to get clear of Cyprus. But I think we must try to reduce our liabilities in an orderly way. I am not persuaded that we need more than an airfield, either on long lease or in sovereignty (like Gibraltar). Then the Turks and Greeks could divide the rest of the island between them. . . .[30]

Given Macmillan's condemnation of what partition had achieved for India, and later Palestine, it seems improbable that he seriously countenanced a partition except perhaps as a last resort in Cyprus, but regarded it as a threat with which to push the Greeks into agreement. With hindsight, it may perhaps be thought that it was unwise ever to let the genie of partition out of the bottle.

Two weeks later came the decision to return Makarios to Cyprus on the 'terrible day' of Salisbury's resignation. It now became accepted that, whatever the Archbishop's connections with EOKA terrorism, this wily prelate, who had been the epicentre of so much storm, was the man with whom Britain would have to deal. On meeting him for the first time (when the Cyprus deal was actually agreed, in February 1959) Macmillan was frankly disappointed:

> . . . I had thought of him as a big man – like Archbishop Damaskinos.[31] Not at all; 5'8" or so, at the most. Without the beard, *not* a strong face. Good hands, flexible and artistic. I would have said agreeable, subtle, intelligent, but *not* strong. This explains, perhaps, his hesitation. . . .[32]

The 'Cyprus Tangle' continued to be, for Macmillan, 'one of the most baffling problems which I can ever remember',[33] and dealing with all the factions and variables involved reminded him of one of those children's puzzles where three or more balls had to be got into the right holes, from which one would always pop out. After the 1957 Bermuda Conference with Eisenhower, however, the Americans adopted a more helpful stance towards the problem, with the tide turning slowly more towards an appreciation of the Turkish point of view. With Makarios back, violence instead of decreasing increased, and Macmillan began to move further towards self-determination, but proposing an interval of seven years. Inevitably this plan was rejected (this time by the Greeks, who saw it as leading to partition), which brought Spaak and NATO on to the scene as mediators. With them came the first ideas of independence that eventually were to win the day.

In December 1957, Macmillan took the imaginative – but risky – decision to replace the hard-line Governor and wartime hero, Field-Marshal Sir John Harding,[34] with the more conciliatory and liberal Sir Hugh Foot,[35] to whom he would turn at conferences and say teasingly, 'Now wheel on the idealists!'[36] But Foot's first plan failed in the spring of 1958, this time with the Turks rejecting it in fear that it would lead to Enosis (union with Greece) as soon as Labour came to power in Britain, which was then regarded as almost a certainty within the next year and a half or so. Macmillan now came up with a 'Tridominion' plan, incorporating a constitution that would satisfy Greeks and Turks, and safeguard the remaining British bases, while conceding sovereignty over the rest of the island. By the time this was formulated in the summer of 1958, the Hashemite dynasty had fallen in Iraq, the British and Americans had landed in Jordan and Lebanon respectively, and events in Syria had made the Turks feel extremely vulnerable – and, therefore, more inclined to be conciliatory to their British allies. Meanwhile, with Algeria now beginning to dominate world headlines, the heat additionally was off Cyprus in the anti-colonialist lobbies of the US and UN – especially since Macmillan was making it plain that Britain now saw Cyprus as an international problem, and no longer a purely colonial one. But still months of haggling lay ahead.

In August 1958, in the midst of the Jordan crisis, there was bad news of increased terrorism from Cyprus, with the murder of two more soldiers,[37] one a colonel, and Macmillan decided to make a flying trip to Athens and Ankara, as well as Cyprus. His stay at the British Embassy in Athens brought back some poignant memories from the Second World War.

It has been repainted and the marks of the bullet holes – which were many – removed. Otherwise, it had not changed much since the days of the siege in 1944–45. How well I remember those extraordinary scenes! The evacuation of the front rooms; the snipers' shots if one ventured into the garden; the midnight

> communion on Christmas Eve 1944; the telegram (given to us immediately after the service) announcing the arrival of Churchill and Eden on Christmas Day. . . .[38]

Macmillan started off by lecturing the Greek leaders, expressing his disappointment that they had not accepted the original British plan: 'They had rejected Radcliffe's plan two years ago; now they wished devoutly that they had not. For the Turks had accepted Lord Radcliffe's constitution, which could by now have been in force – with a *single* legislative assembly. . . .'[39] Menacingly, he warned the Greeks that, if they now rejected the new plan, the result would be 'partition in its worst form – territorial partition, with Turkish bases, etc . . .'. It was, indeed, tragically what the more distant future would have in store, following the disastrous interlude of the Greek colonels. Macmillan ended by reminding the Greeks how, as Churchill's representative, '. . . I had seen something of Greek heroism in war, and helped them to the best of my ability in their struggle against Communism, which (without our aid) would have overwhelmed them in 1944–5. . . .' Prime Minister Karamanlis became 'quite emotional', but friendly; in contrast to his last memories of Athens, as Macmillan left for the airport he found the people in the streets 'not hostile, but not particularly friendly'.

In Ankara Macmillan (who, in common with many Britons of his generation, perhaps allowed a classical education anyway to incline him instinctively more towards the Hellenes than the Turks) took an instant dislike to Zorlu, the Turkish Foreign Secretary: 'one of the stupidest – except for low cunning – rudest, and most *cassant* men I have ever met . . .'.[40] Although he found the Prime Minister, Menderes (who was, as well as Zorlu, hanged two years later by the Turkish military), 'certainly more civilised' than Zorlu, he thought the Turkish arguments reflected 'the rather primitive way of thinking which they still follow. Everything is black or white. . . . You are friend or enemy. . . .'[41] Exploiting the Turks' new sense of vulnerability following events in Iraq, and with it the collapse of the protective Baghdad Pact, Macmillan more or less handed them a *fait accompli*: 'we intended to implement our policy, and . . . there was really nothing more to be said.' Back in England a fortnight later, Macmillan was able to note with satisfaction that, following his visit, 'this time the Turks have behaved with great moderation and good sense. . . .'[42]

Moving on to Cyprus itself, amid top security precautions, he visited with delight his old regiment, the Grenadiers, its battalion currently commanded by the son of his old friend from 1915, Charlie Britten. An impromptu parade was mounted in his honour, and he made a brief speech to the Guardsmen. '. . . I found all this very moving and I almost broke down in speaking, for it all recalled so many memories. . . .'[43] After some splenetic speechifying by leaders of the two communities, which Macmillan declined to take too seriously, he left Cyprus with the feeling that agreement looked at last within reach.

In February of the following year, the final act of 'untangling' Cyprus moved to London, when a nearly fatal tragedy occurred: on his way back from an audience with the Queen, Macmillan heard the news that the plane bringing Menderes and the Turkish party had crashed outside Gatwick. Ten or twelve of the Turks were reported to have been killed, though miraculously Menderes had escaped, very shaken. Together with Greece's Karamanlis, Macmillan went to the London Clinic personally to enquire about Menderes; an act that was clearly appreciated by the Turks. When the talks were at last able to proceed, it was the intransigence of Archbishop Makarios that nearly torpedoed the agreements at the eleventh hour, with everything turning on whether he said yes or no; 19 February was, Macmillan recorded, 'An extraordinary day. Colonial Secretary rang at 9 am (followed quickly by Foreign Secretary). The answer is "Yes". The Cyprus agreement is therefore made!'[44] The Greeks, Macmillan noted, were 'delighted' – 'although they realise that they have *not* had the best of the bargain. They could have done better by accepting the Radcliffe plan *or* the Macmillan plan. . . .'[45] They had abandoned their claim to Enosis; the Turks (for the time being) had abandoned thoughts of partition; the British had renounced overall sovereignty, but had retained key bases. Everybody had sacrificed something. Cyprus would be a republic, with its own flag, under a Greek president and a Turkish vice-president; legislation would be vested in a House of Representatives elected every five years, and composed of 70 per cent Greeks to 30 per cent Turks, proportional to the island's population. Overall Britain came out of the 'Cyprus Tangle' fairly well, internationally as well as in terms of her own interests. The prolonged negotiations clarified to the world exactly what the problem of Cyprus had involved, and in doing so why also it had been such a tricky but crucial one for Britain. Macmillan was well satisfied with the outcome. It was, he told the House, 'a victory for reason and co-operation. No party to it has suffered defeat. It is a victory for all.'[46]

Certainly at the time the Cyprus settlement seemed like a model one. Alan Lennox-Boyd, the Colonial Secretary who at one moment had been on the point of resignation, wrote Macmillan a personal letter declaring that, in exorcising Greek and Turkish animosities, he had 're-established the Concert of Europe'. Even Anthony Nutting, no friend of Macmillan's since Suez, acknowledged that it was he who had broken the deadlock through his 'quiet diplomacy', while his previous master, Eden, would almost certainly have endeavoured to hang on to Cyprus as a colony at any cost.[47] With the exception of the Beaverbrook press, the British media as a whole heaped praise on Macmillan, and undoubtedly the resolution of the 'Cyprus Tangle' earned him valuable points for the approaching General Election. But Macmillan himself was also generous in his commendation of Selwyn Lloyd, who – as Foreign Secretary and with his lawyer's background – had patiently handled much of the detailed negotiations between the explosive Greeks and Turks with what Macmillan rated as 'commendable skill'.[48] In effect, it was really Cyprus that provided Lloyd with his first test as Foreign Secretary in his own right. Macmillan had given him his head and full backing, and Lloyd had fully repaid Macmillan's confidence in keeping him on after Suez. Cyprus ensured Lloyd's continued survival, to the confounding of his critics in the press and the Party.

'Chinese Puzzle'

At exactly the same time as the Lebanon and Jordan interventions, as well as the decisive phase of the Cyprus talks, a totally unexpected – and, for a brief time, highly alarming – crisis suddenly flared up at the other end of the world. Without any warning, and after three years of inactivity, on 23 August 1958, the Chinese Communists began a massive artillery bombardment of the offshore islands of Quemoy and Matsu. As it continued day after day, this looked as if it must presage a full-scale invasion attempt. Taiwan, where Chiang Kai-shek had withdrawn with the defeated remnants of his Kuomintang Army after Mao's victory on the mainland, is a comfortable eighty-five miles distance across the Formosa Strait, but the offshore islands (also held by the Nationalists) lie so close to the mainland that with binoculars from Quemoy you can actually see the faces of Chinese People's Army troops on the mainland. In 1954 Mao had threatened to seize the islands, and Eisenhower had responded with a formal declaration that Taiwan and the islands would be defended by the US against any attack – thereby committing the US to a policy that still persists to the present day. Although the islands were in no way strategically essential to Taiwan's survival, and would have been untenable against any determined attack without the US commitment, Chiang had rashly – and perhaps provocatively – placed some eighty thousand of his best troops (out of half a million) on Quemoy.

This posed a serious dilemma to the British because, with the vulnerability of precious Hong Kong very much in mind, they had already re-established relations with Peking, as soon as it was decently possible in the wake of the Korean War, and (in 1955) Eden had gone on record as saying that, juridically, the Chinese Communists had a good case for claiming the offshore islands. Macmillan saw the problem clearly:

if we abandon the Americans – morally, I mean, they need no active support – it will be a great blow to the friendship and alliance which I have done so much to rebuild and strengthen. If we support them, the repercussions in Far East, India and through the Afro-Asian group in the Middle East may be very dangerous. At home, Parliament and public will be very critical of any change from our public position three years ago.[49]

In early September the crisis escalated when Dulles, giving what Macmillan described as 'the most brilliant exposition of the art of "brinkmanship" in his career',[50] issued a warning that the US might use nuclear weapons against China, if it invaded Quemoy. The world held its breath. Meanwhile Selwyn Lloyd and four other senior ministers were away on holiday, and in Britain Macmillan was left to handle the crisis by himself. In his heart he was sure Dulles was bluffing and that Eisenhower would not countenance what might inevitably lead to the risk of nuclear war with the Soviet Union, but (on 6 September) he wrote a long letter to Dulles and

Eisenhower, saying that he shared US fears of a 'Munich' in the whole Far East (in effect, an early resort to the later famous 'Domino Theory'), but warning of strong British and Commonwealth reservations. He suggested a compromise whereby 'all the friends of the US', together with recourse to the UN, might try to exert pressure to demilitarise the islands, at the same time denouncing any resort to force to alter the *status quo*. The immediate response from neither Washington nor Peking was encouraging.

Week by week the crisis simmered on. Then, in October, China's Marshal Peng unexpectedly announced that the devastating bombardment of Quemoy would continue only on the odd days of the month.[51] Macmillan thought this was rather like parking alternately on one side of the street. The following March the bombardment ceased as suddenly as it had begun. Why it had begun at all, and why it ended without the anticipated invasion (except perhaps through the Chinese running out of ammunition) remains indeed something of a 'Chinese puzzle', as Macmillan entitled the relevant chapter of his memoirs, to this day. One reason advanced at the time was that the shelling was instigated by the USSR as a distraction from events in the Middle East, where the Anglo-American intervention had grabbed the initiative from Soviet hands; to some extent this was supported by a recent visit made by Khrushchev to Peking. In any event, it would – if the theory was tenable – be the last time that the Chinese would pull Russian chestnuts out of the fire for them. On the other hand, this dangerous episode may equally well have resulted from some unknown subterranean pressures within the Chinese domestic scene. To the end Harold Macmillan, at any rate, remained mystified as to what was 'the moral to be drawn'.

France and De Gaulle

1958 was also a year of crisis for France. In May, Macmillan was recording in his diary: 'There has been a great flare up in France, still in a state of political confusion. The Generals in Algiers had set up a committee of public safety. Whether it is to be followed by an attempt at a *coup d'état* in Paris is obscure. . . .'[52] Twelve years had passed since de Gaulle had summarily abandoned the presidency. Withdrawing to Colombey-les-Deux-Eglises, he had observed disdainfully 'the convolutions of this absurd ballet . . . seventeen prime ministers, representing twenty-four ministries',[53] and bided his time, waiting for the *moment juste.* In response to the conspirators of May 1958 who clamoured for his return as the only solution for strife-torn France, he made it clear that he would come back only on his terms; only if a vast majority of the French nation wanted him, and *not* as the prisoner of any one faction, especially not on the bayonets of the French Army in Algeria.

That moment finally came on 30 May, when de Gaulle agreed to form a government – and a long sigh of relief swept over France. On Sunday, 1 June, he presented himself to the National Assembly, the first time he had entered it since January 1946, to receive a vote of confidence by a large majority. Macmillan promptly sent off a message of 'warm congratulations', evoking the Algiers days 'when as President of the committee of Liberation you were leading France to victory . . .'. De Gaulle replied in a similarly courteous vein, ending with the words: 'We shall, I know, have much to do together and I look forward to this.'

De Gaulle quickly invited Macmillan over to Paris. The first Western chief to make the pilgrimage, Macmillan was met at Orly on 29 June by a guard of honour, and de Gaulle in person. He was:

> all affability and charm – quite remarkable. I made a little speech in French, which seemed to please him. . . . It was a beautiful Sunday afternoon – and a very large crowd was out the whole way from Orly to Paris. . . . I have never seen a French crowd cheer in such a friendly way. . . . I think really it was the sign of the popular feeling of hope. At the moment, everyone is confident that the General's policy will succeed. No-one knows what it will be – all the same it commands general confidence. . . .[54]

It was a momentous occasion for Macmillan, meeting again the man who had first come into his life in the dark days in Algiers fifteen years previously, and for whose cause he had fought so hard then. But for Macmillan's support for de Gaulle, against Roosevelt and Churchill, almost certainly de Gaulle would not have been in Paris, at the helm, in 1958. In the intervening years, he found de Gaulle had grown old, resentfully – for, as he once remarked of Pétain, 'old age is a shipwreck'. In order to preserve his deteriorating eyesight, he had given up smoking, but had still had to undergo recently an operation for cataracts. This gave him a kind of agora-phobia, and made him uncertain in public without thick spectacles at hand. The belly had sagged, the face was greyer, the voice had lost something of its resonance. He was sixty-seven years old – three years older than Macmillan. Macmillan noted in his diaries: 'It was astonishing to me to see de Gaulle in his present mood. . . . His manner is calm, affable, and rather paternal. But underneath this new exterior, I should judge that he is just as obstinate as ever. . . .'[55]

Macmillan at once got down to brass tacks on the European Free Trade Area (EFTA), as he said in his memoirs 'in a hopeful though not a confident spirit', adding:

I had to confess to myself that the prospect did not seem very favourable. I knew from my many intimate talks with de Gaulle during the war how obsessed he was by his almost insane hatred for Roosevelt and even for Churchill; by his jealousy of Britain, and by his mixture of pride in France's splendid history and humiliation by her ignoble fall in 1940. . . .

It was plain to Macmillan that getting out of the Algerian jungle and French constitutional reform were preoccupying de Gaulle's mind; EFTA would remain very much a low priority, at least for the time being. He returned to London, knowing that he would have some rough passages with de Gaulle, but little guessing just how far de Gaulle's Gallic pride, fiercely nationalist passions and that resentment of *les Anglo-Saxons* – carried over from wartime days – would lead him in what, finally, for Macmillan would seem like an act of rankest ingratitude to the man who had saved his bacon in the 1940s. Of all the Western leaders of the 1950s and 1960s, he had known de Gaulle the closest; but none would suffer more from that 'obstinacy' which he detected in de Gaulle in June 1958 than Macmillan himself.

In the course of re-reading Philip Guedalla's *Life of Palmerston* that summer, Macmillan observed in the privacy of his diaries how much the problems of the 1850s resembled those of his own in the 1950s. The Russians had 'not changed much – grasping, lying, taking everything they can, and only responding to physical pressure. Nor have the French changed much. De Gaulle is Prince President. It is not so much the duplicity, as the vanity of the French which is so alarming.'[56] Nevertheless, at this stage, Macmillan was still supporting de Gaulle to Eisenhower in a way curiously similar to those days belonging to such a different era in the wartime Algiers of the 1940s. Referring to the talks currently under way in Geneva on nuclear testing, he wrote to President Eisenhower on 20 August:

> . . . I am seriously troubled. . . . I feel that after all our difficulties with de Gaulle over recent events, while he is still suspicious of our intentions towards him, it would be a serious mistake to force the French Government into a position of dissociating itself from our proposals. The trouble which we are having with them already at Geneva shows how suspicious they are on this question. We really must consult them fully and give them time to come to a conclusion. . . . I do feel strongly that the whole economic future of Europe, and perhaps its political future too, may be jeopardised if we allow the French to feel isolated or roughly treated over this question. . . .

This was an important letter because it goes some way to refuting French charges that Macmillan was always conspiring together with *les Anglo-Saxons* across the Atlantic to the disadvantage of France.

In early October, at Adenauer's instance and in the hope of getting the Germans to lend more active help over EFTA, Macmillan flew off to Bonn. The meeting was dominated by an unexpected initiative from Paris. De Gaulle had suddenly sent a private memorandum to Macmillan and Eisenhower about the defence structure of the West. Strongly critical of NATO, de Gaulle proposed replacing its command structure with an Anglo-American–French triumvirate, whose powers would be spread across the world, instead of just confined to Europe. As Macmillan noted correctly, 'Of course, the whole purpose is to claim for France "as a coming nuclear power" a special position, with Britain and America. . . .' He added that, to place France on a par with the USA and Britain, de Gaulle's '"nuclear" claim is absurd'.[57]

The 'triumvirate' proposal ran directly counter to the private agreement that Macmillan and Eisenhower had reached at Bermuda the previous year to exclude any third country from the bilateral exchanges on nuclear weaponry; while at the same time it would in effect give the French a veto on the deployment of US nuclear weapons anywhere in the world. De Gaulle's proposal would, by definition, exclude and demote West Germany, as well as the rest of the NATO powers, like Italy. It is hard to believe that de Gaulle himself was not aware that his terms would be unacceptable, his motives being simply to stake out an early claim for France's new importance in the world.

For some inexplicable reason, de Gaulle then leaked this private memorandum to the Italian and German ambassadors in Paris, as well as to the Belgian, Spaak. Adenauer was enraged; to Macmillan in Bonn 'he showed his disgust and resentment. He had trusted de Gaulle. They had met for confidential talks only a few weeks ago. De Gaulle had seemed to be loyal and open. . . .' Macmillan tried 'to calm him as much as I could. I had a much longer experience of de Gaulle than almost anyone. He was apt to treat his friends with this curious ineptness and rudeness. It was because of his mysticism and egoism . . . a proof of clumsiness but also of innocence. . . .'[58]

Yet Adenauer was by no means mollified by Macmillan's excuses for de Gaulle's behaviour. The following day Macmillan recorded in his diary 'The Chancellor is still very hurt and angry. I do not think he will ever trust de Gaulle again. . . .'[59] There was irony in the fact that, within a period of so few months, it would be Macmillan who would be the focus of Adenauer's suspicions, rather than de Gaulle. Macmillan admitted that his chief purpose in Bonn had been to get Adenauer to help over EFTA. He went on, 'The Germans have up to now been very good. . . . I think I can exploit his [Adenauer's] anger with the French over the de Gaulle memorandum to some account. . . .'

Macmillan was to be proved wrong – on both the above surmises.

Back in London, Macmillan instructed the Foreign Office not to snub de Gaulle over his 'absurd' 'triumvirate' proposal, because the EFTA talks were 'the most important matter to be decided in Europe during the next few months';[60] thus he was to be told, mildly, that HMG's line was that tripartite discussions to talk about the functions of NATO were perfectly in order – so long as the other Allies were kept fully informed. Predictably, this polite brush-off did not enthuse de Gaulle. On the 21st, Macmillan received via the Foreign Office a communication from the British Ambassador in Paris, the brilliant but haughty Gladwyn Jebb, describing de Gaulle as having talked 'rather despairingly' about the consequences if

America would have nothing to do with his proposals. He considered that 'the whole future of the alliance would probably be called in question. . . . if he got absolutely no satisfaction he could tell me straight away that France would cease to play any particular role in NATO and would, in other words, cease to be an active member. . . .'[61] This seems to reveal that de Gaulle was already contemplating his withdrawal from NATO a good deal earlier than has generally been accepted.

Adenauer's Seduction by De Gaulle

At the beginning of November Macmillan was recording in his diary: 'The outlook for the European Free Trade Area seems bad. The French are determined to exclude the United Kingdom. De Gaulle is bidding high for the hegemony of Europe. . . .'[62]

Macmillan hoped to resist de Gaulle's plans with the help of West Germany. But he counted without the extraordinary sea-change that de Gaulle had been able to bring about in the ageing Adenauer between September and November. In September 1958, de Gaulle invited Adenauer privately to his home in Colombey.

Both the General and Madame de Gaulle went out of their way to be warm and welcoming, and by Adenauer's own account[63] that first visit was an instant success. He was impressed by de Gaulle's toughness of mind, in contrast to what had now already begun to seem to him the wobbly and undependable British. De Gaulle actively encouraged Adenauer in his criticisms of Macmillan's Britain. It was already a hobby-horse with Adenauer that the British, having acquired an easy way of life through the wealth of their Empire, had lost the urge to work. De Gaulle did not disagree. Adenauer remarked that Britain was 'like a rich man, who has lost all his property but does not realise it'.[64] De Gaulle declared that Britain should not enter the Common Market so long as she 'remained politically and economically as she was'.[65] Stressing his interest in a united Europe, he added that it would have to cease to be 'the tool of America'. He then told Adenauer, with solemn emphasis that, although it had been said in Germany that his policy towards her 'was one of might and vengeance, I can prove the contrary to *you*.'

Adenauer seems to have returned to Bonn worried at de Gaulle's almost dictatorial powers, but already captivated by his charm. Then, in November, he repaid de Gaulle's hospitality at the small watering-place of Bad Kreuznach. De Gaulle flattered his host by calling him in front of the German press 'a great man, a great statesman, a great European and a great German'.[66] According to the British Ambassador in Bonn, Sir Christopher Steel, it was at Bad Kreuznach that de Gaulle gained Adenauer's support for vetoing the 'Maudling Plan' (the creation of the European Free Trade Area). The old Rhinelander was clearly surprised that de Gaulle should now appear to be the man who most truly appeared to represent his own rooted ideals of the 'European Concept', and the first French leader with the power now to do something about it.

De Gaulle Blocks EFTA Initiative

What Macmillan could expect from Adenauer was now as clearly defined as the lines of confrontation with de Gaulle, and that meant, in particular, no agreement over a Free Trade Area. 'I am deeply disturbed', Macmillan wrote to de Gaulle on 7 November,

> at the position we have reached in our negotiations for a Free Trade Area. We have always well understood that France had specially difficult economic problems. . . .
>
> But the Treaty of Rome, taken by itself, can easily lead to a division in the European ranks rather than a bond of unity. If the industry of the other Western European countries is progressively excluded from the markets of the Six, how can we prevent political antagonisms as well as economic rivalries from springing up?
>
> We thought the idea of a Free Trade Area provided the solution. We saw it as something which in no way interfered with the aims of the Common Market. . . .

Yet, continued Macmillan, French Foreign Minister Couve was now insisting that not only was France refusing to accept a regime of free trade in Europe, despite all the safeguards offered by the British,

> but that such a regime must inevitably destroy the objectives of the Common Market. If this is really so we have been negotiating

at cross purposes. In less than two months' time, an economic cleavage will occur which the present negotiations will be powerless to prevent. . . . It is no secret that even among the Six the conception of a large free-trading area in Europe is generally welcomed for its political sake alone. . . .

After this thinly veiled threat of divide-and-conquer tactics, Macmillan then ended his letter with an appeal to 'our old friendship'. The appeal, however, had little effect. On 14 November de Gaulle rejected Macmillan's appeal for EFTA outright. On 21 December he was elected President of France. Macmillan did his best to keep his temper. As so often it found an outlet in his diaries; on 19 December he was writing acidly of de Gaulle, after a visit Selwyn had just made to his court at the Matignon: '. . . "Rip Van Winkle" is clearly the right name for him. He talked about the "Concert of Europe" and seemed not to have quite realised what had happened to the world since the end of the Second War. . . .'[67]

At the end of his second year in power Macmillan was recording how 'depressed and frustrated' he felt, not least because 'De Gaulle is determined to break up NATO.'[68]

The following day, New Year's Day 1959, an historic date, the Treaty of Rome came into force – for all that those mandarins of Whitehall had convinced themselves that it never would.

Thus ended, in effect, the first phase of what Macmillan in his memoirs described bleakly as 'a long and sterile negotiation'. This was Britain's vain effort, stretching from 1956 to the end of 1958, to get the Six (and notably France) to agree to a Free Trade Area that would embrace themselves, Britain and all the OECD nations. And although negotiations were to continue for another five years, as far as de Gaulle and France were concerned it could be said that the definitive lines of battle had already been laid down by the end of 1958, no more than six months after de Gaulle returned to power.

Chapter Five

No Mr Chamberlain
1958–1959

As a great Russian revolutionary, Alexander Herzen, wrote, 'reconciliations are only possible when they are unnecessary'.

(HM, Riding the Storm*)*

'One of the most highly publicised Odysseys since the Greeks,' said Bevan, and, alas, despite [Macmillan's] own claim he had not brought back the golden fleece.

(Michael Foot, Aneurin Bevan 1945–60*)*

'I am said to have lost touch with public opinion in England,' Macmillan grumbled to himself at the end of his first year in office, 'because I have not already set out for Moscow to see Khrushchev. All this is pure Chamberlainism. It is raining umbrellas.'[1] Yet, in fifteen months' time and while the Communist Chinese shells were still raining down on Quemoy, he was setting up a precedent as the first Western leader to visit Moscow in peacetime.

In the 1950s, as in the 1980s, the notion of 'summitry' obsessed the Western media as a panacea for the world's ills: it was only necessary for the leaders of the great powers to talk, and the threat of war would automatically and miraculously fade away. Furthermore, Macmillan's memories of the great wartime setpiece encounters at Casablanca and Cairo imbued him with some nostalgic optimism (albeit that it was from such 'summitry' as Teheran and Yalta that some of the West's worse reverses had flowed).

By the middle of his Commonwealth tour, Macmillan had already formulated 'a perhaps crazy idea of offering to go myself to Moscow to discuss (a) agenda (for the proposed "Summit"); (b) procedure, with Khrushchev . . .'.[2] Communicating his 'crazy idea' to the Cabinet back in London, Macmillan recorded, 'My Moscow plan did not please the Cabinet. . . .'[3] But he was not going to let it go. On 3 February, Macmillan had also found the Americans 'negative' and 'almost threatening'[4] about his latest draft reply to the Russians, with both Dulles and Eisenhower taking the fairly consistent line of being hostile to a summit – unless there were grounds for thinking it would be productive. Following the first launching of their own space satellite, Macmillan, however, found his Allies 'in a better temper'[5] and more self-confident.

At the same time, in the Soviet Union, Khrushchev had assumed ultimate power when he was made premier in March; and, by 1 April, Macmillan, after a conversation with UN Secretary-General, Dag Hammarskjöld, was sensing Khrushchev to be now 'supreme, without challengers, and very confident of his own and Russian strength'.[6] Here perhaps was a leader one could 'do business' with. As Macmillan studied the new Russian leader's personality, he thought that Khrushchev might be amenable to his persuasiveness and charm.

Macmillan also felt – and not without reason during this year of crises – that there were pressing issues on which he was well qualified to act as a link between America and Russia. Meanwhile, there already existed an outstanding invitation, extended by Bulganin at the time of the Soviet visit to Britain, for a return engagement in May 1957 – though after Suez and Budapest the sudden freeze in the climate had caused it to be shelved *sine die*.

During the summer Macmillan had conducted an exploratory correspondence with Sir Patrick Reilly, the talented British Ambassador in Moscow and an old friend from Algiers days, about the climb towards the summit, about his projected visit to Moscow and about the nature of Khrushchev. Reilly's views on the visit were, and remained, measured. He warned Macmillan that, seeing it against the background of a forthcoming British election, the Russians might try to exploit it for all they could get out of it. They would probably try to use it to isolate Adenauer from his Western allies. If Macmillan came, the visit should not be a hurried one. At the same time the Ambassador warned him that Khrushchev's most dangerous feature seemed to be megalomania. Picking up the hint, Macmillan commented that, whereas he thought Lenin and Stalin had been 'pretty cold fish', 'megalomania frightens one because people who get it can do very stupid things and lead to great disasters. . . . Could Khrushchev do as foolish things as Hitler did?'[7] As Dulles had noted in an earlier letter (19 September 1957):

Khrushchev is a Ukrainian, and has more of the characteristics of Mussolini or Hitler. He may make risky, impetuous decisions, and may miscalculate. I think the future will call for very high statesmanship on our side if, on the one hand we are to avoid war, and on the other hand, avoid unacceptable losses.[8]

The Berlin Crisis

Whether it stemmed from 'megalomania' or preparedness to take a calculated risk, on 10 November 1958 Khrushchev suddenly demanded the withdrawal of Allied troops from Berlin.[9] He followed this up ten days later with the Russian Ambassador in Bonn informing Adenauer, with some brutality, according to Macmillan, that his government intended 'to liquidate the occupation statutes concerning Berlin'.

A shaken Adenauer sent Macmillan a personal message the next day, begging him to 'make representations' to Moscow to dissuade Khrushchev from carrying out this threat. Macmillan did; but the following week, 27 November, the three Western occupying powers received an official Soviet note, stating that the Soviet government now regarded as null and void the existing arrangements on Berlin. Henceforth, the Soviet government was going to sign a peace treaty with East Germany, and it would negotiate with the Western Allies on the basis of Berlin being a 'demilitarised free city'. There followed a clear ultimatum that, unless some solution was reached, within six months military traffic between West Berlin and the Federal Republic might be cut. As Khrushchev wrote to Macmillan on 5 December 1958:

> You will not, I think, disagree that today there is no other place in Europe and indeed anywhere in the world, where the Cold War is taking such acute and dangerous forms as in Berlin. Here the sensitive contradictions and differences which now divide the leading powers of NATO and the Warsaw Treaty converge. . . .[10]

Macmillan's immediate reaction was to write to Ambassador Caccia in Washington, expressing fears about any American plans to keep the route to Berlin open, on the grounds that:

> The whole art of dealing with an opponent who is indulging in 'brinkmanship' consists of not allowing him to get into a position in which he has to choose between war and humiliating retreat. This would be precisely the choice which would be imposed on the Russians under the American plan. . . .

He expressed hopes to Caccia that the American attitude might become more flexible – without their thinking that Macmillan was being defeatist.

Thus was born the 'Berlin Crisis', which was to dominate diplomacy over the next six months and to rumble away during the five succeeding years of Macmillan's premiership. Immediately it was to give a final fillip to Macmillan's intent to carry out his 'Mission to Moscow'. He was himself persuaded that Britain's role as an intermediary had never been of greater value. On 7 December, Macmillan noted, Chancellor Adenauer 'suddenly invited himself to London. He, of course, wants to talk about Berlin. I shall talk to him about European Trade. . . .'[11] Adenauer was, apparently, fobbed off with *politesse*. Instead, the following month, the British Ambassador in Bonn, Sir Christopher Steel, came over to talk to Macmillan, who complained that he 'did *not* get much illumination',

> except that Chancellor Adenauer is in a bad way and aging rapidly. . . . He is still, it appears, fond of me!
>
> About Berlin, etc. he stands (officially) for absolute rigidity and a solid front against Soviet Russia. Behind the scenes, he wrings his hands and says that Russia and the West are like two express trains rushing to a head-on collision. . . .[12]

Macmillan was perhaps counting too much on the durability of Adenauer's 'fondness' for him; in fact it was from this date that the crucial decline in their relations stems. While Eisenhower was kept constantly in touch with Macmillan's intentions, Adenauer (and de Gaulle equally) was not informed until the very last moment, just three days before the trip was actually made public.

There were strong feelings in Germany that Macmillan had treated Adenauer, as an 'ally', shabbily; certainly it is doubtful whether this treatment was sensible, given the support that Macmillan was bound to need, in return, from Adenauer when it came to the forthcoming struggle to resolve Britain's dilemmas with the Common Market. On the other hand, it has to be remembered that this all took place less than fourteen years after the defeat of Hitler. Macmillan's thinking on the two separate but virtually interrelated issues of Berlin and the division of Germany were straightforward and constant. The Potsdam Agreement of 1945 furnished the British–American–French continued occupation of West Berlin with, he thought,

> a very tenuous and spurious basis on which to found our rights . . . just a temporary agreement between generals. . . . I always told them [i.e. the Western Allies] it was not an agreement that

we could press too far, but a *modus vivendi* awaiting a Versailles Treaty. . . .[13]

On the reunification of Germany, Macmillan was not alone in thinking 'we always had to talk about it to strengthen Adenauer (it's fair to say that Adenauer *did* create the modern Germany), and it was an issue which had to be put forward . . . but it was something of a fraud. . . .' The 'fraud' was that few in the West were genuine in their desires to see Germany reunited; certainly not Macmillan, with his personal recollections of both World Wars fought against the might of unified Germany. Adenauer, the Rhinelander, himself was always accused of being lukewarm in espousing a reunited Germany that might once again come under the heel of Prussia. But – a fact to which Macmillan particularly should perhaps have been more sensitive – Adenauer too had to face elections, in which at least lipservice to *Wiedervereinigung* had to be paid.

From his own disagreeable experience of humiliation at the hands of Khrushchev, Adenauer had personal reasons for questioning the wisdom of Macmillan's Moscow initiative. In September 1955 Adenauer himself had paid his first visit to Moscow, cap in hand, seeking the return – ten years after the war – of an estimated 130,000 missing Germans still held in the Soviet Union. The Russians insisted there were less than ten thousand, all of them war criminals. When Adenauer persisted, Khrushchev with unmoderated ferocity shouted a reminder of the fate of the Italians who had invaded Russia. They had all been 'coffined'. Deeply shocked, Adenauer had returned to Bonn empty-handed but for the lives of the ten thousand POWs, which he had been bludgeoned into trading against the establishment of diplomatic relations between Bonn and Moscow. But Macmillan's unilateral initiative to Moscow infected Adenauer with a deep-seated, fundamental mistrust of Macmillan's intentions towards Germany – fearing that he would prove 'soft' towards the Russians, and open to do a deal with them at Germany's expense. These suspicions would henceforth never quite leave him.

Macmillan comforted himself, however, that his No. 1 ally, Eisenhower, had reacted 'in most friendly terms. They say, in effect, that they have complete confidence in me and I must do whatever I think best. . . .'[14] From the subsequent release of American documents, one now knows this was not quite how Eisenhower viewed things:

TELEPHONE CALLS
January 20, 1959
The Secretary called the President – he had a note saying that Macmillan and Lloyd wanted to visit Russia. He thinks it is because Macmillan faces an election, probably in the fall, and wants to be the hero who finds a way out of the cold war dilemma, particularly about Berlin. Neither the President nor the Secretary felt they could – at least their offhand reaction was this – say 'No' – but they pointedly said that of course the Prime Minister would be speaking only for himself, not for the United States or Germany or France. . . .

The President said that he doubted that they would be able to make a dent in the granite – and the trip would therefore react adversely. . . .

However, both are going to think the matter over. . . .[15]

Macmillan endeavoured to reassure his Allies by promising to visit Paris, Bonn and Washington (in that order) to report back immediately following his return from Moscow.

Meanwhile, throughout the last days of January Macmillan had been 'sweating it out' to see whether, in fact, the Russians were going to come through with a firm invitation at all. It was, manifestly, all part of standard psychological warfare on Khrushchev's part:

31 January: I feel rather depressed and frustrated. . . . No answer from the Russians; my proposal has clearly surprised them. . . . We must not *run* after them; but we must not let them insult us by too long a delay. . . .[16]

At last, on 2 February, the Russian reply came. Macmillan was cock-a-hoop:

All my anxieties are removed. They have accepted the date, the length of the visit, and the terms of announcement. . . . This is an immense relief, for we rather 'stuck our necks out' in making the proposal, and a rebuff (which would have been leaked) would have been damaging as well as embarrassing. . . .[17]

When the announcement was released three days later, it came as a bombshell in Britain. Cautiously Macmillan stressed (especially for the benefit of his doubting allies) that the voyage represented 'a reconnaissance not a negotiation', but the news was widely applauded with warm enthusiasm by the British press at large.

'Voyage of Discovery'

With a team of over a dozen the Macmillan caravan set off on 21 February. Macmillan's private physician, John Richardson, who had been with him since Algiers, thought that – with a bout of chest trouble – he was not fit to go. But knowing his patient's tendency to mild hypochondria, Richardson 'didn't tell him, because I knew he *had* to go, and it would just worry him'.[18] Otherwise, he set off in the most exuberant of good spirits, almost at times to the point of frivolity. (According to his Parliamentary Private Secretary, Anthony Barber, Macmillan asked one of the interpreters to be given 'a word or two in Russian'. It was suggested he might try for a start *Dobrodjen* or 'good day'; whereupon Macmillan, with much hilarity, addressed all and sundry Russians with a boisterous 'Double-gin!' 'Double-gin!'.)[19] His clothes, too, had a certain almost calculated eccentricity about them; he annoyed Malcolm Muggeridge by wearing plus-fours to visit a Collective farm outside Kiev, 'as if he were at Chatsworth!';[20] from his very limited stock of ties, he carefully selected his Brigade of Guards tie when visiting a nuclear plant (insofar as that represented military matters), and his Old Etonian when going to the ballet (equals culture). Perhaps more unfortunate was the conspicuous white fur hat, one foot high, with which he arrived in Moscow. It had come out of a drawer, an old relic of his visit to Finland during the Soviet–Finnish War of 1940; as its *provenance* must have been obvious to his hypersensitive hosts, they could conceivably have seen in it an implied dig at them. Macmillan admitted it was perhaps not his most tactful choice, and later changed his Finnish extravaganza for a more conventional and sobre Russian model in black. Problems also arose from Macmillan's use of the word 'reconnaissance', employed in his announcement, which – in Russian – has some sinister espionage connotations; Reilly, the Ambassador, however adroitly substituted 'a voyage of discovery' in the Russian text.

Despite these pitfalls, the ten-day 'voyage' began on an encouragingly happy note. Macmillan made a diplomatic, formal opening speech, reminding his hosts of the signal precedent of it being the first time a British Prime Minister, or any Western leader, had ever visited the USSR in peacetime, and recalling his own earlier tour of thirty years previously. He then stressed that he had *not* come to negotiate on particular subjects, but that he hoped that 'in our talks together we shall at least reach a better understanding of our points of view . . . [and] help to alleviate some of the cares that at present bring anxiety to the world. . . .' Macmillan and entourage were then whisked off on a tour of the sombre Kremlin, where a great banquet was given for him that evening. There then followed a whirlwind ten days divided between Moscow, Leningrad and Kiev, which – apart from the working sessions – included visits to universities, shipyards, industries, farms and – three times – to the ballet. Never a music-lover, Macmillan would have much preferred the famous Russian circus, but 'some idiot in the FO said ballet!'[21] During Prokofiev's *The Stone Flower*, however, when the Demon King made a spectacular aerial entrance instead of popping up conventionally through a stage trapdoor, Macmillan pleased his hosts by remarking 'I liked the sputnik!'[22]

After the Kremlin banquet, the party was driven out to the Soviet government *dacha* at Semenovskoye, where the next day, Sunday, the Ruler of All the Russians indulged in some horseplay, principally at the expense of the British Foreign Secretary. The sedate Lloyd was despatched down a chute in a round basket, to spin across a frozen lake, to the accompaniment of gusts of peasant laughter. Lloyd's embarrassment was made fun of at various moments over the ensuing conferences, as a means of scoring diplomatic points. That morning the discussions began in earnest, and in relatively good humour, starting with Berlin – where Khrushchev made the seriousness of his intent abundantly plain – and moving on to disarmament. For Macmillan it was nevertheless a 'strange but agreeable' day. The following day the talks were resumed, more formally, within the Kremlin. After that session, Macmillan sent off a letter to Eisenhower, noting how:

in spite of their great new power and wealth, the Russians are still obsessed by a sense of insecurity. The old bogy of encirclement has not yet been laid. Whenever Khrushchev mentioned the Germans it was possible to sense his hatred and distrust. . . .

That night there was a banquet at the British Embassy, when Macmillan in his toast gratified Khrushchev by referring to his administrative brilliance during the Battle of Stalingrad. Khrushchev accepted this flattery with 'almost Pickwickian smiles'.

So far, thought Macmillan, the visit had been an outstanding success. Then the honeymoon began to disintegrate. On Tuesday, the 24th, while Macmillan and Selwyn Lloyd were visiting the Nuclear Research Station 120 miles out of Moscow, Khrushchev without any warning to his guests delivered what seemed like a keynote speech, in which he harshly criticised Dulles and Eisenhower; was brutally offensive about Adenauer; but – a complete surprise – offered an immediate non-aggression pact with Britain. It seemed like a deliberate attempt to separate Macmillan from his allies as ministers and diplomats in Washington and Bonn had feared and predicted. He and Selwyn Lloyd sought to have a private exchange of views to discuss how to deal with Khrushchev's offensive speech.

It was not easy. Reilly had warned him in advance of the skill of Soviet bugging and other forms of eavesdropping. For reasons of security, Macmillan had abandoned keeping his diary while in the USSR, just as he had during the 'action' period of Suez. Barber noted how he found 'ten days without being able to gossip in the evenings with Selwyn and his entourage very galling – it was so much in his style – he couldn't even gossip in the cars, which were Russian. . . .'[23] Inside the Embassy, Reilly had had technicians construct what Macmillan could only describe as 'a kind of bug-proof' tent; but the effect of it was so inhibiting even on Macmillan that, when he and Lloyd stepped inside for a confidential talk, 'we simply found nothing to say to each other!'[24] Out at the *dacha*, which it was assumed must have been bugged up to the chimney pots, the only way they felt they could converse safely was by walking out in the snow, well away from trees that were (presumably) festooned with microphones:

> You must imagine two middle-aged, not to say elderly, politicians, clothed in fur coats, fur hats and above all the inevitable but essential galoshes, tramping up and down with their advisers and engaged in long and earnest discussion – *sotto voce* – about a situation which if not immediately dangerous, threatened to become ludicrous. . . .

Because of lack of information on which to act, they decided to 'play it by ear'.

Resuming talks after a liberal lunch on Wednesday, the 25th, Khrushchev appears progressively to have worked himself up into a rage over Germany. With measured calmness, Macmillan stressed that he hoped Khrushchev would 'take careful note' of two points which he felt it was his duty to emphasise: 'The first is that the German situation is full of danger and could develop into something tragic for us all. The second is that it must surely be possible to avoid this by sensible and cooperative work.' Khrushchev replied that he could not understand why the West wished to preserve a state of war with Germany:

> Nor did he understand why we wished to preserve the dangerous character of the Berlin situation. Was it because we wanted to maintain the possibility of moving from the state of armed truce which now existed to a state of real war? Were we arming the West Germans to make use of them in a future war . . . ?

Reverting to his intention to sign a peace treaty with the German Democratic Republic, Khrushchev declared that it was obvious the West wanted to help Adenauer to liquidate the GDR, but that, if there was any violation of the GDR after conclusion of the peace treaty, then 'the consequences would be very grave and it would be the fault of the West'. It seems to have been somewhere at this point that Macmillan also bridled and retorted 'if you try to threaten us in any way, you will create the Third World War. Because we shall not give in, nor will the Americans. . . .'[25] Whereupon Khrushchev leaped to his feet and shouted: 'You have insulted me!' The British delegation were taken aback by this intemperate display of rage. Macmillan reckoned that Khrushchev had been drinking heavily before the storm burst, and was 'rather drunk' at the time; many years later he admitted that perhaps 'we had *all* got rather drunk'.[26] The talks adjourned for the ballet, appropriately *Romeo and Juliet*, with Khrushchev's humour seeming to have returned.

The next day, however, Khrushchev resumed the row over Germany, blaming Macmillan for having created the situation by what he had said the previous day. He then thumped the table and said, 'That is all!'[27] There was a pause when Macmillan felt Khrushchev was uncertain whether to work himself up into a new pitch of rage or let things calm down. He followed up with some offensive remarks about Suez, which stung Macmillan but he kept his temper. Khrushchev observed cynically that there was not much on which to base a communiqué; Macmillan retorted 'that our colleagues had wide and imaginative minds'. There was another pause, then Khrushchev rose and said he understood the British party was leaving for Kiev, and he had hoped to accompany them there and introduce them to his daughter who lived there; however, he had now decided not to come, 'because you've insulted me'. 'Then he altered his line and said "and moreover I've got the most terrible toothache. . . ." He would be sorry to disappoint his daughter. . . .'[28]

Thus ensued the famous story of Khrushchev's tooth; what Macmillan described in his memoirs as 'one of the most whimsical diplomatic episodes in history'. Considerably dismayed, Macmillan and Lloyd withdrew into the bug-proof Embassy tent to discuss how to react to this apparently calculated discourtesy. Predictably there would be some hefty criticisms from Britain's allies, saying 'I told you so,' and the British press were swift to pick up the story with such headlines as 'The toothache insult' and the *News Chronicle* already writing off the trip as a 'monumental flop'. Acting in character, Macmillan decided to put on the mask of 'unflappability', to continue on to Kiev and Leningrad as if nothing had happened, and await events. There was nothing to lose. Bishop was impressed by how 'very philosophical' Macmillan was at this moment: '. . . I remember him talking deliberately to the chandelier in the middle of the room, assuming that it was bugged: "Of course we will have to recall the Ambassador and order the plane. . . ."!'[29]

The strategy was obviously the correct one. Before leaving Kiev for Leningrad on the 28th, Macmillan received from Khrushchev the kind of message that might equally well have come from Peter the Great, or any other earlier Russian despot: 'he said he felt sure that I would be glad to know that his tooth was better. The dentist had used an excellent and newly designed British drill!'[30]

But, in Macmillan's absence, Khrushchev had made a 'helpful speech' and the final discussions resumed on amicable terms – leading to what Macmillan recorded in his diary as 'a really useful and constructive discussion'. On Germany, however, Khrushchev once again made his position quite clear; he wanted the West to accept the existence of the GDR with its existing frontiers. He was not interested in *de jure* recognition. If West Berlin was to become a free city, as Khrushchev had already proposed, then he would offer the Western Allies fullest guarantees for access. On that last day, somewhat to his surprise, Macmillan was allowed the unique privilege of making an uncensored broadcast over Russian television.

In the final communiqué, Macmillan succeeded in getting Khrushchev to agree to declaring that a common objective remained the ultimate prohibition of nuclear weapons, and stressing the importance of an interim agreement on halting nuclear tests – a topic that would continue to be top priority with Macmillan through to the end of his premiership. On Berlin, the best that the two leaders could say was that they had agreed to disagree, but that talks would continue with some urgency.

What Did It Achieve?

As they flew back to England after eleven gruelling days, in the unbugged security of the British plane, Macmillan and his team pondered over what had been behind Khrushchev's extraordinary behaviour. Immediately on the heels of the event, Macmillan found it hard to divine the motives behind Khrushchev's explosion, but felt that it had 'helped me enormously', in that it had made it easier for him to say the tough things he had to say about any unilateral Soviet threat to Berlin. In retrospect long afterwards, Philip de Zulueta reckoned there was no 'pre-calculated motive of Khrushchev trying to humiliate Macmillan; it was just his Russian spontaneity; heavy jokes like Peter the Great, and also an element to see if this new Prime Minister who appeared to be ready to make concessions could be broken down. He wasn't. . . .'[31] The same treatment would be tried, with rather more success, on the green young President Kennedy two years later. For Macmillan's own personal satisfaction, he came back from Moscow feeling that he understood the Russian leader a little better, and – for all his obnoxious faults – rather liking him:

He was a very clever man, very well informed. But he was interesting to me because he was more like the Russians we'd read about in Russian novels than most Russian technocrats are.

They all seem to be made in Germany – rather stiff and . . .
you couldn't really converse with them. But you could with
Khrushchev. . . . He had the true peasant humour. . . .

To his colleagues and allies in the West in general, Macmillan
brought back the view that Khrushchev:

is a curious study. Impulsive; sensitive of his own dignity and
insensitive to anyone else's feelings; quick in argument, never
missing or overlooking a point; with an extraordinary memory
and encyclopaedic information at his command; vulgar, and yet
capable of a certain dignity when he is simple and forgets to
'show off'; ruthless, but sentimental – Khrushchev is a kind of
mixture between Peter the Great and Lord Beaverbrook. Anyway,
he is the boss, and no meeting will ever do business except a
Summit meeting. . . .

Macmillan told his first Cabinet meeting after his return on
4 March that, while he wanted a negotiated settlement over Berlin,

we [Britain] must not get into the position we got into at Munich
[1938]. I will be no Mr Chamberlain. We must therefore talk
ourselves quite boldly about preparations for war and see what
de Gaulle and Adenauer say in response. What would be the
worst thing of all for the West would be a humiliating climb-down
after talking big.[32]

So just what had Macmillan's 'voyage of discovery' achieved? In
retrospect, years later, Sir Patrick Reilly, the British Ambassador
in Moscow who originally had been lukewarm about the visit, felt
that the 'voyage of discovery' had been projected 'for the wrong
motives – with electoral advantage in view':

in those days it was generally believed that the public would vote
for anybody who was seen to make an effort to come to terms
with the Russians. . . . But what was remarkable was the truly
dramatic effect that HM's obvious sincerity and his hatred of
war, his memories of 1914–18, had in defusing what was undoubtedly a dangerous situation over Berlin. . . . I think that
this was Macmillan's great contribution with the Russians, and

undoubtedly had its effect over the negotiations with Berlin later on. . . .[33]

When Macmillan made his first appearance in the Commons on his return, he was delighted that 'All the Conservative party rose when I came in, led by Winston Churchill.'[34] Grumpily Aneurin Bevan wrote it off as 'one of the most highly publicised Odysseys since the Greeks', which had, 'alas, despite Macmillan's own claims, not brought back the golden fleece'.[35]

The Aftermath of Moscow

To allay any possible criticisms by his allies that he had gone to Moscow in 1959 as a kind of latterday Chamberlain, Macmillan had immediately set off on a whirlwind round to reassure them – starting with de Gaulle in Paris. Macmillan had come back from Moscow thoroughly reinforced in his view that the only way to head off a dangerous confrontation over Berlin was to call at once a summit meeting with Khrushchev. But he was isolated in his determination. In Paris de Gaulle – in a monologue that Macmillan was already becoming readjusted to – had seemed to share his misgivings over the weakness of the Allied position in Berlin:

> by admitting right away that one could not have a nuclear war in Europe on the question of who signed the pass to go along the autobahn or the railway to West Berlin – a USSR sergeant or a DDR sergeant. In his view the only question which would justify war would be an actual physical blockade. . . .[36]

Macmillan asked de Gaulle point-blank whether he had said this to Adenauer: 'He admitted that he had not. It would depress him. . . .' It was not until a considerable time later that Macmillan began to realise that de Gaulle was already playing a double game with Adenauer, to recruit him to the Gaullist concept of Europe – at Britain's expense.

In Bonn two days later, Macmillan was met by an indeed rather depressed Adenauer, who 'then launched quite an attack upon us about "disengagement", which they seem to think we had agreed in principle with the Russians. . . . The Chancellor was slow to understand and seemed to cherish some resentment. . . .'[37] Macmillan put to Adenauer what later became known as the 'Macmillan Plan', which embraced the notion of a 'thinning-out' of military hardware on either side of the Iron Curtain. It was his hope that this first step might lead ultimately to general, controlled disarmament – especially in the nuclear field. Adenauer, however, would have nothing to do with the inchoate Macmillan Plan, even if it were to open the door to an inspection of forces beyond the *Interzonengrenze* in East Germany. They were, Adenauer wrote in his memoirs, 'agreed on one principle; no concessions without concessions in return . . .'.[38] Where East–West relations were concerned, the German leader derided 'flexibility' as an illusion.

Following the emergence of the new Paris–Bonn axis, the March 1959 Bonn meeting between Macmillan and Adenauer only marked a steady worsening in their relations. This was reflected in the pungent opinions Macmillan recorded of Adenauer privately:

4 April: . . . The Germans are behaving in a very crude and silly way and the French are joining them in attacking Britain for 'defeatism'. . . .

9 April: . . . I would judge that Adenauer has gone a bit potty. I saw signs of this in Bonn a few weeks ago. How Mr. Khrushchev must laugh at us all! It is rather sad.

Moving on to Ottawa after Bonn, however, Macmillan had been received with 'great applause' in the Canadian House of Commons, where an evocative speech on the common destiny had struck the most powerful of chords. It was also his first visit to Canada, with Dorothy, since their courtship there in 1920.

On reaching Washington, Macmillan's first engagement was to visit Dulles, accompanied by Eisenhower, in his bed at the Walter Reed Hospital. Though clearly in the terminal stages of cancer and under debilitating X-ray treatment, Dulles was still clinging on to office with tenacity and extraordinary fortitude in the face of considerable pain. Macmillan found him 'very thin and emaciated', but 'he was *against* almost everything. He was strongly against the idea of a *Summit*. . . .'[39] Macmillan thought it was a 'strange scene', with Eisenhower seated on a sofa, Macmillan and Selwyn Lloyd on low armchairs, while the dying Secretary of State from a higher chair discoursed in a monologue on Communism, Germany and Berlin. Eisenhower was silent, and Macmillan later regretted having argued 'with this dying man', with whom he had been so much at odds in the past.

The sombre death-bed scene rather set the mood for the rest of the visit, which was neither as happy nor as fruitful as Macmillan's previous encounters with Eisenhower. He was nervous of anything that might indicate to the Russians a weakening of the Allied position on Berlin. To Dulles, two days later, Eisenhower expressed himself equally lukewarm in the face of Macmillan's proposal to draw up an agenda for a summit before any agreement on 'substantive matters'.[40]

From Washington Eisenhower flew Macmillan to his beloved hide-out at Camp David, where Ike seemed to be more his old friendly self. But not much business was achieved. Macmillan was amused by the presidential 'Shangri-La':

> The President showed me the underground fortress which has been built – a sort of Presidential Command Post in the event of atomic war. It holds fifty of the President's staff in one place and one hundred and fifty Defence staff in another. The fortress is underneath the innocent looking huts in which we lived, hewn out of the rock. It cost 10 million dollars![41]

Macmillan recalled that, while Ike had 'never much liked business',[42] now he had to rest '*before* a meal';[43] then, said Macmillan, 'we disappeared for lunch, or went for a walk, and then we had a film . . . the worst! Always the same film about sheep and horses – *Under Western Eyes* or some such thing. . . .'[44]

In the course of the visit Macmillan also had an opportunity to study Eisenhower's possible successor, Vice-President Nixon. He was not impressed, then or later. In Washington the previous summer Macmillan had recorded acidly how, after a dinner one night, the Vice-President had:

> poured out a monologue which extinguished any spark of conversation from whatever quarter it might arise. This spate of banalities lasted for 3 to 4 hours. We withdrew – battered and exhausted, about midnight. Janet Dulles kept her head better than most of us. Whenever the Vice-President had a pause for breath . . . she

said to the company in general 'When we were in Saigon we had Bird's Nest Soup.' But even this failed to stop Nixon for more than a moment. I felt sorry for the Americans. . . .'[45]

From his earliest encounter with Nixon, Macmillan distrusted him; 'not a man you'd buy a car off, as the Americans say'[46] was his verdict in 1959. 'Ike always hated him . . . always regarded him as a sharp lawyer. . . . he would have been all right in Sir Robert Walpole's time. He missed his period. . . .'[47]

On the key, interrelated issues of Berlin and the summit, the gap in Washington was wide, and Macmillan from the start was hard put to dispel American misgivings about what he might have said to Khrushchev in Moscow.

Macmillan was not much more successful in his other endeavour, to get the Americans to agree to a restriction of nuclear testing. They were, he noted in his diary after the Washington visit was over, 'very unwilling to abandon anything *unless* the Russian side of the agreement can be effectively policed . . .'.[48]

On leaving Washington a disappointed Macmillan had to 'agree to the somewhat ambivalent formula proposed by the President to the effect that "as soon as developments in the Foreign Ministers' meeting warrant a Summit Conference" the Heads of Government would be glad to participate . . .'. The 'formula' made the Promised Land of the summit seem far away indeed. Nevertheless, the French and Germans also agreed to it, and a joint note was despatched to Moscow on 25 March.

Macmillan's Washington visit was to be the last time that he would deal with Dulles. Three weeks later, on 15 April, Ike's doughty Secretary of State finally resigned. He died on 24 May. Characteristically Dulles had kept up his volume of work until the very last minute that he was physically able, complaining of the discomfort but never of the pain of the cancer. Macmillan wrote in his diary with magnanimity, 'With many faults, he was a great man, and a great support to the whole Free World. If he was weak and vacillating over Suez and Nasser, he has done all he could since then to repair the damage. . . .'[49] His formal tribute in the Commons was gracious and nonetheless sincere: 'a figure whose very bigness is hardly realised until we are threatened with its absence . . .'.[50] Although it was indisputably Eisenhower who was running foreign policy at the time of the Suez crisis, in the last years of his Presidency he seemed strangely lost without Dulles at his side.

Dulles's successor, his former deputy and one-time Governor of Massachusetts, Christian Herter, was a cripple who could walk only with the aid of crutches, a disability which initially caused Macmillan to wonder whether he would be up to the job. After Herter had been in office some three months, Macmillan was passing to Selwyn Lloyd (at the Geneva Foreign Ministers' talks) the observation that 'Looking at it from a distance, I get the impression that Herter, although honourable and friendly, has not much force. . . .'[51] It was not an unfair summing up. On the other hand, this also meant that Herter was more flexible, more ready to seek compromise than the austere Dulles. But the gap left by Dulles made Macmillan feel that it devolved on him to move in and assume at least the moral leadership of the West.

On 11 May 1959, the Foreign Ministers' Conference – Herter, Gromyko, Lloyd and de Gaulle's Couve de Murville – began in Geneva, *pari passu* with the continuation of the disarmament talks, notably on suspension of nuclear testing. At once, so Macmillan noted, it threatened to bog down on an absurd argument about the shape of the table. Finally, it was agreed that there should be a round table, with – two inches away from it – two separate tables for the opposing German delegations, who were excluded from 'High Table' as a continuing legacy of the lost war.

In a style familiar to watchers of the art in subsequent decades, the two sets of Geneva talks rumbled on through the summer, inconclusively – except that the impulsive Khrushchev now seemed prepared to give his ultimatum over Berlin an extra year's grace.

Frustrations with Adenauer . . .

As domestic pressures piled up on the way to his crucial General Election in the autumn of 1959, Macmillan tended to vent his frustrations over Geneva in the form of pungent comments about his principal allies into the discreet receptacle of his diaries; Konrad Adenauer in particular continued to draw Macmillan's fire.

28 May: . . . Adenauer has become – like many very old men – vain, suspicious, and grasping. . . . [He] has been carrying on a great campaign of vilification of Her Majesty's Government and especially of me. I am Neville Chamberlain reincarnate, and so on. . . .[52]

18 June: . . . De Gaulle will not play with me or anyone else. Adenauer is now half crazy. . . . Eisenhower is hesitant and unsure of himself. . . .

27 June: . . . De Gaulle and Adenauer are just hopeless. Adenauer because he is a false and cantankerous old man. . . .

23 July: . . . a half crazy Adenauer. . . .[53]

Although Macmillan had good reason for deeming Adenauer obstructive over talks with the Russians (and 1959 did mark the beginning of the eighty-three-year-old titan's final decline), the particular harshness of some of his private remarks seems curiously excessive. Central to any argument over Berlin, or East Germany, Adenauer was ever faithful to the Dulles line of negotiating only from strength – and thus set, immediately and philosophically, at odds with Macmillan. If Macmillan thought that Adenauer's inflexibility might spike a chance of detente with Khrushchev, Adenauer – by 1959 – regarded him with suspicion as a 'wet', almost an appeaser, prepared to sell out Germany's vital interests. As Macmillan recognised, there was something specious about Adenauer's attachment to reunification – to which he, the Catholic Rhinelander, was in truth no more attached than his allies. Thus, recalled Macmillan, whether he was Foreign Secretary or Prime Minister, the issue always produced:

a certain unreality, because unless you put as Item One in any agenda – the Reunification of Germany – either amongst ourselves or with the Russians – you would be thought to have 'betrayed the cause'. On the other hand, it was quite clear that the Russians were not going to give up the defensive glacis they had built up by seizing Poland and East Germany . . . certainly not while they suffered from nuclear inequality.[54]

Perhaps neither of these astute politicians fully appreciated the other's electoral necessities; as it was, both won massive majorities on their respective, and opposed, policies.

Nevertheless, none of the above can fully explain the extent of personal animosity that had, regrettably, grown up between the two – and which was to affect considerably more than just the 'climb to the summit'. In theory, they should have got on splendidly together. They had much in common – elegance, a shrewd wit and enjoyment of good conversation and wine. Both politicians also combined high idealism with a good deal of scepticism, sometimes amounting to cynicism. The Rhinelander Adenauer was a devout Catholic, which would have made him at least as sympathetic to Macmillan as his steadfast anti-Communism, and they both had been founder members of the club for European reconciliation. Above all they shared that sense of the ever-present mantle of history, so intrinsic to Macmillan. After their first tête-à-tête in Bonn back in June 1954, Macmillan had been fascinated by a long discourse by Adenauer covering the whole history of the Germans back to Roman times. *But*, recorded Macmillan acridly in his memoirs, 'during the next nine years I was destined to listen to it on every occasion when we met. . . .' (Possibly Adenauer might have shared the same feelings on hearing Macmillan's No. 1 record, always produced with devastating effect, on the tragic significance of the First World War!) As observed by his sister, Madame Pandit, Nehru – with whom Macmillan shared both a low threshold of boredom and often similar view of people – had a give-away trait of crumbling bread at a meal whenever boredom seized him; 'the greater the pile of crumbs, the greater the boredom. . . !'[55] Competition for producing the greatest pile was evidently disputed between Adenauer and the Canadian Prime Minister Diefenbaker. Like the Indian grandee, Macmillan too was frankly bored by Adenauer's conversation, often parochial and especially repetitive in old age. 'A man of great courage' (a virtue to which Macmillan always accorded top marks whenever he recognised it) was Macmillan's final summing-up on Adenauer, but 'he struck me as artful'.[56]

Yet, on top of these disabilities in 'personal chemistry', there was a more fundamental element at work – Macmillan's ambivalence towards Germans as a whole. Although, back in 1947, it was Macmillan who at the Council of Europe had called out 'bring on the Germans', as these defeated Germans became progressively more powerful, and competitive in world markets, Macmillan found it difficult to suppress deeply inculcated mistrusts and indeed aversions. On returning from Adenauer's funeral in April 1967, he remarked on the powerful *frisson* that the sight of the guard of honour clad in coalscuttle helmets had inescapably aroused in him.

However hard Macmillan might try to dissemble his anti-German instincts, Adenauer too had highly sensitive antennae. Moreover, he also had his own motives for not being over-fond of the British. These dated back to the early days of the Occupation when he had been dismissed from his beloved post as Burgermeister of Cologne by a lowly British administrator, for incompetence. Shortly after the event he remarked to a journalist[57] that his three chief dislikes were 'the Russians, the Prussians and the British'. More important, he was highly mistrustful of Britain's disruptive intentions towards his precious dream of European integration. Britain's European policy, he once remarked to a German diplomat in London, was 'one long fiddle'.[58]

Chapter Six

Electoral Triumph
1958–1959

Never in this century did a new Prime Minister take office under such a cloud of doubt as did Macmillan at the beginning of 1957. None stood higher than he did when the Queen granted his request for a dissolution and General Election in the autumn of 1959 . . . a matter mostly of confidence, patience and personality. . . .

(Daily Telegraph, *22 April 1971, review of*
HM, Riding the Storm)

I am, I think, what is called clubbable. I rather like talk. I like characters. I like a pub, I like a club. . . .

(HM, *9 April 1979*)

To all politicians all elections are matters of consequence, but that of 1959 was to assume quite transcending importance for Macmillan. Never to be forgotten was the horror with which senior Tories like Macmillan still recalled the shattering defeat of 1945, and some might claim that Macmillan had started planning the next election from the day he entered office in 1957; certainly the mammoth Commonwealth tour of 1958, and the Moscow 'voyage of discovery' were undeniably planned with at least one eye on the electorate; and great vote-getters they had turned out to be – as had Macmillan's two successful breach-healing visits to Eisenhower. But an expanding economy was a necessary foundation to electoral success. Back in March 1958, Macmillan had delivered a major economic policy restatement to the Conservative Political Centre, entitled 'The Middle Way – 20 Years After'. In tone, it struck listeners who remembered the original work as being more polished and aware of the politically possible than the original, rather heavy work, with its charts about milk distribution and marketing schemes. His speech began with an attack on the evils of egalitarianism; it was 'wrong morally' 'to deny the bold, the strong, the prudent and the clever the rewards and privileges of exercising their qualities', which could only 'enthrone in society the worst and basest of human attributes; envy, jealousy and spite . . .'. It was also 'wrong politically, because I do not see how Britain, with all its rich diversity and vitality, could be turned into an egalitarian society without, as we have seen in Eastern Europe, a gigantic exercise in despotism'.[1] Macmillan then, however, restated his views of twenty years previously (and to which he would still be vociferously loyal some three decades later); namely that the Tories should always 'occupy the middle ground'. His critic, the Labour MP Emrys Hughes, reckoned though that:

Had Macmillan proposed in 1958 many of the measures he had advocated twenty years before, his popularity among the Tory big business supporters would have disappeared overnight and

they would have immediately begun a campaign to get rid of
him.[2]

This was at best only partly fair – in the intervening twenty years
much had happened. Notably, under the Attlee government aspects
of the more radical planning elements proposed by *The Middle Way*
had been put into effect – with fairly disastrous results. But the
champion of the planned economy had by no means disappeared
without trace; for example, in the summer of 1957 Macmillan had
created the Council on Prices, Productivity and Incomes. In effect
a forerunner of the Prices and Incomes Board set up in the 1960s
under a Labour government, it consisted of 'Three Wise Men' – a
judge, an accountant and an economist. The aim was to obtain
what Macmillan described as 'restraint without tears', and though
the Council had swiftly run up against Frank Cousins's veto it did
in fact achieve a measure of success. This was followed by the
policy of the 'guiding light', which laid down that under prevailing
circumstances a rise of 2 per cent in wages and salaries might be
acceptable, 3 per cent in certain circumstances, but with flexibility
for special groups and, in particular, for incentive bonuses.

Macmillan's fear of recession was as strong as ever. To the end
of his life, Macmillan remained fond of his Lewis Carroll image,
that inflation and deflation were 'like caterpillar and Alice, one side
of the mushroom makes you grow, the other side shrinks you . . .
all part of the same mushroom, very much my whole view of
economics. . . .'[3]

The key figure in control of the economy at this juncture was the
new Chancellor of the Exchequer, Heathcoat Amory. Macmillan
much preferred him to his predecessor, Thorneycroft. In a diary
entry in October 1958 he observed trenchantly: 'The former is *very*
intelligent, flexible and courteous. The latter was fundamentally
stupid, rigid, and *cassant*.'[4] The former Minister of Agriculture was
a unique figure in British Tory politics, already one of a dying breed
– the lovable and caring paternalist, devoid of all personal ambition.
He had spent most of his life immersed in his native Devon, in local
government, family business and good works. Originally a Liberal,
he had been 'converted' by Macmillan's *The Middle Way*, though he
did not meet the author until after the war. During the Second
World War he rose to the rank of lieutenant-colonel, fought at
Salerno, and then – although, in his late forties, he should have

been exempted on grounds of age – insisted that he drop into Arnhem with the troops he had trained. He was severely wounded, with injuries that caused him much subsequent pain. Returning from the wars, he distinguished himself as the 'good' employer in the family textile business, and came to national notice with his views that the evils in industry, and within the Tory Party equally, were chiefly the result of the bad employer; he believed strongly that co-partnership was the only practical alternative to state control, and criticised the excessive burden of taxation for penalising initiative and enterprise. Elected to the 1945 Parliament, his views put him unhesitatingly in the Macmillan camp.

A bachelor and a man of great simplicity and frugality (he had no housekeeper, lived off hurried meals in teashops, and took his mending home to an aunt in Tiverton), he was also engagingly shy. When, in 1951, Churchill summoned him to be Minister of Pensions, he is said to have replied, 'you must have got the wrong Amery [i.e. Leo Amery],' which received the gruff retort: 'No. A-M-O-R-Y. . . .'[5] Diligently painstaking, and esteemed for his complete integrity, as a countryman he was perhaps even more successful as Macmillan's Minister of Agriculture in the 1957 government.

Amory regarded Macmillan as having been 'always very friendly to me'; he never:

> bullied me, as I think he did bully Selwyn. . . . He was terrified of one thing, a slump. . . . he did ring me up occasionally. 'Don't you think there might be a slump in a month?' – that was the influence of Roy Harrod. He was always pleased by anything that was expansionary, almost a wild inflationist at that time. . . . It was his instinct to be rebellious against the restrictive actions of the Treasury – he never liked the Treasury: 'What is wrong with inflation, Derry?' I'd reply 'You're thinking of your constituency in the 1930s?' – 'Yes, I am thinking of the under-use of resources – let's over-use them!' . . . He believed in import controls, but the Treasury wouldn't let him. . . .[6]

Macmillan himself spoke of his second Chancellor with warmest affection:

> sweet and Christian nature . . . very good . . . not conscious of his great gifts. Very simple, humble man . . . and a charming

man; very great, generous character. A little eccentric . . . well, he lives like me. . . . Absolutely unselfish . . . he would have been a monk, I think, in the Middle Ages. He was a real Franciscan type. . . .[7]

Macmillan's affection blended with the satisfaction of having a Chancellor more malleable than Thorneycroft. In fact, as Harold Wilson notes, during his whole premiership – later with Selwyn Lloyd, and finally Maudling – Macmillan never lost control of the Treasury (Wilson added sardonically, 'which he saw as the means of creating a favourable financial system for winning elections').[8] For his first Budget of 1958, Amory had produced what Macmillan called a 'good, but humble little package'[9] in which a modest £50 million (the same amount that Thorneycroft had sought to trim three months earlier) of tax cuts was injected, more for its 'psychological effect'[10] than any other. Though it was accepted as cautiously neutral, immediately after the Budget his fears of recession caused Macmillan to begin pressing harder for reflation, removing controls on bank lending and hire purchase. At the end of July he was praising the new Chancellor as 'really handling the economy with great skill. Cautious where necessary, but not afraid of bolder action. He is worth 20 Thorneycrofts!'[11]

Yet, as a Cabinet minute of 27 October 1958 shows, Macmillan was always far from being unaware of the dangers of inflation; the 'corrective measures needed', he recognised in pious hope,

> must not entail commitments for the future which are either indefinite or excessive. The current need is for action which will give a quick and selective stimulus to production and employment without imposing a fresh strain on the balance of payments or over-loading the economy with long-term expansionary plans which will lead in future years to a recurrence of inflationary pressure. . . .[12]

All through 1958 and 1959, Macmillan – with those painful memories of the impact of Suez during his time as Chancellor – was anxious about Britain's dependence on the USA and her prosperity. The importance of sterling, tightly interrelated with international confidence, was uppermost in his mind. Throughout his premiership he recognised the value of fixed exchange rates, added to the fact that a large part of the world still banked with Britain; 'We are so vulnerable,' he had written to Roy Harrod in February 1958, 'given the role of sterling, to the confidence factor, that we seem to be inhibited from making the proper use of the classical methods of monetary control. . . .' And international confidence was a key ingredient for victory at the forthcoming polls. Although an exchange of letters with Amory in January 1959 shows Macmillan still weighing up the essential dilemma of 'boom or slump?', under strong pressure from his *éminence grise*, Roy Harrod, as well as his adviser, Lord Mills, but opposed by some equally strong resistance from a reluctant Amory and the Treasury, the die was cast for reflation. Bank rate was reduced to 4 per cent (in November 1958); targets were set to slash taxation by £200 million; the 1959 Budget date was brought forward from 7 April to 17 March; and a bold move towards limited convertibility (long an ambition of Macmillan's) was taken at the end of December.

Budget 1959; Too Much Reflation?

Amory was, however, already unhappy about inflationary pressures at the beginning of 1959. On 12 January, Macmillan found him, 'urged on by the Treasury', 'rather stiff. He still fears another inflationary boom. . . .'[13] Macmillan (who thought the Treasury was giving Amory 'as bad advice as it has to every Chancellor in turn. . . . I have greater belief in Roy Harrod . . .')[14] countered in a letter (of 19 January), pointing out that industrial production was still falling, and proposing a programme of public investment, especially in housing and education – though recognising that this would of necessity increase government spending figures. When the 1959 Budget was finally produced, it struck Macmillan as being 'simple and attractive'. Income tax, which had stood for some years at 8s 6d, was reduced by 9d (it remained at this figure until 1965) with further reductions on the lower rates. Purchase tax was cut, and 2d taken off a pint of beer; investment allowances were restored. In delivering this pre-election Budget to the Commons Macmillan noted how Amory 'got rather tired at the end of his 2 hours speech and we thought he was going to faint. But he got through. . . .'[15] The following day Macmillan was gratified to learn that the Budget had been '*very* well received in the country and by the Press'. On the backbenches Thorneycroft and his allies fumed. One economist at the time rated it as 'the most generous Budget ever introduced in normal peace-time conditions';[16] while twenty years later Mrs Thatcher (when she and Macmillan still saw largely eye to eye on economic issues), commented: '. . . I must tell you that I think part of our post-1959 problems arose from an extremely over-generous Budget in 1959. . . .'[17]

The results were swift. Coming on top of the wave of an international boom, which – instead of the slump predicted by Harrod, and by Macmillan – had just started, production in Britain rose by 10 per cent in the year. It was a level that the economy could not safely maintain for long. By the end of May Macmillan could record in his diaries that unemployment figures showed a '50,000 decrease (4,000 above the estimate which I had been given). This is good. At the same time, the cost of living has remained unchanged for a year. So we have really brought off the double. . . .'[18] But Heathcoat Amory was still, evidently, not entirely happy; coming to dine with Macmillan alone that same night,

He seemed rather low. I believe it is partly because he lives this strange hermit life and (unless he remembers) hardly eats. . . . He is very sensitive and very conscientious and rather a man to worry. He is now worried about . . . generally having had a too reflationary Budget. . . .[19]

Amory put it to Macmillan that he would like to retire, in due course, after the election. Looking back at his 1959 Budget years later, Amory admitted:

We went a little too far, didn't realise the boom ahead on a Tory victory. . . . Then, for 1960, I realised it had to slow down – we would have to go for a lower annual growth rate. I think he [Macmillan] would have lost his joy of me; I was much more cautious than he was, I foresaw our paths would have diverged in one or two years' time. . . .[20]

But, whatever the long-term economic perspective, the 1959 Budget certainly worked to Macmillan's short-term political advantage. The encouraging upturn in the economy in the spring of 1959 decided Macmillan against holding a snap election. In February of the previous year Rochdale had been lost with a shattering swing of over 16,000 Tory voters, but the end of the year had shown first indications at last of an apparent reversal in the glum trend of lost by-elections, with Aberdeen East held by a 6000 majority. They would wait at least until the autumn, going virtually the full length of the mandate. Heathcoat Amory's 1959 Budget and its reception had been a fundamental factor in this decision.

Macmillan in Command

Although the popular 'give-away' Budget of 1959 unmistakably provided the last key tumbler in the combination lock of Macmillan's election strategy, in the final analysis it was his own personality that was the decisive factor. After two and a half years it had blossomed into something quite different to the figure friends and colleagues remembered from the 1930s, different even from the man who had apprehensively taken over from Eden in 1957. Gone was the diffident publisher, the insecure Duke's son-in-law, the MP who with his pompous, pedantic speeches and heavy humour could empty the House of Commons. Even, or perhaps especially, since his successful Commonwealth tour of 1958, there was a new self-assurance. And somebody (it may have been Edith Baker, the redoubtable housemaid at Birch Grove, who doubled with being Lady Bowls Champion of Hampshire) had changed his whole appearance. When Michael Fraser, head of the Conservative Research Department, first met Macmillan – on a train to Newcastle in the bitterly cold winter of 1947 – he found him:

> wearing an ancient sort of driving coat, with huge pockets, with his feet up on the opposite seat, as in the front bench of the Commons, wearing an old Edwardian kind of cloth cap with a button on top, and reading *Rouge et Noir* . . . pince-nez and shaggy moustache . . . a picture of a kind of bizarre Edwardian academic. . . ![21]

Though the eccentric Edwardian stylishness was still maintained in the voluminous plus-fours on the grouse-moor, the baggy trousers that might once have dismayed any high-street tailor in Stockton had been replaced by spruce new suits from Savile Row. Gone were the little Commissar-like spectacles; the 'Colonel Blimp' moustache had been ruthlessly pruned; the disarrayed teeth fixed – which somehow transformed the toothy, half-apologetic smile; the hair had assumed a more sophisticated shapeliness. Here was a new, almost dapper figure, with instant authority; the television 'personality' had arrived.

On 8 September 1959, Macmillan informed his Cabinet that he had asked the Queen for a dissolution and that the General Election would be held in exactly one month's time. Elected in May 1955, the government could have run for another six months, but the timing had been carefully thought out and the path supremely well prepared. The Prime Minister was thoroughly at ease in his job (his personal Gallup Poll rating had reached a high of 67 per cent), supported by a consort who had had time to become well known, and viewed with affection in the country at large. In contrast, the Opposition had seldom seemed less happy or more divided. By the summer the Macmillan diaries were betraying some rare notes of optimism, following a rapturously received speech he had made at the Albert Hall: '*30 June:* The Press is excellent. Even *The Chronicle, The Manchester Guardian*, etc., admit the Government triumph last night. . . .'[22] A few days later, Boothby – who always had a good feel for the groundswell – wrote to Macmillan recording Labour disarray: 'the impression I have been getting is one of an immense and increasing disintegration which is not yet appreciated by the public, or even by the Tory Party; and that this applies not only to the nuclear bomb issue, but over the whole field. . . .'[23] His instinct was to cash in on this 'state of intellectual chaos' and go for an early election. Macmillan replied in a rather more cautious vein, agreeing that Labour's difficulties were 'fundamental', but that a fickle desertion of Tory 'good luck' could easily swing things around. The Boothby letter seems, however, to have helped fix his mind on an early election date in the autumn.

With the title suggested by Macmillan from his early pre-war endeavours, but much aided by Butler (who, incidentally, in one of his famous leaks to the press had let the cat out of the bag in September 1958 that there was going to be no election that year), the Conservatives hoisted their colours to the mast with a manifesto called *The Next Five Years*. In tone mildly left of centre, and sparkling with confidence, it summarised the main issues as follows:

Do you want to go ahead on the lines which have brought prosperity at home?

Do you want your present leaders to represent you abroad?

The introduction to the 1959 election handbook, prepared by the Conservative Research Department, listed the main economic points that the party intended to emphasise. It began by stressing prosperity:

Seven years of sound policy and good government have brought our country to a high level of prosperity. Progress has not been unchecked, but it is a tribute to the underlying strength of our free and flexible economy that we have weathered . . . the economic effects of the Suez crisis, and the recession of world trade in 1957–58 with so little effect on our commercial position.

It continued:

The Standard of Living is higher today than ever before in our history. It is no accident that today the British people are earning, eating, producing, buying, building, growing and saving far more than ever they did under a Socialist Government. As Mr Macmillan has said: 'National solvency is the foundation on which all our achievements to date rest. And it is the foundation on which all our plans for the future must rest too.'

Exploiting a Friend

Meanwhile the campaign gained a boost by the extraordinary stage management with which Macmillan – like a conjuror out of a hat – had managed to produce Eisenhower in London just a few days before the election began. Macmillan had not read Trollope for nothing, and no one understood better than Trollope the art of leaving no weapon unused, nor any principle uncompromised in pursuit of winning a crucial election. In his exploitation of his closest ally, Macmillan was quite shameless – and Eisenhower was fully aware of it, even to the point of some irritation. In advance of the March visit to Washington by Macmillan, Dulles had warned that he was 'trying to get all the domestic mileage he can get'. Dulles added that 'we are not unsympathetic to this since we don't want to see Bevan win the election,'[24] and that there was no objection to giving Macmillan 'an important role' – though he was suspicious that he might be prepared to compromise on the Berlin issue for an electoral advantage. Three days later Dulles was recording that the 'Pres. was pretty hot' about Macmillan: 'All the publicity he is seeking is outrageous – press conferences, appearance on the Hill – it looks like a publicity tour. . . .'[25]

Nevertheless, by adroit manipulation of the US media Macmillan was able to extract the maximum advantage from the trip – and was forgiven by his old friend, Ike. All through the spring and summer Macmillan then angled for Eisenhower to visit London in the course of his projected world tour. Up to the last minute, it was a cliff-hanger. By 27 July, 'He proposes to go on his travels in *October*, with visits to Japan, India, Pakistan, and Russia. . . . If he does not come to U.K. this will be an insult to the Queen and to our whole nation which will never be forgiven. . . .'[26] Only by implication did Macmillan suggest what such an omission might also do to his electoral plans. However, by 22 August Eisenhower – under considerable pressure from Macmillan – had been persuaded 'to make up for his folly', and Macmillan with delight was recording, 'Everything seems now to be more or less arranged for the Presidential visit. It will be quite amusing, but I do not think we shall get much work done!'[27]

In the event, Eisenhower's visit, his first to England since the war, was a roaring – and rather moving – success, not only for the Macmillan election campaign. Macmillan picked him up at London airport on 27 August, and such were the throng, the route all the way from the airport that, crawling at snail's pace, it took their car two hours to cover the seventeen miles. Eisenhower, in his memoirs, records with amusement how his host assured him that he had given 'a minimum of publicity to our route'; hence he had been quite surprised to find such an amazing turnout. Never has a US President had such a welcome before or since: everywhere he went there were the same warmly cheering crowds along roads and in the villages. The next day he flew to Balmoral to spend two days with the Queen, returning for the weekend with Macmillan at Chequers. Here there were a few hours of serious talk, though Macmillan noted that his guest 'got somewhat restless', and wandered off to hit golf balls in the grounds: 'Unhappily, since the grass was long, a large quantity of balls were struck in proportion to those ultimately recovered. . . .' The visit ended with Ike hosting a 'nostalgic' dinner party at the American Embassy for all his British wartime collaborators. With a deferential touch much appreciated by Eisenhower, Macmillan requested him '*not* to put me next to him, but to rank me only as "Political Adviser" AFHQ . . .',[28] which enabled Eisenhower to place Field-Marshals Alanbrooke and Alexander on either side of him.

Before Eisenhower departed he featured in a joint television appearance at No. 10 with Macmillan, stressing their old friendship and the new excellence of the Special Relationship. (With No. 10 in an advanced state of dilapidation,[29] Eisenhower was amused by the thought that both could have disappeared through the floor: 'It might have been curious, with both principals falling out of sight of the viewing public while expressing confidence in the future.')[30] Even though Macmillan could not get Eisenhower publicly to endorse his 'summitry' ploys, as an opening shot in the election both the broadcast and the visit as a whole were an unqualified triumph. Macmillan's old adversary, Herbert Morrison, growled that the 'slight, if understandable, exaggeration which gave the public the idea that the two men enjoyed a long, intimate association . . . offered wonderful election propaganda on the eve of the announcement of the polling date . . .'.[31]

The Macmillan Electoral Machine

As soon as a glowing Ike had continued on his voyages, the election began with a vengeance. More staid members of the Tory old guard were shocked by the vulgarity of the campaign. There were times when even Macmillan himself was concerned whether his ebullient Party Chairman, Hailsham, had gone too far ('very foolishly – made an attack on the Liberals . . . done a lot of harm to us. I am beginning to wonder whether his lack of judgment does not outweigh his brilliance . . .', he had written some time previously) but on the whole he was unashamed; the main thing was to *win the election*.

Since 1957, under the aegis of Hailsham and his deputy, Oliver Poole, banker and director of the *Financial Times*, the Tory Party had been gearing itself to fight the first modern, media-age election campaign. Macmillan had been closely involved, all the way along, attending all but four out of some seventeen planning sessions, which was something rare for any Prime Minister. At the unprecedented cost of half a million pounds, the advertising firm of Colman, Prentis and Varley had been brought in to saturate the public with such slogans as 'Life's Better Under the Conservatives. Don't Let Labour Ruin It'. The constant harping on the theme of the new, 'You've-never-had-it-so-good' prosperity was to pay off. Richard Crossman, with acerbity not untinged with envy, remarked that the Prime Minister was being sold 'as though he were a detergent'.[32]

Since the last General Election in 1955, the number of British homes with television sets had nearly doubled and Macmillan had set to adapting his own brand of showmanship to this potent new medium – despite his very real distaste for the British press, and despite his having warned Harold Evans gloomily, back in 1957, that he 'was too old to learn new publicity tricks and would do nothing out of character'.[33] His first breakthrough as a 'television personality' had come with a full-length interview staged by a young, brash and virtually unknown journalist called Robin Day, on 23 February 1958, immediately on his return from the Commonwealth tour. This had been followed three months later by an impromptu interview with the world-famous Ed Murrow, from which Macmillan emerged established as (in the words of the *Spectator*) 'every inch the favourite fireside politician'.[34] One experienced political observer, and later head of the BBC, Charles Curran, reckoned this was the moment when 'for the first time the man in the street saw and heard the real Macmillan – not the comic Edwardian dandy of the caricatures but the masterful, dominating, self-confident statesman.'[35] The Opposition had tried to hit back with such jeering slogans as 'Macwonder', 'MacBlunder, the mothball Prime Minister', and the cartoonist Vicky's 'Supermac'. But 'Supermac' in particular had thoroughly rebounded to become, instead of a term of opprobrium, one of affectionate admiration making the intended victim something of a folk hero.

By the end of the 1959 election Macmillan had got together a powerful little team for his own performances. Apart from Harold Evans and Michael Fraser at Conservative Central Office, who kept him supplied with the vital ammunition of facts and figures, the key personality was his speechwriter, George Christ. Macmillan had great affection for Christ (pronounced with a flat 'i'), and placed total reliance upon him. His campaign, he reckoned, 'would have been quite impossible without George Christ. This man has real genius. He is also a most agreeable friend and companion.'[36] Macmillan found Christ always full of ideas and aphorisms – supplemented by phrases from the latest pop-songs provided by his election driver. 'Who is "Lenny-the-Lion"?' he would ask. He also consulted that great comedian, Bud Flanagan, for help. An immense amount of work always went into each throwaway and apparently spontaneous remark. Speeches were tried out, *fortissimo*, in the East Grinstead garden of his Private Secretary, Freddie Bishop, who found the neighbours raptly listening to these 'perorations over the hedge'; and Dorothy claimed that he used her 'as the man in the street; if I can understand it, he says anyone can!'[37] By the end of September he had overtaxed his vocal cords; the indispensable Dr Richardson prescribed 'some good stuff', but Macmillan found liberal inhalations of vintage port to be more effective than the doctor's medicine.

After the initial flush of enthusiasm, the second and third weeks of the campaign threw some cold water on Tory optimism. In his last diary entry (28 September), Macmillan noted 'Daily Mail polls bad – down to 2% lead. But I still feel confident' – though, lying in his bed at No. 10, he wondered whether he would still be there in ten days' time. He was worried that Gaitskell had made rather too good a start; about the same time Oliver Poole confided to Woodrow Wyatt, 'You've got us on the run. . . . I think you may win. . . .'[38] But much would depend on the last Conservative television broadcasts. For Macmillan's final performance Poole asked John Wyndham to seek out Norman Collins, the novelist and television expert, to help produce it. Meeting in Macmillan's hotel room in Nottingham, with Dorothy bustling about 'in a woolly dressing gown' and the room cluttered with posters, handbills, full ashtrays and empty bottles and glasses, and filled with tobacco smoke, Macmillan apologised deferentially for the 'horrid scene', remarking 'how dreadful to think that the affairs of a great country were being conducted from a room like this . . .'.[39] Noting Macmillan's guardsmanlike way of holding himself, Collins decided he should do the broadcast standing up. 'Oh I see,' said Macmillan. 'But am I allowed to?' After he had run through what was supposedly a 'dummy rehearsal', he remarked diffidently that he hoped he would be better when doing it live later that night. Collins replied, 'Mr Macmillan, you have already done it and you have been recorded!' Astonished by the sleight-of-hand, Macmillan told Collins he was a 'remarkable man', and that it was 'like going to the dentist to have a tooth out and to be told that it has already been drawn'.[40] There was a brief row with the BBC, who had been promised a 'live' performance, but it was the recording that went out – bringing praise even from the *Daily Mirror*.

A Personal Triumph

Macmillan had stumped the country with energy, travelling 2500 miles and speaking at some seventy-four meetings; and gave every appearance of enjoying himself. He tried to strike a mean between what he liked to describe as 'a jaunty and detached attitude'[41] and 'a humble note, stressing the need for national unity'.[42] He was at his best when speaking informally, to groups of party workers, boosting their morale. For, right to the last, the election was by no means a foregone conclusion. The *Guardian*, the *Observer* and the *Spectator* had all come out against the Tories, and some telling television broadcasts had been orchestrated by a young Anthony Wedgwood Benn. Then Gaitskell began making a rash, and panicky, electoral promise about vast sums of money which would be earmarked by Labour for pensions and other social reforms, and which would be raised by cutting the allowance on business expenses – *without* threatening any increase in taxes. The blandishments mounted daily. 'This is absurd,' Macmillan remembered thinking:

> . . . I was reading about it in the car, with George Christ, on the way down to Birch Grove. . . . I remember exactly where it was. I said to George, 'We've got him!' And we got out of the car, and called a meeting on Wandsworth Common. . . . There were a few people following, and we had a sort of press conference, and I said 'if this is an auction, I am not in it!' And that finished it. . . .[43]

Macmillan later felt that those were probably the words that won the election. Certainly in the last days, it was apparent that Gaitskell's bid had been seen, the bluff called, and the mood in the country had swung. A telling Vicky cartoon at the time (and one of Macmillan's favourites) showed Macmillan running off with a working-man's clothes, Gaitskell left in a bath towel, with the caption: 'Wot? ME trying to pinch YOUR clothes? Cor, it's obvious they're mine, ain't it. . . ?' The image stuck; it was obvious Gaitskell had lost his clothes.

The Macmillans spent polling evening quietly at No. 10 watching the television results. One of the earliest personal satisfactions was the returning of Maurice Macmillan at Halifax with an increased majority. Coinciding with his final triumph over drinking, after a hard battle, the news gave his father particular pleasure. At 2 a.m., when the verdict seemed clear, he and Dorothy went down to Central Office where an excited crowd gave them both 'a fine ovation'.[44] Macmillan's own majority had risen by 2000, polling 27,055 against his Labour opponent's 11,603; the overall Tory lead over Labour was 107, compared with 67 in 1955. The Stock Exchange reacted with delight. It was, said Macmillan with no false humility, 'a staggering result' – and unprecedented; 'No party has been victorious three times running increasing its majority each time.'

Both friend and foe alike united in acclaiming the 1959 General Election a great personal triumph for 'Supermac'. It was, wrote his future Chief Whip, Martin Redmayne, 'the sudden genius of the new Prime Minister that clinched it'. Acquired over the previous two years, it was his new 'lively confidence which took the electorate by storm . . .'.[45] Even Herbert Morrison was forthright in recognising that the overcoming of the Tory Party's setback over Suez 'was largely due to the skilful politics of Harold Macmillan, together with his intuitive understanding of a large proportion of the British people . . .'.[46] Nobody doubted that Macmillan, with his hundred-seat majority, was now one of the most powerful Prime Ministers in British history, and nobody doubted that here was a man who revelled in his power.

The 'Actor–Manager'

Perhaps the most important factor explaining Macmillan's new-found confidence was that, for all the headaches and the 'balls' that had to be juggled in the air, Macmillan genuinely – and increasingly – enjoyed being Prime Minister. No one, he wrote in his memoirs,

> has any sympathy with the self-pitying statesman, going about like poor Ramsay MacDonald, complaining that he felt like 'a weary Titan'. After all, the answer is easy. Nobody asked you to hold up the world. If your shoulders are tired, there are others ready and anxious to sustain the burden. . . .

Macmillan loved the acting that being at the summit of power seemed to call for; the sudden switches from the Duke's son-in-law to the man-of-the-people; from the West End clubman to the shrewd Scottish publisher; from the academic to the soldier; from the visionary to the pragmatic; from the Edwardian to the man of the space age. It was not undeserved that Enoch Powell, deprecatingly, dubbed him the 'old actor–manager', and the speed with which he could effect his changes of costume delighted him as much as it baffled his audience as to where the real man ended and the actor began – a bafflement that served only to fuel his own delight.

The House of Commons provided full scope for his acquired histrionic skills and his speed on his feet. The verbose and ornate grand generalisations of the past, the laboured wit, had been replaced by something much more devastating – a supreme skill at catching a questioner off-balance with an incisive, and sometimes brusque, riposte. His timing had become almost impeccable, and so had the speed of his footwork. Having studied performances from the backbenches for so many years, and having received the advice of real professionals like Lloyd George and Winston Churchill, Macmillan had by now come close to perfecting the art of dominating the Commons. Talking about the advice he would like to give a new young minister, he once gave this admonition, 'You have to sympathise with the House, and like it.' He continued:

> rather like those Italian lakes, one moment it's calm, the next moment there is suddenly a tremendous storm. . . . you have to study it closely. . . . usually when the press would say that something big was going to happen, it always petered out. . . . you have to know the man who is your questioner. . . . like a prep school, there are boys who are popular, whom you must

never slap down, even if they are asking a silly question, on the other side. . . . then there are the unpopular, the tiresome, and the House rather enjoys their being slapped down. . . . You must remember that, like a school, on the whole it dislikes the front bench (the masters). . . . often you can turn an enemy into a friend, by some slight recognition. . . .

Always keep your temper . . . and always have a good control of questions and supplementaries. . . . in many ways, this is the most anxious work; I would never have lunched out on question day.[47]

The most important factor in dominating the House, thought Macmillan, was 'never to give in, never to show how nervous and awful the whole business is. . . . I think I did seem to have what was called unflappability – if only they knew how one's inside was flapping all the time, they wouldn't have said that. . . .'[48] Repeatedly he confessed that, on a question day, or before a major speech, he would feel physically sick and seldom eat anything. For all his acquired expertise, which made him arguably the most brilliant speaker of his age in the English language, it was a nervousness that plagued him all his life.

Nigel Nicolson, a Tory MP by no means endeared to Macmillan in consequence of his hawkish line over Suez, noted with approval how in the House Macmillan managed 'to conserve energy, by standing like an island in the middle of the road and letting the political debate run round him like traffic'. Another observer who studied Macmillan's performance with notable insight, Norman Shrapnel, the parliamentary correspondent of the *Guardian*, considered that 'Of all the players who have appeared on the Westminster stage over the last two decades', Macmillan was the one who intrigued him most:

By turns blind and aware, sensitive and chillingly cynical, he was perhaps the most complex of them all. . . . He understood, if anybody did, the art of serious political acting. He of all men knew the necessity and the potency of the mask. . . . Behind it, the patience and complexity of the man had a chance to operate. . . . He built himself his Edwardian façade and it provided him with enough cover to get on with a strictly contemporary job.

Shrapnel noted the particular quality, too, of the Macmillan voice.
It was:

> the sort of voice that goes well with disdain. That was something
> else irrevocably lost to the Commons when Macmillan went. He
> was often disdainful, or sounded it, in dealing with offensive,
> unreasonable or just plain awkward questions. It was a weapon
> no subsequent Prime Minister could hope to use to the same
> effect. . . . The ambiguity of the total mix had a panache, a lofty
> grandeur all its own. . . .
>
> His masks were working masks, not for pride or vanity. They
> enabled Macmillan to distance himself, get on with the job with
> minimum distraction. . . . Sometimes the mask would slip and
> we would glimpse the real, thin skin behind. . . . Behind the
> mask, through the skin, one could occasionally catch hints of the
> inner workings of a carefully protected emotional life.[49]

Probably no one had studied Macmillan's parliamentary technique more closely than his critical deputy, Rab Butler, no mean
performer himself. 'He had absolute mastery,' admitted Rab,
'because everything was very carefully prepared, he took the most
immense trouble – for example, his speeches had an asterisk marked
in, meaning "careful pause for extemporary comment"!'[50]
All those who saw Macmillan in action regularly attested to the
extraordinary power of his sensitivity to parliamentary moods.
Harold Wilson (the two Harolds formed, to the end, a curious
mutual admiration society for each other, based chiefly on parliamentary prowess) echoed the views of many of Macmillan's own
entourage, in finding him to resemble in this respect 'a powerful
cat': 'not an alley cat, but a patrician cat, perhaps Persian – not
Siamese, because they're savage – which he was not. . . .'[51] It was
perhaps this feline sensitivity that enabled Macmillan, right to the
end of his life, to swing his audience, in a matter of moments, from
uproarious laughter to tears.
Not all of his opponents, however, agreed with Harold Wilson.
James Callaghan thought the Macmillan style 'altogether too
mannered and too artificial . . . too far removed from real life . . .'.[52]
Woodrow Wyatt was even more critical of the Edwardian music-hall
image, and sometimes found that 'the temptation to knock the
imaginary top-hat off the old trouper was almost irresistible'.[53]

Gaitskell

Whether his opponents liked the style or not, however, one fact was undeniable; so long as Hugh Gaitskell was in charge – and not only because of the internal quarrels that were currently rending the Labour Party – Macmillan's command of the Commons remained absolute. There was something about the worthy Gaitskell which brought out the least attractive characteristics in Macmillan. He heartily despised him and was successful in projecting his personal contempt to the electorate. The middle-class, Cheltenham-born son of a Burma civil servant, Gaitskell never felt at ease with the working class; 'he would travel first class to avoid the awkwardness of contact with them,' remarked his supporter, Lady Longford.[54] This was perhaps also an element that Macmillan recognised, but disliked in himself. Gaitskell had been to Winchester, then going on to New College, Oxford. Macmillan had more than the average Etonian's disdain for Wykehamists. Through no fault of his, Gaitskell had spent the war as a clerk in the civil service.[55] After Gaitskell had 'made a vulgar and violent attack on me'[56] during the 1959 May Day rally to Trafalgar Square, Macmillan exploded in his diary: 'He is a contemptible creature – a cold-blooded, Wykehamist intellectual and *embusqué*.'[57] It encapsulated all his feelings about Gaitskell.

At least, all but one; that was his professional contempt for Gaitskell (in marked contrast to Wilson) as a performer and adversary in the Commons. Though he recognised that Gaitskell spoke well,

He might have been a lecturer in Economics. He made the mistake, which Lloyd George warned me about, of making too many points. . . . he would ask ten, or fourteen, questions – one of which was unanswerable, without telling him a direct lie. . . . I soon learned that you only answered the easy ones. . . . If he had asked one question which he knew I couldn't give the answer to truthfully, it would have been much more effective. But he asked so many questions, it was like one of those exams where you know that the candidate need not attempt more than any four! So you attempted the four easy ones. Poor man. I did it over and over again to him; he never spotted it. . . .[58]

Macmillan himself regarded Gaitskell, not only in technique, as 'an incompetent man, too much the middle-class liberal. . . . a nice fellow, but rather a weak man. . . . He would open a great wound in the Labour Party, and then – most obligingly – place a tourniquet below the wound.'[59]

The Macmillan diaries abound with such references as when, after Gaitskell had written him a 'governessy sort of letter' over Quemoy,[60] he had – with unkind relish – sent him a reply deliberately by hand to Gaitskell's house in Hampstead, which had 'kept him up pretty late. Then the Press mercilessly rang up Gaitskell all the rest of the night, asking if he would send a further reply.' Macmillan rejoiced when the Labour Party Conference of 1958 firmly reinforced Gaitskell's leadership – knowing that he could trounce him the following year.

Macmillan recognised Harold Wilson as a different kettle of fish. To observers, the mutual admiration society between the two Harolds was always an odd one, but it was largely based on professional esteem. When Wilson made a speech attacking him, Macmillan would as often as not rate it in his diaries as 'very amusing',[61] or else treat it with the cautious respect it deserved. He always felt that, had Wilson been Leader of the Opposition, the 1959 election would have been a much tougher contest. Gaitskell, as he remarked on the BBC in April 1971, 'wasn't the kind of man who would drive a Government out'.[62] On his side, Harold Wilson claimed,

> There was absolutely no malice. After we had savaged each other in the House, we would then meet for a drink. . . . I think he liked my crack about his being 'First in, first out' at Suez, and when he was moving in for the kill in the House he invariably kicked the table under the despatch box with his right foot. Such courteous intimations have become rare since then![63]

Wilson would also admit that his admiration led him to emulate the Macmillan technique with some success, thereby acquiring the art of the carefully prepared impromptu and a general air of relaxation.

Managing Men, and Cabinet

Performance on the floor of the Commons, however, constitutes only one part of the success or failure of a Prime Minister. Deft parliamentary operator that he himself was, Harold Wilson once estimated that the really successful British Prime Ministers were those who bothered to visit the Smoking Room, Tea Room or Members' Dining Room. Even Nigel Birch, who bore little love for Macmillan, admitted how he excelled at chatting to MPs of all conditions in the Smoking Room. It came naturally to him: '. . . I am, I think, what is called clubbable. I rather like talk. I like characters. I like a pub, I like a club. . . .'[64] Peter Carrington recalled warmly how, 'whenever you made a speech, even as an under-secretary, you would always get a note saying "Well done," or some such thing. These things matter so much in politics. . . .'[65]

Carrington, who served under all Tory administrations from Churchill to Thatcher, added that he found Macmillan 'a marvellous boss, and a most courteous man; I was deeply fond of him.' The affection was reciprocated. Macmillan once described him to the author as 'the last of the Whigs' (which, in the Macmillan lexicon, was the highest of possible praises); 'full of common sense, a sense of history, and very good nerves . . . any government of the nineteenth century would have been full of Carringtons – always able to bugger off home to his estates if Parliament no longer wanted him. . . .'[66] This was several years before the Falklands compelled Carrington to resign and 'bugger off home'.

Something of the same personal affection was shared by Christopher Soames, often a prickly individual:

> . . . I loved working with him. He was really great, in the sense that he commanded devotion as well as respect. . . . I really loved that man; he was always fun, always very relaxed, reading a novel when you came to see him. That was the great thing about Harold as a boss – it was always such fun, jolly jokes in the Cabinet – rather like Winston – as opposed to today – no, it's all too serious! . . . He also had a great vision of the world. . . . [67]

Macmillan himself made no secret of the fact that he allowed of only the narrowest of margins between what was flippant, or even frivolous, and the deadly serious. Consequently, there were those, even among his closest Cabinet colleagues, who thought him devious, but this was – in Carrington's view – often because 'they couldn't always follow the flippancy, and see what was underneath. What *was* underneath was big views, always consistent, and they never seemed to me to deviate at all. . . .'[68]

Macmillan's skill in the appointment of subordinates has frequently been commented on, but he was equally skilled in managing them, the art of which lies greatly in securing affection and devotion. Affection and loyalty were, to Macmillan, always a two-way flow. His total confidence assured ministers and humbler subordinates alike that they would be backed to the hilt, and that – at least until the bloody 'Night of the Long Knives' in the summer of 1962 – a single error would not lead them to the guillotine. On the other hand, Macmillan's affection for his entourage did have its possessive side. Almost all of his private staff stayed on beyond the call of duty, and Macmillan himself later admitted that he had probably ruined for Philip de Zulueta – who was just thirty-two when he went to work for Macmillan in 1957 – a brilliant future in the Foreign Office.[69]

Predictably, by 1959, Macmillan had imposed his own clear stamp of management. In Sir Norman Brook,[70] the all-powerful Secretary to the Cabinet, Macmillan inherited an outstanding civil servant who had been in the business ever since the Churchill era and was a highly tuned political operator in his own right. His deputy, and successor, Burke Trend,[71] who prepared the Cabinet agenda and briefs, was a more formal individual and on somewhat less intimate terms with Macmillan, but he nevertheless observed his managerial technique acutely: 'He ran the Cabinet very gracefully – no sign of great effort. Sometimes he would show signs of impatience, but just enough to get things done. . . .'[72] A man of considerable intellectual power himself, Trend was constantly awed by the way in which Macmillan almost intuitively sensed the issues, and weighed them up, as he came into the room, and the speed with which his mind could flick from one aspect of a problem to another. Like Harold Wilson, Trend saw Macmillan in action as a big cat. When vexed, the eyes would flash, the right foot would tap the floor: 'just as animals don't get angry, Macmillan seldom did; when he did he turned and he really swiped. But it was all over quickly. . . .' There was never a formal vote taken in a Macmillan Cabinet; instead Trend would occasionally keep 'a quiet little tally of views expressed; if it was a close thing, then Harold would say, "Well, perhaps we had better have more time to think it over; put it on next week's agenda."'

Rab Butler, the long-suffering, loyal deputy, agreed on Macmillan's competence in managing the Cabinet: 'He was very good, only exceeded by little Attlee, who had a habit of biting people in the pants. . . . When Harold got bored, he would dismiss the Cabinet. . . . He was definitely a ruler.'[73] He also remembered occasions when Macmillan had been seized by the Black Dog depression, when he had had to go and bury himself alone in Jane Austen; 'Sometimes I had to step in and take over the Cabinet, telling them that "I told the PM to go away for a few days". . . .' It was a debility which his private staff too came to recognise sympathetically; though the habit of losing himself in a book was seen differently by his grandson, Alexander – who had once been recorded as saying that he wanted to become Prime Minister, 'and sit under a tree and read a book'.

In the course of his premiership, Macmillan altered the conventional, boardroom shape of the Cabinet table to something like a lozenge (although some of his colleagues also thought it more closely resembled a coffin). This was designed to make it easier for ministers at the far end of the table 'to hear and to talk and to see'. One of his other innovations in running the Cabinet was the introduction of a small table behind the pillars in the Cabinet Room of No. 10 at which were seated the private secretaries, Bishop (later Bligh), de Zulueta and Evans. The idea was to save time, and Macmillan – like Field-Marshal Montgomery – believed in the principle that his intimate staff should be kept fully 'in the picture' of all that was going on. He used his private secretaries somewhat as 'Monty' used his liaison officers, as his eyes and ears, and sometimes called them his 'major-generals'. Access to the Prime Minister was normally controlled by the private secretaries, and when they were not in Cabinet they protected him from an ante-room outside his office, where the egregious John Wyndham also held sway. 'Everything was done there,' explained Macmillan, 'they knew everybody, everything.'[74] The devoted John Wyndham, unpaid millionaire landowner, apart from his anomalous functions as court-jester and personal ADC, also worked in the private office and did all the party political work for Macmillan so that none of this should fall on the civil service employees. The owner of Petworth, Wyndham when being positively vetted for his security clearance was asked if he had any debts. 'Yes,' he replied. 'Two million.' Unable to find a taxi late at night at Victoria, he once bribed the driver and conductor of a bus (a form of transport with which Wyndham was unfamiliar) with £5 to each to drop him home – an anecdote vouchsafed for by the meticulous senior 'Garden Girl', Jane Parsons.[75]

The Prime Minister's 'Team'

Freddie Bishop,[76] the head of Macmillan's team, had worked in government ever since he was demobilised from the RAF in 1946. A subtle, diplomatic figure, he had briefly filled the same role as Principal Private Secretary to Macmillan's predecessor, Eden. In 1961 Bishop was succeeded, somewhat against Macmillan's wishes, by Tim Bligh, a much decorated ex-naval officer (and, like Macmillan, a Balliol man) who saw everything in much more black-and-white terms. Then there was Philip de Zulueta, the professional from the Foreign Office who handled all foreign affairs work, a former Guardsman of considerable intellectual agility and self-confidence, speaking Russian and flawless French. In addition to the Press Secretary, Harold Evans, this triumvirate was later augmented by John Hewitt, son of a clergyman, as Secretary for Appointments, and by Philip Woodfield, who was brought in from the Home Office to find the answers to awkward questions in the Commons. Finally, another important component of the entourage was the Prime Minister's Parliamentary Private Secretary, his eyes and ears in the Commons. Up to 1959 this role was filled by Tony Barber, an ex-POW, who later became Chancellor of the Exchequer during the Heath government. A small, wiry man described as resembling 'a terrier, going down into every hole',[77] Barber was succeeded – in notable contrast – by a heavy-weight Ulsterman, Knox Cunningham, a fifteen-stone, six-foot-six rugger blue, who to some suggested the image of Macmillan's secret service gunman.

Bishop noted how, whereas Eden had been most punctilious about never asking any of his private secretaries for policy advice, with Macmillan it became a habit to be consulted, and to give views – especially on foreign affairs: 'He liked to throw out ideas and provoke ideas. . . .'[78]

As part of the ritual of keeping informed his 'major-generals', before lunch most days and again in the evening at the end of the working day Macmillan would hold a sherry session. It was highly unorthodox; Foreign Office officials from across the road, Treasury men or politicians would drift in, while the private secretaries commented on the day's events. Thus a highly intimate relationship was built up between Prime Minister and private secretaries. Yet, at the same time, as John Wyndham noted, the quality of authority was never far absent; like Queen Victoria, Macmillan 'always took it for granted that the chair would be there . . .'.[79] In dealing with his most senior colleagues, the principle of 'you know my mind' applied equally. Unfailing courtesy and unflappability were the norm, and hugely appreciated.

His long-time personal physician, John Richardson, who knew what made Macmillan tick as well as anybody, was acutely aware of just how much it took out of him to maintain the façade of unflappability in private as in public, but with colleagues it was not only put on as part of the act. It paid rich dividends. Anthony Barber probably spoke for the vast majority of those who worked for Macmillan at all levels when he said:

> . . . I never saw him show worry or testiness – which is probably why he did inspire so much confidence. . . . I can think of very few men who evoked greater affection among those who worked for them; in contrast to Ted [Heath], Harold was very undemanding, very considerate. . . .[80]

Barber recalled what he considered a case typical of Macmillan's considerateness, when a junior minister about to be disgraced on homosexual charges (as the law then stood) had come discreetly through the back-garden gate of No. 10, wishing to resign. 'Harold said, "No, it might prejudice your case – don't worry about the Government . . .".'[81] And, however much Macmillan himself might be currently afflicted by the Black Dog, it was evident that he never let it interfere in his dealings with a subordinate.[82]

Macmillan was an uncompromising owl. Into his nineties he would keep dons up long after dinner, into the small hours if given a chance, drinking them under the table, the anecdotes flowing, his intellectual strength and allegresse growing with the night until most of his youthful audience had crept away, broken like old men. The same routine applied while he was in office. He would seldom go to sleep before 2 a.m.; night was a time for work and contemplation. Before he had turned out the light in his single bedroom simple as a cell, with a green telephone by the bedside, he would have gone through a great pile of the red despatch boxes that dog all ministers – and written up at length the copious diaries, the existence of which was unknown to all his slumbering staff – as well as setting aside at least an hour for reading old favourites such as Jane Austen, Dickens, Thackeray and especially Trollope. The boxes consisted of:

> things you must get rid of. Perhaps quite easy, just signatures, or approvals, a rather obvious thing but requires approval. . . . But if you don't do the boxes they can't start work the next morning. If you are lazy and go to bed, you hold up a lot of stuff because the boxes tend to be things approved by other departments, all waiting for your final approval. . . .[83]

Unlike Mrs Thatcher, who gained a reputation for being both owl and lark – to the respect and distress of her staff – rising at 6 a.m. after a late night on the dreaded boxes, Macmillan would wake at a leisurely 8 a.m. and be brought breakfast in bed, followed by the papers. With his distaste for the British press ever mounting, Macmillan often affected never to read the newspapers ('except for Flook [the cartoonist]', he told a credulous Diefenbaker to annoy, 'in which I have a commercial interest').[84] In fact, he read them all with great speed, absorbing them in minute detail within the privacy of his bedroom. Calling in on him at nine, Harold Evans, the Press Secretary, would as often as not find him still in bed, wearing over his pyjamas a brown cardigan well darned at the elbows, and surrounded by despatch boxes and newspapers.[85] He would descend leisurely in mid-morning, well prepared for the day, to quizz the Chief Whip, already in attendance, 'What do you think of the leader in the *Daily Herald*?'[86] Thoughtful of his 'team', Macmillan also had a solicitous purpose in his late rising:

> because if you come to the Cabinet Room at 9.30 and start ringing bells, you only upset them all. It's much better to let them have the boxes. . . . If you come down too early, it's rather like an office, too; all the work piles up and you must let them have time

to open the new letters, the urgent ones, the urgent telegrams, otherwise you become rather a nuisance. . . .[87]

Dorothy Macmillan in No. 10

Compared with the more pretentious residences of other Western leaders, No. 10 Downing Street – built as a private house in the early eighteenth century – still remained a positively cosy establishment by the 1960s. To Julian Amery, who as both a minister and a son-in-law visited it regularly, in atmosphere it was like a cheerfully informal officers' mess, or a club. Others thought it resembled even more closely a family house. Like most other London family houses, there was no back door and bustling impatient Cabinet ministers had to skip past the familiar obstacles of milk bottles on the front doorstep. The dozen or more Macmillan grandchildren wandered in and out with complete freedom (in those carefree days, security checks were almost unheard of); the only rules being that:

> neither tricycles nor bicycles could be allowed in the front hall on Cabinet days. And . . . if you played you mustn't play dominoes *in* the front hall, you must go and play with the police in the police room. . . . Yes, it was like living over the shop in my grandfather's time. . . .[88]

The influence of Dorothy was paramount, and all loved it that way – not least the Prime Minister. There was no one better placed to observe the domestic workings of the Macmillan household than the two head 'Garden Girls' at No. 10, Miss Sheila Minto and Jane Parsons, who between them spanned all incumbents from Baldwin to Thatcher.[89] Miss Minto was categoric that of all the PMs she had worked for, including Churchill, Macmillan was the one she had most enjoyed serving. Both agreed, in unison, that it was because No. 10 was 'such a happy place when the Macmillans were there – a real family house, for which you need a happy family in it.' In common with virtually everybody else who ever came in contact with Dorothy, they loved her for her forthrightness and the way in which they were automatically made party to all that was going on in the household – like any member of a large family: 'so basic, so earthy; she would frequently shout out "Oh that bloody Ministry of Works . . .".'[90]

In Macmillan's own words, in one of those rare personal references to Dorothy in his memoirs:

> Perhaps the clue to her success was that she treated everybody exactly the same; whatever their rank or station, they were all to be regarded as friends and as people in whom she took a deep personal interest. Of course, it would have been better if they had all been children, for it was with children of all ages that she was supremely at her ease. If they must be adults it was just too bad; and the best thing to do was to treat them also more or less as children. Nor did she ever show the slightest change of spirit, whether in good times or in bad. When our popularity stood high she thought it odd, but pleasant. When it was at a low ebb she thought it odder, but still to be endured.

In the course of time Dorothy came to acquire something approaching the popular image later bestowed on the Queen Mother, qualifying – in the words of one newspaper – 'for the title of Britain's most super grannie'.[91] She made a virtue of having never passed any examinations at all, but – in common with the Queen Mother – was both less simple and tougher than she seemed. She would refer to the press as 'such nice friendly people',[92] while her comments in private would often be blistering. On the other hand there was absolutely nothing contrived, and she was being totally herself, when she confessed at a Ladies' Carlton Club tea party shortly after arriving at No. 10 that she felt 'a little lost. I don't know what invitations to accept or reject. And some people ask me to do the maddest things. . . . I am afraid I don't know anything about political history. . . .'[93] Nor was there anything contrived in her lack of interest in clothes (which was total); or in her remark on opening a home for old folks, 'Romance blossoms in places like this. I am pleased, therefore, that you have some double rooms here!';[94] or, when caught chatting to a navvy down a hole in Horse Guards Parade shortly before entertaining Commonwealth wives to tea, in her explanation 'I'm spending 10 minutes relaxing. Otherwise I'd be in a flap, sitting in my flat and waiting. . . .'[95]

The relationship between the Macmillans had always been a

thoroughly unsentimental one, perhaps not altogether uncommon to the British upper classes then. On his coming to power, gossip columnists were intrigued to discover that Dorothy had never bought Harold a tie in thirty-eight years of marriage; that he had never given her a bunch of flowers.[96] All the No. 10 entourage were regularly entertained by her revelations of the Prime Minister's little foibles. Of his austere, prep-school diet, which included a lifelong passion for cold meat that Macmillan assumed should be constantly on tap, she would laugh, 'I had to explain to him that meat must be hot before it got cold!' He was renowned in the family for his impracticality, which (despite his passionate interest in modern innovations) extended to his total inability to master a motor car. The last time he had tried, according to Dorothy, was shortly before the war when, on trying to get the car out of the garage, confusion with the gears had resulted in his driving it straight through the garage wall. Surveying the mayhem, Macmillan remarked calmly, 'Perhaps *you* had better take the *other car* out'; from that moment on he was never allowed near the wheel.[97] In the carefree days when a CND demonstrator prostrate before the official car was still the greatest danger facing a Prime Minister, Dorothy generally drove Macmillan everywhere herself. On one occasion, when confronted by CND demonstrators, she drove straight at them, rolling down the window and swearing at them in colourful terms. The chauffeur riding alongside asked nervously, 'Where did you learn that language, m'lady?' 'From the grooms,' came the unabashed reply.[98] Probably the last Prime Minister's wife to drive, because of security problems, Dorothy was thoroughly expert – though the entourage often wondered how she never had an accident, in that she was continually looking to left and right, pointing out things in the countryside.

But her most passionate interest in life was gardening. She replanned both the gardens at No. 10 and No. 11 Downing Street, and rooted up the staid yellow and white flowers planted at Chequers by Clarissa Eden, to replace them with roses of bright 'normal colours'.[99] At Birch Grove, after the de Gaulle visit had introduced a new modicum of security awareness, a patrolling night guard noted a suspicious light bobbing back and forth outside the house. On investigating, he was amazed to find the Prime Minister's wife, wearing only a slip and gumboots, trowel in hand, a miner's lamp on her forehead and two hot-water bottles strapped to her ample midriff. 'I got a bit behind on the bedding-out,' she explained apologetically.[100] For secretaries and ministers alike coming down on duty to Birch Grove, the atmosphere there was equally friendly, though, the house being notorious for the restraint of its heating, the warmth was more psychological than physical.

Since the Commonwealth tour of 1958, a new warmth had entered into the relationship between Macmillan and Dorothy. It was almost as if, made manifestly aware of the way in which all whom they had met on the trip had opened their hearts to Dorothy's uncontrived charm, he had begun increasingly to appreciate her worth as a consort. Like him, she found herself enjoying the sudden responsibility of life at the top, and threw herself into it with all her infectious enthusiasm and energy. She was an invaluable premier's wife, and all Macmillan's remarks and diary entries (few though they were) reveal a new gratitude and affection. Anthony Barber, like most of the entourage, noted that in his time at No. 10 he 'never saw any remoteness between them'. Although she never ceased to see Boothby, time, prudence and the gentleness of approaching old age had removed most of the pain for Macmillan as well as the reproaches for the suffering of the past.

Yet, despite all the enjoyment of office and this resuscitated family warmth, there was an essential loneliness that went with the job. Macmillan himself often recalled the isolation of his old friend, Alex, as Supreme Commander:

> You suddenly discover your old friends are a bit nervous of you . . . nobody comes to see you any more, just dropping in – except possibly the Chancellor and the Foreign Secretary. . . . I very seldom went to Pratts, or the Beefsteak. . . .[101] You have to have time schedules – that's why private secretaries are so important; they keep you in touch. . . . I used to go to shoot with Philip Swinton[102] – more to get away than anything. (You know, like Winston and his painting.) The chief benefit was meeting different kinds of people. And people with no possible interest to gain from you. . . .[103]

Lord Swinton was one of those with nothing to gain from the Prime Minister. Macmillan also genuinely loved shooting as a recreation (and had an excellent eye) but he was also not averse to the grouse-moor image, enhancing as it did the backdrop of the Prime Minister's unflappability.

One of the few people to fulfil this requirement of disinterest (and certainly the only woman) was Ava, Lady Waverley, the widow of Macmillan's old friend, the former Sir John Anderson. One of those small women whose (considerable) power of attraction lay more in her dynamism than in any more obvious physical attributes, she certainly suffered no 'nervous' inhibitions about people in high places. One of London's more famous hostesses, and widowed in 1958, she had relentlessly pursued such eligible figures as Alexander, Montgomery and Heathcoat Amory, and even Macmillan himself – to the extent that she had allegedly once been 'warned off' by members of the Macmillan clan – possibly Dorothy herself. With her Macmillan had established, not even what would qualify as an *amitié amoureuse*,[104] but an affectionately close friendship that endured from just after the war until her death in 1966. Persistent in her invitations to the ballet (even though it bored the Macmillans), lunches and dinners, Ava was a correspondent renowned for her discretion, and afforded Macmillan a unique sounding-board throughout the premiership.

The Queen

An even more important confidante for Macmillan was the Queen. In his own essential loneliness at the top, 'the Queen was a great support, because she is the one person you can talk to . . .'.[105] Initially, there was a romantic element involved; if the ageing Churchill had fulfilled the role of Melbourne to the young monarch, Macmillan, inevitably, would be her Disraeli. But he swiftly realised that he was also dealing with a strong personality of intelligence, knowledgeability and – when the occasion called for it – sharp wit. Defining the official relationship between Crown and Prime Minister, Macmillan with his profound sense of constitutional precedent recognised the Queen's 'absolute right to know', and – on her side – 'to advise, to encourage and to warn' (as expressed by Bagehot). As soon as he came to power, Macmillan determined to do what he could to strengthen the Queen's prerogative. The principal contact between the two came at the long-established weekly audience, on Tuesday afternoons, at Buckingham Palace.

At first Macmillan found these 'somewhat difficult' and the dialogue forced, and when delivering his formal report, '. . . I could not help remembering Queen Victoria's description of Mr Gladstone addressing her as if she were a public meeting. . . .' Gladstone was never Macmillan's ideal, so he initiated the principle of sending the Queen an agenda of the points he wished to raise each Tuesday. This gave Her Majesty an opportunity to consider the issues involved, and frame her own views (by custom, generally put in the form of questions) on them. Macmillan thus found that the ensuing discussions became much easier; the agenda routine introduced by him has remained operative to the present day.

Macmillan looked forward hugely to his weekly audience; apart from his instinctive reverence towards the monarchy, he was also genuinely impressed by the depth of the Queen's knowledge, the assiduity with which she absorbed the vast mass of documents passed to her, and – even after so few years on the throne – her remarkable accumulation of political experience.

He delighted in discussing with her Church politics and personalities. Though probably more keenly interested in the subject than any other recent Prime Minister, Macmillan reckoned 'She knew much more about the Church than I did. . . .'[106] At the end of one long letter dealing with Church appointments, Macmillan finished with an entertaining anecdote of how Queen Elizabeth I had dealt with a bishop who had protested at her evicting him from his palace:

> 'Proud Prelate. You know what you were before I made you what you are. If you do not immediately comply with my request, I will unfrock you, by God.
>
> (sgd.) ELIZABETH'
>
> I feel sure that Your Majesty is conscious that I have never advised you, as yet, to take any such drastic action, in Your capacity as Head of the Church. . . .[107]

It was not untypical of both style and content of Macmillan's extensive correspondence with the Queen.

Throughout his premiership, Macmillan received letters from the Queen written in a very informed and informal style. Unfortunately for the contemporary biographer royal protocol prevents their publication. But, in this age of security and of prying eyes, what impresses is the number, in those days not only written but addressed in the Queen's own hand and posted while on holiday in Sandringham or Balmoral. One is also astonished that, with her immense pressure of work, such a busy person should indeed find time to write without recourse to a secretary.

Macmillan's relationship with the Queen also embraced a variety of duties, many consonant with the role of a family trustee – such as advising whether or not a member of the royal family should be discouraged from spending an extravagant sum on a new flat. Of much greater importance was the occasion when Macmillan was consulted on the Duke of Edinburgh's proposal (evidently egged on by his uncle, Lord Mountbatten) to change the family name. Macmillan liked to make a good story out of a visit to Sandringham, at the end of 1959, to be greeted by the late Duke of Gloucester:

> greatly disturbed. 'Thank Heavens you've come, Prime Minister. The Queen's in a terrible state; there's a fellow called Jones in the billiard room who wants to marry her sister, and Prince Philip's in the library wanting to change the family name to Mountbatten. . . .'[108]

What he whimsically dubbed the 'Queen's Affair'[109] was finally resolved by Macmillan's recourse to historical precedent. He recalled how the Marlborough family name had been altered to Spencer-Churchill, but in a brief course of time the 'Spencer' had simply disappeared. Consequently he offered a solution of renaming the royal dynasty 'Mountbatten-Windsor'. He predicted that it would not be long before the first barrel disappeared similarly from public usage. (In fact, Macmillan may have been slightly misleading here, in over-simplifying an extremely complex constitutional issue; three decades later, the double-barrelled surname has still not yet come into use, and by the 1960 declaration it will only come into use when the present Queen's *great-grandchildren* arrive on the scene and require a surname. Thus the first Mountbatten-Windsor might be the offspring of Prince Harry, if not given another title, and he could perhaps drop the 'Mountbatten' if he so wished.)

Apart from his own personal attachment to the Queen, Macmillan felt passionately about the pomp and circumstance, and the 'romance', of the British monarch. 'Imagine', he once exclaimed, if at this moment, instead of the Queen, we had a gentleman in evening clothes, ill-made, probably from Moss Bros., with a white tie, going about everywhere, who had been elected by some deal made between the extreme Right and the extreme Left . . . ! Then we would all wait for the next one, another little man, who is it going to be? . . . 'Give it to "X", you know he's been such a bad Chancellor of the Exchequer, instead of getting rid of him, let's make him the next President. . . .' Can you imagine it? I mean, it doesn't make sense, that would be the final destruction of colour and life and the sense of the past in this country, wouldn't it . . . ?[110]

What, on her side, the Queen thought of her First Minister will long remain shrouded in the discretion of protocol. For all the inherited veneration due, the ageing Winston Churchill must occasionally have irritated her with his avuncular manner; 'Lovely – she's a pet,' he was quoted as saying shortly after the Queen's succession. Macmillan himself always reckoned, on the other hand, that she 'liked Harold Wilson very much. He amused her, and he stood up for her Civil List against his Left . . . and I think she had a restraining influence on him. . . .'[111] With his capacity for anecdotes, and asides on the foibles of his contemporaries, Macmillan too could make Her Majesty laugh. From the emotion she was to betray at her leave-taking of him in 1963 if nothing else, one can assume that the Queen regarded Macmillan with respect, and considerable affection, as well.

Chapter Seven

Winds of Change
1959–1960

The wind of change is blowing through this continent, and, whether
we like it or not, this growth of national consciousness is a political
fact.

(HM, in Cape Town, 3 February 1960)

. . . few men I have met have been so capable of disguising their
true feelings.

(Roy Welensky on HM)

The 'Hola Massacre'

In March 1959, six months before the autumn General Election, two events had occurred almost simultaneously in two different parts of faraway Africa that cast a momentary cloud over Tory prospects. These events prefaced storms – not just a 'wind of change' – from Africa that would present Macmillan with some of the most difficult, frustrating and energy-consuming moments of his entire premiership.

The first of these events took place in Kenya. The barbaric Mau-Mau revolt there had been largely suppressed before Macmillan arrived in No. 10, but by 1959 some 1000 of the 'hard-core' terrorists were still held in special camps. At one of these, Hola, a riot took place on 3 March – the day Macmillan was returning from his visit to Moscow – during the course of which eleven detainees were beaten to death. No one seriously argued that the Kenya government or the camp commandant had wished the detainees to die or to be maltreated; but the riot had broken out while the prisoners were being made to work. The Opposition argued that the Kenya government should have foreseen that the new policy of compulsory rehabilitation work would lead to serious trouble. Many of those directly or indirectly involved had been prominent during the years of the Mau-Mau uprising. There was a closing of the ranks in Kenya and one white officer was required to leave a few months before his normal retirement date. The Opposition claimed that a disgraceful cover up was taking place. The Colonial Secretary backed the Governor, Sir Evelyn Baring (a somewhat lofty paladin of Empire); other members of Macmillan's government thought that Sir Evelyn should have taken a tougher line with his officials, and the story of the 'Hola massacre' received wide coverage in the press. An enquiry was called for, and the subsequent White Paper was published in early June. Although Macmillan did everything to play down the report's impact in public, he recorded in his diary on 9 June, 'we are in a real jam.'[1] Gaitskell was threatening a vote of censure, and had put down a motion demanding a 'public enquiry'. Macmillan foresaw 'a serious split' in his own Cabinet over this, and set up an 'African Committee' which – meeting every week – was to endeavour to keep a grip on the situation. The heaven-sent gift to Labour, with the scent of a good pre-election scandal in their nostrils, was acutely apparent to him; as he had written in March, '. . . I must . . . take a hand in this affair, or it may prove really difficult as well as politically damaging at home. . . .'[2]

After further ministerial talks on 10 June, Macmillan thought he was 'beginning to see a line of approach. We must have no Cabinet split; we must not open too much of a flank to our critics; we must be firm but fair with the Kenya administration. . . .' Nevertheless, by the 15th, things had 'not been made easier by the incredible folly of the Colonial Office in recommending an M.B.E. (announced on Saturday) to one of the men whose conduct has been impugned. Colonial Office is a badly run office [a sentiment which Macmillan would echo in years to come], but there is really no excuse for this. . . .'[3]

The following day the debate on the White Paper in the Commons was conducted in a bitter and emotional key, with some fierce personal attacks on the Colonial Secretary, Macmillan's good friend and much respected colleague, Alan Lennox-Boyd. Lennox-Boyd pressed his resignation on Macmillan, who rejected it: '. . . I kept telling him that it would be a fatal mistake and quite uncalled for. But (with all his extraordinary charm and real ability) he is a highly strung, sensitive, and rather quixotic character. I tell him that to resign now over this affair would . . . be a great blow to Her Majesty's Government at the most critical period before the General Election. . . .'[4]

Hola rumbled on for another month, with the Opposition endeavouring to exploit it for the maximum pre-election mileage. On 18 July Macmillan was noting, 'The Attorney General may well drive the Colonial Secretary to resignation and so break up the Government. However, at this moment of time let us hope that the instinct of self-preservation is strong.'[5] Eventually, Lennox-Boyd was persuaded to stay on, at least until after the election; the press accepted the White Paper's vindication of the government; adroitly handled by Macmillan, Hola was put into its proper perspective, and that storm subsided. But in the final House of Commons debate, which ended without a vote, Enoch Powell made a powerful and critical speech which enhanced the feeling at Westminster that the African *status quo* could not continue.

Nyasaland Riots and the Central African Federation

Meanwhile, in early March, at the same time as the 'Hola massacre', serious riots had broken out in Nyasaland (now Malawi), resulting in the declaration of a state of emergency by the Governor, Sir Robert Armitage. By the time order was restored, fifty-two Africans had been killed and sixty-six members of the African National Congress party had been arrested, including the colony's most prominent black leader, Dr Hastings Banda. Behind the riots lay increasing African discontent with the white-controlled Central African Federation (CAF); this consisted of the three neighbouring territories of Nyasaland and Northern Rhodesia (subsequently Zambia) – both of which were predominantly African and came directly under the control of the Colonial Office – combined with Southern Rhodesia (subsequently Zimbabwe), where three and a half million Africans were dominated by 220,000 white settlers who had been given semi self-government since 1923, under the nominal aegis of the Secretary of State for the Commonwealth.

The idea of a Central African Federation had been nurtured in the last years of the Attlee administration; but it was set up in 1953 under the Churchill government. It had been based on sound economic theory: Northern Rhodesia, with its rich copper belt, had great mineral wealth, Nyasaland had excess labour resources, and Southern Rhodesia had considerable industrial potential and agricultural wealth. Behind this economic experiment in racial partnership lay the unspoken assumption that Africans would acquire an increasingly large say in the conduct of their own political affairs. A 'no secession' clause had been built into the Federation's constitution – otherwise no capital loan money could have been raised for the Federation on the City of London's money markets – but provision was made for a constitutional review to be held after not less than seven years and not more than nine; it was in fact planned for the shorter end of the time spectrum, in 1960.

The omens were already not very good when African delegates from both Northern Rhodesia and Nyasaland had opted out of the preliminary conference setting up the Federation. Kenneth Kaunda, a powerful opponent of Federation, had taken control of Northern Rhodesia's main African party, and at the end of 1957 the leading black political parties in all three territories of the Federation reaffirmed their opposition to federation and their intention to boycott any elections. That same year Ghana – and Malaya – had become independent Commonwealth states, and Nigeria was moving towards full self-government. There was also the French factor: both before and soon after de Gaulle's return to power in May 1958, Macmillan (via his son-in-law, Julian Amery) had received warnings of what Gaullist attitudes towards France's African empire might turn out to be. On one occasion, de Gaulle's Prime Minister, Michel Debré, had observed to Amery that, in Africa, either the French and the British – as the two principal colonial powers – had to decide *jointly* to stay, or *both* to clear out. There could be no halfway house, or one future for the British and another for the French. Thus, when in September 1958 de Gaulle offered the French Commonwealth free option of association or independence,* and exactly a year later he shocked the French Army by offering self-determination to the Algerians, the writing on the African wall could not have been plainer to Macmillan. De Gaulle's African policy was to be profoundly influential upon the Macmillan government – and vice versa.

It was against this background that the Africans in the Federation territories felt in particular that the highly restrictive franchise qualifications were unjust, and were impeding their progress towards real political power. Large sections of the white population of Southern Rhodesia were also beginning to demand full independence. The Federation elections of November 1959, duly boycotted by the major black parties, were won by the Federal Party, led by Roy Welensky. All through his dealings with the Federation, Macmillan was to find the volatile personality of Welensky one of the hardest crosses he had to bear. A remark Welensky made in his autobiography, 'I am a fighter,' thoroughly epitomised him.[6] Born in 1907, the thirteenth child of a Jewish father who had emigrated from Russian-ruled Poland and of a mother who came of nine generations of Afrikaner stock, Welensky had been brought up in a rough world very much on the wrong side of the railway tracks which eventually provided his livelihood. When asked on British television

* Sekou Touré's left-wing Guinée alone chose the path of total independence.

whether he claimed to know the African mind, he replied character-istically: 'Considering that when I was a lad I swam bare-arsed in the Makabusi with the piccanins, I think I can say I know something about Africans. . . .'[7] He had gone into the railways, ending up as an engine-driver, and at nineteen became professional heavyweight boxing champion of Rhodesia. The aggressiveness acquired here, plus a tendency to talk in terms of 'knock-outs', never quite left him, and he would amuse Lord Home by recounting how he used to hire young African sparring partners for a penny each, getting through fifty before exhaustion set in. Although he had not a drop of British blood, he was intensely proud of British traditions, and loved with a fierce passion the beautiful, hard country into which he had been born. He was imbued with a paternalistic view of the Africans typical of a White Rhodesian of his age; anything else would have been unnatural. Predictably, his staunchest supporters were to come from the artisan class of Rhodesian whites who composed the vast majority of the electorate.

In 1958 he had gone into politics, and three years later was appointed wartime Director of Manpower in Northern Rhodesia. It was about this time that he first came to the attention of Macmillan, then at the Colonial Office, as a 'Trades Union leader of the white employees . . . demanding enormous wages out of the war, and getting them. Then, of course, doing down the blacks. . . .'[8] After the war he had come strongly under the influence of Godfrey Huggins, later Lord Malvern, Prime Minister of Southern Rhodesia since 1933 and the architect of federation. When Huggins retired in 1956 as the Federation's first Prime Minister, Welensky naturally assumed his mantle. Welensky's attitude towards African 'partnership' and political advancement was en-capsulated in the slogan of 'a vote for every civilised man'; the rub, of course, lay in the Rhodesian whites' definition of a 'civilised man'. In reality, it meant that Welensky was not prepared to accede parity, or anything like it, in the Federation, nor would he contemplate an African majority in any one of the territories.

In October 1958, Macmillan had noted that 'A great row is brewing in Rhodesia, partly because of Welensky's character, partly because the Colonial Office and the Commonwealth Office are at daggers drawn. . . .'[9] This split between the two government departments separately handling the three disparate territories of the Federation lay at the root of most of Macmillan's headaches over the Federation in the next few years. Against all his principles of delegation in the Cabinet, he found himself becoming arbitrator between the two ministers and their rival sets of bureaucrats and their irreconcilable differences.

On 5 March 1959, within a couple of days of the riots that had broken out in Nyasaland, Macmillan foresaw that 'a most troublesome situation' was going to develop. 'It looks as if the Federation plan, although economically correct (since Nyasaland is not "viable") is regarded with such great suspicion by "advanced" native opinion as to be politically unacceptable.'[10] The Cabinet had already, in Macmillan's absence in Russia, decided on a public enquiry into the riots; this was put in the hands of Mr Justice Devlin. After a Cabinet discussion the following week, with the Prime Minister back in the chair, Macmillan concluded that 'The wider problem – can the Federation continue in its present form? – must be studied further *before* the Constitutional Conference agreed for 1960. . . .'[11]

The Monckton Commission and the Devlin Report

On 17 March, the Cabinet decided to set up a Royal Commission, as soon as possible, 'to advise upon the future of the Federation'. This would, in fact, not be *the* constitutional review promised for 1960 at the earliest, but just a review for the review. Macmillan explained blandly to the public that it would aim to 'dispel widespread ignorance of the purpose and working of the Federation'. At least as far as Africa was concerned, it looked to some as though the Macmillan regime was rapidly becoming a government by White Paper and Royal Commission.

To head the new Royal Commission, Macmillan invited his old Oxford contemporary, Sir Walter Monckton. A courteous and unusually uncombative lawyer, Monckton was considered to be a first-class negotiator (but also renowned for his championship of lost causes: he had advised the Nizam of Hyderabad just before Nehru invaded, he had advised Edward VIII during the abdication crisis, and he had settled with the unions as Minister of Labour in the Churchill 1951 government – perhaps too generously). Macmillan hoped that Monckton's reputation in this last post, coupled with the fact of his subsequent resignation as Minister of Defence over Suez, would make him acceptable to Gaitskell and the Opposition – if not to the Africans he would be dealing with in the Federation. Asked to give up the lucrative chairmanship of the Midland Bank to take on this important task, Monckton was given a brief more cosmetic than dynamic: he was to hear local evidence and clear the air of misunderstandings, then use his great powers of persuasion, combined with his famous charm, to encourage a positive climate of opinion on federation as a whole.

From the very first, and unremittingly, fierce opposition to the commission came from Welensky, who saw it as opening a Pandora's box, the contents of which would inevitably destroy the Federation. In April, Lord Home, the Secretary of State for Commonwealth Relations, flew out to Southern Rhodesia to persuade him, with – *inter alia* – the argument that, if Labour came to power that autumn, they would be certain to allow Nyasaland to secede and destroy the Federation; but they might be hampered from doing so if the Monckton Report were at hand. Reinforcing this fear was Macmillan's view at the time that 'So long as the Conservatives are in power here, Roy Welensky can be held back from anything very foolish. If the Socialists get in, 1960 may be a fatal year in Central Africa. Unhappily, African opinion is all the time being inflamed. . . .'[12] Hence there was every urgency to get Monckton off the ground as soon as ever possible.

To Macmillan, it was also of considerable importance – if the Monckton Commission were to carry weight – that it should be bipartisan. Accordingly, on 8 May he wrote to Gaitskell, urging him to nominate some Labour representatives for the Commission: 'Unless we can succeed in creating a common mind on the next stage of evolution for the Federation there is a prospect of real trouble. . . .' On Labour's side, Gaitskell was committed to pressing Macmillan that the Monckton terms of reference be widened to include freedom to consider not only changes in the Federation but its actual liquidation, and throughout 1959 he and his party havered over collaborating with Monckton – causing Macmillan angrily to feel that they were using 'the problems of Africa to reunite their divided party'.[13]

Meanwhile, in July – as the temperature continued to rise in the General Election run-up – Mr Justice Devlin delivered his report on the Nyasaland riots. Macmillan was at once appalled at its content, and furious with the author. 'Why Devlin?' he queried testily in the privacy of his diaries:

> The poor Lord Chancellor [Lord Kilmuir] – the sweetest and most naive of men – chose him. He was able; a Conservative; runner-up or nearly so for Lord Chief Justice. I have since discovered that he is (a) *Irish* – no doubt with that Fenian blood that makes Irishmen anti-Government on principle, (b) A *lapsed* Roman Catholic. His brother is a Jesuit priest; his sister a nun.

Macmillan felt that Devlin had also been 'bitterly *disappointed* at my not having made him Lord Chief Justice. . .'.[14] He was not therefore surprised that the Devlin report was 'dynamite', and 'may well blow this Government out of office'. To Welensky, it was also 'one of the most controversial State Papers of modern times'.[15] Although in the years ahead Welensky and Macmillan would find little to agree about, they were immediately at one in disagreeing with many of the basic assumptions of Devlin and his colleagues. Chief among these was that no evidence had been found to support the government's assertion that the Nyasaland Congress Party had been plotting massacre and assassination – the motive for imposing the state of emergency; second was the provocative statement that 'Nyasaland is – no doubt temporarily – a police state, where it is not safe for anyone to express approval of the policies of the Congress Party.'[16]

The Macmillan Cabinet rejected the Devlin Report, calling on the heavily criticised Governor of Nyasaland, Sir Robert Armitage, to submit a rival document. This was largely written at Chequers in two days – compared with the several months taken by Devlin and Co. Both were then published simultaneously, on 24 July. Macmillan was agreeably surprised by their public reception:

> The so-called 'serious' Press has been excellent. . . . The party seems pretty steady. The 'frondeurs' – who make the mistake of opposing on everything – are quite active – Lord Lambton (one begins to realise what poor Lord Grey suffered at the hands of his son-in-law in the Reform Cabinet),* Enoch Powell (who is a sort of Fakir) and one or two others. . . .[17]

* A reference to 'Radical Jack', the Earl of Durham, an ancestor of Lord Lambton famed for radical reform of the Canadian Constitution, proposed in the Durham Report of 1839.

Nevertheless, hidden from public gaze and minimised by Macmillan, the danger in the Cabinet had been considerable. Lennox-Boyd had once more asked to resign, and with him in all probability would have gone the two other Colonial ministers – Lord Perth and Julian Amery, Macmillan's own son-in-law – plus the Governor of Nyasaland. Nothing could have been more embarrassing to a Tory government in the run-up to a general election, with the wounds of Suez only recently cauterised. Macmillan put the issues squarely to the Cabinet, calling upon each member in turn to give his unprejudiced view, before giving his own. Thus drawn, the Cabinet to a man backed Armitage and Lennox-Boyd. Gratified, Macmillan recorded it as 'a fine performance and most impressive. Mr Gladstone used to call his last Cabinet "the Blubbering Cabinet". This is a "Manly Cabinet". I told them, *after* the decision had been taken, that had it gone otherwise, I should have *not* continued as Prime Minister. . . .'[18]

The Devlin Report was, of course, much more serious than the fracas over Hola. The deaths at Hola were an accident, while the Devlin Report was a direct and authoritative condemnation of government policy. Even so, Macmillan's response seems surprisingly strong. But MPs and ministers alike were restless and fatigued after a long parliamentary session; having had its run on Africa, the press were scampering off after other Silly Season prey; Macmillan himself was immediately plunged back into his predominant concern over the summit. Nevertheless, the despised Devlin seems to have sowed the first strong seeds of doubt in Macmillan's mind as to whether the Federation had any future at all.

A Shift in Policy . . . Iain Macleod

During the summer of 1959, with Parliament in recess, Macmillan continued to ponder on the problem of Africa. On 22 August he wrote a careful brief to Monckton defining how he saw his task and stressing its great importance:

> . . . I am sure that this is one of the most important jobs in our long history for, if we fail in Central Africa to devise something like a workable multi-racial state, then Kenya will go too, and Africa may become no longer a source of pride or profit to the

Europeans who have developed it, but a maelstrom of trouble into which all of us will be sucked.

These were to prove indeed prophetic words over the ensuing decades. He continued:

The cruder concepts, whether of the left or of the right, are clearly wrong. The Africans cannot be dominated permanently (as they are trying to do in South Africa) without any proper opportunity for their development and ultimate self-government. Nor can the Europeans be abandoned. It would be wrong for us to do so, and fatal for African interests. . . .[19]

Somehow the African was to be allowed to advance politically, but not at the expense of the European.

After the Conservatives had been safely returned to power in October, Macmillan recognised in a letter to the Secretary of the Cabinet, Norman Brook, that 'Africa . . . seems to be the biggest problem looming for us here at home. We just succeeded at the General Election in "getting by" on this.'[20] A new approach was called for, and with the retirement of the Colonial Secretary Lennox-Boyd, Macmillan chose the dynamic Iain Macleod to succeed him in what Macmillan rated as 'the worst job of all'.[21] His task was to 'get a move on Africa'.

Macleod was not quite forty-six when given the Colonial Office in 1959. A key product of Butler's post-1945 Research Department, and intellectual High Tory, Macleod had been spotted by Churchill for his humbling of Aneurin Bevan in the House on NHS costs, and at thirty-eight Macleod had become the first of his parliamentary generation to be made a minister; though as one of his critics noted, his one piece of legislation as Churchill's Minister of Health 'was to make it possible for dental assistants to scale teeth'.[22] Nevertheless, Macleod did much to set the fashion for Conservatives – especially the Young Conservatives – and Harold Wilson came to rate him as the Tory most feared as potential successor to Macmillan; although his Party would 'never have the sense to choose him'.[23]

While Lord Home at the Commonwealth Office (for whom Macmillan had great, and increasing, respect) was a Border Scot, Macleod, the son of a doctor from the Western Isles, was (like his chief) a Highlander, 'which means that he is easily worked up into an emotional mood; it also means that he is proud and ambitious. But he has great qualities – a soaring spirit and a real mastery of Parliamentary speaking. . . .'[24] Although possessed of a 'fierce gaiety',[25] he suffered constantly from migraine and crippling arthritis – probably caused by severe war wounds; all of which must have increased the irascibility of a normally emotional nature. Macmillan described him as 'very high-minded, very excitable, often depressed',[26] seeing in him many of the attributes of the Highland race from which Macmillan himself proudly claimed descent.

Macmillan was not to find him 'an easy colleague',[27] but Macleod certainly possessed the qualities for the job now at hand. He did not however have the breadth of experience in colonial affairs that many earlier Conservative Colonial Secretaries had acquired. When he stopped at Malta on his way to Kenya soon after his appointment, it was the first night that Iain Macleod had ever spent in a British colony. On the other hand, he did have a brother who was both a policeman and a farmer in Kenya, and, a strong supporter of the moderate white settlers there, Iain Macleod intended to deal firmly with the obstructive behaviour of those who wished to retain political power in their own hands. He would later write: 'It has been said that after I became Colonial Secretary, there was a deliberate speeding-up of the movement towards independence. I agree. There was. And in my view any other policy would have led to terrible bloodshed in Africa. This is the heart of the argument. . . .'[28] Alan Lennox-Boyd was certainly no racist but while he was at the Colonial Office there was an assumption that the colonies of East and Central Africa might take ten or twenty years to evolve into full independence. Macleod seemed to think that the time span for independence could be compressed into twenty months.

In the Central African Federation, Macleod saw himself as the protector of the people of the two northern territories. Welensky, in the language of the boxing ring, admitted mildly that he found himself instantly in 'a different corner from Macleod';[29] 'I doubt if we ever talked the same language. . . . to me his mixture of cold calculation, sudden gushes of undisciplined emotion, and ignorance of Africa was perplexing and discouraging. . . .'[30] Welensky got on better with Home, with his relaxed, skilful manner of handling people. But Home (not unlike most people) never had a very clear idea of what 'partnership' entailed. He felt very strongly that there should be increased African representation based on educational qualifications; he did *not* believe in the principle of 'one man, one vote'. Macmillan would find himself increasingly drawn in as mediator in this triangle of relationships, underlying which were the divergent views of the Colonial and Commonwealth ministers.

By 1 November 1959, within weeks of his re-election, Macmillan had decided to visit Africa himself at the start of the new year. As he wrote to Norman Brook, 'young people of all Parties are uneasy about our moral basis. Something must be done to lift Africa on to a more national plane, as a problem to the solution of which we must all contribute, not out of spite . . . but by some really imaginative effort. . . .'[31] He continued his efforts to involve the Labour Party in the Monckton Commission, and on 17 November he recorded 'A tiresome and inconclusive interview with Gaitskell, who was accompanied by Bevan and Callaghan [Shadow Colonial Secretary]. . . . They are torn between joining and refusing to join. . . . They will make a decision on purely political grounds – at least Gaitskell. . . .'[32] The Labour leader was, however, irked when Macmillan jibbed at inviting Jim Callaghan to join the Commission. Macmillan was under the strongest pressure from Welensky, who regarded the future Labour Prime Minister as a fomentor of trouble among the Africans and had written to Macmillan on 31 October, stressing that 'Callaghan is quite unacceptable as an individual. . . . I must make it quite clear that under no circumstances could I agree to his inclusion. . . .'[33] Welensky had gone on to say that he had never been enthusiastic about Labour participation as a whole; he regarded the Party as bent on destroying the Federation. To Harold Wilson, Macmillan's exclusion of Callaghan rated as 'one of Macmillan's few churlish actions'.[34]

With some regret, Macmillan at last received the Labour decision on 4 December. '. . . Mr Gaitskell has now at last made up his mind. The Opposition refused to join the Central African Commission. This is disappointing, but it is perhaps better that they should stay out than join with merely wrecking tactics. . . .'[35] From motives that Macmillan considered contemptible party politics, the Labour refusal placed the whole Central African problem firmly in the British party political arena, which was greatly to weaken Westminster's hand in years to come. Home would always reprove himself 'for not scrapping the Commission when Gaitskell wouldn't play'.[36]

At the last minute, Macmillan did, however, succeed in gaining the support of one eminent Labour grandee, Sir Hartley Shawcross, a former Labour Cabinet minister. But the price of Shawcross's willingness to serve was a private, and crucial, assurance from Macmillan that no solution to the Federation would be ruled out, *even secession*. Meanwhile, Welensky continued in his belligerent attitude to the Commission. On 24 November Macmillan 'found Lord Home much alarmed by a message from Salisbury. . . . Welensky is very angry. . . . we are both worried lest, with his high temper and excitability, he will make some foolish statement which will bring everything to a halt. . . .'[37] Two days later, however, Welensky's 'cautious acceptance in principle' was gained by a message 'as soothing as cream and as sharp as a razor' from Macmillan himself.[38] What clinched it, in Welensky's eyes, was an assurance from Macmillan that the British government had *no* intention of extending the Commission's terms of reference to include the possibility of secession.

The margin between the two assurances, to Shawcross on the one hand and Welensky on the other, was large enough for Macmillan to claim good faith, but narrow enough for the pugnacious Welensky later to cry treason; certainly, it was to provide plenty of ammunition for later accusations of disingenuousness. But whatever their beliefs in the ideals of federation, there was nothing the Macmillan government could do (short of rejecting the Monckton findings, as per Devlin) to prevent Monckton interpreting his terms of reference ultimately as he wished, with the possibility of secession as a means whereby federation might be maintained. This was an argument Welensky could never see.

Macmillan Takes Off

On 5 January 1960, Macmillan – accompanied by Dorothy – set off on a six-week tour of Africa. In his memoirs he remarked that it was a journey that he had long intended, if returned to power in 1959, to make one of his most immediate priorities; it would be a logical extension of his Commonwealth tour of 1958. Now, however, his motivation was more pressing: there was not just Welensky and the future of the Federation, which would continue to provide one of the main topics of debate on the Tory backbenches, but the whole question of independence for Britain's remaining colonies in West, East and South Africa. As Macmillan once commented, Africa was 'like a sleeping hippo in a pool . . . suddenly it gets a prod from the white man and wakes up; and it won't go to sleep again . . .'.[39]

During the six weeks they were to travel 13,360 miles by air, 5,410 by sea and about 800 by road, returning on 15 February, a few days after Macmillan's sixty-sixth birthday. Given the exigencies of air travel, then in the pre-jet age (they travelled out on a leisurely turbo-prop Britannia, the so-called 'Whispering Giant'), it would have been a demanding itinerary in the best of circumstances. But – although the mileage covered was less than in 1958 – it was to prove 'mentally and morally more testing'. Macmillan was certainly not outstandingly equipped for the experience. He had never been to black Africa before; but then neither had any other British premier while in office. Wartime Algiers, Casablanca and Cairo had previously been his sole venture on to the continent, and until the previous few months he had in no way been emotionally involved in its problems. Like many of his generation, he regarded the Dark Continent as secondary to Asia, and isolated from the rest of the world. In the past, he had never declared much interest in colonial affairs, once asking Alan Lennox-Boyd for a profit-and-loss account of what each colony cost and what benefits Britain got out of it. He had never said much about his views on Africa, but if anything it was plain that his sympathies were on the side of the African. In Britain one of his pet anathemas was 'your retired colonels in the golf club and their ladies', giving their instinctive support for the reactionary right wing of the Tory Party, and with them he not unnaturally identified the diehard settlers of Kenya and Rhodesia. During his brief period at the Colonial Office in 1942, he had suggested that the big, and rich, European farms of Kenya should be bought by the Crown and run as state companies, for the ultimate benefit of both whites and blacks, concluding with ominous prescience, over a decade before Mau-Mau raised its ugly head, that 'it will be less expensive than a civil war.' Macmillan's revolutionary proposal was never taken up; under Mau-Mau in the 1950s Kenya was stricken with civil war of the most ghastly kind. But it did at least show that Macmillan, rare among his political generation, had given some thought to the long-term future of the Africans as well as the need for fundamental change in colonial Africa.

Though no empire enthusiast, Macmillan – especially since his tour of 1958 – was very conscious of the Commonwealth, that optimistic legacy of the imperial past which so bemused the Tory Party. Equally he, and Lord Home, had become painfully aware of just how much Britain's role in the world had changed as her relative power diminished. Strategically, Macmillan always had an eye on the global impact of the withdrawal of British control from key areas; it was for this reason, he said, that he had 'clung in Cyprus, in Aden and in Singapore'. But he realised that, if he clung too tenaciously for too long to those areas where Africans predominated, dislike and discontent would increase. He too was aware that all depended on timing and on the handling of the recalcitrant white settlers. 'Africans are not the problem in Africa, it is the Europeans,' he had written to Norman Brook at the end of 1959.[40]

The white settlers had excellent contacts in England, not only in the City and St James's but in both Houses of Parliament. Whenever these settlers felt that their position and their capital were being threatened, they vociferously lobbied the right wing of the Tory Party to considerable effect as they were determined to retain the political initiative. Macmillan would find their noisy clamour unnerving and feared that they, their friends and relations and the Lords Lambton and Salisbury might split the party. At the back of his mind would also nag the constant worry that Welensky's steady needling might lead the right wing of his party to oust him personally.

It was against this background of conflicting interests – he could not possibly please all peoples of all races in all territories all of the time – that Macmillan undertook his tour of Africa. Besides Dorothy, he was accompanied by Norman Brook, his new Principal Private Secretary Tim Bligh, Press Officer Harold Evans and the ever faithful John Wyndham, plus two officials from the Commonwealth and Colonial Offices.

Ghana and Nigeria

Ghana was the first leg of Macmillan's journey. His host was Kwame Nkrumah, 'a colourful if somewhat exotic Prime Minister' whom Macmillan had met for the first time at the Commonwealth Conference of 1957, the year Ghana had become independent. For all their differences over South Africa, Macmillan liked Nkrumah for his engaging charm and courtesy ('when he cared to display those qualities'). He thought Ghana then was 'corrupt – *reasonably* corrupt, but I don't think it was *badly* corrupt. Not more corrupt than is absolutely necessary – but it became so later. . . .'[41]

With the Ghanaian's advanced sense of the ridiculous, Nkrumah and his guest shared a joke when some over-fed British photographers got stuck in a lift. Otherwise the Ghana visit was not a particular success; there was not the friendly warmth encountered on the Commonwealth tour of two years previously; Dorothy had toothache ('One of my last three teeth, on which everything else hangs,' she confided to Harold Evans);[42] frequent unscheduled stops by the Prime Minister led the accompanying press cavalcade to diagnose 'Accra tummy' – though, in fact, as was to become comprehensible later, Macmillan's discomfort had a more psychosomatic cause, reflecting the nervous tension of the approach of a major speech. Harold Evans noted his chief's distraction when, in an unpleasant little scene conspicuous by its rarity, Macmillan sharply rebuked Tim Bligh publicly in front of Ghanaian government officials for involving him in an unwelcome press conference. Nkrumah, who consistently showed more interest in the liberation of Africa than in Ghana's own considerable economic problems, subjected Macmillan to a noisy anti-colonial speech; while at a banquet Macmillan slipped in an apparently impromptu reference to a 'wind of change'. It went unnoticed by the attendant press.

Macmillan was more enthusiastically received in Nigeria, his next stop. At Ibadan University he was confronted with crude student placards – 'MacButcher Go Home', 'MacNato, we who are about to be atomised salute thee' and 'LORD MALVERN IS AN ASS. TELL HIM SO' – but on the whole the protesters were good-natured. Up in the northern region, he was attracted by its flamboyant premier, the Sardauna of Sokoto, who had an Eton-style fives court and whom he described to Peregrine Worsthorne of the *Sunday Telegraph* as a 'great character – a local swell . . . not unlike Trollope's Duke of Omnium'.[43] The pace allowed him no time to keep up his diary during the tour as a whole, but he was able to reflect later on how Nigeria, more than most African colonies, had suffered from the arbitrary frontiers imposed on her, which he thought were often 'criminal' in the way they cut through tribal territories. All through Nigeria he sensed a regional and federal crisis looming up; eventually this was to lead to the murder of Premier Abubakar and ultimately to a bloody civil war.

In the retiring British Governor-General, Sir James Robertson, a man who had spent all his life in the Colonial Service, Macmillan found a kindred spirit, and warmly appreciated some wise advice he gave:

> after attending some meeting of the so-called cabinet, or council, I said, 'Are these people fit for self-government?' and he said, 'No, of course not.' I said, 'When will they be ready?' He said, 'Twenty years, twenty-five years.' Then I said, 'What do you recommend me to do?' He said, 'I recommend you to give it to them at once.' I said, 'Why, that seems strange.' 'Well,' he said, 'if they were twenty years well spent, if they would be learning administration, if they were getting experience, I would say wait, but what will happen? All the most intelligent people, all the ones I've been training on will all become rebels. I shall have to put them all in prison. There will be violence, bitterness and hatred. They won't spend the twenty years learning. We shall simply have us twenty years of repression, and therefore, in my view, they'd better start learning [to rule themselves] at once.' I thought that was very sensible.

Macmillan was fond of repeating the Governor-General's wisdom at regular intervals; it was certainly something he carried with him on to Salisbury.

Before leaving Nigeria, Macmillan decided on one of his more inspired appointments – to make Anthony Head, whom he had sacked as Minister of Defence after Suez, the first High Commissioner of an independent Nigeria. It was an excellent choice; the Nigerians were appreciative that so senior an ex-minister should be sent to them; Head proved a sage counsellor over three difficult years, and both he and his wife departed as much loved figures.

Yet there were times when Macmillan still seemed preoccupied and ill at ease. He got places and faces mixed up. At Enugu, recalled Harold Evans, 'with his hand on Premier Okpare's shoulder, he said to the surrounding group, "He gave us a fine dinner last night and made a wonderful speech." But alas, last night the place was Ibadan and the speaker Premier Akintola. He realised later what he had done and was laughing about it. . . .'[44] A more significant gaffe was when, asked by journalists about his plans for Nyasaland and Northern Rhodesia, he replied in an unguarded moment that 'the people of the two Territories will be given an opportunity to decide on whether the Federation is beneficial to them. This will be an expression of opinion that is genuinely that of the people. . . .'[45] In Salisbury, the ever explosive Welensky hit the roof. The impact of Macmillan's unguarded remark was aggravated by Lord Shawcross, back in England, having suggested on television that he felt quite free to recommend to the Monckton Commission the break-up of the Federation, if need be. It was, recorded Welensky, 'certainly a dramatic prelude to Mr Macmillan's first and last visit to the Federation. He arrived, bland and unrepentant, on the evening of Monday, January 18th. . . .'[46]

On to Salisbury

Before leaving West Africa, Macmillan had time to scribble off one of his doom-and-gloom letters to Ava Waverley: 'The problems of the world grow more and more intense. Perhaps it really is now about to come to an end. . . .'[47] Passing from Ghana (already independent) and Nigeria (about to become independent), 'with all their hopes and fears, and to reach Salisbury, the capital of the Federation, was to enter a different world'. Here, there was still a colonial atmosphere: 'The Governor-General, Lord Dalhousie, and his wife received us with the greatest hospitality in their beautiful residence, typical of a vice regal tradition. . . .' During the nine days he spent in the Federation, Macmillan was 'struck by the sense of uncertainty, whether among Europeans or Africans. This uneasiness spread from the political to the business world. . . .'

He tried to pacify Welensky by claiming that his Lagos gaffe had been misreported (according to British journalists present, it had not), and by reassuring him that 'it is certainly not the function of the [Monckton] Commission to destroy the Federation: on the contrary, it is to find means by which the Federation can go forward. . . .'[48] To a group of journalists, Macmillan – when quizzed whether it was conceivable that the Commission could recommend the break-up of federation – gave the jocular reply:

Well, I suppose if they all agreed that nothing could be done, they might have to say so. It would be like that rhyme from Belloc:

> They answered as they took their fees
> There is no cure for this disease.[49]

When he rose to address an unfriendly white audience, 'he had his own methods,' recorded Henry Fairlie:

within a minute he was talking gravely to his audience of the ebb and flow of civilisations, especially those which have touched the African continent; there was even time for a word about the influence of the Phoenicians on the Mediterranean world. It was the effortless superiority of the Balliol man being displayed before an audience which every moment became more helpless. By the time he reached the 20th century – and the Lagos declaration – they were ready to believe anything. . . .[50]

There is little doubt, nevertheless, that – as he arrived in Salisbury – Macmillan still wanted to preserve the fabric of the Federation, while knowing that its form would have to be changed to improve the terms of partnership for the Africans. But *how*? No other leader, before or since, black or white, would be able to find the formula for a multi-racial black and white society – inside or even outside Africa. The message he brought from London, as he wrote in his memoirs, 'did not at all imply African rule on a "one man, one vote" basis – it implied some genuine system of fair partnership with fair representation of the different elements in an agreed system. . . .' But what, precisely, did this mean? Welensky claims he was unable to find out; nor could he pin Macmillan down on his intentions about releasing Dr Banda, still imprisoned following the Nyasaland riots of the previous March.

Nothing Macmillan saw in the course of his two-day side trip to Nyasaland encouraged him. He found officials 'dispirited', imbued with a sense of failure, and came away 'saddened'. Reflecting later on what he saw, he confessed that if – at the time of the conception of the Federation – he had realised 'or had indeed any of us realised, the almost revolutionary way in which the situation would develop and the rapid growth of African Nationalism throughout the whole African continent, I think I should have opposed the putting together of three countries so opposite in their character and so different in their history. . . .' Over the short term, it was clear to Macmillan that nothing could be achieved until Banda was let out; and this would be bound to unleash a new storm from Welensky.

Meanwhile, at the other end of Africa, during Macmillan's sojourn in the Federation, Algeria had been confronting de Gaulle with the gravest challenge to his authority to date. In protest against liberal policies imposed from Paris, the Pied Noir 'ultras' had taken to the streets of Algeria, killing fourteen French gendarmes and wounding 123. For the first time in the bitter five-year-old war, Frenchmen were being killed by other Frenchmen; more ominous yet, the elite paras had shown signs of siding with the 'ultras' behind their barricades. And here was not just a handful of settlers, as in Nyasaland, but a million white colonists with roots going back 130 years. Always with one eye on Algeria, and the experiences of his friend de Gaulle, Macmillan ended his first and last visit to Salisbury with the lessons of 'Barricades Week' resting heavily on his thoughts. 'I could not but view the future with apprehension,' he later wrote. 'Indeed, even amidst the many other problems that were to face the Government during the years of my premiership, the complications, confusions and conflicts of Central Africa seemed never to be absent from our minds and were destined to absorb an immense amount of effort with little corresponding result.'

South African Climax

And so, on 27 January, he flew on to South Africa, then still a full member of the Commonwealth, where parallels with Algeria seemed even closer than those presented by the 200,000 white minority of Southern Rhodesia; it was Macmillan's last port of call, a new set of problems and the climax of his trip – and the most difficult part. In Durban, amid warm sunshine, bathers, tennis players and Union Jacks, a few Africans brandished home-made placards, 'We've never had it so bad'. In Pretoria, Macmillan gave Harold Evans a five-minute exegesis about the South African foolishness 'of elevating segregation into a doctrine. If they didn't make an ideology of it they would almost certainly succeed in getting the results they seek with a minimum of concession. Economic differences between black and white would alone be sufficient to achieve practical separation. . . .' Evans found the Prime Minister 'in his gayest mood. . . . He even gets up from the table to give a personal demonstration of a Morris dance in evidence that the English also have tribal dances. . . .'[51]

Arriving in Cape Town on 2 February, the Macmillans were guests of Prime Minister Dr Verwoerd at 'a delightful house called Groote Schuur', built by Cecil Rhodes. Consistent to his principles, Verwoerd refused to have a single African servant in the house, and the Macmillans were looked after by 'an old and rather incompetent Dutch butler'. Macmillan had by then found nothing congenial in South Africa, or the Afrikaner outlook; he detested Verwoerd's 'horrible ideas', but was impressed by the extraordinary biblical learning that he brought to them. For light relief, Macmillan turned the conversation round to theology. To Verwoerd, noted Macmillan, apartheid:

> was more than a political philosophy, it was a religion; a religion based on the Old Testament rather than on the New. . . . he had all the force of argument of some of the great Calvinist leaders of our Scottish kirk. He was certainly as convinced as John Knox himself that he alone could be right, and that there was no question or argument but merely a statement of his will. . . .

In their lengthy discussions, Macmillan had 'the unusual experience of soon noticing that nothing one could say or put forward would have the smallest effect upon the views of this determined man . . .'.

The morning after his arrival in Cape Town, Macmillan addressed the South African Parliament. It was a signal honour, designed to mark the 'Golden Wedding of the Union'. Macmillan himself simply said of this, his most famous speech, 'I had approached this ordeal with much trepidation and I had taken the greatest care in the preparation of my speech.' This was a considerable understatement. The authorship of the speech is generally attributed to Sir John Maud, then the British High Commissioner to South Africa and a former Dean of University College, Oxford, who had a spectacular career in the civil service during and after the war. But at least half a dozen other people – including Sir Norman Brook, Lord Home, Julian Amery and David Hunt of the Commonwealth Office (who was accompanying Macmillan on the African tour) – also claimed to have had a hand in it. It was certainly shown to Home and Julian Amery before Macmillan left England; Amery recalled adding two paragraphs on Afrikaner successes, 'which were then pulled out'.[52] Macmillan and Norman Brook polished the draft all the way from London to Cape Town, and it seems certain that the speech distracted and nagged away at Macmillan throughout the tour. On the actual day of the speech, one of Macmillan's entourage recalled him having to be led to the lavatory, to be physically sick.[53]

All across Africa hints had been dropped by Tim Bligh to the accompanying press corps that 'something was cooking which would astonish and satisfy us all'.[54] Now, sitting up in the gallery, Anthony Sampson observed how 'members were at first dazed by the rhetoric and historical scope of the speech'.[55] Macmillan began with elaborate compliments to South African progress, and courage in two World Wars, and then quietly led on to an exposition of black African nationalism, which – 'with a wide sweep of history, and with superb deftness' – he compared to Afrikaner nationalism:

> Ever since the break-up of the Roman Empire one of the constant facts of political life in Europe has been the emergence of independent nations. . . .
>
> Today the same thing is happening in Africa, and the most striking of all the impressions I have formed since I left London a month ago is of the strength of this African national consciousness. In different places it takes different forms, but it is happening everywhere. The wind of change is blowing through this continent, and, whether we like it or not, this growth of national consciousness is a political fact. We must all accept it as a fact, and our national policies must take account of it.

It was the phrase 'the wind of change' that would become most associated with Macmillan's speech – a phrase that in fact derived from Stanley Baldwin's utterance in 1934: 'There is a wind of nationalism and freedom blowing round the world.' Subsequently, Home said that 'he rather wished the phrase hadn't been used, but it only seemed dramatic later.'[56] At the time, its impact was softened as Macmillan went on, dwelling meaningfully on the words 'nationalism' and 'nation', to appeal to his audience's pride in creating 'a new nation', 'the first of the African nationalisms'.

He stressed the importance of keeping the African nations away from the Communist bloc, and then, with courtesy but firmness, came to the nub of the speech, the dissociation from South Africa's policies:

> It is a basic principle of our modern Commonwealth that we respect each other's sovereignty in matters of internal policy. At the same time we must recognise that in this shrinking world in which we live today the internal policies of one nation may have effects outside it.
>
> In our own areas of responsibility we must each do what we think right. . . . Our justice is rooted in the same soil as yours – in Christianity and in the rule of law as the basis of a free society. . . . it has been our aim in the countries for which we have borne responsibility, not only to raise the material standards of living, but also to create a society which respects the rights of individuals, a society in which men are given the opportunity to grow to their full stature – and that must in our view include the opportunity to have an increasing share in political power and responsibility, a society in which individual merit and individual merit alone is the criterion for a man's advancement, whether political or economic. . . .

Though spoken in Cape Town, it was clear that Macmillan was equally addressing Welensky and the white leaders of Salisbury. They were, as much as Verwoerd and the Afrikaner whites, his real target. 'It may well be', he warned, 'that in trying to do our duty as we see it we shall sometimes make difficulties for you. If this proves to be so we shall regret it. . . .' He recognised that the Union of South Africa faced 'complicated and baffling' problems that were very different to those of countries with homogeneous populations; for three million people of European origin it had been their home for many generations – and 'the same is true of Europeans in Central and East Africa'. But, he concluded, pulling no punches and with no ambiguity:

> As a fellow member of the Commonwealth it is our earnest desire to give South Africa our support and encouragement, but . . . there are some aspects of your policies which make it impossible for us to do this without being false to our own deep convictions about the political destinies of free men to which in our own territories we are trying to give effect. I think we ought, as friends,

to face together, without seeking to apportion credit or blame, the fact that in the world today this difference of outlook lies between us. . . .

'I certainly do not believe in refusing to trade with people,' he continued, 'because you may happen to dislike the way they manage their internal affairs at home. Boycotts will never get you any-where. . . .' It was a view that he continued to hold as firmly in the 1980s as in 1960. After speaking for nearly fifty minutes, he closed on a rousing note: 'Let us resolve to build, not to destroy, and let us remember always that weakness comes from division, strength from unity. . . .'

The South African parliamentarians applauded Macmillan warmly as he sat down, seeming to be more flattered by his praise of their country's achievements than aware of the implications of the speech. Anthony Sampson, who thought at the time that the speech was brilliant, probably the finest of Macmillan's career, found years afterwards that it was still 'marvellous reading' and he always admired Macmillan's courage in going to South Africa to make it.[57]

At a banquet the following day a photograph – which always amused Macmillan – showed Verwoerd and himself with an empty chair between them, but this seems to have been a curious accident of protocol, rather than symbolic of any deeper *froideur*. In fact, as Harold Evans noted, the burghers of Cape Town 'showed no public signs of being disenchanted with their guest, and turned out in large numbers to line the streets when he drove to the harbour to board the *Capetown Castle*, and it was an emotional leavetaking. . . .'[58]

It was in the British and world press, however, that the message appeared loud and clear. As far away as Canada, the *Ottawa Journal*, praising Macmillan's courage, commented that 'It could not have been easy' for him 'to stand up in South Africa's Parliament and tell the authors of racial segregation that Britain would have no part of it . . .' and that 'No South African listening to these words could be in doubt about them. . . .' The speech, it concluded, 'may well find an honored place in history books of the future'.[59] Norman Brook later summed up world comment on the tour as a whole in a letter of warmest congratulations to the Prime Minister: 'When you first mooted the idea of your African journey, I said that it was a tremendous risk but offered a great prize. You took the risk and you have won the prize. You steered a most skilful course, through very great difficulties, and you came through triumphant. . . .'[60]

Was Macmillan responsible for the 'wind of change'? Some of his more right-wing critics blamed the speech for unleashing the hurricane that was to come. Lord Colyton (who as Henry Hopkinson had been a minister at the Colonial Office under Churchill and Eden) spoke for these when he condemned it as coming 'twenty-five years too early . . . it precipitated everything – Algeria, the Congo, etc. . . .'[61] Even Lord Hailsham felt 'It may be that he went too far; if he had gone slower, the results in Africa might have been the same, but at least at lesser cost in human lives . . . but that's purely my judgement.'[62] Or did Macmillan, with his capacity as a Cassandra, simply see and define those storms that lay ahead, inevitably, in Africa? For, even while he was actually in South Africa, a conference in Belgium was deciding to give independence to the Congo in four months' time, with all the whirlwind that that was to unleash. Certainly, after 3 February 1960, nobody in the West looked at Africa in the same way, and the storms followed with mounting rapidity – and violence.

Macmillan Returns Home

Once aboard the *Capetown Castle* on 5 February, an atmosphere of the carefree pleasure cruise reigned, led by the Prime Minister himself, for the ten days of the voyage home. Most marked was the sudden relaxing of tension, so typical of Macmillan after delivering a major speech; he finally (noted Harold Evans) got round to apologising to Tim Bligh for his rudeness in Accra; tieless and in his elderly brown cardigan, he chuckled to Evans 'at the thought of the world seeing his African tour as a move of profound wisdom, whereas (he says) it was just to get away from London in the middle of winter . . .'. There was mirth at the expense of John Wyndham, who had gone to sleep in one bed while in Government House in Nyasaland, and woken up – inexplicably – in another. The stately Norman Brook was teased at finding lipstick on the lapels of his white dinner jacket after dancing too closely with the ladies of the court. Dorothy, who 'took a lively interest in boat drill yesterday, being much struck by the piratical appearance of the crew', complained, like any long-suffering but affectionate wife, of how Harold 'simply won't use new things when she buys them for him. For example, she bought him a new toilet case to bring on the tour but he said it was much too good to use and put it away. . . .'[63]

Nevertheless, within two days of sailing, Macmillan was recording that 'A tremendous new storm has blown up in Salisbury. . . .' Welensky was 'sending intemperate telegrams, threatening secession and the break-up of the Federation, all because of Her Majesty's Government's wish to release Banda . . .'.[64] It was somewhat more complicated than that. While Macmillan was actually in the Federation, Dr Banda had been visited in his cell by the Liberal MP and QC, Dingle Foot, brother of Michael and Hugh (currently Governor of Cyprus). Referring to talks he had had recently with both Monckton and Macleod, Foot told Banda that both wanted him released and had suggested a 'deal' whereby this would be effected if, in exchange, Banda would give evidence to the Monckton Commission. Banda replied that he would accept this only if all his colleagues were released in advance. Banda's cell was bugged, and a transcript of the conversation was on Welensky's desk in Salisbury within forty-eight hours. Welensky regarded it as the height of disingenuousness that Macmillan, while in the Federation, should have so assiduously avoided discussing Banda's future, when his early release was already being actively planned in London.

Macmillan arrived back in England on 15 February, the day that the Monckton Commission started its work in the Federation, to find the usual accumulated sea of troubles awaiting, apart from 'one agreeable interlude' of the campaign for the Chancellorship of Oxford, of which more later. There was an impending railway strike, new threats of inflation, and the Governor of the Bank of England in a funk; there was a possible constitutional tangle over Princess Margaret wishing to announce her engagement to 'a commoner called Jones'; there was discord with the Americans regarding the projected summit and the Nuclear Tests Conference; there were worries about Berlin and Khrushchev's next move; de Gaulle had exploded his first atomic bomb, and there were rumbles from the Chiefs of Staff about abandoning Britain's Blue Streak. Finally, the painfully negotiated settlement in Cyprus was 'going "on" and "off" – like a dish at a cheap restaurant'.[65]

At the eleventh hour, that turbulent priest, Makarios, had thrown his spanner into the works. It all revolved round the size of the base areas that were to be retained by the British forces, and their protection; Makarios was bent on reducing them to a minimum. In his memoirs, Macmillan described how 'a long and wearisome negotiation' with the Cypriot Archbishop continued throughout the first half of 1960. To conduct these negotiations, on his return to London in February Macmillan despatched his son-in-law, Julian Amery, then Under-Secretary at the Colonial Office. Amery was warned that he would find himself up against a wily negotiator, but that he had one ace up his sleeve: Makarios wanted independence as soon as possible; thus, if he stalled, 'our reply was to postpone the date from month to month'. Flying backwards and forwards, Amery, said Macmillan, proved in the event 'to have as robust an endurance as his episcopal opponent' – and did a superb job. A full agreement was reached by July, and the transfer of power took place formally on 16 August, when Archbishop Makarios moved in as President of the new Republic of Cyprus.

Cabinet Crisis

Nevertheless, despite the final Cyprus interlude, the gravest problem within the Commonwealth remained the Central African Federation. The proposed release of Banda created what Macmillan described in his memoirs as 'a real clash of opinion' within the Cabinet. Macleod wanted to let Banda out as soon as possible; Macmillan, perhaps recalling the advice of Governor Robertson of Nigeria, agreed – on the grounds that it would be farcical for the Monckton Commission to deliberate on constitutional reforms for Nyasaland without Banda. But the Commonwealth Office sided with Welensky in opposing this. Home flew to Salisbury, to confront this latest crisis, and his telegram back to London revealed 'a growing sense of something like panic. Unless we are careful, the Europeans [in Southern Rhodesia] will do something rather desperate. . . .' He had 'tackled Welensky direct', and had been told about the bugged conversation: 'Welensky is deeply offended. . . . They conclude from all this that Iain is treating their serious affairs with indifference and worse and that he and the Government are in league with their enemies. . . .' Home managed to reassure the Welensky government, and gain their acquiescence in releasing Banda *on the day* Monckton left the Federation, 'but I see little

chance of carrying them further without the complete break. . . .
Please do *not* say anything to Iain until I arrive home as I must talk
to you alone.'[66]

Events, however, were precipitated by Macleod the following
day, 23 February, when 'Suddenly – and to everyone's amazement
– Colonial Secretary announced at *end* of Cabinet that although he
thought we had taken the only possible decision [i.e. Home's
proposal above], he could not possibly be associated with it and
must resign. . . .' Macmillan was baffled as to Macleod's motives:
'Is it a plot? (à la Thorneycroft) Is it nervous strain?' he wondered.
'. . . I do not know what to do about Colonial Secretary. . . . He
seems merely to repeat that his honour is involved. . . .' The crisis
continued to deepen the next day, and it was apparent that Macleod
had given some embarrassing half-promises to Banda, behind the
back of Home, and the Cabinet:

> . . . I fear he has got into an emotional, Celtic position. He
> certainly looks very unhappy. . . . I am now pretty sure that he
> has said (or perhaps, worse still, written) some foolish things to
> some of these Africans. He is *very* clever and *very* keen and
> enthusiastic – but he is also very inexperienced in this sort of
> thing.[67]

Finally, Macmillan himself came up with a Salomonic Judgement
that Banda should be released three days *before* Monckton left
Nyasaland, instead of three days *after*. This would give him the
chance of 'giving evidence *in his own country* and as a *free man*' – if he
wished to do so. Macleod was 'quite excited by this and said it
would solve this problem. So I rang Lord Home and asked him if he
thought there was any chance of getting Welensky and Whitehead
[Prime Minister of Southern Rhodesia] to agree. Alec Home is a
really splendid fellow. He fully understood the political dangers
which would follow Colonial Secretary's resignation. . . .'[68]

Still in Salisbury, Home – with some skill – persuaded the
Welensky Cabinet to agree. On the 27th Home returned, and
confirmed Macmillan's suspicions about Macleod's 'naivety'. On
1 April, Banda and his colleagues were released and (excepting
Banda) gave their views to the Monckton Commission; the disorders
predicted by the Commonwealth Office did not take place – though,
six days later, Banda was announcing on television his intention to

demand immediate self-government and secession from the Federation. Macmillan mused that 'We would have done better to throw him back earlier into the river. He has grown into a bigger fish by gorging safely in our fish-pond. . . .'[69] Later, in his memoirs, Macmillan would write of Banda as 'an admirable leader and ruler of his people. . . . I formed an intimate friendship with this attractive and courageous man, which has lasted through many years.'

But, far from being the 'minor crisis' Macmillan wrote it off as in his memoirs, the Banda episode had confronted Macmillan with his first serious Cabinet split since the triumphant election the previous year. Not for the first time, nor the last, either the Colonial Secretary or the Commonwealth Relations Secretary – or both – had come close to resigning. 'Iain's resignation', as Macmillan admitted in his diaries, 'would have been (at this particular moment) a most damaging, if not mortal, blow. . . .'[70] One small consolation ('This comforts me a little . . .') was the total success in keeping the crisis out of the press; a success which, by comparison with the unhappy experience of subsequent Tory leaders, spoke volumes for the intrinsic loyalty of Macmillan's colleagues. Nevertheless, the end of the Banda crisis came as a 'great relief': 'It is difficult after so many years to realise the nervous strain which can develop over such delicate issues.'[71]

The tension had been aggravated by the anomaly of having two Secretaries of State with fundamentally conflicting briefs. But it is questionable whether it was not perhaps Macmillan's own worst fault not to have appointed a 'supremo' in charge of both departments immediately after the 1959 election, instead of waiting another two and a half years before creating the post for Rab Butler. There is no satisfactory answer; or was it, possibly, that there was no single pair of hands to whom he felt he could entrust such a concentration of power?

The Sharpeville Massacre . . . and the Commonwealth Conference

Meanwhile, in South Africa, on 21 March – less than two months after Macmillan's visit – sixty-seven Africans were killed and another 180 wounded when police fired on demonstrators outside the police station of the Sharpeville African township. A state of emergency was proclaimed, and 1700 people detained. Recording this 'tragic incident', Macmillan noted that 'The British Press has "gone to town" . . . with all sorts of dreadful pictures, etc. . . .' There were also worldwide protests, and the massacre was brought before the UN Security Council. Macmillan foresaw that there would 'now be a tremendous effort to stoke up similar riots in Rhodesia or Nyasaland or Kenya, in order to put the United Kingdom in the dock . . .'.[72] On the ensuing UN resolution condemning apartheid and its consequences, Britain – joined only by France – took the 'not very noble but very sensible, course' of abstaining.

To Macmillan, more important than US resolutions was 'the reality of the situation in South Africa'. As he wrote to the Queen on 3 April:

> The rigidity, and even fanaticism, with which the Nationalist Government in South Africa have pursued the apartheid policy have brought about – as I feared when I was there – a dangerous, even ominous, situation in that country. How it will all end we cannot tell.
>
> Meanwhile, I fear that I must warn Your Majesty that I see a very difficult period facing the Commonwealth. . . .
>
> . . . I feel my supreme task is to try to . . . avoid anything in the nature of disintegration. After all, the South African Government will not last for ever. . . .[73]

Within a week, there was news of a further drama in South Africa; Macmillan's former host, Dr Verwoerd, was shot in the neck and narrowly escaped death. According to first reports, 'he was shot by a white man. I devoutly hope this part is true,' wrote Macmillan, noting later that the would-be assassin proved to be 'both a madman and a Liberal' (the two were occasionally synonymous in Macmillan's vernacular). The value of South African shares plummeted by £650 million; then rebounded. No one at the time suggested that Sharpeville, let alone the attack on Verwoerd, might in any way have been sparked off by Macmillan's remarks in Cape Town; and in any event the train of powder had been lit long before. Nevertheless, it was clear which way the signposts were pointing, and Macmillan looked forward to the annual Commonwealth Prime Ministers' meeting in early May 'with considerable apprehension'.

His friend, Tunku Abdul Rahman of Malaya, had written a rough message following Sharpeville, condemning 'a rule of terror where the poor Africans are shot down in cold blood. It is unthinkable and unbelievable that a Commonwealth country should have employed the same method as that of the Russian communists in Hungary. . . .' He wanted the matter taken up at the forthcoming Conference.[74] To Rab Butler, Macmillan wrote anxiously, 'Once the Commonwealth begins to disintegrate I feel it is really finished. . . . I do not want to play the role of Lord North. Mr Gaitskell, both by temperament and appearance, is much more suited for it. . . .'[75]

The first session of the ten-day Conference went badly. Eric Louw, South Africa's dour Minister of External Affairs and the convalescent Dr Verwoerd's stand-in, was 'rude and ill-informed'. There could be no doubt that – drawing the fire from Central Africa (which was, of itself, a minor relief) – the problems caused by apartheid in South Africa would dominate the agenda. 'The prospects are pretty bad,' Macmillan recorded the following day: 'If we *do nothing*, the Commonwealth will seem to have no faith and no purpose. If we *do too much* South Africa will secede and this may mean the beginning of a general break-up. . . .' Meanwhile, news of Gary Powers and Eisenhower's U-2 débâcle had just come in: 'Quite a pleasant Saturday,' was Macmillan's cheerful diary entry: 'the Commonwealth in pieces and the Summit doomed!'[76]

His Commonwealth peers were 'very nice', but their general idea was 'to leave it all to me to find a way out! I thought Nkrumah very sensible. He is absolutely against trying to force South Africa out of the Commonwealth. . . .' Of the rest, Nehru seemed to have 'hardened' his line on South Africa, and was 'rather sour'; Ayub Khan (of Pakistan) a 'serious figure'; Welensky 'excellent – wise and generous'; Menzies 'a tower of strength'; Nash (of New Zealand) 'a nice, good natured, well-intentioned old-fashioned Liberal'. Only Diefenbaker from Saskatchewan, of whom Macmillan had already begun to form an increasingly poor opinion, was 'woolly' and 'very disappointing': 'deaf, ignorant, and little more than a "tub-thumper". He never forgets "party" politics, and talks of little else. . . .' At the critical stage of the Conference, while Nkrumah was 'most statesmanlike', 'Poor Diefenbaker nearly wrecked the agreed formula at the end, so I had to close down on him most firmly. . . .'[77]

It was tight-rope walking all the way. At the end of the Conference, a fifteen-clause communiqué filled with double-think and
double-talk was issued, which concluded that the participants had
'emphasised that the Commonwealth itself is a multi-racial association and expressed the need to ensure good relations between all
member states and peoples of the Commonwealth'. Macmillan
recorded in his diary that 'we have saved the unity of the Commonwealth (at least for the time being) *without* any sacrifice of principle';
while in his report to the Queen he admitted: 'The official text is
weak but has the advantage of being agreed. . . . it does at least
keep the Commonwealth for the time being from being broken
up.'[78] No one knew better than Macmillan that it was at best a
papering-over job, deferring the moment of decision at latest to the
following year's meeting. Barely was the ink dry on the 1960 Prime
Ministers' communiqué than Macmillan had to take off for the
doomed Paris 'summit', with little to cheer him.

Moreover, however 'wise and generous' Welensky had been about
Commonwealth difficulties at the Conference, he and the Federation
still provided Macmillan's main source of worry in Africa. They
were far more dangerous to him in the political scene at home than
was South Africa. Following the Banda episode, suspicions in
Salisbury about the good intentions of the Macmillan government
went from bad to worse. Welensky concentrated his energies more
on trying to influence British opinion than on wooing the Africans,
lobbying right-wing Tories and industrialists with considerable
success, and raising a storm of protest at every adverse turn of
events. Tory fears about the pace of decolonisation in Africa had
been fuelled by the Kenya constitutional conference which laid
down a timetable for full independence in 1963. This giant step had
produced cries of alarm from many of the most moderate white
settlers in Kenya. Nonetheless Harold Macmillan recorded that the
outcome of the conference was 'a great triumph for the Colonial
Secretary'.[79]

In July, with considerable competence and ingenuity ('juggling',
as Welensky put it, 'with never fewer than three balls in the air'),[80]
Macleod speeded through a conference on political advancement
for Nyasaland. Attempting to satisfy African demands without
outraging the whites, the Nyasaland constitutional Conference enabled elections to be held in August 1961. Welensky's delegates
accepted that the outcome would be an African majority in the

Legislative Assembly, but behind this was the knowledge that Banda was committed to secession. The implication was that Welensky himself was no longer averse to letting Nyasaland leave the Federation; and with hindsight it is difficult to see why Welensky and his colleagues should have been so adamant that Nyasaland, with its large black population and weak economy, should stay in the Federation at all.

The Congo Erupts

Suddenly, also in July, a new bombshell exploded on the scene – in the shape of anarchy and civil war in the Belgian Congo neighbouring the CAF. Immediately it brought about an influx of refugees into Northern and Southern Rhodesia, with – noted Welensky – 'far-reaching psychological and political consequences'.[81] At the beginning of the year, the Belgian government had agreed to give Belgium's immense colony, bigger than all the Federation put together, independence within six months. No other colony was less prepared for independence. It was said that no more than twenty Congolese had received higher education; and certainly there had been little administrative training, as in the British colonies; in effect, the fourteen million Congolese had been ruled directly from Brussels, and no agreement had been reached among the new nationalist leaders as to what constitutional forms should be adopted. On 10 July, Macmillan recorded that the Congo:

> has fallen into chaos; murder, rape, intertribal warfare, mass flight of Europeans, etc. The Belgian Government doesn't quite know what to do. The Prime Minister (Congolese) called Lumumba (or some such name) is a Communist and probably a Russian agent; the Premier of Katanga (where the mineral wealth is) is a moderate, and wants to be independent. . . .[82]

The south-eastern province of Katanga (now Shaba) produced 60 per cent of the world's cobalt and ranked fifth in the world in copper production, not to mention uranium, cadmium and zinc; without its wealth the Congo would have lost its economic lifeline. The Belgian government, which did not wish to lose the revenue from the Belgian-owned mines there, could have declared that

Katanga was a separate state before independence but the Belgian government dithered, and it was left to a popular and wealthy tribal leader, Moise Tshombe, to declare Katanga independent on 11 July. As the Katangan mines ran contiguously with Northern Rhodesia's, it was vital to Welensky, and to Macmillan, that whoever held power in Katanga was pro-white, and anti-Communist, and would protect the European mines and property. As Tshombe fulfilled all these requisites, and enjoyed strong local support, they backed him, with Welensky even wanting to send in troops.

The Belgians airlifted in paratroopers from Europe; while Prime Minister Patrice Lumumba and the new Congolese President Joseph Kasavubu asked the United Nations Secretary-General, Dag Hammarskjöld, for military aid to help them control the Congo and expel the Belgians. Lumumba also made a direct appeal to the Soviet Union for troops – to the considerable alarm of both Macmillan and Eisenhower. It soon looked as if the unhappy Congo was going to become a dangerous cockpit for world conflict.

On 13 July, Welensky was appealing to Macmillan to try to keep the UN out of the Congo, 'and thus minimise opportunities for Communist penetration. Could we not work for a "buffer state" in Katanga. . . ?' The irony of Welensky, so dedicated to ruling out any secession in the Central African context, now urging Katanga to do just that, was compounded, as Macmillan noted, by the fact that 'Our own left-wingers, who demand secession for Nyasaland, are characteristically against independence of any kind for Katanga. . . . It is a very tricky situation. . . .'[83] In the turbulent months to come, the Congo would turn upside down a great many preconceived ideas, stances and principles.

Macmillan's own view was that the only way to keep the Russians from a direct intervention was to work through the UN; to help Ghana – whose deteriorating economy and internal difficulties left the danger of Nkrumah turning to Eastern Europe; and to try to keep Welensky quiet. 'Meanwhile, the Russians are making a tremendous propaganda attack on all of us – France, Belgium, US, UK . . . etc. . . .'[84] On 4 August Macmillan was gloomily reporting that the Congo was now moving to a new crisis. With the exaggerated pessimism that sometimes accompanied his late-night diary entries, he thought 'Civil war in Africa might be the prelude to war in the world. Ever since the breakdown of the Summit in Paris I have felt uneasy about the summer of 1960. It has a terrible similarity to 1914. Now Congo may play the role of Serbia. . . .'[85] As he admitted later, he was at the time excessively concerned lest the Congo turn into an 'immediate confrontation with the Russians. But they ran out, as they always will if you stand up to them. . . .'[86] He was also deeply unhappy about the American hand: 'as long as Cabot Lodge is at UN, the Americans are quite unreliable. . . . Lodge is Boston – and fundamentally anti-British – not the Irish sort, which sometimes forgets; but the "Colonial" sort, which has to hate England out of snobbism – to prove that their ancestors were at the tea-party.'[87]

De Gaulle, too, was angered by the American vacillations, sending a sharp personal reproof to Eisenhower over the lack of Western political solidarity in the face of the anarchy in Africa and possible Soviet intervention there: 'the Atlantic Alliance, as it exists . . . seems to France inadequate to realities and incompatible with her world responsibilities. . . .'[88] Eisenhower, meanwhile, was swiftly becoming disenchanted with Lumumba; alarmed by Lumumba turning to Khrushchev for military aid after the UN's refusal to help him against Tshombe, the President decided after all to give US financial backing to the UN peacekeeping force. Then, on 14 September, with American encouragement and UN connivance, the young, unknown Colonel Joseph Mobutu staged a coup in Leopoldville, declaring that Lumumba had been deposed, that he was 'neutralising' all politicians until the end of the year, and that he was expelling all Soviet-bloc personnel. Macmillan, watching the ever changing Congo situation, likened it to the Crazy Gang. Khrushchev, attending a session of the UN in New York, was thrown into a rage and ferociously attacked Hammarskjöld. The coup also caused further rifts within the Congo, for Mobutu and his Congolese 'army' were not sufficiently powerful to overthrow Lumumba in his Stanleyville base.. The Congo seemed to be split three ways between the forces of Tshombe, Mobutu and Lumumba's left-wing adherents: all prey to any power which wished to move in.

The Monckton Report – At Last

Early in September, while the Congo was still in a state of flux, the Monckton Report finally reached Macmillan's desk. It was a powerful document, and it was not unanimous. All but two of its twenty-six members considered that the Federation had proved of great economic value to all concerned, but recognised that this could not make up for the lack of political freedom, and that the weight of African opinion was strongly opposed to its preservation. The Commission called for 'prompt and far-reaching reforms'. There should be swift moves to provide Northern Rhodesia with an African majority in the Federation's legislature; while in Southern Rhodesia the franchise should be significantly broadened. 'The strength of African opposition in the Northern Territories', the Report recognised, 'is such that Federation cannot, in our view, be maintained in its present form.' And 'African distrust has reached an intensity impossible in our opinion to dispel without drastic and fundamental changes both in the structure of the association itself and in the racial policies of Southern Rhodesia.'

All in all, it amounted to a fair indictment of the way in which the Federation was being run. A minority report of two (African) members recommended that the Federation 'should be dissolved forthwith', but much the most serious was the conclusion reached by the majority 'that Her Majesty's Government should make a declaration of intention to consider a request from the Government of Nyasaland to secede from the Federation'. This was exactly what Welensky had feared all along, and when he read the Monckton Report Macmillan knew that there would be a major storm in Salisbury.

Two months earlier, Home had succeeded Selwyn Lloyd as Foreign Secretary and it was his replacement as Commonwealth Secretary, the tough and able Duncan Sandys, whom Macmillan now sent out to Salisbury to sugar the pill. For Welensky, the Report was 'a terrible piece of high explosive, with a four weeks' time-fuse attached to it . . .'. As he wrote to Macleod, 'The secession proposals are the final straw and I consider them to be a complete breach of the understandings upon which I agreed to the appointment of the Commission. . . .'[89]

There followed a volley of telegrams to Macmillan, who reported on 3 October that Welensky 'is in a terrible state about . . . the reference to "secession". Commonwealth Secretary is doing his best. . . . I sent a telegram to Welensky urging him to make the best of Monckton. After all, it is a *unanimous* report in *favour* of Federation continuing. . . .' The report would not necessarily have to be accepted or rejected, argued Macmillan, perhaps not with strongest conviction; 'it was a contribution to the problem and was presented for the consideration of the Review Commission, to which all were committed.' None of this carried much weight with the outraged Welensky.

It was no use pointing out, as Welensky did, that Monckton, by including the secession clause, had breached the terms of reference to which he had originally agreed – and on which Welensky felt he had been categorically assured by the British government. Once the Report was published, the deadly word 'secession' would be out, and, once the principle had been mooted, it was only a matter of time before it became reality. Welensky called on Macmillan to 'honour the agreement between us', and repudiate the Report. Returning to London from New York on 6 October, Macmillan had 'long talks with Sandys and Macleod about Welensky', admitting that 'No doubt the Monckton Commission *has* gone beyond the strict terms of reference in one respect – the suggestion of a possible right to "secede" at some future date. . . . But the main recommendation should please Welensky, for it declares that "Federation" must continue. . . .'[90] Far from 'pleasing' him, such exhortations relayed by Welensky made him feel he was 'being enveloped by clouds of chilly cotton-wool', 'the customary thick coating of Macmillan treacle and cotton-wool'.[91]

On 11 October, the Monckton Report was published; the British government refused to repudiate it; Welensky protested publicly. In his memoirs, Welensky declared that this was the moment when 'those who had created the Federation of Rhodesia and Nyasaland . . . passed sentence of death on it'.[92] While nationalists like Dr Banda in Nyasaland and Kenneth Kaunda in Northern Rhodesia grasped at the secession clause in the report, acrimonious communications continued to flow between Macmillan and Welensky, who declared in a long and angry letter on 7 November, 'To put it quite clearly, I feel that I have been let down.'[93] He requested, menacingly, permission to publish the telegrams between them, to illustrate the bad faith of Her Majesty's Government. Macmillan refused. At home, the Prime Minister was also coming under considerable fire – commenting stoically on 8 November, 'The *Daily Express* has rather an offensive leading article about my alleged mishandling of Welensky. However, I must put up with this. . . .'[94]

Before the Lancaster House Review Conference on the future of

the Federation in early December, Welensky withdrew his impu-
tations against Macmillan personally. But the Conference itself was
a stormy affair, with first Banda walking out, then Joshua Nkomo,
one of the African delegates from Southern Rhodesia.* Banda was
later reconciled, and persuaded to read the lesson in church at
Chequers over the weekend, together with Duncan Sandys, which,
Macmillan commented, 'was thought quite symbolic'.[95] Nkomo in
turn was dismissed from his delegation by Sir Edgar Whitehead,
the elderly Prime Minister of Southern Rhodesia, without either
Sandys or Macmillan being warned; 'he gets blinder and deafer
every day,' wrote an exasperated Macmillan.[96] At almost the same
time as this was going on, de Gaulle paid his most disastrous visit
to Algiers, booed by Europeans and Algerians alike. Macmillan
noted gloomily in his diary entry for 14 December: '. . . Central
Africa is really our Algeria, on a smaller scale. . . .' Three days
later, Macmillan adjourned the Federal Review Conference, and
also postponed the two constitutional conferences on Southern
and Northern Rhodesia until the New Year. At least a complete
breakdown was avoided.

So ended the year of the wind of change.

---

* Nkomo later became one of the principal guerrilla leaders in the war against
Ian Smith, and – later still – Mugabe's chief opponent once independence had
been achieved.

Chapter Eight

Eruption at the Summit
1959–1960

The Americans have created a great folly. . . . One of their machines has been shot down by a rocket (it is said, a few hundred miles from Moscow). . . .

(HM, Diaries, 7 May 1960)

There was now little to be done except try to conceal as best I could my disappointment amounting almost to despair – so much attempted so little achieved.

(HM, Pointing the Way)

When Macmillan awoke on 9 October 1959, he stood at the apogee of power and the peak of all ambition. His vast parliamentary majority made him, at least on paper, one of the most powerful British premiers in living memory. All options were open to him; there seemed to be nothing 'Supermac' could not achieve. The future looked promising for his Britain. What was to follow was a series of disappointments of tragic proportions.

Predictably, Macmillan's major preoccupation after the election centred on foreign affairs. During the last year that his friend Ike was still in office, he wanted to press full steam ahead towards a 'summit'. But, as always happens in politics, unexpected winds would blow from unexpected quarters to buffet him off course; they would blow from the Soviet Union, from Europe, and they would begin to blow, now, from several parts of Africa.

But his first task had been to recast his team. Certain senior ministers wanted to retire; heading the list was Heathcoat Amory, whose unhappiness had continued to the point where he asked to give up the Treasury as soon as possible. Macmillan was able to talk him into staying on over one more Budget, so as to minimise all suggestions of dissent over Government financial policy. Alan Lennox-Boyd, Colonial Secretary over the previous five years, had also had enough of the stresses and strains of government; in Cabinet the previous summer Macmillan recorded that he and Eccles (Board of Trade) 'have ceased to be on speaking terms – they are only on bawling terms . . .'[1] over a matter of colonial cotton imports. A man of independent means married to a Guinness heiress who wanted him to take over the family firm, Lennox-Boyd (to Macmillan's considerable regret) now intended retiring from politics altogether. To fill his post – which Africa was to make even more of a hot seat than Cyprus had done – Macmillan had chosen a fellow Highlander, Iain Macleod.

In the game of musical chairs that ensued, the Chief Whip Edward Heath succeeded Macleod as Minister of Labour – a job for which, according to Macmillan, he had advanced a claim. Heath, whom Macmillan had regarded as a 'first class chief whip', was replaced by Martin Redmayne – who was not to prove in the same category. Hatchet-man Duncan Sandys had moved from Defence to the Ministry of Supply, with the brief of breaking it up and forming a new Ministry of Aviation, to try to infuse new life into the ailing British aircraft industry. Macmillan moved another man of action, his old friend Ernest Marples, into the Ministry of Transport, to start building the motorways Britain so woefully needed; while another self-made entrepreneur, Harold Watkinson, took over from Sandys at the Ministry of Defence. Reginald Maudling (described by Macmillan as 'one of the younger suc-cesses') was promoted to replace Eccles at the Board of Trade. Eccles moved back to his former position as Minister of Education, to which his talents were possibly better suited.

But – citing the charges of nepotism that it would arouse – a post for his own son Maurice was one he could not find, for all the real delight that Maurice's success at the polls had evoked. Given his own capability and the fact that he had now cured himself of the scourge of alcohol, Maurice (despite being a dull speaker, just as his father was in the 1930s) was well fitted for junior office – certainly more so than some Macmillan kinsmen whose appointments did draw the inevitable criticisms – and his passing-over was yet another source of sadness and discord within the family. Maurice himself never complained. Meanwhile, Macmillan noted that his 'chief problem' had been over the chairmanship of the Party. With Poole having left to return to business, Hailsham was 'really not safe'.[2] After the election Macmillan found that he was 'in a very over-excited condition and keeps giving ridiculous "Press Con-ferences" . . .'. Macmillan felt that Hailsham had quietened down; nevertheless the chairmanship of the Party had been given to the more sober Butler, a choice that Macmillan thought would be '*very* good symbolically'. It would show the world that 'after our great victory, we intend to remain progressive and not slide back into reaction. . . .' Hailsham was placated with the new post of Minister for Science.

At the most important post of all, however, Macmillan kept Selwyn Lloyd – to the surprise of his critics, and, perhaps partly, to confound them. Back in February 1958, Lloyd had given such a dismal performance in the Commons against an attack by Bevan that the press had widely called for his resignation. Macmillan had spent 'two or three very difficult days' dissuading the discouraged

Lloyd from resigning, on the grounds that he had lost his authority. It was an example of Macmillan's principle of rewarding loyalty with loyalty. The following June *The Times* picked up the pursuit again, in an 'extraordinary article . . . stating, among other things, that I have decided to replace Selwyn Lloyd as Foreign Secretary "shortly"'.[3] Macmillan went on to note that, although it would not have mattered much normally, the article had 'made a tremendous row at home and overseas', which worried him. Noting the next day how 'Poor Selwyn is naturally rather upset,' Macmillan determined more than ever not to be pushed into making a change. Besides, he had still had uses for 'poor Selwyn' at the Foreign Office – the scaling of the 'summit'.

In September 1959, to a full accompaniment of American razzmatazz, Hollywood extravaganza, earthy aphorisms (coming excessively close to some starlets dancing the can-can Khrushchev quipped that the 'face of humanity was better looking than its backside'), Khrushchev had carried out his visit to the US. Eisenhower was persuaded that he detected something of a thaw. Compared, certainly, with Ike's triumphal visit to London the previous month, there was something forced, however, about the cordiality; the *New York Times* described it as 'more like a funeral procession than a parade'.[4] But, following their talks at Camp David, Khrushchev had suspended his threat against Berlin. On 9 October, the day after his re-election, Macmillan received from Eisenhower – at long last, and after much delay – a message proposing a summit meeting of the Western heads of government to take place in December. To Macmillan this was an essential preliminary to a summit with the Russians, the goal to which he had been working ever since coming to power. But now it was the enigmatic de Gaulle who dragged his feet. Macmillan was vexed, but amused to note sardonically that 'Poor Adenauer, who usually "sucks up" to de Gaulle, accepted the American invitation to the Western Summit, before he heard that de Gaulle was going to refuse. . . .'[5] Meanwhile, there seemed to be little manifest movement in the Russian position. In August Macmillan had received a long communication from Khrushchev about Berlin:

How is it possible to speak about 'the forcing of a crisis' by our side? Are we really doing anything which could threaten your interests? What is West Berlin to you, if you do not want to fight against us. . . ?

We can come to an agreement about the time when a Peace Treaty should be signed. But you must bear in mind that this signature of a Peace Treaty would mean that you would lose your right to occupy West Berlin. This you must clearly understand. This is not an ultimatum – logical common sense leads to this conclusion.

Not an ultimatum, perhaps, but certainly an adroit gambit in the skilful Soviet chess-game, which Macmillan found difficult to answer.

Through most of the rest of October, matters over the Western summit seemed to hang fire, and pessimism overtook Macmillan again: 'De Gaulle is mysterious; Adenauer changes his position every day; and I fear the President may be losing heart. . . .'[6] Then, on 29 October, de Gaulle came up with a proposal fixing the meeting for 19 December – and in Paris. Macmillan noted, '. . . President Eisenhower is disgusted at the delay, but not disposed to argue any more. To this I have agreed. . . .'[7]

Meanwhile, on 20 November 1959, the European Free Trade Area agreements were finally initialled in Stockholm. Pressed on by his Scandinavian associates, coupled with his mounting fear of finding Britain excluded, commercially if not politically, from Europe, Macmillan had wrestled throughout 1959 with the creation of EFTA. There were many technical problems which had to be resolved by Maudling and his team, and squared with the Commonwealth – such as Norwegian fish and Danish bacon and butter. The negotiations hardly offered exciting reading. And the birth of EFTA made a growing number of Britons aware that it was a poor substitute for joining the Treaty of Rome. It was easily said that Europe was at 'Sixes and Sevens'. Macmillan, however, stuck to his view that EFTA was but a stopgap on the road to unity.

The Western Summit

By the time the Western heads of state met in Paris, Eisenhower's resistance to the summit with Khrushchev had all but been worn down. A major factor had been the dogged persistence and pressure applied by Macmillan. 'I had no intention of bickering with one of my best friends,' wrote Eisenhower in *The White House Years*,[8] which was revealing of just how much that intangible Special Relationship had played in Eisenhower's final summit decision. In Paris, de Gaulle conducted the proceedings with utmost dignity and grace, referring graciously to 'the good old days' in Algiers. When he pointed out that it was in fact in Algiers that the three had last met, there was an element of self-inflation; de Gaulle was no longer a defeated supplicant, *les anglo-saxons* chiefs were now his guests. Recalling his first summit – at Casablanca – Macmillan also found himself making private comparisons between the highly intelligent but devious Roosevelt, with his insincere charm, and Eisenhower the straightforward soldier, dedicated to golf and poker rather than to more intellectual pursuits, who was now President. At the beginning, Macmillan could also not help deriving amusement at the contrast of French and American style at the Conference; de Gaulle, 'the "Grand Monarch", speaking the French of the 18th century, beautifully spoken . . .'; Eisenhower, with his few and simple political beliefs, put forward in an often garbled syntax, 'almost unintelligible to de Gaulle'. When it came to discussing a date and venue for the grand summit, Eisenhower made heavy weather about having to clear his 'skedool'; which the hard-pressed interpreter could only translate as '*Le calendrier diplomatique est très chargé – mais je ferai de mon mieux. . . .*' Geneva seemed the logical venue, but de Gaulle grumbled, according to Macmillan: '*Ce n'est pas très gai. Le lac. Et puis toute cette histoire de ce Monsieur Calvin. Non. Ce n'est pas très gai. Tout de même . . .*'[9] Macmillan then suggested Paris.

It was a singularly adroit stroke, because if neutral Geneva had been chosen this would commit the participants to no more than a single, one-off summit. But Macmillan's ambitions had already moved on beyond just the forthcoming conference; he was:

anxious that the Summit should not be considered, as both the President and de Gaulle seemed to regard it, as a unique occasion. I was anxious to promote the concept of a series of meetings moving steadily forward from point to point in which 'peaceful co-existence' (to use the jargon of the day) – if not peace – could reign unchallenged in the world.[10]

Choosing Paris therefore meant that it would have to be followed by London, Washington, Moscow, in effect accepting the notion that Macmillan was now cherishing of a series of summits. Predictably, de Gaulle seized the bait; he was 'pleased by the idea of Paris and consequently accepted the *series* concept without demur. President Eisenhower agreed quite readily, and Adenauer less willingly. However, the decision was made. . . .'

Macmillan was also gratified that Eisenhower treated Adenauer roughly for his obstructiveness over Berlin: 'very firm and almost rude. He was thoroughly exasperated. . . . the German Chancellor collapsed and did not speak again.'[11] The old Rhinelander got a second barrel from Macmillan, after he had cynically suggested that the proposal for a series of summits was 'helpful in elections'. 'I replied rather angrily that I was not thinking of elections but of our duty to God and to mankind. Eisenhower came to my support. . . .' Macmillan was concerned at the appearance of his old friend: '. . . I did *not* think the President very well. He looked terribly flushed and seemed very restless. . . .'[12] Nevertheless, Macmillan could go back to London well satisfied with what had been achieved. The invitation to the summit had been sent off to Khrushchev.

On returning home, he sent off a long, perceptive and distinctly cheerful letter to the Queen. Referring to Eisenhower, he wrote,

> The fact that he does not stick to his brief, and has forgotten most of what he has been told by his advisers, leads many people to under-rate his fundamental strength, and indeed nobility of character. I sometimes feel that when he says the exact opposite of what he has been told – and even apparently agreed to say – he is not acting from weakness, nor from the forgetfulness of age, but is following his own instinctive judgment. In many cases I would think this better than that of the State Department or the Pentagon.[13]

Macmillan went on to report how, after an extremely good lunch, Adenauer 'delivered for nearly an hour a lecture on the danger of Communism . . .'. 'I regret to inform Your Majesty that I fell asleep during the latter part of this oration. . . .' He also expressed some optimism about how the meeting seemed to have distinctly improved his standing with de Gaulle:

He clearly thought that the President's acceptance of the tripartite meetings was the result of my pressure, and was correspondingly grateful. Thus, by a piece of good luck, what I would not have dared to do on my own for fear of being disloyal to the Americans, President Eisenhower had done for me and I really feel that, as a result, our chance of getting closer to France and the French Government has been considerably enhanced. . . .

On the whole, therefore, I think Your Majesty may feel that whatever dangers lie ahead – and they are many – the Conference has succeeded in its immediate objectives. . . .

Macmillan had every reason to rejoice. His last but one diary entry for 1959 noted that Khrushchev had sent 'a very friendly letter',[14] accepting the Western invitation to the summit. A date was now fixed – 16 May 1960, in Paris. The long, uphill struggle to the summit looked like being a major personal triumph for Macmillan, almost single-handed. His patience and calm had been noteworthy, and the omens were now that they were about to be rewarded, setting a crown on his role of statesman.

One needs to be reminded, however, that Eisenhower's 'conversion' had been lukewarm and decidedly reluctant. He remained full of scepticism and misgivings about the prospects of the May summit. To what extent had he acceded out of regard for his old friend? Macmillan's thoughts entered the New Year on a distinctly pessimistic note. Perhaps he had some premonition of the sad sequence of events that were to ensue. In the meantime, the six months preceding the summit passed in a flurry of diplomatic activity. In November Adenauer came to London. On 5 January Macmillan took off on the 'winds of change' tour of Africa, not returning until 15 February, for him a major digression from summitry and the European scene.

While Macmillan was away in Africa, Khrushchev had come out with an aggressive and discouraging declaration, to the effect that, if the summit got nowhere, he would go ahead with a separate peace treaty that would leave access to West Berlin to be controlled by the German Democratic Republic. However, the Nuclear Test Conference, which resumed in Geneva in January, seemed more promising. The Russians had suddenly seemed to become more amenable to the entry of Western inspection teams. Macmillan was glad to accept Eisenhower's invitation to fly to Washington to discuss the matter in March.[15]

Macmillan's diary entries are indicative of just how much his expectations see-sawed in the months preceding the summit. '. . . I do not feel very hopeful,' he wrote before leaving for Washington. 'The Americans are divided, and with an administration on the way out, the Pentagon and the Atomic groups are gaining strength. . . .' Once in Washington, he found Eisenhower 'definitely decided' to go along with him on the moratorium, but the military keen 'to go on *indefinitely* with experiments (large and small) so as to keep' refining upon and perfecting the art of nuclear weapons . . . '.[16] Thus even if the President gave the nod, any agreement could be so hedged about with 'ifs' as to render it ineffective. However, 'the President stood very firm,'[17] and on 29 March a joint communiqué accepted the Russian disarmament talks proposals. Meanwhile, on 19 March, Macmillan had received a most friendly and positive letter from Khrushchev. Altogether, it made him feel that 'All the omens are good' for the summit just six weeks ahead.

In a more relaxed mood, Macmillan recalled with delight how, at the Capitol, he had been accorded the signal honour of addressing the Senate, introduced by Vice-President Nixon. Characteristically, his immediate reaction was: 'How pleased my mother would have been. She regarded a Senator of the United States as almost the highest degree of dignity and felicity to which mortals could aspire.'[18] Finally, before he left Washington (which, incidentally, was to be his last visit while Eisenhower was still in office) the President confided to him, apparently almost *en passant*, some troublesome thoughts about Cuba. The New Year of 1959 had begun with a minor event, the repercussions of which were certainly not predicted at the time – the ousting of Batista in Cuba by Fidel Castro. As Macmillan reported to Selwyn Lloyd on his return: 'He [Eisenhower] said that the position there was becoming intolerable, but he realised the difficulties of *overt* action. . . .'[19]

De Gaulle's State Visit – April 1960

Hardly had Macmillan returned to England than de Gaulle arrived on a state visit, the first since his return to power in 1958. As Macmillan emphasised to the Queen in his long letter at the end of

1959, 'in the present state of Europe, if we are to reach agreements helpful to this country, so long as de Gaulle remains in power the French are the key.'[20] Then, by way of underlining his remark, on 14 February 1960, Macmillan recorded that, deep in the heart of the Saharan wastes of wartorn Algeria, de Gaulle had exploded his first atomic bomb, 'and now claims equal partnership with Britain. Yet another problem. . . !'[21] He recalled de Gaulle's sour comment after he had visited him on his return from Moscow the previous March – '*Je ne peux pas faire la guerre – on ne me donne pas les bombes atomiques!*'[22]

Macmillan began actively to contemplate ways in which he would woo the man who, at AFHQ during the war, had appropriately been given the codename of Ramrod, as evocative of one who had 'all the rigidity of a poker without its occasional warmth'. Meanwhile, to prepare for the state visit, in March Macmillan had flown to see de Gaulle again in Paris, where he found him 'mellowed', his charm great.[23] In an expansive mood, de Gaulle had reflected on the war, 'about Yalta (and the betrayal of Europe) and all the rest . . .'. Having just read the last volume of de Gaulle's war memoirs, Macmillan probed as to why he 'continually harped on the theme of the "Anglo Saxons" . . .'. De Gaulle declared that he 'believed in NATO, but its "set-up" was absurd.' The French Army within it was 'demoralised'. Once his army was back from Algeria, 'he would raise the whole issue' at NATO, was Macmillan's accurate forewarning. De Gaulle was scornful of American general-ship and organisation, but nevertheless he felt that America should constitute the 'grand reserve'. When Macmillan asked de Gaulle whether he was afraid of '12 German divisions on their own', he said he was not – at least for another generation, but thought it necessary to keep Germany firmly allied to the West to avoid any revival of German militarism. Speaking about France's history, de Gaulle indulged in a note of wry humour, recalling to Macmillan after one dinner how 'in this very room Charles X had abdicated. He went to England – Louis-Philippe went off in a *fiacre* – also to England. Napoleon III went to England, too. He paused – and said that he would no doubt be welcomed. . . .' Macmillan, of course, nodded assent gracefully.

Macmillan left Paris on a fresh note of optimism, believing that the meeting had succeeded 'in revitalising our old friendship. I feel that there is just a chance that I can get him to act in this dreadful

The new PM; returning from the Palace, 10 January 1957.

'Little Local Difficulties'; Birch, Powell, Thorneycroft.

The Commonwealth Tour, 1958; with Pandit Nehru and daughter, a young Indira Gandhi.

Making new friends Down Under, 1958.

Back from the Commonwealth; a happy and relaxed homecoming.

Friends again; with President Eisenhower, Washington, June 1958.

Makarios; on and off in Cyprus.

Journey to Muscovy, February 1959. The smiles disappeared later; so did the white hat, a perhaps too pointed reminder from the Finno-Soviet war of 1940.

General Election, 1959; canvassing at Oldham.

General Election, 1959; a helping friend sets a precedent, President and PM
before the cameras at No. 10. (*Centre stage*, Harold Evans, Press Secretary.)

General Election, 1959; utilising all the media.

General Election, 1959; winners (and, four years later, rivals) – Hailsham and Butler.

Together, at Birch Grove, 1958.

At home in No. 10, before rebuilding began.

Moving out – temporarily.

Winds of Change; Welensky, the fighter, January 1960. (This hat was a gift in Northern Rhodesia, later Zambia.)

Winds of Change; rallying the troops, Basutoland (later Lesotho).

Winds of Change; South Africa. Prime Minister Verwoerd and the spectre at the feast – a conspicuously empty chair.

Left in charge while the PM travelled; Rab once more brings him back from the airport, February 1960.

At the UN, September 1960.

An unexpected interruption from the floor – Khrushchev, shoes on.

Rambouillet, March 1960. Negotiating with de Gaulle; the smile a little forced?

Adenauer visits London, April 1958. Allies, but hardly friends.

London, April 1960. A warm welcome. The Duke of Edinburgh and Foreign Secretary Selwyn Lloyd. But de Gaulle goes his own way.

De Gaulle says, 'No', January 1963.

A happy interlude; Chancellor of Oxford, June 1960 (attended by his
fifteen-year-old grandson, Alexander, future Earl of Stockton).

6–7 [i.e. EEC versus EFTA] economic situation. . . .' On his return
to London, Macmillan sent off a detailed report to the Queen in
which he relayed de Gaulle's belief 'that France can and must lead
Europe', and added that the 'Anglo Saxons' were 'not sufficiently
sympathetic to French ambitions or to the traditions of
Europe . . .'.[24] He thought, however, that he had succeeded in
persuading de Gaulle of Britain's desire to play her full part in
Europe, and that the test would lie in whether France was prepared
to assist in avoiding a permanent economic division of Western
Europe.

Speaking of the forthcoming state visit, Macmillan ended his
letter by reporting that de Gaulle was much looking forward to it,
and that

> . . . Madame de Gaulle is very shy and speaks practically no
> English. She is a woman of considerable character: I have even
> heard it said that she is the only human being of whom the
> General stands mildly in awe – but I can scarcely believe this. . . .

The visit would be pointedly evocative of the Free French leader's
days at Carlton House Gardens in the grim 1940s, and Macmillan
determined to spare neither expense nor effort in making it a major
event that would, he knew, appeal to de Gaulle's sense of grandeur
– and vanity.

No one could have orchestrated it better than Harold Macmillan,
and it was to stand out as the most magnificent reception accorded
a visiting ruler in the post-war era. It would not have escaped de
Gaulle's eye that it was considerably more lavish than that even
bestowed on Macmillan's beloved Ike the previous summer. Louis
XIV would not have been displeased. Huge Crosses of Lorraine,
lit by a myriad of fireworks, illuminated the front of Buckingham
Palace. After a fanfare by the massed trumpeters of the Household
Cavalry, de Gaulle was accorded the signal honour of addressing
the Lords and Commons jointly assembled in Westminster Hall.
When he caught sight of the ageing Winston Churchill in the front
row, the haughty and turbulent leader of the wartime Free French
was observed to brush a tear from his eye, while Churchill too
'faltered'.[25] De Gaulle rose to the occasion with an address of
moving grandeur, and speaking without notes, in resonant French:
'What people', he asked in closing, 'know better than France and

Great Britain that nothing will save the world if it is not those qualities in which they excel; wisdom and firmness?'[26] An elaborate tribute was paid to Churchill, accompanied by a 'most friendly' reference to Macmillan himself.[27] It was – to use Macmillan's own words – 'a wonderfully impressive ceremony'. The *metteur en scène* had every reason to be highly satisfied by his artistry.

'The Summit That Never Was' (Eisenhower)

Unfortunately, Macmillan's mood of euphoria generated by the flamboyant success of the de Gaulle state visit was not to last long. By 9 April, he was voicing his misgivings in a letter to Selwyn Lloyd, that the Pentagon and 'the atomic energy people', regardless of the President's decision, might do everything in their power to make the disarmament conference fail.[28] At the same time, in Washington, Herter was setting down his own doubts whether the summit would prove 'a great success'.[29] Then, literally out of the blue, a most extraordinary event occurred.

On the afternoon of 1 May, Eisenhower was telephoned by his aide, General Goodpaster, and told, 'One of our reconnaissance planes, on a scheduled flight from its base in Adana, Turkey, is overdue and possibly lost.'[30] In operation spasmodically since 1956, the U-2 was a fragile aircraft, more like a glider than a conventional plane, with a vast wing-span which enabled it to hover at altitudes of 70,000 feet – or almost a mile higher than the existing world record. It was the temporary answer to the Soviets' Sputnik success, which had so alarmed the US with its evidence of the USSR's superiority in rocket technology. Eisenhower had been assured by both Dulles brothers that its high altitude put it well beyond the reach of Soviet anti-aircraft weapons; but, if it should be hit, such was its fragility that the unfortunate CIA pilot would not survive to tell any tale; and, finally (a somewhat specious argument), so ashamed would Khrushchev be that the US had been capable of surveying Soviet territory over such a long period that he would never admit it – even though he had been fully aware of the flights. In the event, all three arguments were to prove false. Eisenhower approved the flights (it was said that the CIA had persuaded the President by showing him a U-2 photograph of himself playing golf in Augusta, Georgia, in which he had actually been able to pick out the ball), on the ground that they 'produced intelligence of critical importance to the United States',[31] notably on the actual state of Soviet missile technology, and nuclear testing.[32] However lukewarm Eisenhower may have been about the May summit, no serious suggestion has ever been made – even by Macmillan at the depths of his despair – that the U-2 flights were continued in 1960 with the *deliberate* intent of sabotaging the summit. Rather, it seems to have been just one more instance of a failure of diplomatic sensitivity on the part of the Americans – and a colossal one at that.

The first Macmillan heard of the loss of the U-2 and its pilot, Gary Powers, was on 7 May, 'a glorious day – warm and sunny',[33] during the Commonwealth Prime Ministers' Conference at Chequers. He was then involved in reporting on his recent tour of Africa, and endeavouring to head off a crisis over South Africa. The news came, not from Eisenhower (who had known about it for the best part of a week), but from an angry speech by Khrushchev. As Macmillan noted in his diary:

> The Americans have created a great folly. . . . One of their machines has been shot down by a rocket (it is said, a few hundred miles from Moscow). . . . It seems to have . . . had a failure (perhaps of oxygen), lost height and been shot down. Worse still, the pilot did not go by his ejection chair (which would have automatically blown up the machine in the air) but by parachute. He did not poison himself (as ordered) but has been taken prisoner (with his poison needle in his pocket!). The Russians have got the machine; the cameras; a lot of the photographs – and the pilot. God knows what he will say when tortured![34]

Khrushchev in his speech added that Powers had in his possession among other things a poison pin, a silenced pistol, French gold francs, two gold watches, and '"seven gold rings for ladies"'. Unwelcome as it was, however, the news was not as strange to Macmillan as it might have been. Under the closest veil of secrecy, the U-2s had also been carrying out photographic spy flights from bases in Britain, under British auspices, for some time. Macmillan went on to admit in his diaries (though the admission was omitted from the memoirs) that the British themselves:

actually have done some very successful ones [photographic flights] (with aeroplanes which the Americans gave us). We called the exercise 'Oldster' but with the Summit negotiations coming on, all ours have been cancelled by my orders. The Americans were to do the same, but made their ending date the end of April. . . .

What Macmillan did not know, and could not have guessed at the time the U-2 was shot down, was that the CIA – with or without the knowledge of the President – had permitted the flights to continue so close to the start of the all-important summit. His diary entry continued: 'Khrushchev has made two very amusing and effective speeches, attacking the Americans for spying incompetently and lying incompetently too. He may declare the Summit off. Or the Americans may be stung into doing so.' He ended on a sardonic note: 'Quite a pleasant Saturday – the Commonwealth in pieces and the Summit doomed!'[35]

Via his wartime friend Bob Murphy, he evidently attempted to drop a hint to the beleaguered President that he follow British custom and decline to discuss intelligence activities in public.[36] Nevertheless, on the Sunday, 8 May, he had to record that:

The Americans have now had to come clean about their aeroplane. But it is still a very odd story. The pilot could *not* (say the experts) have parachuted from 70,000 feet and landed alive. . . . Why did he not shoot or poison himself? Why did he tell his whole story and route etc.? Is he perhaps a traitor?[37]

In fact, the Americans had erred by not 'coming clean', pretending initially that the U-2 had just strayed a little off course from its base in Turkey; a lie which infuriated Khrushchev, and which Eisenhower in his memoirs subsequently confessed was 'the big error'.[38] Macmillan continued his own diary with another note omitted from his own memoirs, and which perhaps made his case for indignation against Eisenhower just a shade weaker, writing with manifest relief, 'Nothing has yet come out about British flights into Russia. . . .'

There followed some hours of suspense as fears grew that Khrushchev might cancel the summit. Then, at six o'clock that same evening, Macmillan was informed that an urgent letter had come from Khrushchev, but – coolly – he decided it could wait till the morning; then:

> . . . I was relieved to find that it was all about how to conduct the Summit most profitably. So he hasn't called it off! I do not see how Ike can, unless the Russians shoot the unlucky pilot. But, nowadays, they are more likely to make him appear at a Press conference. . . .[39]

It looked as if the summit would take place, after all. But meanwhile the Americans continued to issue unfortunate and somewhat equivocal statements, which made Macmillan think that they had 'become quite distracted'. His knowledge of Khrushchev's mentality led him to the opinion that, at that point, he 'might well have accepted either silence or some formal disclaimer'. But 'Unhappily, with characteristic honesty, Eisenhower stated, at a Press conference, that the U-2 flights had been made with his knowledge and approval.' From then on, Macmillan detected, there was a distinct hardening of the Soviet line.

On the morning of 15 May, Macmillan set off to Paris, 'full of apprehension' but still not entirely without hopes. That afternoon Khrushchev called to see him, and the first sight of the Soviet leader confirmed that 'We are in for trouble.'[40] The Russian leader came 'in full state', accompanied by Gromyko, Marshal Malinovsky (the Soviet Defence Minister, whose first sight of France had been as a young soldier with the Russian division on the Western Front in 1917) and several others. Malinovsky stuck to Khrushchev like a leech throughout the Conference, and his presence helped persuade Macmillan that Khrushchev was acting throughout under heavy pressure from the army and hardliners in the Kremlin. Reading out a formal declaration to Macmillan, Khrushchev stated that it would be impossible to continue the summit, unless Eisenhower (a) condemned what had been done, (b) apologised, (c) undertook not to do it again, and (d) 'punished the criminals'. Macmillan tried to reason with Khrushchev, 'but did not succeed in appeasing him . . .'.[41] Equally, the humiliating terms were quite unacceptable to Eisenhower.

That night Macmillan slept badly. His diary for the next day contained only the briefest entry:

16 May: It is impossible to describe this day. It started at 7.15 am and ended at 1.00 am the following morning. I cannot 'write it up' – I am too tired. I must stop till later.[42]

That day of 16 May was, for Macmillan, as he later wrote in his memoirs, 'one of the most agonising as well as exhausting which I have ever been through except, perhaps, in battle'. He resumed his diary with a long account, in retrospect, five days later; in the meantime, '*The Summit* – on which I had set high hopes and for which I worked for over 2 years – has blown up, like a volcano! It is ignominious; it is tragic; it is almost incredible. . . .'[43]

Macmillan began the day (16 May) with a private breakfast with Eisenhower. He struck Macmillan as being 'depressed and uncertain',[44] and – much later – Macmillan recalled how much 'weaker, physically weaker' he had found his friend Ike in those last months of his presidency, compared with its earlier years.[45] He tried to console him by making it clear 'that we absolutely stood together. Most of our intelligence work was joint, and it was just bad luck that the Americans, after a great run of successes, had suffered this set-back. . . .'[46] This seemed to cheer the President, and Macmillan asked him what he was going to say to Khrushchev at the Conference later that morning. When Herter came in, a text was produced, but Macmillan thought it '*not* very good and much too truculent. . . . I felt the Americans were in considerable disarray. . . .'

The day's conference then opened on a slight note of farce, with Khrushchev pulling out of his pocket a large wad of typed notes, with a gesture that made Macmillan think of Mr Micawber assailing Uriah Heep, and began to read a set speech. Eisenhower, too, at one point 'could not help grinning' at Khrushchev's vehemence. 'He happened to notice this, and thereafter kept his eyes glued to the text of his speech.'[47] But Eisenhower's and Macmillan's amusement did not last long. Khrushchev added two points to his previous day's demands, 'both intended to be as offensive as possible to Eisenhower', noted Macmillan. They were that (a) the summit should now be postponed for six to eight months (i.e. until Eisenhower's presidency was ended), and (b) that Eisenhower's visit to Russia (proposed in return for Khrushchev's to the USA) be cancelled. Macmillan then appealed eloquently to Khrushchev to accept that 'espionage was a fact of life, and a disagreeable one', and rise above it for the sake of humanity. De Gaulle, with his usual lofty irony, made a telling point: 'At the present time, anyway, a Soviet satellite passes each day over the sky of France. It flies over at an altitude much higher than an airplane, but it still flies over it.'

Eisenhower sat in a cold rage; he scribbled a note to Herter, 'I am going to take up smoking again.'[48] It seemed to him an outrage that the representative of a government which 'had been so notoriously involved in spying, especially in the United States',[49] should speak to him like this. Later he commented that if the Russians simply wanted a four-power statement deploring and denouncing espionage, he would have no objection. He would also be prepared to renounce use of the U-2s – 'in the right circumstances'.[50] But this would not be enough for Khrushchev. It was generally agreed that it would be better for Khrushchev to walk out of the summit than for Eisenhower to do so.

Almost desperately, Macmillan still tried to salvage something from the wreckage, visiting each of the other three leaders in turn. Khrushchev, he found, 'was polite, but quite immovable'. Macmillan tried to make light of it, commenting *sotto voce* to his entourage on Khrushchev's tailoring as he left the Soviet Embassy: 'They may know how to make sputniks, but they certainly don't know how to make trousers.'[51] The next morning, 17 May, what little hope Macmillan had left was dashed by Khrushchev giving an impromptu press conference outside a Parisian vegetable market, in which he reiterated all his demands on the Americans. It was plain that the Conference was doomed. In private, Eisenhower told Macmillan that he 'planned to stay around Paris for at least a couple of days . . . to avoid any impression that he was the one breaking up the Summit Conference . . . '.[52] Eisenhower asked his old friend to go for a drive with him in an *'open car'*.

He obviously wanted this very much and my agreement gratified him. . . . Ike's object was clear – ingenuously clear. But it suited me. If Khrushchev must break up the Summit Conference, there is no reason to let him break up the Anglo-American alliance. . . .[53]

Later that evening the stone-faced Gromyko, recorded Macmillan, 'made it clear that they had fully decided to break up the Conference.

But he was quite hopeful about going on with the "Test" Conference at Geneva. . . .' Khrushchev came to see Macmillan before returning to Russia, but made no attempt to see Eisenhower. On the afternoon of the 18th Macmillan spent a farewell hour *à deux* with Eisenhower. 'He seemed very upset at the turn of events, so I tried to comfort him. . . .'[54] Eisenhower conceded one thing: that until the US had satellites aloft, they would carry out no more U-2 flights.[55] There was a final meeting of the three Western leaders at the Elysée at which they discussed 'our line *if* and *when* Khrushchev signs a peace treaty [with the GDR]. In itself, we cannot object. But if he says that this automatically and unilaterally destroys our (Western) rights what do we do next. . . ?' In an important passage omitted from the Macmillan memoirs, he recorded that Eisenhower:

> made it very clear that in his view we can do very little. All last year's talk about an armoured division going down the autobahn to Berlin is bunk. That is a gain. But since, in the end, we shall have to negotiate, it makes it all the more tragic that we are not doing so now, owing to the Summit failure. *De Gaulle*, in the absence of Adenauer, talked some good sense. Berlin cannot be recaptured or defended without major war. But de Gaulle does not believe that the Russians will force the issue. . . .[56]

So it was over. There was no disguising the shattering personal disappointment to Macmillan; a 'disappointment amounting almost to despair – so much attempted so little achieved', he wrote in his memoirs. It was the first major reverse in the more than three years of his administration – the first of several. Harold Evans recalled how, at the gloomy dinner following the collapse of the summit, Macmillan had tried to relieve the glum atmosphere by 'wry jokes all round'.[57] Lloyd was the butt; 'Well, I suppose to cover up the disaster, we'll have to give you the sack, Selwyn!' (His insecure Foreign Secretary was almost certainly not amused, having expressed several times vexation at the Prime Minister's tendency to act as his own Foreign Secretary.)

As was his wont at moments of extreme stress, Macmillan withdrew into himself, and plunged into reading *Pride and Prejudice*. But various observers saw the mask of unflappability slip momentarily; an American present at the summit reckoned that it left him 'in a highly emotional state. . . . World peace, he pleaded, hung in the

balance. . . .'[58] Years afterwards, Macmillan himself admitted that
the fiasco in Paris 'was the most tragic moment of my life'.[59] The
summit had been, he believed, the most important goal to which
he had been working ever since coming to office, and especially
since his visit to Moscow the previous year. Now there was nothing
left in the ruins on which to build. Of those closest to Macmillan,
Philip de Zulueta confirmed:

> . . . I never saw him more depressed. He was really cast down
> and glum after it. Apart from all the effort he had personally put
> into it, this was the moment he suddenly realised that Britain
> counted for nothing; he couldn't move Ike to make a gesture
> towards Khrushchev, and de Gaulle was simply not interested.
> I think this represented a real watershed in his life. . . .[60]

Curiously enough, however, it was not in terms of personal failure
that the outside world tended to see Macmillan after the collapse
of the summit. In its perverse way, the British public (as per Gallup)
accorded Macmillan a peak popularity rating of 79 per cent; it was
not only the highest he would achieve, but was also exceeded only
by Churchill at the height of his wartime popularity. The débâcle
in Paris may have deprived him of his role as the architect
of East–West rapprochement, but as the end of Eisenhower's
reign approached Macmillan was seen more as the strong man
of the shaken alliance, stepping in to restore some balance and
sang-froid.

After Paris, Macmillan immediately set to work to analyse precisely what had gone wrong. Partly he thought it might be explained
as a 'simple human reaction' by Khrushchev. Though he never
bore a grudge against his old friend Ike, he always felt that, if he
could only have made the right statement at the right time, it might
have let Khrushchev 'off the hook'.[61] It was 'such a childish
thing'. On the other hand, events in Paris also persuaded him that
Khrushchev, in sharp contrast to his predecessor, Stalin, did not
have as much power and independence as he had thought when
they met in Moscow.[62] '. . . I find it very difficult to explain these
events, and cannot therefore see the pattern of the future,' he wrote
in a letter to the Queen, and then went on with this thoughtful
conclusion:

It may be that there has been some internal change in the balance of power in Russia which has caused Mr Khrushchev to retreat from his policy of detente. It is significant that he never spoke to me alone, but was, throughout all his talks in Paris, accompanied by Marshal Malinovsky, the Soviet Minister of Defence, and Mr Gromyko. . . . Moreover, he appeared by his demeanour to be less in command of the situation than eighteen months ago. He often looked towards his colleagues as if seeking to carry them with him. It may be, therefore, that the Russian Government used the American aircraft incident as a convenient excuse for a change in their policy. . . .[63]

In the passage of time, more and more did this last interpretation of Macmillan's seem to hold water. In the meantime, a few days later, a letter arrived at No. 10 from Macmillan's loyal Commonwealth colleague, Tunku Abdul Rahman of Malaya, advancing another theory, that the Russian purpose in coming to the Conference at all had been:

mainly to make a boastful display of their arrogance for the benefit of the peoples in their own particular world without an honest intention to come to any understanding. I have a feeling that China had something to do with this breakdown. . . .[64]

It was, certainly, at about this time that the split between Russia and China first reached a significant level. Macmillan replied to the Tunku, expressing interest in his theory – which he had not considered before – and remarking, 'How absurd it is that one should know so little about what really moves these people. . . !'[65]

Meanwhile, in Washington similar post-mortems were being held. President Eisenhower sharply refuted press comment to the effect that Macmillan might have 'lost standing' with him, as a result of Paris.[66] In support of Macmillan's thesis about the limitations on Khrushchev's independence, the President told his Cabinet how Macmillan had relayed to him a 'jest' made by Khrushchev on his farewell call, when he had arrived accompanied by Marshal Malinovsky:

. . . Khrushchev had said he supposed that Macmillan wondered why the Marshal was always with him, and that was because the Russian people felt that Macmillan was such a skilled diplomat he could twist Khrushchev around. The Marshal was there to see that Mr Macmillan didn't, Khrushchev exclaimed. . . ![67]

Apart from being a sample of Khrushchev's sense of humour, Eisenhower thought that there could be 'perhaps just a little truth in it, for Khrushchev's self-confidence might not be as great as it was when he visited the US. . . .'

Out of it all, Eisenhower in his memoirs (written five years later) admitted that his 'big error' had lain in his issuing 'a premature and erroneous cover story'. But he still stuck to his belief that the summit, if held, 'would have proved to be a failure and thus would have brought the Free World only further disillusionment . . . .'.[68]

The remainder of Eisenhower's last term passed in an atmosphere of ice in East–West relations. Khrushchev's 'peaceful line was gone', noted Eisenhower; 'in its place was a Kremlin attitude reminiscent of the days of Stalin'.[69] On 30 June, the Russians stalked out of the Disarmament Conference on which Macmillan had also set so much store. The following day a US survey plane, flying from a British base, was shot down over international waters in the Arctic. A storm arose in the Commons and the press over the use of US bases in Britain, which gave Macmillan some of his 'most difficult and anxious' moments in the House since Suez. To Khrushchev's protest Macmillan replied with equal coldness: '. . . I simply do not understand what your purpose is today.'[70] Following the collapse of the Disarmament Conference, he accused Khrushchev frontally: 'you chose to break off negotiations as if you did not want to know what we were going to propose. . . .' About the same time, Macmillan wrote gloomily in his diaries:

We are only now beginning to realise, as the weeks go by, the full extent of the Summit disaster in Paris. For me, it is perhaps the work of two or three years. For Eisenhower, it means an ignominious end to his Presidency. For Khrushchev, a set-back to his more conciliatory and sensible ideas. For the world, a step nearer ultimate disaster.[71]

Writing to the Queen on 17 September, he remarked: 'We have fallen from the summit into the deep crevasse.'

Chapter Nine

'Stagflation': The English Disease
1960–end of 1961

The new Progressive Conservatism will turn out to be a policy of alternation between Benzedrine and Relaxa-tabs. I don't like it at all.

(*HM,* Pointing the Way)

They are very bitchy, some of those old dons. . . .

(*HM on Oxford University*)

While he was juggling with the balls of the summit and détente, with Africa and de Gaulle, since the triumphant 1959 election Macmillan's domestic problems had swiftly intensified. The famous remark, 'You've never had it so good,' so often quoted out of context, became the easy butt of cartoonists. Meanwhile, a new word was entering the jargon of Westminster economists – 'stagflation'. It meant that baffling combination, special to Britain at that time, of a stagnant economy and simultaneous inflation.

The end of 1959 had seen a fall in Britain's vulnerable currency reserves. On 19 January 1960 while Macmillan was still in the middle of his African tour, Heathcoat Amory had fired off to him a long warning letter. Drawing attention to Britain's declining reserves, he had pointed out how British interest rates were lower than in either the USA or Germany. He also noted how recent economic expansion (thanks to government policy over the past eighteen months) had also led to pressure on resources and an increasing demand for labour. This meant low unemployment, more demand for labour, and hence higher wage demands from the unions. He concluded:

> None of the foregoing factors *taken by itself* would . . . point to the necessity for immediate action. But, taken together, they reveal conclusively to my mind a situation and still more perhaps a trend in which an early warning signal is most certainly called for. . . . Psychologically it seems to me of great importance to make such a warning signal early rather than late.[1]

Two days later Macmillan had agreed that the situation was serious enough to warrant raising the bank rate from 4 per cent to 5 per cent – high in those days. On the day after his return from Africa he was noting in his diary, a not unfamiliar statement: '. . . I have certainly come into a great log-jam of problems. . . . Chancellor of the Exchequer at 10.00 a.m. He is worried – almost nervously so – about inflation. . . .'[2] Heathcoat Amory had his reasons. One of them was a nasty wages bill, nastier than usual, that was about to be presented by the railways. As part of the 1958 settlement with the railways unions, the Guillebaud Committee had been set up to try to work out a fair wage structure. Before its report was due out at the end of February 1960, however, the unions had demanded an interim pay award; General Sir Brian Robertson, Chairman of the British Transport Commission, had offered 4 per cent; the unions had refused, threatening yet another all-out strike. All this had brewed up while Macmillan was on his way back from South Africa. To avert a strike, Macmillan had cabled back raising the offer to 5 per cent; it was, he admitted, 1 per cent more than the Cabinet had hoped, and 'this additional 1 per cent was fiercely attacked by the financial pundits' – notably ex-Chancellor Thorneycroft and his supporters.

All in all the prospect of increased railway payments, sparking off in turn further wage demands, combined with increased estimates from the spending departments, of £340 million, had all begun 'to reappear like familiar spectres from the past' as preparations began for the 1960 Budget. As Thorneycroft never ceased to point out (in fact he was still doing so in the 1970s and 1980s), since his resignation from No. 11 government expenditure had increased, not by the bitterly fought-over £50 million, but by £750 million.[3] On 17 February, his first working day after returning from Africa, Macmillan spent an hour with Amory and the Governor of the Bank of England together. He was met with 'a sudden mood of despondence and alarm', and came away 'worried – not so much about the boom but the loss of nerve . . .'.[4]

Macmillan hardly needed detailed briefing from the Bank of England about the basic ingredients of the new crisis; during the short-lived boom of 1958–60, the British had gone on a 'refrigerator spending spree', lavishing money on imported goods instead of savings or investment. Over the previous year imports had risen by a dramatic 10 per cent, exports by only 4 per cent. The economy, as he put it mildly to a television interviewer in 1973, had got 'slightly overheated'.[5] The Governor of the Bank of England, Mr Cameron Cobbold,[6] and the Chancellor viewed it in graver terms. On 26 February there was a further meeting at which Macmillan found them both 'suddenly very pessimistic about the future', and foresaw 'another row looming up': 'inflation, too much imports, balance of payments difficulties, loss of gold and dollar reserves, etc. etc. – the same old story. So they want violent disinflationary measures and a fierce Budget (£100 million extra taxation). It's 1955 all over again. . . .'[7]

Amory's 'Stand-Still' Budget

Macmillan was determined to fight such violent remedies tooth and nail, and the next day he followed up with a cool personal letter to his old friend Amory, saying,

> The more I think about our conversation yesterday the more depressed I am.
>
> Max Beerbohm once said that history does not repeat itself; it is the historians who repeat one another. This is certainly true of the economists and professors. They are very apt to make the same diagnosis and apply the same remedies although the circumstances may differ in character. . . .

He continued:

> Following the Budget of last year and the Election last autumn, a deflationary Budget would either be very foolish or very dishonest. Unless it is supposed that we would be thought very modern and up-to-date, like those young ladies who oscillate daily between the stimulant and the tranquilliser. The new Progressive Conservatism will turn out to be a policy of alternation between Benzedrine and Relaxa-tabs. I don't like it at all.
>
> For these reasons I still think that you should consider a *stand-still* Budget. . . . A gentle squeeze may be right; but it cannot be sensible to cheer the economy on vigorously one moment and then push it violently back the next. . . .[8]

A 'stand-still' Budget it was indeed when 3 April came round; twopence on tobacco and 2½ per cent on Profits Tax would bring in a modest £80 million over the next two years, and a tightening on hire-purchase credit. This would be matched by some £30 million of concessions, ranging from an end to the tax on cinema tickets upwards. No one would have called it an exciting Budget, let alone a radical or reforming one, given the great new political power Macmillan now possessed in Parliament. He wanted it to be known as the 'Consolidating Budget'; he also reckoned that, once again, he had won the battle 'quite definitely'[9] against the combined weight of the Treasury and his Chancellor.

'Budgets, like babies,' proclaimed Macmillan's hero, Trollope, in *The Prime Minister*, 'are always little loves when they are first born. But as their infancy passes away, they also become subject to many stripes.' The stand-still, 'Consolidating' Budget was not badly received by the Conservative backbenches – nor, indeed, by the Opposition – but in its aftermath Macmillan received a few 'stripes' from private correspondents. On 26 April, the intrepid Bob Boothby wrote to Macmillan in his forthright way:

> . . . I really do think you must take steps to dispel the impression, now rapidly gaining ground, that there is a total lack of assurance and decision at the Treasury. The hand may be on the tiller. But it is becoming clearer every day that it doesn't know where the hell it is steering.[10]

The implied criticism here was almost as much directed at the Prime Minister as at his Chancellor. Macmillan replied with more than a touch of heavy irony:

> Alas . . . it is the fault of an economy balanced like ours. Of course, if we succeeded in losing two wars, wrote off all our debts – instead of having nearly £30,000 millions in debt – got rid of all our foreign obligations, and kept no force overseas, then we might be as rich as the Germans. It makes one think a bit. . . .[11]

Always adventurous, Boothby came back the following day on a line diametrically opposed to Amory and the Treasury 'deflationists': 'My constant fear is that, by holding demand below productive capacity, we may become a low-investment high-cost economy. This is no way to achieve competitive prices in world markets, or indeed to combat a cost inflation. . . .'[12] Through the spring of 1960, matters worsened, with the trade gap widening even more alarmingly, and by the end of April Macmillan had agreed that Amory should give the economy 'a touch on the brake'. Hire-purchase regulations were further toughened, and 'Special Deposits'[13] of 1 per cent were introduced. By the beginning of June

Macmillan found himself forced to push bank rate up again from 5 per cent to 6 per cent, and the Special Deposits regulator from 1 per cent to 2 per cent. This time public reception was more critical. It was clearly time for Amory to be replaced.

Amory Goes: the 1960 Reshuffle

As early as January 1959, Amory had made no secret of his own unhappiness at the Treasury. Harold Wilson recalled how, 'if you attacked him, poor old Derry Amory would look like a wounded stag.'[14] After the 1959 election he had made known to Macmillan his own desire 'to exchange the fierce conflicts of national politics for the comparative calm of business and philanthropy', but had been persuaded by Macmillan to stay on to see through one more Budget. Macmillan recognised later his error in keeping on, too long, a Chancellor who was both tired and unhappy, when a fresh mind was badly needed. Meanwhile, the delight which Macmillan had expressed in dealing with Amory after the intransigent Thorneycroft had progressively given way to disenchantment:

> *11 March:* . . . a sweet man – a really charming character. But he is tired and overdone. He feels his responsibilities almost too much. Fundamentally, he lacks nerve.[15]

Macmillan decided to replace Amory by the faithful Selwyn Lloyd, who had 'had five years as Foreign Secretary, which is an immense strain . . .'.[16]

Explaining these moves to the Queen on 30 July, in a tone typical of the uninhibited way which, by his mid-term of office, he had come to confide in her, Macmillan wrote:

> . . . I must frankly tell Your Majesty that I believe Your Majesty's interest will now be better served by the resignation of Mr. Heathcoat Amory and the transfer of Mr. Selwyn Lloyd to the Treasury. I felt for some time that Mr. Amory, with all his charm, had lost his buoyancy and resilience and entered into a permanent quietism more suitable to a monastery than to the busy life of every day. I do not say he was defeatist. He just seemed overwhelmed. . . .[17]

But, as Macmillan was to discover even more painfully just two summers later, the replacement of such a key figure as the Chancellor of the Exchequer inevitably unleashes with it a major reshuffle of the government. First of all, a new Foreign Secretary had to be found to replace Selwyn Lloyd. While deliberating this complicated game of musical chairs, Macmillan had calculated that bringing him on to the 'Home side' might offend Rab's susceptibilities, in that it would make him 'a possible rival to Butler in considering the succession. Although he is not ambitious in any wrong sense, he [Selwyn Lloyd] is conscious of Rab's weakness and oddness (which seems to grow not lessen). . . .'[18] Consequently, Macmillan says that his first act was to consult Rab himself, who 'had no desire either to return to the Treasury, or to take on the Foreign Office'. Later he also refused, twice, the post of Commonwealth Secretary. 'So he should feel well treated.' 'I think he will decide to remain Home Secretary, but I should really like him to take Commonwealth Secretary. He would be particularly good at dealing with Rhodesia, etc. . . .'[19] It would be two years before the offer would come round again; Rab, on the other hand, always disputed Macmillan's recollection, claiming that he had not been granted the option of going to the Foreign Office, but would – still – 'like to have gone there and assumed one hat instead of three. But Alec Home was chosen. . . .'[20]

Alec Home was one of Macmillan's boldest appointments, fiercely criticised from all directions at the time. 'What have we done to deserve this?' was how, with detached amusement, Home himself recalled the *Daily Herald*'s reaction, while even the Tory *Daily Mail* observed that Macmillan still had time 'to stop making a fool of himself'.[21] In what Macmillan then rated as 'the cleverest and most effective speech' he had ever heard Gaitskell make,[22] the Leader of the Opposition had denounced the choice, pointing out that Macmillan himself had only come to the Foreign Office through Eden's reluctant decision that Lord Salisbury was debarred by his peerage, a decision which Macmillan was said to have endorsed warmly at the time. In fact, Macmillan regarded Home's being in the House of Lords a positive advantage: it 'gave him much more freedom to move about the world, and all that kind of thing which you have to do as Foreign Secretary'.[23] Home was far from being an obvious choice for Macmillan; the criteria by which he harshly judged men like Rab – having been an *embusqué* and a *Munichois* – applied with equal force to Home, who had *not* fought in the war (for reasons of poor health) and who *had* been Parliamentary Private Secretary to Neville Chamberlain at the time of Munich. But temperamentally the fourteenth Earl and the Crofter's great-grandson had a lot in common. He was, Macmillan once remarked,

> not a steely professional, but he was more than an amateur. Quite tough, yes; but he didn't reveal his strength . . . shy, retiring – rather like me in many ways. We got on admirably – he was extremely agreeable and easy to deal with; but he was also quite firm. Wasn't a stooge of mine, by any means. I didn't want that, of course. . . .[24]

Selwyn Lloyd might have disagreed.

There was another dimension. Martin Redmayne, Macmillan's new Chief Whip who took over from Ted Heath at the same time as Home's appointment, reckoned that it was the one 'which gave him [Macmillan] most pleasure', because it 'appealed to both his sense of history in real terms, and to his love of Trollope'.[25] Home himself was naturally diffident about his qualifications, as well as his being in the Lords and his not very robust health. For a week Macmillan was kept waiting for Lord Home's decision; then, on 17 June, Macmillan recorded: 'lunched with Lord Home. *He will take the Foreign Office*. I am delighted. . . . Alec Home has been so good [as Commonwealth Secretary] and has the confidence of all. . . .'[26] Strangely, there was virtually no comment in the press about the important appointment of Edward Heath to be Home's number two, shortly to supervise the EEC negotiations – beyond praising him as a 'Man of Action'. With this appointment, Macmillan promoted a new star in the Tory firmament. Years later, at the beginning of the Thatcher era, and in some disillusion at what he construed to be a lapse of party loyalty, Macmillan described him with a tartness that he might otherwise not have expressed when Heath was working for him:

> . . . Hengist and Horsa were very dull people. Now, as you know, they colonised Kent; consequently the people of Kent have ever since been very slightly – well, you know . . . Ted was an excellent Chief Whip . . . a first-class staff officer, but no army commander. . . . He was brilliant on Europe; the job didn't want somebody who was a good orator, but he had an infinite capacity

for details and was very patient and very good with the continental mind.[27]

Most of these virtues Heath certainly displayed; in addition he was more energetic, and ambitious, than Maudling – and abrasive. But he seemed to be distinctly lacking in 'sensitive finger-tips', and had no particular liking for the French, nor any conspicuous empathy with foreigners as a whole. Viewed with hindsight, was he in fact the ideal negotiator for dealing with the prickly Gaullists of the 1960s? On the other hand, given that – a decade later – he was the man who *did* finally bring Britain into the Common Market, after the departure of de Gaulle, it may well be that there was in fact no one who could have done better at the time.

Inter alia, the 1960 reshuffle also threw into question the Leadership of the House of Lords. 'Lord Hailsham', noted Macmillan on 17 June:

> came at 5.00 pm and talked about his own future for an hour or more. He thinks he might do better by going back to the Bar now.[28] Before this, Alec and I (with the Lord Chancellor) had been discussing whether Lord Hailsham could lead the House of Lords without disaster. . . .[29]

Given the critical choice that Macmillan would have to make during the succession stakes three years later, this juxtaposition of his views about Home and Hailsham in 1960 is not without interest. But, a much higher priority than the Leadership of the Lords, moving Home meant that the increasingly important job of Commonwealth Secretary would be vacant. Macmillan offered it, once again, to Rab, who finally refused, and Macmillan appointed his 'hatchet-man' Sandys – to be opposite number to Iain Macleod. Among the lesser new Cabinet appointees, Macmillan broadmindedly (and shrewdly) brought back in the two fallen angels, Thorneycroft and Powell; Enoch Powell to Health and Thorneycroft as Minister of Aviation. The offer to Thorneycroft had required 'much reflection', as Macmillan still regarded the 'little local difficulty' of 1958 to have been 'rather a "bad show"', but he enjoyed a private chuckle at the thought that the parsimonious Thorneycroft would find the Ministry of Aviation 'a great spending department, which he obviously didn't much like . . .'.[30] During the 1960 reshuffle the talented John Profumo was also promoted to take over the War Office.

From Pretoria in January of 1960, Macmillan had written to Maurice, in the whimsical style he often reserved for his son, 'According to the *Sunday Express* my existence is your chief handicap, but time will overcome this. . . .'[31] Yet in the autumn when there was final instalment of the government (non-Cabinet), Maurice was passed over again. Macmillan made his son-in-law, Julian Amery, Secretary of State for Air, and his wife's nephew, the eleventh Duke of Devonshire, Under-Secretary at the Commonwealth Office, to the accompaniment of 'a little mild fun in the newspapers about "nepotism" and "happy families" – but all in very good tone. I think everyone recognises that Maurice has suffered, rather than gained, by being my son. A Duke, of course, is always fair game.'[32] Macmillan justified the latter, perhaps not very inspired, appointment to his biographer, Nigel Fisher, with one of his throwaway remarks, 'Andrew is awfully good with the natives. The Devonshires have always been good with the natives.'[33] To some of the Macmillans, it was also regarded as 'Handing out patronage – his revenge on the Cavendish clan!'[34] Yet, for those inside and outside the family, who recognised his political talent to be well in excess of those of his noble kinsman, this passing-over of Maurice, yet again, was seen as one more sad blow in the awkward father–son relationship; particularly sad at a time when he was successfully struggling out of his period of alcoholism. When, at the beginning of November, Maurice was chosen to move the address at the opening of Parliament, his father recorded that he did so 'in an admirable speech': 'After all the talk in the newspapers about my "family" appointments . . . he delighted the House by his opening sentence "as the only back bench member of the family". . . .'[35] Too loyal to his father, and too generous-spirited ever to show bitterness, Maurice must nevertheless have suffered then more than just a little twinge of disappointment – yet again; and this was probably felt even more keenly by his family.

With the departure of Heathcoat Amory from Macmillan's Cabinet, so went also a certain gentleness. Equally, with the intransigent Thorneycroft and the dissenting Amory replaced by the compliant Selwyn Lloyd, Macmillan to a large extent – and against all his instincts for delegation – would find himself becoming, willy-nilly, his own Chancellor, in addition to being his own Foreign Secretary (certainly on the major issues) and his own 'Minister for Africa'. Was it all too much for one man? It was a dilemma that other British leaders had faced previously and would have to face again. Something had to suffer; in Macmillan's case, it would be the British economy – which was, perhaps, where the most serious damage of all could be inflicted, in the long term.

Selwyn Lloyd at the Treasury; Growing Economic Problems

It was plain to his colleagues that Selwyn Lloyd was no keener to leave the Foreign Office for the Treasury than Macmillan had been five years previously (with reason, because – in contrast to Macmillan – he had had absolutely no experience of the world of finance), and was justifiably diffident about his capacity for the job. Nevertheless, he threw himself into the Treasury – with an energy that was unmatched by any original ideas. A lonely man, he continued to weekend at Chequers, thanks to the grace-and-favour of the Macmillans, with a labrador as his sole companion. It proved to be Macmillan's least successful appointment, the Treasury being the one place where Britain in the 1960s most needed ideas. With a more imaginative mind than Selwyn Lloyd's there, many of the subsequent disasters might have been avoided. Macmillan clearly hoped that a personality as malleable as Selwyn Lloyd's would permit him to be his own Chancellor too. But this was not to be; in fact Macmillan just went on being his own Foreign Secretary, and the transfer of Selwyn Lloyd was what marked the beginning of his downfall. Nevertheless, at first Macmillan expressed the same high hopes of Lloyd as he first did of Amory:

> . . . I was very glad to find him in capital form, full of confidence, buoyant, and with many practical ideas. A great contrast to the last few months of poor Don Quixote, his predecessor. Derry Amory was absolutely splendid for two years. After that, he was somehow worn out. The truth is that, unless one has the right temperament, the strain is too great for either a Foreign Secretary or a Chancellor, year after year. After all, we shall soon have had *ten* years of it. . . .[36]

Macmillan resisted any allusion to the strain on Prime Ministers. Undoubtedly, one of the relaxations which helped him to stay sane was being able to escape to Birch Grove whenever possible. 'This morning it is very beautiful and I am about to go for a walk in the woods,' Macmillan wrote to his confidante, Ava Waverley, from Birch Grove on 16 August, while Britain and Parliament were away on holiday:

> Tomorrow back to London and a day of worry and trouble. We have got through the Power Strike but the Seamen's Strike is still running; and there are troubles in the Docks and the motor works which threaten us. It is apparently the inevitable result of prosperity. . . .

He hoped, however, that things would improve enough to allow him to 'go away at the end of this week to shoot some grouse . . . '.[37] A new railway strike was called off, but a stoppage by tally-clerks paralysed the London Docks in September; partly as a result of which the October 1960 trade figures proved to be 'alarming – £122m gap [up] from £76m in September. . . . the bad trend is there. . . . '[38] In November a major row brewed up over an offer by Ford USA to buy up Ford UK, with the resultant *malaise* spreading through the British motor-car industry, and spilling into the autumn of the following year; strikes involving thousands of men were called over such matters of life-and-death as the length of the morning tea-break. The 'tea-break' strikes also hit the building industry – including Mowlem's, who were at work on the rebuilding of No. 10.

Towards the end of 1960, Macmillan was worrying about the wider, international implications of Britain's dilemmas. Was there a sufficient base from which international credit could finance a greatly increased volume of international trade? If there was a general deflationary movement in the free world, how was this to be countered? Should the dollar and the pound be devalued, or the Deutschmark up-valued?

The arguments in Cabinet continued: 'two and a half hours on the Economic situation,' Macmillan recorded on 30 November; it was:

> really baffling. We are borrowing short and lending long; exports are stable or falling; imports leaping up – yet the £ is strong and

money – some 'hot', some genuine investment (e.g. Ford) – keeps flowing in. 'Everyone believes in Britain – except the British.'[39]

The New Year of 1961 was celebrated by 160,000 Post Office workers with a month of 'working to rule' in protest at rejection of their demands for a 4 per cent increase. The spring brought further unofficial strikes in the London Docks – this time unmistakably Communist-led. On 17 January, Macmillan recorded a 'difficult Cabinet'[40] on the economy and on Powell's proposed 'economies' in the Health Service.[41] This was followed up, in February, by a fairly forthright résumé on public opinion and economic trends from the Conservative Research Department. It reckoned that, had the Labour Party then been a more effective opposition, it could have mounted a 'formidable case' against the government's economic policy in 1960 when Britain's balance of payments was the worst since 1951. Fortunately, however, the Opposition had been in a 'chaotic state'. The Report continued in a critical vein, clearly pointed at Macmillan himself:

> we have virtually exhausted the Neo-Liberal seam in economic policy. The existing armoury of economic weapons – Bank Rate, hire-purchase restrictions, credit squeezes – is admittedly deficient. Yet apart from the introduction of special deposits last year, we have tried out no new ones and, much more important, we have done nothing visibly to examine the problems and search for new ones. . . .[42]

In March speculators made a serious 'bear' attack on sterling, with Macmillan noting, 'We lost £67m in *one day* (£26m was the worst post-Suez day)' from Britain's slender reserves.[43]

Shortly before the Budget, Macmillan's 'old and trusted adviser', Roy Harrod, came to him as a 'prophet of woe. He says the £. will crash in the summer. We *must* restrict imports. Treasury and Board of Trade say the opposite. What is a poor Prime Minister to do?'[44] Harrod's advice represented a 180° swing, and it marked the beginning of Macmillan's disenchantment with this long-standing *éminence grise*.

Balance-of-payments figures published on 1 April were so discouraging that Macmillan and Lloyd found it 'not easy to frame a Budget, certainly not a popular Budget'. Macmillan succeeded in pressing Lloyd to make substantial concessions on surtax for higher incomes, raising the level from £2000 to £5000, which was, indeed, hardly popular in the nation at large, especially as Powell had just doubled National Health prescription charges, while all pressures to introduce a tax on capital gains had been sturdily resisted. A 10 per cent tax (long overdue) was imposed on television advertising, while 'regulators' were introduced whereby – without summoning Parliament or framing an interim Budget – the Chancellor could vary duty on tobacco, alcohol and petrol, as well as increasing the weekly National Insurance stamp. Like a doctor, he could now administer small doses of medicine when needed. These 'regulators' were, Macmillan claimed, the 'outstanding innovations' of Selwyn Lloyd's first Budget: but, in the eye of the public, it was altogether about as lacklustre, unexciting and unradical as the last Budget.

In June and July trade figures continued bad, with Macmillan reporting to Ava Waverley: 'The economic situation needs some strong action – and that means a lot of difficulty. Everyone is in favour of someone else making sacrifices. . . .'[45]

By the end of the month Lloyd had to produce another packet, a 'little Budget'. Bank rate went up again, this time (temporarily) to 7 per cent; consumer taxes were raised; government spending and bank overdrafts fiercely squeezed. Over the past year, Selwyn Lloyd told the Commons, wages and salaries had soared by 8 per cent, national production by 3 per cent. The nation was becoming uncompetitive; 'a pay pause was now essential'. Thus was born a famous expression: the 'pay pause' was a first clumsy and rather 'amateurish' (as Macmillan himself admitted) forerunner of an incomes policy, a system of controls over wage settlements which would be used by both Conservative and Labour governments, but which invariably proved to be divisive.[46] William Haley at *The Times*, for one, was not satisfied. Whereas he had welcomed one of the new Chancellor's earliest speeches as being 'forthright and courageous', by July *The Times* was expressing extreme pessimism:

It is as well to say now that the task is beyond him. It is beyond any Chancellor of the Exchequer. No matter what the measures may be they will not, on their own, cure the deep-seated ills of the British economy. Nothing short of an effort by the whole nation can do that.[47]

And, following Lloyd's 'little Budget' and the introduction of the pay pause,

> . . . Britain's economy has been sick for years. The malady has outstayed all too many Chancellors. They come; they apply their nostrums at some feverish moment; they declare the patient will now recover; they go. Before the public have had time to know much about their successor the trouble starts all over again. . . . Every British Government since the war has funked the consequences of really fighting inflation. It is hard to believe that at long last Britain has come to the turning point. . . .[48]

Nevertheless, as a result of Lloyd's new measures, by August the immediate run on sterling seemed to have been met and held. 'We had thus won the first round,' claimed Macmillan. To give sustenance and credibility to the pay pause he and Selwyn Lloyd worked through the rest of the summer on a scheme, to be presented to both sides of industry, proposing the creation of a National Economic Development Council, drawn from the unions, management and government. Macmillan gave Lloyd full credit for 'this forward-looking scheme', and Lloyd himself evidently came to regard it as his most important contribution in government. But 'Neddy', as it became known, also had central planning features foreshadowed more than twenty years earlier in Macmillan's book *The Middle Way*.

After considerable divergence in the Cabinet, 'Neddy' got the go-ahead on 21 September. But would it have the clout to do the job? In October Lloyd was able, cautiously, to reduce the bank rate to 6½ per cent, but the following month – to Macmillan's considerable anger – the Electrical Trades Union was handed a wage increase twice as high as they should have, thereby driving a coach-and-horse through the pay pause. Even *The Economist* turned and rent Macmillan: 'the Government', it declared, 'deserves the deepest censure for its contribution to the electricity wages surrender; and it is no good the Prime Minister wringing his hands like an impotent Pontius Pilate. . . .'[49] Macmillan ended his diary for the year on what had become an almost ritualistic note of gloom about the economy: 'The problems which now confront Britain, internally and externally, are really terrifying. No one seems to realise their complexity. . . .'[50]

Robens and the Mines; Beeching and the Railways; Eccles and Education

One surprising economic success story, however, was the mining industry. It had been nationalised under the 1945 Attlee government, and in 1961 Macmillan 'poached' from Labour Alfred Robens to cleanse the Augean stables at the Coal Board. Macmillan thought it was a 'lucky' choice; others might think it inspired. Very much of the old school of Labour, Robens had been Parliamentary Under-Secretary at the Ministry of Fuel and Power from 1947 until he became Minister of Labour in the last months of the Attlee government. As an anti-Bevanite and anti-left Labour Party moderate of the old school, Robens out of office had been progressively more disillusioned with the internecine wrangling within his Party, and in 1961 happily accepted Macmillan's offer of chairmanship of the Coal Board, plus a peerage, 'much to the annoyance of my Party'.[51] For the next ten years he managed Britain's troublesome mining industry with a rare degree of harmony – particularly so during the three Macmillan years, 1961 to 1963.

Macmillan faced even more intractable problems with British Rail. By 1960 its accumulated debt stood at £1600 million, and it was running at an annual deficit of over £100 million; strikes, or threatened strikes, were an almost annual event; and a Robens – or a Hercules – was urgently needed here, too.

While Macmillan was away in Africa, publication of the Guillebaud Report – the result of a study lasting two years which tried to work out lasting wage structures for the railways – had only resulted in a fresh round of wage claims. Macmillan on his return decided that it was time for a thorough and radical look at the railways – and transportation as a whole. In March 1960 he stated publicly that the government would accept the Guillebaud recommendations on 'fair and reasonable' wages, *but*, in return, the railway workers, the British Transport Commission and the public would have to accept a radically reduced railway system that could operate without imposing an endless, and unacceptable, burden on the national economy. The British Transport Commission ran not only the railways but a 'vast hotch-potch of enterprises', hotels, docks and canals, as well as a considerable amount of road transport, and much of it was unprofitable. Accordingly Macmillan set up a Commission, composed of experienced industrialists and financiers, chaired by Sir Ivan Stedeford (another associate of Macmillan's from the wartime Ministry of Supply), to settle the fate of British Rail. On the Commission was also the portly Technical Director of ICI, Dr Richard Beeching, and over it presided in the background the Minister of Transport Ernest Marples, Macmillan's protégé from his days at the Ministry of Housing, whose 'agile mind and his thorough grasp of business principles and methods' he thought admirably fitted to the immense task ahead.

It took the Stedeford Commission the best part of 1960 to set out a plan, and – with the unions fighting it much of the way – it was not until the last year of Macmillan's administration that the proposed changes were actually implemented. The cumbersome British Transport Commission was split up into the four boards respectively running Railways, Docks, Inland Waterways and London Transport. Beeching, whom Macmillan had by now come to regard as 'one of the most able and fertile brains in the industrial and commercial world', took over the Railway Board. He and Marples discovered some amazing anomalies in the railways – whose deficit had, by 1962, now risen to a record £159 million. In September 1962, Beeching's proposals provoked a strike by the National Union of Railwaymen, who wanted to 'continue to build wagons which are not wanted and steam locomotives which are not required. . . . This is fantastic and everyone knows it. . . .'[52] Pointing out that half the passenger stations contributed only 2 per cent of the revenue, Beeching recommended closing no less than half the stations altogether; abandoning one-third of the total route mileage; slashing the number of goods depots; and introducing 'liner trains', to carry containers which could be transferred from road to rail, and fast intercity passenger and freight services. All this would lead, eventually, to a cut of some 70,000 railway personnel. It would also lead, inevitably, to vastly increased traffic on Britain's antique road system. Marples meanwhile was set to work (barely in time) to build the first motorways (the M-1 had opened in November 1959).

Opposition to the 'Beeching Cuts', from all quarters, was intense. Macmillan recalled Marples telling him of a railway service in Wales that was used by only one man: ' "If I gave him a Rolls Royce for life, we'd make £150,000, but there would be a terrible row in the press. . . !" '[53] There were indeed many 'terrible rows', and concessions that had to be made before the Beeching programme went through, although Macmillan himself probably drew more personal invective over a misguided decision determining the fate of the Doric Arch at Euston Station than over all the rest of the Beeching Cuts.[54]

Beeching's efforts were, however, indeed 'Herculean' and the results inevitable; and Macmillan reckoned the nation owed him 'a deep debt of gratitude'.

It all meant a vast change in the quality of British life, with crumbling railway embankments shorn of rails and sleepers and overcrowded roads epitomising the disappearance of the heritage of the Industrial Revolution that had made the nation great. It was ironic that Macmillan, with his profound sense of the past, should have had to preside over such changes, in the interests of modernisation. That Britain's railways, decades later, were still in the red and still not competitive with their continental rivals was probably not the fault of Beeching, Marples or Macmillan.

Apart from transport, one of the most important areas of change during the Macmillan era was in Education, where David Eccles had presided first from 1954 to 1957 under Churchill, and then again from 1959 to 1962. A highly cultured man, Eccles was to prove certainly the most effective of the post-1939 Ministers of Education since Rab Butler, performing miracles for the educational system. Under the 1951 Churchill administration, Eccles had not found much support, but, returned to Education after the 1959 election and given a free rein from a sympathetic Prime Minister, he achieved some remarkable results. He obtained from Macmillan increased funds sufficient to raise standards, even though the school-age population was spiralling rapidly; raised teacher qualifications and reduced the pupil–teacher ratio; and radically improved both the standing and quality of higher technical education. These were decisions which, says the highly critical John Vaizey, though 'none of them sufficient to achieve national headlines, affected deeply the way of life of millions of young . . . .'[55]

Eccles's policies were carried on subsequently by his brilliant disciple, Edward Boyle – until all was turned upside down by Labour and Shirley Williams. Though little mention was made of education reform by Macmillan himself in his memoirs, undoubtedly tacit support from the top played an essential role in Eccles's successes.

Political Fortunes

Martin Redmayne, the new Chief Whip, was to recall that the autumn of 1960 'certainly stands out in my mind as the beginning of the end of the "Supermac" era'.[56] Despite the government's economic problems, however, Macmillan's political support did not actually decline in 1960. In November by-elections were still all won by the Tories, most by comfortable margins. Macmillan noted with satisfaction that the Liberals had taken a lot of Labour votes, finishing second in four places: it was 'a very good result for us, by and large'.[57] Macmillan was also amused to learn, *en passant*, that at Bolton East the Labour and Liberal candidates had both directed personal attacks against the Conservative on grounds of his '(a) not having been to a Public School (b) on being NON-U!! The Tory Party has certainly evolved in the last 40 years.'[58]

For a while, continuing into 1961, Macmillan's popularity was undoubtedly protected from the buffeting of fickle British public opinion by internal storms that were rending the Labour Party, and acting as something of a lightning conductor for the Tories.

Gaitskell's troubles stemmed from his courageous stand on two issues that had riven the Party from top to bottom; first, in opposing the CND and the left in their demand for unilateral nuclear disarmament (he would not be the last Labour leader to have to face such a challenge); secondly, in calling for the redrafting of the famous 'Clause Four' of the Party constitution, which theoretically committed the Labour Party to the wholesale nationalisation of shops, farms and factories. Gaitskell's own future was at stake, and as the first Conference of the defeated Party approached in October 1960 he looked doomed. Then, working on it through the previous night, on 5 October Gaitskell pulled out all the stops and produced at Scarborough what was generally rated as the greatest speech of his career.

The executive lost the ensuing vote, but by a far smaller margin than previously anticipated; at Blackpool the following year Gaitskell succeeded in reversing the vote, with vastly increased support. Though he never ceased to condemn Macmillan as a man who 'cheated at politics',[59] and avoided his company whenever possible, after Gaitskell's victory over the unilateralists at Blackpool in 1961, Macmillan recorded it as 'a great and deserved triumph for Gaitskell and will increase his stature in the country. He has been very persistent and courageous. . . .'[60] Nevertheless, the fact was that, for all his courage, Macmillan's rival would never acquire the charismatic gifts of an Aneurin Bevan, who died in July 1960.

In May 1961, Hugh Gaitskell's close confidante, Ann Fleming, wrote to Evelyn Waugh recalling a dinner party at Petworth given by John Wyndham to entertain his chief:

> It was a splendid occasion to observe Mr Macmillan, he was suave with impersonal eyes, he ate and drank with extreme moderation and he talked from eight o'clock to one a.m., the only pause at midnight when he advanced to the door and we humbly followed expecting the great man's bedtime – but no, it was for a natural purpose – and in a trice he had returned to us and was at it again. Except for a weakness for anecdotes about the Peerage, everything he said was interesting, indeed very interesting. . . . I was impressed by him and wouldn't care to play poker with him.[61]

Macmillan himself certainly would not have echoed her view of his supremacy at the poker table. Privately, there still remained a deep lack of political self-confidence in Macmillan, which always seems extraordinary when one recalls his smashing personal victory so recently at the polls. For here, in effect, was a Prime Minister constantly grateful for the kind of psychological massage regularly applied by his friend Ava Waverley. When she had written to him, in August 1960, trying to encourage him with a reference to the appreciation felt for him by 'simple people', he replied:

> Can it really be true that you feel I have done some good, or, at least, am trying to do so? If humble people (not, of course, the clever, worldly politicians and diplomatists and 'hommes d'affaires') think that, it is a great reward.
> But I fear that it is that you are too kind and pick on anything that is of good repute, forgetting all the mean and paltry things that people say. . . .[62]

After each important division in the Commons, his diaries would show him totting up his majority like a Silas Marner counting his gold:

the Economic Debate went very quietly. We got a majority of 92 (on a *Two-line* Whip) which shows that the Party is beginning to recover its balance. . . .

6 February 1962 [following a Debate on the Common Market]: . . . majority 98 (4 of our chaps, coming from Yorkshire, were two hours late – or we would have had 102). . . .[63]

There were many more entries in this vein.

Whereas Churchill and Eden had made do with majorities of 17, and 58, and Attlee after 1950 only 5, Macmillan's was never to fall below 90. Yet it fretted him constantly; as did the loss of a by-election, such as Paisley, where the Liberal revival pushed the Tories down to 'a bad third': 'Everyone is rather depressed. . . .'[64] Private anxieties alternate with external unflappability: '*16 May:* 10 a.m. Chief Whip. He is rather worried about Party discipline. I told him to ride the Party on the snaffle and keep the curb for great issues. . . .'[65] Thoughts about a 'palace revolt' were also readily aroused by the indiscretions of ministers, generally centring around the person of Rab Butler. (At a lunch, *à deux*, with Rab in the run-up to the 1959 election, Macmillan had recorded, 'He is in good form, full of ideas. His hope is that we shall win by twenty or so. I suppose his further hope would be for me to resign after a year or two. . . .')[66] On 22 May 1961, Macmillan was recording a comment by the *Sunday Express*'s 'Crossbencher' column:

that the Home Secretary, R. A. Butler, has definitely decided to play the role of Disraeli – break the Government and lead the orthodox 'Country Party' to the defence of British agriculture and the Commonwealth. I don't think this is true – as yet. . . .[67]

But obviously the doubt lingered.

It was thus with some relief when, in September 1961, Macmillan recorded that Rab had agreed 'to yield the Leadership of the House and the Chairmanship of the Party to Iain Macleod . . .'.[68]

14 October: . . . I am amused at the way legends grow or are created. Butler is putting about that it was he (not I) who suggested Macleod's appointment to Leader of the House [etc.]. . . . Although this bears no relation to historic truth, it may be useful myth. . . .[69]

The EEC – Persuading the Cabinet, the Party and the Commonwealth

Macmillan was particularly worried at this time about his campaign to get Britain into the Common Market. The collapse of the summit had left his European policy in a state of some considerable flux. Back in July 1960, he was reflecting gloomily in his diaries about the options confronting Britain:

> Shall we be caught between a hostile (or at least less and less friendly) America and a boastful, powerful 'Empire of Charlemagne' – now under French but later bound to come under German control? Is this the real reason for 'joining' the Common Market (if we are acceptable) and for abandoning (a) the Seven (b) British agriculture (c) the Commonwealth? It's a grim choice.[70]

But during the course of the year a post-summit equation began to take shape in Macmillan's mind: a Europe plus Britain, acting 'in a harmonious leadership',[71] would be equal to the USSR and the USA. The sense of weakness left by the summit had persuaded Macmillan that Britain had to belong, comprehensively, to that larger and more powerful grouping. By the end of 1960, after much delicate testing of the water, both at home and abroad, and as part of what he called 'The Grand Design', Macmillan had committed himself to apply for full membership of the Six. It was perhaps the biggest single decision of his premiership. He was very conscious of being well ahead of British public opinion, while at the same time trying to carry along a divided party – not to mention the British Commonwealth. Beyond all pragmatic considerations, it was however also clear that Macmillan felt that full entry into Europe would provide a great psychological boost to the British people, and would have an energising impulse – impossible to quantify – on the economy, which was already once again looking sickly. But had he taken too long to come to this 'biggest decision'? Had he already missed the bus that would convey him into Europe?

The extent of the continuing pressures most close at hand to Macmillan seems to be revealed in a memorandum of 16 September 1960 to his new Private Secretary, Tim Bligh. Macmillan was replying to some observations made by Sir Frank Roberts, currently the UK Permanent Representative with NATO, the tenor of which suggests that the Foreign Office was still harbouring its old divide-and-rule illusions about the Six:

> . . . I think he [Roberts] is still too tempted to play the role of the friend of NATO as an institution without regard to other situations. From his account the Germans, the French, and even the other members of the Six are on the point of having a God-Almighty row. . . . I do not think Sir Frank Roberts realises that we are a country to whom nothing else matters except our export trade. Without our revival our strength disappears. . . . Our only hope of an agreement on Sixes and Sevens, which is the vital British interest today, is by a political situation arising which brings about the economic solution.

The memorandum continued on a note indicating that Macmillan himself was not yet immune to the wishful-thinking hypothesis of the Foreign Office: 'Internal stresses among the Six are on the whole more likely to lead to that than anything else. It is only since they have begun to quarrel that there has been any question of meeting the British and the EFTA point of view. . . .'[72]

As far as the 'key', President de Gaulle, was concerned, Macmillan entered the New Year of 1961 with modest optimism. After a meeting at Rambouillet, he wrote to Adenauer reporting how de Gaulle 'told me that he has no intention of excluding us from Europe or creating a political organisation inimical to us . . .'.[73]* He went on to beseech Adenauer to press de Gaulle at their next meeting on the 'desirability' of 'restoring the economic unity of Europe'. In a letter to the Queen of the same date, Macmillan mentioned an observation which – for obvious reasons – he had refrained from putting to Adenauer: '. . . I detected a distinct change in the President's [the recently inaugurated Kennedy] attitude towards the Germans and he was quite frank that his enthusiasm for the Common Market was largely caused by his desire to fence the Germans in. . . .'[74] Who was deceiving whom? Was de Gaulle

---

* This reflected a hope of Macmillan's which, to the end of the Common Market negotiations, he would never completely abandon. Answering the author's questions in September 1979 he was emphatic: 'Why did we persist? I felt once he had let us start, he couldn't say no; he didn't want us in, but I felt we would leave him no excuse to exclude us . . .' (AHC).

practising that skill which, as a consequence of his devious handling of the Algerian War had earned him among his critics the nickname of this 'Prince of Ambiguity'?

In April 1961, de Gaulle himself faced the most dangerous challenge to his authority when four senior French generals raised the standard of revolt against him in Algiers. Yet, when this was quelled, it left him stronger than ever before; with Algeria off his hands the following year, he would be left free to pursue the goal of hegemony in Europe – at Macmillan's expense. Nevertheless, that same April Macmillan felt confident enough to broach 'The Grand Design' to his Cabinet, after which there followed 'an excellent discussion on Europe'. Yet, within the Cabinet, there remained doubters about Britain joining the EEC – and some important ones. The following month the old suspicions about Rab Butler had been raising their head again, to the effect that he was planning to break the government by rallying 'to the defence of British agriculture and Commonwealth. I don't think this is true – as yet. But I do not hide from myself the magnitude of the decision that's soon going to face us. . . .'[75] On 22 July 1961, the Cabinet made a *'unanimous* decision in principle'[76] to apply formally to enter the Common Market, though it is important to note that the application simply asked for negotiations with the Six to enquire if Britain could get terms on which it could then decide to join. The obliqueness of the application was, in fact, to make it easier for de Gaulle to project his ultimate veto. On the other hand the distinct possibility that de Gaulle would veto Britain's application made it difficult to implement the new policy with energetic enthusiasm. While de Gaulle had to be convinced of the magnitude of the British conversion, Macmillan had to reassure the Conservative Party, the Commonwealth and other members of EFTA that nothing irrevocable had happened. In his statements to both the country and the Commons, he deliberately played down the full significance of the application, remarking, in low key, only of this monumental decision: '. . . I believe that our right place is in the vanguard of the movement towards the greater unity of the Free World, and that we can lead from within rather than outside. At any rate, I am persuaded that we ought to try. . . .'[77]

Within a fortnight of the Cabinet decision, there was a debate in the House to approve the British application. The timing itself was risky. If the debate went badly the start of the summer recess would

mean that there was little opportunity to repair the damage – and
the end of July, a time when parliamentary tempers are normally
frayed – is not usually the best moment for launching a major new
initiative. But the fact that Macmillan felt it safe to launch the
application only when there was no possibility of immediate
counter-attack before the October Party Conference again suggests
how risky he still considered the new policy to be.

Conscious of the occasion, Macmillan however put everything he
had into preparing his expository feat in the Commons on 2 August.
He had been greatly helped by his son Maurice, who had written
him a long letter the previous day. It was characteristic of his sense
of filial duty, and of his (too often unrequited) affection for his
father.

> Dearest Papa,
>   I hope that you will not think it impertinent if I put a few points
> about your Common Market speech and about the broadcast. In
> its present mood and with its present composition I think that
> the House is unfortunately no more capable collectively of rational
> thought than the country. . . .
>   . . . Who am I to write all this to you? I do so out of great
> affection and love, as well as from deep respect and great
> admiration.
>   Your devoted son,
>   Maurice[78]

The result was, in the opinion of many in the House that day,
one of the finest and most persuasive speeches of Macmillan's whole
career. There was in this country, he reminded his listeners,

> a long tradition of isolation. In this, as in most countries, there
> is a certain suspicion of foreigners. There is also the additional
> division between us and continental Europe of a wholly different
> development of our legal, administrative and, to some extent,
> political systems. If we are basically united by our religious faith,
> even here great divisions have grown up.
>   Nevertheless, it is perhaps worth recording that in every period
> when the world has been in danger of tyrants or aggression,
> Britain has abandoned isolationism. But it is true that, when the
> immediate danger was removed, we have sometimes tried to

259

return to an insular policy. In due course we have abandoned it. In any case, who could say today that our present danger has been removed, or will soon disappear? Who doubts that we have to face a long and exhausting struggle over more than one generation if the forces of Communistic expansion are to be contained? . . .

Expressing his preference for a confederalist rather than a federalist solution to the problem of sovereignty, Macmillan declared: 'Here again, unless we are in the negotiations, unless we can bring our influence to bear, we shall not be able to play our part in deciding the future structure of Europe.' He concluded:

A great responsibility lies on the Six as well as on ourselves. Hitherto, although there has been this economic union in Europe, while the rift was wide there has also been the hope of healing it and thus the position has become bearable. But if it should become clear that this rift will continue and perhaps deepen then I fear that the consequences will be grave. As I said in the United States earlier this year, 'It will be a canker gnawing at the very heart of the Western Alliance.' I am sure that this consideration is in the minds of our continental friends.

To sum up, there are, as I have said, some to whom the whole concept of our working closely in this field with other European nations is instinctively disagreeable. I am bound to say that I find it hard to understand this when we have accepted close collaboration on other more critical spheres. Others feel that our whole and sole duty lies with the Commonwealth. If I thought that our entry into Europe would injure our relations with and influence in the Commonwealth, or be against the true interest of the Commonwealth, I would not ask the House to support this step.

I think, however, that most of us recognise that in a changing world if we are not to be left behind and to drop out of the main stream of the world's life, we must be prepared to change and adapt our methods. All through history this has been one of the main sources of our strength.[79]

In fact, the hostile reaction in the Commons proved remarkably feeble. At the end of the Debate, less than thirty Tory abstentions were counted. Only one right-wing Tory voted against the government: Anthony Fell, who termed Macmillan a 'national disaster'[80] and was in turn dismissed (in the Macmillan diaries) as a disciple of Lord Beaverbrook.[81] Not even the most junior minister defaulted.[82] Macmillan, with his sense of history, noted down that the debate fell on the forty-seventh anniversary of the start of the First World War: 'the beginning of the end of Europe's supremacy . . .'.[83] Later, in October, a motion to join the Common Market was passed at the Party Conference at Brighton.

Meanwhile, Macmillan also had to overcome the objections of the Commonwealth. Of the 'old' Commonwealth countries, who were likely to be most affected, it soon turned out that the key figure would be the veteran Prime Minister of Australia, that sturdy friend of Britain, Bob Menzies. Holyoake of New Zealand was deeply concerned about the fate of his country's butter and lamb products; but from the very beginning it was clear that Diefenbaker of Canada was going to be 'difficult'.[84] Macmillan noted that Diefenbaker paid 'too little regard to the great underlying movements of world affairs', and he continued to be a thorn in Macmillan's side right to the end.

The essence of the Commonwealth case was that, if Britain abandoned the old system of imperial preferences and disappeared behind the high EEC tariff wall, the loss of trade would be immense. The European riposte to this was that, if Britain had joined the Treaty of Rome in the first place, the pain of readjustment would have been far less for the Commonwealth – as indeed it had been for the former territories of the French colonial Empire. Temperate foodstuffs and manufactured goods from the 'developed' Commonwealth countries (Canada, Australia, New Zealand) were particularly vulnerable. With all his persuasive power, Macmillan put to them the argument that in the course of time British access to the bigger European market would enhance trade prospects for the Commonwealth. In Brussels, Heath, doggedly and with brilliant mastery of detail, was pressing the EEC to compensate Commonwealth trade losses with 'comparable outlets'. Meanwhile, at home, apart from the substantial political worries in the Party about the abdication of political sovereignty involved in joining the EEC, Macmillan's main task was to reconcile the British farmers to the gradual loss of government subsidies.

While the negotiations, ranging from Indian tea and Australian kangaroo meat to cricket bats and coconuts, hardly made for exciting headlines they were much easier to attack than defend, a fact that the Beaverbrook press swiftly exploited. In a letter to his former subordinate at the wartime Ministry of Supply, Lord Beaverbrook made the position of his newspapers admirably clear:

> There is every intention to support you in everything but that blasted Common Market, which is an American device to put us alongside Germany. As our power was broken and lost by two German wars, it is very hard on us now to be asked to align ourselves with those villains. But you know I wish you well, and wish you out of the Common Market and in Downing Street for as long as you want to stay there. . . .[85]

Unforgiving to the grave about the unspeakable Hun, Beaverbrook was more or less as good as his word: relentless in attacking the government over the EEC, but restrained (generally) in criticism of Macmillan personally. Macmillan made various attempts to woo the 'Beaver', but in vain; 'As well ask us to repudiate the Presbyterian Church as give up this cause . . .' came back the uncompromising retort.[86]

Macmillan and the Press

The 'mean and paltry things' written about him by the press affected Macmillan more than he ever cared to admit. His aversion to the press (which, in turn, exposed his own personal vulnerability) mounted steadily through his premiership, and beyond. 'The Press is lousy,'[87] became a repeated refrain. He detested the personal intrusion of the press, particularly at moments of family tragedy, as when, later, his daughter Sarah died prematurely and a grandson Joshua died, accidentally, by drinking after a period on drugs. Macmillan soon decided that he would encourage no close relations with any of the 'press lords':

> There was that great lady, Pamela Berry[88] – a very tiresome woman; she wanted to be the Egeria of the Prime Minister, and have him to lunch with her, and I wouldn't have it, so she was angry and attacked me ever after. . . . Then The Times – Haley –

used to come round every week, or every fortnight, but I didn't ring him up. He came, and I told him what was happening; but he obviously wanted it to be on the old *Times* relationship. . . . He would like to have been consulted; but I did not want to consult anybody. . . .[89]

The powerful Berrys, proprietors of the staunchly Conservative *Daily Telegraph*, did indeed not like Macmillan; in the opinion of Harold Evans, 'probably because he *had* rebuffed Lady Pamela'. With the editor of *The Times*, Sir William Haley, Macmillan had a prickly relationship of long antecedence. He would never forgive 'The Thunderer' its pre-war policy of appeasement under Dawson, and had not forgotten how 'bad', under Barrington-Ward, it had been in opposing Churchill's policy in Greece in 1944. According to Harold Evans, Macmillan's able and devoted Press Secretary all through from 1957 to 1963, Haley – a man with a somewhat thin social skin – felt he had been snubbed by Macmillan in the Mediterranean during the war, and had nourished a resentment ever since. Haley had left school at fourteen and started life as a ship's wireless operator, became Director-General of the BBC and – in 1952 – Editor of *The Times*. 'Haley hated his guts,' claimed Evans; 'It was very evident there was a personal dislike; to Macmillan, Haley was really the arch-enemy.'[90] Haley even went so far as to say to one of his associate editors once, 'Make no mistake, this man Macmillan is a thug.'[91] Haley distrusted Macmillan's political opportunism, and in particular his unleashing of the pre-election economic boom in 1959.

Macmillan, on his side, thought that Haley's persistent attacks on his efforts to control inflation were 'completely irresponsible'. They were 'an appeal to pure sentiment; he was an old-fashioned liberal sentimentalist. . . .'[92] Macmillan told Haley, on at least one occasion, that the thing he most admired about *The Times* was how 'every twenty-five years you publish a book to show how on every great public issue you have been wrong!'[93] It was not a remark likely to endear Macmillan to a man of such tender sensibilities as Haley. While he respected the integrity of 'Halier-than-Thou', as he frequently dubbed him (and not always in private), Macmillan often fumed at the moralising of *The Times*. Haley, he recorded early in 1957, 'seemed to approve of the Government but nevertheless lectures us daily in the best grandmotherly style. The trouble with

The Times is that the proprietor[94] is a nonentity and the Editor is a prig. . . .'[95]

Macmillan was fully aware of his shortcomings in dealing with Fleet Street: '. . . I have always had a bad, or at the best a grudging Press – I think because I do not cultivate sufficiently their rather unpleasant proprietors (Beaverbrook; Rothermere; Roy Thomson; David Astor . . .).'[96] Apart from Macmillan's principal worries in the 'serious press', the so-called 'popular press' ranged from eulogy to damnation, depending on circumstances, and Macmillan was generally happy to write them off as having 'lost their heads'.[97]

Another faction of critics came from that phenomenon of the late 1950s and 1960s, the Angry Young Men, intellectuals who attacked the lack of moral values of the affluent society – and some Angry Old Men. 'He is a very empty man,' pontificated Malcolm Muggeridge in 1961.[98] The more severe critics among the young intellectuals included the wealthy and patrician Ian Gilmour, owner of the *Spectator*, who in 1959 urged his readers to vote Liberal, or Labour, rather than for Macmillan. Subsequently, as a senior but dissentient 'wet' minister under Mrs Thatcher, critical of her right-wing policies, he found Macmillan's consensus, 'Middle-Way' philosophy rather more congenial. On to the *Spectator* Gilmour brought a comparatively unknown twenty-nine-year-old, Bernard Levin, who under the pseudonym of 'Taper' launched some acrid criticism of the parliamentary foibles of the day.

'What an immense advantage de Gaulle has over me,' Macmillan wrote enviously in May 1961. 'No parliament – and a Press that carries little influence!'[99] To Ava Waverley he wrote later in the same year:

> The Press here still as petty, ill-informed and spiteful as ever. Fortunately I think its political power grows less and less. The radio and TV have become the medium by which the modern Sophists speak (happily with conflicting voices) to the people. . . .[100]

He wondered, briefly, whether 'a monthly Press Conference on American lines would be a good thing for me to try'. The idea, however, was never pursued; Macmillan's conjecture about the waning power of the press was, however, wishful thinking and would rebound to strike him grievously in the last year of his premiership.

Macmillan's alienation from Fleet Street is perhaps all the more extraordinary, given his recognition of television as the 'instrument' where influence in the 1960s truly resided, and the skill – even relish – with which he had already adapted himself to exploiting this media. He once told the television cameras that 'old dogs have to learn new tricks', and then set to showing that this was possible. As the first (and the one who travelled the most) of the jet-age leaders, he became an expert in the art of the airport interview ('The place where television chooses to lurk . . . that hot, pitiless probing eye . . .'). With a brilliant pre-election stunt in 1959, he had set a precedent by inviting the cameras into No. 10, to show himself at intimate ease with President Eisenhower; equally, when visiting Khrushchev, he was perfectly aware of how well his funny white hat from Finland would come over on television screens at home. As his Minister of Information, Bill Deedes, observed, Macmillan totally 'entered into the part – like charades in a country house';[101] perhaps it was because it appealed to the 'actor–manager' in his make-up.

Moving House and Illness

Compared with the pleasure that Macmillan had derived from his office in the first three years, 1960 was not a good year, 1961 even worse. They brought the collapse of the summit, and the beginnings of fresh headaches over Africa, de Gaulle and the economy. Nor, in personal terms, were they particularly joyous years for Macmillan. While in Africa in 1960, he received the grievous news that his revered older brother, Daniel, had been stricken with cancer. (Though a frail figure, Daniel too had the Macmillan toughness of mind over matter, and in fact survived for another five years.) That summer brought unsought dislocation when family and staff had to leave No. 10 (before it collapsed)[102] for their temporary quarters in Admiralty House, while Downing Street was being rebuilt. The last Cabinet Meeting at No. 10 was held on 29 July, and the move began the following week. Macmillan found his new quarters 'still in a frightful mess. There are no rooms yet available except the Cabinet Room, Office, etc. No upstairs rooms have been done. Office of Works have been incredibly slow and vague. . . .'[103]

Predictably, as anyone with Macmillan's experience of British building methods could have foreseen, the rebuilding of No. 10 took many months longer than estimated and the family were not to be back there until the summer of 1963, only a few weeks before his resignation. Macmillan's own sitting room in Admiralty House had a splendid view of the dome of St Paul's, but otherwise he was not very happy in his new quarters; it was much larger, the temporary Cabinet Room seemed at first 'intolerably big compared with the old cosy room in Downing Street'. The 'Garden Girls', like Misses Minto and Parsons, also dreaded leaving the 'family atmosphere' so carefully created by the Macmillans at No. 10; while Dorothy sorely missed her garden.

During his days of relaxation aboard the *Capetown Castle* as he returned from Africa, Macmillan talked jokingly (to Harold Evans) of going on till he was eighty,[104] but soon the burdens of office were beginning to press on him physically. In July in a chatty letter from Dorothy to Harold (then at Bolton Abbey), full of news about shopping, weddings, gamekeepers, tennis weekends, grandchildren and other vital family matters, she expressed concern that he was overdoing things, and had not had a proper holiday for far too long: '. . . I really think you will have to try and do a bit less. It's these awful meals that kill one. I don't feel that I am very adequate in helping in all the ways I might!'[105] Returning from the UN in October, he found his old war wounds plaguing him – and he frightened Tim Bligh with the suggestion 'we'd really better start thinking about the succession'.[106]

The following year, 1961, there was more cause for concern about Macmillan's health when he was afflicted by some kind of virus throughout most of June.

15 June: . . . I am writing this in bed, after taking some of the Doctor's drugs, so perhaps the mood is blacker than it ought to be. But the Trade Figures are really awful. . . .

21 June: . . . Sir John Richardson has been to see me. I have no more 'élan vital'! I am finished! In other words, I ought to have a month's holiday. As it is, I am to have four days, starting tomorrow evening. . . .

25 June: . . . My 'rest cure' failed. . . . Sir John Richardson came and was encouraging – *if* I can rest. But when and how can I rest? I am beginning (at last) to feel old and depressed. . . .[107]

By August even the Queen had begun to express concern about the reports of Macmillan's health, so that at one of his weekly audiences he had to 'remind her of what Mark Twain said of reports of his death – "they are much exaggerated" . . .'.[108] The year ended in similar vein, with Macmillan noting the 'terrifying' problems that faced Britain: '. . . I lie in bed and brood about all these things, rather sadly, for the Veganin and the other drugs make one depressed. . . .'[109] In his memoirs, Macmillan claims that at this point he was 'seriously contemplating resignation'.

While the ever present element of a certain hypochondria should not be discounted, Macmillan's store of resilience was, however, always remarkable. Although, under the prevailing pressures, he was occasionally drinking more, on the whole he led a frugal life. Preparing an important speech, he would note:

> . . . I stayed in my bedroom – reading the papers, reading *Sense and Sensibility* and lounging . . . a sandwich; Barley water, and a pill which Sir J. Richardson had given me. (I took two, actually.) This is *much* better for me (and my race) than alcohol, which makes us truculent and prosey. . . .[110]

Dorothy was increasingly proving a great support to him:

> She has not spared herself since I became PM. She has been *all over* the country, for simple and friendly meetings for women of all types. Now (when they come together at their conference) very many of them know her personally. Neither Mrs N. Chamberlain nor Lady Churchill, or Clarissa Eden, attempted anything of the kind. . . .[111]

Apart from Trollope and Jane Austen, for distraction and relaxation there were the grouse-moors and Swinton or Bolton Abbey, and an occasional day's pheasant-shooting at Petworth, which never failed to work magic with the jaded Prime Minister. As he once wrote to Lady Swinton:

> I think one of the reasons why one loves a holiday on the moors is that, in a confused and changing world, the picture in one's mind is not spoilt.

If you go to Venice or Florence or Assisi you might as well be at Victoria Station – masses of tourists, chiefly Germans in shorts. If you go to Yorkshire or Scotland, the hills, the keepers, the farmers, the farmers' sons, the drivers are the same; and (except for the coming of the Land Rover etc.) there is a sense of continuity. There is also the country and the neighbourliness that goes with people who live in remote and beautiful country. . . .[112]

Chancellor of Oxford

While the years 1960–1 suggest already a turning point in Macmillan's fortunes, certainly on the home front, they had also brought him one of the greatest joys and consolations of his life, one that could provide a source of both interest and satisfaction to his very last days. It also gave him a role that he was able to fill with more consistent and conspicuous success than perhaps any other.

In December 1959 Lord Halifax, who had been Chancellor of Oxford for twenty-five years, died and this prestigious life appointment fell vacant. Two years earlier in 1957, Macmillan had selected Hugh Trevor-Roper,[113] the historian and a Macmillan author, to be Regius Professor of History at Oxford[114] in preference to A. J. P. Taylor, whom Macmillan regarded as being too controversial and too left-wing. Awarding the post to Trevor-Roper, a combative figure who made a hobby of collecting enemies and was regarded as a High Tory, aroused animosity in certain quarters. Out of a sense of gratitude (and admiration), Trevor-Roper astonished the Oxford Establishment by putting forward the name of an active party politician – Harold Macmillan. The conventional candidate was Sir Oliver Franks, Provost of Queen's and Chairman of Lloyds Bank. Professor of Moral Philosophy at Glasgow aged thirty-two, then a brilliant wartime civil servant who in five years rose to become head of the Ministry of Supply, subsequently appointed by Attlee to be Ambassador in Washington, Franks had many qualifications; but many (including Harold Macmillan) considered him to be stodgy, and too open to left-wing pressures. There had never been a contested election for the Chancellorship since the time of Asquith in 1925.

Macmillan was away in Africa on the 'wind of change' tour when he received Trevor-Roper's invitation, and at first he was profoundly flattered, but equally reluctant. Pre-1914, Oxford and Balliol had given him the two happiest years of his life, but for anyone who had not known Oxford before 1914 it was – he often said – like those who (as Talleyrand had remarked) had never known *le plaisir de vivre* before the French Revolution. After the First World War '. . . I would not go near it for years – everybody was dead. It was a terrible place, terrible atmosphere. . . .' Also 'they are very bitchy, some of those old dons. . . .'[115] Further despatches from Trevor-Roper followed in quick succession, as in Oxford the campaign began to hot up. Leading the Franks camp was the legendary Warden of Wadham, Maurice Bowra, with whom Trevor-Roper had crossed swords on many occasions. An eminent antagonist of Franks, the gloriously indiscreet Isaiah Berlin, felt that Bowra 'always led the "immoral front" – homosexuals, Evelyn Waugh . . . while he [Bowra] thought that Macmillan stood for pomposity and priggishness . . . '.[116]

Such was the tenor of feelings at Oxford, while the temperature was to rise steadily as personal animosities surfaced and old university scores were settled. Franks (who voted Liberal) had one supreme disqualification, wrote Macmillan with heavy irony in his memoirs: 'he was still young and active and there was a possibility that he might actually "do" something, perhaps even too much. . . .' On board the homeward-bound *Capetown Castle*, Macmillan considered the proposition. It appealed to that element of the *condottiere*, which had once made him want to drop with the planned airborne landing on Rome in 1943, as well as to his life-long attachment to Oxford. He would have a go.

The campaign had opened with a vengeance; as one paper observed, 'Even Tammany Hall was never like this!'[117] Trevor-Roper himself, who first came to fame through his early book, *The Last Days of Hitler*, revealed himself as having a secret Walter Mitty passion to be an Army Chief of Staff; and, judging from the tactical skill, expertise and ruthlessness with which he conducted the campaign, he would have made an excellent one.

Senior members of the Cabinet, notably Heathcoat Amory and Kilmuir, the Lord Chancellor, and the Cabinet Secretary, were aghast when they heard of the Prime Minister's intentions. An agitated Kilmuir sped down to Oxford, quizzing Trevor-Roper and Robert Blake secretly. 'Can you guarantee he'll win, otherwise it could be politically very damaging?'[118] The two dons did their best to be reassuring. If Macmillan lost (which seemed not improbable), it would also be a considerable personal humiliation for him. But he was not to be deflected: 'they said "it might be dangerous". I said "that might be said of foxhunting. . . . You chase something you don't really need at the risk of breaking your neck. . . ."'[119] Under Trevor-Roper's harassing fire, Bowra quickly 'retired into neutrality',[120] his place as Franks's champion taken by the Master of Pembroke, R. B. McCallum (charitably described by Trevor-Roper as 'a sanctimonious Scottish ass').[121] With consummate tactical skill, Trevor-Roper contrived to emphasise Macmillan's appeal as the 'anti-Establishment' candidate, as he put it in his military-style situation-report to Macmillan's office on 21 February:

> The University Establishment – those nameless, faceless, self-important Provosts of This, Masters of That, and Principals of the Other – are on the side of colourless, successful mediocrity. . . . we are going flat out for the young and the gay, to whom, I think, the PM has a greater appeal than to the staid and respectable. . . .[122]

As polling day on 5 March approached, the Cabinet was biting its nails with nervousness at the anticipated humiliation of the Prime Minister. Macmillan himself (from whom Trevor-Roper thoughtfully concealed some of the more savage aspects of the campaign in-fighting) covered over his own apprehensions when writing about the election years later, dismissing it laughingly as 'the most corrupt we've ever had!' 'Balliol, which was solid for me, ran a buffet with free drinks all day long (MAs only!). . . . a lot of my friends took MAs, just to vote, and a special train was run from London.' It was filled primarily with Conservative MPs, who had been leaned upon heavily by the Whips. 'There was open voting, and the voters were bullied and booed. . . . It didn't look at all well, until *The Times* attacked my candidature . . . ("Halier-than-Thou" wrote a pontifical leading article the day before the poll). . . .'[123]

The Franks camp was filled with foreboding by the influx of 'exiles'. It was a fine, spring-like day, and Oxonian members of the Cabinet appeared, properly begowned, in force to support the Prime Minister. The Senior Proctor, Robert Blake, had to lend his own gown to an improperly dressed Chancellor of the Exchequer, Heathcoat Amory. There were the anxious Lord Chancellor, Lord

Kilmuir, Sir David Eccles, Duncan Sandys, Lord Hailsham, Reginald Maudling and Sir Edward Boyle. Political names of the future included Sir Keith Joseph, and a bright young woman MP called Margaret Thatcher, whom years later Oxford would deplorably snub in refusing to grant an honorary degree to the university's most distinguished female graduate and the country's first woman Prime Minister.[124] The voting sometimes cut across party political allegiances. Richard Crossman and Thomas Balogh (later Harold Wilson's economic adviser) voted for Macmillan; Woodrow Wyatt admitted he voted against Macmillan 'out of pure political prejudice and for absolutely no other reason'.[125] Gaitskell himself, wearing a blue pullover and orange tie, later admitted to Randolph Churchill that it was 'not the first time I have voted against Macmillan'.[126] Others had equally mixed motives; Evelyn Waugh always opposed Macmillan because he held him personally responsible, as Minister of Housing, for tearing down the Clarendon Hotel and replacing it on Cornmarket with the largest Woolworths in England; while another worthy son of Oxford voted for the PM purely in the hope that he would ban the wearing of corduroy jackets in Common Rooms. There was also at least one don who, having bitterly opposed Suez, voted for Macmillan because he had terminated the Anglo-French operation. One American television newscaster, incongruously clad in cap and gown as befitting a former Rhodes Scholar, was observed explaining into a microphone that this was the 'only foreign election in which American citizens were entitled to vote'.[127] When Bowra (who stood scowling at anti-Franks supporters and smiling at the faithful as they entered the Divinity Schools) spotted a black voting against Macmillan, he nudged Blake: 'Ha ha! The Winds of Change haven't blown all that far!'[128]

At the end of a day the like of which Oxford had never seen before, or probably ever will again, an unhappy Maurice Bowra – in his capacity as Acting Vice-Chancellor – was forced to read out, in Latin, a thumping majority of 279 (out of a record poll of 3673) for 'Mauricius Haraldus Macmillan'. For the university, £1500 was reaped on MA purchases.[129] When Jane Parsons brought Macmillan the news in No. 10, adding 'May I be first to congratulate you,' 'he just said "Oh, how very nice," typically non-committal, "snarling" with his teeth.'[130] But his true delight was not to be disguised; Robert Blake recalled how 'remarkably excited, and very moved' he was: '"It's wonderful, absolutely the nicest thing that has happened to me all my life," and he was really genuine. . . .'[131]

The new Head of Oxford was duly installed on 1 May, wearing the Chancellor's gown of elaborately brocaded black silk – with his cap on back to front. He spoke half in English and half in Latin which, for a classical scholar, always astonished the *cognoscenti* by its schoolboy pronunciation,[132] declaring: '. . . I have always loved Oxford with a true and deep affection. I can never repay the debt that I owe my college and my university. . . .' He went on to reminisce that, in his undergraduate days, Oxford had no industry save printing and a marmalade factory, and turning to Latin: '*Hic mihi dies semper recordandus erit, hic candido calculo notandus*' ('This is a day I shall always remember – a red letter day').[133] With a typical Macmillan throwaway, he observed in his memoirs that he reckoned those who had voted for him did so in the expectation 'that as a Prime Minister I should not be able to interfere, and that when I retired I should be too old to do so . . . '.

If this was so, his supporters certainly miscalculated. He was to turn out to be one of the most energetic and dedicated Chancellors Oxford ever had. Even while Prime Minister, he amazed dons by seldom refusing an invitation, giving particular priority to the less fashionable colleges and humbler occasions.

At his inaugural Encaenia in June 1960, the new Chancellor bestowed his first honorary degrees. They included Selwyn Lloyd and his successor, Lord Home; Dame Evelyn Sharp, from his Ministry of Housing days; Sir Lewis Namier, whom he greatly admired as a historian, and a Macmillan author; and his old friend from Eton and the trenches, Harry Crookshank. At a very festive Gaudy at Christ Church that evening, Macmillan admitted, 'I rather enjoy patronage; at least it makes all those years of reading Trollope worthwhile.'[134] It was the first of the Oxford speeches that, over the next twenty-six years, were to win him a new fame, and much affection.

In his memoirs Macmillan himself played down his election to Chancellor of Oxford as just 'one agreeable interlude'. In fact, amid all the sea of troubles closing in on him, it was much more than that, and a very considerable source of consolation – then, and for the remainder of his life.

Chapter Ten

'A Very Special Relationship'
1960–1961

. . . I do not feel Kennedy will be bad for us. He will perhaps have ideas and be attracted by ideas. . . .

(HM, Diaries, 2 November 1960)

And so we had a very special relationship.

(HM, July 1980)

When the founding fathers of the USA, in their eighteenth-century wisdom, devised the US presidential system, with all its ingenious checks and balances designed to safeguard it from a despot like George III, it seemed a masterpiece of enlightenment. Two hundred years later, however, the checks appear to outweigh the balances. The first year of a new President is spent learning the job; then follow two years of business, while the fourth year is spent preparing for the next election. Since 1945, more US Presidents have spent that last year in disarray than the reverse, provoking inevitable concern among America's allies. For Macmillan, the final months of his old wartime friend of twenty years' standing, Eisenhower, were imbued with personal sadness, tempered with alarm and occasional annoyance. In domestic policy as in the world at large, America seemed to have gone to sleep, while Eisenhower gave the appearance of an 'aged monarch', escaping with increasing regularity to the golf course, and with no John Foster Dulles to activate US foreign policy.[1] In contrast, Khrushchev stood at the peak of his brash and unpredictable powers. Since the collapse of the Paris summit of 1960, following the U-2 incident, he had become coldly belligerent, and a new Ice Age in East–West relations seemed to have begun. Meanwhile it was painfully clear to Macmillan that no new initiative over such dangerous issues as Berlin could be taken until Eisenhower was replaced by a new President, elected in November. In considerable apprehension he had recorded in his diary in June 1960 his fear that nothing could be done 'to reverse the dangerous drift' until after the US elections, and then: 'If the Republicans win, one might begin some work *before* Christmas. If the Democrats win, nothing can be done till the Spring of 1961. . . .'[2] Berlin remained the principal worry, but on balance he thought the odds were against Khrushchev starting anything there until he had a chance to sum up Eisenhower's successor; to Eisenhower Khrushchev had made it plain, with maximum discourtesy, that he had no intention of wasting time in discussing the matter any further with a 'lame duck' President.[3] In this hiatus, after all he had done to try to save the Paris summit, Macmillan's

own stock remained high within the Alliance – and perhaps particularly so in America.

Blue Streak and Skybolt

If the East–West dialogue had become frozen in uncertainty and
peril at the upper altitudes, Macmillan continued to work away on
the lower slopes, persisting with his earlier endeavours to get an
agreement on ending nuclear testing. Since the collapse of the
summit, he noted that the atmosphere had altered, and in June the
Russians had walked out of the long-running Geneva Disarmament
Conference. But Macmillan, though downcast, refused to give up
hope. Meanwhile, under the 1958 agreement repealing the Mac-
Mahon Act which Macmillan had signed with Eisenhower (to the
great distress subsequently of de Gaulle), Britain uniquely had
received the know-how to manufacture her own smaller and more
sophisticated nuclear warheads. As a vehicle to deliver them, the
Ministry of Defence had devised first of all a 'guided bomb', a kind
of primitive forerunner of the Cruise missile, Blue Steel. But, after
much money and effort had been expended, Blue Steel had been
scrapped in favour of Blue Streak, a surface-to-surface missile
operating at a long range, which had been backed by Duncan
Sandys while Minister of Defence. By February 1960, however,
after much soul-searching, Macmillan had been persuaded by the
unusually cogent technical arguments of the Chiefs of Staff that
Blue Streak too was a loser. Already £60 million had been spent on
Blue Streak, and its production would have cost at least another
£500 million.

As one of the spin-offs of the Special Relationship which Macmillan had so assiduously pursued with Eisenhower, Britain was
now (in March 1960) offered Skybolt by the Americans – on very
advantageous terms. Currently under development in the US,
Skybolt was projected as a stand-off, long-range missile, with a
highly complex guidance system that was designed to be fired from
aircraft, rather than from land or sea. Its great attraction to the
British defence chiefs was that it would keep the RAF's increasingly
obsolescent V-bombers going for another 'generation'. By way of a
gift Skybolt, however, was to prove something of a Shirt of Nessus
for Macmillan; yet he had in addition received from Eisenhower what

he conceived to be a much more valuable 'half-promise' of Polaris, the sophisticated submarine-based missile which the Americans believed would be a deadlier and more advanced strategic weapon. Macmillan explained his philosophy in a letter to the Queen that may still bear relevance in the 1980s:

> for political and morale reasons I am very anxious to get rid of these fixed rockets. This is a very small country, and to put these installations near the large centres of population – where they have to be – would cause increasing anxiety to Your Majesty's subjects. A bomber is somehow accepted on its bombing field; and a mobile weapon, either on a truck or better still in a submarine, is out of sight. It was made clear to me that no strings – to use a technical expression – will be attached. . . .[4]

In the April debate over the scrapping of Blue Streak, Macmillan was relieved to get away lightly, largely through the usual divisions within the Opposition as to whether Britain ought to have a nuclear force at all. In June, however, there were already questions in the House (notably from Macmillan's *bête noire*, George Brown), on the future of Skybolt. By October 'disquieting rumours' had reached the government, through unofficial channels, that the Americans were contemplating abandoning Skybolt.[5] On 1 December, Macmillan was pondering in his diary: 'are the Americans going to let us down, and (if so) what can we do?'[6] It showed Macmillan already anticipating the serious confrontation that, in fact, was not to break for exactly another two years. On the other hand, as of December 1960, Macmillan was now surprisingly describing Polaris – the eventual substitute for Skybolt – as 'ill-thought out' and a 'dangerous' weapon. Not for the last time, Britain's nuclear defence seemed to dangle on a tenuous string, the other end of which lay firmly in American hands.

Part of the Skybolt 'deal' agreed by Macmillan 'in principle' during his Camp David visit of March 1960 was to provide the new US Polaris bases in a Scottish loch.[7] There were, of course, substantial local political risks: 'A picture could well be drawn of some frightful accident which might devastate the whole of Scotland. . . .' It was a decision not lightly to be taken, and in ratifying it the Cabinet expressed considerable anxiety. Macmillan voiced his own private misgivings in his diary of 12 June:

it turns on whether we are just to give our allies facilities – more or less as a satellite – or whether we can make it a joint enterprise. Can we get one submarine from U.S. and start to build another? The whole problem is full of uncertainties and dangers. . . .[8]

Macmillan put the 'uncertainties' squarely to Eisenhower in one of his last official exchanges, addressed to his 'Dear Friend'. First, there was the location, proposed by the Americans to be on the River Clyde near Glasgow:

it would surely be a mistake to put down what will be a major nuclear target so near to the third largest and the most overcrowded city in this country. As soon as the announcement was made, Malinovsky[9] would threaten to aim his rockets at Glasgow. . . .

For Macmillan, Loch Linnhe in his native Highlands was preferable: 'From a security point of view, a robust population of three or four thousand highlanders at Fort William is much more to my taste than the rather mixed population in the cosmopolitan city of Glasgow. . . .' Macmillan went on to press that it 'should be seen to be a joint enterprise designed to strengthen the deterrent forces of the West. We must run the affair as a partnership. . . .' He saw this as Britain supplying floating dock and tender facilities, and – eventually – coming in with her own Polaris submarines. Raising the question of control, he urged that, beyond the existing agreement that the US Polaris missiles should not be fired from Britain's territorial waters, without her consent, the Zone should be extended to one hundred miles – 'for presentational purposes'.[10] The ensuing complicated negotiations were not helped by the heavy-handedness of Pentagon generals who 'add to the general dismay in UK by giving ridiculous Press interviews of a "sabre-rattling" kind . . .'.[11]

In October Macmillan received a grateful letter, signed 'Ike', appreciative of the British having approved (in September) the Holy Loch base off the River Clyde, but going no further than the following general assurance, which was 'not intended to be used publicly':

In the event of an emergency, such as increased tension or the threat of war, the US will take every possible step to consult with Britain and other Allies. . . .[12]

Thus was an important commitment, and a principle, resolved.

Macmillan

Confronting Khrushchev at the UN

At the end of September, with the Congo boiling over, Khrushchev announced that he was intending to lead personally a Soviet (and satellite) delegation to the UN. After discussing it with the Queen at Balmoral, and strongly encouraged by Home, Macmillan decided to go himself to New York to confront Khrushchev – 'if only to rally the West'. The Soviet leader's appearance was of course given maximum coverage by the American press. Making a three-hour speech to the General Assembly, 'directed to excite and inflame the Afro-Asians', he attacked Eisenhower and Hammarskjöld, called for the abolition of the post of Secretary-General of the UN, and proposed that the UN leave New York. Then came Macmillan's moment. In a carefully prepared, moderate and constructive speech designed to contrast with the melodramatic posturing of Khrushchev, Macmillan addressed an unusually well-attended and attentive General Assembly five days later. He had taken the precaution of not circulating his speech in advance. Defending both the UN and Hammarskjöld over the Congo, he struck directly at Khrushchev and his polemic, declaring that:

> the sponge of public opinion is almost saturated with the persistent flood of propaganda. It can pick up no more. . . .
> . . . Words like 'colonialism' and 'imperialism' have been slung about here without much regard to the facts, at least of modern colonial and imperial history. . . .

He then launched into a brief review of the British record, and, after one of his superbly timed pauses, pointed around the hall demanding:

> Gentlemen, where are the representatives of these former British territories? Here they are, sitting in this Hall. Apart from the older independent countries, Canada, Australia, New Zealand, South Africa – here are the representatives of India, Pakistan, Ceylon, Ghana, Malaya. Here, here in this Hall. In a few days' time, Nigeria will join us. . . .
> . . . Who dares to say that this is anything but a story of steady and liberal progress. . . .

At about this point, Khrushchev, who had been making periodic, oafish interruptions, began banging on the desk with his shoe. Macmillan, at his most unflappable, stopped and asked quietly: 'Mr President, perhaps we could have a translation, I could not quite follow.'[13]

The remark brought the house down, gained points notably with the Afro-Asians, visibly discomfited Khrushchev, and established for Macmillan a reputation for style that would never be forgotten in the US. It would serve him well when it came to breaking the ice with the future President.

Taking Leave of Ike; the New President

During his UN visit, Macmillan breakfasted with Eisenhower. The conversation was general, but he came away feeling that the President looked 'rather ill and tired'.[14] It was in fact to be the last time that they would meet while he was still in office. On his departure from the White House, Macmillan wrote to Eisenhower on 13 January 1961:

> As I think over the history of our collaboration which has now lasted some eighteen years, and especially over the last four years, one thing stands out. Whether we agreed or disagreed on particular policies we had I think a deep unity of purpose and, I like to feel, a frank and honest appreciation of each other's good faith. . . . This was something which one does *not*, alas, often find between Heads of Government even of Allied countries; personal friendship and trust cannot be manufactured, they just grow. So it is not surprising that this ending of an official connection with an old friend causes me so much regret.[15]

Some years later, as the reputation of Eisenhower began to be revised in the US, he added '. . . I think people now realise what a fine man Ike was. He was a sort of Duke of Wellington of America. I was lucky to have him. . . .'[16]

In the January 1960 issue of *Esquire*, Professor Arthur Schlesinger Jr, an ardent supporter of John F. Kennedy for President and later his biographer, castigated the 1950s as an era of 'torpor' in the US, and looked forward to a new decade with 'a sense of motion, of leadership and of hope'.[17] But, as the elections approached, that sense of hope was by no means universally shared – and certainly not in Britain. Macmillan's early view of Senator Kennedy (the Senator of Massachusetts) was that he was young and inexperienced, and occasionally given to excessive diatribes against British imperialism. His main reservation concerned the character and influence of Joseph Kennedy Senior. While the US primaries were under way in June, Bob Menzies had written to Macmillan a long personal appreciation, in which he quoted one Democrat as saying, 'I am not afraid of the Pope. I am afraid of Papa.'[18] It was a view entirely echoed by Macmillan himself. Although Dorothy's nephew, the Marquess of Hartington,[19] had married Jack's sister, Kathleen ('Kick'), Macmillan had never met any of the Kennedy clan; but he had heard a great deal from Churchill about Joe Kennedy while he was Ambassador in London at the beginning of the war:

> and we regarded him with some contempt, as being a man of low character whose view was that Britain was beaten. It may not have been at all fair; he may have expressed a perfectly objective view that there was no way we could win. But it was generally thought that he was unfriendly, and defeatist. So therefore I had no particular reason to have any affection for the President. . . .[20]

In his suite at the Waldorf Astoria while he was attending the United Nations, Macmillan had watched on television a pre-election confrontation between Nixon and Kennedy, the presidential candidates. Shortly afterwards Eisenhower asked him what he thought:

> . . . I said 'Your chap's beat'. And he said 'What do you mean?' And I said 'One of them looked like a convicted criminal and the other looked like a rather engaging young undergraduate. . . .' Well, you know, Nixon had that curious sort of furtive, dark face. . . .[21]

Although it was to be one of the closest presidential races, by the end of October Macmillan's political antennae were telling him that Kennedy looked set to win, and he was already looking ahead. '. . . I do not feel Kennedy will be bad for us. He will perhaps have ideas and be attracted by ideas. . . .'[22] When the election results came through on 8 November, Kennedy was shown to have won

by just over 100,000 votes out of nearly 69,000,000. He was the first
US President to have been born in the twentieth century.

The reaction in America, spontaneously and quite suddenly, was
the release of a great pent-up surge of energy, and euphoria.
America's elation at the promise of youth and vigour offered by
forty-three-year-old Jack Kennedy was soon shared by half the
world, jaded and anxious for a new direction. Though he had
foreseen the result, Macmillan's own first thoughts were mixed with
apprehension, and some gloom. Some journalists at home wasted
no time in making invidious comparisons. On 12 November, Harold
Evans found his boss:

> feeling his age. . . . I found him brooding in the Cabinet Room
> on Wednesday morning over the *Mail* cartoon showing the young
> and eager Kennedy and Nixon hauling the bathchairs of Mac-
> millan, de Gaulle and Adenauer 'into the twentieth century'. He
> had torn it out of the paper. 'I don't think it's quite fair,' he said,
> and then as an afterthought, 'They don't even seem to know
> which century we're in. . . .'[23]

Something of his apprehension came through in the last words of
his official valedictory message to Eisenhower on 10 November,
when he said, 'I cannot of course ever hope to have anything to
replace the sort of relations that we have had.' 'Happily, for me,'
said Macmillan, 'the last sentence proved not to be true.'

What could not be foreseen by anyone then was that, against all
prognostications (and greatly to Macmillan's own credit), he was
in fact about to enter into a relationship that – although totally
different in kind – would be even closer than that which he had had
with Ike. For Macmillan, the romantic, this was to prove one of the
most fulfilling passages of his life, despite the moments of private
exasperation and misunderstanding, and its tragic brevity. 'I had
with two Presidents this extraordinary relationship: I was sort of
son to Ike, and it was the other way round with Kennedy. . . .'[24]

For the moment, however, few of the preliminary reports coming
out of Washington were encouraging. The week after the election,
Macmillan recorded Jock Whitney, Eisenhower's Ambassador (and
a staunch Republican) coming to 'gossip' about the new President's
'character and probable ways of doing business'. 'Kennedy must
be a strange character according to Jock Whitney. Obstinate,

sensitive, ruthless and highly sexed. . . .'[25] Obviously the Ambassador had imparted to Macmillan 'gossip' about Kennedy's private life that was beginning to be known in a fairly wide circle in the States, though not yet abroad. None of it would have been much to the liking of the puritanical Scot. At the end of November he entertained Lyndon Johnson to dinner, and was not deeply impressed: 'a Texan, an acute and ruthless "politician", but not (I would judge) a man of any intellectual power . . .'.[26] A few weeks later, Jock Whitney returned for another chat: 'He seemed to think the new President's appointments were "conservative" – therefore reassuring to him (but, as I did *not* say, correspondingly depressing to me).'[27]

'The Grand Design'

Macmillan the pragmatist realised that to get to know and win round this new American leader he would have to start from square one. The original Special Relationship between Churchill and Roosevelt had been engendered and nurtured by the common bond of the Second World War, and his own friendship with Eisenhower stemmed from the same background. How was he going to persuade this unknown young President to play the 'Roman' to Macmillan's 'Greek', as he liked to think he had induced Eisenhower to do during those days in Algeria in 1943?

The very day after the election, he was trying out his thoughts on how to 'handle' Kennedy with Home. Noting how while with Ike there was always the 'appeal to memories':

> With this new and comparatively young President we have nothing of the kind to draw on. We must, therefore, I think make our contacts in the realm of ideas. I must somehow convince him that I am worth consulting not as an old friend (as Eisenhower felt) but as a man who, although of advancing years, has young and fresh thoughts. . . .[28]

With it he sent the draft of 'a possible letter', already sketched out well before the election. After much advice and redrafting, it was finally sent off in mid-December. Macmillan started, with the utmost deference and deft expertise of the publisher, by appealing to the vanity of an author:

as I have just read the collection of your speeches called *The Strategy of Peace* I am looking forward with special pleasure to discussion of some of these things. If I may say so, I much sympathise with your approach and your determination to put the immense strength of your position and of your country behind a new effort to face the problems of the second half of this century. . . .

The policies of the Western Alliance were, he thought, 'not properly adjusted to the realities of the 1960s'. He set down 'the first and most important subjects' as:

what is going to happen to us unless we can show that our modern free society – the new form of capitalism – can make the fullest use of our resources and results in a steady expansion of our economic strength. . . . If we fail in this Communism will triumph, not by war, or even subversion, but by seeming to be a better way of bringing people material comforts. In other words, if we were to fall back into anything like the recession or crisis that we had between the wars, with large scale unemployment of men and machines, I think we would have lost the hand. . . .

He then turned to 'the immense problem of disarmament' with emphasis on the Geneva Nuclear Test negotiations: '. . . I still cannot quite make out whether Khrushchev has misunderstood or misrepresented what we have been trying to say to him. Perhaps we may be able to make him realize that we really do want disarmament. . . .' Paying homage to the need for leadership from the United States, he ended by stressing the 'special ties' afforded by Britain and the Commonwealth. Finally, '. . . I am sorry to inflict all this on you when you have so much to think about. . . . I await our first meeting with great eagerness.'[29]

That Macmillan, in his first letter to the new President, should have put, as his top priority, concern about the long-term economic health of the free world, with all its undertones of pre-war Stockton and the Middle Way, indicates the extent to which he was still preoccupied with fears of an international recession. At the same time, by way of restating the family connection (always particularly

close to the heart of a clan like the Kennedys) he shrewdly despatched Dorothy's nephew, Andrew, the Duke of Devonshire and
younger brother of 'Kick' Kennedy's dead husband, to attend the
President's inauguration. 'To his astonishment, he was put on the
platform in the best place, next to the President. . . .'[30]

All through the Christmas holidays, led by what he modestly
described as 'that fatal itch for composition which is the outcome
of a classical education', he mulled over an expansion of his letter to
Kennedy into a major 'think-piece'. What Macmillan half-jokingly
dubbed 'The Grand Design'[31] turned out to be in effect his blueprint
for 1961, setting out – at considerable length – all the economic,
political and defence problems confronting the free world. It was
carefully phrased so as to capture the imagination of the young
President: 'this *must* interest him and put out one or two exciting
ideas – yet it must not be pompous, or lecturing, or *too* radical! I
spent the morning on trying my hand at various drafts. . . .'[32] He
tried it out first on Norman Brook and Freddie Bishop; then, on
getting their approbation ('rather to my surprise'),[33] passed it to
the Foreign Secretary and the Chancellor, for onward circulation.

'The Grand Design' showed Macmillan at the peak of his powers
as a thinker on the wider canvas, with echoes from the tract-writer
of the 1930s. Its main purpose was 'to call attention to the need to
organise the great forces of the Free World – USA, Britain and
Europe – economically, politically and militarily in a coherent effort
to withstand the Communist tide all over the world', and it began
by stating baldly, 'The Free World cannot, on a realistic assessment,
enter on 1961 with any great degree of satisfaction. . . .' He went
on to note how the West had now lost its overwhelming nuclear
superiority, and how formidable – in the economic field – the
challenge of Communist production and technology had become.
In the face of the monolithic strength of the Kremlin, the West had
a number of groupings, in Europe, and in the Middle and Far East,
but 'which have nothing like the same unity of purpose or of
practice'. Britain no longer had either the economic or the military
power to take the leading role. But '. . . I am an unrepentant
believer in "interdependence". . . .' He thought that a 'united Free
World' was more likely to be achieved through joint monetary and
economic policies than via any political or military alliances. In
this context, he felt it incumbent on the British to urge on the
new American administration the need for extending world trade,

'including the expansion of credit by whatever means, orthodox or novel'. He also argued that the economic power of the free world should be more effective at providing aid to the Third World (though this was not an expression then widely current). 'There ought to be more of an overall plan and less rather "hand-to-mouth" giving of aid. . . .'

Macmillan lingered at length on the problems of France, and de Gaulle's aspirations. It was imperative to prevent the Six–Seven split in Europe getting any worse, which meant reaching an 'accommodation with de Gaulle', which in turn was primarily a political and not an economic problem. Particularly for Kennedy's benefit, he set it out as follows:

> *De Gaulle wants the recognition of France as a Great Power, at least equal to Britain.* He suspects the Anglo Saxons.
>
> So long as the 'Anglo-Saxon' domination continues, he will not treat Britain as European, but as American – a junior partner of America, but a partner. . . .

De Gaulle, Macmillan went on to explain, felt excluded from the Anglo-Saxon NATO 'Club'. 'Hence':

> (a) his persistent efforts towards 'Tripartitism' – which the Americans and the British have accepted 'en principe' to a limited extent, but have never really operated;
>
> (b) his determination – whatever the cost – that France should become a *nuclear* power. For it is France's *exclusion* from the nuclear club that is the measure of France's inferior status. It is particularly galling for him that Britain should have an independent nuclear capacity; he accepts that the United States is in a different category.
>
> . . . Can what *we* want and what *de Gaulle* wants be brought into harmony? Is there a basis for a deal. . . ?[34]

Macmillan made it abundantly plain to President Kennedy just how important all this was to his future intentions of joining the Common Market.

Throughout his extensive travels in 1961, Macmillan was to press the main themes of his 'Grand Design'. His first trip abroad, at the end of January, was to Rambouillet, where he found de Gaulle 'relaxed, friendly'. He seemed 'genuinely attracted by my themes – Europe to be united, politically and economically; but France and Great Britain to be something more than European Powers, and to be so recognised by the United States. . . .'[35] After dinner they were subjected to a French film about Stone Age tribes in New Guinea; Macmillan recalled them being 'naked and unashamed', enjoying the primitive, and priapic, happiness of man before the Fall, and he asked de Gaulle what could be done with these simple people. De Gaulle replied at once, mordantly: 'they ought immediately to be elected to the United Nations!' Macmillan, with his recent experiences at that body, concurred.

In his private diaries, the British Ambassador in Paris, Pierson Dixon, noted how Macmillan was not then really a popular figure in France.[36] Dorothy, on the other hand, with her rustic simplicity, stole many hearts. (Long after the event, Lady Dixon, an elegant Greek woman, recalled how, when accompanying Dorothy to the French television studios for an interview, she had been taken aback to find the Prime Minister's wife wearing a silk white blouse and a priceless Cavendish necklace, but combined with an old tweed skirt; 'Oh, but my dear, I know these TV people,' she explained, 'they only want to photograph you from the waist up!')[37]

Macmillan's encounter with Adenauer and the Germans in London the following month was less encouraging: 'the large economic issues which face the world they affect not to understand. In other words, they are rich and selfish. . . .'[38] Disappointing messages were also reaching Macmillan from Washington. It was clear that Kennedy and his new team at the State Department did not admire de Gaulle's general political philosophy, and were unreceptive towards Macmillan's proposals for limited tripartitism. It looked as though the 'Grand Design' might have fallen on stony ground; indeed, it narrowly escaped disappearing altogether. According to the economist Professor J. K. Galbraith, he was summoned to the White House to discuss the paper, but on arrival a flustered Kennedy told him that the document could not be found. A frantic search through the White House subsequently located it in three-year-old Caroline Kennedy's nursery. Galbraith wrote a characteristically witty minute, suggesting the creation of a child-proof filing system in the White House.[39]

More seriously, Kennedy had other things to think about, and was – evidently, and despite all Macmillan's redrafting – not particularly drawn by the circumstantial style of the ageing British Prime Minister. Macmillan decided he had to press for an early meeting with Kennedy, but – as with Ike in 1957 – was determined not to appear too ardent a suitor. In the event, the first pass was made – quite unexpectedly – by Kennedy.

'This Young Cocky Irishman'

Macmillan was scheduled to have his first encounter with the new President in Washington at the beginning of April, and on 24 March he and Dorothy took off for a short trip to the West Indian Federation, with the over-worked Prime Minister looking forward to a rest, or at least a 'not particularly testing time'. But at 4 a.m. on the morning after their arrival in Trinidad there was an urgent telegram from Kennedy, asking to see Macmillan 'without delay' to talk about Laos, which was now causing the Americans deep anxiety. Could Macmillan fly to meet him at the Key West naval base in Florida the next day – Sunday? It was a five-hour flight in those days, and though Macmillan's entourage may have felt it somewhat cavalier of the much younger man to summon in this way a sixty-seven-year-old who had only just completed a long flight from London, Macmillan's only comment was that he had never flown a round trip of 3600 miles just for a hamburger lunch. Tactically, however, he was delighted; it was most gratifying that, for this consultation, the initiative had come from Kennedy, and Macmillan's spontaneous acceptance was bound to leave the new President somewhat beholden to him. It was an advantage he would play to the full.

Macmillan could not help but be nervous about the personal chemistry at the meeting, on which so very much depended. Here was, he reminisced on television many years later: 'this young man, the hope of the youth of the world, and here was an ageing reactionary Prime Minister bringing ten or eleven years of Tory misrule to its end. . . .'[40] To Kennedy he thought that he would inevitably appear as a 'stuff-shirt', or square.

Unexpected as the Key West meeting was, however, Macmillan for one had been assiduously doing his homework on his host ever since Jock Whitney had represented him as being a 'strange character'. He had tapped every possible source: Foreign Office reports; observations from Harold Caccia, the British Ambassador in Washington; itinerant Americans in Britain; relatives, like Andrew Devonshire, and – more notably – David Ormsby-Gore, who was then Minister of State at the Foreign Office and who had been a close personal friend of Kennedy's from pre-war days in Britain; he even consulted journalists, like Henry Brandon, the *Sunday Times*' veteran correspondent in Washington. Brandon recalled a conversation very soon after Kennedy had come to the White House revealing Macmillan's preoccupation. 'Look,' he said, 'I've known Eisenhower for years.'

> We belonged to the same generation. We had fought the war together. We had common experiences. And now there is this young cocky Irishman . . . how am I going to deal with him? How on earth am I going to preserve the kind of relationship between the US and Britain that I was able to preserve under Eisenhower, with Kennedy? . . . You've known him for a long time. Tell me more about him.[41]

Brandon did his best to be reassuring. Macmillan discovered that, while his father was in London before the war, young Jack Kennedy had studied under Harold Laski, the socialist economist, at the London School of Economics, where he had developed a fascination for British political society and a particular love for the late eighteenth and early nineteenth centuries. He admired William Pitt for his subtlety, and Charles James Fox for his conciliatory talents. But – despite his father, or perhaps because of him – Churchill was always his greatest British hero; this much he shared with Macmillan.

Much of his life after 1939 seemed to offer atonement for Joseph Kennedy's isolationism. Disqualified from the US Army because of his chronically bad back, he had persuaded the Navy to take him in 1941, and after Pearl Harbor had pulled every string to get to sea. In the Solomon Islands in 1943 his torpedo boat, PT-109, had been sliced in two by a Japanese destroyer and Kennedy had displayed considerable heroism in rescuing crew members from a flaming sea. Courage (according to his brother Robert) was the virtue he most admired; here, automatically, was ground that

Macmillan could share to the full. With the pain from his bad back exacerbated by injuries sustained on PT-109, Kennedy suffered almost constant discomfort; which equally was something that Macmillan with his own war wounds could sympathise with. Like Macmillan, Kennedy was given to deflationary understatement about himself; when asked how he became a war hero he replied, 'It was involuntary. They sank my boat';[42] and Kennedy too was a deeply emotional man.

From the cradle, all the Kennedys had been brought up in a febrile political atmosphere; Jack Kennedy himself was renowned for his inexhaustible intellectual curiosity, and his voracious reading. He would even sometimes take a book while out walking. He was particularly gripped by history and works of political biography, like David Cecil's *The Young Melbourne*, which was also one of Macmillan's favourites. He enjoyed reading, and talking, about families and dynasties. Like Macmillan, too, he had a somewhat fatalistic view of history, shaped – as he saw it – by forces beyond man's control, which in turn drove him on to confront his own destiny. In course of time, the radical right in America came to hate him more and more, but – as he once remarked to David Ormsby-Gore – one of the 'rather sad things' about political life was that 'you discovered that the other side really had a very good case'.[43] This unpartisan aspect of Kennedy was yet one further quality he shared with Macmillan.

Possibly even more important as their relationship developed was their rather special sense of humour. Kennedy's biographer, Schlesinger, reckoned that if Roosevelt was a 'man of humour', Kennedy was 'a man of wit'. Irony was his favourite mode, and a remark such as 'Washington is a city of southern efficiency and northern charm' might almost have been made by Macmillan too. Kennedy's sense of humour had a strong element of the 'black', and the Celtic; with a finely tuned ear for the ridiculous he relished the irreverent, and resembled Macmillan to a remarkable extent in his capacity to talk lightly of matters about which he felt very deeply. As members of the Kennedy entourage like Theodore Sorensen came to recognise, the façade of great self-assurance also concealed a degree of shyness.

Where the two shared no common ground was, of course, in Kennedy's ferocious appetite for women. In the middle of a working lunch on nuclear arms during their third or fourth meeting,

Kennedy, his attention wandering, turned to Macmillan and enquired casually, 'I wonder how it is with you, Harold? If I don't
have a woman for three days, I get a terrible headache. . . .'[44] The
sixty-seven-year-old, monogamous Prime Minister was nonplussed.
Late in life, in one of his rare fits of impatience with the late
President he excoriated him for 'spending half his time thinking
about adultery, the other half about second-hand ideas passed on
by his advisers'. (A throwaway remark, the second part was not a
view seriously held by Macmillan.)[45]

Nevertheless, for all Macmillan's apprehensions, the area of common ground already staked out by the time of that first meeting
was not unpromising, and – on the American side – had doubtless been to some extent cultivated by the retiring President,
Eisenhower, briefing his young successor with the commendation:
'You'll find Macmillan a good friend whose counsel you should
listen to.'[46]

Key West and Laos

The war in Laos had been fizzing ever since Macmillan came to
power, reaching an apogee by the end of 1960. Laos was one of the
four entities which comprised Indo-China following the French
withdrawal.[47] At the Geneva Conference of 1954 Eden (then
Foreign Secretary), by what Macmillan rated 'almost a miracle of
patience and diplomatic skill', had achieved a tenuous neutrality
for Laos. It was tenuous because the land-locked kingdom was
flanked by both Communist China and Ho Chi-minh's triumphant
and aggressive North Vietnam. In 1959 civil warfare had broken
out between the weak, neutralist government of Prince Phouma
and the Communist Pathet Lao, who were then provided with
substantial supplies of arms from North Vietnam. The US had
already spent $300 million over five years trying to keep Laos
out of Communist hands. Pressed by Allen Dulles of the CIA,
Eisenhower had come to regard Laos as the key to all South-east
Asia, and at this point the US became involved for the first time,
sending 'technicians' to advise the Laotian forces. The danger
signals were clear to Macmillan; on 8 December 1960 he had
recorded:

The situation in Laos is bad – the Americans are anxious to intervene overtly as well as covertly. . . . Outside this foolish internecine war, the Communists are waiting hopefully for their chance. The Thais want intervention by the SEATO powers.[48] It is easy to see the dangers. China must react and perhaps Russia. Yet if Laos goes, what chance is there for South East Asia . . . ?[49]

Here was an early statement of the 'domino theory', later to become so derided in the US during the Vietnam War; in fact what happened over Laos in 1961 was a vitally important overture to Vietnam.

Mindful of France's disaster at Dien Bien Phu, and the equally disastrous rift between Dulles and Eden which had followed, Macmillan had done his best to counsel Eisenhower against further US commitment. Instead he urged that the International Commission, which had drawn up the peace settlement in Indo-China, be reactivated. This had provoked Eisenhower's 'strangely hysterical reply', urging intervention by SEATO:

It looks as if Allen Dulles's policy has been accepted altogether by the State Department and the President. This is a most dangerous situation for us. If SEATO intervenes (Thais, U.S. and ourselves) it will cause trouble in India, Malaya and Singapore. If we keep out and let U.S. do a 'Suez' on their own, we split the alliance. But what is much worse, our Chiefs of Staff do not think that military intervention is really feasible, or likely to be successful. . . .[50]

By return Macmillan had signalled Eisenhower, stating his fears in grave terms:

. . . I am much disturbed at the trouble that we are both getting into over Laos. For the first time for many years it seems that our policies, although of the same strategic purpose, have been a little divergent on tactics. This we must surely remedy as soon as we can. . . .[51]

A week later Macmillan had been able to report to the Cabinet that the Americans seemed to have yielded to the British view that

SEATO intervention 'would bring in North Vietnamese and Chinese volunteers', as had occurred during the Korean War; and, he went on to predict, 'Fighting would probably extend to Vietnam.'[52] But now, provisionally, Eisenhower had agreed to Macmillan's proposal to reconvene the International Commission. Macmillan felt that, during the last weeks of Eisenhower's administration and the first of Kennedy's, the US would be unlikely to launch any military action. Meanwhile the Russians, who were an essential party to the International Commission, stalled as the Pathet Lao clearly appeared to be winning.

Then, on the eve of his departure for Trinidad, Macmillan received the disquieting news from Washington that Kennedy had been persuaded that, if SEATO would not intervene, the US might have to 'go it alone' to save at least part of Laos. In Japan, 2000 marines, performing as extras in a film, vanished from the set. Macmillan suddenly saw Britain caught between a grim Scylla and Charybdis; it would, he reckoned, have been 'tragic to separate ourselves from the Americans. We had suffered enough in a previous crisis from an Anglo-American schism. . . .' He made it clear to the Americans that 'at the end of the day, whichever decision they took, we would support them. . . .' This, he was sure, was right 'if we are to have influence in future with the President and the new administration . . .'.[53] Accordingly, he had embarked willingly on the long trip to Key West.

That meeting on 26 March was, he recalled, one of the strangest of all his experiences. The British 'team' consisted only of himself, Tim Bligh, a detective and two Garden Girls from No. 10, and they were joined by Harold Caccia, who had flown down from Washington on the President's plane. In marked contrast, the President was accompanied to Key West by a vast panoply of Pentagon brass, of all services and ranks, and this first encounter took place in a US Navy fortress. It began with an elaborate exposition accompanied with maps and a blackboard. Macmillan was impressed by the intentness with which Kennedy listened in silence, asking only a few questions 'while bridges were flung across rivers, troops deployed on a great scale and the rest'. The two then adjourned, alone, to another room for lunch, which consisted of a hamburger ('not a form of lunch I'm very fond of!').[54]

The first impression Kennedy made on Macmillan was of 'a curious mixture of qualities – courteous, quiet, quick, decisive –

and tough . . .'.[55] Writing to Jackie Kennedy one of many letters following the assassination he recalled 'the very first time we met to talk – I felt something had happened. Naturally I "fell" for him. But (much more unexpectedly) he seemed to warm to me. . . .'[56] At Key West, Kennedy was distracted, unbeknown to Macmillan, by a more immediate and closer problem – the project to land in Cuba at the Bay of Pigs, which may have accounted for a certain reserve. Nevertheless, this remarkable instant rapport evidently affected Kennedy equally. Although, in political terms, the opening bars in the concerto were cautious and tentative, it encouraged both to begin speaking in very direct language to each other. According to Macmillan, the two leaders had barely begun to munch their hamburgers before Kennedy asked him what he had thought of the morning's exposition. Macmillan replied, 'Not much. It is not on,' and then went on, with a forthrightness that, of itself, might have seemed surprising after so brief an acquaintance, to give advice that might have aided subsequent US leaders over Vietnam – 'DON'T.'[57]

The Americans, he told Kennedy, had three options in Laos: they could put in a puppet government, 'which would be useless, and corrupt, and then you'd have to take it over.' Kennedy interjected that that option would be impossible, 'because that's imperialism'. 'Well, then,' Macmillan continued, 'you will have it on your back, you will have to finance it, and send armies that will get bigger and bigger . . . and produce an inflation that would practically destroy the domestic economy of Laos; or, thirdly, you stay out altogether. . . .' Kennedy's only comment was 'Well, that's very interesting.'[58] Macmillan was encouraged to sense that the young President already 'was evidently in control of the Pentagon, not the other way round. . . .'[59] He did *not* want to "go it alone". . . .'[60]

Without saying so, Kennedy seemed to indicate to Macmillan that he shared his doubts, significantly scaling down the contingency plan produced by the military.[61] Under strong pressure from Kennedy and his imposing entourage, Macmillan however agreed that 'it might be *politically* necessary to do something, in order not to be "pushed out" by the Russians. This I thought might well be their intent at the beginning of his Presidency. . . .' In view of the hammering that Kennedy was shortly to receive from Khrushchev in Vienna, this was sound enough reasoning, but Macmillan made it clear that the British would be unlikely to do more than 'join in the appearance of resistance'.

Typing up to the last minute, the No. 10 'Garden Girls' had to run for a moving plane and the British party arrived back in Trinidad very late that night. Kennedy returned to Washington disappointed that he had got nothing stronger than a moral commitment from Macmillan. Macmillan found the exceptional heat of Trinidad uncongenial, and on Good Friday was stricken with a sharp attack of gout. On 4 April, as per schedule, he flew on to Washington.

Washington, April 1961

Macmillan at once found that his Washington visit, which he had anticipated with some apprehension, was made much easier by the breaking of the ice at the unscheduled meeting at Key West. He and Dorothy were greeted with the utmost courtesy by the Kennedy family and the whole apparatus of Washington official hospitality. Before a working lunch in the White House on the first day, the President 'took me upstairs to introduce his wife, who is charming. Also to drink some strong cocktails. . . .'[62] It was the beginning of a very warm friendship with Jackie, continuing long after the President's death. The next day the two leaders were taken on a river cruise aboard the *Honey Fitz*, down the Potomac to Mount Vernon, a combination of pleasure and work: 'About six a side – subjects, Berlin, the Nuclear Tests, and more Laos.'[63] As they passed a small flotilla from a local high school, struggling raggedly against the current, Macmillan remarked, 'Looks like the Laotian Navy!'[64] It was the kind of crack that immediately struck a chord with Kennedy, defused the seriousness of the discussions, and helped set the tone of the whole visit. 'In the past,' reported James Reston of the *New York Times*, 'the visit of a British Prime Minister to Washington was usually a solemn procession, full of hands-across-the-sea clichés, formal meetings and dinners and vapid communiqués. . . .'[65] But, in contrast, a Macmillan visit to Washington became 'like a house-party and at times almost like a spree'. Macmillan himself was quoted as saying that there was 'something very eighteenth century about this young man . . .'. 'He is always on his toes during our discussions. But in the evening there will be music and wine and pretty women.'[66]

The Laos crisis was simmering down; following his meeting with

Macmillan in Key West, Kennedy had received similar advice separately from two very eminent Americans supporting Macmillan's point of view; that veteran counsellor of many US administrations, Averell Harriman, after a trip to Laos advised that the Pathet Lao could not be beaten 'without very large American intervention';[67] while General Douglas MacArthur, his fingers badly burned in Korea but still a 'hawk', warned Kennedy forcefully against the commitment of American footsoldiers on the Asian mainland. Meanwhile the Russians too had shown themselves to be more willing to help with a ceasefire and negotiations. (As Khrushchev put it to the US Ambassador, Llewellyn Thompson, in an expansive moment: 'Why take risks over Laos? It will fall into our laps like a ripe apple.')[68]

Macmillan was somewhat disconcerted by the young President's apparently excessive reliance on his vast, and ever present, team of advisers. Therefore he set particular value on two lengthy private talks he had with the President, alone. It was here, he wrote in his memoirs, that the foundations of his ensuing intimacy with Kennedy were laid. He was able to have a sympathetic discussion with Kennedy about 'The Grand Design', and the problem of France and British entry into the EEC. 'How far he will be able to go with de Gaulle to help me, I do not know,' Macmillan recorded in his diary, 'but he will try.'[69]

At the end of the Washington talks, Macmillan went away encouraged by the strength of Kennedy's support for Britain joining the EEC; economically, the new President thought it would make bargaining on trades and tariffs that much easier; politically, he hoped that once Britain was safely inside the EEC she would be able to steer and influence her new partners. This was to lend a powerful impetus to Macmillan's campaign to galvanise British initiatives on his return. Kennedy, who was to visit Paris the following month, already harboured few illusions about de Gaulle; he thought he was 'more anxious for the appearance than the reality', but when it came to practical discussions, 'the French were very negative.' With some foresight, he calculated that, if the French Army returned from Algeria, 'de Gaulle would certainly disorganise NATO.' When Macmillan broached the possibility of de Gaulle being helped to establish an independent nuclear force, however small, Kennedy seemed unenthusiastic and thought it would be 'difficult' for the Americans to accept.

On some of the wider issues, there was perhaps less instant rapport. Kennedy was resistant to Macmillan's hints about bringing Communist China into the UN; it would take another decade and a Republican President to swing America around to this. He inherited to the full State Department misgivings that Macmillan was 'soft' on Berlin, and doubts about the validity of Macmillan's residual enthusiasm for summitry. He declined to invoke Macmillan's first-hand experience on how to handle Khrushchev. In fact Kennedy made Macmillan somewhat brusquely aware that he was not going to call on Macmillan's services as an 'honest broker' to try to set up a summit with Khrushchev; Kennedy had already made plans to fly to Vienna to meet Khrushchev alone in June. On his side, Kennedy was also disappointed at Macmillan's general lack of support over South-east Asia (although David Ormsby-Gore was later to reckon that Macmillan's advice on Laos had definitely influenced the position finally taken by Kennedy).[70] In private, the President talked very openly about all the internal pressures on him – his lack of a majority in Congress, and all the domestic reforms he wished to achieve. But there was still a defensive reticence there; at times Macmillan found him 'detached', just as he had been in Key West.[71] In just ten days' time, the CIA would be unleashing its secret action in the Bay of Pigs. Kennedy seems to have hinted at what was ahead, referring obliquely to the problem of the Cuban exiles in Miami:

> What did I think about it? I said I thought they were more of a nuisance in America than they would be in Cuba. What would he do with them if he kept them? He said that was just the point that worried him. He thought it would be better to let them go to Cuba and become guerrillas. . . .

Perhaps Kennedy was sounding out Macmillan; what is clear is that he revealed no details of the impending operation, nor did he consult his British opposite number. Things would be different in a year and a half's time with the next Cuban crisis.

In a long letter to the Queen, Macmillan noted how Kennedy's 'honeymoon with the American people is still continuing . . .'. This might have described equally well his own feelings about the overall impact of the visit. In their final communiqués, both leaders significantly used the word 'happy'. The American press were equally enthusiastic. Writing from London, Joseph C. Harsch of the *Christian Science Monitor* remarked how Macmillan 'is one of the very few living British politicians who can manage to sound convincingly patriotic without sounding Anti-American . . .'.[72] *Time* noted that the two had arrived at few real decisions, but 'they had achieved a measure of the personal understanding vital to the troubled months ahead. . . .'[73]

After a short stay in Canada (which provided the best 'take-home' anecdote of the tour; Dorothy had found a bemused Prime Minister wandering in the corridor outside his bedroom in Rideau Hall, clad only in shirt and underpants, but no trousers, and asking plaintively, 'Where is the office? I want a young lady'),[74] Macmillan returned home to the usual full measure of domestic problems. On 12 April came the news that, with Gagarin, the Soviet Union had put the first man in space. It was a blow to American prestige. Then, hot on its heels, followed the first accounts of the Bay of Pigs.

Bay of Pigs

Eisenhower had kept Macmillan fairly well appraised of his intentions towards Castro. After his visit to Washington in April 1960, Macmillan had reported back to Selwyn Lloyd how Eisenhower, speaking of Cuba, had 'said that the position there was becoming intolerable, but he realised the difficulties of *overt* action. . . .' Nevertheless, many Latin American countries had 'given the impression that they would be pleased if the United States took action against Castro . . .'.[75] With his bitter memories of Suez Macmillan's judgement at the time had been that Eisenhower would have been 'Less enterprising about this sort of operation than some of his advisers, since he has a highly developed moral sense about all this sort of thing . . .'. Therefore Macmillan had come away doubting (correctly) whether action was imminent, 'unless some dramatic change in the situation takes place'. Things had then gone from bad to worse, with Macmillan noting in his diary for 17 June that Castro was

confiscating all the American properties and threatening to seize the oil refineries, including that belonging to Shell. The

Americans are pained and uncertain. (What a pity they never understood 'Colonialism' and 'Imperialism' till too late!)[76]

On 12 July, a six-page letter came from him, setting out the whole background of the Castro take-over, and US attempts to come to terms with it. 'The critical element' now, said Eisenhower, was 'the degree to which Cuba has been handed over to the Soviet Union as an instrument with which to undermine our position in Latin America and the world . . .'. As there now seemed no chance of reforming Castro's attitude, 'we must rely, frankly, on creating conditions in which democratically minded and Western orientated Cubans can assert themselves and regain control of the Island's policies and destinies. . . .'[77] The letter had gone on to discuss economic measures to bring home to the Cuban people the cost of Castro's policies, by heavily cutting down, for instance, on the Cuban sugar quota; the letter had also contained broad hints, but nothing more, of eventual military action.

Macmillan had replied with a personal, sympathetic and rather 'hawkish' telegram: '. . . Castro is really the very devil. He is your Nasser, and of course with Cuba sitting right on your doorstep, the strategic implications are even more important than the economic. I fully understand your apprehension. . . .' Macmillan thought it would be legally difficult for Britain, in response to any specific US request, to compel British tanker owners in peacetime to cease carrying oil to Cuba. However, speaking in no uncertain terms, he continued, '. . . I feel sure Castro has to be got rid of, but it is a tricky operation for you to contrive, and I only hope you will succeed. . . .'[78] Three days later this was followed up with a more detailed and somewhat more cautious telegram, saying that he now had 'some doubts as to the success of the new policy';

furthermore everything I hear of the state of feeling in other Latin American countries confirms the importance of avoiding any action which might create the impression that the United States was actively intervening in Cuba. . . .

Macmillan went on to wonder whether it might not be wiser to let the counter-revolution in Cuba rise of its own accord. 'Or at least let them be very unobtrusively supported from the United States. . . .'[79]

On 8 August, Eisenhower replied thanking Macmillan for his general agreement and support and continuing:

> You ask quite understandably how we really mean to achieve our aim in unseating Castro and in replacing him by a more suitable regime. . . . we expect to move ahead with further economic measures designed to bring pressure on the Cuban economy. . . .[80]

This, in effect, appeared to be the last of the correspondence. As it turned out, the operation Eisenhower passed on to Kennedy would combine the worst of all worlds.

On 17 April of the following year, the landing on the Bay of Pigs took place. It was based on a plan laid down under the Eisenhower administration in March 1960, and drawn up by the CIA in the utmost secrecy. Both as a military commander and as President, Eisenhower had a habit of drawing up plans covering a wide range of contingencies, without necessarily implementing them. Macmillan would not have been informed of these plans in advance, nor would he have expected to be. Thus the operation against Castro was pigeonholed until the installation of President Kennedy. As of March 1961, it called for military landing of a brigade of anti-Castro dissidents who had found refuge in Florida and the neighbouring states, trained covertly by the CIA. The force numbered fifteen hundred men and was equipped with tanks and supported by its own air force; or should have been. But, on pressure from outside, Kennedy suffered a major loss of nerve and refused to permit the use of Cuban-manned strike planes – until it was too late. He then rejected the CIA's pleas to use US planes to salvage the disaster. The informed view now is that the Bay of Pigs landing would probably have succeeded, if Kennedy had supported it. The day after the landings, 18 April, Macmillan noted in his diary:

> . . . I have not great hopes of their winning and if they fail it will be a blow to American prestige. . . .
> *19 April:* . . . the counter-revolution doesn't look too good. . . .
> *20 April:* . . . Cuba is over. . . .[81]

The Bay of Pigs was probably the worst blunder of Kennedy's career.[82] From it was to flow many evils, among them perhaps

Khrushchev's preparedness to confront Kennedy over Berlin, and to risk nuclear war over Cuba the following year.

Privately Macmillan was disappointed. He had not been consulted or informed, as he might have hoped to have been by his friend Ike, at least before the operation became imminent. He felt, hawkishly, that Kennedy should have committed US air power to support the landings, rather than let it fail; or Kennedy should not have accepted the CIA plan in the first place.[83] But, though shaken, Macmillan was strongly impressed by the way the young President (at least publicly) shouldered all the blame. He assured him, jokingly, at the time, 'I'm not going to attack you in the United Nations!'[84] and, when they next met, quipped that he could have performed 'my ultimate service to mankind if those Cubans would only have shot down my plane;[85] then you could have had your little invasion!'[86] Beneath the jokes, Macmillan showed himself 100 per cent loyal in support of a colleague in adversity.

Kennedy in Europe

Barely had the dust settled on the Bay of Pigs than de Gaulle faced a revolt by four rebel generals in Algeria.[87] But it was all over in four days, presenting de Gaulle with – as Macmillan noted in his diary – 'a complete and overwhelming triumph. He is now supreme. . . .'[88] Almost simultaneously France exploded her fourth atomic bomb in the Algerian desert. Though the synchronisation was accidental, its historic significance was not lost on Macmillan. The contrast between the fortunes of Kennedy and de Gaulle at the end of April 1961 was pointed, and Macmillan was left highly sceptical whether de Gaulle's new supremacy would be 'a good augury for the Grand Design'.[89]

On 31 May Paris welcomed the Kennedys, and – predictably – Jackie Kennedy stole the heart of Paris. The youthfulness and dashing good looks of the couple were paraded against a series of dazzling sets – the Hall of Mirrors at Versailles, the *grands salons* of the Elysées, and Paris in springtime. Macmillan could not help being a little disappointed that, amid all the razzmatazz of Paris, 'the time given to serious discussion was not very considerable.'[90] Nevertheless, it was clear that Kennedy 'played up loyally'; had pleaded for Britain's entry to the EEC as a factor to increase

Western stability; and had in fact done 'everything I had asked him to do . . . with the exception of the actual delivery of nuclear information on nuclear weapons . . .'.

It was, however (and especially from de Gaulle's point of view), an exception of prime importance. This was reflected in a key exchange of letters between Kennedy and Macmillan not mentioned in the Macmillan memoirs. Following up strongly on the doubts Macmillan had expressed in Washington, Kennedy wrote on 8 May:

> After careful review of the problem, I have come to the conclusion that it would be undesirable to assist France's efforts to create a nuclear weapons capability. I am most anxious that no erroneous impressions get abroad regarding future US policy in this respect, lest they create unwarranted French expectations and serious divisions in NATO.
>
> If we were to help France acquire a nuclear weapons capability, this could not fail to have a major effect on German attitudes. . . .[91]

As one of a number of sops to de Gaulle, Kennedy suggested that more US and UK nuclear forces might be committed to NATO command in Europe. On 15 May, Macmillan wrote back to the effect that he was very sceptical about this last proposition, or of 'giving SACEUR [Supreme Allied Commander in Europe] a strategic nuclear force of his own'. He agreed that the nuclear question was 'the most difficult part of the French problem', and that perhaps:

> The only alternative is to find some means of persuading de Gaulle to forgo his ambitions for complete independence in this field – and thus discourage other countries [i.e. West Germany] from pressing for this. In my judgment this might be done by giving him a formula about consultation and control which would satisfy his honour and in which he could join. . . .[92]

Later that summer Kennedy endeavoured to sweeten the pill by licensing to the French American information on strike aircraft. However, he was adamant that this foreshadowed no change in 'basic policy' regarding the French nuclear programme: 'We continue to feel that assistance for either of the key components of the French program – warheads or ballistic missiles – would be undesirable for the reasons indicated in my letter to you of May 8.'[93] This Anglo-Saxon exchange certainly allowed no suggestion of treating France as an equal partner, as far as nuclear weaponry was concerned, and in it would reside the seeds of de Gaulle's rejection of Macmillan's overture to join the EEC – or at least his excuse for so doing. At the end of their talks in Paris, de Gaulle had little encouraging to say to Kennedy about Macmillan's prospects for getting into Europe.

The contrast between the incandescent triumph of Paris and what Kennedy now encountered in his first meeting with Khrushchev could hardly have been more dramatic. The grey and rainy weather as Air Force One touched down in Vienna was symbolic. Throughout the two days of discussion, Khrushchev showed himself at his coarsest and most blustering, his contempt for Kennedy's recent Cuban débâcle implicit. Neither the charm of Jacqueline Kennedy, nor the Vienna Ballet dancing amid the glories of the Schönbrunn Palace could make any impact. Tough, cynical and ruthless, Khrushchev danced rings around the young man inexperienced in diplomacy. Rashly Kennedy allowed himself to be drawn into a discussion on Marxism, for which he was ill prepared. When Kennedy referred to the danger of 'miscalculation' triggering off a nuclear war, Khrushchev flew into one of his rages such as Macmillan had been subjected to in Russia two years previously.

On the nuclear test ban, Kennedy got nowhere, but it was on Berlin that Khrushchev was toughest and most menacing. A rearmed West Germany signified the threat of a third world war; whatever the West did, he intended to sign a peace treaty with East Germany by December. And that would be the end of American rights in Berlin. Kennedy hit back; Berlin was a vital concern of the US; she was not there on anyone's sufferance; she had fought her way there, and her continuing presence rested on contractual rights. Khrushchev replied that if the US wanted to go to war over Berlin, 'that is your problem.' Kennedy said, 'It is you, and not I, who wants to force a change.' Khrushchev repeated that his decision was irrevocable. Kennedy snapped, 'It's going to be a cold winter,' turned on his heel and walked out. To his entourage, Kennedy confided that it was the hardest work he could ever remember; in his political experience he had usually found that some compromise could be reached, but with Khrushchev there was no 'area of accommodation'.[94]

When the Kennedys arrived in London on 4 June, Macmillan noted that the crowds were not quite as large as they had been for Eisenhower in 1959, but there was no mistaking the warmth – mingled with a curiosity to set eyes on this glamorous young couple who were now so much at the focus of world news. The President made a brave show of being 'in good form', but Macmillan was at once aware how deeply troubled Kennedy was by his savage mauling in Vienna. He was also suffering acute pain from his chronic back trouble. For the first working day a formal session had been arranged, replete with all the usual advisers sitting opposite each other 'like a set of boxers', as Macmillan described it: 'These sort of meetings are the most boring in the world.. . .' With his usual acute sensitivity to mood, Macmillan immediately perceived that this was not what a tense and fatigued Kennedy wanted:

So I said, 'Mr President, you have had a tiring day, don't let's have this. . . . Why not come up to my room and we will have a little chat?' He seemed rather relieved, and he came up at about half past eleven, and we sat down till about three in the afternoon.[95] I gave him some sandwiches and whisky, and that was all. He just talked. . . .[96]

For the first time together, Kennedy really let his hair down. Macmillan observed at the time how 'surprised' he had been:

by the almost brutal frankness of the Soviet leader. The Russians are (or affect to be) 'on the top of the world'. They are now no longer frightened of aggression. They have at least as powerful nuclear forces as the West. They have interior lines. They have a buoyant economy and will soon outmatch Capitalist society in the race for materialist wealth. It follows they will make no concessions. . . .[97]

He found Kennedy 'rather stunned – baffled would perhaps be fairer' and 'impressed and shocked'.

In a long letter to the Queen some months later, Macmillan explained: 'the President was completely overwhelmed by the ruthlessness and barbarity of the Russian Premier. It reminded me in a way of Lord Halifax or Mr Neville Chamberlain trying to hold a conversation with Herr Hitler. . . .' He thought that, for the first time in his life, Kennedy had 'met a man who was completely impervious to his charm'.[98]

Macmillan tried to give Kennedy heart by being both sympathetic and light-hearted. When Kennedy added a complaint about the way the press had treated himself and Jackie during the Vienna interlude, exclaiming, 'How would you react, if somebody should say "Lady Dorothy is a drunk!"?' Macmillan's answer was 'I would reply, "You should have seen her mother!"'[99] But, once again, he was filled with admiration at the courage the new President displayed in shouldering all the blame, recognising his mistakes and facing up to unpleasant realities. Macmillan was also more than gratified at the way Kennedy had now expressly sought out his counsel, and consolation.

Much more important, however, was his appreciation of a significant turn in his friendship with Kennedy, whose visit he rated:

a success from the point of view of our personal relations. He was kind, intelligent and *very* friendly. I find my friendship beginning to grow into something like that which I got with Eisenhower after a few months at Algiers. . . . Kennedy, with an entirely different mental background, is quick, well-informed, subtle; but proceeds more by asking questions than by answering them. . . .[100]

Several years later, in one of his many letters to Jacqueline Kennedy after the assassination, Macmillan wrote:

. . . I shall never forget our talk alone (in London) when he was back from the first (and *bad*) visit to meet Khrushchev. He seemed to *trust* me – and (as you will know) for those of us who have had to play the so-called game of politics – national and international – this is something very rare but very precious. . . .[101]

On his return to America, Kennedy himself wrote to Macmillan

. . . I value our open and friendly conversations more and more. London felt near home to us all. . . . And so I am sorry to see that one or two crabbed minds have suggested that somehow, in

trying to get on better with de Gaulle America is getting on less well with England. It's not so, as we both know, and I'll find the chance to clear the point up soon.
    Sincerely,
    JFK

Underneath was scribbled in the President's own hand: 'Many, many thanks.'[102] The postscript spoke volumes. Some time later Kennedy apparently confided to Henry Brandon, the veteran Washington correspondent of the *Sunday Times*, 'I feel at home with Macmillan because I can share my loneliness with him. The others are all foreigners to me.'[103]

'The Usual Advisers, Ambassadors and Experts . . .'

The concern expressed by Kennedy about appearing to get on better with de Gaulle at the expense of the Special Relationship was by no means without point. After three encounters (and particularly after London), Macmillan had got to know something about the new Kennedy team. Writing to the Queen after his return from Washington in April Macmillan had observed how the new President had already 'surrounded himself with a large retinue of highly intelligent men – young and old. . . . There is a saying in Washington that "all the egg-heads are in one basket".'[104] Five months later he was following this up with a more considered view to the Queen, contrasting the new regime sharply with the 'constitutional monarch' style of government as practised by Eisenhower, in which (at least during the time of Dulles) he seldom interfered with the day-to-day running of the administration:

In President Kennedy you have a man of great charm, great energy, great intelligence and, I would judge, considerable caution. He does not say much, he asks many questions, and treads rather warily. He thinks all the time about politics. . . . He has surrounded himself with a team of extremely able young men,[105] largely drawn from university life. The Secretary of State is a professor with very little experience of anything except the academic world. . . .[106]

The result of this 'immense collection of egg-heads', so the recently elected Chancellor of Oxford University went on to note, was 'a considerable rivalry not only between them individually but collectively between them and the more solid figures in the Pentagon. . . .' This led, as Macmillan was beginning to discover, to one of the fundamental difficulties in dealing with Washington, which was 'not so much the duplicity but the duality of American policy as it is conducted through the strange complex of power that is distributed between the White House, the State Department and the Pentagon. . . .' It was a sagacious observation of perennial validity and as relevant to American Presidents in the 1980s as to the Kennedy era.

Kennedy's choice of Secretary of State, Dean Rusk, had more than a little in common with Selwyn Lloyd. An academic and a Rhodes Scholar, he was a quiet and reticent Southerner who never pushed himself, and had none of the colour of, say, Secretary of Defense Robert McNamara. This unobtrusive modesty often did not impose itself either on Congress, or on the rather uncoordinated State Department. He was not long on imaginative thought, and – though much respected by Kennedy for his good mind – was never one of the inner circle.

Rusk's period as a Rhodes Scholar had endowed him with a love for Oxford, but this had been overshadowed by some unpleasant experiences he had had with the British during the war, when serving in the Far East. He was left with a resentment of British arrogance, and was certainly no particular friend of the Special Relationship.[107] Under Rusk in the State Department, and with considerably more influence than they would have enjoyed with a more forceful Secretary of State, was a powerful lobby of 'Conceptualists', or 'Europeanists'. Under the vigorous and attractive George Ball, Francophiles like William Tyler and other such influential figures as Walt Rostow, Robert Bowie and McGeorge Bundy of the National Security Council hoped to achieve a withering away of the British nuclear deterrent and a downgrading of the Special Relationship.[108] Their aim was to place France and West Germany on a more equal footing with Britain. All this was to have potent repercussions in the final year of the Macmillan–Kennedy era.

A weighty counterbalance to any awkward or unfriendly lobby within the Kennedy administration was the advent of the 'two Davids' – David Ormsby-Gore (later Lord Harlech) in Washington, and David Bruce in London. At their very first meeting in Key West, the question had been raised as to who would succeed Harold Caccia, who was about to complete a distinguished term as Britain's Ambassador to the US. Kennedy was immediately (according to Macmillan) 'emphatic for David Gore. "He is my brother's most intimate friend" (and, of course, "my brother" is thought by many to be the Grey Eminence). . . .' The Hon. David Ormsby-Gore, MP, Eton and New College, had been a junior minister in the Foreign Office ever since Macmillan came to power; as brother of Maurice Macmillan's wife, Katie, and further linked through marriage to Dorothy Macmillan's side of the family, his appointment then had provided additional fuel for the charges of nepotism. Coming from a family with more than a streak of Welsh eccentricity, David Ormsby-Gore shared with Jack Kennedy a rather special and engaging quality, most endearing to his vast circle of friends; in his many enthusiasms he appeared never entirely to have grown up. But beneath an exterior of genuine, rather than cultivated bohemianism, coupled with the kind of toothiness that Americans tend to associate with upper-class vapidity in a Briton, there lay an impressive and deadly serious intellect, as well as considerable toughness. Exactly Jack Kennedy's contemporary, they had become friends in London in 1938. The friendship had been cemented by 'Kick' Kennedy marrying Lord Hartington, a cousin of Ormsby-Gore, and later becoming godmother to David's eldest child.

Macmillan had no hesitation in acceding to Kennedy's wish:

> You see, the President had three lives; he had his smart life, dancing with people not in the political world at all, smart people, till four in the morning; then he had his highbrow life, which meant going to some great pundit (like Professor Ayer), and discussing his philosophy; and then he had his political life. And David belonged to all three. . . . that was unusual in an Ambassador (well, what is diplomacy?). . . .[109]

As things turned out, among Macmillan's many inspired appointments, he probably never made a better one, and equally Britain was probably never more successfully represented in Washington.

Ormsby-Gore's privileged entrée to the White House soon became the (sometimes acute) envy of his fellow envoys; while it even caused some resentment with the self-effacing Dean Rusk, who occasionally felt he was being bypassed in the channels of communication between Kennedy and Macmillan.

In London, Ormsby-Gore was admirably well matched by the other David, Ambassador David Bruce. A wealthy man of great taste, charm, intellect and wit, Bruce was also a skilled and experienced professional, having been Ambassador in Paris (1959–62) and Bonn (1957–59). Drafted in a literary style rare to the State Department, his despatches were a delight to President Kennedy, for whose eyes they were generally intended, and they showed considerable insight into, and sympathy for, Macmillan. 'I am neither an intimate nor a friend of the PM,' he wrote apologetically after several months en poste; but he then continued:

> Few apparently are. His play, to use a gambling expression, is close; and his inmost thoughts are seldom open to penetration. He is a political animal, shrewd, subtle in maneuver, undisputed master in his cabinet house. . . .
>
> At times he gives the impression of being shot through with Victorian languor. It would be a mistake to infer from this that he is lacking in force or decisiveness, as it would be to deduce from what is called his 'Balliol Shuffle' that he is not capable of swift action. . . .
>
> . . . He has charm, politeness, dry humour, self-assurance, a vivid sense of history, dignity and character. To what extent he would bend conviction to comport with expediency one cannot say. . . . Realizing that a revival of the classical balance of power in Europe with Great Britain weighing the scales is no longer possible, my guess is that he will go far to suit otherwise discordant notes to the US President's harmony. . . .[110]

David Ormsby-Gore and David Bruce thus provided the third and fourth sides in the very remarkable new rectangle of the Special Relationship, with Kennedy and Macmillan at each end.

Chapter Eleven

Facing Up to Khrushchev and De Gaulle
October 1961–October 1962

*We have not forgotten the lessons learned so painfully in the thirties
and we are not prepared to accept acts of force. . . . This is an
issue on which the peoples of the Western World are resolute.*

(*HM*, Pointing the Way*)*

*. . . if Hitler had danced in London we'd have had no trouble
with de Gaulle. . . .*

(*HM, 20 October 1978*)

After Kennedy's meeting in Vienna, Macmillan passed the next weeks in some apprehension, wondering how the inevitable first 'testing out' of the new President by Khrushchev would manifest itself; and wondering how his own freshly forged entente with Kennedy would handle a first trial by fire. During a bout of the Black Dog at the beginning of June, he gloomed in his diary: 'Will 1961 be the end? Who can tell? War in Laos and/or war over Berlin are both possible. . . .'[1] In Geneva, the Nuclear Test Conference seemed to be degenerating into 'a farce',[2] with the Russians becoming more and more aggressive. By 25 June, after a brief 'rest cure' that had not worked, a fresh fit of pessimism caused him to

> 'feel in my bones' that President Kennedy is going to fail to produce any real leadership. The American Press and public are beginning to feel the same. In a few weeks they may turn to us. We must be ready. Otherwise we may drift to disaster over Berlin – a terrible diplomatic defeat or (out of sheer incompetence) a nuclear war. . . .[3]

The following month, Macmillan's fears of a drift into war by error were given further impetus by an absurd, and bloody, conflict that had broken out in Tunisia: 'The French and Tunisians are at war in Bizerta – a terrifying example of the result of both sides bluffing and both bluffs being called! What an example and how easily it might be repeated in Berlin. . . .'[4] Meanwhile, speaking at a political rally in Wiltshire, he had taken a tough line – for Khrushchev's benefit. Western rights to be in Berlin 'cannot be in question', he declared: 'We have not forgotten the lessons learned so painfully in the thirties and we are not prepared to accept acts of force. . . . This is an issue on which the peoples of the Western World are resolute. It is a principle which they will defend. . . .' He was relieved, however, when Kennedy let it be known that he favoured an early 'negotiation' with the Russians. (Meanwhile Khrushchev had achieved yet another feat in space – Major Titov had circled the planet seventeen times; Macmillan thought it 'a

wonderful feat of science and technology, although . . . rather dull
for the man . . .'.[5]

Then, suddenly in the small hours of Sunday, 13 August, the
East Germans sealed off East Berlin, throwing up a monstrous wall
through the middle of the divided city. On the Soviet side, Germans
jumped from their windows to get to the West before guards
and bricklayers could brick up their windows. This brutal action
followed, as Macmillan recorded sardonically in his memoirs, 'a
record number of refugees leaving the Marxist Heaven of East
Germany for the Capitalist Hell (or at least Purgatory) of West
Berlin – 2,400 in a single day . . .'. The timing was good; most
Western leaders were away on vacation; the West Germans were
distracted by being in the middle of federal elections, while the CIA
appears to have been thoroughly taken by surprise.

Adenauer, pressed on by electoral considerations and by de
Gaulle, made belligerent noises; Mayor Willy Brandt condemned
the feebleness of the Western ripostes; other Germans spoke angrily
of a 'stab in the back'. From Paris de Gaulle was able to make more
useful mileage in his efforts to woo Adenauer by taking the toughest
possible line over Berlin – in implicit contrast to 'wobbly' Macmillan. He could point to the essential hypocrisy of Anglo-American
rhetoric about supporting German reunification, yet being ready to
accept her permanent division – as symbolised now by the Berlin
Wall. He could also maintain, then and later in his memoirs, the
(unprovable) thesis that Khrushchev was bluffing all the time on
Berlin. But, as Macmillan later noted acidly to Kennedy, it was all
very fine for de Gaulle to strike such a hawkish posture over Berlin
and 'to seem to contemplate war with equanimity';[6] neither he nor
Adenauer bore any of the real responsibility, and he would not be
called upon to pay the bill in the event of 'miscalculation'. (In fact,
as he foresaw, de Gaulle swiftly backed away.)[7]

As for Macmillan himself, when the crisis broke he was under
doctor's orders to get a rest. This meant taking a week's holiday
to shoot grouse at Bolton Abbey and Swinton, and to play golf
at Gleneagles. From the north, he wrote to his confidante, Ava
Waverley:

A tremendous lot of telephoning and telegraphing about the
'Berlin crisis'. Everyone (except my admirable colleague, the
Foreign Secy.) had been very excited. You can imagine what has

been coming hourly out of Washington. However, I hope we are through the first stage, when the most important thing is to do nothing foolish. . . .[8]

Among 'all the telephoning and telegraphing' was a message from Kennedy saying that he was reinforcing the Berlin garrison with a 'battle group', totalling 1500 men. In terms of what the Russians had on the ground,[9] Macmillan thought that 'militarily this is nonsense'. But he agreed to 'send in a few armoured cars, etc, as a gesture'. (De Gaulle, on the other hand and for all the brave talk, despatched neither an infantryman nor a tank.)[10] But Macmillan continued to fret that 'with both sides bluffing, disaster may come by mistake. . . .'

Nevertheless, he refused to abandon his short holiday in the north, though he predicted (correctly) that the British press would criticise him for being on holiday during the crisis, 'but actually this is nonsense'.[11] Meanwhile, however, through judicious unofficial guidance from the Elysée (and the usual spate of confidential leaks from Washington), the press had got wind of discord among the Allies. Playing golf with Dorothy at Gleneagles, Macmillan was beset by journalists and photographers popping out of every bunker. The game was made impossible, and Macmillan admitted to having 'rather lost my temper'. The result was an impromptu remark, on the eighteenth fairway, which he at once regretted, to the effect that the crisis had 'been got up by the press'. He added no less crossly: 'Nobody is going to fight about it.'[12] The next day the Sunday papers followed up with some acrid comment. But at a press conference judiciously held in the same relaxed surroundings of Gleneagles, Macmillan (pressed by Home) climbed down, showing himself once more at his most imperturbable, and putting the earlier golf-course outburst 'in its proper place'.[13]

In Washington, Arthur Schlesinger recalled it as being a time of 'strange, moody days'. A (British) poll had showed that 71 per cent of Americans were willing to fight for Berlin (though precisely what commitment this implied was not clear), against 46 per cent of the British – and 9 per cent of the French.[14] Macmillan's finger on the nation's pulse was accurate, reflecting as it did his own sentiments about the Germans. There were Americans who still thought, not for the first time, that Macmillan was 'soft' over Berlin; but Kennedy was coming to realise that Britain was in fact the only reliable ally the US had in this crisis. On 21 August, he asked Dean Rusk to draft a proposal to Khrushchev, in which he listed as objectives: 'Protect our support for the *idea* of self-determination, the *idea* of all-Germany, and the *fact* of viable, protected freedom in West Berlin. . . .'[15] The reunification of Germany he now accepted as an unrealistic negotiating objective. As Macmillan summarised it in his long letter to the Queen of 15 September 1961, just as he had cautioned Eisenhower against 'being what is called "tough" over Berlin', so he had

> warned President Kennedy that this policy would lead either to a nuclear war or to a great diplomatic defeat. If we continued to be 'tough' there was a risk of war. If we shrank back from a nuclear war at the last moment and made some kind of accommodation, the more we had talked up 'no surrender' the greater would be the loss of dignity when it was clear that some concessions must follow. I think President Kennedy has accepted this. . . .[16]

In personal terms, the Berlin Wall was a disappointing setback for Macmillan, representing as it did one more failure in his attempts for detente with Khrushchev.

The running crisis over Berlin was aggravated through 1961 by the rapid alternation with which Khrushchev blew hot and cold, and which kept the Western powers constantly on the defensive, reacting piecemeal to his changing whims and ploys. Macmillan could see how skilfully Khrushchev was seeking to frighten, and exploit divisions between the Western Allies. There were moments when Berlin looked infinitely dangerous. On 9 September, there were jittery messages about a possible Russian attempt to stop Western aircraft reaching the city. In his diary for that day, Macmillan recorded, 'I rather doubt.'[17] He was right; another anxious day passed without incident. A week later – it was also the day that the US resumed H-Bomb tests underground – he was reflecting on a solemn anniversary.

> *15 September:* 45 years ago, today, I was taking part in the September 15th attack by the Brigade of Guards in the Battle of the Somme. This was the first time that Tanks were used. I was

severely wounded – for the third time – and spent most [of] the last two years of the war in hospital.

Last night I went to dine with my oldest friend – Harry Crookshank – who was wounded in the same battle. He – alas – is very ill. We talked of old times mostly. He is wonderfully brave, but I fear he is a dying man.[18]

Such grim recollections never failed to concentrate his thoughts on the horrors of what a third world war would do to the Europe he loved.

In October 1961 there was another ugly alarm when American and Soviet tanks moved up to the border in Berlin, and faced each other muzzle to muzzle. Macmillan made apparent to Kennedy his disapproval of such brinkmanship. It reminded him of Dulles at his worst, and only served to heat up further the already explosive situation. By and large, Kennedy was increasingly coming round to share Macmillan's viewpoint.

Converted to Macmillan's thesis that, so long as he was kept talking, Khrushchev could be deflected from carrying out his threats, Kennedy initiated a series of his own proposals to Khrushchev on the threatened city. They included adjudication by the World Court, an all-Berlin Free City, a five-to-ten-year *modus vivendi*, the use of Berlin as a UN headquarters, and so on.[19] This 'battle of notes', as Macmillan dubbed it, in which Berlin was closely enmeshed with the wider issue of nuclear testing, 'went merrily on' through the autumn and winter of 1961.

'A Country House Party'

If the Berlin crisis had aligned Macmillan and Kennedy more closely together, it had also done the same for de Gaulle and Adenauer, while at the same time widening the gulf between them and *les Anglo-Saxons*.

At the end of November, when de Gaulle was due to come to England to continue talks on Berlin and the Common Market, he let it be known that – for reasons of his own – he would rather not stay at Chequers. He wanted to meet Macmillan as '*vieux copains*', and dropped strong hints that it would be agreeable to be invited to Birch Grove. Macmillan's deduction was that de Gaulle was seeking the informality that Birch Grove would impose advisedly so that nothing detailed and comprehensive could emerge.

Whatever the motive, Macmillan found it flattering, but 'inconvenient'. The normally nonchalant Dorothy was thrown into a major spin. Gravest of all was the security problem, which, though later to become a grim everyday fact of life for Western leaders, was unheard of in Macmillan's Britain of 1961, and assuring the safety of de Gaulle's life in rural Sussex presented a considerable headache.

As Macmillan tells the story, first Dorothy came to him on the night before de Gaulle's arrival, 'in a state of uneasy concern':

'I have been rung up,' she declared, 'by a young man from the Foreign Office with a short black coat and fancy pants.' 'How on earth can you tell what he wore?' I asked. 'Oh,' she said, 'he spoke like it.' 'Well, what did he say?' My wife explained that what he said in a high plaintive voice was this: 'Lady Dorothy, what are we going to do about the General's blood?' Faced with this unexpected problem, I said, 'I think you had better tell him we will ring him back'. . . .

It turned out that, in case of his being wounded in an assassination attempt (there had already been several), de Gaulle was required to carry with him a stock of transfusion blood – which had to be kept in a refrigerator. Approached by Dorothy, Mrs Bell, the family cook, retorted that there was no room in the kitchen fridge; 'it's full of haddock and all sorts of things for tomorrow.' So an additional fridge was obtained, and set up in solitary grandeur in the squash court, like 'an altar to Mithras'.

Meanwhile, French and British police with dogs swarmed in the gardens and surrounding woods; and Macmillan recorded: '(One Alsatian happily bit the *Daily Mail* man in the behind.) Altogether a most enjoyable show.'[20] Then, during the first morning of talks, a pontification by de Gaulle on the world situation and American influence was suddenly interrupted by loud knocks on the library door. Macmillan sent de Zulueta to deal with it:

'As I was saying when I was interrupted,' said the General somewhat nettled, 'we must take great precautions to preserve Europe from this dangerous predominance.'

Now came more knocks, more and more insistent. Thinking

the house might well be on fire, or some murderous attack about to take place, I went out to find our head keeper, Mr. Blake, calm, respectful but indignant. 'What has happened?' I asked. 'Why, sir, these police, French, Sussex, London, they are all over the place with Alsatian dogs, walking through the woods and park and into the coverts. They have been all through Gitlands, Binghams, Wickens, and they are now into Wheelers. We are going to shoot on Monday, and there won't be a bird in any of them. This has got to stop, sir.' I remonstrated, 'This is a great international occasion.' 'I don't know what it is, sir, but it has got to stop.' Happily it stopped the next day. With that true sense of the value of things that is the mark of a countryman, the keeper was right. . . .

It would have been a good shoot – and 'the meeting led to nothing' recorded Macmillan. When later he recounted to his guest the interlude with the gamekeeper which Macmillan thought highly diverting, de Gaulle assumed his most imperial expression and 'did not seem amused'. Beneath all the hilarity, however, there had been some serious and forthright talk, little of which made happy listening for Macmillan.

Over Berlin, de Gaulle remarked to his host that, even more than Britain or the USA, France was determined to see Germany firmly tied to the West. This would be endangered if the West were to make concessions to the Soviets at Germany's expense, and France was determined to prove Germany's one good friend. The Russians had made no concessions to the Western point of view, and therefore the time to negotiate had not yet come. Macmillan queried how one could be sure what the Soviet attitude was if one was not prepared to discuss the matter with them. Throughout the weekend de Gaulle remained unbending.

Afterwards, Macmillan reflected with more than a little irritation:

He does not want war. He does not believe there will be war. But he wants to pretend to the French and the Germans that *he* (de Gaulle) is the strong, loyal man. He will not 'do a Munich'. But he only dares take this line, devoutly praying that the British and Americans will get him out. He readily admitted this to me. . . . If de Gaulle thought there was a real danger of war, he would be in a panic. . . .[21]

When Macmillan relayed all this to Washington, Kennedy was infuriated by the cynicism of de Gaulle, who, for all his professed support for Adenauer, had already recognised the Oder–Neisse frontier, shied away from using force to defend Berlin, and nursed dreams of an eventual deal with Russia – at Germany's expense.

De Gaulle was no more conciliatory over the Common Market. The British government was now fully committed to joining the EEC, but the possibility of a French veto was still a huge obstacle to overcome. On the second day of their conversations at Birch Grove, Macmillan had told de Gaulle that he would like to 'speak quite frankly' to him. 'European civilisation', he declared, 'was what we must at all costs preserve. It has survived for 3000 years, but it was menaced from all quarters, Africans, Asians and Communists, and, in a quite different way, even by our Atlantic friends. . . .' He then went on to warn de Gaulle with some force:

> that this was a turning point in history and for Europe. If the United Kingdom could not enter the EEC in 1962, the chance would not recur. The circumstances were uniquely favourable; the President was in power in France; Dr. Adenauer had been re-elected in Germany for a further period, and he, the Prime Minister, was in power in the United Kingdom. In a manner of speaking, they were men of destiny. . . .

If agreement could not be reached 'over a few thousand tons of wheat, people would think that the real cause of failure was that the United Kingdom was not wanted in Europe. Her Majesty's Government would then be forced to set out on another course, which meant turning away from Europe. . . .' In Dullesian language, Macmillan was confronting de Gaulle with the prospects of an 'agonising reappraisal' by the British, who would not 'agree to go on paying vast sums of money, amounting next year to something like £100 million, to keep British troops in Europe . . .'. If de Gaulle's idea 'was to set up a new Empire of Charlemagne, obviously it must defend itself'. Here was a thinly veiled reference to British support for France in two world wars: 'The United Kingdom could not be called upon to help only when times were bad. . . .' Macmillan could not say what course the United Kingdom might then follow, but 'History would regard it as a repetition of the story of the city states of Greece which could not unite or could only unite occasionally as at Marathon. The dream of French and British leadership of Europe would be gone for ever. . . .'[22]

In reply, de Gaulle admitted that he was 'very impressed by what the Prime Minister had said'. He agreed that 'Europe must be made to live' and then went on, somewhat dismissively, 'As for the British, they had a long history and they were also Europeans in their own special way. . . . Canada, Australia and New Zealand may have been Europeans once but they were no longer Europeans in the same sense as the British. . . .' But France 'did not want to change the character of their Europe, and therefore did not want [the British] to bring their great escort in with them. India and African countries had no part in Europe.' He feared that, if Europe let the rest of the world in, 'they would lose themselves; Europe would have been drowned in the Atlantic. . . .' He cautioned against trying to settle things too quickly. To this Macmillan declared that this was where he differed with his guest; 'the problem must be settled next year or the courses of the two groups would begin to diverge.' 'The President should understand that, if present negotiations fail, a reaction against Europe would set in in the United Kingdom, and all possibility of agreement might be lost for a generation.' De Gaulle had ended that particular conversation on a studiously vague note, saying that he 'believed that all the problems would be successfully solved'.

This was all plain speaking, and set the philosophic gap between the two statesmen as clearly as it was ever to be stated.

Yet Macmillan could not 'find myself able to resent the characteristic egotism of my old friend . . .'. As he had done so often in the Algiers of two decades previously, in the aftermath of the 'country house party', Macmillan stood back to take stock of de Gaulle's enigmatic personality:

The Emperor of the French (for he is now an almost complete autocrat, taking no notice of any advice and indeed receiving little of independent value) is older, more isolated, more sententious, and far more *royal*. . . . He is well informed, yet remote. His hatred of the 'Anglo-Americans' is as great as ever. While he has extraordinary dignity and charm, 'unbends' delightfully, is nice to servants and children and so forth, he does not apparently listen to argument. I mean this almost literally. Not only is he not convinced, he actually does not listen. He merely repeats over and over again what he has said before. And the doctrine – almost dogma – is based on intuition, not ratiocination. He talks of Europe, and means France.[23]

Again, as in wartime Algiers, his view of de Gaulle oscillated between admiration and extreme exasperation. There were times when Macmillan ranked de Gaulle with Churchill among the greatest men he had known. But, observing the curiously small size in *képis* worn by this unusually tall Frenchman, he would also note how Churchill, 'with that vast head of his, was constantly thinking forwards, as well as backwards', whereas the 'little pinhead' of de Gaulle 'could only look backwards – to Louis XIV'.[24] Macmillan frequently reflected on how deeply injured de Gaulle's deep national pride had been – and still was – by the humiliating events of 1940 onwards.

> Things would have been easier if Southern England had been occupied by the Nazis – if we'd had Lloyd George for Pétain, then we would have been equal. . . . that's why he found Adenauer, who'd also been occupied, an easier ally than me. . . . I may be cynical, but I fear it's true – if Hitler had danced in London we'd have had no trouble with de Gaulle. . . .[25]

He wrote in his diary at the time,

> The tragedy of it all is that we agree with de Gaulle on almost everything. We like the political Europe (*union des patries* or *union d'états*) that de Gaulle likes. We are anti-federalists; so is he. We are pragmatists in our economic planning; so is he. . . . We agree; but his pride, his inherited hatred of England (since Joan of Arc) . . . above all, his intense 'vanity' for France – she must dominate – make him half welcome, half repel us, with a strange 'love–hate' complex. Sometimes, when I am with him, I feel I have overcome it. But he goes back to his distrust and dislike, like a dog to his vomit.[26]

Megaton Nuclear Testing; Bermuda, December 1961

One of the most serious repercussions of the Berlin crisis was that the Russians decided to resume H-Bomb tests. What was clearly the first of a series was exploded in the atmosphere at the end of August, but it seemed probable that preparations for the tests had been under way since the end of the previous year. Macmillan was deeply disquieted. Powerful lobbies in the US, like the Joint Atomic Energy Committee of Congress, reckoned that the Russians were gaining an unassailable lead in nuclear weapons, and had also been cheating by exploding bombs in 'Big Holes' – or deep underground caverns. Sympathetic to the idea of a test ban for some years already, Kennedy, as a candidate in 1960, had pledged not to be the first to resume testing in the atmosphere, and not test underground at least until he had had time 'to exhaust all reasonable opportunities'[27] for agreement. Kennedy described the Soviet decision as 'primarily a form of atomic blackmail, designed to substitute terror for reason in the present international scene'.[28] Then, on 3 September, he and Macmillan despatched a joint appeal to Khrushchev proposing that the three powers should cease all atmospheric tests. Khrushchev's reply was to explode another bomb.

Kennedy now came under increasing pressure to respond in kind. On 6 September, Macmillan recorded glumly, 'The President gave in and has announced his decision to resume underground tests, *not*, repeat *not*, atmospheric tests. . . .'[29] Khrushchev followed by boasting (before the 22nd Party Congress) of a fifty, and even a one hundred, megaton bomb – a devastating weapon five thousand times as powerful as the original Hiroshima weapon that had killed 100,000 people. Between 1 September and 4 November 1961, the USSR carried out thirty major tests, nearly all in the atmosphere, and of a peculiarly 'dirty' kind. The climax of the test series came on 30 October with one of over fifty megatons, the most powerful ever. It had obviously required many months of detailed preparation. By this time, though there had been fewer Russian than Western tests since testing began, the Soviet Union had discharged more radioactive poison into the atmosphere than the US, Britain and France combined.[30]

Under constant barracking from the Labour benches, Macmillan declared that Britain would not restart her own tests, but would reserve her right to do so, if it seemed her security was at risk; but they would, if possible, be underground. Twenty-five years before Chernobyl, Macmillan called a meeting of experts to discuss plans for countering the threat of contamination from the vast Soviet explosions, which resulted in 'a complete scheme for dried milk for infants, if the iodine contamination from fall-out should become serious . . .'.[31] Meanwhile, Macmillan, too, was under mounting pressure from his nuclear technicians to arrange an underground test of the warhead designed for Skybolt. Privately, he wished he could 'find some way of seeing the President'; but decided that, under the circumstances, this might look 'panicky'.[32] A serious discussion would have to be deferred until the meeting already scheduled for mid-December, in Bermuda. He asked Kennedy to agree that experts on both sides might be present, to report jointly on what the proposed US tests would be designed to achieve.

Bermuda was the fourth meeting between Kennedy and Macmillan in less than a year. In effect, both leaders arrived pushed by their advisers in directions where they philosophically did not wish to go. On his side, Macmillan was being pressed to restart underground nuclear testing to try out the new warheads designed for Skybolt. This would require American collaboration, as the ideal testing sites lay in the great caverns many hundreds of feet beneath the Nevada desert. He himself, as he always had done and would continue to do, placed his highest priority on achieving at least a limited test ban, on nuclear explosions in the atmosphere.

Though Macmillan's latest proposals, in the autumn of October 1961, had been turned down – on the urging of the US Atomic Energy Commission – Kennedy thoroughly shared the same philosophic views as his British opposite number. One of his 'egg-heads', Science Adviser Jerome Wiesner, recalled first explaining to him, in his office in the White House one day, how radioactive particles could descend as fall-out on areas far removed from an explosion: '. . . I told him . . . that it was washed out of the clouds by the rain, and he said, looking out of the window, "You mean, it's in the rain out there?" – and I said, "Yes"; and he looked out the window, looked very sad, and didn't say a word. . . .'[33] Kennedy endorsed the strategy of his new Secretary of Defense, McNamara, which incorporated a switch from the 'massive retaliation' doctrine of Eisenhower to one of 'flexible response', with much heavier reliance on conventional forces. But, while he was sceptical about the value of tactical nuclear weapons, Kennedy was also determined to close the strategic missile gap.

Analysis of the new Soviet explosions (by an impartial panel of US scientists) concluded that important progress had been made, particularly in the development of larger weapons of low weight and high explosive content.[34] Kennedy was also warned by his experts of their suspicions that the Soviets might be on their way to developing anti-missile missiles (or ABMs) in space; which would dramatically alter the 'balance of terror'. On both scores, the US nuclear scientists could meet the threat only by reopening their own testing in the atmosphere. By the time of Bermuda, Kennedy himself had been brought round by this line of argument: 'If they [the Soviets] fooled us once,' he said, 'it's their fault. If they fool us twice, it's our fault.'[35] Eniwetok Atoll, where the first US H-Bomb tests had taken place, was now a United Nations Trust Territory – which ruled it out – and the only testing ground reckoned to be suitable was Christmas Island, a remote Pacific reef. It was a British territory. Headed by Glenn T. Seaborg, chairman of the US Atomic Energy Commission, the US negotiators at Bermuda proposed to 'parlay one for the other';[36] that is, the US would facilitate underground testing in Nevada for the British, in return for use of Christmas Island.

According to American sources, on this issue Kennedy was 'very, very vacillating'.[37] But, to Macmillan in Bermuda, he put a compelling case. In his turn, Macmillan resisted with an emotional eloquence that became fixed in the memories of the Americans who were present. He began by evoking the horror of a nuclear holocaust, and the awful prospects of an indefinite nuclear race. It was a 'rogue elephant' against which all must act. You and I, he said to Kennedy, 'could not sit in an ordinary little room four days before Christmas and talk about these terrible things without doing something about it'.[38] He recalled the great efforts that both the United States and Britain had made in the test ban talks. David Ormsby-Gore, for instance, had spent three years in Geneva, 'the dullest city in the world'.[39] And the talks had almost succeeded. Once again, Macmillan proposed a summit with Khrushchev, and a major push for disarmament – as well as a solution to Berlin; 'we might fail, but we would have lost only a few months'. Macmillan added that his reading of Russian literature, plus his own first-hand observations, inclined him to think they might come round; moreover, the nuclear effort was a terrible drain on Soviet resources. 'I made a tremendous appeal,' Macmillan recorded in his diaries, '. . . that we should make another effort – in spite of the Russian trickery and bad faith – to put a stop to all this folly. . . .'[40]

Kennedy was moved, but he had to face realities and rejected

Macmillan's summit proposal on the grounds that the Russians would only stall. Hints were dropped to the British scientists present to the effect that, by participating in the Christmas Island tests, they might pick up invaluable technical information that was otherwise still highly secret. Playing for extra time, Macmillan said he would have to refer the Christmas Island request back to his Cabinet for a final decision; but this, the Americans saw, was a technicality. The end result of Bermuda was a sad disappointment for Macmillan.

Nevertheless, neither allowed the grim substance of the talks, or disappointment with the results, to affect their personal relationship, which, remarked David Ormsby-Gore, 'blossomed very considerably during the course of that meeting, and after that it was almost like a family discussion when we all met . . .'. This was, so Ormsby-Gore reckoned, 'the first occasion on which they really sized each other up and decided that they very much liked each other's company. There was no doubt about it. . . .'[41] Macmillan himself found Kennedy (apart from worrying about 'Old Joe' Kennedy, who had just had a violent stroke):[42]

> *very* friendly and rather humble. He is courteous, amusing, and likes a joke or a neat turn of a phrase. He is *very* sensitive. He seemed particularly pleased by the present which I brought him (a copy of the William and Mary ink stand on the Cabinet table) and by Debo Devonshire's present (silver buttons – of the footmen's coats – with ducal coronet and crest).
>
> In health, I thought the President *not* in good shape. His back was hurting. He could not sit long without pain. . . .[43]

Macmillan observed that Kennedy's restlessness also had something to do with the set-up of the Conference. Once again neither felt comfortable surrounded by scientists pontificating in their own arcane language; once again, both were comfortable conversing to each other à deux. To lighten the proceedings at Bermuda, Macmillan took pleasure in twitting the scientists about the mischief their handiwork caused, and amused the Americans by imitating to perfection the Cockney accent of the eminent nuclear physicist, Sir William Penney. Macmillan, in deadly seriousness, had asked Penney how many of Khrushchev's hundred-megaton bombs it would take to destroy Britain completely: 'Five or six will knock us out,' came the reply; 'to be on the safe side, seven or eight' – then, without any change of tone, 'I'll have another gin-and-tonic, if you would be so kind!' The refrain – 'I'll 'ave another gin-and-tonic, if you would be so kind' – at Sir William's expense lent considerable light relief to the ensuing discussions on nuclear holocaust. There was probably never any better example of the Macmillan style of not having 'too rigid a distinction between the flippant and the serious'.

Following the Bermuda Conference, the Americans had also moved very close to the Macmillan position over Berlin. At Bermuda, Macmillan had 'got the feeling that the President is getting impatient with Adenauer and really angry with de Gaulle'.[44] In a long letter to Kennedy after the meeting, Macmillan reassured Kennedy by reminding him how Khrushchev had first announced his intention to sign a peace treaty with the East Germans as many months previously as November 1958, but had deferred it subsequent to Macmillan's visit to Russia the following February. Although he had resurrected the spectre after the summit débâcle of 1960, 'he is still showing some degree of moderation by refraining from implementing it even at the end of this year. . . . we have been given a breathing space. . . .'[45] Indeed, the red-letter month of December passed by without Khrushchev fulfilling his threats of signing his separate peace treaty with East Germany or of sealing off West Berlin. Apart from one brief crisis in February, when the Russians 'buzzed' Allied aircraft over the Berlin corridors, the situation in Berlin was to remain a stalemate throughout 1962, until it was eventually overtaken by the Cuban missile crisis in October.

As far as an agreement on nuclear testing went, it was certainly in a deadly serious and disappointed mood that Macmillan returned from Bermuda. In the *New York Times*, James Reston headlined his account, 'Success in Bermuda'.[46] This was not how Macmillan saw it; Seaborg of the US AEC reckoned that the British 'had been forced to bow to the determination of their more powerful ally', and had given the Americans virtually everything they had asked for.[47] Macmillan felt, rather despondently, that he had detected 'a marked contrast between President Kennedy "in action" on a specific problem (e.g. Congo, West Irian, Ghana), and his attitude to larger issues (the nuclear war, the struggle between East and West, Capitalism and Communism, etc). In the first, he is an extraordinarily quick and effective operator – a born "politician" (not in a pejorative sense). On the wider issues, he seems rather lost. . . .'[48]

After a Christmas (habitually a glum time for him anyway) which was plagued with a severe chill, depression and sombre thoughts, Macmillan 'pondered and brooded in bed and produced by last night a new plan for trying to get a general detente . . .'.[49] His 'plan' was developed in a long and personal letter to the President.[50] Capitalising on Kennedy's longing to make a breakthrough towards peace, its aim was to provide him with the essential ammunition. Macmillan followed up some of the emotive appeals he had made already at Bermuda, especially noting the irony that he should have spent Christmas Day pondering how to commend to his Cabinet the 'dedication' of Christmas Island for American purposes. To him, the nuclear race was 'at once so fantastic and retrograde, so sophisticated and so barbarous, as to be almost incredible'. Ultimately nuclear weapons turn up in the hands of all kinds of 'dictators, reactionaries, revolutionaries, madmen . . .'. 'Then, sooner or later, and certainly I think by the end of this century, either by error or folly or insanity, the great crime will be committed. . . .'

Thinking years ahead of his time, he wondered whether there was 'any real justification on technical grounds for believing that an effective anti-missile system could be developed . . .'. Although he felt 'morally bound' to support US requests, he pleaded for one more personal overture to Khrushchev, to agree to convert the direct Eighteen-Power Conference on Disarmament, which was due to meet in March, into one final try for a test-ban treaty leading on eventually to general disarmament. He ended his letter, 'on the whole, it is not the things one did in one's life that one regrets but rather the opportunities missed.'

As Arthur Schlesinger has it, Macmillan's letter received a 'dusty answer' in the State Department, with one high official declaring contemptuously, 'We can't let Macmillan practice emotional blackmail on us.'[51] The response was, however, much modified by Rusk and Kennedy, who now – though determined to go ahead with testing on Christmas Island – agreed to give Khrushchev until April to agree a comprehensive test-ban treaty; in which case the US would drop the tests. Khrushchev brusquely refused. On 25 April 1962, the US testing in the atmosphere began with the minimum of publicity, but nevertheless accompanied predictably by worldwide condemnation. The 'rogue elephant' dreaded by Macmillan was loose again. Without attempting to hide the bitterness of his disappointment, Macmillan declared to the Commons: 'We have done everything we possibly could. . . . We made proposal after proposal. We are discouraged but not defeated. . . .'[52] At least for the moment, it looked as if – once again – his efforts had come to nothing, and there was the added ignominy of the tests taking place on British territory.

Champs, June 1962

Meanwhile, the specific issue which found de Gaulle and Macmillan most at odds (and which therefore most threatened Britain's chances of joining the EEC) also happened to be nuclear weapons, coupled with de Gaulle's renewed call for a tripartite relationship which presumed parity with Britain as an independent nuclear power. Throughout much of 1962, as a result of de Gaulle's inscrutability, Macmillan was to be found once again vacillating between optimism and downright pessimism, but coming down – usually in the strictest privacy of his diaries – more and more on the side of the latter. In early June Macmillan and de Gaulle were due to meet at the Château de Champs in France, as a return engagement to the Birch Grove visit. On 19 May, a communication from the British Ambassador in Paris, Sir Pierson Dixon ('who has the most subtle mind in Whitehall'),[53] left him with the impression that de Gaulle 'has now definitely decided to exclude us [from the EEC]. . . . Others (and I am one) do not feel that de Gaulle has definitely made up his mind. I think he may still be torn between emotion and reason.'

About the same time, he was observed by a grandchild to be rereading *War and Peace*; when asked why he replied, only half-joking, 'It's instructive to see how another French general was defeated!'[54] Apart from outwitting or defeating de Gaulle, Macmillan reflected long on what *douceur* he could offer him to lubricate Britain's way in. As he noted on 14 May, 'the real crux of all this lies in the French nuclear ambitions';[55] but, under strong pressure from Kennedy, committed to preventing any further nuclear proliferation, Macmillan had very little room to manoeuvre here. In a letter to Home of 16 May, which showed the limitations of what Macmillan might be able to offer, he wrote:

It is possible that my talks with President de Gaulle at Champs on June 2 and 3 will represent the last opportunity of convincing the General. . . . I should like to be ready to speak about the possibilities, or impossibilities, of Anglo-French arrangements for joint targeting of nuclear forces in a hypothetical situation in which the United States might not be involved.[56]

He went on to mention the possibility of France being incorporated in the nuclear-armed Multi-Lateral Force, a baby of the American 'Europeanists' sold to Kennedy as a way out of Britain and France possessing their own independent nuclear deterrent, and which was to generate much heat at the Nassau Conference later in the year.

The position to be taken by Macmillan was further debated in a session at Chequers, from which the concerted view emerged of France being considered, in nuclear matters, as a rather tiresome junior partner to the US and UK, but who, somehow, would have to be accommodated.[57] A few days later, Dixon at a working supper with Macmillan and Home in London, on the eve of the Champs meeting, reported that de Gaulle had been severely shaken by a series of unrelated setbacks in France, including a savage last flare-up of OAS and FLN terrorist killings in Algeria. Macmillan recorded (perhaps not entirely without an element of wishful thinking):

So we *may* be approaching the end of the regime. On the other hand, no one man and no group of politicians wants to displace him with Algeria really unresolved. All this may make him more difficult to deal with. The General seems now to have turned definitely *against* Britain. Yet no one can be sure. The Ambassador feels that 'folie de grandeur' – the familiar disease of dictators – is beginning to be more marked. He simply cannot believe that any other view than his own could be arguable, much less tenable. He pontificates more and thinks less. . . .[58]

It was on this pessimistic note that Macmillan and Dorothy, accompanied by Philip de Zulueta, departed for the Château de Champs. The omens were not improved by a joint statement by Menzies of Australia and Marshall of New Zealand, criticising the EEC arrangements for replacing imperial preferences, a statement which was – naturally – heavily written up in the Beaverbrook press. At the same time, on the day the Champs talks began, *Le Monde* quoted Macmillan as having stated plainly that there would be no 'nuclear bargaining between Britain and France'.[59]

Macmillan arrived at Champs determined, however, not to be discountenanced. The Château was, he discovered, a lovely eighteenth-century house of modest size close to Paris, which had once belonged to Madame de Pompadour, with a wonderful garden by Lenôtre. Its classical style seemed admirably suited to de Gaulle's 'natural courtesy and old-world manners'. The visit began with a 'small family dinner', with de Gaulle playing the 'role of a stately monarch unbending a little to the representative of a once hostile but now friendly country'. After dinner there was a film in the pretty eighteenth-century dairy, which had been converted into a little theatre. It was all perfectly agreeable. In the course of their conversations, de Gaulle, having all but put the war in Algeria behind him,[60] struck Macmillan as being relaxed and confident. He repeated his preference for a Six without Britain; first, because British entry would entirely alter the character of the Community, in political as well as economic terms; and, secondly, because Britain was too tied to America.

De Gaulle mused that though perhaps it might be better for Britain not to join the Six, he wondered whether it would then still be possible to have a common policy on such matters as Berlin and defence. Berlin must clearly have been thrown up with a thought of its impact on his ally, Adenauer, and on defence de Gaulle then went on to press his suit for British support in developing France's nuclear missiles. The British official account has Macmillan simply saying, 'If there was an attack against Europe at some future date the United States might perhaps hesitate to use her nuclear forces. Some European deterrent was therefore perhaps necessary. . . .'[61] Given the importance of precision here, this seems unsatisfactorily vague, and was to become the source of one of the most crucial Anglo-French misunderstandings (or, at any rate, what de Gaulle's entourage subsequently claimed as a misunderstanding – or worse). The French Ambassador to London, de Courcel, who was present at Champs and was a meticulous diplomat, insisted ever afterwards that Macmillan *did* go so far as to make a direct offer of Franco-British nuclear collaboration as an implied *quid pro quo* for France supporting British EEC entry.[62]

On his side, however, Macmillan's recollection (as written in his memoirs ten years later) was that de Gaulle had 'seemed to understand that, while we might co-operate in some of the details which were within our own control, we could not part with those secrets which we only received from America as heirs of the original founders of nuclear science in the war . . .'. Here was a clear stumbling block to any ambition of de Gaulle's for an Anglo-French missile. In any case, Macmillan's letter to President Kennedy, reporting on the 'fairly satisfactory discussions' at Champs, stated baldly, 'We had no discussion about nuclear matters except that de Gaulle several times repeated his determination to secure a small deterrent force for France. . . . I did ask him if he would feel, as I did, that a tripartite meeting with you might be useful. But he did not seem particularly attracted by the idea. I think that he would like to see the organization of Europe proceed a stage further. . . .'[63]

After Champs, Macmillan returned home feeling 'reasonably satisfied'.[64] At least the General had not shown 'the rather brutal attitude which had been attributed to him, and predicted as likely . . .'. He was able to report to the Queen the encouraging belief that 'the danger of the French opposing a resolute veto to our application has now been avoided, at least for the time being.'[65] From the existing record it is difficult to see the grounds for Macmillan's optimism.

Macmillan's courtship of de Gaulle was not helped, however, by a keynote speech made by Kennedy's forthright Secretary of Defense, Robert McNamara, at Ann Arbor, Michigan, almost immediately after the Champs meeting. McNamara condemned all national nuclear forces (except those of the United States) as 'dangerous' and 'lacking in credibility'. Macmillan (who already regarded McNamara as one of the President's associates whom he did not entirely trust) castigated this at the time as a 'foolish speech' which had 'enraged the French . . . and put us in a difficulty, which the Opposition here will try to exploit . . .'. With more than usual irritation against his principal ally, Macmillan continued: 'In NATO, all the allies are angry with the American proposal that we should buy rockets to the tune of umpteen million dollars, the warheads to be under American control. This is not a European rocket. It is a racket of the American industry. . . .'[66] Macmillan's irritation flowed over in a sharp note to the Foreign Secretary, of 24 June 1962:

We have an independent deterrent and the French are going to get one; these are facts which the Americans cannot alter. There is therefore no point in their going on talking about them: the moment to take stock will come quite soon after our talks with the Six have ended . . . so I hope we can persuade Rusk, and even McNamara through him, to stop making speeches and launching plans for the time being. If the Americans have a 'grand design' for Europe, they are much more likely to achieve it if they talk less now. . . .[67]

Macmillan, however, was unsuccessful in this bid to muzzle the Americans. In a press conference of 27 June, Kennedy went so far as to be openly critical of de Gaulle's nuclear policy, describing it as 'unfriendly'. On 4 July, Independence Day, Kennedy marked it by proclaiming his own 'Grand Design' in which, mingling the 'Europeanist' theme, he spoke movingly of a 'Declaration of Interdependence', in which Europe and North America would stand as equal pillars holding up NATO. But de Gaulle had no intention of allowing independence to be confused with interdependence; without the one gift – nuclear know-how – which he required from America, and which could not be given him, any idea of Atlantic interdependence was meaningless to him. Nevertheless, the Americans went on pursuing their campaign for the 'non-dissemination of nuclear weapons' right through the autumn of 1962.

Chapter Twelve

Night of Long Knives
July 1962

I fear the truth is that after ten years of unparalleled prosperity, the people are bored. . . . we have made it possible for people to gratify their exasperation at minor difficulties by voting against the Government. In a word, we have made England safe for Liberalism!

(HM, Diaries, 25 March 1962)

A scrupulous man is impractical in politics.

(Anthony Trollope, Life of Cicero*)*

It was not only Khrushchev and de Gaulle who were worrying Macmillan in 1962. He had ended 1961 distinctly puzzled, and distressed, by the dramatic downturn both in the fortunes of his Party and in his own popularity since the electoral triumph of just two years previously.

Quintin Hailsham, with his experience as Chairman of the Party (1957–9) that had afforded him an acute ear for its moods, put the problem squarely to Macmillan in a memorandum of 2 October 1961. 'A feeling of fecklessness and disunity seems to be infecting the Party at the moment,' he wrote; 'and this is reflected in the curious, contradictory, irresponsible and I would say extremely dangerous state of public opinion. . . .' Hailsham defined the 'secret of parliamentary leadership' as contained in 'timing, conciliation, moderateness'.

> But the *Party* can only be moved by a sense of *direction*, a central theme – or rather a pattern of interlocking themes easily understood, acceptable but sufficiently controversial, with an underlying motif of the urgency of action by party workers to ensure success and ward off danger. . . .[1]

To anyone of Macmillan's sensitivity, the implied dissatisfaction with his leadership was unmistakable. The following month, at a meeting of the Tory Finance Committee, considerable backbench unease was expressed at the bad breach in the pay pause that had resulted from the Electricity Board settlement.

When Parliament was opened by the Queen on 31 October, Macmillan in his diaries recorded that it had been 'a bad day', and that he had made 'rather a mess of it'.[2] Opposition jeering had been led by his Labour *bête noire*, George Brown. Following the critical Finance Committee meeting of November, Macmillan noted down his awareness 'that after ten years the Conservative Party has got pretty restive . . .'.[3] A number of ministers had already had to be sacked for 'incompetence', and his diary indicated that several more dismissals were contemplated. Meanwhile, earlier that autumn he had persuaded poor Rab Butler to give up the chairmanship of the Party to 'a younger man'; that younger man turned out to be Iain Macleod, replaced in his controversial role as Colonial Secretary by Maudling. Macleod, reckoned Macmillan, was the embodiment of 'Progressive Toryism'.

Liberals and Labour; Strife Within the Tory Ranks

While the Liberals were making inroads in all directions, 1961 ended with the opinion polls showing that the Tories had fallen behind Labour for the first time in three years. Since his fighting speech at Scarborough in 1960, Gaitskell had quietly, and rather remarkably, beaten back the challenge to his leadership. He had begun to command more respect in the House (just as Macmillan's personal dominance was weakening) and morale on the Labour benches was recovering. Labour Party unity was also helped by the escalating verbal excesses of the CND movement, since Gaitskell's renunciation of it. CND had reached its climax with its Easter March of 100,000 in 1960. The following August, the venerable Bertrand Russell indicted Kennedy and Macmillan wildly as being 'much more wicked than Hitler . . . the wickedest people in the story of man . . .'.[4] At the 1961 CND rally, in the largest mass arrest in British history to date, 1314 marchers, including John Osborne and Vanessa Redgrave, joined Russell in the cells; but on 30 October Khrushchev obligingly detonated, in the atmosphere, the biggest explosion in history – a Soviet fifty-seven megaton bomb. December saw a major CND flop, with 6000 instead of an expected 50,000 turning out to picket nuclear airbases.

For Macmillan, the New Year of 1962 began on a note of fatigue; two years of trouble-shooting voyages (which had earned him the reputation of being 'the most travelled Prime Minister') had left him 'beginning to find that my constant journeys tired me more each time'. Indeed the numerous journeys recorded in these pages had clearly exacted a political as well as a physical penalty. Macmillan's preoccupation with summitry and the various threats to world peace meant that there was less time – and a decreasing amount of mental energy – to devote to domestic problems. In 1961 he had arguably thought more about the problems of Berlin than about the parochial problems of his constituents in Bromley. And Macmillan's foreign preoccupations were not as rewarding politically as his earlier efforts to restore the Special Relationship with President Eisenhower had been. Theoretically the application to join the Common Market could have provided the theme for which so many Conservatives yearned. But the threat of a French veto inhibited a wholehearted campaign in favour of entry. Meanwhile, the problems of Africa, which were beginning to take an increasing amount of his attention, were always likely to divide rather than unite the Conservative Party.

In Cabinet, there seemed to be more strife – real, or sometimes inflated by Macmillan's own imagination, which was, in itself, perhaps a symptom of fatigue. Early in January, he found his new Colonial Secretary, Maudling, being even 'more "African"' and 'more difficult and intransigent' than his predecessor, Macleod. First Maudling threatened resignation; then it looked, by instalments, as if Maudling, Macleod and Sandys – accompanied by Lord Perth and Hugh Fraser – might all flounce out in different directions. If they all went, feared Macmillan, 'it will be very hard (with all our other difficulties) to prevent the break-up of the Government. This is a very bad situation.'[5]

At about the same time, Macmillan thought that – in a protest at financial cuts to the school building programme – the Minister of Education, Eccles, and his Parliamentary Secretary (Kenneth Thompson) were 'clearly preparing for a dramatic exit from the Government, which Eccles is clever enough to see [is] in great difficulties and slowly breaking up. However, I don't think anyone, however disgruntled, will turn to him.'[6] This was an unfair misjudgement of Eccles, who had not the ambition, the capacity nor the backup to bring down the government, but it revealed once again that underlying insecurity of Macmillan's.

In February 1962 latent discontent within the Tory ranks actually burst into the open, for the first time, with an overt (albeit not very menacing) palace revolt: 'An agreeable, but somewhat crazy M.P. (Legge-Bourke, Ely) has made a speech, full of praise of me, but saying I should retire, exhausted, in favour of a younger P.M. . . .'[7]

The popular press gave the speech banner headlines, 'REVOLT AGAINST MACMILLAN'; and Harry Legge-Bourke, who was elected Chairman of the 1922 Committee in 1970, was no run-of-the-mill publicity-seeking rebel. Nor did many of his colleagues think he was 'somewhat crazy'. At a major Foreign Affairs debate two days later, Macmillan was relieved to be able to count a majority of 98, with Churchill making a show of leaning heavily on Macmillan's arm as they left the Chamber together. The unfortunate Legge-Bourke withdrew in some disarray; but the point had been made. Macmillan fell to reflecting on the impossibly exhausting burdens (which 'nowadays would astonish a trim City tycoon')[8] that fell upon the government, and wondering how long its individual members could take the strain.

On the economic front, January was 'a very disappointing month',[9] with a trade gap of £67 million and no increase in production. The Chancellor's spending estimates looked like ending up £111 million above his target. Thus, while the credit squeeze was hurting, and antagonism to the pay pause – in its inevitable unfairness to certain sections of the electorate – was swelling, none of it seemed to be working. Something was going to have to be done – but what? Then, in March, discontent erupted demonstrably in a series of by-elections. At both Lincoln and Blackpool, the Conservatives fared badly – in the latter only narrowly holding a safe seat against the Liberals. At Middlesbrough East, Labour won (as expected) but the Liberals moved into second place. The real shock came at Orpington, Kent, adjacent to and similar in its neat suburban prosperity to Macmillan's own constituency at Bromley, and regarded as one of the safest seats in the country. Just before polling day Macmillan had hoped that Orpington might be won by a small majority; but, in fact, a Tory majority of nearly 15,000 was turned into a loss to the Liberals (Eric Lubbock) of some 8000.

To Macmillan, this was 'an overwhelming defeat',[10] for Orpington was exactly the sort of seat which had flourished in the Macmillan era. There were some cynics who argued that the Liberal, Eric Lubbock, who had briefly served in the Welsh Guards, looked like the sort of candidate that the Conservatives should have put up. But Peter Goldman, one of the brightest of the exceptional team recruited by the Conservative Research Department after the war, fought an energetic and capable campaign. The sheer size of the swing discounted the notion that the result was in any way attributable to latent anti-Semitism in the electorate, but the fact that the Labour vote had all but disappeared was a further blow rather than a consolation for Macmillan. The emergence for the first time of tactical voting, with Labour voters deserting their own candidate to support the better-placed Liberal candidate, meant that scores of traditionally safe Conservative seats might now be at risk. Orpington, the most significant post-war by-election to date, issued the warning that the Conservative Party henceforth had to face a war on two fronts. In the privacy of his diaries, Macmillan admitted 'we have been swept off our feet by a *Liberal* revival. . . .'[11] A 'real' movement, he saw it as representing a revolt of the middle classes, hit by the credit squeeze and resenting the vastly improved conditions of the workers, while at the same time envious of the apparent prosperity of the 'rich' – whom they saw as living on expenses, capital gains or capital. In more personal terms, he also saw Orpington as denoting a victory for the right-wing Tory 'enemies of the leadership'; '. . . Lord Salisbury is working hard, with growing power. He genuinely believes that the loss of our Conservative voters to the Liberals is due to our having followed too "liberal" policies! He thinks *reaction* is the cure, and he regards me as the arch-enemy of reaction. . . .' Old battle lines were being redrawn.

Following Orpington, Macleod wrote Macmillan a ten-page assessment, in which he declared that 'Incomparably the leading factor was the dislike of the pay policy. . . .' He reckoned that voters felt that the government's emphasis was upon restraint when, rightly or wrongly, they were in the mood for expansion. He thought the pay pause had been particularly hard on groups like the nurses, that it had done great harm, and that it was hard to project the image that 'Conservatives care'. Meanwhile, in the press, cartoonists, leader-writers, columnists and gossip-writers all kept up an unremitting fire. Martin Redmayne, the Chief Whip, was however able to reassure Macmillan that the assault was 'concentrated not on him but on the need to revitalise the government with new and younger men . . .'.[12] At the end of 'a very rough ten days',[13] Macmillan confessed himself increasingly 'perplexed':

We must *not* abandon our economic policies. . . . But we must, even if we can 'expand' again with more vigour, try to impose our 'incomes policy'. Otherwise, we shall merely fall into another sterling crisis. . . . I fear the truth is that after ten years of unparalleled prosperity, the people are bored. . . . we have made it possible for people to gratify their exasperation at minor difficulties by voting against the Government. In a word, we have made England safe for Liberalism![14]

Although Orpington was to prove a false summer (the first of many) for the Liberals, Macmillan took the threat very seriously indeed. Bemoaning the fact, in April, that '. . . Conservative Party gets weaker and the Liberals eat into our position like rats . . .',[15] the following week he had to record another humiliating electoral reverse. This time, at Derby, the General Election Conservative vote of 20,000 in 1959 dwindled to 10,000 with their candidate coming third. 'On paper,' Macmillan reckoned, it looked as if the Conservatives might well emerge from the next General Election as the smallest party: '. . . I shall have led it to its greatest victory in 1959 and its greatest defeat in 1963 or 1964. It is very puzzling. . . .' He found himself recalling Browning, read at Summerfields school 'with the Reverend Henry Bowlby in "Sunday Private" in 1906', and the lines 'It was roses, roses all the way'; 'If I were not so old, I would be very cynical. But it is the young who are cynical – or at least believe themselves to be so. . . .'[16]

On 25 April Macmillan was only too pleased to take off on another trip (of a week) to the US. Before leaving he was greatly cheered up by the Foreign Secretary, recently returned from his home in the Border country. Macmillan asked him

> if there was any news. 'Yes – very bad news indeed.' 'Oh dear! What's happened?' 'There's no cover at all, owing to the late spring. The wild pheasants are nesting practically in the open, and as soon as an egg is laid it's taken by a crow or a jay!' I found this comforting.

For all the recent slings and arrows, it was evident that Macmillan had not entirely lost his sense of humour.

In Washington, Macmillan was further cheered up by some 'all-star entertainment', including Peter Sellers and the world's best jazz players, followed by a 'take off' of the two leaders ('a very American scene . . . a sort of hilarious school-boy crudity which was engaging . . .');[17] Kennedy, he noted, had gone out of his way 'to do me honour':

> He met me at the airport; he put on a very impressive guard of honour; he took me to the White House in his helicopter; he came

to dinner at the British Embassy on the Saturday night – all these are really a breach of protocol for anyone not a head of state. . . .[18]

As British visitors to the US not uncommonly find, Macmillan returned to London with his batteries greatly recharged. But at home he found that the local government elections, fought on national rather than municipal issues, had continued the run of political misfortune; the swing away from the Tories and towards the Liberals was 'spectacular'. Then, on 12 May, Macmillan was enraged to learn that the dockers had been given a wage increase of about 9 per cent, as against the pay-pause 'guiding light' of 2½ per cent. By capitulating to the bluster of Frank Cousins, the employers ('a very weak lot') had struck 'a *great* blow to our incomes policy, [which] makes it difficult to see where we go now . . .'.[19]

In the meantime, Selwyn Lloyd's second (and last) Budget in April had been no great success. The press found it feeble, and about the kindest thing they could say of it was to dub it the 'Sweets-and-Ice-Cream' Budget, because a 15 per cent tax had been walloped on to sweets and soft drinks (increasing the revenue by £40 million). There were minor adjustments to Purchase Tax rates; it was increased on clothing and furniture (which was not popular)and reduced on cosmetics. No major tax reliefs were offered, except for some trifling changes to the lower scales of 'unearned income', aimed at helping old people living on their investment dividends. The most striking measure was the introduction, by a Conservative government, of Capital Gains Tax (Macmillan would have preferred calling it 'Tax on Short-Term Speculative Profits'), which has stuck ever since. On the other hand, Macmillan was gratified to record that Selwyn Lloyd had been able to cut the 'crisis' bank rate of 7 per cent established the previous July to 5 per cent, and then (under constant pressure from Macmillan himself) to 4½ per cent by the end of April. Most of the financial journalists, he observed, had 'asked for an expansionist and reflationary Budget'.[20] He himself could barely be more than lukewarm at the mouse which the Chancellor and the Treasury officials had managed to produce between them, while – for the first time – a strongly critical line on Selwyn Lloyd's own performance appears in the diaries: '. . . Selwyn, though an admirable Minister and a splendid colleague, somehow fails to "put it across". He has not the appearance of having "Fire in his belly". . . .'[21]

The Night of Long Knives

On returning from his trip to Washington in May, Macmillan became increasingly dismayed at the lack of any new energetic or imaginative suggestions coming from the Treasury, or the Chancellor. On the government's incomes policy, the Cabinet as well as the Party in the House alike were 'all confused'.[22] Confusion was compounded by a collapse of prices on Wall Street, and the dissatisfaction which President Kennedy had voiced to Macmillan while in Washington over the existing international monetary system. Everybody seemed to expect the Prime Minister himself to produce some new idea out of the hat. The pay pause, with Selwyn Lloyd's barely incandescent 'guiding light', had not really worked; nor had his personality been able to sell it to the electorate. Daily it was becoming clearer to Macmillan that Selwyn Lloyd, like Heathcoat Amory before him, had now failed and would have to be replaced. But when, and by whom, and to implement what new measures?

These were the questions Macmillan addressed to the Cabinet in a twenty-page 'think-piece' on 28 May, and all through June he pondered these problems. He was not helped, as much as he had been in the past, by his own circle of personal advisers. The deft Freddy Bishop had been replaced by Tim Bligh, an ex-naval hero who tended to see everything in much more black-and-white terms. He was also perhaps missing the counsels of the former Chief Whip, Ted Heath, whose awareness of currents within the Party was not matched by his successor, Redmayne. Macmillan's Parliamentary Private Secretary Anthony Barber had also been replaced by a less stimulating successor, Knox Cunningham; and the advice he was receiving from his old friend, Roy Harrod, seemed increasingly Delphic. Harrod, he noted, on 12 June:

> thinks the economy is on the decline and should be expanded, but *without* increasing wages (which merely increases costs). There seemed no answer to *how* this was to be done, except by increasing enormously the salaries of dons and professors, whose wages do not enter into costs, since they produce nothing. . . .[23]

Macmillan's growing disenchantment with the eminent academic was barely disguised. In the midst of all this, at the beginning of the month Macmillan had had his discouraging talks with de Gaulle

339

at Champs, which offered no good omens for the British EEC application. Mid-June brought 'another *very* bad by-election in West Lothian, and our stock is low . . .'.[24] The Conservative candidate actually lost his deposit.

All these factors – coupled with his own growing personal unpopularity and physical fatigue – combined to cloud Macmillan's judgement at a critical juncture. At the same time, he was being subjected to maximum pressure by Party Chairman Iain Macleod to take vigorous and visible action.

By the summer of 1962, Macmillan reckoned that, like the human body, the British economy had developed a certain resistance to most medicines: 'Thus doubts arose both as to the diagnosis and the cure.' Accordingly, he sat down and drafted out his own paper on an incomes policy, the first instalment of which was delivered to the Cabinet on 20 June and discussed on the 22nd. It contained four main proposals. First, the 'guiding light' relating the rise in personal incomes to the increase in national wealth (or, currently, about 2½ per cent per annum) would have to be maintained. Secondly, a standing National Incomes Commission (later known as 'Nicky', as opposed to 'Neddy') was to be set up. This implied more central planning of the variety which Macmillan had expounded in *The Middle Way* in 1938; the crucial question, long to be debated, was what teeth it should be given to make itself effective, where the pay pause had failed. Thirdly, to protect the consumer against price rises, Macmillan wanted to abolish Resale Price Maintenance. (This measure was eventually passed just before the 1964 General Election and alienated many small shopkeepers.) Fourthly, Macmillan proposed the setting up of a Consumer's Council (finally established in 1975).

Macmillan felt satisfied by his paper; 'it is very bold.'[25] But Selwyn Lloyd's first reaction to it was 'rather chilly', while Macmillan himself was distinctly irked that it was he, the Prime Minister, who had had to do the Chancellor's work for him. Yet again (as over Central Africa), it ran counter to all his principles of delegation and non-interference, even though the best explanation of Selwyn Lloyd's original appointment as Chancellor of the Exchequer lay in Macmillan's hope that Selwyn would be a pliant master of the Treasury. It made him 'angry with the Treasury and the Chancellor for their delay and lack of initiative. A whole year gone, and then the P.M. has to do it himself, at the last minute. . . .'[26]

On 21 June, Rab Butler came to lunch. He was 'as always calm and helpful', and Macmillan found him thinking along the same lines, namely:

> that the present grave political position is due entirely to the bad handling of the economic problem (or rather its bad presentation) by the Chancellor of the Exchequer and the Treasury. He felt that drastic action was necessary to save the situation. This means the problem (an immense human and political problem) of replacing the Chancellor of the Exchequer.[27]

There then followed what Macmillan admitted to have been 'some of the most unhappy days of my whole administration'. He kept the decision to drop Selwyn Lloyd very close to his chest. Only Rab, and to a lesser extent Macleod, shared the secret. Macleod (who was himself an obvious candidate to replace Selwyn Lloyd) kept up a constant pressure on Macmillan for change; Rab, as everyone knew (and not least Macmillan), was not capable of keeping a secret for very long – to the constant delight of the political correspondents. Meanwhile, Macmillan's decision was complicated by the fact that, under mounting public pressure to inject some new, younger blood into the Cabinet, he was also contemplating, but *only* contemplating, a major reshuffle. Lords Kilmuir and Mills, both approaching seventy, had intimated several times that they would like to retire; John Maclay, the Secretary for Scotland whose wife had been very ill, and was not well himself, also wanted to go; Watkinson (Defence) had suggested that he would like to return to private business – and Macmillan had not been unduly impressed by his performance at the Ministry of Defence; Eccles wanted a change from Education (but what?); and Charles Hill, the old 'Radio Doctor' who was currently Minister of Housing, had perhaps also been around too long, and he too had let Macmillan know that he would be content to depart – in due course. Macmillan's inclination was to carry out such a major reshuffle, at his own timing, probably at the end of the summer of 1962.

His diaries reveal that by Sunday, 8 July, Macmillan had still only barely made up his mind about Selwyn Lloyd alone. Referring to the necessity of making 'the vital change at the Treasury', he noted, '. . . Selwyn – of whom I am very fond and who has been a true and loyal friend since I became P.M. – seems to me to have lost grip. He is, by nature, more of a staff officer than a commander. But lately, he seems hardly to function. . . .'[28] He had failed to 'put over' his policy; although 'whether anyone can, may be doubted. But whether at Foreign Office or at Treasury, Selwyn (although an excellent operator in many ways) has never spoken "as one with authority".'[29] He also recognised the signs of battle fatigue: 'he had had all these years at the FO, and Suez, then two years at the Treasury; nobody can stand it. . . . He was very good to start with, but then he lost his nerve; he was worn out, he was tired out, he was finished. . . .'[30] As Macmillan often pointed out subsequently, Foreign Secretaries or Chancellors, unlike company directors or academics, could not simply take off for six-month holidays, and then return. Equally, once announced, the retirement of a senior minister – unlike that of a captain of industry – could not be deferred to some future date; it had to take effect forthwith.

> if (as I must) I decide that he must go, *when* and *how*? It will be personally terrible and I shrink from it. It will be said to be a 'panic' measure. I will be accused of gross 'disloyalty'. Yet all those I trust – Alec Home, Norman Brook, Chief Whip – agree that it is right. I am to talk with him on Thursday, and try to give him fore-warning in a nice way, with a view to the changes (which should be on a large scale) being announced at the end of the Session (August 3rd).[31]

The actual replacement of Selwyn Lloyd alone he intended to announce the week after his 'talk' with him on Thursday, 12 July.

On that very day, however, his hand was forced. Anthony Royle,[32] then a backbencher who compiled a detailed log of events, noted that up till then, apart from speculation in the press over the previous two months, no rumours of a reshuffle had been heard in the lobbies of Westminster. Then, on the 11th, Rab lunched with Lord Rothermere and some of the leading executives of the *Daily Mail*. Among them was the paper's Lobby correspondent, Walter Terry.[33] The next day, under Terry's byline, there appeared a major 'scoop' authoritatively predicting the sacking of Lloyd and the promotion of Butler. Terry let it be known that he had received his information 'from the highest possible source'.[34] Swiftly the word ran round the lobbies of Westminster; 'Rab has blabbed.'[35] Macmillan was appalled. Coming on top of the cumulative effect of all the other stresses and pressures on him, the *Daily Mail* story had the effect of triggering off one of his rare losses of nerve, leading to a reflex reaction. One is tempted to recall other crisis moments when a swift decision had to be taken – Suez in November 1956, and possibly the Paris débâcle of May 1960. In July 1962 the consequence was a disastrous misjudgement.

The Thursday morning began with a thoroughly unhappy Cabinet, discussing Macmillan's incomes-policy paper. 'Selwyn took little part,' recorded Macmillan; 'Brooke (Chief Secretary) [at the Treasury] seemed embarrassed. . . .'[36] Still Macmillan gave no clue as to his intentions. In retrospect, it was clear that he was dreading the task that lay ahead; something for which, in his own innate shyness, he was singularly ill equipped. The 'fatal hour of 6pm', fixed for his interview with Lloyd, came: '. . . I did my best – but it was a terribly difficult and emotional scene. It lasted ¾ hour. . . .'[37] In a state of obvious nervous tension himself, Macmillan put all the familiar reasons, which he had rehearsed with Rab, for requiring a change of Chancellor; he then added that there was a danger of a split in the Cabinet, implying a conspiracy against himself.[38] He admitted that he did the hatchet work clumsily. Selwyn Lloyd took it all extremely badly. A lonely man, with no wife and no other life, he dismissed Macmillan's suggestion that he could make a new career in business ('about which he had often talked to me') and surprised him by refusing a peerage; he 'said he would stay in the House and support his financial policy (or, I suppose, criticise any deviation from it) . . .'. Later, Macmillan told Bligh 'to ring up Selwyn and say that in the emotion of our talk I had forgotten to offer him a C.H. Would he like it. . . ?'[39] Though Selwyn Lloyd accepted, this was clearly not much balm in the wound.

Leaving Admiralty House very distressed, Selwyn Lloyd, instead of returning home to his flat, 'went to the Smoking Room at the House of Commons where', according to Anthony Royle,

> in a perfectly honourable manner, he naturally told his friends of this shattering blow to him. It would perhaps have been wiser for him to have gone home. Within a very short space of time the news had gone round the House of Commons and filtered through to Fleet Street. . . .[40]

343

There was considerable personal sympathy for Selwyn Lloyd, loyal and solitary figure that he was. He then spoke to Nigel Birch, one of the three Treasury ministers who had resigned in 1958 over the 'little local difficulties', who remained an ardent deflationist and one of Macmillan's most openly bitter enemies. Together they drafted a letter of resignation for Selwyn Lloyd (which Macmillan regarded as 'rather stiff'),[41] asserting that his policies had 'been right and have had a considerable measure of success', as well as stressing his continuing anxiety that the growth of public expenditure 'should not outstrip our resources'.[42] Birch pushed Selwyn Lloyd into ensuring that his letter was published (unlike Thorneycroft's of four years previously), then despatched his own salvo to *The Times*:

> Sir
>
> For the second time the Prime Minister has got rid of a Chancellor of the Exchequer who tried to get expenditure under control.
>
> Once is more than enough.
>
> Yours truly,
> NIGEL BIRCH[43]

Later that same night, over dinner, Selwyn Lloyd poured out his heart to his friend John Hare,[44] the Minister of Labour who had strongly supported him over the pay pause. Hare was deeply shocked by the suddenness, and the manner, of Selwyn Lloyd's dismissal.

Early the following morning, Friday the 13th, Macmillan was rung by Alec Home, who relayed to him that Hare 'had reported to him that Selwyn had told him that he (Hare) ought to resign in sympathy at his rough treatment – or, at least, should demand that the policy (Pay Pause, etc) with which Hare had been so closely associated should not be abandoned . . .'.[45] The resignation of Hare, an influential man for whom Macmillan had great personal respect, would have been a major disaster, and could have brought down the government. So thought Macmillan anyway. Meanwhile a weekend of speculation in the press could have a catastrophic impact on sterling. 'All this confirmed in me the need for speed.' The speed was indecent; the whole reshuffle programme would now have to be accelerated into one day.

Could we complete a list and get it to the Queen for her signature by 6pm (for publication at 7pm)? This would stop intrigue in the House and the party. . . . If we could not act, the whole Government and Party might be split from top to bottom. . . .

In the end, things worked out pretty well. . . .[46]

It was not a view widely shared.

Lord Mills had already been dealt with on the Thursday afternoon, and had gone quietly. But on Friday the 13th, mayhem took place. According to Royle, after a banner headline in the *Evening Standard* at lunchtime, 'Ministers who later on during the afternoon were to be sacked were still continuing to dictate memoranda and hold meetings in Whitehall, quite clearly under the illusion that they were continuing safely in office. . . .'[47] That same afternoon there was a Garden Party at Buckingham Palace, attended by Macmillan, who only a few hours previously had informed the Queen of his changes. While surviving ministers strolled about the lawns eating cucumber sandwiches, newly appointed members of the government were arriving at another entrance to kiss hands.

Watkinson, the Minister of Defence, like Mills went quietly. So did Maclay, though the abruptness of his dismissal distressed some of his friends like Anthony Nutting. As for the Radio Doctor, 'poor Dr. Hill was very upset,' noted Macmillan, 'it was painful. But he is really *not* up to it. . . .'[48] In his memoirs, Hill repeated the unhappiness he had felt: 'the way a thing is done is much more important than what is actually done. . . .'[49] Kilmuir, an old friend, fellow Guardsman and neighbour who enjoyed the pomp-and-circumstance attached to the office of Lord Chancellor, never forgave Macmillan for the lack of dignity with which he had been despatched. In his own memoirs, Kilmuir claimed he had expected to go on until early 1963, and remarked of his dismissal:

. . . I got the impression that he was extremely alarmed about his own position, and was determined to eliminate any risk for himself by a massive change of government. It astonished me that a man who had kept his head under the most severe stresses and strains should lose both nerve and judgment in this way. . . .[50]

In later life, Macmillan – who had always sympathised with Kilmuir over the unhappiness of his domestic life (Lady Kilmuir had been living openly with a fellow peer, 'Buck' De la Warr, whom she subsequently married after Kilmuir's death) – bit back; 'He was always a "beta minus"; the stupidest Lord Chancellor ever . . . hopeless in Cabinet – that's why I got rid of him. . . .'[51]

Perhaps the most distressed of all, apart from Selwyn Lloyd, was David Eccles, the Minister of Education. Macmillan, who had not forgotten the contretemps over departmental cuts at the beginning of the year, asked Eccles if he would go back to the Board of Trade (whence he had been transferred to Education after the 1959 election). Eccles made it plain that the only job he would accept was Chancellor of the Exchequer. This was not on offer. In the distance of time, Macmillan recollected that at the interview Eccles had been 'very upset', but had 'over-played his hand' ('very vain . . . frightfully bumptious . . . very high opinion of himself . . .').[52] Macmillan's reason then for not offering Eccles the Treasury was that 'he did not have a good enough reputation in business'. Perhaps a more honest explanation would have been that Eccles would have been much more 'awkward' and independent-minded at No. 11 than Amory, Selwyn Lloyd, or Selwyn Lloyd's successor, Reginald Maudling, especially in view of the (unwarranted) suspicions aroused by him in January. According to the Macmillan diaries, Eccles 'preferred (not being Chancellor of the Exchequer) to go altogether (with a Peerage).[53] I was glad about this solution, which enabled me to bring in Sir E. Boyle (a *very* clever young man) to Education. . . .'[54]

Possibly Eccles, whose shrewd business acumen had enabled him to build up a personal fortune from nothing, would have made an energetic, and resourceful Chancellor. Butler, for one, 'questioned whether Eccles, whose intellect was valuable in any cabinet and who had rendered distinguished service in a variety of posts, could be spared . . .'.[55] The whole Eccles episode added yet another unhappy undertone to the 'Night of Long Knives'. Eccles had always venerated Macmillan as the politician he most admired, and in the days in Opposition they had stood shoulder to shoulder in the pro-European vanguard. Sadly, this veneration was not requited; the two stood somewhat in the same relationship that Macmillan had suffered with his old chief, Churchill. But Eccles had always regarded Macmillan as a friend who would not let him down. Like Kilmuir, Eccles was unforgiving; he had, he told his friends, been 'sacked with less notice than a housemaid'. In their valedictory audiences with the Queen, various of the sacked ministers made evident their extreme distress.

So Selwyn Lloyd was replaced by Reginald Maudling, brilliant, young, ambitious, with a (possibly exaggerated) reputation for laziness, but certainly more compliant than either Eccles or Macleod would have been. The indiscreet but indispensable Rab who had triggered it all off was promoted to be Deputy Prime Minister with the new and peculiar title of First Secretary of State; more important was the function given him, at last, to co-ordinate all government policy over the Central African Federation. To replace Rab at the Home Office came Henry Brooke, a former subordinate of his at the Treasury. Brooke was a decent man, but short on sensitivity, who was to prove very accident-prone over such forthcoming issues as the deportation to Nigeria of the dissident Chief Enahoro.[56] At Education Eccles gave way to Boyle; while 'another clever young man'[57] – Sir Keith Joseph – was introduced by Macmillan to take over from the Radio Doctor at Housing. Peter Thorneycroft was promoted to become Minister of Defence. William Deedes became Minister of Information, but – though he was a practising journalist of distinction* – the presentational problems remained unresolved. Kilmuir was replaced by Manningham-Buller (widely known as 'Bullying Manners'), the Attorney-General, who was not a noticeable improvement.

Of the Macmillan clan, Julian Amery was offered promotion from Secretary of State for Air (under the Minister of Defence) to Minister of Aviation, but was told rather brusquely that he could not be in the Cabinet and was given five minutes to reflect;[58] he observed that it seemed to be 'a poisoned chalice'[59] that he was being given, but accepted nonetheless. Still there was nothing for Maurice; and still there were as many Etonians in the Cabinet (ten out of twenty-one), although, if anything, it had moved marginally to the left. On the other hand, it had a happier, more cohesive look about it, and among the ten new faces some useful younger talent had been brought in at the intermediary level. But what in effect was to be his last team left the Prime Minister looking rather isolated, minus his old friends and seventeen years older than the average age. In twenty-four hours he had sacked one-third of

---

* He later became editor of the *Daily Telegraph*, and subsequently Lord Deedes.

his Cabinet, an act of carnage unprecedented in British political history.[60]

For Macmillan personally the whole 'Night of Long Knives' had been profoundly painful, and – worse than the preparation of any difficult speech – the brutal execution of so many old friends and colleagues had made him physically sick. The French Ambassadress, Martine de Courcel, vividly remembered his dining during the crisis and throwing her cuisine into consternation by asking weakly, 'May I just have a little cold chicken?'[61] On the Saturday (14 July) after it was all over, he took to his bed, writing up his diary at Birch Grove: 'in mother's old bedroom, looking out into the garden and the woods. It is all very peaceful. . . .' But he was left 'exhausted, almost shattered by the events of the last two days . . .'.[62] Only Dorothy was with him, and he was probably never more grateful for her company and comfort. Characteristically, she had been 'very robust' throughout the ordeal. On the eve of the purge, she had got stuck in theological conversation with the wife of a condemned minister, who had observed, 'Fortunately there's One above who knows all the answers'; 'Yes,' replied Dorothy absent-mindedly, 'Harold will be down shortly.'[63] Grace Thomson, wife of a Labour shadow minister,[64] recalled how, when she had commiserated at a fête after it was all over, 'It must be a nerve-racking time for you,' Dorothy had replied: 'Terrible . . . I can't keep my mind off those four grandchildren in the swimming pool. . . .' It was upon her kindly instinct for human feelings that he had been prompted to write long personal valedictory letters to the fallen without delay.

The 'Night of Long Knives' produced Jeremy Thorpe's best-known witticism (though it was somewhat to backfire on him in years to come): 'Greater love hath no man than he lay down his friends for his life.'[65] Reading the papers in bed at Birch Grove, Macmillan noted that the *Daily Mirror* on the Saturday (14 July) was '*very* violent against me. *Times* servile . . . *Sketch* puerile and vulgar . . .'.[66] The Sunday press the following day (15 July) was – as Harold Evans recorded – almost universally 'sour',[67] with almost the sole exception of William Rees-Mogg (then a dedicated Rab supporter). 'HIS OWN EXECUTIONER' was the headline in the *Sunday Telegraph*; 'MAC THE KNIFE' and 'FOR MAC THE BELL TOLLS' were other more obvious ones. Macmillan did his best to make light of the press reaction, writing a memorandum to Harold Evans:

. . . I see one of the papers has the headline 'Macmillan at crisis of his career – whole future staked'. . . . It is terribly good to be able to talk about staking one's future at the age of 68. The crisis of my career was a long time ago. We might have some fun about this. . . .[68]

What most seriously, and immediately, worried Macmillan was the effect on sterling if the idea got around that 'we are going to reverse engines and go in for a dangerously "expansionist" policy. . . .'[69] Accordingly he instructed Maudling forthwith to put out a statement reassuring foreign investors. He was also worried that there might be a rally of 'extreme restrictionists' to the sacked Chancellor, as presaged by Nigel Birch's bitter letter to *The Times*.

His fears were not groundless. Charles Hill, the sacked Radio Doctor, later warned Harold Evans that an effort had been made to persuade forty to fifty backbenchers to abstain on the Opposition's Censure motion, in the hopes that this would cause Macmillan to resign without actually bringing down the government. When the dejected Selwyn Lloyd first appeared to take his seat on the back-benches after the purge, he was cheered resoundingly by Tories, while Macmillan was greeted in chilly silence and to Opposition jeers. Lord Avon emerged from retirement to declare in a speech his opinion 'that Selwyn Lloyd has been harshly treated',[70] and the ghost of Selwyn Lloyd was to haunt Macmillan throughout the rest of his administration. Deprived of the solace of Chequers which Macmillan had generously accorded him throughout the past five years, the lonely man left behind him, in charge of the housekeepers, his labrador – his only companion. When the annual Cabinet photograph was next taken there, the unhappy dog wandered through the group of posing ministers, looking for his lost master, and a minister remarked wanly: 'That's Selwyn's dog. . . .'[71]

The considered view of Macmillan's colleagues was almost universally critical. At the time, Rab – whose indiscretion had played so important a part – was characteristically equivocal. Harold Evans recalled being telephoned by him shortly after the purge, in a Rab-like fashion, with a purpose that was not immediately apparent. 'I haven't been in it all,' Rab protested;

'I feel quite calm about it all because it *is* a revolution; I feel my neck all the time to see if it is still there.' But then, quickly, 'I do understand the Prime Minister's motives and I am behind him. I know why he got rid of Selwyn after six years. But it wasn't done properly. . . .'[73]

Much later, in his memoirs, Rab observed that 'the spilling of so much blood did serious damage to the Prime Minister's hitherto unbroken image of "unflappability".'[73] Few would disagree. Lord Hailsham considered that 'his handling was very inept, and left a nasty taste in the mouth,'[74] while Mrs Thatcher a few months after she had come to power herself and before her own 'Night of Long Knives', found Macmillan's brutality in 1962 out of character: 'No one who thought about individuals and was thinking about them at the time could do what he did then. . . .'[75] She was then a Parliamentary Secretary at the Ministry of Pensions, and the only explanation she could find was that the prostate illness, which laid Macmillan low the following year, was already beginning to affect him. Macmillan's successor, Home, also remained mystified as to why Macmillan had carried out quite so extensive a blood bath that July: 'why not wait till September before the Party Conference? Or he could have sent Selwyn to the Home Office. There was a bit of panic there, he reacted too strongly. . . .'[76] In common with most, Home felt that the 'Night of Long Knives' had constituted a watershed in Macmillan's fortunes.

If this was an exaggeration, it was one in scale only. The Gallup Poll noted that, although the government changes were not in themselves unpopular, they brought a sharp increase in the unpopularity of the Prime Minister. On 11 July, his personal rating was:[77]

Satisfied: 47%   Dissatisfied: 39%   Don't know: 12%

After the purge (20 July), the figures read:

Satisfied: 36%   Dissatisfied: 52%   Don't know: 12%

It was a devastating peripeteia from the high of the 79 per cent satisfied of May 1960, after the Paris summit reversal. Certainly Macmillan, once he had been seen to let drop the mask of unflappability, was never quite able to regain his reputation for sangfroid – at least at home. Macmillan himself made no bones about admitting, subsequently, that he had 'made a great error. I think I should have contented myself with this one change. . . .'[78]

The Dust Settles: New Policies

For the short term, the scars seemed to fade with remarkable speed. None of the sacked ministers excited much personal enthusiasm among the electorate, who, in any case, as Woodrow Wyatt observed, 'like the drama of executions in high places'.[79] On 26 July, the Opposition tabled a vote of Censure, and Gaitskell directed some bitter words at Macmillan, 'a desperate man in a desperate situation': 'His Government will be remembered not for the leadership they gave the nation, but as a conspiracy to retain power. Men and measures have been equally sacrificed for this purpose.' But, once again (though perhaps it was less telling than heretofore), Macmillan trounced his opponent in debate, noting scathingly that 'Gaitskell was a lecturer by nature, not an orator.' Bringing home backbenchers from all over the world, the Whips managed to achieve a majority of 98; 'not an abstention from our side', Macmillan noted with satisfaction.

When, in the course of the debate, he accused Gaitskell of concentrating his attack on personalities, rather than policies, he had a point. Both press and politicians had dwelt so much on the exciting events of the purge that they neglected the new measures behind them; and these were not unimportant. Chief among them was the setting up, in place of the abandoned pay-pause machinery, of a National Incomes Commission, to join the planning bodies already created by Macmillan. It began on a voluntary basis, and initially the TUC (*'very* unfriendly')[80] declared – predictably – that they would have nothing to do with any incomes policy. Nevertheless, the Labour government that succeeded the Tories, as Macmillan recorded with satisfaction, 'became converts', replacing 'Nicky' in 1965 with the more authoritative Prices and Incomes Board. By his legislation of summer 1962, Macmillan believed that he had established an incomes policy as a 'permanent feature of our economic life'. But behind it lay a clear determination that 'we were now definitely set upon an expansionist course'. The question was, with the world facing what looked like a recession, and British unemployment figures set to soar to 500,000 by the autumn and reaching 800,000 by the beginning of 1963 (the highest since 1947), had the change of course come too late? Or were the Enoch Powells justified in accusing Macmillan of opening the Pandora's Box of inflation?

In August Macmillan was able to go away for the parliamentary

351

recess with the immediate storm blown up by the purge apparently abated, the Party faithful rallied. After a bout of sleeplessness, he wrote from his much loved Swinton to Ava Waverley, in a hand even more erratic than usual:

> . . . I have been reading a lot about Napoleon and Talleyrand and all that. This period has always fascinated me. (Not the battles which I don't understand, but the politics.)
>
> . . . Altho' it was a terribly painful job to make these recent changes, I am more and more convinced that I was right not to shrink from my duties. . . .
>
> My hands are getting very stiff and I find it more and more difficult to hold a pen. My right hand (which was shot through at Loos) is very weak.
>
> And my eyes are deteriorating – stupidly.
>
> However, I hope to still be able to see – and kill – a few grouse. . . .[81]

After four days there he moved on to Bolton Abbey and returned to London much refreshed. There were even patches of good news on the economic front; 'after two years of battling with them and the former Chancellor', the Treasury had finally come round to adopting Macmillan's views about the need for increasing world 'liquidity'.[82] In the autumn, his plans for expansionism began with a cut in Purchase Tax on motor cars from 45 per cent to 33⅓ per cent; a short while later the Treasury, 'now in quite an expansionist mood', agreed to lower Purchase Tax across the board in the 45 per cent category; while bank rate was reduced again from 4½ per cent to 4 per cent. At the end of 1962 the inflation rate was 1.9 per cent.[83] In October the Tory Party Conference in Llandudno had gone off without a hitch. Dorothy Macmillan 'received a tremendous welcome'; the Prime Minister's speech was greeted with customary enthusiasm. Most of it dealt with Britain and the Common Market.

The EEC – Persuading the British and the Commonwealth

Although Macmillan had already begun the tricky negotiations with the Commonwealth leaders, and had successfully negotiated both the Commons debate on the EEC application and the Party

Conference in October 1961, he was acutely conscious that his Common Market policy was still opposed by a substantial section of British public opinion, while he had to carry along both a divided party and a hesitant Cabinet.

He did not even have the support of his Deputy Prime Minister. In July new rumours were reaching Macmillan about Rab:

> that (a) if we reach agreement in Brussels, Butler will lead a revolt in the Party on the cry of 'selling out the Commonwealth'; (b) if we fail, the PM's Common Market policy . . . will be humiliated and he must resign.[84]

It was not until August that Rab finally came off his fence, at a dinner at Buck's to which he had invited Macmillan several weeks in advance:

> It was clearly to be an occasion. And it was. He told me that in spite of (a) the farmers; (b) the Commonwealth; (c) the possible break-up of the Conservative Party, he had decided to support the Common Market. It was too big a chance to miss, for Britain's wealth and strength. But we must face the fact that we might share the fate of Sir Robert Peel and his supporters.[85]

Even so, in the Cabinet the next day, Macmillan found Rab 'rather gloomy', his gloom shared in full by Christopher Soames, the Minister of Agriculture, who was prophesying 'great trouble from our farmers'.[86]

As for the Opposition parties, the Liberals had ranged themselves firmly on the side of Macmillan, and during the Commons debate of August 1961 the influential Labour MP Roy Jenkins had made a pro-European speech of 'luminosity' and 'sincerity'. For over a year the Party leader himself remained uncommitted, but by June 1962 Denis Healey and Harold Wilson had jumped overboard into outright opposition. Their desertion, he reckoned, would probably provoke 'a new battle *against* Gaitskell' within the Opposition ranks. Meanwhile Gaitskell himself had explained his apparent indecision as follows:

> . . . Macmillan is a very crafty man. This is one reason why I am determined not to let the Party get committed on the Common

Market. If we try to reach a decision ourselves I am pretty certain we would remain hopelessly divided while the Tories reluctantly decide to unite behind whatever Macmillan decides to do. . . .[87]

It seemed like fairly low-level party politics in face of an issue of grandest proportions, and it enabled Macmillan to mock Gaitskell unsparingly at the Party Conference of October 1962. '"She didn't say yes, she didn't say no,"' he quoted the Jerome Kern song to the delight of the Tory Party faithful gathered at Llandudno:

> 'She didn't say stay, she didn't say go
> She wanted to climb, but she dreaded to fall
> So she bided her time and clung to the wall. . . .'[88]

The mirth continued as Macmillan compared Gaitskell to a Frenchman who had recently sat on a tightrope for 174 hours and then given up: 'Poor deluded man, he thought he had set up a world record!' But by then Gaitskell had in fact come off his tightrope.

On the eve of the critical Commonwealth Conference of September 1962, Gaitskell, so Macmillan noted with some disgust,

> issued a statement *against* entering the Common Market on present terms. . . . The effect of this cannot yet be assessed. He also demands a General Election on the issue if the parties are not agreed. . . . I stayed in bed in the morning. . . .[89]

Gaitskell's biographer, Philip Williams, who explores at length his subject's tortuous, but no doubt honourable, route to a decision, blames Macmillan for having 'never made the smallest gesture' towards bipartisanship during the EEC talks.[90]

Macmillan's failure to put out a hand towards the Opposition over the EEC talks doubtless reflected those deep-seated personal animosities, and Gaitskell's tergiversation so late in the day provoked fresh reactions of contempt:

> *10 September:* . . . I'm afraid he is a poor creature, without any real breadth of view or sense of values. Or perhaps he has them and is consciously false to them. . . .[91]
>
> *12 September:* . . . Gaitskell going about smiling and smirking, as if he had just kissed hands. . . .[92]

But whatever his personal feelings about Gaitskell, the defection of the Labour Party came, undeniably, as a bitter blow to Macmillan. More than that, the decision of September 1962 was to represent a major turning point in the Labour Party's relationship with Europe – and, indeed, Britain's. Paradoxically it also struck an echo among Macmillan's critics on the right of his own party, the elderly ladies and the colonels of the shires, Empire Loyalists and other doubters right across the Tory spectrum.

Meanwhile, another 'crunch' had come with the Commonwealth Conference, which began on 10 September. Macmillan opened with a 'carefully prepared speech', which lasted over an hour. He explained the 'complete transformation' that had taken place in Europe since the war; then went on to re-emphasise the 'hard, but inescapable fact' that in order to be able to import the foodstuffs and raw materials essential to her, Britain had to be able to find markets for exports of her manufactured goods; and the British market alone was no longer big enough to absorb the growing production of the Commonwealth. He tried to persuade the Commonwealth Prime Ministers that British entry into the EEC would 'not be incompatible with the Commonwealth; the two associations being complementary', and assured them that Britain's value to the Commonwealth lay in the expanded markets, and capital, she would be able to offer through joining the Europeans; while, if she were to become isolated from them, 'our general political influence in the world would inevitably diminish.' It was perhaps not Macmillan's most powerful address, but he was followed by Edward Heath, then at the peak of his very formidable powers, with an exposition that Macmillan rated as 'really a masterpiece – from notes, and not from a script'. This hour-and-a-half description of the negotiations from Heath left the Commonwealth Premiers 'exhausted – and I hope impressed'.[93] But there then followed two days of 'a broadside attack'[94] on the British negotiating position, which Diefenbaker had led off 'in a false and vicious speech'. Even that trusted friend of Britain, Bob Menzies, whom Macmillan had considered would be the key to the whole situation, had made a '*very* damaging speech'. Nehru (Macmillan found him looking old, tired and peevish) had little to say.

At their weekly audience, the Queen had been 'sympathetic', Macmillan noted, but 'worried about Commonwealth feeling'. By the night of 12 September, Macmillan admitted that he was feeling shaken, Butler was 'disgusted', while 'Poor Ted Heath', 'who is only accustomed to Europeans who are courteous and well informed even if hard bargainers, was astounded at the ignorance, ill-manners and conceit of the Commonwealth . . .'.[95] As the Conference progressed (or rather the opposite), so Macmillan's impatience with his Canadian opposite number reached new heights, as Diefenbaker in particular pressed insistently for Canada to retain privileged access to the British market for her foodstuffs, notably wheat from his own prairie provinces. Although this was, inevitably, a cause close to Diefenbaker personally, in Macmillan's eyes the Conservative demagogue from Saskatchewan revealed himself as 'something of a mountebank',[96] 'a very crooked man . . . so self-centred as to be a sort of caricature of Mr Gladstone', and to whom the only test of a question was 'the political advantage of himself and his party . . .'.[97] Macmillan derived some satisfaction in discovering that Diefenbaker was now so deaf that it was doubtful whether he had 'heard anything of our speeches'.[98]

None of this personal vexation was allowed to appear in the Macmillan memoirs, but, by the beginning of the second week, tempers were fraying all round and it looked as if the Conference faced deadlock, with each premier adamantly pushing forward his own shopping list.[99] Macmillan, admitting that both he and Heath were 'very depressed' (and, his diary comments, 'overstrained'), buried himself in *Kenilworth* ('a splendid story') for distraction. At the eleventh hour, however, a plan worked out overnight between Norman Brook and Macmillan, which involved scrapping the proposed 'long' draft of a final communiqué, laden with points of dissent, in favour of a more neutral 'short' one, achieved unexpected success.[100] Macmillan noted that Diefenbaker's deafness now helped him to 'pass from one clause to another fairly rapidly . . .'. 'Menzies (having, I suppose, made a sufficient demonstration for home politics) was reasonable. He reverted to his favourite sport of teasing Diefenbaker. . . .'[101]

When the communiqué was issued on the afternoon of 19 September, Macmillan was 'so exhausted that I went to bed at 5pm and slept for 2 hours!' The laboriously patched up communiqué stated baldly that the 'greater part of the meeting' had been given over to discussing Britain's EEC application (what else, indeed!) and that 'Although this discussion had disclosed many differences of viewpoint and many uncertainties, all the exchanges have been conducted in the frank and friendly atmosphere which characterises Commonwealth meetings. . . .' The Commonwealth Prime Ministers acknowledged the 'strenuous efforts' the British government had made to ensure that the Six understood the 'safeguards' necessary, if British entry were 'not to be on such terms and conditions as to impair their vital interests'; but the communiqué revealed their continued 'anxieties about the possible effects of Britain's entry into the European Economic Community'. Finally, it had been agreed that, when negotiations were resumed, British ministers would 'take full account' of the Commonwealth views and 'would continue their efforts to safeguard essential Commonwealth interests'.[102] This was *not* going to please de Gaulle; or else it was going to give him fresh pretexts for closing the door. To anyone who could translate the language of diplomacy the communiqué revealed that internal dissensions were unresolved.

In his memoirs, Macmillan assessed the results of the Commonwealth Conference as having been 'satisfactory', from the British point of view. But only just. It seemed that the effort of trying to carry Britain into Europe had blunted Macmillan's normally sensitive antennae so that he frequently minimised the problems posed by de Gaulle. The heat of the debates had made it abundantly plain that the Commonwealth leaders felt that, after so many delays and hesitations, the price Britain was being called upon to pay to join the EEC club was too high – from her own, as well as the Commonwealth's, point of view. Gaitskell, swiftly reading between the lines of the communiqué, was able to make political capital by declaring that it confirmed the Commonwealth leaders' fears that, on the terms so far negotiated, 'much damage would be done to their countries'. He pressed Macmillan to honour the pledge made to safeguard Commonwealth interests: thus 'it follows that we must either obtain better terms or stay out.'[103]

The dissatisfaction was infectious, even among Macmillan's closest supporters. On 21 September, he recorded wanly:

Poor Roy Harrod and Juliet Rhys-Williams (dear, trusted, loyal friends) who used to be strong 'Europeans', have now changed round, and become *violent* opponents. This saddens me, for I am devoted to them both. . . . The controversy is now beginning to crack the old Party alignments. Where it will end, no one can tell. Of course, it all depends on the final terms which we can get at Brussels. . . .[104]

Nevertheless, with a display of his old resilience, he succeeded in leading his followers triumphantly through the Tory Party Conference of the following month. It was, some observers thought, possibly his last great triumph. He took immense trouble with his own speech, running through no less than eight separate drafts; it was 'shorter than customary, and perhaps for that reason enthusiastically received', he observed modestly.

To have got through both Commonwealth and Party conferences relatively unscathed, Macmillan remarked to Harold Evans, was 'a miracle, a miracle'.[105] On the course of the debates he was able to sum up to the Queen:

At any rate it has elevated political discussion from the rather small beer which often concerns us. . . . The Labour movement now seems to be moving towards a strange combination of what used to be called 'Little Englandism and Jingoism'.

That, at least, was a fair prediction. He continued: 'The Conservative Party are being asked, and I think will agree, to turn their minds from the old Imperialism which no longer has its old power, to a new concept of Britain's ability to influence the world.'[106] Few could dispute that this was a noble sentiment, reflecting how – within the past two years – Macmillan had swung Tory foreign policy through just about 180 degrees. From now on, as he wrote in his memoirs, Britain and her application to join the EEC were 'in the straight' in Brussels; 'and if we were to be prevented from reaching the winning-post somebody would have to trip us up and take the full responsibility for our fall. . . .'

The trouble was that the British reservations had become so manifest in the course of their domestic debates, the overtures to the Europeans in Brussels so cautious, the delays so prolonged, that the 'somebody' who might seriously want to 'trip us up' now had no shortage of pretext. The faith of even the loyalest of Britain's friends in Europe (not to mention the US) had been sorely taxed over the past long year of negotiations. None of this was missed by de Gaulle. On 3 October, Macmillan was noting a despatch from his Ambassador in Paris: '. . . Bob Dixon reported a *bad* interview with de Gaulle – who was gloomy, cynical, and harsh. . . .'[107] It recalled to Macmillan his experiences with de Gaulle in Algiers twenty years previously: 'He will be an obstacle to progress at Brussels. Whether he can, in the end, stand out against the will of all Europe, I cannot tell. But this will have to be put to the test. . . .' The important thing was, to 'fail honourably'.[108]

Meanwhile, before de Gaulle could be 'put to the test', all thoughts were suddenly distracted by the explosion of an infinitely more menacing crisis on the other side of the Atlantic: Cuba.

Chapter Thirteen

'A Trial of Wills': Cuba October–November 1962

Kennedy and Macmillan are the wickedest people in the story of man.

(*Bertrand Russell, September 1961*)

These things which seem world shaking at one moment you can barely remember the next. . . .

(*JFK after the Bay of Pigs, 1961*)

On Sunday, 21 October, Macmillan received an urgent, top-secret signal from President Kennedy:

> I am sending you this most private message to give you advance notice of a most serious situation and of my plan to meet it. . . .

He went on to state that photographic intelligence had 'established beyond question, in the last week', that the Soviets were planting medium-range missiles in Cuba. Six sites had already been identified, with two possibly in operational readiness. The US government had decided, he informed Macmillan,

> to prevent any further build up by sea and to demand the removal of this nuclear threat to our hemisphere. . . . This extraordinarily dangerous and aggressive Soviet step obviously creates a crisis of the most serious sort, in which we would have to act most closely together. I have found it absolutely essential, in the interest of security and speed, to make my first decision on my own responsibility, but from now on I expect that we can and should be in the closest touch, and I know that together with our friends we shall resolutely meet this challenge. . . .

As far as the Special Relationship was concerned, it is important to note that the first, crucial decision had been taken on Kennedy's own responsibility, and *before* consulting Macmillan or any other ally. Kennedy went on to stress, by way of reassuring Macmillan, that, though 'Khrushchev's main intention may be to increase his chances in Berlin', the US would be ready to take a full role there as well as in the Caribbean. 'What is essential at this moment of highest test is that Khrushchev should discover that if he is counting on weakness or irresolution, he has miscalculated. . . .'[1]

Kennedy's message did not come entirely as a bolt from the blue to Macmillan. Ever since the Bay of Pigs débâcle in April 1961 tension had remained high in the Caribbean, and with the heating up of the Berlin crisis Khrushchev had shown signs of raising the pressure over Cuba; although he had pledged to Kennedy that the Soviet government sought no advantage in Cuba, had no bases there, and no intention to establish any. But from late July 1962 Soviet shipping to Cuba had increased and US intelligence reports showed (defensive) surface-to-air missiles (SAMs) being installed with the help of several thousand Soviet technicians. In September Kennedy warned the Russians that the introduction of any surface-to-surface (offensive) missiles would be viewed very gravely. On 13 September, he told a news conference that if Cuba were to become a significant military base of the Soviet Union 'this country will do whatever must be done to protect its own security and that of its allies.'[2] On 1 October the Foreign Secretary Lord Home had told Macmillan that the President 'simply couldn't understand why we couldn't help America by joining an embargo . . .' on trade.[3] Kennedy had also voiced fears that immediately struck a chord with Macmillan; namely that Khrushchev was seeking to 'provoke' an intervention by the United States in order to wipe out Berlin. In his diary of 3 October, Macmillan recorded his judgement that 'the Russians are clearly using *Cuba* as a counter-irritant to Berlin. . . .'[4]

News of a Cuban crisis had already begun to circulate in Washington, that city of open secrets, and Ormsby-Gore had alerted the Foreign Office (on 19 October) to expect 'an impending crisis, probably about missiles in Cuba'.[5]

In the White House, Jacqueline Kennedy was entertaining the Maharajah of Jaipur and his glamorous wife to dinner, and her first intimation of the crisis was when she found 'upstairs, David and Jack squatting on the floor, looking at the missile pictures. . . . I had to rush backwards and forwards, to keep the party going. . . .'[6] As it was, the presence of David Ormsby-Gore at that early stage of the story was to assume particular significance.

Hidden from Macmillan at that time was the long and bitter debate which had taken place among Kennedy's inner councils as to what action to take. As reported by Ormsby-Gore (for some reason his telegram did not reach Macmillan until late in the evening of 22 October) Kennedy had said that there were really only two alternatives open to him.

(1) They could order an all-out air strike first thing Monday morning [22 October] to take out all the known missile sites and

363

the missiles themselves . . . which would then be followed by the imposition of a blockade of Cuba. . . . (2) they could impose almost immediately a blockade without first carrying out an air strike. . . .

The President then asked me for my views as to which of these two courses I felt was the correct one. I said that I saw very serious drawbacks in the first course of action he had outlined to me. Very few people outside the United States would consider the provocation offered by the Cubans serious enough to merit an American air attack. I thought that in the circumstances America would be damaged politically, and in any case I could not believe that the missiles so far landed constituted any significant threat to the United States. . . . Therefore, of the two alternatives he had put to me I was certainly in favour of the second, although this too would have far-reaching political implications including the probability of a maximum Russian reaction perhaps in the Berlin context.[7]

Fortunately the President and his colleagues came to the same conclusion.

Macmillan later reckoned, with considerable relief, that if the President had known what became clear a few days later, namely 'that the missiles themselves were largely in position and that the force deployed a great part of the available nuclear strength of the whole Russian economy', Kennedy might have been unable to resist the arguments for an immediate 'take-out' action.

'The First Day of the World Crisis'

On the morning of Monday, 22 October, Macmillan recorded in his diary 'the first day of the world crisis!' It did in fact look as though the world was closer to war than at any time since the Berlin blockade of 1948. That morning, Ambassador David Bruce came to see Macmillan with a long letter from Kennedy, and a 'great dossier'; '. . . Ambassador Bruce, in his detached and quiet way, did not attempt to conceal the excited, almost chaotic atmosphere in Washington. . . .'[8] Unbeknown to Macmillan, something of that febrile atmosphere had also been passed on even to the suave David Bruce. On receiving Truman's former Secretary of State, Dean

Acheson, on his way as Kennedy's special envoy to brief de Gaulle, Bruce had told Acheson to feel his pocket, and had shown him a revolver, saying, 'I was told by the Department of State to carry this when I went to meet you!'[9] This was substantiated by Chester Cooper, then CIA liaison officer in the White House, whose role in Suez will be recalled and who accompanied Bruce when he went to see Macmillan on the 22nd: 'he was the armed escort.'[10] Cooper recalled Macmillan's reaction on receiving the deadly information:

> . . . Bruce saw Macmillan alone for a few minutes, and then called me in. Macmillan's reaction when he saw the pictures was very interesting. He looked at them for a little while and then said, more to himself than to us, pointing at the missile sites, 'Now the Americans will realize what we in England have lived through for the past many years.' Then he was concerned that this remark, which was quite spontaneous, would indicate that he was either unsympathetic or perhaps even chortling over our difficulties. He hastened to assure us that it was an instinctive reaction, and that he was terribly worried about the missiles and would, of course, provide the United States with whatever assistance and support that was necessary. . . .

Bruce told Macmillan that the photographic material from U-2 reconnaissances provided 'incontrovertible military evidence, on the Soviet installation of offensive nuclear missiles in Cuba'. According to Cooper, Macmillan then went on to remark:

> that he was going to have considerable trouble with the Commons and with the British public because there was great suspicion in England at that time that the United States exaggerated the Castro threat. The pictures satisfied him, but might be regarded as a bit of fakery unless somehow they could be shown to the British people generally. . . .

In the first draft of a message to Kennedy, Macmillan's immediate reaction was to advise invading Cuba 'and have done with it; at any rate to avoid drifting into the situation which we had done at Suez . . .'. With some prescience (the trade-off of the Turkish Jupiter bases was not even under consideration at this point) he was alarmed lest Kennedy might '"miss the bus" – he may *never* get rid of Cuban rockets except by trading them for Turkish, Italian or other bases. Thus Khrushchev will have won his point. . . .' But the more Macmillan reflected, the more he saw Cuba as a possible feint, the main danger being that Khrushchev's real purpose:

> was to trade Cuba for Berlin. If he was stopped, with great loss of face, in Cuba, would he not be tempted to recover himself in Berlin? Indeed, might not this be the whole purpose of the exercise – to move forward one pawn in order to exchange it for another?[11]

Macmillan put these points to Bruce, and they were to form the basis of his advice to Kennedy throughout the crisis; his main fear, as he encapsulated it many years later, was simply that '. . . Khrushchev might have suggested a swap of Cuba for Berlin – how could the Americans have resisted?'[12]

In his first response to Kennedy, Macmillan assured him that Britain would of course give all possible support in the Security Council. He then reminded Kennedy how Europeans had lived for so long in close proximity to the enemy's nuclear weapons that they had 'got accustomed to it, so European opinion will need attention . . .'. Macmillan followed this up later with a remark about 'if you live on Vesuvius, you don't bother much about eruptions. . . .' The import of the last remark – don't fuss so much – did not delight Kennedy; who was also, initially, disappointed by Macmillan's apparently sceptical request for the publication of photographic evidence. De Gaulle by contrast had been prepared to accept the President's word, without supporting evidence.[13] But Macmillan's point was a valid one; for the sake of public opinion it was essential to have the U-2 photographs for publication, as incontrovertible proof. 'No one will believe this unless they see these,' he said.[14] At the same time he also rejected urgings from General Norstad of NATO to place British forces on a higher state of readiness. Macmillan, with his own tragic personal memories, pointed out that mobilisation sometimes led to war.

Macmillan immediately invited Gaitskell to see all the documents the Americans had sent. Gaitskell was dubious whether the identified missile sites were 'offensive' in character: 'he did *not* take a very robust attitude. He thought his Party "would not like it". I doubt if they would like any decision – firm decision – on any subject. . . .'[15]

(Gaitskell, accompanied by George Brown and Harold Wilson,

came to see Macmillan again the following day: 'they hadn't much to say. Brown was more robust than Gaitskell. Wilson looked very shifty. Fortunately, they all distrust each other profoundly.'[16] Macmillan's own Cabinet 'seemed rather shaken, but satisfied' by the Kennedy revelations. 'I take it for granted', was Macmillan's own immediate response when shown the photographs himself by David Bruce, 'that the statements made by your government are unchallengeable.'[17]

Late on the night of the 22nd, Kennedy telephoned Macmillan personally, the first of a series of calls between the two leaders during the crisis. ('You know how Americans love telephones,' Macmillan would remark years later.)[18] The new scrambler line had a 'Press to Speak' button which both found difficulty in operating, and the transcripts make slightly comic reading. They took the form of the President largely holding a monologue, with Macmillan contributing sympathetic interjections that, read subsequently, often sounded rather vapid. But, in the opinion of Home among others,[19] Macmillan's calmness undoubtedly helped bolster the President, and Macmillan admitted that the conversations 'were a great comfort to me'. On the first night, Kennedy seemed 'rather excited, but very clear. . . . He could not tell what Khrushchev would do. . . . He is building up his forces for a *coup de main* to seize Cuba, should that become necessary. . . .'[20] That same day Macmillan had sent out messages to the Commonwealth leaders, putting them in the picture ('the only faint-heart', he noted, proved to be Diefenbaker),[21] but most particularly to de Gaulle (who had already received a personal message from Kennedy), addressed to 'My dear friend', and inviting his thoughts.[22] De Gaulle's first reply was simply to observe 'we are entering into a difficult period';[23] he followed this up on the 25th to say that he agreed with Macmillan's view that 'for the moment this remains primarily a Russo-American dispute about Cuba. . . .'[24] Thus de Gaulle had no cause to complain that he had not been kept informed, any more than Macmillan.

Two British Contributions

True it is that the initial decision to meet Khrushchev's challenge by naval blockade had in effect been taken *before* Kennedy first communicated with Macmillan, on the appreciation that US

367

interests were involved in a much more direct manner than Britain's. The famous Kennedy telephone calls were purely informative, and in no way seeking advice, only the comfort of affirmation. Though other US allies (like de Gaulle, Diefenbaker and Adenauer) were also kept informed, none received the same blow-by-blow account of developments, or the same degree of heart-to-heart unburdening to which the British Prime Minister was to be treated. It was not insignificant that none of the members of ExComm (Kennedy's inner war cabinet of the National Security Council, set up on 16 October) was aware of the extent of the transatlantic calls.[25]

There was another important dimension, the figure of Sir David Ormsby-Gore, the closeness of whose involvement with President Kennedy as personal friend and trusted adviser, as well as British Ambassador, was suggested by Jacqueline Kennedy's observation noted earlier. By October 1962 their dealings had attained a degree of intimacy quite resented by other ambassadors, as well as by senior members of the administration. At the peak of the crisis, contingency arrangements were made for the Ormsby-Gore family to be brought to the safety of the presidential nuclear shelter beneath the Appalachians; the prevailing mood in Washington, he recalled long afterwards, '*was* frightening. . . . I never felt nervous talking to Bobby, or the President, but I was with some of the others . . .';

> . . . I always remember our children being at school, with orders to bring their rations and clothes, and prepare to take off for the shelters, if necessary. We dusted off the Embassy evacuation orders. . . .[26]

Kennedy, on his lonely pinnacle of power at that moment, had (in his own words) come to 'trust David as I would my own Cabinet'.[27] As a result, the British Ambassador was accorded the unprecedented honour of being invited to sit in on top-level sessions of the National Security Council. A straw-vote held before Ormsby-Gore and the British had been informed of the crisis had shown six (chiefly the military) in favour of a surgical strike, and eleven (headed, most articulately, by Bobby Kennedy, and behind him Secretary of Defense McNamara) for a 'quarantine' blockade. But there remained a strong lobby (chiefly the military) in favour of action, and Ormsby-Gore's voice in support of Bobby Kennedy lent significant weight to the less militant, blockade faction. He told the President on that first night of 'Missiles Week', Sunday the 21st, 'that I thought a bombing – an immediate strike – would not be understood in the rest of the world, and that some form of blockade was probably the right answer . . .'. Kennedy replied, according to Ormsby-Gore, 'as a matter of fact, that is what we have decided. . . .'[28]

It was at a subsequent meeting of the National Security Council, on 23 October, that Ormsby-Gore – acting entirely off his own bat, and without referring back to Macmillan, but with his total support *ex post facto* – made a crucial suggestion. He recommended that the proposed 'quarantine line' of the US naval blockade be modified from 800 miles to 500 miles off the Cuban coast. This would give the Soviet ships approaching from Europe more time to react, and provide Khrushchev with a face-saver. The suggestion was accepted by Kennedy and ExComm, and the blockade went formally into effect the next day. At the UN, the Soviet representative, Zorin, had the effrontery to deny that there were either missiles or launching pads in Cuba. Given the European disbelief in the word of the CIA ('it had a bad name'),[29] Ormsby-Gore pressed Kennedy to take Macmillan's advice and have the photographs immediately released to the press. This was done, with telling effect.

Meanwhile, in Florida and the gulf ports the US Navy was assembling a massive conventional force, the extent of which was not appreciated by Macmillan or the US public until well after the crisis had passed. Some 25,000 marines aboard navy vessels and more than 100,000 army troops were ready for an invasion of Cuba; while some 45 ships, 240 aircraft and 30,000 men were also deployed directly in enforcing the blockade.[30]

Britain's second important contribution during Cuban Missiles Week took the shape of Colonel Oleg Penkovsky. Regarded by well-placed intelligence operators, on both sides of the Atlantic, as having been *the* most important agent within the Kremlin since 1945, Penkovsky[31] was recruited (in April 1961) by MI6, but handed to the CIA for debriefing. Over a period of sixteen months he produced a range of intelligence items that were unprecedented in quantity and quality, including reports on Soviet intentions over Berlin. His valuable material included details on the installation of the Soviet missiles in Cuba, as well as information suggesting that the state of Soviet rocketry was in fact far less advanced than Khrushchev boasted. It was this intelligence that helped bolster significantly Kennedy's resolve to confront Khrushchev over the Cuban missiles. Penkovsky was arrested by the KGB on 22 October, the day Kennedy publicly revealed existence of the missiles; this might have been coincidental – or a direct consequence of the intelligence delivered. Penkovsky was not a cautious man. He was sentenced to death the following May. Officers of both MI6 and the CIA had little doubt of the 'supreme importance'[32] of Penkovsky's role during the missiles crisis. It was a view consistently shared by Macmillan.

The $64,000 Question

On Wednesday, the 24th, the world held its breath; 'that terrible Wednesday morning when we all sat with our hearts in our mouths to see whether any of the Russian ships did turn around', recalled Ormsby-Gore.[33] Twenty-five Soviet ships were reported on their way to Cuba; fourteen were believed to be carrying rockets. A rumour reached Macmillan that some of them were stopping and turning about. At 11 p.m. that night Kennedy telephoned Macmillan a second time:

> *Prime Minister:* Well, I'm all right. What's the news now?
>   *President Kennedy:* Well, we have no more word yet on what's going to happen out there. As you have probably heard, some of the ships, the ones we're particularly interested in, have turned around. . . .[34]

Macmillan wondered whether this did not represent a 'great triumph' for Kennedy. The President was not certain; it was possible that the turning was tactical, to avoid the US laying hands on the secret and incriminating missiles; meanwhile work on the sites was still continuing. Then, 'rather unexpectedly', recorded Macmillan in his diary,

> President asked me straight out the 64 thousand dollar question 'Should he take out Cuba?'[35]

Kennedy actually put the crucial dilemma that had been perplexing him and ExComm as follows:

We're going to have to make the judgement as to whether we're going to invade Cuba taking our chances or whether we hold off and use Cuba as a sort of hostage in the matter of Berlin. Then any time he takes an action against Berlin, we take action against Cuba. That's really the choice we now have. What's your judgement . . . ?

Macmillan replied that he:

would like to think about it. I think it is very important because I suppose the world feels that we shall some time or other have to have some sort of discussion with them, but we don't want to do that in such a way that he has all these cards in his hands.

Kennedy continued, in a monologue like a chess-master thinking out loud: 'He has Cuba in his hands, but he doesn't have Berlin. If he takes Berlin, then we will take Cuba. . . .' Macmillan said he thought the issue 'very well put', but again said he would like to think about it and would send back a considered message. At the time it struck him that, but for the deadly seriousness of the situation, the dialogue was all 'just like a revue called "Beyond the Fringe" which takes off the leading politicians . . .'.[36]

Kennedy went on to ask Macmillan if he was having trouble in Parliament with the Opposition. Macmillan replied no; he had to make a brief statement the following day, and answer questions, but he felt that – armed with all the supporting intelligence material that David Bruce had given him that morning – he could handle it without difficulty. He then continued,

I feel myself pretty sure that we ought not to do anything in a hurry. We ought just to let this develop a day or two.
   President Kennedy: Right, Prime Minister. As I say we are mobilising our force so that if we decide to invade we will be in a position to do so within a few more days. . . .

Turning to the function of the UN, Kennedy told Macmillan of a conversation he had had that day with Hammarskjöld's successor as Secretary-General, U Thant, which he read out slowly at dictation speed. U Thant had in effect appealed to Kennedy and Khrushchev to call off both arms shipments and the blockade for a two-to-three-week 'truce' period while talks were being conducted. Macmillan thought it 'rather tiresome of him, because it looks sensible and yet it's rather bad . . .', and he went on to warn Kennedy that he thought it a 'very dangerous message'. Kennedy accepted this, recognising that the U Thant proposal carried no guarantees in it. Macmillan asked: 'Well now, how do you think we shall get out of this in the long run? Do you think we ought to try to do a deal, having a meeting with him, or not?' Kennedy thought that Khrushchev's reaction to the 'quarantine' over the next twenty-four hours would prove vital; he was doubtful about a 'meeting' at this stage, because '. . . I don't quite know what we will discuss at the meeting because he'll be back with his same old position, probably offer to dismantle the missiles if we'll neutralise Berlin. . . .' Macmillan offered to fly to Washington to see Kennedy; would it be 'advisable', or 'disagreeable'? Kennedy suggested that they should talk again on Friday, two nights later, when he would know whether the quarantine was going to work or not. Macmillan said he would be happier if they could talk each evening. Kennedy agreed to telephone again at the same time on the morrow.

Of all the Kennedy–Macmillan transatlantic telephone conversations during Missiles Week, this was probably the most important. Did it constitute, on the President's part, 'consultation' or merely 'information'? Historians of the Special Relationship would argue the toss long afterwards. If it was not actually 'consultation', then it was something very close to it.

After mulling on it overnight, the next day Macmillan sent Kennedy his considered answer to the '$64,000 question'. As far as 'taking out Cuba' went, he felt that 'events have gone too far. While circumstances may arise in which such action would be right and necessary, I think that we are now all in a phase where you must try to obtain your objectives by other means. . . .' In his reply to U Thant's proposal, which Macmillan stressed would be of utmost importance to world opinion, Kennedy he thought should point out that events had proved Russian promises worthless; that the missiles *in situ* must go, and that only 'some system of inspection' could replace blockade.

Macmillan's telegram was very firm in tone. If the above requirements were achieved, he reckoned, it would:

enable you to say that you had in fact obtained your objectives. For if there are no ships arriving, then the purpose of the quarantine is served; and if there is no more construction the purpose of largely immobilising this threat is also served. In other words, such an approach as I suggest fits in with the answer to last night's question which I feel I must give.

At the same time you will no doubt continue with your military build-up for any emergency. This may be as important a factor for persuading the Cubans to accept inspection as in other directions. . . .

As expected, Khrushchev accepted U Thant's proposal. On the 25th, a second proposal arrived from U Thant suggesting that Khrushchev keep his ships out of the quarantine area and asking Kennedy to avoid a confrontation. Propped by Macmillan's advice, Kennedy responded with a wisdom and adroitness that Macmillan found 'extremely ingenious', 'that if he keeps his ships out of there of course we will avoid a confrontation . . .'. That same day Parliament was prorogued; as Macmillan told Kennedy in their nightly telephone conversation, his statement was 'very well received on all sides'.

Gaitskell, as usual, said he would ask 2 questions and proceeded to ask 10. But his tone was helpful. He was most damaging about 'consultation'. His memories are, of course, of Suez. Wade (Liberal Deputy Leader) was weak and futile. . . . There was a mild demonstration, but it amounted to very little. . . .[37]

Macmillan also sent off firmly worded communications to the Commonwealth nations, and to de Gaulle, stressing the necessity for the US to be seen to '*act*' if confidence in the US was to remain among her allies. The lesson of Russian duplicity was that disarmament could not be left to depend on Khrushchev's assurances. Meanwhile U Thant, pushed further by Kennedy's message, asked Khrushchev specifically to keep his ships out of the quarantine area – something he had not done in his earlier message.

On Friday night, the 26th, Macmillan had 'two *long* telephone talks with the President. The situation is very obscure and dangerous. It is a trial of will.'[38] At the back of Macmillan's mind was the constant fear of Kennedy being influenced by the Bay of Pigs; 'just as we were by Suez' – he 'couldn't have risked another failure'. On the second of the two conversations (there appears to have been no record of the first), Macmillan probed what seems to have been the first intimation of a 'deal' by Kennedy:

> *Prime Minister:* The idea that you have just mentioned is that Cuba might be made like Belgium was by international guarantee – an inviolable country and all of us would guarantee its neutrality and inviolability. Is that a possibility . . . ?

Kennedy replied that this was 'a matter which seems to me we ought to be thinking about . . .'. Later in the conversation Macmillan followed up with a further proposition: 'If we want to help the Russians to save face would it be worthwhile our undertaking to immobilise the missiles which are here in England during the same period – during the conference?' Kennedy was hesitant:

> . . . I think that the prospect of a trade of these missiles for some guarantee for Cuba is still so vague that I am not really in a position to say that there is any possibility of an easing up. Maybe by tomorrow evening at this time I'll know better.
>
> *Prime Minister:* Yes, because of course at this stage any movement by you may produce a result in Berlin which would be very bad for us all. That's the danger now.
>
> *President Kennedy:* Well, we are not going to have any problems because he is keeping his ships out of there. . . . On the other hand, if at the end of 48 hours we are getting no place and the missile sites continue to be constructed then we are going to be faced with some hard decisions.
>
> *Prime Minister:* And, of course, in making those decisions one has to realise that they will have their effect on Berlin as well as on Cuba.
>
> *President Kennedy:* Correct, and that is really why we have not done more than we have done up till now. . . .

In their turn, the Russians now made what Macmillan regarded as a 'rather dangerous but specious proposal'; namely, to bargain the missiles they had placed in Cuba against the US Jupiters stationed in Turkey. It was specious, thought Macmillan, because it would be trading like with unlike, and under unacceptable pressure; it was dangerous because 'the weaker brethren, at home and abroad', immediately fell for it. (*'The Times* and the *Manchester Guardian*', he recorded on the Sunday, were 'particularly gullible. The Press today – *Observer* and *Sunday Times* especially were awful. It was like Munich. The *Sunday Telegraph* was very good and firm. . . .')[39] Despite arguments about the obsolescence of the Turkish Jupiters, Macmillan said that he would never have consented to any such trade-away, 'as a permanent deal'. Such a sign of weakness by the US would have demoralised other NATO members, and not just the stalwart Turks; which was why he had suggested to Kennedy, as an alternative, the *temporary* defusing of the sixty Thors (established by Eisenhower) in Britain. As events developed, very swiftly, over the next hours, any such potential deal disappeared off the negotiating table.[40]

The Blackest Hour

Saturday, 27 October, was filled with deadly menace; it was the most agonising day of the week-long crisis, and – in Britain as well as in the US – the most frightening day that anyone at the hub of matters could remember. A U-2 was shot down over Cuba (piloted, in fact, by the courageous Major Anderson who had first photographed the missile sites two weeks previously). The whole system of aerial reconnaissance, essential to protecting US interests, was placed at risk. The military in Washington were poised to launch a retaliatory air strike on the SAM bases that had killed Anderson, which would have been bound to lead to escalatory action. Kennedy issued a statement, tantamount to an ultimatum, pointing out that the crisis had been entirely caused by Soviet offensive weapons sited in Cuba. Work on the missile bases must stop; offensive weapons must be rendered inoperable; further shipments must cease; and all this must be done under effective international verification. Kennedy informed his allies that, if 'satisfactory responses' were not received within forty-eight hours, 'the situation is likely to enter a progressively military phase.'[41] The threat was implicit; an invasion of Cuba on Tuesday. From New York and Washington there were ominous reports that Russian diplomats were destroying confidential documents. Yet there were straws in the wind. A Soviet-inspired *démarche* had been made to Macmillan to the effect that, if he would issue an appeal for a summit conference to settle the issue, the situation might still be saved. At first Macmillan and Home regarded this as a 'trap', an attempt to drive a wedge between London and Washington.

Meanwhile, in Washington two conflicting signals had arrived from Khrushchev. The first, long, diffuse and characteristic of Khrushchev in its emotional style, proposed that if the US would not 'participate in an attack on Cuba and that [if] the blockade would be lifted', he would agree to send in no more weapons and allow those already in Cuba to be withdrawn or destroyed. This, says Macmillan, 'in effect, met Kennedy's demands in full, and amounted to complete capitulation'. But it was followed up by a second signal, couched in more formal and harsher terms, proposing the exchange of the Cuban missiles for the Turkish Jupiters, and much less compromising. All day ExComm pondered what reply to give. Theodore Sorensen, who was present, noted:

> Our little group seated around the Cabinet table in continuous session that Saturday felt nuclear war to be closer on that day than at any time in the nuclear age. . . . Fatigue and disagreement over the right course caused more wrangling and irritability than usual. . . .[42]

Then, after an evening of intolerable suspense, Robert Kennedy came up with what Schlesinger described as 'a thought of breathtaking simplicity and ingenuity; why not ignore the second Khrushchev message and reply to the first . . . ?'[43] By now it was the small hours in London. Though there were a number of calls between Bundy and de Zulueta during that night of maximum suspense, there appears to have been no further conversation then between Macmillan and Kennedy. But Macmillan then despatched a teleprinter message as follows:

> The trial of wills is now approaching a climax. Khrushchev's first message, unhappily not published to the world, seemed to go a long way to meet you. His second message, widely broadcast and artfully contrived, adding to the Turkey proposal, was a recovery on his part. It has made a considerable impact. We must now wait to see what Khrushchev does. . . .[44]

To what extent Kennedy may have been influenced by Macmillan's messages at this point is not clear, but his mind was working along the same lines. He agreed to make one last effort for a peaceful settlement, welcoming and accepting the suggestion made in the first Russian letter.

Defence Minister Peter Thorneycroft recalled an almost sinister tranquillity as he walked across St James's Park on that Sunday morning. '. . . Whitehall deserted. It was very quiet. . . . rather a lovely morning. . . .' Walking into the Ministry of Defence, he thought '"My God, I wonder whether this really is it"; not the real feeling that we were going to be devastated, but the possibility did occur.'[45] The tension was not reduced at a meeting held later that morning at Admiralty House between Macmillan, Butler, Home, Thorneycroft and Heath. Before any news of Khrushchev's reaction could reach London, Macmillan decided to send his own message to Moscow: 'We *supported* the American demand that the missiles should be taken out of Cuba. I appealed to [Khrushchev] to do this, and then turn to more constructive work – disarmament and the like. . . .' The message was sent off at noon. An hour or so later, as the ministers were finishing lunch together, the news came over the radio that 'the Russians had given in!'

> First, they admit to the ballistic missiles (hitherto denied by the Communists *and* doubted by all good fellow-travellers in every country) then they said they would be 'packed up, crated and taken away' – a complete climb-down (*if* they kept their word).[46]

The rider to Khrushchev's letter was that Kennedy promise not to invade Cuba, either by the US or other nations of the Western hemisphere.

Recoiling from the Brink

'So it was all over!' Macmillan received the historic news in a state of total exhaustion, having been up throughout Friday and Saturday nights. Harold Evans remembered him, flopped down in a chair by the ticker-tape machine in Admiralty House as the ministers and staff trickled away, and managing to quip that it was like the aftermath of a wedding, 'when there is nothing to do but drink the champagne

377

and go to sleep'.[47] Macmillan himself recalled how relief and gratitude came 'almost with a sense of anti-climax, after days during which it was difficult to restrain yet necessary to conceal our emotions. . . . We had been on the brink, almost over it. . . .' In Washington when President Kennedy announced the news to ExComm, 'We all stood up,' recorded Sorensen; 'He had, as Harold Macmillan would later say, earned his place in history by this one act alone. He had been engaged in a personal as well as national contest for world leadership and he had won.'[48]

In Washington as in London, it was a beautiful day and Arthur Schlesinger remembered the President making a Macmillan-like aside, in what little more than a year later might have seemed like the blackest of black humour: 'This is the night to go to the theatre, like Abraham Lincoln.'[49]

Macmillan signalled to Kennedy that day:

It was indeed a trial of wills and yours has prevailed. Whatever dangers and difficulties we may have to face in the future I am proud to feel that I have so resourceful and so firm a comrade.[50]

By letter, Kennedy replied the same day:

Dear Friend,
I am grateful for your warm generous words. Your heartening support publicly expressed and our daily conversations have been of inestimable value in these past days.
Many thanks.
John F. Kennedy[51]

It was not quite the end of the Cuban crisis. In November there was a brief flare-up when Castro refused to give up the Soviet Ilyushin bombers that the Americans also held to be part of the 'offensive' weaponry in Cuba. On the night of 14 November there was another anxious telephone call between Kennedy and Macmillan, which began on a jocular note:

Prime Minister: Is that you, Mr President?
President Kennedy: It is, Prime Minister. How are you getting on?
Prime Minister: We have had a very good day in Parliament. We have knocked out the Opposition.

President Kennedy: But you do that all the time. We are still not too far along on the Cuba matter and the bombers.

Prime Minister: What about the bombers?

President Kennedy: We might get the bombers out but they want us to withdraw the quarantine and the over-flights and have inspection of Florida as well as Cuba. . . .

Macmillan was firm: 'You must not give in to him. . . .' There was a follow-up the next day.

President Kennedy: . . . we still want to go ahead on the IL-28s and we want to get something from them on that before we withdraw our blockade and formalise our guarantee against invasion. It is a major political question here.

Prime Minister: You must get the bombers out before you give any guarantee of non-invasion. . . .[52]

After much further diplomatic manoeuvring, and with Kennedy under strong domestic and international pressure to let the Russians off the hook, the US blockade was formally lifted, and the last of the Russian bombers removed on 6 December. On 27 November Macmillan received from Khrushchev an uncharacteristically piano letter:

I fully share your view, as well as that of President Kennedy, that the Cuban crisis has led to a better understanding of the need for prompt settlement of acute international problems.

It was, said Macmillan, in the postscript to the crisis he wrote in his memoirs, 'An admirable sentiment – but leaving quite a lot unsaid.' Khrushchev's letter went on:

In your message of 28 October you say that the normalisation of the situation in the Caribbean area opens up for all of us an opportunity to work towards the solution of the disarmament problem. We welcome your statement on this score and we hope that it will find reflection in the British stand in the disarmament negotiations.[53]

The last paragraph was particularly grist to Macmillan's mill. Out of all the appalling danger of the past week, here it looked as if there might be a glimmer of light, after all Macmillan's own strivings for some kind of a halt to the nuclear race.

Macmillan's Role?

After the most immediate danger had passed, Macmillan had spent the following Sunday trying to compile in his diary his own analysis of events: 'The trouble with a first-rate crisis,' he found, evoking memories of another world drama of just six years previously, 'is that it is physically impossible to keep the diary going, just when it would be really interesting! (The same thing happened during the Suez crisis.)' Already, in retrospect, there seemed to him something unreal about all that had happened, since the world had stood on the brink:

> It's now a week away – still difficult to realise. In Secretary Rusk's words 'We looked into the mouth of the cannon. The Russians flinched.' (I don't think, myself, that it's as simple as that. All the same, the President was very firm and his will prevailed.)

During Missiles Week, beset by 'all those messages and telephone calls', Macmillan had felt urged on by 'the frightful desire to *do* something, with the knowledge that *not* to do anything (except to talk to the President and keep Europe and the Commonwealth calm and firm) was probably the right answer . . .'. He still felt 'tired out', and longing for some days of continuous rest, 'which is impossible. At 68 I am not as resilient as when I was a young officer. . . .' On the whole, however, he felt his government had 'played our part perfectly. We were "in on" and took full part in (and *almost responsibility*)[54] for every American move. Our complete calm helped to keep the Europeans calm.' The French, he added in parenthesis, 'were anyway contemptuous; the Germans *very* frightened, though pretending to want firmness; the Italians windy; the Scandinavians rather sour. But they *said* and did nothing to spoil the American playing of the hand. . . .'[55]

At the time, Macmillan confessed to have been puzzled as to Khrushchev's motives in sending in the Cuban missiles. A great deal had been at risk; it had cost him a lot – 'probably £300–£400m'.

When he reviewed his conclusions eleven years later, Macmillan saw it in terms of a chess game; if Khrushchev had been able to keep his 'pawn' permanently in Cuba, 'it would have been a very powerful weapon against American intervention in Eastern Europe. He could have then swopped Berlin for Cuba, which was perhaps his idea from the start. . . .'[56] Otherwise Khrushchev's ploy could be seen as a brilliant, if dangerous, *démarche* which, had it succeeded, would have drastically altered the nuclear strategic balance, as well as perhaps helping ease Khrushchev's domestic problems.

Why did Khrushchev finally withdraw, and cut his (very considerable) losses? Macmillan, in 1973, thought it was 'Probably owing to the same pressures that I think brought him down'; meaning, it was the forces of conservatism in Russia, notably the Old Guard in the Red Army, which disapproved of Khrushchev's 'adventurism' over Cuba, much as it had disapproved of his 'adventurism' in being prepared to risk negotiations with the West at the (aborted) summit of 1960. Macmillan remained puzzled as to why Khrushchev never made a 'counter-move' on Berlin, which he had fully expected even once the maximum danger of Missiles Week was past. On balance he came down on the side of the argument that Khrushchev really believed Kennedy would invade Cuba, on either 29 or 30 October. '*This American invasion could not be stopped by conventional means*';[57] but the Russians were not prepared to face being the first to squeeze the nuclear trigger. In fact, the threat to Berlin ended once Khrushchev had backed down over Cuba. In June of 1964, after both Macmillan and Kennedy were no longer at the helm, Khrushchev did sign a form of peace treaty with East Germany, but it tacitly accepted the West's contractual rights in West Berlin. Macmillan's policy of firmness, with flexibility, had won the day.

Macmillan himself described the Cuban missile crisis in the Commons as 'one of the great turning points in history'.[58] Certainly after it there came the establishment of the 'hot-line' between the Kremlin and the White House, and the reopening of the door to discussions on nuclear disarmament. For the remaining year of the Kennedy–Macmillan era, Khrushchev also showed a new cautious respect for the young President he had previously held in such manifest contempt. On the other hand, it could be argued that the massive build-up of the Soviet nuclear armoury during the Brezhnev era was a consequence of Khrushchev's 'flinching'; the Soviet Deputy Foreign Minister, Vasily Kuznetsov, warned John J. McCloy in November 1962, 'You Americans will never be able to do this to us again.'[59] One question that has never been satisfactorily answered is just what Kennedy, and Macmillan, would have done had Khrushchev not 'flinched' on that Sunday, 28 October.[60] Macmillan himself refused to believe in nuclear conflict over Cuba.

Macmillan never relinquished his profound respect for the 'extraordinary skill'[61] with which President Kennedy had handled the crisis. In his diaries at the time he praised him for having:

> played a firm *military* game throughout – acting quickly and being ready to act *as soon as* mobilised. This was Eden's *fatal* mistake – in which we all share the responsibility. You cannot keep an 'army of invasion' hanging about. It must invade or disperse. President K. did not bluster – but everyone knew that (if no other solution was found) there would be an invasion. . . .[62]

In his foreword to Robert Kennedy's book on the crisis, *13 Days*, Macmillan paid the President this glowing and heartfelt tribute:

> he had the supreme quality, shared only by very great men, of refusing to evade or cushion his final responsibility by an attempt to spread it out upon the backs of his colleagues. . . .
> . . . For President Kennedy really did preserve both Peace and Honour. . . .[63]

Just how important was the influence Macmillan exerted on Kennedy during the Cuban crisis? No one was better able to judge than the late Lord Harlech, David Ormsby-Gore, who admitted it might have become exaggerated: 'I can't honestly think of anything said from London that changed the US action – it was chiefly reassurance to JFK. . . .'[64] Macmillan himself, with engaging modesty, confessed many years later that, over the significance of the telephone calls, he had perhaps 'played the cards above their face value';[65] one must never show off, but on the other hand it never did any good to go round professing to be 'second rate' in terms of influence. But if those lengthy and unprecedented transatlantic telephone calls between Prime Minister and President

at the height of the drama fell short of 'consultation', in the strictest
sense of the word, they were certainly more than just 'informative'.
For there had already emerged a deep, almost instinctive harmony
of views between the two; it was no coincidence that, since the
Macmillan visit to Washington that April, both had been profoundly affected by reading the same book, Barbara Tuchman's *The
Guns of August*, and each had drawn from it the same cautionary
conclusions on the political miscalculations that had precipitated
the First World War. In his foreword to the Robert Kennedy book,
Macmillan praised the way in which the President had 'remained
calm and firm',[66] but undoubtedly, in his role almost of a father-
figure, Macmillan's own quality of hard-won 'unflappability' had
communicated something to Kennedy. In this time when the dreadful responsibility for the survival of mankind seemed to rest on his
shoulders alone, the sixty-eight-year-old Prime Minister had been
the only person, with the exception of his brother Bobby, whom
JFK could really be open with, and he had found him an invaluable
sounding-board.

It was for his support, if nothing else, that Macmillan gained
Kennedy's lasting respect and gratitude. Equally, Macmillan's
own sang-froid had, as he himself reckoned, 'helped to keep the
Europeans calm'.[67] In the words of Robert Kennedy, if the US had
not found unreserved 'trust and mutual respect' among its NATO
allies, and had Khrushchev been able to drive a wedge between
them, 'our position would have been seriously undermined.'[68] Dean
Rusk in retrospect reckoned that, 'in terms of mobilising the una-
nimity of NATO', the British attitude had been 'very important'.[69]
Predictably here the joker in the pack had been de Gaulle. When
Acheson had come to brief him on the missiles at the beginning of the
crisis, de Gaulle had asked pointedly whether the former Secretary of
State had come to consult him about a decision to be taken, or
inform him of one already taken. De Gaulle had then drawn himself
up to his full height and declared that if there was a war, 'France
will be with you. But there will be no war.' He then added, typically:
'I must note that I have been advised, but not consulted.'[70] When
the Soviet Ambassador, Vinogradov, had come to warn de Gaulle
of the dire consequences of siding with the US, de Gaulle stretched
out his hand dismissively and uttered the famous words:
'*Hélas, Monsieur l'Ambassadeur, nous mourirons ensemble! Au revoir,
Monsieur l'Ambassadeur.*' Kennedy appreciated de Gaulle's forthright

committal, but equally realised that he could risk being tough in that his finger was on no button.

As the dust of Cuba settled, Macmillan and Kennedy were both angered by the columnists (largely British, such as Michael Foot in *Tribune* and Wayland Young in the *Guardian*)[71] who were suggesting

> that the Americans not only failed to consult us, but have treated us with contempt; that the 'special relationship' no longer applies; that we have gained nothing from our position as a nuclear power; that America risked total war in a US/USSR quarrel, without bothering about us *or* Europe. . . .[72]

Macmillan dismissed these attacks as being partly initiated by 'ignorance of what really happened', and 'desire to injure and denigrate me personally'. In congratulating Ormsby-Gore for his inspired performance during the crisis, Macmillan was able to observe how glad he was that it 'leaves us with strengthened ties with the Administration'.[73] Ormsby-Gore replied:

> The President has, I know, already told you how much he appreciated your support and advice during that critical week. In this he was being deeply sincere and has repeatedly said the same thing to his closest friends, adding that he has no similar close contacts with any other ally. He is furious with newspaper commentators who suggest that recent events indicate that there is little value for the US in the special Anglo-American relationship.[74]

On appraising Macmillan's role in retrospect, McGeorge Bundy (seldom one to gloss over realities) reckoned, on Cuba as on Berlin, over the really big issues 'he was a pretty tough guy.'[75]

What Kennedy really felt about Macmillan's role could hardly be better epitomised than by the following telegram of 19 December from Secretary of State Rusk to the President, on the eve of the potentially explosive Nassau Conference:

> Should you be seeking a suitable gesture with which to end your meeting with Macmillan, the thought has occurred to us that you might wish to consult with him regarding an invitation from you to Queen Elizabeth and Prince Philip to stop off in Washington

on their way to, or returning from, their trip to Australia this winter. . . .[76]

Rusk's 'thought' was to prove impracticable at such short notice, but it indicated eloquently how, if anything, the Cuban missiles crisis had probably brought the intimacy, and trust, between Macmillan and Kennedy to a new peak.

Chapter Fourteen

The Continuing Burdens
of Empire
1961–1963

Harold Macmillan's mind was the most complicated I have encountered in my political life. . . .

(Roy Welensky, 4000 Days)

What sufferings we go through to try to keep the Commonwealth together. Bed at 3 a.m. Slept badly.

(HM, Diaries, 27 March 1963)

The Central African Federation

When Macmillan complained, as he so often did, of having 'too many balls in the air at once', invariably at least one of them stemmed from the heritage of Empire – generally from Africa, and most specifically from Central Africa, and particularly coupled to the name of Roy Welensky. The last years of his premiership, he admitted, 'were haunted, not to say poisoned', by the tensions and passions emanating from the Central African Federation. The Federal Review Conference of December 1960 had been deferred indefinitely by Macmillan, after it became clear that nothing would be achieved, but in February 1961, a year after the wind of change had been pronounced, the two conferences to amend the constitutions of Southern and Northern Rhodesia, postponed from December, were held in Salisbury and London.

At the former, Duncan Sandys managed to achieve what Macmillan designated 'a great triumph' by pushing through a double-roll electoral system, which gave the Africans a minor advance in representation and (so Macmillan reckoned) opened the door for further progress. Neither the Africans nor the right-wing Dominion Party of the Europeans were satisfied; but, claimed Macmillan, it 'stood the test of time' until illegally repealed under Ian Smith.

Over Northern Rhodesia, with its large African majority, but valuable copper-mining assets that provided the basic wealth of the Federation, a fierce battle raged over many months. In January 1961, Macmillan had suggested to Welensky a plan for giving the Africans sixteen seats as against fourteen Europeans in the Legislative Assembly – plus (a crucial 'plus') some six nominated officials, who would in effect hold the casting vote. Macleod, once again, wanted to go faster. Macmillan reckoned that anything less would fail either to satisfy African demands or to meet world opinion. But Welensky rejected this scheme, on the grounds that anything like parity would 'mark the end of Federation'. When the Northern Rhodesian Conference opened in London at the beginning of February, Welensky and his United Federal Party boycotted it.

The British government nevertheless went ahead and issued a White Paper, putting forward its own proposals.

Welensky threatened to call up troops to meet eventualities in Northern Rhodesia. For a moment, Macmillan feared that the pugnacious Welensky might be intending some kind of unilateral action; this was indeed anticipating events by several years, but Macmillan admitted to being 'in a somewhat pessimistic mood at the time'. He confided to his diary on 22 February, 'I am very tired and anxious. . . . All these African troubles have so absorbed my time that I have not done much other business. . . .' It was typical of the demands that he allowed Africa to impose upon him. He went on to criticise Macleod for having 'undoubtedly leaned over too far towards the African view', and to express his fears of 'a Boston Tea Party . . . or an African blood bath. . . . the curious thing is that the British public and press have not got hold of the true state of things. We cannot send British troops to fight British settlers. There will be no battle of Bunker's Hill. . . .'[1]

Macmillan admitted himself surprised that so little had leaked of this 'exhausting crisis', but he was convinced that if Macleod had resigned over it, the government would then have fallen – a perhaps curious judgement, for if Macleod had departed it was doubtful whether more than a handful of MPs would have abstained in any subsequent debate and division. After a grave Cabinet meeting on 24 February, he recorded: 'We are preparing for the worst event in Rhodesia – that is, open rebellion. We are drawing up the necessary legislative, administrative, and military plans, if the worst should occur. . . . I am very tired.'[2]

At a dinner à deux with Macmillan on 5 March, Welensky, so he claimed in his memoirs, mentioned the British concentration of aircraft and troops in Nairobi. Macmillan seems to have been caught off balance, and (still according to Welensky) assured him, Welensky felt somewhat evasively, that the Nairobi force had been collected 'in case you needed help'.[3] This was one of several occasions when Macmillan gave the impression of having been taken aback by the high quality of Welensky's 'inside information'. He knew that Welensky had established close links with Lord Salisbury and the right wing, and that he missed no opportunity of stirring up their sympathies. He also suspected Welensky of being briefed by sympathisers close to his own government. The Cabinet (with Butler, in his capacity as Home Secretary, activating the measure) had Welensky's rooms at the Savoy Hotel 'bugged'. Macmillan later admitted readily to the 'bugging': '. . . Welensky always thought he was clever . . . would say to his entourage, "We pulled a fast one on the British Government." But this was immediately relayed to me . . . so he was not so clever as he thought. . . .'[4] And Welensky, in his turn, had of course 'bugged' Dr Banda while in jail. It was all indicative of how deep the mistrust between London and Salisbury had become.

Macmillan observed that Welensky's 'behaviour while in London has been very bad'. He had made a bitter attack on Macleod's policy ('and by implication on me') before two hundred Tory MPs, and had intrigued with Lords Salisbury and Lambton: 'The former (like his grandfather) has proved master of "flouts and gibes and jeers" in the House of Lords. The latter (who is ineffective as a speaker) has published a series of rather poisonous articles in the Beaverbrook Press. . . .'[5] If anything, Welensky's frontal tactics were proving counter-productive, with Southern Rhodesia becoming gradually classed, in the public mind, with South Africa – greatly to the detriment of Welensky's cause.

In Westminster, the socialists, and the Liberals, were against federation, so were Africans in all three territories; while Whitehead of Southern Rhodesia was 'ready at any moment to abandon it to save his own skin'. As Macmillan was able to write on 24 March in all sincerity, and with some bluntness, 'about the only friend of Federation is Her Majesty's Government.'[6]

During all this, inside the Federation, cut off – or cutting itself off – from the changing realities of the outside world, life thrived with extraordinary ebullience. Money flowed in, and so did new settlers, from places like Kenya where there now seemed little future for Europeans, from South Africa, and even from full-employment Britain. In the early 1960s, Salisbury – and only to a lesser extent, Bulawayo and Ndola – were sparkling boom towns. Even though institutions such as the Post Office and bastions like Meikles Hotel (at least in name only) had 'gone multi-racial', the White Rhodesia attitude still flourished in such bastions as the Salisbury and Bulawayo Clubs – on the segregated benches of Stanley Square – and on the farms. Yet it was there for all to see, those who had not been blinded by the expansive self-confidence of Roy Welensky, that the dazzling prosperity was built on sand – upon cheap labour from Nyasaland, upon copper sales from the North Rhodesian copper belt, and upon the compliance of the Southern Rhodesian Africans, for whose standard of living Federal prosperity had already done much but promised more. Macmillan recognised these false premises, wanted the Federation to continue somehow, but knew in his heart that it was doomed by the irreconcilable stresses within. It was these perceived contradictions that led him into irresolution, through 1961 to 1963, patching and fudging, and into what at least Welensky held to be downright prevarication.

South Africa Leaves the Commonwealth

While worries over the Federation continued, Macmillan was faced with the final showdown over South Africa. At the Commonwealth Conference of May 1960, which took place only a few weeks after the Sharpeville Massacre had outraged opinion throughout the world, and particularly within Commonwealth countries, Macmillan had used all his skills to prevent the Commonwealth from breaking up and to keep South Africa within it. He was abundantly aware of having achieved at best a papering-over job; the real decision would have to be faced at the Commonwealth Conference of March 1961.

In the meantime, both Malaya and Ghana had boycotted South African goods, and there was strong pressure on other countries to do the same. In August 1960 Macmillan wrote a diplomatic letter to President Nkrumah of Ghana, which – in the light of subsequent history – seems particularly sagacious:

> It is in the nature of things harder for any Government to modify its way at the behest of outside critics than under pressure from within. There is a danger that extremes of pressure from outside could tend to harden opinion in South Africa. . . . For our part we favour a policy of understanding patience, and persuasion. . . .[7]

In South Africa a referendum was held in October on whether or not the Union should become a republic; in advance Macmillan warned Prime Minister Verwoerd that, if the result was 'yes', South Africa would have to reapply for membership to the Commonwealth and that, as feelings were, this would certainly be opposed by some members. Verwoerd in turn appreciated that if the republic was unacceptable to the Commonwealth, then South Africa would have to be a republic outside. In the event, out of a poll of 90.7 per cent and a total vote of 1,626,336, the majority in favour of a republic was only 74,580. Verwoerd told Macmillan that South Africa nevertheless wished to remain in the Commonwealth, but would not permit any attempt to interfere in her internal affairs. 'He never gave a single inch on anything,' said Macmillan many years later.[8]

In contrast, the august Tunku of Malaya and – even more surprisingly – Nkrumah showed themselves prepared to take a moderate line on South Africa's 'readmission'. Macmillan's 1960 visit to Accra (and his letter of August) seemed to have paid off. Of the 'white' Commonwealth, however, the threat came from Canada's Diefenbaker, who, in November 1960, warned Macmillan that, 'unless significant changes occur in the Union Government's racial policies', Canada's support could not be counted on.[9] 'John Diefenbaker is going to be troublesome,' Macmillan noted wearily in his diary. 'He is taking a "holier than thou" attitude, which may cause us infinite trouble. For if the "Whites" take an anti-South African line, how can we expect the Browns and Blacks to be more tolerant?'[10]

Recognising that Diefenbaker's position could be decisive at the coming Conference, Macmillan wrote him (and Nehru) a long letter, pleading for moderation, and warning – prophetically – that to turn South Africa out of the forum of the Commonwealth would be to condemn 'the country to further years of apartheid and ever-growing bitterness'.

When the Conference began, on 8 March, however, Diefenbaker was unmoved, and Verwoerd unyielding. For a week Macmillan struggled, under what he admitted to be acute nervous strain, with often no more than two or three hours' sleep a night, pleading, but in vain. The stumbling block came over Verwoerd's obdurate refusal to allow a black High Commissioner in Pretoria. Macmillan noted that 'Even President Ayub [of Pakistan], usually so moderate, was deeply offended by some of Dr Verwoerd's remarks . . .',[11] such as the suggestion that there would have to be a special hotel for the African representatives, if admitted at all. After it was clear that no compromise proposals by Macmillan would be acceptable, he suggested to Verwoerd the face-saver (apparently devised by Iain Macleod)[12] that he should withdraw his application to be readmitted to the Commonwealth, rather than face 'an almost overwhelming vote against'. Verwoerd accepted.

On 14 March, Macmillan announced to the Commons, in 'a grim and painful silence', the news of South Africa's withdrawal. Macmillan says that he felt 'weighed down by a sense of grief and foreboding . . . almost a sense of despair'. Welensky, however, who dined with him a few days before the announcement, accused Macmillan of false sentiment:

> He was always one of the most accomplished actors in public life, and in the three hours I spent with him then he put on a truly magnificent performance. As he spoke of his deep sympathy and understanding of us in Africa, his eyes were moist and shining and his voice vibrated with emotion. . . .[13]

Welensky recalled the tears rolling down Macmillan's cheeks as he evoked the horrors of 'Britishers shooting down Britishers'. But Welensky dismissed this as crocodile tears, and damned Macmillan's speech as 'one of naked appeasement'.

Others closer to Macmillan did not share Welensky's opinions about his sincerity. Lord Kilmuir reckoned that he had 'never seen Macmillan so utterly miserable and distressed'.[14] Harold Evans found him in an equally emotional mood, recalling the South Africa visit of the previous year. '. . . "I can't help thinking about all those people in Durban. . . . It wasn't me they were cheering. It was the old country – 'home' they called it. It is those people I care about."' Then he remarked on the effect on his own position. '"Don't think I am under any illusion about it" – putting his hand on my arm. "It is a defeat. Perhaps my first real defeat. You can imagine the things Gaitskell will have to say. I could retire, of course. But I won't. This makes me all the more determined to go on."'[15] To Sir John Maud, the British High Commissioner in South Africa, Macmillan wrote: 'There it is – the wind of change has blown us away, for the time. But peace will come one day, although perhaps after much sorrow and tribulation. My faith is not dimmed. . . .'[16]

In the ensuing parliamentary debates, Lord Salisbury criticised Macmillan on the ground that it would have 'been wiser to stand firmly, even rigidly, on the principle that there should be no interference . . . in the domestic affairs of member states' within the

Commonwealth. To the Commons, Macmillan, in an eloquent speech, blamed Verwoerd squarely; had he:

> shown the smallest move towards an understanding of the views of his Commonwealth colleagues, or made any concession, had he given us anything to hold on to or any grounds for hope, I still think that the Conference would have looked beyond the immediate difficulties to the possibilities of the future. For, after all, our Commonwealth is not a treaty-made league of Governments; it is an association of peoples. . . .[17]

But, privately, he was also unforgiving about Diefenbaker. In contrast to Australia's Menzies ('a great imperial statesman'), Nehru, Ayub and even Nkrumah, Diefenbaker seemed once again to be playing domestic politics:

> It might have been said of Diefenbaker what Disraeli so naughtily said of Gladstone – 'intoxicated by the exuberance of his own verbosity'. . . . poor old Dief. would have read the leading article in the Winnipeg something-or-other, and he would suit his actions to that. Without him, we could have got through – though we might have failed at the next conference. . . .[18]

Spotlight on Northern Rhodesia

South Africa's departure from the Commonwealth served only to increase Macmillan's concern over the Central African Federation; its future, he wrote on 8 April, 'is anxious and obscure'.[19] The focus remained on the government's White Paper proposing change for the constitution of Northern Rhodesia; by June Macmillan was noting in frustration that 'Every idea we put up is opposed either by Welensky or by Governor Hone – usually by both. . . .'[20] Behind the opposition of Sir Evelyn Hone, Governor of Northern Rhodesia, lay the hand of Macleod and the Colonial Office; the fundamental antipathy between Macleod and Welensky had now grown to a point where '. . . Welensky hates Macleod and vice-versa, and each hope to destroy the other. . . .'[21]

Macmillan recorded on 3 June that 'the Colonial Secretary is in unhappy mood. We seem to be back in an atmosphere of crisis and "resignation".' Macleod's excitable temperament and his repeated threats of resignation were in great contrast to the personality and behaviour of Duncan Sandys: 'as cool as a cucumber, methodical; very strong in character, has gradually mastered the art of Parliamentary speaking, tremendously hard working; not easily shaken from his course – ambitious, and rather cruel . . .'.[22]

It was a relief to Macmillan that Sandys, of whose toughness he was becoming increasingly appreciative, was on hand to control Welensky; from the latter he received on 18 June 'a terrible message . . . rude, blackmailing, coarse, and silly . . .'.[23] The following day, the Cabinet 'agreed – though with some hesitation – to stand firm on a "package" deal with Welensky, based on a fair interpretation of the White Paper . . .'. Aimed at finding ways of broadening the franchise, the point at issue was a complex one; it all turned around the weighting of the 'Upper' and 'Lower' rolls. Welensky was demanding 'Upper-roll predominance', while the Africans – though in theory insistent upon the 'one man one vote' principle – were prepared to accept (at least temporarily) an equality of strength between the two rolls. 'In other words,' as Macmillan explained it, 'it is fifty–fifty (as the White Paper says) or sixty–forty (as Sir Roy Welensky demands). There are, however, points where we can fairly meet the Federal Party [i.e. Welensky's]. . . .'[24]

In the haggling that ensued, Welensky once again accused the British government of bad faith; 'slithering out from major agreements in principle', and he damned its 'obdurate insistence' in handing to Kaunda and his allies, 'pledged to break up the Federation', a majority in the Northern Rhodesian councils.[25] Dining with Alec Home, now Foreign Secretary, at Buck's Club, on 19 June, Macmillan found him 'very distressed about Rhodesia'. Macmillan did not minimise the gravity of the situation, and recorded – once again – the serious fear that Welensky might end 'in open rebellion and Her Majesty's Government put in a ludicrous as well as impossible position . . .'. He foresaw a time when Southern Rhodesia might become 'the scene of strife and conflict on a terrible scale, white versus white, black versus black, all against all'.[26]

The stress of the protracted crisis was beginning to have its effect on Macmillan, physically. The following day, Question Time in the Commons 'went badly. My voice is so bad that I can hardly speak.' His faithful doctor, Sir John Richardson, came to see him: '. . . I have no more "élan vital"! I am finished! In other words, I ought to have a month's holiday. As it is, I am to have four days, starting tomorrow evening. . . .'[27]

But Rhodesia and Welensky would not go away. On 25 June Macmillan noted: 'My "rest cure" failed – for on Friday afternoon I had to come down and preside over a number of ministers who spent nearly all Friday – morning, afternoon and evening – in the Cabinet Room. . . .' It was rumoured that Welensky was going to descend suddenly on London. A Feydeau-style farce now ensued, the humour of which Macmillan – despite his sickness – was able to savour:

Rumour kept changing – Sir Roy Welensky *would* come to London after all. He would *not*. No: he *would*. And so this threat (or promise) was played, backwards and forwards, like a ping-pong ball. Sandys kept his head; Macleod overplayed his hand; Alec Home was so disgusted by Macleod's tactics that he nearly resigned himself; Lord Chancellor tried to keep the peace; then they sent for me – practically in pyjamas![28]

On the Saturday morning, Sir John Richardson came again and was 'encouraging – *if* I can get rest. But when and how can I rest? I am beginning (at last) to feel old and depressed.' Nevertheless, with all his pills, he managed to sleep for eleven hours. 'Then the telephones began. Welensky presses for more concessions. I have said *no*. . . . I sent a final telegram to Roy Welensky of rather insincere "good wishes". Actually (as the children say) this *may* be a real turning point *if* Sir Roy Welensky *acquiesces* (and does not either crow or lament); if he makes no foolish threats. . . .'[29]

Meanwhile, in Salisbury, according to Welensky, he had been called to the telephone by Sandys who, 'against the hubbub of the airport and the roar of the engines warming up', pleaded with the Federal Premier and begged him not to come. Welensky, persuaded, had his 'bags unloaded' and went home.[30] The following day an agreement was announced in the House of Commons, though Welensky made it plain that 'it was a compromise which, like all such solutions, would probably please nobody,' and was being imposed on him by the British government.

In London, as the last-minute compromise over Northern Rhodesia had been reached, Macmillan noted that his ministers were:

'all on edge'. In spite of all the threatened resignations (a daily event with Macleod) no resignation has actually become effective. . . . Macleod, with many faults, has been persistent, imaginative and ingenious. Sandys has been most loyal to me and absolutely tireless. Nor have we, in making some concessions to Welensky, surrendered any principle. . . .[31]

By 8 July, Macmillan was able to rejoice: 'By a miracle, we have achieved a solution of the immediate crisis. Both Sandys and Macleod have agreed and so – under pressure – has Welensky. . . .'[32]

In a matter of weeks, however, all was torpedoed by Kaunda leading violent riots of protest in Northern Rhodesia, in demand of 'one man one vote'. Kaunda's party was banned, and the 'solution' so painfully hammered out was set in abeyance once again. When Welensky's Federal High Commissioner in London, A. E. Robinson, saw Macmillan at Admiralty House on 12 September, he observed that – despite the summer recess and a spell on the grouse moors – his face was 'drawn with fatigue' and he was 'a good deal less than cordial'.[33] Reporting to the Queen on his latest attempt to achieve a compromise over Northern Rhodesia, and revealing the opposing pressures to which he was constantly subject, Macmillan observed tartly:

. . . Sir Roy Welensky will, of course, be upset by it, but then everything upsets him. The left-wing Press here interprets our statement as a strong measure against Kaunda and a defeat for Mr Macleod. The *Daily Express* says it is a sell-out to extremists. The more moderate Press say, quite truly, that it is reasonable and fair. . . .[34]

The Queen to Ghana

At this time Macmillan was also advising the Queen on another African issue, Ghana, where the Queen was scheduled to make a state visit in November. This had already been unavoidably postponed for two years, and now unrest and threats against Nkrumah's life raised serious doubts in Whitehall as to the advisability of her going at all. In September Macmillan was noting that Nkrumah had returned from a trip to Russia 'in a dangerous mood',[35] and had thrown out all his British officers, and most of his non-left-wing British advisers. In October, the situation deteriorated with the arrest of fifty of Nkrumah's political opponents. Macmillan, however, recommended to the Queen (who needed no urging) that she go; otherwise cancellation, following the inner tensions provoked by the issue of South Africa, might be interpreted as signifying that 'we did not want Ghana in the Commonwealth. That would be a very grave step. . . .'[36]

Macmillan also wrote to Kennedy, who was then considering a massive injection of cash for the multi-million dollar Volta Dam project, pointing out that cancellation of the visit might push Ghana out of the Commonwealth and into Russian hands. Adroitly, he recalled to American memories the consequences of John Foster Dulles's repudiation of Egypt's Aswan Dam in July 1956. Would he therefore either (a) announce American participation in the dam *before* the Queen set forth, or (b) if the verdict was negative, delay announcing it until the Queen was safely back on 20 November?

At the same time, Macmillan was faced with the serious contingency that Nkrumah might equally decide to leave the Commonwealth immediately after the Queen's visit, which would 'put us in a ludicrous position'. Meanwhile, after several bombs had exploded in Accra, Macmillan found himself faced by mounting concern within the Tory Party, which was vigorously expressed by John Morrison, the powerful Chairman of the 1922 Committee. Macmillan decided that Sandys should go out to Ghana to test the water. Sandys 'cajoled or forced the reluctant President' to do a dummy-run with him over the royal route, in an open car; 'he emerged to tell the tale'. Still opposition mounted in the Commons, and (though he thought the threat exaggerated) Macmillan felt it his duty to warn the Queen that, if he were outvoted:

. . . I would *not* repeat not alter my advice. I would resign – at (say) 11 p.m. The Queen (who was to leave at 9 a.m. [the next day] for London Airport) would no doubt have retired early. But she would no doubt see me. She could refuse my resignation, and ask me to carry on. I could agree, but I could not alter my advice. So the Queen would leave, with a *hostile* vote from House of

Commons, and flouting *their* advice. I should no doubt be im-
peached. What would happen to her?
    . . . It all seemed too absurd to be true.[37]

And indeed so it turned out.

The Queen, characteristically courageous and determined to do
her duty for the Commonwealth, was impatient with the fainthearts
in Parliament and the press, and insisted on going ahead with the
visit. In the event, it was an outstanding success, with the local
press pronouncing her 'the greatest Socialist monarch in the
world'.[38] When she returned, safely, and covered with laurels for
her courage, Macmillan promptly telephoned Kennedy to say, 'I
have risked my Queen; you must risk your money!' Kennedy replied,
in kind, that gallantry demanded he match the Queen's 'brave
contribution' with his own.[39] On 12 December 1961, the US formally announced participation in the Volta project; a few days later
Kennedy wrote to Barbara Ward:* 'We have put quite a few chips
on a very dark horse but I believe the game is worthwhile.'[40] Ghana
remained in the Commonwealth; there was no constitutional crisis.
It was perhaps one more case of the Special Relationship working,
in practice.

The Congo: On the Boil Again

Meanwhile, the situation in the Congo remained grave, creating
further headaches for Macmillan, and producing differences with
Kennedy. Macmillan fully shared Kennedy's fear that Soviet involvement in the chaos of the Congo might lead to a Russian base
in the heart of Africa. Where they differed was over the means of
keeping the Soviets out. Both were in agreement that it was essential
for the central government in Leopoldville to possess full authority.
Here, on the one hand, matters were complicated by the Organisation of African States, which had declared in January 1961 for the
remnants of the left-wing Lumumba regime in Stanleyville. This
threatened Macmillan with fresh rifts in the Commonwealth.
On the other hand, to provide Leopoldville with authority meant

---

* Barbara Ward's husband, Robert Jackson, was one of Nkrumah's principal
advisers.

bringing to heel Tshombe's secessionist Katanga, which produced nearly half the tax revenues and foreign exchange earnings of the Congo, and which was supported by powerful lobbies in Britain and France – and Welensky in neighbouring Rhodesia. It was Katanga's revenues that enabled Tshombe to recruit white mercenaries and buy weapons.

The murder in January 1961 of Patrice Lumumba, the left-wing leader, under circumstances which remain mysterious, and Tshombe's arrest in April were followed by Kennedy introducing a new actor, a previously little-known labour leader called Cyrille Adoula, to the Congo scene. With a certain amount of bribery organised by the CIA, Adoula was duly elected Prime Minister in the summer of 1961, with Lumumba's deputy, Gizenga, as his Vice-Premier, and with the full support of the United Nations. Tshombe was freed, signing a pledge to reunite Katanga with the rest of the Congo; which, on returning to Katanga, he promptly repudiated. Kennedy increased US financial commitments to the UN in the Congo, but was chagrined when Secretary-General Hammarskjöld – at Adoula's request – used his new mandate and increased financial support to try to reintegrate Katanga by force. Macmillan was even more shocked, especially by accounts of atrocities committed by the UN troops. He regarded Kennedy's man, Adoula, with apprehension as a potential Kerensky to whom Gizenga ('more or less a Russian agent')[41] would play Lenin.

In some agitation, Macmillan telephoned Kennedy on the new direct secret line which had just been installed, 'to persuade him to act firmly with us . . .'. Meanwhile, he had sent Lord Lansdowne, a Parliamentary Under-Secretary of State at the Foreign Office, to mediate on the spot. On 17 September, Macmillan was encouraged to learn from Lord Lansdowne the '*very* good news' that Hammarskjöld, under pressure from Lansdowne, had agreed to fly that evening to Ndola (just inside Northern Rhodesia). There he would meet Tshombe personally, in an attempt to achieve a ceasefire. 'Lansdowne has done well,' recorded Macmillan.[42] Then, almost immediately, came the news that Hammarskjöld had been killed when his plane crashed on its approach to Ndola; Lansdowne had narrowly escaped.[43]

Criticism that the UN had exceeded its charter in Katanga ran strong in Britain and France; while Macmillan, too, came under heavy fire from his own backbenchers. His declared aim was, ideally, to achieve a 'united Congo' but not a 'Communist Congo'; he felt that no good would come out of destroying Tshombe, but that he must be made to join a Congo federation while persuading Adoula to respect states rights. He noted, with some irony, how the Americans, despite their own history, 'appeared to regard this as a somewhat rash and even novel proposition'. But, in his attempts 'to preserve the middle position between the extremes', Macmillan found himself getting tied in more of the kind of knots that Central Africa peculiarly seemed to generate for him.

Bombs for the UN; an Explosion at Home

In the autumn of 1961 following Hammarskjöld's death, the situation in the Congo deteriorated once again; in Stanleyville, Congolese troops went on the rampage, killing thirteen Italian pilots of the UN forces, while in Katanga Tshombe seemed to be losing control over his troops and white mercenaries. Although in spirit (and moved by right-wing Tory pressures), Macmillan was with Katanga over its struggle for independence, he continued to pay lipservice to the United Nations, and – at the beginning of December – rashly agreed to a request from the Indian air force contingent with the UN for twenty-four 1000-pound bombs, for deployment against airfields used by Tshombe's mercenary flyers. The bombs seemed to many Tory MPs to be a wholly inappropriate contribution. To Welensky and his supporters in Britain, this was one more example of Macmillan's duplicity in that (so Welensky claimed) the government had specifically assured him that the UN would *not* be permitted to take over Katanga by force. Welensky saw it as 'a typically oriental stratagem which would commit Britain irrevocably to the UN attack on Katanga . . . ';[44] Macmillan had fallen into a trap. Many of the Macmillan Cabinet were equally unhappy about the decision taken on 7 December, even though Home told Dean Rusk that actual delivery of the bombs would be withheld until the UN had its troops under control, and they ceased committing atrocities.

Suddenly the bombs blew up in Macmillan's face. Macmillan first realised 'we were in for a row' after shooting with John Wyndham at Petworth over the weekend of 9 December. There followed 'an internal political crisis', which Macmillan saw at the time as being 'both acute and dangerous'. The mood in the Tory

Party Macmillan described as being 'very tense'; the backbenchers were up in arms, and the reaction of the influential 1922 Committee (with Lord Salisbury hovering implacably in the Lords) profoundly shocked him. A debate was set for the 14th. The sudden storm told on Macmillan's nerves: 'For some reason (I suppose, age and infirmity) I have felt this "crisis" more than I should have done – have worried, and slept badly, and so on. All the same forces are being mobilised as were at Suez. . . .'[45] In fact, of course, the line-up of the factions was exactly the reverse of the Suez controversy. The Labour Party and the Liberals and the left wing of the Tory Party all broadly supported the UN intervention. The right wing and a large section of the centre, including a number of officers of the 1922 Committee, thought that the government had temporarily taken leave of its senses.

In something approaching a 'flap', or even a panic, Macmillan rang Kennedy. He told him that he was in dire trouble, and needed every vote he could get the following day. A similar message came from Alec Home, via Dean Rusk. That same night (13 December) Kennedy dined alone with David Ormsby-Gore, who put it to him that Macmillan was facing his most serious challenge in the Commons, and that to save himself he needed 'a request from the United Nations to cease fire – in 12 hours – 24 hours at the most . . .'. Ormsby-Gore described this as one red-letter occasion 'on which Kennedy was wonderful at appreciating the difficulties of his friends and allies. . . . he threw the full weight of his authority behind getting the results that Harold Macmillan required.'[46] After dinner, Kennedy telephoned his representative at the UN, Adlai Stevenson, and instructed him to tell U Thant (Hammarskjöld's successor) that the reconciliation process between Tshombe and Adoula should begin immediately. Stevenson protested, but the President was insistent.[47]

The Commons debate of 14 December was indeed one of the most heated since Suez. Macmillan found that, within his own Party, 'in addition to the small group of people who really hate me – Lords Hinchinbrooke and Lambton; Nigel Birch; Mr Turton; and about ten others – the anxiety about United Nations behaviour had spread to the whole *centre* of the Party. . . .'[48] He blamed the UN officials, as well as the 'incredible folly and weakness' of Adlai Stevenson, in not curbing them. Then, at the other extreme to the right-wing Tory rebels, there was the *Daily Mirror* with headlines of 'MACMILLAN BETRAYS U.N.'; while there was talk elsewhere in the press of 'up to 60, or even 100 Tories abstaining – which would have meant the end of the Government . . .', recorded Macmillan after the event.[49]

Fortunately, Macmillan reckoned, the Opposition made 'a fundamental error of tactics', by not leaving most of the debate to the government's own critics, and adopting 'a sympathetic even unctuous attitude towards the rebellious forces'. Harold Wilson, in his first effort as Shadow Foreign Secretary (instead of Chancellor of the Exchequer), made a 'bad speech', so violent as to reunite the divided Tories: 'offensive, vulgar, poisonous. It made the Opposition laugh, but with the laughter one has at salacious jokes in an improper play. They were really ashamed. . . .'[50] The moment Wilson sat down, Macmillan felt comforted. He then wound up – 'in my new style, with *no* set speech but a few notes . . .'. It was extremely effective. Towards the end of his speech, with superb timing, he was able to spring on the House the vital news that U Thant had, within the last couple of hours, informed him he was sending two of his most trusted colleagues to achieve a peaceful reconciliation. Wilson commented acridly that the government was more concerned about a ceasefire with the rebels in its own ranks than with a ceasefire in the Congo. At the same time, Macmillan was able to add the welcome news that Kennedy had telephoned to say he had now been 'persuaded' by Macmillan's arguments to support the important Volta Dam project in Ghana.

Once again Macmillan had dramatically overestimated the threat to the government. Most of the protesters were cross, but would have been appalled at the prospect of defeating the government. When the vote was taken, Macmillan had a majority of 94 with only 10 or so abstaining, instead of the predicted 60 or more. With a quick sleight of hand, Macmillan had succeeded in turning the bombs into doves. When Ormsby-Gore relayed the news to the President, he remarked – with perhaps just a note of sarcasm – 'Well, that was a pretty good majority; I wonder whether we needed to have gone to all that trouble the other night in order to get it?'[51] Macmillan may, once again, perhaps have reacted in an excess of pessimism, though undoubtedly on this occasion the danger of his government falling did, to him, seem very real. In his memoirs, he admits that the incident of the bombs was 'handled clumsily', but is otherwise reticent about his behind-the-scenes dealing with Kennedy.

The episode did not end with Macmillan's victory in the Commons. Tshombe and Adoula met and agreed to a reluctant truce, known as the Kitona accord, but Tshombe, once again, quickly reneged – on the grounds that he had been acting under UN pressure. Atrocities in the name of UN 'peace-keeping' continued; and Macmillan arrived in Bermuda in December grateful to Kennedy for getting him out of the hole (which he felt the UN had plunged him into), but tough-minded, and frustrated that neither Britain nor any European power could really influence what was happening in the Congo. He was openly critical to Kennedy (though none of this appeared in the communiqué) about US support, spiritual and financial, for the UN 'driven on by the Afro-Asians and the "non-aligned", with their bitter "anti-colonial" complex . . .'.[52] Britain, backed by France, would not continue to support the UN in its aggressive policies.

For his part, Kennedy had come to Bermuda hoping to get Macmillan to do some hard talking to Katanga's silent partner, Roy Welensky; the UN had solid evidence that Rhodesia was providing arms to Katanga. Rusk asked Ormsby-Gore if the British government did not, in fact, still control the Federation's foreign relations? Ormsby-Gore replied (rather lamely, he later thought) that if London gave direct orders to Salisbury, this would lead to 'tremendous rows' in Parliament.[53] Kennedy also brought with him a communiqué, endorsing the principles signed at Kitona, which he wanted Macmillan to endorse. But Macmillan would have none of it, and told Kennedy that, regardless of Tshombe's 'indecent dealings' with white mercenaries, he remained the West's best bulwark against Communism in the Congo. Thus, on the Congo, Macmillan and Kennedy left Bermuda roughly agreeing to disagree.

The Congo, 1962–1963

In January 1962, Adoula's central government, with UN support, arrested the pro-Communist Gizenga and defeated his forces. A brittle peace temporarily reigned; but rifts soon began to appear in the vicarious accord between Adoula and Tshombe, and with them the strange tango continued: Macmillan and Kennedy both activated by a desire to keep the Russians out, but dancing to different tunes.

Pressed by Adlai Stevenson, in March 1962, Macmillan agreed – reluctantly – to continue to pay Britain's $12 million subscription to the UN's peace-keeping bill of $500 million a month. But the following month the Americans were puzzled by Macmillan's Private Office hinting that there might be an open split between the two countries, because Macmillan still believed that if Adoula gained the upper hand over Tshombe he might open the door to the Soviets, and Tshombe's position had to be maintained for as long as the UK was responsible for the Central African Federation. At Kennedy's request, tripartite talks were mounted in Belgium, with David Bruce heading the US delegation, on the ground that (as Bundy told the State Department) the British would 'do more for Bruce than they will for anyone else'.[54] The Conference was a fiasco, and relations between the President and Prime Minister became cool, with Kennedy pointedly warning Macmillan that, if talks on reintegrating the Congo failed through Tshombe's fault, Adoula would 'no longer heed or be free to follow the counsels of restraint. . . . the Chief of the Congolese Government will be obliged to reassert his authority. . . .'[55]

Macmillan was coming increasingly to feel a pox on both their houses: 'these particular Africans seem really impossible to deal with – Tshombe and Adoula are equally difficult. . . .'[56] At the end of June, Adoula declared that all peaceful means to a solution were now exhausted. In the middle of his 'Night of Long Knives' crisis, Macmillan noted a new war brewing up, 'owing to the folly of all concerned'.[57] Disillusion with Tshombe was growing; but Macmillan could still not quite accept UN military action against Katanga. He was let off the hook by the UN proposing (under US pressure) economic sanctions – i.e. a boycott on Katanga copper. Since much of the rest of the world's copper was in American hands, this did not entirely please Macmillan, but he recorded his 'real concern' as being 'that Welensky might be driven by United Nations' folly to some folly of his own. He might reach a merger or armed alliance with Tshombe. It would be tempting. The Katanga and the Northern Rhodesian copper belts really form a single system. . . .'[58] It was illustrative of just how little control Macmillan felt he had over Welensky at this juncture. Macmillan continued to haver and – in a rare fit of impatience with his friend – Kennedy summoned

David Ormsby-Gore to 'chew him out' over the chameleon-like behaviour of his chief.[59] Kennedy himself would dearly have liked to pull the US out of the involvement in the Congo altogether; but the Cuban missiles crisis that autumn made him think again, as the danger of Adoula calling for Soviet help looked more of a reality than ever.

Praising U Thant for his 'exemplary patience', Macmillan welcomed the inauguration in October of a Federal Constitution for the Congo, but 'with obstinate folly Tshombe now repudiated the whole plan.' The following month – after the distraction of Cuban Missiles Week had passed – he was recording that the unhappy country was 'boiling up again . . . I suspect the American copper interests in all this. They are equally jealous of Union Minière and of the Northern Rhodesian copper companies. . . .'[60] In December, Macmillan was referring to the Congo as 'the eternal and quite insoluble problem . . .',[61] but he was still holding out strongly against any UN military action, and once again warned Kennedy of the trouble this might bring him in Parliament. Recalling how Macmillan had seemed to cry 'wolf' over his parliamentary problems at the time of the bombs-for-Katanga issue the previous December, the President was unresponsive. It was agreed, however, that no action was to be taken until after Macmillan's meeting with Kennedy in Nassau; meanwhile Macmillan was under great pressure over Skybolt, and direly in need of the President's good offices.

Then, on Christmas Eve, a UN helicopter was shot down in Katanga; Macmillan had come to reckon that Tshombe was now 'a broken reed even to his own supporters'. Reluctantly (and leaned on heavily by Kennedy, who warned him that the Russians were poised to move in), he agreed to military operations against Tshombe. In January 1963, Tshombe fled to Rhodesia and thence to Europe, and Katanga's secession was ended. That July Adoula, now (for the time being) undisputed leader of the Congo, came to London and was received by Macmillan with 'special courtesy'; by the end of November the entire staff of the Soviet Embassy in the Congo was deported.

So ended the sad saga of the Congo, in Macmillan's day. Kennedy at the time reckoned that the US was entitled to 'a little sense of pride';[62] in later years, Macmillan liked to claim expansively that '. . . Kennedy and I, we drove the Russians out. . . .'[63] But, as the record suggests, this may have been more by good luck than by good management. Indisputably, if the Soviets could have established themselves in the Congo, together with – subsequently – Angola next door, it would have provided them with a base lethal to Western interests throughout Africa – however unlikely this might now seem with hindsight. But, on the whole, it was hardly Macmillan's finest hour. Meanwhile, as Welensky noted, 'It was against the background of the Congo crisis that the final act in the life of the Federation was played out. . . .'[64]

Exit Macleod; Enter Maudling

By the autumn of 1961, Macmillan was thoroughly wearied with all the infighting within his Cabinet over Central Africa, and particularly by the highland histrionics of Iain Macleod; 'too clever by half', as Lord Salisbury had dubbed him. The strife between Macleod and Sandys had become invidious. Burke Trend, deputy secretary to the Cabinet under Norman Brook, saw Sandys as 'a very slow, ponderous thinker' and the volatile Macleod as 'very fast'; he reckoned that only Macmillan 'held those two together', thereby maintaining the unity of the Cabinet.[65] Macmillan respected Macleod for 'his high idealism and a deep sympathy with African aspirations', as well as for his capacity to inspire the young; in retrospect, he thought 'he would have been certain to have been elected Prime Minister if he hadn't died; but he . . . needed someone above him. . . . He was argumentative. . . .'[66] Macmillan wanted to retain the cooler and tougher Sandys, but the time had come to shift Macleod; the rows in Cabinet had cost Macmillan too much, in both time and energy. Thus, on 9 October 1961, Macleod was transferred to replace Butler as Chairman of the Party Organisation and Leader of the House, and Reginald Maudling took over as Colonial Secretary.

When Maudling had first come to Macmillan's attention, in 1957, he had rated him, in rather headmasterly terms, as 'very clever, a little lazy; and a trifle vain. But I believe that if he buckles down to it he *will* do very well. . . .'[67] Maudling, like Macleod before him, had no experience of colonial problems before taking up his new office. But Macmillan was mistaken if he thought that, with the more phlegmatic Maudling, there would be less argument and less pressure from the Colonial Office. Very soon Macmillan found Maudling being even more progressive – *'plus noir que les nègres*, more difficult and intransigent than his predecessor. He threatens resignation. . . .'[68]

Once again, the row was over Northern Rhodesia. Maudling wanted the government, in Macmillan's words, in his first diary entry for 1962, 'to go back radically on the June plan, which was "agreed" with Sir Roy Welensky after immense labour then. It is true that in September we referred to "possible changes" – but we are not bound to make any. . . .'[69] Macmillan thought Maudling's new scheme 'quite impossible'. There was renewed talk about both Sandys and Maudling resigning. But, since the previous July when Macmillan had seemed poised to achieve a compromise over the Northern Rhodesian Constitution, the world – and public opinion – had moved ahead, perhaps faster even than Macmillan realised; certainly a great deal faster than Welensky could perceive from Salisbury.

In early February, Sandys flew once again to Salisbury where, at a lunch after Welensky had insisted that Nyasaland could be kept 'peacefully' within the Federation, he had allegedly replied, 'We British have lost the will to govern.' To which Welensky's colleague, Julian Greenfield, had snapped back, 'But *we* haven't.'[70]

Returning to London, Sandys reported to Macmillan that Dr Banda was now quite adamant about the need for Nyasaland to secede from the Federation. Macmillan foresaw 'hideous trouble awaiting us' and three days later, on 26 February, 'a new horror – the United Nations and Southern Rhodesia. A group of countries, of which Poland is one, is to enquire into liberty in Southern Rhodesia!'[71] From then on, however, the Cabinet accepted 'what now seemed the inevitable disintegration of the Federation'.[72] Welensky, he reckoned privately, 'could hardly win one African vote today. By his talk and his brutality he has killed "multi-racialism". . . .' Despondently, Macmillan could see 'no way out from a civil war or an African revolution. All this results from Welensky's intransigence on the one hand and (I fear) our own hesitations on the other. . . .'[73]

Maudling's new proposal for Northern Rhodesia prepared the way for an African majority. Macmillan thought that even Welensky was 'at last beginning to face realities, 2 or 3 years too late. He recognises that Nyasaland cannot be kept in. . . .'[74] When

Welensky flew to London to contest the new Maudling proposals, at the end of February, he seemed to Macmillan 'calm, rather subdued'.[75] When he accused Macmillan of caving in to African nationalist threats, Macmillan (according to Welensky) gave him a lecture on the dangers of using force:

> In Algeria the French have a million men under arms, and they have now suffered a humiliating defeat.* It is too simple a reading of history to think that you can exercise control simply by the use of power. Indeed, I cannot guarantee that British troops would undertake the kind of duties that would be necessary. . . .[76]

Enter Rab; Exit Federation

On 9 March 1962 there was a bad by-election result at Lincoln, with the Tories losing 3000 votes to the Liberals. Macmillan noted: 'The chief difficulty at the next General Election will be the cry "Time for a Change!"'[77] It was the day, after Maudling had been in the job only five months, that Macmillan made a change, taking the step which, he himself recognised, should have been taken many months earlier. The conflicting interests of both the Colonial and Commonwealth Relations office were finally brought under the control of one man – Rab Butler. Back in May of the previous year Macmillan had been expressing wonderment 'that we ever agreed to so difficult a project as "Federation" – which involved two Secretaries of State being responsible for the same territories. . . .'[78]

Why he had not appointed an 'overlord' when Macleod was moved, or even months before, is hard to explain; to say that Rab was the only man up to the job, and that he had refused it the previous year, is only partly satisfactory. It would certainly have saved the Prime Minister himself substantial and unnecessary stress and distraction that perhaps proved disastrous to his premiership. As he wrote to Maudling, on 9 March: 'The division of responsibility between two ministers inevitably threw a great burden on me personally.'[79] Perhaps, breaching for once his own golden rule of

---

* The following month de Gaulle would sign the Evian Agreements, giving wartorn Algeria her independence.

'delegation', he considered himself indispensable in holding the rein over Africa. But in fact Macmillan's lack of previous experience in Africa added to the burden of this self-imposed task.

Not unexpectedly, the recipient of what Macmillan himself admitted was an 'onerous and distasteful task' was rather less than delighted, and Rab's mobile mind must surely have speculated on whether Macmillan had at last hit on a poisoned chalice to hand his rival. According to Rab, he had protested, 'It'll kill me!' 'Nonsense,' came the reply; 'look what North Africa did for me! It'll make you, Rab!'[80] If Rab got the remark right (and he repeated it on many occasions), it was as specious as its innuendo was diminishing. But Macmillan was right that Rab was admirably fitted for the job. Courtauld cousins of his late wife were respected grandees of Southern Rhodesia, while his progressive liberalism commended itself to the African leaders. Banda and Kaunda were both pleased, and Welensky praised him (perhaps rather pointedly) as being 'very flexible in negotiation, but when he has reached his decision he does not change it. . . . The best British Minister I had to deal with . . . and he had the roughest, most unpleasant job. . . .'[81]

It was clear that Rab's brief would be to preside over the liquidation of the Central African Federation, in which capacity he had more to do with actually promulgating the wind of change than Macmillan himself. After visiting the Federation in May 1962, Butler told the Cabinet that secession for Nyasaland could not be delayed much longer. On 19 December, he formally announced the government's agreement; almost simultaneously, elections in Southern Rhodesia brought in the right-wing Rhodesia Front led by Winston Field (later to be succeeded by Ian Smith), instead of Sir Edgar Whitehead. Macmillan said in his memoirs that he was 'deeply grieved by Whitehead's defeat, for he had represented, to the best of his power, a tradition of moderation and even of liberalism'. But Field's victory was predictable. Coming to London in March 1963, for the final Conference on the future of the Federation, he told Macmillan straight out that federation could no longer continue, and that Southern Rhodesia wanted independence – with its existing constitution. Confessing Britain's impotence in the matter, Macmillan wrote: 'It was not nowadays what Her Majesty's Government would like to do. It was what we *could* do.'[82]

It was the end of Welensky's dream. He noted that Butler was 'wan and grey' when he gave him the government decision to liquidate, and refused Macmillan's invitation to an official luncheon: '. . . I don't want to be discourteous, but I cannot accept the hospitality of a man who has betrayed me and my country. . . .' These were bitter words, and Welensky's bitterness was not to diminish over the years. He did not blame Butler, but did squarely blame Macmillan, whose mind was, he concluded, 'the most complicated I have encountered in my political life'.[83] Welensky would have been unlikely to deny that this was a polite euphemism for duplicity.

Macmillan's anxieties did not end with Rab's take-over. The new burden seemed to exacerbate that strong melancholy streak in Butler, which (when it was bad, and it had become especially pronounced at times since the death of his first wife, the beloved Sydney) affected his performance more noticeably even than Macmillan's Black Dog periods did his. 'Rab was rather melancholy and in one of his moods,'[84] was a characteristic Macmillan diary entry during 1963.

On 20 April, the new Field government in Southern Rhodesia demanded their independence, 'without negotiation and without conditions. If we do not grant it,' Macmillan added ominously, 'they will take it. . . .' Three days later he was noting: '. . . Rab seems so tired and even listless. He is, at heart, in favour of granting independence [to Southern Rhodesia] *without* conditions and at once. He may be right. But it would split our Cabinet and our Party. . . .'[85] A few weeks later in May, a serious split threatened the Cabinet once again; this time it was Butler versus both Sandys and Macleod. The glum reality was, so Macmillan thought, 'that we shall either keep Southern Rhodesia in the Commonwealth or lose at least all the *African* countries . . .'.[86] Meanwhile a new storm had blown up to afflict and distract Macmillan – the Profumo affair.

In June, Butler flew out to preside over the funeral arrangements at Victoria Falls. Macmillan congratulated him on terminating what he called 'a noble experiment'[87] with dignity; he wrote in his diaries, without irony, 'His reputation will certainly be enhanced. . . .'[88] Dissolution of the Federation was fixed for 31 December; by then Macmillan himself would have been out of power already for more than two months. There followed the complex work of dismantlement, creating out of the colonies of Northern Rhodesia and Nyasaland the two new states of Zambia and Malawi. A resolution on the future of Southern Rhodesia was deferred. In 1965, Ian Smith led an isolated Southern Rhodesia into the wilderness.

Could it have been otherwise? Had the Federation blossomed, it would have been a brilliant example of racial harmony, but – in retrospect – Macmillan saw its three components as so different in character that it would have been 'like trying to unite under a single system East and West Germany'.[89] Like a shaky marriage of an ill-assorted couple, it was better to dissolve it rather than to soldier on, once the underlying confidence had gone. As regards Southern Rhodesia, Macmillan saw all the questions with the same clarity that he saw so many problems. If it were given formal independence, he wrote on 23 March 1963:

> we shall be blamed by all progressive and even moderate opinion. If we do not, we shall do *no* benefit to the Africans and we shall force S.R. into the hands of S. Africa. This will mean a bloc of White power from the Cape to the Zambesi. Is this a good thing or not? These are questions that pose themselves now. . . .[90]

Macmillan was unable to provide the answer, but so too were five successive British governments, until Mrs Thatcher in 1980. In the intervening years, he repeatedly asked himself, with regret, 'whether by some means or other concessions to African opinion could have been obtained which would have justified a British Government in granting full independence to Southern Rhodesia'? In office, he had been constantly appalled at the agonies which the seven-year-long Algerian War imposed on France, with its one million *pieds noirs* compared to Rhodesia's 220,000 white settlers. Equally, he was determined to keep out of any confrontation with the Europeans there which might lead to a 'Boston Tea Party', or – worse – to a sanguinary 'Bunker's Hill'.[91] Here he succeeded. Otherwise, in attempting to make a circle out of an impossible triangle, by resort to every sort of evasiveness (and often exacerbated by his own ministers), his policy could be reckoned a failure. Not unlike Bismarck's famous saying, Macmillan saw his map of Africa as being in Europe. But he had been forced to devote a disproportionate amount of time and energy on Africa, provoking splits in the Party and the country, and then repairing them. 'What remains in my memory', his last words on the Federation read, 'is the immense amount of time and trouble taken over the future of the African territories amidst so many other baffling problems. . . .'

East Africa . . . and Malaysia

The Central African Federation proved Macmillan's major preoccupation, but it ran alongside other problems of the imperial legacy in Africa – and further east. In East Africa, decolonisation had gone on apace once the wind of change had been pronounced in 1960. Another tidy-minded Colonial Office attempt to produce a federation there had been aborted, but, within four years of Alan Lennox-Boyd's resignation from the Colonial Office after the 1959 General Election, Tanganyika (followed by the island of Zanzibar, the two later forming Tanzania after a bloody insurrection) and Uganda achieved full independence. In Kenya, the headlong rush to independence was complicated by the legacy of Mau-Mau (which had more or less been foreseen by Macmillan back in 1942, when he drafted his radical scheme of land reform) and the presence of a considerable white population. Here in Kenya it consisted largely of an affluent settler class, which had achieved a high degree of agricultural efficiency, concentrated chiefly in the White Highlands. After the Second World War they had been supplemented by a new group of younger settlers, many of them ex-officers. Together they totalled somewhere over fifty thousand. Unlike Rhodesia (and, on a much larger scale, French Algeria) there were few white lower middle-class artisans; in Kenya, as in the two other East African colonies, this stratum was filled by some 170,000 Asians. Hated by the Africans because of their commercial ascendancy, the Asians were driven out, with considerable brutality, some years after independence – to create new wealth, but also new problems, in Britain.

In Kenya the strongest and most articulate tribe was the Kikuyu, whence Mau-Mau had sprung. Much centred on the figure of their leader Jomo Kenyatta, who had been imprisoned at the start of Mau-Mau. Flying in the teeth of Lord Salisbury and the Tory right-wing, as well as of most local advice, Macmillan repeated the risk he had taken with Makarios in Cyprus and, in line with Macleod's urgings, had Kenyatta released. It was a considerable risk; Kenyatta swiftly gathered power around him, while the colony was afflicted with strife, and bankruptcy. At the end of 1961, Macmillan was noting pessimistically: 'If we have to give independence to Kenya, it may well prove another Congo. If we hold on, it will mean a long and cruel campaign – Mau-Mau and all that. . . .'[92]

Under the personal aegis of Reginald Maudling, following Macleod as Colonial Secretary in October 1961, and after much wrangling, a constitution was finally hammered out and elections held in May 1963. A substantial sum of money was set aside to buy out the farms of those white settlers who could not face African rule. On 12 December, Kenya achieved 'Uhuru' (independence), under the premiership of Kenyatta, and during the first twenty-five years of independence – against all predictions, not least Macmillan's – it was to prove one of the more successful endeavours in African decolonialisation, together with a modicum of harmony for the white settlers who continued to live in their beautiful land.

Across the Indian Ocean from Kenya, Britain had also fought a long and tough civil war against Communist insurgents in Malaya. Under General Sir Gerald Templer, the Malayan campaign turned out to be one of the few conspicuous successes against Communist guerrillas of the whole post-war era. But it was a success that was due not least to the fact that Malaya had been promised full independence, and gained it, at the early date of 1957. By itself Malaya looked unviable, and Macmillan and Duncan Sandys, together with the imposing figure of the Tunku, cobbled together a Malaysia Federation, composed of Malaya, Singapore, Sarawak and North Borneo. Singapore, its most prosperous component, in fact seceded in 1965, but the rest of the Federation thrived. Its creation, in July 1963, however, immediately encountered the wrath, and territorial ambitions, of President Sukarno of Indonesia. In Djakarta a mob wrecked the British Embassy, and for the next few years British, Australian and New Zealand troops fought out a 'small war' in the jungles of Borneo until Sukarno was overthrown by General Suharto in 1966.

Macmillan recognised that Sukarno (behind whom lurked an opportunistic Communist menace, never far absent in South-east Asia) could be stopped only if he clearly understood that the Western powers were united. On 23 September 1963 (in one of his last official communications with Kennedy), he powerfully invoked the President's intervention:

There is ... bound to be a most dangerous and unpleasant conflict unless Sukarno can be stopped at the last moment. ... All of this points to the absolute need for our two countries to stand together at this moment, in all respects. I cannot but feel that to allow Sukarno to drive a wedge between us in this matter of the oil companies would give him exactly the sign for which he is looking. ...

Macmillan then asked Kennedy to put pressure on Sukarno, and make him realise that 'he cannot pick off all his surrounding neighbours one by one without encountering united Western resistance.'[93] Macmillan recorded, however, that the reply from Kennedy, who was thought to have made unwise commitments to the American oil lobby, 'was not altogether satisfactory'. Thus, it was 'not on an altogether happy note that my connection with the affairs of South-East Asia was to terminate – although the story was to end happily in the years to come'.

India Under Attack from China

In September 1962, China attacked India, crossing the frontier from the high uplands of Tibet. It turned into a major offensive, with the Indian defenders being pushed back all along the line. A wave of anxiety passed over Western capitals. China was still an enigma; what were her objectives? Where would the attack stop? As head of the Commonwealth, Britain was involved, Macmillan's support invoked. But – a sign of Britain's new impotence in the world at large – there was little he could do.

Macmillan's own sympathy towards India, and Pandit Nehru, was somewhat ambivalent. He greatly admired Nehru for what he had done to create post-imperial India, and for his political skill, and respected his intelligence and learning. At the same time, he observed with detached amusement the snobbishness of the upper-caste Indian; while Nehru found conversation with Kennedy on grand political philosophy frankly boring, he was always at ease with Macmillan gossiping about grand British families. To Macmillan, there was always an element of hypocrisy about Nehru (though it never lessened his liking for him); he would preach Indian support for African aspirations, though making his sense of superiority plain. 'The curious thing about Nehru,' Macmillan wrote after Nehru had lunched with him in November 1961, 'is that all his pro-African ideas are purely theoretical. He looks down on most Asians from the proud position of a high-caste Indian aristocrat. Africans he regards with contempt.'[94] The Africans responded with dislike. At Commonwealth Conferences, Nehru was always 'in the star field'; though 'it was a little as if you had a saint in the Cabinet – all right for a bit, then a damned nuisance. . . .'[95]

The same conflict between theory and practice Macmillan found in Nehru's attachment to anti-imperialism and 'passive resistance', while making aggressive noises towards his neighbours, notably Pakistan, which India was subsequently to defeat in two successive wars. Towards the end of 1961 India had massed her forces on the border of the tiny Portuguese enclave of Goa, declaring (in Macmillan's words) 'in phrases to which we had become all too accustomed, that "India's patience was becoming exhausted"'. Macmillan begged Nehru to hold his hand, reminding him (at the back of his mind, he doubtless recalled the critical Indian line taken over Suez in 1956) of the special respect India had gained 'as a country which, however great the provocation, does not believe in solving problems by the use of armed force. . . . Your example has had an incalculable influence on many other countries.' If this changed, Macmillan speculated, 'I feel sure that President Sukarno would then consider himself justified in making a military attack on New Guinea. . . .'[96]

Little thinking that he might be the next victim, Nehru nevertheless went ahead and invaded Goa. The following year, India began to arm herself with Russian MiG fighters, alleging fear of Pakistan's military superiority; Pakistan and the USA were upset, and so was China – where the consequences of the Sino-Soviet split were being forcefully felt. Thus when, in September 1962, Nehru cried for help, Macmillan was less than entirely sympathetic. In one of their weekly audiences, the Queen, so Macmillan recorded, 'was amused by my picture of the transformation of Nehru from an imitation of George Lansbury into a parody of Churchill . . .'. He was conscious, however, that the Indians were 'having a bad time': 'my guess is that they are doing a bit of a Dunkirk. But when they get more into the plain and abandon the high mountains, the Chinese advantage should not be great. . . .'[97]

There was a further aspect; Macmillan fundamentally disagreed with the US 'China hands' who tried to infect Kennedy with alarm about Chinese expansionist aims. Ever since his rift with Khrushchev, Macmillan had always believed that the key to peace in the Orient lay in the wooing of China. Numerous messages passed between Macmillan and Washington, combined with panicky appeals for military assistance from Nehru. Kennedy's Ambassador in New Delhi, the six-foot-eight economist, J. K. Galbraith, who spoke with persuasion from his lofty altitude, urged the commitment of Western air power to protect Indian cities from Chinese menace. Macmillan countered, on 18 January 1963: '. . . I appreciate the force of Galbraith's argument. . . . At the same time I fear that if the Indians are assured of Western Air Defence they may become more intransigent with the Pakistanis; the latter may then be tempted to flirt with China in their turn. . . .'[98] The President, however, remained much calmer than his advisers; possibly Macmillan's influence played a role. Meanwhile, as inexplicably as it had begun, the Chinese attack suddenly ceased, and the war ended.

One of the enigmas of the Mao era, like the sudden bombardment of Quemoy and Matsu in 1954, the objective of the 'War-on-the-Roof-of-the-World' puzzled Macmillan, but on balance he reckoned it had been simply to advance to a line that was strategically suitable to China, and to establish a military route through to Pakistan; or perhaps, as with the (considerably less successful) campaign in 1979 against Vietnam, it had also been intended, pre-emptively, to 'teach the Indians a lesson'. Comparing 'British scepticism with American alarm', Macmillan felt that Britain, with her longer experience, was vindicated in believing that, though the Chinese would take advantage of troubles in any adjacent area, they would not themselves embark on a policy of adventure. He was highly critical of the view from Washington, where '. . . Chinese expansionist policies were believed to be responsible for all the troubles in South-East Asia. It was this fundamental mistake which later led America into so many years of trouble. . . .' Was Macmillan's philosophy that the Chinese dragon was worse than its roar, and was tameable, ahead of its time – or just premature?

Similar thinking affected Macmillan's view of Indo-China, where, by the summer of 1961, despite the ceasefire in Laos that had succeeded Macmillan's first meeting with Kennedy at Key West in March, the Viet Cong had begun attacking posts in South Vietnam.

The Russian challenge to Berlin was also then reaching its peak, and – as Macmillan wrote to the Queen on 15 September: 'We are thus threatened with the possibility of being asked to intervene militarily in the Far East, just at the time the European crisis is deepening. . . .' With Berlin and its vulnerability the pre-eminent worry in Macmillan's mind, he expressed relief when that month Kennedy showed himself reluctant to get any further involved militarily in Laos, because there were too many other problems 'on his plate'. But the following spring a fresh worsening of the Laos situation brought the Pathet Lao to the border of Thailand. This provoked considerable alarm in Bangkok, and Britain – because of her responsibilities to the SEATO pact – became more closely involved. A small force of RAF Hunters was sent to reinforce the Americans, but by the autumn of 1962 the advent of a neutralist coalition government in Laos enabled them to be removed.

This was just after the ending of the Cuban missiles crisis, and Macmillan recalled discussing the Laos settlement with Kennedy over a new telephone installed since those dramatic transatlantic exchanges, which was '(a) better – you talk as on an ordinary telephone; (b) safer – it would take ninety years to break the code; (c) British. A score for us. . . .'[99] Meanwhile, South Vietnam had begun to look increasingly menaced, and – against Macmillan's better judgement at the time – the US involvement had started; helicopters and training aircraft accompanied by 400 servicemen in December 1961 had risen to 4000 training personnel by the following February. By 1963, Macmillan was shocked to discover that the 'advisers' had escalated to 15,000 troops; and he had not been informed. By the time he left office, the situation in Laos and Cambodia looked deceptively tranquil, but he felt that the prospects of South Vietnam defending herself against the North were 'gloomy'.

At Key West and subsequently, he had warned Kennedy against getting bogged down in Indo-China, but – writing the last volume of his memoirs while the Vietnam War was still dragging on to its tragic conclusion – he thought it was not up to America's British ally 'to indulge in captious criticism'. He himself had no positive solution to offer, except possibly always to play the Chinese card against the Soviets. But when President Nixon did, it would be too late.

Menace in the Middle East

Compared with other news hotspots like the Congo, Cuba and Laos, the Middle East had rather disappeared off the world headlines since the Anglo-American interventions in the Lebanon and Jordan in 1958. But this did not mean an end to the problems facing Britain there – or the disappearance of Colonel Nasser. The turmoil which had begun with the creation of the state of Israel, the Arab challenge to her right to exist and the withdrawal of the British presence ran deep. Nasser remained committed to exorcising the Arab world of British influence. The pivots of British power in the Middle East had depended upon Malta, Cyprus, the Canal Zone and Aden. Cyprus and the Canal Zone were now gone, and the British presence in Malta was now circumscribed. Aden thus suddenly assumed a greatly increased importance; beyond it the remnants of British power in the Arab world lay in a series of loose defence treaties with the sheikhdoms of the Gulf – like Muscat and Oman, Dubai, Bahrain and Kuwait.

In June 1961, General Abdul Karim Kassem, full of the revolutionary fervour that had carried him into power in Iraq after the coup that had murdered King Feisal and his pro-British premier, Nuri-es-Said, laid claim to Kuwait. Now, through oil, one of the richest areas in the world, Kuwait was – Kassem declared – 'a long lost but integral part of Iraq'; without outside help, it was also virtually defenceless. On 30 June, Kuwait called for assistance from both Britain and the Arab League. According to Macmillan, 'the Cabinet left the whole management of this affair to me. . . .'[100] He was strongly supported by Mountbatten, as Chief of the Defence Staff and a wartime expert on Combined Operations. With memories of how dithering had compromised the Suez enterprise, and how the intervention in Jordan in 1958 had nearly been jeopardised, Macmillan acted with swift decisiveness. The first British troops landed on 1 July, and by the middle of the month a brigade group was in position in the blazing desert. Predictably, the Soviet Union in the UN Security Council voted against any international action on behalf of Kuwait. Then, at the end of July, the Arab League offered Kuwait its mantle, and the Iraqi threat dissolved. The rapid and effective deployment of the British 'firefighting force', small as it was, was a significant milestone between the fiasco of Suez and the success of the Falklands twenty-five years later.

Nasser had meanwhile been thwarted in his aspirations to place a ring of steel round Israel when, in September 1961, a coup in Syria resulted in the destruction of his 'United Arab Republic' and the separation once again of Syria and Egypt. He now turned his energies to the Yemen, the turbulent hinterland to Aden. In September 1962 the Imam, a medieval despot, died and civil war broke out over the succession. Because of the commitment of Jordan and Saudi Arabia, Britain supported the royalist forces; Nasser, with Khrushchev behind him, backed the left-wing revolutionary forces; the US at first thought the left-wing rebels would win, but Kennedy felt that, on balance, he should support the Nasser-backed rebels so as to prevent the Russians having the field to themselves. Macmillan wrote to Kennedy on 15 November 1962, declaring that their joint object should be:

> to make the various outside countries disengage from the Yemen. . . . this is clearly important for the internal stability of Saudi Arabia and Jordan. . . . recognition [of the Yemen rebels] especially by you would spread consternation among our friends throughout Arabia, and particularly in the Aden Protectorate where it would be assumed that Britain was not resolute enough to be dependable and that the United States was pursuing a separate policy. . . . our position in the Gulf depends on the Aden Colony and Base. This itself is untenable without the Aden Protectorate. . . .[101]

Macmillan went on to urge Kennedy not to give recognition at least without a firm commitment for Egyptian withdrawal.

Kennedy's reply two days later was 'discouraging'; the rebels were bound to win, and to delay recognition would merely encourage them to turn to the USSR. Macmillan commented: 'So the Americans will risk paying the price (recognition) without effecting the purchase (Egyptian disengagement). This will make our position worse in the Protectorate. . . .'[102] He remained obdurate; Britain would not recognise the rebels unless *they* recognised her position in Aden and the Protectorate.

The New Year of 1963 found the problem unresolved, but by March Macmillan noted that the position in the Yemen was 'deteriorating rapidly'.[103] There were now 28,000 Egyptian troops there – one-third of Nasser's whole army. The Americans began to take fright over the potential threat to their oil interests in Saudi Arabia, and switched support from the rebels. A team of observers were sent from the UN to supervise a truce, though Macmillan was disgusted by their partiality: '. . . Nasser is bombing Yemen and Saudi Arabia day and night with powerful Russian bombers, and is using poison gas. Nothing happens. No protest. No Afro-Asian resolutions in Security Council or Assembly. Imagine what would happen if we were doing one twentieth of this from (say) Aden. . . .'[104]

This was roughly the scene when Macmillan left office two months later. But he reckoned that, such was the Egyptians' 'capacity for being disliked', even the Yemenis might turn against them. Macmillan's prediction came true, and Nasser's prestige in the Arab world was finally destroyed by his defeat in the Six Day War with Israel in 1967. But meanwhile fatal damage had been done to British interests, and Aden was rent with left-wing terrorism. In 1966, under the Wilson Labour government, the decision was taken to evacuate Aden. It was carried out, in Macmillan's view, in a manner 'calculated to produce the maximum of trouble and peril . . . our friends were to be abandoned and our enemies comforted. . . . the Federal Government and Army crumbled away. . . .'[105]

Both Macmillan and Home always considered the Denis Healey policy of disengagement from East of Suez to be 'the most disastrous thing that has happened in twenty years'.[106] Macmillan himself often claimed in later years that, if he had been in office, he would have gone far to support any coup to oust the Marxists from their key strategic position in Aden.

The Immigrants

The other side to the coin of Britain's imperial legacy, which first achieved crisis proportions in Macmillan's day, was constituted by the influx of immigrants from the Commonwealth to Britain – chiefly of black West Indians. The problem had already come to the Cabinet's attention in 1954, during Churchill's last years. Before that, coloured faces were largely to be seen at the universities, but by 1954 the rate of immigrants, pouring in by 'banana-boats', had quadrupled over 1953, and numbered about 40,000. Those coming from the Commonwealth required no papers, though in the West Indies there were restrictions on movement between one island and another. Macmillan recalled the Minister of State for the Colonies in November 1954 answering questions with a statement that the government was 'very well aware of the importance of the problem', and was determined 'to see that a satisfactory solution is evolved'. Macmillan appended a caustic comment that experts in Parliamentary language 'could deduce from this delphic reply that nothing very much would be done about it now . . .'.

In 1955, numbers of immigrants rose to 43,000; three years later public attention was focused sharply on the problem by the Notting Hill 'race riots'. Still there was no clear policy, despite the warnings, to deal with the issue. With full employment in Britain, there was a need for West Indians to do the 'dirty jobs' – in the hospitals, on the Underground, and in cleaning the streets – which Britain's more choosy white workers eschewed. Macmillan (as Churchill before him) was also aware that restrictions on immigrants from the West Indies might rebound against the white settlers still there; he was under pressure from Commonwealth leaders, and from 'liberals' in his government (like the greatly respected Edward Boyle), to avoid any possible suggestion of discriminating against the blacks.

The problem, as with much of the domestic matters that fell into Rab's domain at the Home Office, was one that did not assume highest priority with Macmillan. In 1958 and 1959, the immigration figures dropped, and the problem seemed to recede. But in 1960 the numbers rose to 58,000 and by 1962 they had soared to 136,000. It was a time of the final withdrawal of Britain from much of the Empire, and immigrants were increasingly drawn by the advantages of Britain's welfare state. The total number of coloured immigrants had now reached 350,000, and – for the first time – unemployment was beginning to be a factor. At the end of May 1961, Macmillan recorded in his diary 'a long discussion [in Cabinet] on West Indian immigration into United Kingdom, which is now becoming rather a serious problem . . .'.[107] Rab was detailed to handle it at the annual Tory Conference in October, which he did with no great distinction. Macmillan thought that he 'brought much of his trouble on himself by an appearance of vacillation . . .'.[108]

Meanwhile a Bill was being prepared, one of the principal complications of which was how to preserve non-discrimination while not closing the door on members of the 'white' Commonwealth, and Eire. On 1 November, the Bill was published – and a storm broke. It was attacked from all quarters; Macmillan claimed that he had never seen the Commons 'in so hysterical a mood since the days of Suez'. He also thought that some of the emotion was 'synthetic'. Gaitskell was, he felt, sincere; but he was infuriated by his manoeuvring with the press: 'Gaitskell is the kind of cad that only a gentleman can be,' he declaimed in the privacy of his diaries (a sentiment that was not repeated in his memoirs).[109] Gaitskell (in Butler's words) labelled the Bill 'cruel and brutal anti-colour legislation',[110] but most of Macmillan's wrath was reserved for 'Halier-than-Thou', his *bête noire*, the editor of *The Times* ('which exceeded itself in its self-righteous and unctuous approach').

The Bill, having been fiercely disputed at Committee stage, finally came into force on 1 July 1962. It was (to the fury of Enoch Powell) a pretty watered-down affair.* In retirement, Macmillan was able to derive scant satisfaction from the fact that Labour was subsequently forced to introduce far more stringent controls, and that *The Times* would recant: 'There were widespread misgivings at the passing of the Commonwealth Immigrants Act in 1962. A good many people were reluctant to believe that such restrictions were necessary. Since then it has become evident that they are essential. . . .'[111] It is clear from his diaries that Macmillan, when Prime Minister, devoted ten times as much attention to the problems of the Central African Federation as he did to the problem of Commonwealth immigration.

Chief Enahoro

In 1963, in the midst of all his security problems at home, a new and unexpected facet of the immigration problem in its post-imperial setting landed on the head of Macmillan and his already unpopular Home Secretary, Henry Brooke (who had succeeded Butler after the Night of Long Knives). Chief Enahoro was a leading dissident from Nigeria, and Nigeria wanted him back there to face trial on charges of treachery and subversion. In the Commons on 22 March, Macmillan was caught in the cleft stick that 'If the Home Secretary were to refuse to return this man under the 1881 Act,

* It was six years later that Powell made his famous 'rivers of blood' speech.

Nigeria would at once repudiate the Queen and the Common-wealth. . . .'[112]

The Opposition, who exacted much capital out of the case, claimed that the arguments for deportation used by both Brooke and Macmillan were dishonest and inhumane. The Cabinet was split. On the 27th, the government was routed in the Commons after George Brown had ingeniously brought up a subtle legal point whereby it could be interpreted that to deport Enahoro would be to deliver him to a death sentence. Macmillan was forced to adjourn the debate in disarray, while seeking assurances from Lagos; failing these, he thought it might be hard to carry his own side. Offended by the attitude of the Commons, Nigeria now threatened either to break off diplomatic relations, or leave the Commonwealth, of which it was by far the largest African member.

On 4 April the Cabinet decided to face the storm at home, and send back Enahoro. On 10 April, having been up till 5 a.m. the previous night, writing and rewriting his speech, Macmillan faced a vote of censure in a hostile House. Both supporters and opponents alike 'said it was the most *effective* which I had ever made in the House of Commons . . .'.[113] In a letter explaining to Anthony Head, his popular High Commissioner in Nigeria, what had happened, he stated:

In the early part of the week it seemed that we would probably be defeated or that the figures would be so close as to amount to a defeat. Had we been defeated it would have been difficult for me personally not to have resigned although it is possible that a Conservative Government of some kind might have carried on.

I decided to take this risk simply from the Commonwealth point of view but it was a very great one. . . .[114]

There had been the unusually high number of forty abstentions. In his diary, Macmillan reckoned that 'had the worst happened, I don't think we could have got away with a "vote of confidence" the next day. . . .' He would have had to rise, and 'Whether the Queen would have sent at once for Wilson,* I am not sure. She might perhaps have thought it within her rights to try another Con-servative. . . .'[115]

* After Gaitskell's death in January 1963, Wilson had succeeded as Leader of the Opposition.

In the event, Enahoro soon passed into oblivion. The unfortunate Chief was sent back to Nigeria and imprisoned for treason but was released in 1966 by the military government. He held various governmental posts and became state chairman of the National Party of Nigeria in 1978. The escalation of what would normally have been a small side issue showed to what extent the Macmillan government had become 'accident-prone' by spring 1963, and the debilitating effect on Macmillan of the continuing responsibilities for Britain's imperial past.

As he wrote that March, 'What sufferings we go through to try to keep the Commonwealth together. Bed at 3 a.m. Slept badly.'[116]

Chapter Fifteen

Skybolt Falls and
De Gaulle Says No
May 1962–January 1963

. . . Great Britain has lost an Empire and has not yet found a role.

(Dean Acheson, speech at West Point, 5 December 1962)

. . . de Gaulle is trying to dominate *Europe. . . . It is the end – or at least a temporary bar – to everything for which I have worked for many years. . . . All our policies at home and abroad are in ruins. . . .*

(HM, Diaries, 28 January 1963)

By the end of 1962, the awaited finale on Britain's application to join the EEC was at hand. Macmillan in his memoirs likened it to a steeple-chase, though in terms of length and severity of the obstacles it made the perils of the Grand National look like a local point-to-point. By 1 December 1962, Heath, according to the Macmillan diaries, was reporting ruefully from Brussels: 'The *French* are opposing us by every means, fair and foul. They are absolutely ruthless. For some reason they *terrify* the Six – by their intellectual superiority, spiritual arrogance, and shameful disregard of truth and honour. . . .'[1] Four days later Macmillan was reflecting that de Gaulle, to protect the short-term interests of French agriculture and commerce, 'will bargain as hard and selfishly as any old French housewife in the market. The Brussels negotiations are dragging – but I suppose the crunch must come in February or March at the latest.'[2]

Meanwhile, at the end of the Cuban missiles crisis, on 17 November, Kennedy had cabled to Macmillan suggesting a meeting on 19 and 20 December. Macmillan's reaction was: 'This is good; but I want to see *de Gaulle* first. . . . If I do not at least propose this, de Gaulle will be very suspicious. . . .'[3] Thus two separate meetings were arranged, in close succession in December; the first with General de Gaulle at Rambouillet on the 15th, and the second with Kennedy at Nassau on the 18th. In his memoirs Macmillan observed: 'Both would be of vital importance; and over both now hung dark and disturbing clouds.'

Among these clouds there were also many problems to distract attention from the main issues to be discussed at these two meetings: in Britain the economy was still looking shaky, with unemployment approaching a post-war peak of 800,000; a far-reaching reorganisation of Britain's defence structure was under way; abroad there were anxious worries in Yemen and Aden, Malaysia, the Congo and the Central African Federation; China had just invaded India with disturbingly unclear objectives; while both Washington and Whitehall had barely recovered from those moments in October when the world had seemed to teeter on the brink of the unthinkable.

Then, at the beginning of December, Macmillan's woes were added to by a speech by the revered former American Secretary of State, Dean Acheson, in which he declared:

> . . . Great Britain has lost an empire and has not yet found a role. The attempt to play a separate power role – that is, a role apart from Europe, a role based on a 'Special Relationship' with the United States, a role based on being the head of a 'Commonwealth' which has no political structure, or unity, or strength and enjoys a fragile and precarious economic relationship – this role is about played out.

The comment caused more trouble in the British press for Macmillan, who, stung, exploded in the privacy of his diaries that Acheson was 'always a conceited ass, but I don't really think he meant to be offensive . . .'.[4]

Confiding to his diary two days later (not for the first time), 'I do not recall a time when there were so many difficult problems to resolve and awkward decisions to be made,'[5] Macmillan went on to comment plaintively on the growing hostility and unfairness of the British press. In this crucial run-up to the final decision in Brussels, he was also finding American attitudes less than helpful. At the same time, there were a number of reports emanating from Washington that Skybolt, the US missile promised to Britain, was running into technical difficulties, compounded with the 'anti-proliferation' policy the Washington 'Europeanists' had succeeded in selling to the President: 'The failure of Skybolt might be welcomed in some American quarters[6] as a means of forcing Britain out of the nuclear club. . . .'[7]

On 12 December, the Minister of Defence Peter Thorneycroft returned to report on some 'wholly unsatisfactory' talks with Mc-Namara in Paris. Thorneycroft had little doubt that the Americans meant to drop Skybolt altogether. Macmillan recorded laconically: 'There will be a great row in both countries. And it means a great battle with President Kennedy next week.'[8]

Rambouillet, December 1962

On 15 December, just over a month before France was due to go to Brussels on the British application, Macmillan set forth for

Rambouillet, also anticipating a 'great battle' with de Gaulle. The meeting, at the imposing château where François I died, began with a pheasant shoot at which de Gaulle (who did not participate) stood behind his guests commenting loudly (and disconcertingly) each time they missed. Macmillan (an expert shot) nevertheless got 77 out of a total bag of 385.

> The beaters were soldiers, in white smocks; the loaders were gamekeepers in a sort of military uniform (and very efficient); there was a good deal of trumpet work and much excited shouting. . . . It was an extraordinary and strangely old-fashioned ceremony. I should imagine that Edwardian shoots in England . . . were not dissimilar. . . .[9]

(Macmillan also noted that he had to pay for his own cartridges – with French meticulousness, £5 8s od for 170 cartridges.)[10] After the shoot, the serious talks began, followed by the usual film show. Macmillan found de Gaulle 'older' and 'more difficult'[11] since they had met at Champs. Sweeping Gaullist victories at a general election in November had meanwhile placed de Gaulle securely in undisputed power domestically – more so than Macmillan – and he at once claimed anew that the EEC would be changed by British entry. He piqued Macmillan by repeating charges made at Champs that the Commonwealth and the British people were not ready; Macmillan riposted that over the past six months he had proved just the opposite. As regards the nuclear deterrent, Macmillan, in his memoirs says he warned de Gaulle that it now looked as though the US would abandon Skybolt and he:

> wished to assure the General . . . we were determined to maintain our independent deterrent. I would explain to the President that, if Skybolt broke down, I must have an adequate replacement from the United States, such as Polaris – otherwise Britain would have to develop her own system, whether submarine or aerial, in spite of the cost.

According to Macmillan, he explained in detail to de Gaulle the difficulties that had beset Skybolt over the past few months and added that if it were cancelled he would insist on having Polaris – to which he reckoned he was entitled, under his original agreement with President Eisenhower. De Gaulle, he said, 'quite under-stood'.[12] De Gaulle, however, seemed to have got the impression that, if let down by the Americans over Skybolt, the British would decide to work with France on a nuclear missile. This was not the British recollection. Macmillan apparently made no reference to any further offers on nuclear 'collaboration'. Once again there was a breakdown in comprehension, with the French refusing to accept the official British version of the conference and subsequently alleg-ing linguistic discords. Strolling with de Gaulle in the grounds of Rambouillet, without interpreters, Macmillan spoke in French and, it is said, de Gaulle heard things in a way Macmillan had not intended. His Private Secretary, de Zulueta, who was present, reckoned that the fault at Rambouillet was that Andronikov, the brilliant French interpreter, was seldom allowed by de Gaulle – out of pride – to translate:

This didn't matter to Harold Macmillan, his French was very good, but I really do not believe that de Gaulle entirely under-stood everything that was said – especially on the crucial, techni-cal points. Macmillan did talk elliptically![13]

Both leaders were indeed renowned in their own entourages for their capacity to be elliptic, but the record (the only minutes kept were by de Zulueta; the French made none) seemed to indicate that nothing vital was agreed *à deux* at Rambouillet. There still remains an element of mystery surrounding Champs and Rambouillet but, if de Gaulle misheard at Rambouillet, or even at Champs, it was almost certainly because he wished to do so – as his subsequent action indicated.[14]

On the Sunday, 16 December, de Gaulle became increasingly discouraging about the British application, repeating all his old arguments, but more adamantly. Macmillan recorded that 'our talk became something of a wrangle. This is very unusual in our relationship. . . .' Reverting, 'rather ungraciously', to the difficulties at Brussels, de Gaulle declared that, within the Six, 'France could say "no" against even the Germans; she could stop policies with which she disagreed, because of the strength of her position. Once Britain and all the rest joined the organisation things would be different. . . .' Realising that the chips were down, Macmillan let his anger take control and said with indignation that what de Gaulle had now put forward:

> was a fundamental objection in principle to Britain's application. If that was really the French view, it ought to have been made clear at the start. It was not fair to have a year's negotiation and then bring forward an objection of principle. De Gaulle seemed rather shaken. . . .
>
> . . . On this depressing note our conference ended.

Summing up on Rambouillet (which was in fact to be the last occasion that he and de Gaulle would ever meet), a disconsolate Macmillan recorded that they had 'agreed' on 'the nuclear', but that otherwise: '. . . I thought the discussions about as bad as they could be from the European point of view. . . .'[15] Macmillan admitted, 'We returned to London on 16 December with rather heavy hearts . . . in no doubt that de Gaulle would, if he dared, use some means, overt or covert, to prevent the fruition of the Brussels negotiation. . . .' Nevertheless, deep down, Macmillan still nurtured a slender hope; as he put it years later, '. . . I felt once he had let us start, he could not say no – he didn't want us in, but I felt we would leave him no excuse to exclude us.'[16]

After Rambouillet, Macmillan, however, endeavoured to conceal the extent of his disillusion from the outside world – even from his friend, the President. This would seem to have been less out of any intention to deceive the President than from a natural and deeply ingrained instinct for refusing to acknowledge reverses, and equal disinclination to seek solace for them. That the Americans were uninformed about the extent of the setback to Macmillan also represented a failure of US diplomatic intelligence.

The Skybolt Crisis

Back home on 16 December, Macmillan was immediately plunged into 'a meeting on Skybolt and Polaris, which lasted till late in the evening', and he predicted: 'We shall have a difficult time with the Americans in Nassau.'[17] An atmosphere of 'total gloom' surrounded that meeting, recalled Sir Solly (later Lord) Zuckerman, then Chief Scientific Adviser to the Ministry of Defence.[18] The next day the

Minister of Defence, Peter Thorneycroft, reported on his recent talk in London with McNamara, and warned the Cabinet that the future of Skybolt was in serious jeopardy.

As late as November 1962 Thorneycroft was telling the Commons that, although the first four firings of Skybolt had been only partially successful, there was no change in the development programme.[19] Nevertheless Macmillan had come under bitter and mounting political criticism. There were strong suggestions that Britain should now abandon the independent deterrent altogether. In the States, these were bolstered by McNamara and the State Department 'Europeanists', whose foreign policy priorities embraced a withering-away of the British nuclear deterrent, and a downgrading of the Special Relationship. In December the Special Relationship had received an additional battering from Acheson's infelicitously timed speech, and from McNamara repeating at the NATO meeting in Paris the tenor of his Ann Arbor remarks of June.

By December Macmillan's diary entries show him being subject to a growing sense of perfidy in Washington. For him – it should never be forgotten – retention of the British nuclear deterrent represented a major part of his political platform, whereas to Kennedy, attached though he had already become to Macmillan personally, it represented no more than an awkward plank, highly unpopular to the 'Europeanists'. But, for Macmillan, the unrequited removal of Skybolt would be as if Britain were unilaterally disarmed. Thus, a week before the Nassau Conference began on 18 December, Macmillan was sending a tough message to his Ambassador in Washington, David Ormsby-Gore:

> if we cannot reach an agreement on a realistic means of maintaining the British independent deterrent, all the other questions may only justify perfunctory discussion, since an 'agonising reappraisal' of all our foreign and defence [plans] will be required.

Such language had not been heard in Anglo-American dealings since Suez.

The 'Skybolt Crisis' was both the most complex and most baffling problem ever to beset the Kennedy–Macmillan Special Relationship. When it was over, Kennedy, dismayed at the lethal damage it had come close to inflicting, commissioned an American professor, Richard Neustadt of Harvard, to conduct a full investigation. This was to result in a penetrating report, held classified for many years afterwards, and which subjected the principals on both sides to some devastating comment.[20] According to Neustadt, Thorneycroft claimed that, despite several visits to Washington to stress how essential Skybolt was to British defence requirements, by September 1962 he still had received 'no impression that there was any likelihood of cancellation'. The first intimation came, he thought, via a message from David Ormsby-Gore on 8 November. Thorneycroft said his immediate reaction was to ring up McNamara and ask him for Polaris. The general conclusion of the Neustadt Report, however, in the words of the veteran British correspondent Henry Brandon, was that 'the writings were on the wall, but the British Government didn't believe them and didn't want to.' He felt the two ambassadors, Ormsby-Gore in Washington and David Bruce in London, could between them have done better to explain to Kennedy that 'this was political dynamite' for Macmillan.

> essentially there were two misunderstandings: one, that the British government continuously thought that the US really is not going to abandon the Skybolt in the end; and the Pentagon, which felt that if it said this weapon could not succeed the British would accept that judgement. The judgement was based so much on technical grounds that the political implications were overlooked here at first. . . .[21]

It was not until the crucial meeting with McNamara on 8 November that, Ormsby-Gore claimed, he received a clear warning about the possible cancellation of Skybolt, and in turn passed an equally clear warning that this would be 'a political disaster' for Britain. The mystery remains why, during the next five weeks before McNamara's December visit to Europe, neither side seems to have made a move. Perhaps one should not forget the multitude of pressures and distractions that had by then piled on both leaders. As Sorensen said: 'After Cuba, it seemed a small problem. All problems did.'[22]

Co-operation was not helped by the mutual antipathy between McNamara and Thorneycroft. Years later McNamara claimed, 'If there was any blame attached, the fault was not ours; it was Thorneycroft who knew the British position, and should have squealed. . . .' (McNamara was always forthright in his language;

he described Skybolt as 'proven to be a pile of junk, for which we were paying the whole bill . . .'.)[23]

The British line was, McNamara recalled: '"Don't announce withdrawal of Skybolt until there is a substitute."' Elsewhere McNamara had stressed the basic, and important, difference of approach between the two personalities, with Thorneycroft looking at Skybolt from the point of view of domestic politics, and himself from the point of view of NATO defence.[24] On the latter score, there was no possible excuse for going ahead with Skybolt; on the former, the British had plenty of time to adjust their domestic politics, but did not. McNamara blamed the British squarely for having wasted the five weeks from 8 November. Thorneycroft, however, declared himself to have been shaken by McNamara's 'leak' on arriving at London airport for the key discussions of 11 December, when he let the cat out of the bag about the dropping of Skybolt – an indiscretion that led the British to accuse McNamara of political ineptitude.[25] Neustadt's comment on this, however, is that Thorneycroft's rage was really 'directed to the fact that McNamara did not come offering Polaris'.[26]

Sir Solly Zuckerman – who claims to have been probably the first to have known at top level that Skybolt was a 'dead duck', back in early 1961 – had passed this information on to the British services, and found it 'impossible that Macmillan did not know about the Skybolt failure by the autumn of 1962. . . . but he turned a blind eye on the Skybolt problem – he was interested in other things. . . .'[27] 'Preoccupied' might have been more accurate. Sometimes, Zuckerman confessed, he thought that Macmillan regarded the technicalities of weaponry as an unreal business.[28] It seems incredible, however, that Zuckerman's doubts did not get through to his ministerial chief, Peter Thorneycroft. Perhaps the multiplicity of posts held simultaneously by Zuckerman (they ranged from his stewardship at the Zoo[29] to the BBC, as well as his responsibilities to the MoD) limited their contacts, but the viability of the weapons system that was to carry the British deterrent should have been a regular item on the agenda when the Secretary of State for Defence and his Chief Scientific Adviser talked.

He was convinced that Thorneycroft did not take the McNamara warning to abandon Skybolt seriously until the 11 December meeting, when Zuckerman had whispered to him 'Ask him "Will it work?"' After only a moment's hesitation McNamara, glancing at

Zuckerman, answered, 'No, it won't.' Then, and only then, says Zuckerman, did Thorneycroft 'believe that McNamara meant what he said . . .'.[30] In the apt words of Arthur Schlesinger, Jr, the talks were 'a Pinero drama of misunderstanding: Thorneycroft expecting McNamara to propose Polaris, McNamara expecting Thorneycroft to request it . . .'. Concentrating on the political consequences of cancellation, rather than the technical,

> Finally Thorneycroft asked the hard question: if the United States were cancelling Skybolt for technical reasons, would it be prepared to state publicly that it would do everything possible to help Britain preserve its independent nuclear role?[31]

McNamara was not helpful, and the meeting broke up in frosty deadlock.

Neustadt regarded McNamara as being one of the 'loose nails'[32] in the drama of the run-up to Nassau. He recalls that, after Ambassador Ormsby-Gore had relayed back to London the McNamara bombshell of 8 November, Macmillan had replied calling on him to get three provisional guarantees from Washington. There should be:

1. No publicity before the decision was made.
2. No decision before consultations.
3. Consultations as soon as possible.

Kennedy, having had this fed back to him, had at once said 'Sure, okay.' But, claims Neustadt, he then apparently forgot to tell McNamara 'Be sure to talk to the Brits at once'.

> This was the fatal point. McNamara was supposed to go to the UK, to see Thorneycroft, before any leaks took place. However, he kept on putting off his trip, right into December; finally gets there December 11th – the leaks with the press occur on the 6th. McNamara had no sense of hurry, because he didn't realise that the President had made a *formal pledge* to Macmillan. Hence, Thorneycroft enraged by the non-offer of Polaris. Equally Macmillan must have thought that there had been bad faith. Then there was the misfortune simultaneously of the Dean Acheson speech. . . .[33]

The above seems as convincing an explanation as any – the 'muddle' theory of history generally triumphs over the 'conspiracy' theory.

To Nassau

Nevertheless, the British delegation arrived at Bali-Hai, a sumptuous private house in Nassau on the morning of Wednesday, 19 December 1962, in a not very friendly mood; in fact, in the words of Henry Brandon, they were 'the angriest' British delegation seen at any Anglo-American summit since the war.[34] George Ball of the State Department wondered whether it was purely by hazard that the Bahamas band struck up 'Oh, Don't Deceive Me' as Kennedy arrived on Air Force One.[35]

After the opening courtesies, Macmillan plunged straight in on Skybolt, tracing Anglo-American atomic co-operation back to the wartime 'Tube Alloys' project, and referring pointedly to Eisenhower's original 'broad honourable understanding'. Macmillan went on to note that there had been much talk about a Multilateral Force (MLF), but he was not quite clear what it meant; this was said with some apparent mischievousness, in that Kennedy was also beginning to lose patience with the woolliness of this concept, hatched by his 'Europeanist' lobby within the State Department. Macmillan revealed his strong disapproval of MLF (a seaborne force to be manned by sailors from the European NATO powers, including West Germany, in which the ships would carry nuclear weapons – but under overall US control) by remarking caustically to George Ball, 'Do you really expect our chaps to share their grog with the Turks?' He then reached into British history, back to Marlborough, and recalled cases where British forces had served under foreign generals, but without surrendering national authority: 'Interdependence and independence were the two sides of a coin,' an aphorism Macmillan was well pleased to have invented.

It was at this point that Macmillan delivered one of his greatest, and most moving bravura performances, that remained in the memories of many of his American listeners long after.[36] He invoked his own experiences in the First World War, recalling the courage and heroism as well as the horrors, and noting that men had not died then for the *entente cordiale* but for their own country. The implication was there, of course, subtly touched, of what Britain

437

had suffered in the cause of Western civilisation during her glorious past (and before the US had entered the fray), as well as her resolution now to enter Europe and bury the lethal rivalries of the past. But she was not going to abandon her history, and was determined to stay in the nuclear club – whatever the cost. On this theme of the Great War, with his own harsh experiences, no one could speak with more genuine emotion than Harold Macmillan, and at Nassau it made a deep impact on Kennedy – in whom courage in battle always roused strong echoes.[37] Indeed, the Americans seem to have been even more impressed than Adenauer, de Gaulle and the many Conservative Members of Parliament who had heard Macmillan develop similar themes.

Meanwhile, behind the scenes at Nassau things had been happening. On board Air Force One, Ormsby-Gore (to whom, for his role during the recent Cuban missiles crisis, Kennedy had become particularly indebted) had been invited by the President to sit with him, and for half an hour they had 'conversed as politicians'.[38] For the first time, Kennedy (by his own admission) realised just how devastating, politically, Skybolt could be to Macmillan. On the plane the two close friends devised a new scheme; the US would scrap Skybolt as a weapon for herself, but would carry on development jointly with the British, splitting the costs fifty–fifty. But it was too late; Ormsby-Gore arrived in Nassau to find Macmillan now firmly committed to getting Polaris at any price (this had been previously unbeknown to the Ambassador,[39] and therefore Macmillan's decision must presumably have been made during the flight of Air Force One). When the fifty–fifty offer was formally made at Nassau, Macmillan destroyed it by remarking that 'while the proposed marriage with Skybolt was not exactly a shotgun wedding, the virginity of the lady must be now regarded as doubtful' – in fact: 'the girl had been violated in a public place.' This was just the style of raffish Edwardian wit that particularly struck a chord with Kennedy's own sense of humour. The Anglo-American entourages, so recently at icy loggerheads, witnessed a miraculous thing – the burgeoning and blossoming of the two leaders' personal affection for each other, so recently enhanced by the Cuban crisis, and which was to have a decisive impact on the course of the Conference – and the next two decades of Western defence as well.

On the evening they arrived in the Bahamas, Kennedy and Macmillan walked together for a long time, without advisers. In the meantime, Ormsby-Gore – in the words of Neustadt – 'was engaged in "sitting on" Thorneycroft. If the PM now was bent upon Polaris, the original enthusiast for that approach was more concerned about his stance as fighter of Americans.'

Thorneycroft wanted to leave in a huff, 'rally the country, go it alone, and "let you take the fall-out", as an associate later put it . . .'.[40] But as the two leaders strolled together, disregarding the rough edges of their staffs, talking not only about the Skybolt crisis and politics, but also about their shared interest in history and the things that both found ridiculous or funny, or deadly serious, the whole atmosphere began to change from above.

Now, at Nassau George Ball, the professional diplomat, thought he identified 'one international distress signal recognized by politicians all over the world, and that is the cry of another politician in trouble . . .'.[41] But this was certainly not the principal channel on which Kennedy and Macmillan were communicating. Like all truly warm, close friendships it had moments of rancour and irritation when each could speak of the other in bitter depreciation – but which swiftly passed. 'Much more reliable than President Kennedy,' said Macmillan of McNamara in one fit of pique after Nassau, 'who makes the facts fit his arguments . . .';[42] 'looking at it from their point of view – *which they do almost better than anybody*,' Kennedy remarked acidly to Sorensen in the wake of Skybolt, 'it might well be concluded that . . . we had an obligation to provide an alternative.'[43] (To Bundy Kennedy had privately dismissed Macmillan's cherished deterrent, which had caused all the fuss, as 'a political necessity but a piece of military foolishness . . .'.)[44] Nevertheless, none of this diminished the magic of their friendship, capable of sweeping aside mountains of bureaucracy and more pragmatic considerations.

As the hard talking continued at Nassau, the American entourage – particularly the 'Europeanists' – watched with mounting alarm as it seemed as if Macmillan was going to make off with the President's shirt. Neustadt, who was fascinated by the depth of the Special Relationship, had no doubts that Skybolt 'was a case in point where JFK *did* overrule his subordinates in order to help Macmillan. It was a case of "king to king", and it infuriated the court.'[45] The 'Europeanists' fought staunchly to restrain the President, pointing out the danger that giving Polaris to Britain would cause de Gaulle to bar the door to Europe. Macmillan countered with repeated assurances that, at Rambouillet, he had put de Gaulle fully in the picture, was keeping him informed now, and had received no indication from him that Polaris would be a stumbling block.

Macmillan was offered a substitute missile with the cosily country-style name of Hound Dog; but it turned out that this particular beagle was too obese to fit under the wings of the British V-bombers.[46] (Anyway, Macmillan did not want it.) Macmillan threw out the perennial anxieties that trouble all Europeans, now as then: 'The Americans were willing to defend Europe and had the means to do so. Would they always have the will?' He would trust this President, but what about his successors? Hence Britain's need for an independent nuclear deterrent. Macmillan reiterated that he was 'determined to get Polaris and felt that we had a right to it. In return we would be prepared to make it clear that in normal circumstances we would regard our nuclear power as available to NATO and thus add to its strength.'

The Results of Nassau

Such was the pressure of the last-minute discussions that Ormsby-Gore found himself scurrying across the tarmac to get on Air Force One, its engines already warmed up. (His valet had been left behind three times in the last four flights.)[47] On returning to Washington Ormsby-Gore reported in a letter to Macmillan that Kennedy himself had admitted it had been 'certainly the hardest working conference he had ever attended'.[48] There remained some loose ends and technical details to be tied up, but Macmillan had won. He had got Polaris. He returned home in a state of total exhaustion, and it was something of an understatement when he wrote to Ava Waverley on 24 December: 'I got back yesterday after a very rough time, first in Paris and then in Nassau. We seem to be ploughing through rather heavy seas at the moment, but I daresay we shall get into calmer waters. . . .'[49] As he recorded in his memoirs, the arguments at the Nassau meeting 'were much more violently contested than any previous one', and 'the Americans pushed us very hard . . .'. There were, indeed, last-minute hiccups to reawaken lingering mistrust in the edginess of fatigue. It seemed incredible, but virtually as Nassau adjourned McNamara announced the first 100 per cent successful firing of the disprized, 'violated' Skybolt.

Kennedy claimed, 'it was the first time I have ever known McNamara to do anything silly.' Kennedy 'flew into a terrible rage', Ormsby-Gore recalled.

> He went through the roof. Luckily for poor Bob McNamara, he was flying out to Colorado for a skiing holiday. . . . We were sitting by the pool at Palm Beach behind his [JFK's] house ready to have a swim when the crisis burst. He was having a manicure and the manicurist sitting beside him. . . . This wonderfully sunny scene beside the pool – and suddenly this vast explosion and this violent language going out via telephone while the wretched manicurist went on cutting his nails. . . .[50]

In London the news provoked Macmillan's bitter diary outburst questioning Kennedy's reliability, where he went on to wonder whether the Americans 'may have "out-smarted" us altogether. It is *very* hard to judge whether they speak the truth or not. . . .'[51] But later in the same entry Macmillan comes down on the side of trust:

> It is also clear to me that they are determined to kill Skybolt on good general grounds – not merely to annoy us or to drive Great Britain out of the nuclear business. But, of course, they handled things in such a way as to make many of us very suspicious.

As in other moments when the fabric of the Special Relationship had been preserved, Macmillan breathed in and counted twenty, writing to Kennedy the following day with utmost moderation: 'It was rather provoking that Skybolt should go off so well the next day. It would have been better if it had been a failure. However, those are the chances of life. . . .'[52]

When the final, commercial details of the deal were tied up, Macmillan grumbled to his diaries, 'The American Defence Minister has been very grasping . . .' (this because Washington was now asking for a British contribution to the research and development costs of Polaris, 'a point which had never been mentioned at Nassau'), but 'I have refused to agree to his demands and have been forced to appeal to the President direct. I heard yesterday that he accepted my proposals.'[53]

In fact, though, Polaris was to turn out an extremely generous and beneficial deal for Britain. Britain got the weapon at a knock-down price that cost less than 2 per cent of the total British defence budget (though Lord Zuckerman in his memoirs queried whether at Nassau Macmillan had ever calculated the full financial burden);[54] while France had to struggle painfully and expensively to construct her own underwater deterrent. Rightly or wrongly, the British deterrent was preserved for another generation, and from Macmillan and Polaris to Thatcher and Trident was as from father to daughter. The final agreement was that Britain should be supplied with the Polaris missile, Britain making her own warheads, 'which we were quite able to do'. 'In return, our nuclear fleet was to be "assigned" to NATO, except in cases "where Her Majesty's Government may decide that supreme national interests are at stake".' Writing soon after Nassau in the *Reporter*, Dr Henry Kissinger questioned the 'extraordinary ambiguity' of this reserve clause. 'What happens', he asked, 'when the British Government decides that supreme national interests are at stake?'[55] 'You don't fire it off as if it were July 4th or Guy Fawkes!' Macmillan would explain years later, by way of a reply to Kissinger.[56]

From the American point of view, Nassau was a thoroughly badly organised conference, doubtless reflecting the stresses and distractions of the Cuban crisis, still little more than a month distant. Professor Neustadt, in his report, wrote: 'We "lost" what may be the chance to further our proclaimed concerns for European unity and strategic integration. Nassau *may* have been an opportunity. . . .'[57] For George Ball and the 'Europeanists', it was undoubtedly seen as 'a great victory' for Macmillan; in the opinion of Arthur Schlesinger, 'instead of forcing the British to an MLF commitment, we had saved their deterrent, thrust an issue into the hands of de Gaulle and set back the cause of integration. . . .'[58] Certainly it spelled something like the end for 'The Grand Design', but then – by the close of 1962 – Kennedy's own enthusiasm for it seems to have been running out of steam.

Yet, if France lost out in terms of having to finance, and develop, her own nuclear deterrent after 1962 (and may not that necessity have mothered such brilliant spin-off inventions as Exocet?), it cannot be said that she was entirely the loser in terms of higher political strategy. Of the three leaders, Kennedy, Macmillan and de Gaulle, who except de Gaulle – as of January 1963 – saw all his policies consistently and methodically advanced along the channels he had prescribed?

At Nassau, however, the Anglo-Saxon Special Relationship, in its simplest terms, had been preserved in a remarkable fashion. As Macmillan wrote to the Queen from Nassau,

It has been a hard and at times almost desperate struggle to maintain the two concepts of interdependence and independence. But I must pay tribute to President Kennedy's sense of fairness and willingness to be persuaded by argument and over-rule those of his advisers who were not sympathetic to our views.[59]

As a postscript to Nassau and all the dramas that had so shaken the Special Relationship, what could be more appropriate than this excerpt from a telephone conversation, dated 19 January 1963.

Prime Minister: I say, did you enjoy Nassau? I loved it, didn't you? I thought it was awfully good.
   President Kennedy: Oh, which is that?
   Prime Minister: The Nassau meeting.
   President Kennedy: Oh, yes – very good, very good.[60]

Kennedy's mind had evidently moved on.

Macmillan's government swiftly appreciated that, out of the jaws of defeat, he had carried off a remarkable personal success at Nassau.[61] The Queen congratulated him for having demonstrated that Britain still counted for a great deal, and could hold her head high.[62] Her Majesty was right; but this was not how the British press saw it. On Christmas Eve Macmillan recorded in his diary with some lassitude and depression, 'the Press is *very* bad and I sense that they have been able to whip up *Anti-European* emotions. . . . However . . . I am too tired to do anything more just now. . . .'[63]

He passed Christmas rereading some reminiscences about the Duke of Wellington, and – observing how much his own personal standing had been weakened by the continual media attacks – recorded with a rare note of self-pity: 'Poor Wellington! He was even worse treated by his friends than I have been!'[64]

443

De Gaulle's Veto

There remained the third panel of the triptych – de Gaulle and the 'French Connection'. On 26 December, Macmillan wrote to Heath, beavering away in Brussels,

> . . . I only trust that nothing I have done at Rambouillet or Nassau has increased your difficulties. My impression of de Gaulle is that he is friendly to me personally, not unfriendly to Britain . . . wants friendly relations with Britain, but does *not* want us now in the Community because he is in a mood of sulks about the future of Europe politically and would prefer to stay where he is with France dominating the Five. At the same time I am not sure whether he wants this to be too public. . . .[65]

Excessively pious hopes and Macmillan's habitual optimism when dealing with de Gaulle went hand in hand with some clear-sighted realism. What was to follow was, however, tragically to be the last round in Macmillan's long relations with de Gaulle, begun twenty years earlier when Macmillan had first championed the prickly Free French leader against Roosevelt and Churchill at Casablanca. Macmillan entered the New Year recording pessimistically in his diary: 'We do *not* expect much from de Gaulle except obstinacy and non-cooperation, but we must try. . . .'[66]

From Nassau, Kennedy had tried to sweeten whatever disappointment de Gaulle might have felt from the Polaris deal (notwithstanding Macmillan's asseverances to the contrary) by offering France – rather at the eleventh hour – Polaris on 'similar' terms to Britain. There was some quibbling over the words 'similar' and 'the same', with the French appearing not to appreciate the subtle distinctions, and at first the Quai d'Orsay reacted favourably. It was soon seen that the key difference was, of course, that while Britain was capable of making her own nuclear warheads for Polaris France was not, and was not now being offered the essential know-how by Kennedy. Here was the rub, which was bound to make the Kennedy 'deal' unpalatable to de Gaulle. But, apart from that, there was the all-important factor of de Gaulle's personal pride, in the name of France; could he be expected to accept any 'deal', however favourable, that might have emerged from a meeting to which France herself had not been a party? A vital matter of principle was involved; *Le Monde* said it all in an extended headline, on 3 January 1963: 'President Kennedy Has Decided to Direct the Western Alliance Without Bothering Himself Too Much With Possible Objections of His Allies. . . .'[67]

Therefore, when the final word came through, curtly from Paris, 'the General is no longer interested in that . . . ',[68] there should have been little surprise in Washington and London.

Seeing the unpromising way in which things were going with de Gaulle, Macmillan sent a telegram to Ormsby-Gore on 30 December containing an important and bold initiative to be passed on to Kennedy. Would the President agree to tempting de Gaulle into what would amount to a 'tripartite system' (which de Gaulle himself had been clamouring for ever since his return in 1958), through Britain supplying the warheads (which de Gaulle could not himself manufacture) for the Polaris missiles the Americans were offering the French? In return, de Gaulle should agree to facilitate British entry into the EEC. Macmillan asked that it be put to the President only on the 'kind of secret and personal basis on which we have discussed one or two matters, e.g. Berlin'.[69] It was 'a bold plan', and the most diehard Gaullist could hardly have accused Macmillan of not trying. Had it succeeded, de Gaulle would have had his *force de frappe* for virtually nothing. In Macmillan's view what de Gaulle could, or would, never understand was Britain's basic right to have American technical knowledge on nuclear weapons: 'He thought the French ought to have it, because *we* had it. And he couldn't understand that we had it, because we had invented it . . . during the war. . . .'[70] In response, Ormsby-Gore was not encouraging about the prospects in Washington; Kennedy thought Macmillan's last-minute initiative would have entailed a complete reversal of US policy and, even if he could have overcome his own scruples on nuclear proliferation, there was little chance of his getting such a proposal past Congress.[71]

On 14 January, de Gaulle held at the Elysée Palace a press conference, in what Macmillan described as 'de Gaulle's most majestic and "Louis Quatorze" style'.[72] Dealing first of all with Britain's application to join Europe, in much the same language he had employed with Macmillan at Rambouillet, he said:

Sentiments, as favourable as they might be and as they are, cannot be put forward in opposition to the real facts of the problem. . . . England is insular. . . . In short, the nature and structure and economic context of England differ profoundly from those of the other states of the Continent.

. . . in the end there would appear a colossal Atlantic community under American dependence and leadership which would soon swallow up the European Community.

De Gaulle continued with a reference of almost insulting condescension towards Macmillan, that it was 'a great honour for my friend, Harold Macmillan, to have perceived so early of the need to join Europe . . .'. Having dealt with the British application, he then turned to the Nassau agreements and the American Polaris offer: 'Undoubtedly, no one will be surprised that we cannot subscribe to the Anglo-American Nassau Agreement. It does not meet the principle of disposing of our own right of our own deterrent force.'[73] On 19 January, Macmillan was telephoning Kennedy to report on the dimmer than ever prospects at Brussels:

Prime Minister: Well, I think it's a very bad situation. I think this man has gone crazy – absolutely crazy.

President Kennedy: Well, what do you think it is that's made him crazy?

Prime Minister: He's simply inventing any means whatever to knock us out and the real simple thing is he wants to be the cock on a small dunghill instead of having two cocks on a larger one.[74]

The battle lines were clearly drawn.

Was Nassau, however, cause – or pretext – for de Gaulle? The greater the distance in time, and as more records become available, the less the first hypothesis seems tenable. In retrospect, Macmillan thought that if the French had been offered Polaris on really equal terms, it might 'have made a difference' to de Gaulle's attitude to Britain's EEC application in January 1963, 'but not the whole difference'.[75] Lord Home was convinced that de Gaulle 'would never have accepted an American offer however favourable, because he was pledged by every word and action to the total recovery of France, unbeholden to anyone else . . .',[76] while even the arch-apostle of the American 'Europeanists', George Ball, admitted in later years '. . . I think it more than likely that General de Gaulle would have vetoed British entry into the Common Market even if Nassau and the Skybolt crisis had never occurred. . . .'[77]

Meanwhile the animosity between Adenauer and Macmillan, so skilfully fanned by de Gaulle, also played its role in the French decision. In West Germany British entry into the EEC was supported both by public opinion and by every member of the Cabinet – except Adenauer. But the old Rhinelander's authority was still absolute, and his influence on his former subordinate, Professor Walter Hallstein, at that time President of the European Commission, also remained very considerable. Adenauer and Hallstein both expressed surprise that de Gaulle should block Britain with an outright veto;[78] nevertheless, only a week after de Gaulle's press conference, Adenauer went to Paris for the momentous signature of the Franco–German Treaty of Friendship. He left behind him a chorus of dissent in Bonn, but the treaty of reconciliation he was about to sign with de Gaulle, the summit of his life's aims, was far more important to him than the aspirations of Britain, or Macmillan – whom he never liked, or trusted. The signature of the Treaty by Adenauer provoked his pro-British Foreign Secretary to quote Milton to a British journalist: 'The desire for posthumous fame is the last infirmity of noble minds.'[79]

'We Have Lost Everything'

On 28 January, Couve de Murville, de Gaulle's Foreign Minister, went to Brussels to tell France's five EEC partners that the negotiations had to cease. The following day the French formally vetoed Macmillan's application to join Europe. To Macmillan it was a devastating blow. Up to the last moment he could not quite bring himself to believe that the man whose political existence he had saved, on more than one occasion, from the wrath of Churchill and Roosevelt back in wartime Algiers, should now act with such ingratitude to Britain, and be so personally snubbing. He wrote in his diary with something approaching despair: 'All our policies at home and abroad are in ruins . . . except our courage and determination.'[80] He felt particularly sorry for Heath, and could not stifle his bitterness and anger with de Gaulle: 'No one could have been a better negotiator and Ambassador – but French duplicity has defeated us all. . . .' Couve, he noted, had 'behaved with a rudeness which was unbelievable':

> The final scenes took place Monday and Tuesday. The end – or at least long delay, whether prolonged or final – in all our European policy has had a curious effect. At home, there is the return of the old feeling 'the French always betray you in the end'. There is *great* and *grievous* disappointment (among the younger people especially) at the end of a fine vision. . . .[81]

Broadcasting to the nation on the 30th, Macmillan declared: 'What happened at Brussels yesterday was bad, bad for us, bad for Europe, and bad for the whole Free World. A great opportunity has been missed. It is no good trying to disguise or minimise that fact. . . .' He continued with a gentlemanly but nevertheless hard shaft directed at de Gaulle:

> What has happened has revealed a division. France and her Government are looking backwards. They seem to think that one nation can dominate Europe and, equally wrong, that Europe can or ought to stand alone. Europe cannot stand alone. She must co-operate with the rest of the Free World, with the Commonwealth, with the United States in an equal and honourable partnership. That is why we in Britain need to stand by the Atlantic Alliance. . . .

He concluded: 'What we do must be creative and constructive, not vindictive. . . .' But it was hard to achieve either for the time being. As he continued in his diary entry for 4 February, 'the great question remains "What is the alternative?" to the European Community. If we are honest, we must say that there is none – had there been the chance of a Commonwealth Free Trade area, we should have grasped it long ago. . . .'[82]

With a sense of emptiness, and beset by all the other problems that the winter of protracted Arctic cold had imposed on Britain, he took off on a brief official visit to Rome, and the Vatican.

In Italy, Macmillan found the Italians:

> angry and alarmed. They *hate* the French, especially de Gaulle. . . . They hope . . . to *block* developments – especially those which the French want – in the Community. . . .

All this is good – but I rather fear that the French calculation is right. All this indignation, they believe, will blow over and they will be left undisputed masters of the field. . . .[83]

Macmillan was not far wrong, and a decade would have to pass before post-de-Gaulle France could be persuaded to permit Britain's entry into the EEC – by Macmillan's former negotiator in Brussels, Edward Heath.

Meanwhile, in Britain animosity to de Gaulle and France plumbed the depths. In pique Macmillan allowed himself to be persuaded by the Foreign Office, and public opinion, to cancel an official visit by Princess Margaret to Paris. It was an impulse of the moment; there was (Macmillan recorded) 'a great row'[84] in the media, and looking back on it he regretted the decision. 'It would have been more dignified,' he thought, to let the Princess fulfil her engagement. In the government collapse of the EEC negotiations brought an appalling anticlimax, since in almost every department ministers had been hard at work on it. Even the new Leader of the Opposition, Harold Wilson (Hugh Gaitskell had died suddenly during the same week as de Gaulle's veto) observed how very 'hard hit' Macmillan was,[85] and briefly Macmillan seems to have toyed with the idea of going to the country in a 'patriotic appeal'.[86] Here the shock of the final veto seemed momentarily to have clouded his political judgement. The central plank of the government's policy had just broken and Macmillan had nothing to put in its place in order to fight a viable and victorious election campaign. Harold Wilson would have had a field day, though few on either side of the House held him personally to blame for the EEC débâcle. Even his foe Haley of *The Times*, though not lamenting the failure of the EEC initiative, 'reflected more official sorrow than official anger';[87] while, perhaps as a display of that British sympathy for the underdog, the Gallup Poll reported that only 17 per cent (to 58 per cent) of Britons held Macmillan personally responsible for the failure to get into the EEC.[88] After the Commons debate in February, he still received a majority of 103.

None of this offered much consolation to Macmillan at the time. To his friend, Ava Waverley, he wrote, '. . . I do not remember going through a worse time since Suez. . . .'[89] He felt so low as even to refuse a lunch invitation from her that, normally, he would warmly have welcomed: 'the strain is too great.' Not one to harbour rancour for long (except perhaps against the media), his personal bitterness towards de Gaulle rapidly subsided, and – at the end of his days – any anger he felt towards de Gaulle was always mingled with genuine admiration: 'He was a great and brave man, and he saved France.'[90]

Macmillan's Fault?

Nevertheless, for Macmillan it remained the gravest failure of all his policies, and following, as it did, the débâcle of the 1960 summits there was nothing to put in its place. Certainly, had he succeeded he would have achieved a unique place in history as the Prime Minister who took Britain into a uniting Europe and found her a new role, and it would have been the greatest success, not only of his career but of any British leader since the war. How much, then, was it his own fault that Britain's EEC bid ended in failure? At various times over the years, and by various critics, he has been accused of going too slow, or too fast; of being too late, or too early; of being too cautious, of not trying hard enough to win Adenauer's support, or of being foolish in first canvassing the support of Kennedy; and of failing to gauge the depth of de Gaulle's anti-British and anti-American feeling. A criticism with hindsight more difficult to counter is that Macmillan failed to use his vast majority of October 1959 and the national support he still maintained over the next two years with audacity to sweep the British electorate into Europe. Instead, as has been seen, he delayed, uncertain of support in Britain and the Commonwealth, when a show of less hesitation could have convinced Europe, if not France, of Britain's new determination. There was strong factional opposition to Britain joining the EEC at the time, but Macmillan possibly underestimated his capacity to overcome it. So valuable time was lost, until de Gaulle himself became strong enough to turn what looked like British pusillanimity against Macmillan, and then to impose his one-man veto over the rest of Europe.

Certainly at vital moments both Macmillan and de Gaulle seemed unable to understand each other's words. At Champs and at Rambouillet de Gaulle appears to have misunderstood Macmillan's description of the British nuclear deterrent and the nature of the Anglo-American nuclear relationship. By the same token, in the drawing room at Champs and the library at Birch Grove, Macmillan seems to have underestimated the strength of de Gaulle's vision of a revival of Charlemagne's Holy Roman Empire. Throughout his discussions with de Gaulle and other European leaders, Macmillan had always honestly proclaimed that 'Europe cannot stand alone, she must co-operate with the rest of the free world, with the Commonwealth and with the United States in an equal and honourable partnership.' On the other hand, de Gaulle could claim to have made it perfectly plain at Birch Grove and at every other meeting that 'Canada, Australia and New Zealand may have been Europeans once but they were no longer Europeans. . . . and France did not want to change the character of . . . Europe and therefore did not want Britain to bring this great escort in with them.' The differences were always fundamental and Macmillan can perhaps most justifiably be criticised for not devoting more energy to the preparation of a contingency plan if the French used their veto.

But, when all is said and done, the fact remains that Macmillan was treated monstrously by de Gaulle, from whom he personally deserved better things. On the other hand, to take a fatalistic view, could anything have altered the prospect of de Gaulle's ultimate veto, given that – motivated by *une certaine idée de la France* – nothing was going to move him in any direction in which he did not want to go? But at least Macmillan had pointed the way; he set Britain on a new course from which there could now be no turning back, and he had placed a foot in the European door which even Gaullist France could not keep closed for ever – even though it would undoubtedly have been better both for Britain and for Europe if the door could have been opened in 1963, instead of ten years later.

Finally, out of Rambouillet and Nassau and Brussels, there emerged one factor which time would prove to be just as relevant a quarter of a century later. This was the capacity of the British and the Americans to resolve, by means of old-established channels, the ease of the common language and bonds of close personal friendship, a major crisis within the Special Relationship; while, at the same time, it proved much more difficult, if not impossible, to resolve a Franco-British crisis based on years, indeed centuries, of mutual mistrust, but also to some extent based simply on the age-old problems of linguistic *mésententes*. Here at least history might vindicate a sixty-eight-year-old British Prime Minister in his endeavours to woo a forty-five-year-old American President.

Chapter Sixteen

'Everybody's Darling, Anyway'
January–June 1963

Sir,
Few of our island kith and kin
Are totally immune to sin.
Yet, when some man the public know
Is caught flagrante delicto
With feigned regret and hidden spite
The sepulchres are painted white.
Sometimes the plea's security;
Sometimes it's national purity.
Unleashing bloodhounds: splendid sport
For those who've not themselves been caught.

   I am, Sir, your obedient servant,
     Sir John Colville

   (*Letter to* The Times, *10 October 1983*)

I do not live among young people much myself.

       (*Harold Macmillan, 17 June 1963*)

If the last chapter ended with devastating defeat for Macmillan on the foreign scene, with de Gaulle's veto, we now approach – at home – what was perhaps the saddest, and most humiliating, episode in his long public career; truly a heaping of Pelion upon Ossa. 'No man should ever lose a night's sleep over any *public* disaster,' Macmillan once declared, quoting Gladstone; but the Profumo affair was to impinge painfully on all that was most distressing, though buried deeply away, in Macmillan's own private life. When 1962 was over, he recorded that it had been 'a *bad* year'.[1] But 1963 was to be considerably worse.

Macmillan had passed through Christmas, afflicted by the usual seasonal gloom to which he was prone, but perhaps more fatigued than ever by all the compounded stress of the previous months – the Night of Long Knives, Berlin, Cuba, Rambouillet – and finally culminating, on the eve of the holiday, with Nassau.

Undoubtedly, an exhausted Macmillan, with those famous hooded eyes, the Edwardian languor, the tongue-in-cheek humour and the grouse-moor plus-fours, was all wonderful grist to the mill of the cartoonists and satirists. By this time, no holds were barred in the new world of British satire. 'The ranks are drawn up,' Jonathan Miller had declared gleefully on the opening of the Establishment Club, 'and the air resounds with the armourer's hammer. When battle is joined one can only hope that blood will be drawn. . . .'[2] In a bizarre parallel that seemed to adumbrate the savagery of the satirical instincts now unleashed in contemporary Britain, Kenneth Tynan rated *Beyond the Fringe* as 'the funniest revue that London had seen since the allies dropped the bomb on Hiroshima'.[3] There Peter Cook delighted audiences with his parodies of a tired and broken-down Macmillan contrasted with a young and vigorous President Kennedy, and – indeed – by the beginning of 1963 the Aunt Sally of much of the most savage and destructive satire was Macmillan and his apparent decrepitude.

But Macmillan had been playing the old man for years already, and much of the 'act' was mocking himself. When he was to become a genuinely old man, long after retirement, these were facets which the television viewers loved and which enthralled those who met him for the first time. In the early 1960s, though, they only irritated increasingly his young and not-so-young critics. Often they were blinded by the act, and unable to fathom the astute brain and modern-mindedness behind it. Nevertheless, as his own sixty-ninth birthday approached, Macmillan seemed even to his own entourage to be showing signs of strain once again, and even the climate seemed to have turned against the government.[4] The coldest winter in two centuries dragged on through January, bringing unemployment to a new peak of 4 per cent, the highest since that other appalling winter of 1947. With this background of disruptions and work stoppages, and the further downturn in the economy, Macmillan mused ruefully, 'Our affairs are not properly arranged for cold weather.'[5] Though the sub-zero cold gripped all Europe, it was the already shaky British economy that seemed to suffer most.

Politically Macmillan also noted a disquieting downturn in the Gallup Poll in February; '15% against the Party; as much against me'. The newly created right-wing Monday Club was calling for his resignation, in the wake of de Gaulle's veto, and Macmillan found a challenge from his enemies 'reaching quite formidable dimensions. "Macmillan must go" is the cry. . . .' He was determined, however, that 'We *must* go on at least till May, perhaps to October 1964, in the hope that our economic measures will have produced their results. So we must stick it out. . . .'[6] But an audience at the beginning of February with the Pope, who was suffering from terminal cancer and whose appearance shocked Macmillan, made him forcefully aware of his own mortality, approaching as he was his seventieth year. He was even more shocked by the sudden death, on 18 January, of his principal political opponent, Hugh Gaitskell, from a mysterious virus. Gaitskell was only fifty-six – thirteen years his junior.

Macmillan was deeply affected, and – in a spontaneous gesture – moved the adjournment of the House of Commons. It was the first time this had been done in honour of an Opposition leader who had never been Prime Minister. There was an element of contrition for the harshness of some of his judgements on Gaitskell: 'It is very sad – for although I did not find him a sympathetic character – he was a man of *high* quality. . . .'[7] He was, moreover, soon to realise, once the Opposition succession stakes were settled,[8] that he would find a far more daunting adversary in the shape of forty-seven-year-old Harold Wilson. But, as Harold Evans reveals, the sudden death of Gaitskell inevitably also aroused more subjective speculation in Macmillan. Always highly suggestible when it came to illness, he had been repelled by the morbidity of the press, giving every detail of the progress of Gaitskell's illness. 'Don't let them behave like this when I die, Harold,' was his remark to Evans, as he was being made up for the television cameras, and then *sotto voce*, 'Who do you think they will put up for the succession, Harold?' A few days later, however, Macmillan was confiding to Evans the reassuring news: '"John Richardson came to see me this morning. He said that I have the blood pressure of a man of thirty." Then, in a conspiratorial whisper, "I shan't chuck my hand in, you know. . . . Anyhow, it wouldn't do any good if I did. Of course, if it would help that would be different. . . ."'[9]

Macmillan remained cast down over de Gaulle's veto; in the policy hiatus that followed, marking time despondently to see what de Gaulle would do next, he found it 'terribly reminiscent of the late '30s – waiting on Hitler . . . '.[10] By 9 March, on the issue of his popularity, Macmillan was noting, '. . . Gallup Poll continues unfavourable . . . nearly half the Conservatives think that I should retire. . . .'[11] A fortnight later, he was recording that the Tories were now running 15 points behind Labour, the Labour Party's largest lead in seventeen years.

Spies

It was in this depressing context that Macmillan was plunged into a series of security scandals, first Vassall, then Profumo. Macmillan was neither the first, nor certainly the last, British Prime Minister to be dogged by the issue of spies and security problems. As Foreign Secretary, in November 1955 he had been obliged, by lack of evidence to the contrary, to give 'Kim' Philby formal clearance in the House of Commons against charges of being the 'Third Man' in the Burgess and Maclean case[12] – to the dismay of the intelligence community. What stuck most in Macmillan's mind at the time was what he condemned as a squalid 'hue and cry' in the press. He already was instinctively antipathetic to the whole subject of spies and spying (though he did not seem in any way distressed when Rab Butler had Welensky bugged). He reckoned that, to have a watertight security system, one would have to resort to totalitarian methods 'distasteful to our national sentiment and contrary to our long traditions'; to him the information passed to the Russians by Burgess and Maclean[13] was less damaging than the demoralisation caused by the *fact* of their treachery. Therefore, the less said about spies and traitors in public the better.

During the first three years of Macmillan's premiership no moles surfaced. Then, at the beginning of 1961, tip-offs from a Soviet defector (via the CIA) led to the rounding up of the 'Portland Spy Ring', which had been supplying Soviet intelligence with information from Britain's highly secret Underwater Weapons Establishment. Arrested, and sentenced to long terms of imprisonment were 'Gordon Lonsdale',[14] a mysterious figure believed to be Russian by birth; the Krogers, Polish Jews formerly resident in America and friends of the Rosenbergs, executed in the electric chair for spying; and two Britons employed at Portland, Houghton and Gee.

Immediately after the Portland trial, Macmillan announced the setting up of a committee under Sir Charles Romer to investigate what had happened and to consider what security weaknesses had been revealed. The press, he noted, gave voice to 'great public concern over what seemed an inexplicable affair', and – three months after the court case – he was still having to defend Lord Carrington, then First Lord of the Admiralty, against vigorous calls for his resignation.[15] Then, just before the Romer Committee produced its report, an even more serious blow fell; George Blake, a senior officer of MI6, was tried and found guilty of betraying its secrets to the KGB, dating back to his imprisonment during the Korean War. Vast numbers of agents working for Britain, and America, had been betrayed by Blake and executed, and the enormity of his treason was reflected in the unprecedented sentence of forty-two years imposed on him.[16] Macmillan noted in his diary that the deeply shocked public 'do not know and cannot be told that he belonged to MI6, an organisation which does not theoretically exist. So I had a rather rough passage in the House of Commons. . . .'[17] Such were the problems of dealing with spies in the open.

Macmillan thought it proper to keep the Opposition leaders informed, and he told them that it was not thought that an investigating committee would:

> need to probe into the efficiency of MI5 operations. It seems probable that they will find that MI5's detection work was, in this case, competently carried out. Any need for investigation arises on the other side of the picture, in security procedures and their application in the Admiralty and its out-stations here and abroad. . . .[18]

In the light of the disarray that is now disclosed to have existed in MI5 during the years when Sir Roger Hollis was Director-General,[19] Macmillan's assertion here may seem a trifle bland. It seems most improbable, however, that he would have seen fit to probe deeply into the internal workings of MI5 at that time. It was not his style; instead, he would have left it to Butler as Home Secretary (to whom MI5 was directly responsible), as he did with most domestic problems. On receiving the information, Gaitskell, Macmillan recorded gratefully, had behaved correctly and considerately, but he was nervous lest his deputy, George Brown (who had also been briefed), should 'chatter too much in his cups'.[20] On the other hand, 'The press has been terrible, without any sense of responsibility. They want sensation. . . .'[21] Given the appalling consequences of Blake's treachery, the press had some cause to be 'terrible'.

When published (in June 1961) the Romer Report was critical of the lack of 'security mindedness' at the Underwater Weapons Establishment. Macmillan seemed to think that, to meet public anxiety, yet another enquiry was needed, and he now set up the Radcliffe Committee to investigate all aspects of security in Britain.[22] Lord Radcliffe's findings, made available to the Cabinet in January 1962, were most disquieting in their revelations about the extent of Communist penetration within the civil service and trades unions, the full impact of which was to be felt during the Wilson administrations. It made a range of recommendations, which included a tightening-up of 'positive vetting', and a continuation of the 'D-Notice system' whereby the press were required to observe non-publication of specified security matters. But, on the whole, the Radcliffe Report had nothing dramatic to offer, either in its findings or in its recommendations; Macmillan was satisfied that it 'disclosed no radical defect in the system'. He discussed the Report with the Opposition leaders, Gaitskell and Brown, and – although Macmillan found the latter 'so rude that I could have kicked him out of the room . . . one of those few men who are more disagreeable sober than drunk'[23] – they agreed to associate themselves with the Report, which Macmillan then decided to publish. It was well received by the press, and Macmillan was able to congratulate himself that the government had 'handled the affair with wisdom and good sense'. For another six months there was a deceptive lull on the security front.

Not revealed in the Radcliffe Report were the channels of communication, and responsibility, between the intelligence services and the Prime Minister that prevailed in Macmillan's day. This was of relevance in what was to follow. MI5, responsible for internal security and counter-espionage, was (since the Maxwell-Fyfe re-organisation in 1952 that had followed in the wake of Burgess and Maclean) directly accountable to the Home Secretary personally; while MI6, the organ for active gathering of foreign intelligence, came under the Foreign Secretary. Each was a sacrosanct empire unto itself, and had no official existence. But the director-generals of both services, Sir Roger Hollis of MI5 and Sir Dick White of MI6, had right of direct access to the Prime Minister, which they used with varying discretion. Dick White, a career officer of MI5, and a former Director-General of that service, had been appointed to MI6 by Eden following the Commander Crabb scandal in 1956. He was respected and liked by Macmillan and had an easy relationship with the Prime Minister. In his turn, White always found Macmillan 'marvellous to deal with'.[24] White had palpably done a good job in refurbishing the image of 'Six'. It was not the same with Hollis. In recent years sensational accounts have been published in the course of the 'Great Mole War' that Hollis (who moved into White's slot as Director-General of MI5, on White's transfer to head MI6) was yet another undercover Soviet agent. These charges remain to be substantiated; but, judging from MI5's inept performance during the Hollis years, Hollis – an unforthcoming, reticent and retiring man – had at least a great deal to be reticent and retiring about. Macmillan regarded him dismissively as an 'insignificant man'.[25]

Vassall

Had the whole security affair ended in mid-1962, however, with Radcliffe, 'whose recommendations we began rapidly to carry out', Macmillan wrote in his memoirs,

> all would have been well, and the remainder of my administration would not have been darkened by this cloud which, always threatening, had not hitherto been the prelude to a dangerous storm. But it was not to be; and the last year of my premiership was over-shadowed by a series of difficulties starting with some genuine apprehensions as to security and spreading rapidly into the much wider area of scandal, more easily comprehensible and more generally enjoyable. . . .

It began in September 1962, while Macmillan was drafting his important speech to the Party Conference on the EEC, when Thorneycroft, the Minister of Defence, and Carrington, First Lord of the Admiralty, wanted 'to see me urgently'. He recorded in his diary:

> There has been another espionage case – and a very bad one – in the Admiralty. An executive officer, homosexual, entrapped by the Russian Embassy spies and giving away material (of varying value) for five or six years. Only caught by the help of a Russian 'defector'.[26] There will be another big row. . . .[27]

It was to be bigger than Macmillan anticipated.

W. John Vassall was a somewhat pathetic figure, almost a case study of a homosexual driven by alienation, rather than by any ideological motivation, to become a traitor. He had been a ciphers clerk in the British Embassy in Moscow, where he had felt himself to be socially snubbed and had taken to handing over secret documents to the KGB. He lived ostentatiously beyond his means, and, though a blatant homosexual, was never spotted as a security risk. Macmillan's first reaction was to blame the then British Ambassador for not having 'kept track' of Vassall. 'One ought to know the private life of a staff in Moscow in a way which is quite impossible in London. . . .'[28] When Hollis came to see Macmillan about Vassall and announced (by Macmillan's account, manifestly with high satisfaction), 'I've got this fellow, I've got him!', Macmillan looked glum, and Hollis remarked, 'You don't seem very pleased, Prime Minister.' The reply (and an immortal one) was,

> No, I'm not at all pleased. When my gamekeeper shoots a fox, he doesn't go and hang it up outside the Master of Foxhounds' drawing room; he buries it out of sight. But you just can't shoot a spy as you did in the war. You have to try him. . . . better to discover him, and then control him, but never catch him. . . .[29]

Macmillan pointed out that now there would be

> A great public trial. Then the security services will not be praised for how efficient they are but blamed for how hopeless they are. There will then be an enquiry . . . [which] will say – like the Magistrate in 'Albert-and-the-Lion' – that no one was really to blame. There will be a terrible row in the press, there will be a debate in the House of Commons and the Government will probably fall. Why the devil did you 'catch' him?[30]

This magnificent declamation may possibly have owed something to *esprit de l'escalier*; nevertheless, it was entirely representative of what Macmillan consistently felt about spies and spying. It almost certainly would have made an appreciable impact on an 'insignificant man' like Hollis.

On 22 October, the day the Cuban missiles crisis erupted, Vassall was sentenced to eighteen years' imprisonment. Macmillan – distracted by events in the Caribbean – hoped that the case could then be investigated within the existing Radcliffe review structure. But it would not go away. On 5 November, when the world had barely got over the shock of Cuba week, Macmillan was forced to admit, 'The Vassall case is getting more embarrassing. . . .'[31] The Labour Party, led by Macmillan's *bête noire*, George Brown, declared that – in view of the previous Admiralty lapses – the investigating machinery proposed by Macmillan was totally inadequate.

Meanwhile, a vicious whispering campaign had developed, scurrilously linking Vassall with Thomas ('Tam') Galbraith, a former junior minister at the Admiralty, currently an Under-Secretary of State for Scotland. At the Admiralty, Vassall had once worked in Galbraith's private office. Letters that had passed between them were published as a White Paper, but – in the words of the *Annual Register* – they revealed

> nothing more damaging than the former Civil Lord's interest in his office carpets, crockery, and paper clips. The most that could be said against Mr. Galbraith was that he had suffered a socially pressing and plausible junior colleague a trifle too gladly.[32]

Nevertheless, Britain's popular press, sniffing their two favourite ingredients – spies and sex – linked together were relentless in their pursuit of Galbraith, going from one excess to another. Galbraith was dogged mercilessly, with reporters even cross-questioning his wife's hairdresser as to 'whether she had said anything'.[33] As a result, a reluctant Macmillan acceded to the setting up of a special tribunal – once again under the experienced Lord Radcliffe.

While all this was under way, as Macmillan recalled in his memoirs,

> . . . I had been engaged in facing what seemed the opening phase of a Third World War, involving not merely the intellectual strain of constant talks with the President, but the physical disadvantage of scarcely sleeping more than one or two hours each night. Yet, so strangely is the human brain constituted, this terrible danger seemed to distress me less than the personal and human anxieties.
>
> I do not remember a more worrying time – and so wasteful of effort. I suppose I would have done better to have had a Judicial Enquiry of some kind at the start. Had I known that all this mud would be thrown about, I would have done so. But we cannot have a tribunal every time we catch a spy. Now that the net is closing, we shall probably have some more cases. The public does not regard catching a spy as a success, but as a failure.

In countering the press charges, he made a speech which was – so he thought – 'the most impressive and successful which I have ever delivered in Parliament'. Galbraith and Carrington were effectively vindicated. But, because of the slurs, Macmillan felt it advisable that Galbraith should resign, *reculer pour mieux sauter*. By his own account, Macmillan accepted Galbraith's 'insistent' offer of resignation only reluctantly; but the then Chief Whip, Martin

The new President, a new phase in the Special Relationship, and a new friend.
Washington, April 1962.

Old friends; President Kennedy with Ambassador Ormsby-Gore.

Bermuda, December 1961. Differences over nuclear testing. Secretary of State Dean Rusk, President Kennedy, Macmillan, Foreign Secretary Home.

Admiralty House, June 1961. For the President, a comforting visit after a hard time from Khrushchev in Vienna; for Jacqueline Kennedy, a triumph exceeded only by Paris.

Friends at work; Washington, April 1962. *From left*, Sir Norman Brook, Cabinet Secretary, Macmillan, Ormsby-Gore.

Labour at the seaside, Brighton Conference, September 1962. Not posing for the artist: George Brown, Opposition Deputy Leader, Hugh Gaitskell, Party Leader, his eventual successor, Harold Wilson, Len Williams, Conference Secretary.

Left of Labour. Frank Cousins of the TUC 'declared war on everything and everybody'. (HM, *Riding the Storm*, p.355)

The new Chancellor, Selwyn Lloyd, April 1962.

After the Night of Long Knives, exit Selwyn Lloyd, enter Reginald Maudling;
the Tory Party Conference, October 1962.

'Supermac' takes off; 1959.

Election, 1959.

Grappling with Europe, as seen by Vicky, 1960.

. . . even in retirement.

October 1963. The succession, as seen by Cummings.
Note the absence of Home, the dark horse.

The succession, Act II.

"Mr Kinnock! Would you care to buy some Georgian silver, antique family furniture and an old painting?"

'Selling the family silver'; at odds with Margaret Thatcher, November 1985.

The Derby, 1957; the
'You've-never-had-it-so-good' pose.

In the grouse-butt, August 1959;
a more familiar habitat.

A luncheon visit, May 1959; still deferential to his old chief.

John Profumo MP, June 1963, after resigning as Secretary of State for War.

Returning to London at the height of the Profumo scandal, June 1963.

At the Party Conference, October 1963; the contenders – Hailsham, Home, Butler, Macleod.

The Queen leaves King Edward VII Hospital, 18 October 1963, followed by Sir Michael Adeane. 'She seemed moved: so was I.' (*HMD*, 18 October 1963.)

Retired, and recuperating, Regent's Park, October 1963.

The publisher returns; the author begins, January 1964.

Shooting with Maurice, still convalescent, Birch Grove, November 1963.

Dorothy Macmillan's funeral at Horsted Keynes, Sussex; Harold Macmillan accompanied by Maurice, 25 May 1966.

On *Firing Line*, with William F. Buckley Jr, New York, 1980.

Biographer greets subject; Washington, November 1980.

Mrs Jacqueline Kennedy at Birch
Grove, May 1965.

Bestowing a degree on Prince Charles,
Oxford, May 1983.

Eighty-fifth birthday respects from a new Tory leader, in opposition. Margaret
Thatcher MP, at the Carlton Club, February 1979.

China, with Deng Xiao Ping, October 1979; a new voyage of discovery.

A new role. In the House of Lords on the first day of public television, with former colleagues of the Tory Front Bench, Lords Boyd-Carpenter and Home, 23 January 1985.

Redmayne, differs somewhat in claiming that he had actually had to go, at Macmillan's behest, and ask him to resign. ('It was not my happiest moment. Nor were the wolves diverted for more than a moment.')[34] Macmillan readily admitted later that allowing Galbraith to resign had been a serious mistake, particularly in view of what was to follow over Profumo.

'Getting the Journalists'

The press continued to clamour for the head of Carrington. After the Vassall debate, where he had gained Margaret Thatcher's admiration and had been unsparing in his denunciation of Fleet Street, Macmillan remarked half-apologetically to the man who would bear the brunt, Harold Evans, '. . . I've made a lot of enemies in the press today, Harold. But I am an old man and I don't really care. . . .'[35] About the same time Alan Watkins of the *Observer* recalled Macmillan having been heard to remark, 'Now we'll get the journalists.' Macmillan was not a vindictive man, but there was an element of revenge in what was to follow. He felt that he had become the target for far more than his fair share of slings and arrows from the media. During the recent security exposures, he was angered by the way in which the worst issues got the least publicity and 'were not understood by the Press'; for example, Vassall got vastly more lineage than Blake, who had caused by far the greater damage. But what most outraged him were the personal slurs on Galbraith and Carrington. 'I felt strongly', he wrote in his memoirs, 'that not only should the truth be searched [*sic*], but also that the purveyors of lies should be punished. It was important that an incipient McCarthyism should be stemmed without delay. . . .'

When, after several months, the Radcliffe Tribunal delivered its verdict, clearly and unequivocally, Carrington was completely vindicated, and Galbraith equally absolved of any involvement with Vassall. Meanwhile two journalists, one from the *Daily Sketch* and one from the *Daily Mail*, who had been summoned to give evidence before the Tribunal were sent to prison (in March 1963) for six months. They had refused to disclose their sources of information for articles linking the Portland case with Vassall – if, indeed, there had been any sources; a fact which other journalists questioned. Said Macmillan laconically, 'the Press represented them as martyrs, but the man in the street was more sceptical.' All the way from the *News of the World* to *The Times* the furore was immense. Only a short time previously, following some by-election reverses, *The Times* had pontificated in a long leader, 'The country has moved close enough to a presidential form of government to mean that only a change of Prime Minister will persuade people that they are looking at a new Ministry. . . .'[36] Now open war was declared. Was Macmillan justified, or well advised, to permit such draconian action? He himself remained unrepentant to the end of his life, tending to pass responsibility to the judiciary:[37] it was 'nothing to do with me, it was the judge who took this as a contempt of court,' he told the BBC in September 1973. He insisted that he had been powerless to intervene in the workings of the law, but:

> The Headmaster's always to blame. The boss is to blame. But it was really Radcliffe. I didn't know anything about it. . . . They didn't believe that the P.M. doesn't talk to a judge during the case. I naturally was rather amused! . . . But they never forgave it for the rest of my life. . . .[38]

Certainly Macmillan shed no tears over the punishment of the journalists. Harold Evans reckoned that, by 1963, the press had become 'vicious and really vilified him'[39] but that the court action 'was to sour relationships between the Prime Minister and the Press . . . beyond any expectations at the time'.[40]

Among the politicians involved, Lord Carrington for one never forgot Macmillan's 'generosity'; 'He was personally so kind, wholly honourable and generous – he stuck his neck out through thick and thin, and needn't have done so; he needn't have refused to accept my resignation.'[41]

Fell, Philby, Blunt and 'Peters'

Between the sentencing of the wretched Vassall in October 1962 and the publication of the Radcliffe Tribunal findings the following April, Macmillan had no peace on the security front; the procession of spies continued. First, in November, there was Miss Barbara Fell, a senior official of the Central Office of Information, sentenced to two years' imprisonment for passing intelligence (of a fairly low order) to her young Yugoslav lover; 'apparently in the somewhat naive attempt to convert him to the Western way of life', commented Macmillan; 'not too bad', he wrote in his diaries, 'folly rather than treachery . . .'.[42] Next there came the final act in what Macmillan described as the 'almost historic' case of 'Kim' Philby. 'We think we have at last solved the mystery of who "tipped" off Burgess and Maclean,' he wrote in his diary for 19 February 1963:

> It was a man, much suspected at the time, but against whom nothing could be proved – one Philby. He was dismissed in 1951 from the service and has lived since in the Middle East, chiefly in the Lebanon, where he writes for the *Observer* and the *Economist*! In a drunken fit, he confessed everything to one of our men, so the whole thing is now clear. Maclean and Burgess were worse than mere *defectors* – they were spies, paid by Russians, over quite a number of years. This man Philby seduced them and recruited them to the Russian service. He has now disappeared from Beirut, leaving £2,200 in cash for his wife. Whether he will appear in Russia or not, we do not know. Anyway, it means more trouble. . . .[43]

Macmillan's diary entry described the details of the Philby story with fair accuracy, except that Philby had not been drunk when he had confessed to 'one of our men', Nicholas Elliot of MI6.

Macmillan seems to have been kept uninformed about the disappearance of Philby; this was consonant with his subsequent treatment by Hollis over Profumo, and almost certainly had something to do with his observation about 'shooting foxes' – which had become widely current in the Security Service. It was not until 29 March that Heath, speaking for the Foreign Office, announced it; on 1 July he stated categorically that Philby had been the 'Third Man', and was now presumed to be somewhere 'behind the Iron Curtain'. There was renewed storm in the press and a difficult passage for Macmillan in the Commons. He was agreeably surprised, however, at the staunch support he received from Gaitskell's successor, Harold Wilson. 'I had an hour with Harold Wilson,' Macmillan wrote in his diary for 11 July, 'and tried to explain to him how the so-called Security Services really worked. It seemed to me right to do so, and he took it quite well. . . .'[44] Macmillan recorded the gratitude he felt, after the Commons debate the following day, for Wilson's 'high sense of responsibility ... at a period when I was very hard-pressed ...'.

From Philby the trail of powder led to Blunt. The last of a series of interrogations which led to Blunt's confession, and secret amnesty, apparently took place in 1964 – therefore after Macmillan's own resignation. When the revelations of Blunt's treachery first became known in 1979, Macmillan remarked,

> Yes, certainly we knew about it, but felt we couldn't do anything. Nothing to arrest the man on. No proof. If I'd said in the House, 'X was a traitor,' then I might have been called on to state this out of privilege, and suffer a monumental libel suit. Yes, we did suspect that Blunt was a wrong 'un. . . .

'What was much more serious, in my time, and much more worrying,' Macmillan continued,

> was the warning we had of a possible traitor at the top of MI5.[45] He'd been spotted wandering round the loos in the park ... passing things, probably it was opium or something, he seemed to be somewhat unhinged, probably not working for the Communists. Fortunately he retired before we could do anything, but it was all a great worry. . . .[46]

He continued, eighteen months later, on the same theme:

> First of all we thought it was boys, then he was followed and was observed to meet a foreigner; I think he was probably Japanese, and we watched him.
> My impression was that he was – like so many people in that game – suffering from the fatigue of having been at it too long. . . .[47]

The wanderer-in-the-park was 'Peters', alias Graham Mitchell, Hollis's Deputy Director-General in MI5.[48] On account of his strange activities, Mitchell had been under surveillance, under the codename of 'Peters', as a top-level mole at the head of MI5 since April 1963. Hollis had informed Macmillan about it shortly thereafter, evidently playing it down as much as possible, and refusing initially to request permission to tap 'Peters'' telephone.[49]

Mitchell then suddenly asked for early retirement; the molehunters were disconcerted, as this suggested that another mole might have tipped him off. By December 1963, after Macmillan had retired, 'Operation Peters' was abandoned for want of conclusive evidence. Mitchell died in 1984. The spotlight was then focused on Hollis himself, but on insubstantial and unsatisfying evidence. (Macmillan always held the opinion that Hollis was an inept and 'insignificant' head of MI5, but not a treacherous one.)

In April there were two more security headaches for Macmillan. The first was a 'tiresome "leak"' on Civil Defence, which had enabled the CND to print pamphlets:

> which purport to reveal the various Civil Defence measures, including the Regional HQs. It is *not* very serious from a practical point of view, but it's *another security failure* of the Government, and the Press – smarting under Vassall – has grasped eagerly at a new chance of attacking me and the Home Secretary. . . .[50]

The second case, three days later and presumably related to the first, went unrecorded in Macmillan's memoirs:

> We have caught a spy (or rather a man 'getting ready to spy' – buying equipment etc.). He is an employee of Euratom, doing 'liaison' with the Atomic Energy Authority. . . . It will be rather delicate with the Euratom authorities but rather a triumph for the Security Service. For once, we have 'got' a man *before* he has done us any injury. . . .[51]

This was all illustrative, Macmillan later thought, of how 'by an extraordinary combination of circumstances or an exceptional run of ill-luck, Parliament and the public were being continually stimulated into a sense almost of hysteria. Nor did our critics distinguish between the failures and the successes.' And he went on – perhaps rather revealingly: 'from my point of view, life would have been easier if the counter-espionage work had been less effective. . . .'

It was against this essential backdrop that the Profumo case occurred.

Maudling's First Budget; the Economy

Meanwhile Macmillan was increasingly preoccupied with the pre-paration of Maudling's first Budget. The run-up to it had been hardly encouraging. The bitter winter and a peak of nearly 4 per cent unemployment had been compounded with the serious threat of a national power strike in frozen January. Macmillan did not need the Romer Report to tell him just how strongly the Communists had become entrenched in the Electricians Union, particularly among the key power-station shop stewards: 'These men are simply trying to exploit their blackmailing power, under Communist leadership. . . .'[52] The construction industry had been reduced almost to a standstill by the cold and the power-cuts, and on the 12th he was recording: 'The trade union leaders seem to be losing out to the Communist shop-stewards. A serious situation is upon us. . . .'[53] And two days later, 'The trade unions have an arbitration agreement which they refuse to implement on the ground that since the summer of 1961 arbitrators have been subservient to the Government's Incomes Policy! How I wish it were true. . . !'[54] The precariousness of the situation in Britain was brought home to Macmillan by a prolonged power-cut that plunged Chequers into darkness during one Cabinet working session.

> Anyway, we managed to settle the Electricity dispute *without a defeat*. (Indeed, the extreme trade unions and the shop-stewards complained bitterly about the agreement reached – three-year agreement, and about 4 per cent rise a year – *very* good from the Incomes Policy point of view.) The Communist shop-stewards [have] lost out. But the E.T.U. remains disgruntled. . . .[55]

At the end of February Neddy (the National Economic Develop-ment Council) – which now seemed to be functioning reasonably smoothly – reported that a 4 per cent annual growth figure was still obtainable for the period 1961–6[56] but that the stagnation of 1961/2 now required growth of some 5 per cent in 1963/4 to reach the target. The experts, Macmillan noted, 'regarded national wage increases of some 3 per cent as the maximum which the economy could stand'. But, in fact, the settlement with the ETU meant that this limit was breached. Some economists said that this was a severe blow to Neddy, though Macmillan – writing in the Heath/Wilson era of hyperinflation – commented that 'It must seem strange to a new generation to reflect how modest were the figures which caused us such alarm in a previous decade.'

Macmillan, however, remained more concerned about the stagnation of British industry, especially in comparison to her European competitors. Back in November 1962 he had found time between Cuba and Vassall, and the other concurrent crises, to address a memorandum entitled 'Modernisation of Britain' to both his Chancellor and his Deputy, Rab. It began:

We have now reached a stage in our post-war history where some more radical attack must be made upon the weaknesses of our economy, both productive and structural. We face a situation in which the conditions of trade are becoming increasingly competitive and our commercial rivals increasingly better equipped to compete with us, while our own economy remains sluggish and 'patchy'. If we are to respond adequately to this challenge, we have to do two things:

(a) First, in order to enhance our competitive power and to ensure a level of exports commensurate with full employment at home, we have to increase our productivity by bringing our productive capacity into full use, by eliminating restrictive practices and by developing to the utmost the new methods which technology is bringing within our reach. Whatever the result of the Brussels negotiations, this need is urgent. In or out of Europe, Britain needs to be brought up to date in almost every sphere of life.

(b) Second, we have to re-organise the structure of the island in such a way as to rectify the imbalance between south and north – between the 'rich' areas and the 'poor' regions, the over-employed regions and the under-employed regions – and redress the grave social anomalies which are created by this imbalance. . . .[57]

Macmillan was stating with clarity two fundamental problems that would continue to bedevil his successors. To deal with them he called upon Maudling to preside over a 'steering-committee' to explore specific suggestions. Within the Party, he set about orienting it towards the forthcoming General Election; a spoof slogan, 'Modernise with Macmillan', reflected, with its supposed contradiction in terms, the anxieties felt by many Party activists. On 5 January, he followed up his concern about the depressed North-east – which was his old stamping-ground from Stockton days – by appointing the energetic Lord Hailsham to assume responsibilities ('a politically unremunerative task') for the area. The depressed areas were slow to respond to treatment; the mid-February unemployment figures reached 7 per cent for the North-east, with Macmillan noting that the prospects for its shipbuilding and the heavy industries were bad. He threw himself into sponsoring new projects for Scotland and the North-east, and took off on an exhausting, whistle-stop visit to Glasgow after the Budget.

Under pressure from the polls (in mid-March a *Sunday Telegraph* sampling showed that 62 per cent felt he should resign)[58] sterling continued weak, with a loss (in March) of £100 million in two days. Macmillan was by now thoroughly disillusioned with his former gurus, and in particular he was critical of:

the economists – Harrod, Juliet Rhys Williams, Schwarz, Harold Wincott, Kaldor,[59] and all the rest of this motley crew. Up to now the 64,000 dollar question has been 'How to Boom without Busting'. With the help of the experts and the *Times* newspaper it seems that our immediate future may be to Bust without Booming. . . .[60]

Nevertheless, Macmillan refused to be deflected (as he wrote to the Queen while she was on a tour of Australia and New Zealand), from his determination 'to expand the economy'.[61] The theme of the 1963 Budget was to be 'Expansion without Inflation', and in his new Chancellor, Maudling, he found a 'flexible and ingenious' accomplice, bolder than he had expected. There were tax cuts of nearly £300 million, and – along with 'imaginative' proposals to attract and expand industry in the depressed areas – Macmillan found that his ministers 'were pleased and impressed',[62] 'the professional economists disagreed, sometimes with us, more often with each other. . . .'

The Budget was not, however, greeted with great excitement. Macmillan noted that, in attacking Maudling's Budget, 'Wilson's rather cheap sneers were not effective.' As before, however, it all depended on a partnership between the government, employers and trades unions. 'Will the trade unions play?' wondered Macmillan; 'It all depends on them.'[63]

The question was not to be answered in Harold Macmillan's time; nor in Harold Wilson's. Macmillan, however, was convinced that this last, expansionist Budget was not the cause of the difficulties that followed after the Conservatives left power in 1964. In the last weekend in April, Macmillan held an imposing, and unprecedented, meeting at Chequers of all Cabinet ministers and all ministers who headed departments.[64] *The Times* dubbed it the 'Brains Trust' meeting, and its theme was 'Britain in the 1970s' – an attempt to create a forward-looking economic blueprint for the country now that de Gaulle had closed the door to Europe. But Macmillan was to be out of office (and his successor, Home, too) before any of the Brains Trust's ideas could proceed much further.

With the coming of spring, Macmillan noted both an improvement in the economy and a corresponding rise in Tory morale. By May gold reserves had risen £29 million, exports were soaring, and by mid-June overall unemployment figures had sunk to 2.1 per cent (though they remained stuck at 4.3 per cent for Scotland and the North-east), production was rising and 'Neddy' seemed to be working.

Such was Macmillan's renewed confidence that at the annual luncheon of the 1922 Committee he announced his intention of leading the Party into the next election. It was at this point that the Profumo scandal exploded.

Profumo

Even a generation later, it still seems almost incredible that a Prime Minister who, less than four years previously, had led his Party to one of its greatest electoral triumphs should have been all but ruined by the peccadillo of one junior minister. Perhaps it could only have happened in that strangely hysterical year of 1963, when the British public seemed credulously dedicated to believing the worst fantasies about its leaders, political and social.

Aged forty-eight in 1963, John Profumo had had a distinguished war record in the Household Cavalry, attaining the rank of brigadier; he was elected to Parliament during the war, lost his seat in 1945 and, after his re-election in 1950 he had been steadily promoted, until he had been appointed by Macmillan in 1960 to be Secretary of State for War. He was thus in charge of the army, although under Macmillan's reorganisation of Defence the importance of the office had been considerably diminished. But he looked a candidate for further promotion. Educated at Harrow and with an Italian grandfather (*Who's Who* described him as '5th Baron of the late United Kingdom of Italy'), he was an attractive – though balding – man-about-town. He was well matched by his wife, Valerie Hobson, the actress, who had made her mark starring in *The King and I*, and the Profumos were very much in the eye of the 'Swinging Sixties' society. On a hot weekend of July 1961, Profumo met, and fell for, nineteen-year-old Christine Keeler during a naked frolic around Lord ('Bill') Astor's swimming pool at Cliveden. The intermediary was Dr Stephen Ward, the society osteopath and part-time portraitist, with whom Keeler (euphemistically described as a 'model' but in fact a callgirl) lived from time to time. Ward was a close friend, and tenant, of Lord Astor. The two shared an absorption in sex in all its anomalies, and Ward rented from Astor a cottage on the Cliveden estate. It was neither the first nor the last time that the Astor pool was witness to nude shenanigans, but the scandal might never have reached the proportions it did without the shadowy presence of Captain Yevgeny Ivanov, Naval Attaché at the Soviet Embassy in London, and therefore – *ipso facto* – a recognised intelligence operator. Ivanov had been introduced to Ward by the highly Conservative editor of the *Daily Telegraph*, Colin Coote, at a lunch at the Garrick (Ward was included in the party because he was 'anxious to visit Moscow and to draw Soviet personalities from life').[65] Ivanov also wanted to rent a cottage from Astor. Some time in the weeks following the pool encounter of July, Profumo started an intense affair with Keeler, but this ended apparently before the end of 1961. According to Keeler, two years later, she was also sleeping concurrently with Captain Ivanov (hence the security risk) – but doubts were subsequently thrown on the truth of this by the Denning Report.[66]

None of this might have come to public notice but for the trial of Johnny Edgecombe that began well over a year later, on 14 March 1963, which involved Stephen Ward. A West Indian lover of Keeler's, and a marijuana pusher, Edgecombe was accused of having shot up Ward's flat in Wimpole Mews, Marylebone, where Keeler and her eighteen-year-old friend, an 'unemployed actress' called Mandy Rice-Davies, were living. But during the trial, to the embarrassment of the prosecutor, Christine Keeler, the key witness, disappeared to Spain. Shortly after Christine Keeler returned, another West Indian lover, 'Lucky' Gordon, was charged with wounding her in a London street. The British press were now on to a thoroughly good thing, and it was not long before rumours were abounding about Profumo's involvement. These had already been sniffed out by the long nose of Colonel George Wigg, Labour MP for Dudley. With the pendulous ears and lugubrious eyes of a bloodhound, and a concomitant keen sense of smell, Wigg[67] had risen from the ranks during twenty-five years in the army; he was proud of having 'always been an NCO at heart' and of his 'deep contempt for the incompetence of the British ruling classes'.[68] He also bore a grudge against Profumo, by whom he had recently been slighted in the Commons.

It was in the middle of the Commons debate on the imprisoning of the two Vassall journalists, on 21 March, that Wigg – supported by Barbara Castle – dropped his bombshell. Under the protection of Parliamentary Privilege, he referred to speculation involving a member of the government, and invited them to deny it. Wigg, whose speciality was military and security matters, alleged that he was motivated only by security considerations.[69] The following morning at 11 a.m., after two hours' sleep, a jaded Profumo rose to a packed and hushed Commons to deliver a statement that had obviously been prepared in great haste overnight. Rab Butler was appalled, exclaiming, '"Not on a *Friday morning* surely!"'[70] According-ing to Butler's biographer, Anthony Howard, Rab thought that Profumo should have been given more time, and should have withdrawn from his ministerial post while an enquiry was con-ducted; had it been accepted, Rab's advice might have saved both the government and Macmillan considerable embarrassment. In his statement, however, Profumo declared that he had last seen Keeler in December 1961, but what was a lie was his claim that 'there was no impropriety whatsoever in my acquaintanceship with Miss Keeler. . . .' He continued, '. . . I shall not hesitate to issue writs for libel and slander if scandalous allegations are made or repeated outside the House. . . .'

Until this solemn statement by Profumo, the Chief Whip, Martin Redmayne, among many others, was sceptical about whether Profumo had spoken the truth: 'I am a man of the world, and I

473

know that if you hear a lot of rumours that somebody is sleeping with a girl, there is generally something in it.'[71] Amid all the belabouring which he had taken (and was continuing to take) over Philby and Vassall, Macmillan was relieved by Profumo's absolutely clear-cut denials – especially because they were supported by his threat of libel suits, followed up immediately by actions against *Paris Match* and *Il Tempo*. Here he was bolstered by Dorothy, who, with her abundant common sense, remarked, 'he must be OK, he wouldn't perjure himself in Court. . . .'[72] In his memoirs, Macmillan wrote, 'This categorical statement in my eyes settled the matter. . . . Had I any doubts about Profumo's integrity, I could hardly believe he had both misled the House of Commons and perjured himself in the courts. . . .'

When Did Macmillan Know?

It was not quite the first time that murmurs about the Profumo scandal had been brought to his attention. According to the Macmillan memoirs, it was 4 February, when he had returned from his official visit to Italy and his audience with the Pope, that his Private Office first told him about Profumo and Keeler, and the possible security problem. In his absence, Tim Bligh, the Principal Private Secretary, had handled the information, passing it on to MI5.[73] He and the Chief Whip, Martin Redmayne, had confronted Profumo, who admitted that he had known Keeler in 1961, but 'denied all allegations of impropriety'. Profumo had also explained that, back in 1961, he had been warned to see as little as possible of Stephen Ward, 'because there was a security problem involved, and he had heeded that advice'. Macmillan said he had been 'satisfied with these assurances'.

In fact, it seems that Macmillan's Private Office had already received some forewarning about Ward earlier, towards the end of 1962, from another Private Secretary, Philip de Zulueta.[74] The de Zuluetas had been on the brink of renting a cottage on the Cliveden Estate from Lord Astor, next to Stephen Ward. Meeting Ward at Cliveden, de Zulueta found him 'most agreeable', but had then been warned by an English professor present of Ward's close friendship with Ivanov. Having once served in Moscow ('so I knew the form, otherwise I probably wouldn't have done it') and being a naturally prudent man, he decided to opt out of the cottage and warned Hugh Fraser (currently Secretary of State for Air) – who was then also about to rent a Cliveden cottage. (Years later, de Zulueta reflected what a 'huge scandal' there would have been had the Prime Minister's Private Secretary and his Air Minister also been involved in the Ward scenario.) De Zulueta recalls mentioning his decision to his colleague, Tim Bligh, and he also passed the professor's warning on to MI5. (But, as will be seen shortly, MI5 already had Ward and Ivanov in their sights.)[75] De Zulueta is quite clear that he said nothing about this to Macmillan before the storm broke in March, and then only *en passant*. In the June debate, Macmillan stated that he had not heard of Ward's name before his return from Rome in early February.[76] It seems improbable, however, that some gossip about Profumo would not have reached his ears earlier.

With the many other problems on his plate, of which at the time de Gaulle's very recent veto must have ranked high – plus all the Vassall mud in the air – Macmillan evidently did not attach the highest priority to the Profumo gossip in February. Before Profumo's appearance in the House on 22 March, he had gone through the text of his statement with Redmayne and the Attorney-General, Sir John Hobson, and reckoned that the Profumo 'statement was clear and pretty convincing . . .'.[77] In his diaries (but not repeated in the memoirs) he expatiated at some length on the background of the story, in a tone revealing just how out of touch – and out of sympathy – he was with the world inhabited by the Wards and Astors. Profumo had been:

> alleged to be mixed up in a rather squalid criminal case, about a black man who shot a 'model'. 'Model' is the word which is nowadays used to describe a rather better class prostitute, usually (like Harriette Wilson) under the protection of one patron, but sometimes willing to distribute her favours more widely. It has been widely rumoured for some time that Mr. Ward (an osteopath, suspected of being a pimp) had this girl in his string, and that Bill Astor was mixed up with the affair (having given this Mr. Ward a cottage at Cliveden). Worse still, Jack Profumo, Secretary of State for War, is said to have been an intimate friend of the girl and to have shared her with the Russian Military Attaché! The girl, who should have appeared in the trial of

the black man – another lover – for attempted murder, has disappeared. Bill Astor has also left the country. The old 'Cliveden' set was disastrous politically. The new 'Cliveden' set is said to be equally disastrous morally. All this gossip, grossly exaggerated no doubt if not altogether untrue, has been circulating in the lobbies and the Clubs for some weeks. . . .

Macmillan continued that Profumo by his statement:

had met Ward at Cliveden originally and had called at Ward's flat where the girl was living. He (and his wife) had been friends with both, but he had actually not seen the girl since the end of 1961. Profumo has behaved foolishly and indiscreetly, but not wickedly. His wife (Valerie Hobson) is very nice and sensible. Of course, all these people move in a raffish, theatrical, bohemian society, where no one really knows anyone and everyone is 'darling'. But Profumo does not seem to have realised that we have – in public life – to observe different standards from those prevalent today in many circles. . . .[78]

There was no further mention of Profumo in his diaries until May. In the interim, Harold Evans recorded him as remarking of Lord Carrington, in the context of Vassall, that he was 'an honourable man in whose word he had absolute confidence. He hoped that this would prove no less true of Profumo, and that there had been nothing of a scandalous nature in his relationship with Christine Keeler. . . .'[79] The tone of Evans's diary entry suggests that Macmillan may by then not have been entirely free of doubts about Profumo, for all his asseverations of two weeks previously. Meanwhile, the rumours and gossip continued, growing ever wilder.

Security Aspects

On 9 April, Macmillan received (via Harold Wilson) a memorandum by Wigg, 'based on rather rambling accounts of the social lives of Ward and his friends'. Still Macmillan reckoned that, 'whatever criticisms might be made of Profumo's wisdom in mixing with such people two years ago, there was no question of his being a security risk . . .'. Few would dispute this. 'So', wrote Macmillan in his account of the affair: 'the days passed on and, engrossed by far more important problems, I trusted that we would hear no more of this particular episode. . . .'

On 7 May (the day after the *Daily Mail* had announced an encouraging 2 per cent rise in Tory fortunes), Macmillan recorded in his diaries that ' "C" [Sir Dick White], Hollis and Trend came to see me. . . .' The immediate topic was how to handle the pending Moscow spy trial of Greville Wynne, who had acted as 'courier' to Colonel Penkovsky. No mention whatsoever seems to have been made of the security aspects of the Profumo case, but the day's entry ended: 'Long discussions with my secretaries and Chief Whip about another "scandal" which threatens to "break". I trust it may not, but it is well to be prepared.'[80] On 14 May, Macmillan told Wilson that the 'material' supplied by Wigg had been studied, but that no further action was deemed necessary.

On 24 May, Wilson wrote to Macmillan, enclosing a long communication from Ward, in which he alleged that Profumo had not told the truth in his statement to the Commons. Macmillan promised to look into it.

The previous day, Macmillan had had a further visit from Hollis, who had told him of Keeler's allegations about Ward asking her to find out atomic secrets from Profumo; that is the date when nuclear warheads were going to be deployed in West Germany.[81] Hollis shot down the 'so-called evidence' produced by Wilson that Ward was a Russian agent, and confirmed to Macmillan that 'The security people do not believe this, but believe that he was a pimp, not a spy. . . .' But, as of that date, Macmillan now reckoned that the Profumo case had become 'more serious' than Philby (although Hollis had just told him that Philby was now definitely known to be in Russia: 'When this news comes out (if it does) there will be a new row. . . .').[82] Such was his disquiet about the Profumo rumours that he now asked the Lord Chancellor, Lord Dilhorne (the former Sir Reginald Manningham-Buller) to look further into the matter, and told Wilson – 'who continued to press me' – that he was doing so. He then left for a planned ten-day holiday for Dorothy and himself in Scotland:

31 May: . . . I am handing over to Butler for a week (the first time I have done so since I became P.M., except for my longer visits abroad). I am to get only the minimum of telegrams and papers. It should be a real rest. . . .[83]

He told Harold Evans that he felt 'as excited as a child' at the thought of setting off for Scotland the next evening.[84] Meanwhile, the Profumos set off to Italy on holiday.

The question has been repeatedly asked why Hollis and MI5 had been so slow, and apparently so unemphatic, in warning the Prime Minister about Profumo and the Ivanov connection – and, indeed, Profumo himself.[85] One possible explanation is that Hollis, who never felt at ease with Macmillan, was still smarting from the 'shooting foxes' rebuff over Vassall, as well as all the other recent failures of the Security Service, and was not over-eager to stick out his neck yet again. Still more important was the fact that, once it had decided that Profumo constituted no security risk, MI5 had no responsibility whatsoever to save the government's political bacon, a point well made in the Denning Report. Whatever, Hollis seems culpable at least of serious incompetence in giving Macmillan so little information, and so late – especially the intelligence, brought to him only on 29 May, about the alleged spying-out of atomic secrets, even though Hollis had discarded this as spurious.

Profumo Resigns

While on holiday in Italy, Profumo received a telegram from the Chancellor, Lord Dilhorne, summoning him back to London earlier than planned. On 4 June he returned, having told his wife while in Italy that he had had an affair with Keeler, and having determined to confess, at last, that he had lied to the Commons. Macmillan and his wife Dorothy were in Oban when his 'few days of repose were quickly and rudely ended' by a telephone call from his Private Office, reporting Profumo's decision to 'come clean' and admit his having slept with Keeler. Writing in his diary a month later (because of the pressure of events)[86] Macmillan declared, '. . . I do not remember ever having been under such a sense of personal strain. Even Suez was "clean" – about war and politics. This was all "dirt". . . .'[87] But, since Parliament was not sitting, he did not think it necessary to break off his holiday immediately, and went on to Iona and Gleneagles as planned. He also did not seem quite to realise then just how great the crisis was that was building up over him. According to Rab, standing in as his faithful deputy, he 'rang from Scotland to ask whether we could not fight back . . .',[88] and Rab was taken aback to hear Macmillan say he could 'hardly believe this was a major issue . . .'.[89] On his return (on 10 June), he struck Rab as being 'in a somewhat euphoric state, and said that everything looked so different in the north that he can hardly believe the trouble into which he was coming. It was only the following week that he realised the extent of the tragedy that had occurred. . . .'[90] While he was in Scotland, Macmillan also received a letter from Chief Whip Redmayne, offering his resignation. According to Redmayne, Macmillan replied 'characteristically, "If you resign, I shall resign,"' and went on to say, as he said later in public, that '"we had nothing with which to reproach ourselves, except perhaps too great a loyalty. That is not, in my view, serious accusation against any man." Of course,' commented Redmayne subsequently, 'both sentences were a gross over-simplification of an appalling situation, but they were true Macmillan. . . .'[91]

When Macmillan returned to London on the 10th, he found that 'Lucky' Gordon was on trial at the Old Bailey for wounding Keeler; Ward had been arrested and charged with a variety of offences under the Sexual Offences Act of 1956, including brothel-keeping, procuring a living on the earnings of prostitutes, and so on; and the *News of the World* had begun serialisation of Christine Keeler's life story. Prurience and gossip were having a heyday, which was making Britain a centre for world news in a way that she had not been since Suez. 'Every part of the Profumo story', recorded Macmillan,

> was used against the Government by an exultant Press, getting its own back for Vassall. The 'popular' Press has been one mass of the life stories of spies and prostitutes, written no doubt in the office. Day after day the attacks developed, chiefly on me – old, incompetent, worn out. . . .[92]

The press was indeed 'getting its own back' for the recent imprisonment of the two journalists, as well as settling the scores of more long-standing and deep-rooted animosities against Macmillan. To Macmillan, *The Times* particularly was 'awful . . . really nauseating . . .'.[93] Haley, knowing his moment had come, led the assault with his most memorable and damning editorial, entitled 'It *is* a moral issue', which declared sententiously:

> Eleven years of Conservative rule have brought the nation psychologically and spiritually to a low ebb. . . . The Prime Minister and his colleagues can cling together and be still there a year hence. They will have to do more than that to justify themselves. . . .[94]

When the House reconvened on the afternoon of Monday, 17 June, the parliamentary day began with the Joint Parliamentary Secretary to the Ministry of Pensions and National Insurance, a bright young woman called Margaret Thatcher, fielding some dreary questions about unemployment benefits. Harold Wilson led the attack by declaring portentously: 'This is a debate without precedent in the annals of this House,' arising from 'disclosures which have shocked the moral conscience of the nation . . .'. 'We are not here as a court of morals,' he went on, carefully concentrating his assault on the security risk, and Macmillan's neglect of it.[95]

For Macmillan there followed 'the most difficult and wearisome task';[96] it was probably the greatest test of his parliamentary career, and he faced it with disarming frankness. (As he once quoted his favourite, Trollope, 'The fact is if you "own up" in a genial sort of way the House will forgive anything.')[97] There were none of the 'actor–manager' embellishments his critics ascribed to Macmillan when he began, on a note of high personal emotion, and unsparing of Profumo:

> On me, as Head of the Administration, what has happened has inflicted a deep, bitter and lasting wound. I do not remember in the whole of my life, or even in the political history of the past, a case of a Minister of the Crown who has told a deliberate lie to his wife, to his legal advisers and to his ministerial colleagues, not once but over and over again, who has then repeated this lie to the House of Commons. . . .
>
> . . . I find it difficult to tell the House what a blow it has been to me, for it seems to have undermined one of the very foundations upon which political life must be conducted.

He continued with a detailed account of Profumo's acquaintance-ship with Ward, and Ward's connection with Ivanov. He denied as 'completely untrue' allegations that he had known of Profumo's association with Ward as long ago as August 1961, and 'did nothing about it'. With conspicuous openness, he answered the question why he had not tackled Profumo himself:

> . . . I think that that is an extremely fair question and I will tell the House why. I did not do so for two reasons. First, I thought he would have spoken more freely to the Chief Whip and the Law Officers than to me, his political chief. Secondly, for me personally to carry out an examination of this kind, in the probing detail necessary, would have made it difficult, if not impossible, for him to feel in future, however innocent he might have been, that he enjoyed my confidence. . . .

He went on to stress to the House the consequences that the innocent Galbraith had suffered during the Vassall case: 'I have been re-proached for accepting the resignation of my hon. Friend, when I did, when rather similar rumours were circulating. . . .'

When it came to the revealing *lettre de congé* written by Profumo to Keeler, and beginning 'Darling', he drew a first laugh from the House by remarking that Profumo had explained 'that in circles in which he and his wife moved it was a term of no great significance'. He then went on to make an observation that was widely and long held against him, as evidence of his being out of touch with the facts of life: '. . . I do not live among young people much myself. . . .' Coming down to the specific reports that the Security Service had received, about Keeler being asked by Ward to give information from Profumo on the nuclear secrets, he was contrite:

> The Security Service did not pass either of these reports to me. [Hon. Members: 'Oh!'] I am only giving the facts. . . . as things have turned out, I think it very unfortunate that this information was not given to me, but the head of the Security Service, in considering these reports, did not take that as of great importance. . . .

This was an unmistakable backhander to Hollis. Although, Macmillan went on, investigations established that there had been no breach of security, 'Yet I must repeat that I strongly regret that this information, which came originally from the police, was not, through the files of the Security Service, passed on to me. . . .' He ended his statement by throwing himself upon the compassion of the House:

> . . . I said at the beginning that it was my duty to act honourably, to act justly, and to act prudently. My colleagues have been deceived, and I have been deceived, grossly deceived – and the House has been deceived – but we have not been parties to deception and I claim that upon a fair view of the facts as I have set them out I am entitled to the sympathetic understanding and confidence of the House and of the country.[98]

Macmillan's frankness had taken much of the wind out of the Opposition's sails, and their attack was hampered by Harold Wilson's somewhat shoddily hypocritical pretence at concentrating on the security risk, which had been proved to be not very great. (Wilson would have been more effective had he pressed his charge that the Minister of War had laid himself open to blackmail.) The most savage attack came from Macmillan's own side, through the person of Nigel Birch, who had harboured a deep bitterness against Macmillan ever since his resignation over the 'little local difficulties' in 1958. Pouring scorn on Macmillan's trust for Profumo, he declared:

> We cannot just have business as usual. I myself feel that the time will come very soon when my Right Hon. Friend ought to make way for a much younger colleague. I feel that ought to happen. I certainly will not quote at him the savage words of Cromwell, but perhaps some of the words of Browning might be appropriate in his poem on 'The Lost Leader', in which he wrote:
>
> > '. . . let him never come back to us!
> > There would be doubt, hesitation and pain,
> > Forced praise on our part – the glimmer of twilight,
> > Never glad confident morning again!'
>
> 'Never glad confident morning again!' – so I hope that the change will not be too long delayed . . .[99]

But the Whips had been out in force, warning Tory MPs that there was a serious threat of Macmillan resigning, if his majority at the ensuing division was much reduced, which in turn might well lead to a premature general election. No Tory backbencher would welcome this. Jobs were at risk. The threat significantly reduced the scale of the revolt against Macmillan's leadership; nevertheless, when the House divided, there were twenty-seven abstentions, from the left as well as the right of the Party, including Nigel Birch, Lord Lambton, Humphry Berkeley[100] and Harry Legge-Bourke. ('Not only the usual malcontents,' admitted Macmillan, '. . . but a lot of worthy people who had been swept away by the wave of emotion and indignation. . . .')[101] The result was a much reduced majority of 57; Redmayne had warned him that it might have shrunk to as low as 40 – at which point he would have considered resignation.[102] It was, given the circumstances, more than a close shave, and certainly the worst result Macmillan ever obtained in the Commons.

Ambassador David Bruce sent a telegram the following day to President Kennedy, commenting:

> . . . Macmillan's admission that he did not know what was going on at critical times was in circumstances pitiable and extremely damaging. He did not try to shirk responsibility, but on his own account did not give impression that he knew how to exercise it in unfolding developments of case on which nearly everyone in Parliament appeared to be better informed than the Prime Minister. . . .

Bruce thought that the final vote would not end 'the Profumo affair' and concluded that the Macmillan government was mortally wounded: 'in Embassy opinion, no move to replace Macmillan will be made before President's visit [at the end of June]. On present indications, however, his replacement cannot be too long delayed, for . . . Prime Minister has become . . . an electoral liability.'[103]

That so astute an observer of the British scene as David Bruce should believe that the Macmillan government was on its last legs is one reminder of just how bleak the situation looked for Macmillan at the time.

The Impact on Macmillan

Macmillan was described as leaving the House 'looking bowed and dispirited'.[104] The Chief Whip, Martin Redmayne, thought he had spoken well, 'though obviously under great strain',[105] but critics like Christopher Booker regarded it (and notably his admission about not living 'among young people') as 'the most broken performance of his career'.[106] His former Parliamentary Private Secretary, Anthony Barber, who saw him after the debate, remembered it as the time when he had seemed 'most crestfallen'.[107] To Rab Butler, Macmillan admitted shortly afterwards that 'his heart was broken, but his spirit was still strong';[108] while his successor, Alec Home, recalled the Profumo debate as being 'the only time I remember him being worsted – he so fundamentally hated the whole thing.'[109]

It was the low ebb of the Macmillan administration. Only 23 per cent of voters polled by Gallup thought Macmillan should stay on as Prime Minister. The Gallup Poll showed Macmillan reaching the nadir of his personal popularity, compared with the Leader of the Opposition (35 per cent to 54 per cent) in his time as Prime Minister, and the lowest since Neville Chamberlain. MPs noted, too, that when Macmillan left the Chamber and went to the Smoking Room after the Profumo debate, only two people joined him there – his son-in-law, Julian Amery, and his son, Maurice. Not one of his Cabinet colleagues went to speak to him.[110] Knox Cunningham, the successor to Anthony Barber as Macmillan's Parliamentary Private Secretary, warned him that there was 'disloyalty to him at a very high level'.[111] Rab Butler was shocked to hear Major John Morrison, Chairman of the 1922 Committee, talking about a new government, and says that he was 'surprised at the Conservative Private Members' rush to get rid of a trusted leader in a moral crisis, and one who had proved himself a great Prime Minister . . .'. Visiting Macmillan that same evening, he found him 'more worried about the continued revelation of moral disturbance than he was about his own future'. Clearly contemplating resignation, he told Rab that he did not wish to do so 'on the basis of this one sordid case but would wish to do it in an orderly manner . . .'.[112] In what Macmillan designated the 'second week of the crisis', from the 17th onwards, gossip and speculation burst through all the river banks, and there was no telling where the grubby waters would not reach. 'A kind of Titus Oates atmosphere prevailed,' recorded Macmillan, with the wildest rumour and innuendo against the most respectable Ministers. Altogether, partly by the blackmailing statements of the 'call girls'; partly by the stories started by or given by the Press; and partly (I have no doubt) by Soviet agents exploiting the position, more than half the Cabinet were being accused of perversion, homosexuality and the like. . . .[113]

Years later he recalled how he had 'chaffed' his colleagues that he was 'the only man who's absolutely all right because every hour of my day is written down by the detective who never leaves me, even when I go to play golf or shoot, he's there, so . . . there's nothing I can do, I haven't got the opportunity. Alas!'[114] But it hardly seemed a subject for much mirth in June 1963. At a fête in Bromley, where he was seen to move among the coconut shies and lucky-dips like a sleep-walker, when he posed for a photograph with the small daughter of a constituent, a heckler hissed obscenely in his ear: 'Take your hand off that little girl. Don't you wish it was Christine Keeler?' Rumours were rife about Macmillan's own imminent departure. What also caused him passing concern, however, was that the tide of gossip might even lap around the Royal Family; the Duke of Edinburgh had once been treated by Stephen Ward and had sat for a portrait by him. That was all; but, so Macmillan feared, it would have been enough for the scandal-merchants in the foetid atmosphere of 1963.

On 21 June Macmillan announced the appointment of Lord Denning to undertake a 'Judicial Enquiry into the security aspects' of Profumo, which he hoped would check 'the flood of accusation and rumour'. Two days later he addressed an almost painfully apologetic letter to the Queen, suggestive of a truly stricken man. Expressing his 'deep regret at the development of recent affairs', he felt he 'ought to apologise for the undoubted injury done by the terrible behaviour of one of Your Majesty's Secretaries of State upon not only the Government but, perhaps more serious, one of the great Armed Forces. . . .' He admitted that, with hindsight, 'following the unjust attacks on Lord Carrington and Mr. Galbraith', he had perhaps given too much weight to not being unjust to Profumo, and repeated the apologia of his statement to the House: to whit, '. . . I had of course no idea of the strange underworld in which other people, alas, besides Mr. Profumo have allowed themselves to become entrapped. . . .' He said that he had begun 'to suspect in all these wild accusations against many people, Ministers and others, something in the nature of a plot to destroy the established system. . . .'[115]

Back came a charmingly consoling letter from the Queen, sympathising with her Prime Minister over the horrible time he had been experiencing, and supporting his view of the need to act justly; she recognised how difficult it was for people with high standards to suspect colleagues of unworthy conduct.

The Macmillan Government had indeed come closer to falling than most people realised. One senior minister, Duncan Sandys, who felt himself about to be tainted by allegations arising from the divorce case between the Duke and Duchess of Argyll, actually came to a Cabinet meeting with resignation letter in hand, and was only prevented from delivering it by Christopher Soames, his former brother-in-law. Had he resigned, that would almost certainly have proved the last straw for the tottering Macmillan administration.[116] But, during the third week of the crisis, beginning 24 June, Macmillan began to detect a 'massive reaction', and an upswing in his popularity, as that British sense of sympathy for an underdog asserted itself. Messages flowed in 'on a scale never equalled (I am told) in the history of No. 10'.[117] At one time they totalled five thousand a week, ten times the normal weekly tally, and almost all of them friendly.

Among the letters he kept, one particularly moved him. It came from the mother of a Grenadier corporal. In battle in the First World War, the nervous eighteen-year-old had asked Lieutenant Macmillan if he could 'have a memento' of him. Macmillan had given the boy his silk handkerchief. He was killed later in the war, and, in 1963, his mother sent it back to Macmillan, with a note: 'I hear you are in trouble, I'd like to send you the most precious thing I have. . . . Yours respectfully.'[118]

'Wonderful' was the adjective he used to describe the support he had received within the family. Of Dorothy, Macmillan wrote in his memoirs that without her 'constant daily affection and support . . . I might have succumbed to melancholy brooding in the midst of all these troubles'. From Maurice, Macmillan received several long letters conspicuous for their affection and concern, informing him of what was afoot in the backbenches. One is left with the feeling that, had the relationship between father and son only been closer, Macmillan might have been forewarned earlier about Profumo. The obscene unfairness of some of the press attacks also seemed to reunite the Party in the country at large in the Prime Minister's defence: 'To attack Dorothy and me as loose and degenerate (as *The Times* does) infuriates them. . . .'[119]

The wave of moral recrimination reminded Macmillan of Macauley's famous invective from the Victorian era (which he quoted in his memoirs):

> We know of no spectacle so ridiculous as the British public in one of its periodical fits of morality. In general, elopements, divorces, and family quarrels, pass with little notice. We read the scandal, talk about it for a day, and forget it. But we cannot suffer the laws of religion and decency to be violated. We must make a stand against vice. . . . At length our anger is satiated. Our victim is ruined and heart-broken. And our virtue goes quietly to sleep for seven years more. . . .[120]

With the wretched Profumo now disgraced and stripped of all public dignities, and with sympathy for Macmillan multiplying, wrath now descended on the head of Dr Stephen Ward.[121] On 22 July he appeared for trial at the Old Bailey; he was absolved from any security offences, but found guilty of living on the immoral earnings of Christine Keeler and Mandy Rice-Davies. On 3 August, abandoned by his friends, he died of an overdose of Nembutal, leaving a valedictory note: '. . . I am sorry to disappoint the vultures. . . .'[122] Macmillan made no comment in his diaries about either the sentencing of Ward or his suicide.

Catching up at last on his diary on 7 July, Macmillan noted that the 'fourth crisis week' had 'Proved rather good' – though, with characteristic understatement, 'of course, I cannot and have not given any picture of the agonising weeks which I have been through . . .'.[123] That night he and Dorothy made a rare appearance at the ballet, for the first night of the Bolshoi ('Swan Lake – very good, and pleasantly old-fashioned'). He was still mulling over resignation, and finding it difficult to make up his mind: 'Of course, if things go badly with the Denning report, there will be no choice. I shall have been destroyed by the vices of some of my colleagues, which were (naturally) unknown to me. . . .'[124] The June visit of President Kennedy to Birch Grove ('a great success') had given his popularity a renewed fillip; but still, on 12 July, Macmillan noted that the Gallup Poll was bad again, with the Conservatives trailing

17 per cent behind Labour. He sensed a deep restlessness within the Party: 'Only 3 more weeks to the end of the Session. If we can get through these without disaster, we can breathe. . . .'[125] But, he was far from being out of the wood on other security worries, not just Profumo. Early in July, Philby surfaced in Moscow:

> *11 July:* . . . A very long Cabinet 10.30–1.30. . . . The 'Philby' Case has been very difficult, chiefly because of the problem of answering the questions asked by the Press and Public without injuring and even hamstringing the work of the Secret Service. . . .[126]

Nor was Philby the only headache; there was the rumbling worry about 'Peters', then still 'unresolved'.[127] He referred to it discreetly in his diaries:

> *23 July:* . . . The Denning Report continues. . . . The other 'security' enquiries are proceeding. I am beginning to wonder whether all this game of espionage and counter-espionage is worth the candle. . . .
> *27 July:* . . . it does look as if the Service is 'Penetrated' at a high level. . . .
> *12 August:* . . . I worry all the time and cannot get these two dangers out of my mind. . . .[128]

By the end of the parliamentary session, the reaction had truly set in with the August Gallup Poll showing 'a tremendous swing back to us'.[129] The 'Great Train Robbery' was providing the press with some new distractions.[130] Labour was now only 6 per cent instead of 18–20 per cent ahead, and Macmillan learned that he too had risen:

> equally or more in public favour. How strange it all is. If only we can avoid more ministerial scandal. But, alas! I fear that Lord Denning's report (or rumours we hear) will condemn one important and one unimportant minister. . . . This will be another great shock and may make my position impossible. . . .[131]

On 16 August he spent half an hour giving his own evidence to

Lord Denning; from what he could glean from the energetic judge he continued to fear there was going to be 'trouble about *two* ministers, but how formidable this will be, I don't know . . . '.[132]

August passed, with Macmillan reading Ashley's 1879 *Life of Palmerston* and taking off to the Yorkshire moors of his friend Lord Swinton. But somehow the unflappable grouse-moor image did not come off in the summer of 1963. The irrepressible Cummings lampooned him savagely in a cartoon in the *Daily Express*, of 19 August 1963, as a broken-down figure with his back full of arrows inscribed 'from the 1922 Committee', 'from *The Times*', etc., holding his gun pointed at himself, to the relief of two happy grouse: 'We're in luck! He can't get used to the idea that for once he's not the target!'[133]

Denning Reports

At last, on 17 September, Macmillan received the Denning Report. With relief he noted at once that the allegations specifically against 'the two ministers'[134] had been dismissed as unfounded rumour, and that – in general – Denning had educed 'nothing sensational'.[135] Owing something to the style of a 'penny-dreadful', with sub-headings like 'The Borrowed Car', 'The Cup of Tea', 'The Man in the Mask', 'The Man without a Head', the report started by damning Ward as 'utterly immoral', given to 'sexual orgies of a revolting nature' and a Communist sympathiser, a dabbler in intelligence, but nothing more. It referred (and this particularly caught Macmillan's attention) to the possibility 'of winning over Captain Ivanov (of the Russian Embassy) to be a defector and the possible use of Mr. Profumo for this purpose . . .'.[136] Denning doubted that Keeler had ever been Ivanov's mistress, and rejected the notion of both Ivanov and Profumo 'sharing her services'. He gave MI5 a very clean bill of health; they had not known that Keeler was having an affair with Profumo, and it was not their business anyway; they had acted properly in reckoning that it was 'essentially a political matter which was now in the hands of the politicians and not the concern of the security service . . .'.[137] The police were mildly criticised for not having taken a full statement from Keeler at the beginning of February, which 'might have led to further enquiries and brought everything to a head earlier . . .'.[138]

But Denning, with his highly developed personal belief in private liberties, thought it right that – whether under the police or MI5 – there should be 'no machinery for reporting on the moral misbehaviour of ministers'.[139] He condemned unscrupulous papers for irresponsibly purchasing at high prices, and purveying, the 'marketable commodity' of scandal, and he concluded: 'There has been no lowering of standards. But there is this difference today. Public men are more vulnerable than they were; and it behoves them, even more than ever, to give no cause for scandal. . . .'[140]

Macmillan's relief at Denning's findings were, however, diminished by the one paragraph, 286, 'which puts the blame on us for having been deceived by Profumo. But that's an old story. . . .'[141] In Lord Denning's words,

> the fact remains that the conduct of Mr. Profumo was such as to create, amongst an influential section of the people, a *reasonable belief* that he had committed adultery with *such* a woman in *such* circumstances as the case discloses. It was the responsibility of the Prime Minister and his colleagues, and of them only, to deal with this situation: and they did not succeed in doing so. . . .[142]

On the 19th Harold Wilson (who, according to Macmillan, had been 'launching a great personal attack on me – for "debauching and corrupting public life . . ."')[143] came into Admiralty House having read the report, 'and commented rather sadly to Bligh that there wasn't much in it. I suppose', added Macmillan sardonically, 'he meant "not much for me". . . .'[144] The Macmillan Cabinet decided to 'publish and be damned', in full, and despite misgivings expressed by Wilson. At 7s 6d (39 pence) a copy, it was an immediate and record-breaking bestseller, with the lubricious-minded queuing up outside the Stationery Office on 26 September. They were deceived. Macmillan noted that the press was 'so disappointed by the lack of scandals in Denning, that they all turn on me. It was to be expected. . . . I hope the "Party" will stand firm – though I doubt it,' Macmillan noted critically. 'They haven't much courage. We shall see. . . .'[145] But the swing-around was swift. On the 27th, 'All day long came messages of congratulation. I feel somehow that the tide is turning and that the people as a whole will support me. The American Press headlines (curiously enough) are "Macmillan vindicated"...."[146] Yet he then had no more than three weeks' time left in office to look forward to.

Post-Mortems

This was, in effect, the end of the Profumo affair – though the post-mortems lingered on. The Macmillan government survived – but, without it, would Harold Wilson have won the following year, by four seats? Of the unhappy, talented man whose lapse gave rise to the whole affair, as Denning wrote: 'the House of Commons held him to have been guilty of contempt of the House.[147] His name was removed from the Privy Council. His disgrace is complete....'[148] Had it not been for the preceding spy scandals and the enforced resignation of Galbraith, Profumo might never have felt constrained to lie, or the press drawn into escalating the scandal, which might so easily not have happened. Profumo himself disappeared from the public arena, spent the rest of his life admirably dedicated to valuable good works, most loyally supported by his wife. At regular intervals, some journalist writing 'in the public interest' would rake up the old story to plague the ruined man and cause him renewed suffering. His haunted, unsmiling face was a living epitaph to the 'Swinging Sixties', and a constant reminder of the penalty of his major sin: lying to the House of Commons – an aberration not unknown there, but in this instance compounded with the other deadly sin, that of being found out. More even than Stephen Ward, who chose not to live with the consequences of his offence, Profumo became a scapegoat for the British 'fit of morality' in 1963.

Both in his memoirs and on television Macmillan paid tribute to the 'dreadful forfeit' paid by Profumo, and the selfless and 'courageous' manner in which he had set about 'regaining not only his own respect but that of his fellow men'.[149] But in his heart Macmillan remained bitter, finding it hard to forgive Profumo for the lasting damage his action had wrought on the government. *If only* Profumo had come clean to the Law Officers and the Chief Whip, he could have honourably resigned (like Galbraith) and then – once it had been shown that no security risk was involved, and he had been forgiven by the Commons for his peccadillo – been returned to a ministry in due course; at least this was always Macmillan's opinion in retrospect. With so many *real* and deadly serious security problems at hand, Macmillan saw Profumo as representing the 'Suetonius, or Tacitus' side of events – a frivolity not strictly relevant to the main course of history, or necessary. As he remarked repeatedly to Harold Evans, he regarded the Profumo affair as being utilised by the press as part of a systematic 'plot to destroy the system'[150] – much as the Stavisky scandal in the 1930s had ruined the Third Republic, which in turn had helped lay France low.

There remains only Macmillan's own responsibility in the story.

The Denning Report exonerated Hollis and MI5, insofar as the morality of ministers was no business of theirs – given that there was no security risk involved. But, if Hollis had been encouraged to have a closer relationship with Macmillan, he could well have tipped him off (or at least Butler, to whom he was directly responsible), in a friendly and unofficial way, before Profumo became inextricably committed to his lie. And how well served was Macmillan by his own immediate advisers? Should not Norman Brook have informed him that he had warned Profumo about Ward back in 1961? A number of Tory MPs were strongly critical of Martin Redmayne, the Chief Whip, as it was his job to have known the facts of Profumo's private life, and kept the Prime Minister apprised. Should he have advised Macmillan to confront Profumo himself? Redmayne was much criticised for giving the contrary advice; Macmillan, though, 'found it distasteful',[151] claimed Redmayne, 'yet he asked me more than once whether he should not see Profumo himself. Personally, I saw no point in it. . . . If we could not shake the story, the Prime Minister certainly would not. It was not in his character to do so. . . .'[152] He added, Profumo 'had been seen by all of us, and said exactly the same thing; if Harold had seen him, he would have said exactly the same again, and then the Prime Minister would have been involved in the mess, and we wanted to keep him above it.'[153]

Peter Rawlinson, the Solicitor-General at the time, supported Redmayne, but twenty-four years later said, 'I still can't understand why Profumo lied,'[154] and wondered whether it would have made it easier for Profumo to tell the truth had he been questioned personally by the Prime Minister. On one of the very rare occasions when he broke his dignified silence lasting so many years, Profumo himself made plain his conviction that he would have been unable to tell a lie to Macmillan. He had indeed hoped that he would have been sent for, but only learned later that Macmillan had been advised not to see him, on any account.[155]

As far as Macmillan's own motivation was concerned, he once explained to his son-in-law, Julian Amery, that he had avoided seeing Profumo so as not to be in danger of repeating the error of judgement he felt he had made during the Vassall case after seeing 'Tam' Galbraith himself.[156] Speaking many years after the event, however, Macmillan said that he thought it would have been 'a lot easier' for Profumo to speak to his contemporaries, rather than to a man of nearly seventy; 'I dislike all this kind of thing. But secondly, I thought, well, he might be shy. . . .'[157] Perhaps this was a misjudgement on the part of both Redmayne and Macmillan; with his highly sensitive antennae, Macmillan was never an easy man to conceal things from, let alone lie to. Some MPs felt that Redmayne's predecessor, Ted Heath, would have served his Prime Minister better than Redmayne; he would not have missed the innuendoes in the Commons Smoking Room, and would not have been afraid to push Macmillan into a confrontation with Profumo. Equally, not for the first time, Macmillan may have been at a disadvantage in the replacement as his Parliamentary Private Secretary (the Prime Minister's 'eyes and ears' in Parliament) of Anthony Barber by Knox Cunningham, the six-foot-six ex-boxer and rugger player, who (in the words of Michael Fraser) 'had a bad habit of getting things wrong';[158] Barber, in contrast, would have been 'like a terrier, going down into every hole'. Maurice Macmillan tried hard to warn his father of the facts about Profumo, but this would not have been easy for any member of the family, and especially so in their sadly remote relationship.

The one person who might well have known, having his ear to the ground in London clubland and society, and who possibly might have been able to say to Macmillan, 'Profumo *did* commit adultery with Christine Keeler, and he's lying,' was John Wyndham – so close to the Prime Minister as to have become almost a surrogate son.[159] There is no evidence to suggest that he did; or, if he did, it was in such muted terms as not to be heard by Macmillan. Why? The key words in Martin Redmayne's statements were that Macmillan 'found it distasteful' – and it was the adjective Macmillan himself used. This would have been something of an understatement – or, as Lord Home saw it, 'he so fundamentally hated the whole thing.'[160]

It has recently been suggested that the American Ambassador, David Bruce, might have tipped off Macmillan from American information, but the evidence is circumstantial and flimsy.[161] There is no record that Macmillan had an audience with Bruce before 4 March, about which Macmillan had nothing else to note in his diary apart from Washington gossip. Had Bruce told Macmillan anything about Profumo, judging from the content of his later diary entries on Profumo, it seems almost certain that he would have made some reference to it. Equally, it would have been against the character of David Bruce to have initiated the subject with Macmillan, even assuming that he possessed special knowledge. Like Macmillan, Bruce revelled in political gossip, but was not interested in sex scandals. If he had heard anything of this nature that he thought the Prime Minister should know, he would almost certainly have had it channelled through Macmillan's Private Office, via Philip de Zulueta, or particularly John Wyndham. There is no evidence that he did; while his widow, Evangeline Bruce, is categoric that Bruce had 'no previous knowledge, before what we read in the papers'; and further, 'even if he had, the last thing he would have done would have been to talk about it to Harold Macmillan; he knew that sex was a "forbidden subject". . . .'[162]

Yet, as we have seen, it does seem probable that, from time to time before the storm burst, and during it, more fragmentary warnings about Profumo reached Macmillan's ears than he would ever admit, but something deeply rooted in his character inhibited him from hearing them. The pain and distaste he felt for the whole story, his deep hatred of incursions by the outside world into private life, was implicit in almost every line of his statements during the 17 June Commons debate. Though in different words, opponents like Wilson, Shinwell and Wigg, close colleagues like Anthony Head, Butler, Home and Carrington, Freddie Bishop and Philip de Zulueta, members of his family and his own doctor of many years, John Richardson, all agreed on one thing: that it was all deeply repugnant to what was essentially puritanical in him, and personally painful to him. In years to come, he could bring himself to speak almost flippantly about the Profumo affair: 'everybody's darling, anyway',[163] and 'what are call-girls for, except to be called?', or 'Profumo should simply have said, "Of course, I took a well-known courtesan to bed, and I cannot tell you how agreeable she was . . .".

That would have been all right. . . .'[164] But it was certainly *not* how he felt at the time.

There were, of course, other personal motivations for his 'deafness', for his reaching so eagerly for Profumo's categoric denial in March – despite any doubts he harboured. His conscience was still painfully plagued at having very recently been unfair to a colleague in accepting, too readily, Galbraith's resignation over Vassall. (Profumo's own denial struck a chord here, when he protested to the Solicitor-General, Peter Rawlinson, that 'it would be grossly unfair that he should be driven from public life and into ruin when he was totally innocent.')[165] This did influence his actions over Profumo, reckoned Lord Carrington: 'He was determined not to pillory a good man.'[166]

But there was something much more fundamental. Macmillan declared, as he repeatedly did, that Profumo belonged to a 'different world' to his, which he did not understand:

> In the old days you could be absolutely sure that you could go to a restaurant with your wife and not see a man that you knew having lunch with a tart. It was all kept separate but this does not seem to happen these days . . . and Profumo was incapable of keeping the two sides of his life separate. . . .[167]

The 'different world' was the world of adulterers, to which he did not belong, but to which Profumo – and Boothby – did. It was a world which comprised the half-heard, half-imagined sly innuendoes of the Commons Smoking Room and the St James's clubs. It was a world to which, for the past thirty-odd years and more, Macmillan had resolutely closed his mind as well as his ears; and it went grievously against his nature to have to open both now, over Profumo. It was here that he was perhaps overprotected by someone as close to him as John Wyndham, who, more than anyone, would have become aware of his deep vulnerability over the many years he had spent with him, from 1942 onwards. To underestimate the 'Boothby factor' in Macmillan's handling of Profumo would be as misguided as to fail to comprehend just how grievously it hit him. As so often, the one reference to his personal feelings in his memoirs comes right at the end of the chapter where he mentions (almost *en passant*) how he had nearly 'succumbed to melancholy brooding'. This must have been a gross understatement. For the whole Profumo case touched the most vulnerable layers, indeed the very centre of Macmillan, almost certainly reawakening memories that he had sought for so many years to repress.

Perhaps if it had happened at a time when Macmillan had possessed more ebullient vigour, in the confident years between 1959 and 1961, he might have weathered the Profumo storm more successfully. As it was, coming in the wake of so many other misfortunes and reverses, he never quite got over it. To colleagues, he suddenly seemed older, and more alone, and never regained his former deftness.[168] It may well also have exacerbated the illness that finally drove him from office only weeks later. 'It brought the premiership to an end in rather a sad way,' he said later: 'It was a wounding thing, oh, it was. . . .'[169] Consistently puzzling to him in later years was the irrationale which had led the British public into such a state of credulity, in 1963, whereby it would believe almost any accusation 'against leading men of unblemished integrity'. To turn the episode into 'an extravagant campaign', he declaimed, 'which by its very lack of proportion became ridiculous, was to destroy rather than sustain respect for all established government . . .'. Certainly, in its impact on a British government, the Profumo affair was unprecedented. As far as the role of private morals may affect persons and governments in the future, a last word that transcends dates and countries may have been spoken by Harold Macmillan on the BBC ten years later:

> . . . public life, it's quite different to private life. Nobody has any right to enquire into the private life of ordinary citizens and subjects, it's their affair. They're not imposing themselves on you. They live their life. But if you go into public life, become a Prime Minister, become a Foreign Secretary, become a member of a Cabinet, nobody asked you to; nobody asked you to stand for Parliament. Nobody asked you to carry the burdens that I describe here. You have to be very careful about complaining about them. There are plenty of people who will take them from you. But you do set yourself up to do something different to other people. And to take the very great responsibility, moral responsibility of coming into a position of leadership. And I think that does imply certain parallel duties. You can – you owe it, if you step into the front line, and if you can use a very reactionary, an old-fashioned sentence, which hasn't done much harm to our

country through many centuries, you should behave like an officer and a gentleman.[170]

As a final postscript to the story, a few years after Macmillan's retirement, a member of the family invited Christine Keeler down to Birch Grove, as a joke. Macmillan was of course absent, and it was with some difficulty that an outraged retainer prevented her from signing the visitors' book – alongside the names of Kennedy, de Gaulle, Winston Churchill and the Queen; though hers, too, had not been without influence in his career.[171]

Chapter Seventeen

A Last Triumph
June–September 1963

I can see the helicopter now, sailing down the valley above the heavily laden, lush foliage of oaks and beech at the end of June. He was gone. Alas, I was never to see my friend again. Before those leaves had turned and fallen he was snatched by an assassin's bullet from the service of his own country and the whole world.

(HM, At the End of the Day)

I had to go out of the room. I went to tell D. and burst into tears. I had prayed hard for this, night after night. . . .

(HM, Diaries, 27 July 1963)

·'Amid the many disappointments of this period,' wrote Macmillan in his memoirs, 'there was at least one cause for satisfaction.' Effectively obscured though they were at the time, there were glimpses of a silvery lining. Defence was one; arms control another. After his own frustrating experiences in the Ministry of Defence, Macmillan from the moment of his arrival at No. 10 had set about a fundamental reorganisation of the British defence set-up. The Ministry was a legacy from wartime days, when the omnipotent warlord, Churchill, had held all the strings in his hands. In peace-time, as Macmillan himself discovered, it possessed little power and an imprecise brief. Helped by two strong personalities (though they were often at odds with each other), Duncan Sandys as Minister of Defence, and Mountbatten as First Sea Lord and later Chief of the Defence Staff (CDS), Macmillan on coming to power had immediately applied himself to concentrating overall authority under one minister. Opposition had been fierce, with a result that Sandys and Macmillan had had to accept defeat and *reculer pour mieux sauter* on some of their more dramatic schemes for integrating the three services, and in 1959 Macmillan had settled for a minister with a lower profile and certainly less abrasive than Sandys in the shape of Harold Watkinson, a businessman who believed in letting the professionals run things.

It was not until the end of 1962, by which time the more Sandys-like and forceful personality of Peter Thorneycroft had been installed as Minister of Defence, that Macmillan felt able to return to the attack. In October 1962, Mountbatten had handed Thorney-croft what he called '*my* great paper' on defence reorganisation. Mountbatten had 'come to the firm conclusion' that nothing short of 'abolition of separate Service Departments and the creation of a single Ministry of Defence will get to the root of the problem'.[1] This was precisely what Macmillan had been after, for several years already. He had a somewhat ambivalent attitude towards the flamboyant colossus: 'Poor Dickie talks all the time and has (with all his charm) a very limited mental capacity. . . .'[2] But he realised that Mountbatten was the only serving officer with the power and prestige to push through the reforms he had in mind, and – observing 'Dickie's' self-inflation with amused detachment – Macmillan had nothing against Mountbatten, predictably, grasping all the credit for them.

Macmillan had his own very clear, and graphic, ideas of the armed forces; the RAF he saw as 'a small number of mounted knights, fighting single-handed, plus a large number of servants'.[3] There would never be any difficulty recruiting for it; ditto the Royal Navy. The problem was always the army, and here Macmillan – as an old Grenadier – fought vigorously for retention of the regimental system, as a morale factor similar to the shipboard loyalties of the navy. He feared that 'Dickie', in his dreams of fully integrated services, might be going too far here, and recoiled from any suggestion of an amorphous force all dressed in 'mud-grey uniforms', like the Canadians.[4]

Macmillan set forth his aims in a long letter to the Queen on 13 December:

> Of course when dealing with fighting men the most important factor of all is morale. The soldier is more interested in the Regiment than he is in the Army; and the sailor's loyalty is to his ship and not to the Board of Admiralty. The airmen, as the youngest in the three Services, is perhaps even more anxious than his fighting comrades to identify himself with his own show, the Squadron, or the Wing, or the group.
>
> Somehow we have got to meet the two needs. We must unify to be efficient and avoid waste. And we must diversify to keep alive the spirit of the men. . . .

His idea was to 'try to combine the good features of both the single Service concept and the existing three separate Services', while centralising responsibility for planning, operations and weapon development within the Ministry of Defence. On returning exhausted from the Nassau Conference, however, he had run into an anticipated barrage of criticism: 'We still have our Defence Reorganisation plans to launch. Then we shall have *no* friends anywhere!'[5] The service ministers, supported by the respective Chiefs of Staff, were 'putting up a strong reactionary fight'.[6] A large part of the trouble lay in the overweening nature of Mountbatten himself, which instinctively aroused antipathy. On several occasions,

Mountbatten reported decisions of the Chiefs of Staff to the Minister of Defence in terms quite contrary to what had actually been decided. As his own biographer, Philip Ziegler, comments, by 1963 (though he was six years younger than Macmillan) Mountbatten was already beginning to show one of the failings of old age: 'an inability to distinguish between what had happened and what he would have liked to have happened'.[7] To circumvent a dangerous repetition of the earlier stalemate, Macmillan decided once again to resort to his favoured device of an independent enquiry, selecting two old soldiers who would be welcomed as *sans peur et sans reproche*, Generals Lord ('Pug') Ismay and Sir Ian Jacob. By the end of February their findings, modifying some of Mountbatten's proposals but endorsing most, had been accepted by the service ministers and Chiefs of Staff.

At the beginning of April, however, Macmillan sensed that he and Mountbatten were running into new difficulties, and he despatched a forceful minute to Thorneycroft, couched in positively Churchillian language:

> The staff should be cut by at least 20% as a result of the exercise. . . . Pray take no notice at all of any obstruction. You should approach this the way Lloyd George used to approach problems with dashing, slashing methods. Anyone who raises any objection can go, including Ministers. The Service Ministers are not in a very strong position anyway, politically or in any other respect. I beg you to take an axe to all this forest of prejudice and interest.

Macmillan's forceful tactics worked in the teeth of stiff opposition. By the end of July 1963, the Macmillan–Mountbatten Defence White Paper had been published, debated and accepted. 'We had succeeded on all the major issues,' rejoiced Macmillan; 'we had defeated the attempts to weaken the powers of the new Secretary of State for Defence.'

Most of the less radical Ismay–Jacob proposals had been accepted; some of Mountbatten's wishes had not been met, but he was not displeased. There was to be a unified ministry to absorb the old service ministries, to be housed physically in one vast new complex (this was particularly welcome to Mountbatten), which would also house the separate Ministry of Aviation; there would be a single secretary of state (who would eventually emerge as one of the four most powerful Cabinet ministers) and a minister of state for each service, but of secondary rank; the central Permanent Under-Secretary would enjoy primacy; and, finally, there would be a strengthening (albeit in the early stages a marginal strengthening) of the role of CDS. The traditions and battle honours of individual units were to be retained, an issue particularly dear to Macmillan.

'P.M. gave First Lord, First Sea Lord, me and Minister of Defence drinks to celebrate our victory,' wrote Mountbatten in his diary for 30 July 1963,[8] and, as if to set a seal on the victory, the building of a new aircraft-carrier was agreed that same day. Although the Order in Council was not actually approved by the Queen until Macmillan was out of power the following March ('an emotional and historic moment for me', Mountbatten recorded),[9] a new framework for the British fighting forces had been created that would carry them towards the twenty-first century (and triumphantly to the Falklands and back in 1982). By 1970 the new MOD already employed less people than had the three service HQs that had preceded it, together with all the valuable economies that that signified. In his memoirs, Macmillan paid tribute to Thorneycroft's 'remarkable patience', and in years to come he always praised the key role that Mountbatten had played, reckoning that it could 'not have been done without him'.[10] As predicted, Mountbatten claimed the lion's share of the glory; 'The idea did not suddenly dawn on me,' he once claimed; 'it was the result of 20 years' experience in war and peace. . . .'[11] But, as his biographer, Philip Ziegler, recognises, Mountbatten 'could not have done it alone – the championship of the Prime Minister was indispensable. . . .'[12] Wherever the credit falls due, it was Macmillan's initial concept and his indefatigable persistence that finally pushed through the Defence reorganisation, which was to prove one of the most lasting achievements of his administration, praised by subsequent Labour and Tory leaders alike.

Towards a Nuclear Test Ban

To Macmillan the toughening and reorganisation of Britain's defence establishment always went hand in hand with efforts to achieve an international agreement on nuclear disarmament. Both were facets of the same problem which overshadowed all others, and to which Macmillan had attached the highest priority ever since coming to power. The goal of some form of arms control on nuclear weapons had been at the forefront of his thoughts when he went to Moscow in 1959, as it had in all his dealings first with Eisenhower and then with Kennedy. He had watched with gloom as the long-protracted Geneva disarmament talks ended in impasse; he had experienced something approaching despair when the combination of Eisenhower's U-2 débâcle and Khrushchev's intransigence had torpedoed the 1960 Paris summit; and at the end of the following year in Bermuda he had been bitterly disappointed when the new young President had been carried along by his military advisers to launch a new series of atomic tests in the wake of Khrushchev's megaton explosions. It was with unhappy irony that he had seen himself bulldozed into allowing a British territory, Christmas Island (where the first British H-Bomb was detonated), to be used for the new American tests in the atmosphere.

Macmillan's long-term philosophy was simple; something had to be done to curb both nuclear testing and the escalation of weapons, or the human race would be doomed. Despite all the setbacks and reverses, he had never lost faith and had continued to beaver away at both the Americans and the Russians. In Kennedy he had, from the beginning, sensed a kindred soul. Certainly the Cuban missiles crisis had made a most powerful impression on Kennedy. David Ormsby-Gore, who was so close to Kennedy all through that terrifying week, recalled the President as saying on several occasions during it 'that this world really is impossible to manage so long as we have nuclear weapons. . . . This is, I think, what made him deeply interested in disarmament. . . .'[13]

It was evident to Macmillan that Khrushchev had been equally shaken by the implications of Cuba; at the same time, the Russian military establishment pushing him on (in the same way as the Pentagon did Kennedy) could reckon to be reasonably satisfied by the technical advantages that the massive tests of 1961–2 had brought them. Macmillan therefore thought the time was ripe to have another go at both leaders: 'since Khrushchev may be the best type of Russian leader we are likely to get, there *is* some strong argument for trying now to negotiate either some limited agreements or over a wider field,' he had written in his diary shortly after the Cuban missiles crisis.[14] And, indeed, on the same day Macmillan had received a letter from Khrushchev where he proposed that *all* tests should be banned, including underground tests. He reckoned there was no need for inspection teams; modern science could devise ways to effect the necessary monitoring.

Here was the rub – the basic, mutual distrust between the Americans and the Russians. Resorting to the 'big hole' argument, Kennedy's technical advisers expressed fears that the Russians would cheat, carrying out tests underground which could be detected only by expert inspection teams on the spot. Evoking his unhappy memories of the U-2 incident, Khrushchev on the other hand claimed that the US would just use their 'inspection teams' for espionage purposes. Advised by Penney and Zuckerman, Macmillan reckoned all along that scientists would, and sooner rather than later, devise sure seismic detection means by which tremors caused by nuclear explosions could be differentiated from ordinary earthquakes. In the States the Macmillan view was supported by the influential Averell Harriman, who (on Macmillan's instigation) was to play a key role in the negotiations that followed, and developments were later to prove them both right. Macmillan's priority was first to get an agreement in principle with the Russians, then to worry about the small print. But he underrated Kennedy's political difficulties at home, much as Kennedy had failed to comprehend Macmillan's domestic problems over Skybolt.

Winning Over Kennedy

While the two leaders were in Nassau, debating the Skybolt crisis, a well-timed note for Kennedy had arrived from Khrushchev on 19 December. It started by declaring baldly that the time had come 'to put an end once and for all to nuclear tests . . .', and, in the words of Macmillan, it went on to propose one 'real concession'; it 'stated that the USSR would now be willing to consider two or three on-site verification inspections each year . . .'. The American team did not regard two or three as enough, but Kennedy himself 'agreed that this offer marked a substantial advance'. Hitherto the Pentagon had been holding out for up to twenty, while in talks with his Soviet opposite number, Kuznetsov, the American disarmament negotiator, Arthur H. Dean, had only mentioned a possible figure of between eight and ten.

Back in the States, Kennedy ran into darkening domestic weather. In contrast to Britain, there was no widespread public consensus for a Test Ban Treaty in the US, and the Joint Chiefs of Staff came out against it on almost any terms. In the meantime, however, prominent American nuclear scientists had arrived at the opinion that five inspections a year would give the US 'adequate security against clandestine nuclear testing', and by February no less than Robert McNamara, the Secretary of Defense, was ready to settle for six. But partisan opposition, whipped up by various lobbies, had become intense. Particularly acute was the situation in the Senate, where Kennedy faced a hostile majority and required a two-thirds vote to ratify any treaty. The reckoning 'on the Hill' was that Congress would reject anything less than a compromise of seven to eight.

It looked as though impasse threatened again; and there also remained the problem of getting China and France, the other nuclear powers, to join in on the ban.

On 8 March, news came through of a new, and total, stalemate at the Disarmament Conference in Geneva. Macmillan called an urgent 'working lunch' to discuss strategy, at which Sir William Penney was 'quite clear that it's not science but politics which holds back the President . . .'.[15] At a further meeting three days later, Macmillan decided to send off a major letter direct to Kennedy. It was despatched on 16 March. In it, he reminded Kennedy that since the Bermuda Conference in December 1961 the Russians had come to accept the principle of three annual inspections, while the West had moved down from twenty to seven: 'So, from the man-in-the-street's point of view, the two sides have come a great deal nearer. Indeed, to the layman, we would seem so near that it would be almost inconceivable that the gulf could not be bridged. . . .' Macmillan continued: '. . . I have a feeling that the Test Ban is the most important step that we can take towards unravelling this frightful tangle of fear and suspicions in East–West relations. . . .' He then raised with Kennedy the problem which he knew was a constant source of major concern to him – the prospects of Germany claiming control of nuclear weapons: 'It is quite true Germany is bound by all kinds of agreements and undertakings. But these could easily be represented by a bad German in the future as the modern counterpart of Versailles. . . .'

Macmillan thought that the only way of averting this danger

would be to achieve a test agreement accompanied by a 'non-dissemination agreement'. On the subject of the inspections, he pressed his view that, as scientific techniques improved, fewer annual inspections would be needed as time went on: 'So much for the chances of our catching them if they cheated. However I am bound to say that I think they would be at great risk if they did cheat after signing the Treaty. . . .' He put forward five possibilities for resuming the initiative, one of them being that the President, Khrushchev and himself might meet at a summit in Geneva. He thought there was 'something queer' about Khrushchev's move towards accepting the principle of inspection, and – following up on an idea from Ormsby-Gore – he suggested that perhaps it might make sense to send 'some emissary such as Averell [Harriman], or even your brother, Bobby', who could then clear up any misunderstandings and find out what Khrushchev's real intentions might be. He ended: '. . . I am sorry to inflict so long a letter on you, but I feel this very deep personal obligation upon me. . . .'

Macmillan stressed in his memoirs how he had based his appeal on Khrushchev's concession in accepting the principle of 'on-site' inspections. In the event, he noted, the whole concept proved abortive, 'partly due to American intransigence as to the number to be claimed'. Shackled by Congress, Kennedy's reply (on 28 March) was cautious, but 'not unhelpful', and he proposed that Macmillan and he should send a joint letter to Khrushchev, enclosing his idea of a draft. Through April, the drafts and amendments to drafts flowed back and forth across the Atlantic. In Washington, Kennedy revealed something of his despair to his entourage; he was, he said, 'haunted by the feeling that by 1970, unless we are successful, there may be ten nuclear powers instead of four, and by 1975, fifteen or twenty. . . . I regard that as the greatest possible danger. . . .'[16] In London, Macmillan confided to his diary his own special, and enduring, nightmare after reading Wheeler-Bennett's classic account of the antecedents to Hitler, *The Nemesis of Power*:[17]

A terrifying book and everyone in politics or Foreign Office ought to read it again every year. Will the Germans be democratic for long? . . . Will Germany, in spite of her engagements, demand nuclear power? My theory is that unless we can satisfy them by a *general* Test Ban Treaty . . . the Germans are bound to become a nuclear power sooner or later. . . .[18]

Here was the same anxiety that was plaguing Kennedy. But, despite the pessimism of their professional diplomats, Macmillan and Kennedy refused to be discountenanced.

As a sop to Kennedy and his 'Europeanists', on 1 April Macmillan decided to 'give our "support" to the President's "multi-manned" nuclear ships[19] (while secretly hoping the scheme would fall through!) . . .'.[20] Kennedy, however, remained opposed to what would have amounted virtually to a summit (a familiar chord in the Anglo-American concerto); memories of May 1960 'are very strong in this country', he wrote to Macmillan. What he did *not* reveal to his friend was the additional misgivings he voiced inside the White House; namely that the French and the West Germans would be 'aroused' by Macmillan's presence, the British elections would be tied in to it, and his own discussions with Khrushchev would be too formal. Yet, if absolutely necessary, he told Harriman, he would go to a summit.[21] But he seemed keen to follow up the idea, initiated by Macmillan and Ormsby-Gore, of 'special emissaries'. Having accepted some minor amendments to the joint draft, Macmillan realised he had to strike with utmost speed: 'to try to get it settled with President Kennedy and his White House Advisors before the State Department and Pentagon rats get at it . . .'.[22] Macmillan began to feel 'instinctively that at least some agreement was within our grasp'. On 15 April, he wrote to the Queen:

> . . . President Kennedy has certainly behaved very well over this, because reading between the lines of the many messages that have passed and telephone conversations which have taken place, he has clearly overridden both the Pentagon and the State Department on certain important points. Moreover, he seems to have sympathised with and shared our motives. . . .[23]

Meanwhile pressures at home, over Vassall, over Profumo, and his own waning popularity were building up. The long-prepared joint letter was delivered to Khrushchev on 24 April. By now some of the 'rats' in Washington seemed to have been won over, Macmillan noted with some acerbity:

> the State Department (after being sceptical, not to say hostile) have suddenly become enthusiastic about the joint approach to

Khrushchev. I suppose this means that the President's Press boys
are getting ready to represent it as entirely an American initiation,
with the young New Frontiersman in the van and the old British
P.M. being dragged reluctantly at his heels. It is really rather
amusing. . . .[24]

Winning Over Khrushchev

Khrushchev's reply came two weeks later. Couched in his old style,
it could hardly have been ruder. There was no need for inspections,
and no point in going over all the old arguments; the Russians had
learned the Anglo-American test-ban proposals by heart, just as
they used to learn the 'Pater Noster'. The continued demand for
inspection was no more than an attempt to introduce NATO spies
into Soviet territory. He had consented to two or three inspections
back in December, in order to help the President with his Senate;
yet, instead of accepting this offer in the spirit in which it was put
forward, the West had started to haggle. They talked about seven
or eight inspections, covering up to five hundred square kilometres
each. If there was no real hope for an agreement, Khrushchev
threatened, then the Soviet Union had no choice but to take
measures to strengthen its own security. 'I'm not hopeful,' Kennedy
told a press conference on receiving the Khrushchev letter; 'I'm not
hopeful.'[25]

When one considers what was probably at stake, Khrushchev
perhaps had a point in his irritation with the 'haggling'. Macmillan
also thought that the Western position had been 'complicated' by
the ill-conceived US proposal for the 'multi-manned NATO force'
of some twenty-five ships and two hundred Polaris missiles – which
would include the West Germans, thereby giving Russia's deadly,
ancestral enemy at least a little finger on the trigger. Nevertheless,
towards the end the letter contained a glimmer of hope when it
said, perfunctorily, that Khrushchev was prepared 'to receive your
highly placed representatives'. Washington and London brooded
over how to respond to this unpromising message, and a number
of hasty conferences took place at Chequers, for which David
Ormsby-Gore flew back from Washington.

Macmillan's Ambassador now leaped into the breach once again.

He had in his mind the adroitness with which Robert Kennedy had saved the day during the Cuban crisis, suggesting that Khrushchev's first, conciliatory letter be answered and the second, abrasive one be ignored. At first the plodders in Foggy Bottom and Whitehall produced what Arthur Schlesinger described as 'a debater's screed, dealing *seriatim* with Khrushchev's points'.[26] But Ormsby-Gore, picking up Khrushchev's final paragraph, stifled the debate and proposed concentrating instead on the 'special emissaries'. Macmillan strongly supported this, though he feared that 'The Americans will not like this, but David Gore is confident that the President will agree – if only to please me. . . .'[27] Once more, that personal Special Relationship came into play and (according to Schlesinger) 'Kennedy readily agreed.' Thus, on 30 May, 'a brief letter went to Khrushchev, touching lightly on a couple of the familiar arguments but centering on the proposal that American and British emissaries go to Moscow at the end of June or early in July.'[28]

Meanwhile, in the States Kennedy had begun to generate more enthusiasm for the test-ban talks, and decided to make a major pronouncement. As a platform he chose the Commencement ceremony of Washington's American University on 10 June, the same week that Profumo had confessed to his lie to the House of Commons. Two days before, however, a further response arrived from Khrushchev, grumpy, restating in fairly tough language his theme about espionage, with a side-blow at West German 'revanchists' and the proposed creation of the MLF; but, nevertheless, it contained a clear go-ahead to opening negotiations. Speaking at the American University, Kennedy went out of his way to welcome Khrushchev's initiative. In an address restrained and elevated in language, Kennedy spoke of 'the most important topic on earth: world peace'. By this, he did not mean a 'Pax America enforced on the world by American weapons of war'. He reminded his young American audience of how no nation had 'ever suffered more than the Soviet Union suffered in the course of the Second World War', and if world war came again both sides 'would be destroyed in the first twenty-four hours'. Both countries had 'a mutually deep interest in a just and genuine peace and in halting the arms race. . . . We all breathe the same air. We all cherish our children's future. And we are all mortal. . . .'[29] It was a profoundly moving address, the main substantive proposal of which was that the US would effect a moratorium on atmospheric testing, as long as other countries followed suit; at the same time, he announced the early opening of discussions towards 'a comprehensive test ban treaty' in Moscow.

Later, Khrushchev told Harriman he considered Kennedy's address to have been 'the greatest speech by any American President since Roosevelt'.[30] Doubtless it had its effect; in East Berlin on 2 July, Khrushchev offered a limited ban, outlawing explosions in the atmosphere, in outer space and under water. Prospects of a comprehensive ban had vanished under Russian and American niggling over the number of inspections.

Macmillan reached gratefully for this opening, though throughout June – and despite the dispersal of effort caused by the Profumo affair – he continued to battle away at the Americans on underground testing. In his long letter to Kennedy of 16 March, Macmillan, advised by Ormsby-Gore, had proposed he should send as his 'special emissary' Harriman or the President's brother Bobby. To his delight, Kennedy now decided on the former. It was a courageous choice, as Harriman's relations with the orthodox State Department were never easy. A multi-millionaire Democrat and a veteran negotiator whose experience went back to the days of Roosevelt and Stalin, he was one of the Americans Macmillan most admired; and the admiration was mutual. 'Of all the Americans I've ever known or had to deal with,' said Macmillan on television ten years later: 'he's the ablest. He's also got every quality for this kind of thing. Infinitely patient. Slightly deaf, but not quite so deaf as he appears. A great advantage in a diplomat. . . .'[31] On the British side, Macmillan had wanted to send the trusted Ormsby-Gore, but the Ambassador had demurred on the grounds that it would be wiser to have someone of Cabinet rank, and who could not be considered an American 'stooge'. Accordingly, Macmillan settled on Lord Hailsham, currently Minister responsible for the North-east. Apart from his brief experience as Minister of Science, the choice of Hailsham was a curious one; and could have been disastrous. That it was one of Macmillan's least inspired appointments was perhaps indicative of the pressures on him, and his lassitude at the time; while the success of the negotiations subsequently undoubtedly tended to lead Macmillan momentarily to regard Hailsham as his natural successor. Macmillan himself later explained that he thought the ebullient and pugnacious former Party Chairman might 'amuse' Khrushchev: 'Of course he too is boisterous, he could answer his jokes and so on, and he's very shrewd of course, and very determined. . . .'[32] On the other hand, Hailsham would be most ably supported by Sir Humphrey Trevelyan, the British Ambassador in Moscow, who, as Chargé d'Affaires in Peking between 1953 and 1955 had been the first Westerner to negotiate with Mao after the Korean War. Trevelyan's own feelers convinced him that the mood among the Soviet hierarchy was ripe for some limited détente in Europe – on terms, naturally, favourable to Soviet interests.

Kennedy to Birch Grove; a Last Encounter

On 23 June, Kennedy left for Europe; it was to be his most successful visit, and his last. In West Berlin he was acclaimed with the wildest reception of all, with some three-fifths of the population streaming out on to the streets, 'clapping, waving, crying, cheering as if it were the second coming', wrote Arthur Schlesinger.[33] It was here he made his famous utterance:

> All free men, wherever they may live, are citizens of Berlin, and, therefore, as a free man, I take pride in the words *Ich bin ein Berliner!*

From Berlin he flew on to Ireland, and a warm-hearted but calmer welcome – and thence on 29 June to Birch Grove. Following the encouraging experience of de Gaulle, Kennedy had invited himself to stay at Birch Grove briefly, to discuss MLF and the test-ban talks. The news had been withheld to the last minute; Macmillan finding a new source of irritation with *The Times* for drumming up suggestions that the Special Relationship was in disarray:

> The story is that the President has 'snubbed' me – cannot get on with an old Edwardian like me, and longs for Harold Wilson. . . . Perhaps when the President actually announces his self-invitation to stay a day at Birch Grove, the truth will be believed. . . .[34]

With a considerably larger retinue than de Gaulle's in November 1961, the upheaval was proportionately that much greater on the Macmillans' limited resources. Writing like any friend to an older hostess, Jacqueline Kennedy wrote a charmingly thoughtful letter to Dorothy a few days before the visit (which she was not accompanying):

> . . . I came upon our French chef last night happily writing out menus for Jack's stay in Birch Grove. He was writing FRENCH BREAD in large letters after each course – which I thought a bit much.
> . . . I don't know what link in the state trip chain broke. . . . I hate to think of what other things they may have told you the President cannot do without.
> You are most kind to ask – but know so well – these visits can get so out of hand – and really burdensome to the hostess. . . .

Recalling the story of de Gaulle's blood (which 'I shall never forget'), she went on,

> So I thought I would write to you directly and say *please* think of Jack as someone David Gore is bringing down for lunch – and just do whatever you would do in your own house – his tastes are distressingly normal – plain food – children's food – good food – he likes anything.[35]

Had she known the Macmillan cuisine, Mrs Kennedy need hardly have worried; despite the excellence of Mrs Bell, 'children's food' (preferably cold chicken – and ham – and undressed salad) was precisely what the Prime Minister most revelled in.

Hotel rooms were commandeered as far away as Brighton; Maurice Macmillan's neighbouring house, Pooks, was used as a forward communication post, and to house 'various Ambassadors'. As years passed, Macmillan made an excellent story out of it all: 'Helicopters, great machines taking over the whole building . . . Dean Rusk living in the lavatory at Pooks, or somewhere – there were about eighteen of them there, twenty of them . . . and they did nothing. All we wanted to do was to have a talk. . . .'[36] The President's arrival was greeted with crowds of well-wishers, the curious and (in the Profumo context) the prurient. They mingled with children invited by the Macmillans from nearby schools, neighbours, tenants, servants and workers off the Birch Grove estate. There were also 100 CND marchers, demanding the abolition of nuclear tests

– possibly unaware that this was what the meeting was all about. Macmillan recalled the crowd as being mostly inspired 'by a single spirit. To them, Kennedy meant youth, energy, idealism and a new hope for the world. . . .'

Macmillan never forgot the 'feeling of excitement' that Kennedy's arrival imposed on the whole neighbourhood: '. . . I can see him now, stepping out from the machine, this splendid, young, gay figure, followed by his team of devoted adherents. Never has a man been so well or so loyally served. . . .' Macmillan, however, recalled being shocked by the appearance of Kennedy, who was evidently on cortisone for his back. It made him 'very puffed up, very unhealthy. He suffered agony, he was a terribly brave man; I had no idea how much he suffered. He couldn't sit for very long without getting up. . . .'[37] A £3 rocking-chair was swiftly purchased for the President.

The Kennedy visit took place during what Macmillan described as 'the third crisis week' of the Profumo affair and – although he was determined not to allow the visit to be employed as a device to help his friend over his internal problems – the President arrived, in Mrs Kennedy's own words:

> very depressed, at the prospect of what he considered to be a great hero brought down; so Jack wanted to do something really nice, and give him a nice present, and to hell with State Department budget – so he gave Lady Dorothy a golden dressing table set with her initials on it – she was very touched by it and said 'Oh, I have never had one!' – while Harold presented some porcelain blue birds to Jack, saying 'And those are for you,' with lots of chuckles. . . .[38]

On Macmillan's account, inside Birch Grove it seemed 'more like a play or rather the mad rehearsals for a play, than a grave international conference'. There was none of the solemnity which usually characterises such meetings. 'After all, we were friends and many of us intimate friends; and the whole atmosphere was that of a country house party, to which had been added a garden party and a dance. . . .' By mutual preference, all the serious discussions with Kennedy, according to Macmillan, 'took place between him and me alone, with sometimes Private Secretaries to record decisions'. At one point towards the end of the visit, feeling that the vast assembled 'court' of dignitaries had been left out in the cold, with 'nothing to do', Macmillan suggested to Kennedy that they should hold a kind of mock conference. The President, said Macmillan, was 'in a mischievous mood', and the idea appealed to his 'puckish humour'.

> We therefore staged a rather formal conference on orthodox lines, the two protagonists facing each other with a circle of their supporters behind – something like a prize-fight. This took place in the drawing-room, and since we had already settled all the important points it was necessary to think of a subject. . . .

Kennedy suggested the future of NATO, and accordingly they 'embarked on a formal interchange of views, chiefly for the benefit of our advisers'. When Kennedy suggested, impishly, that maybe the tradition of NATO Supreme Allied Commanders being American should be broken by having a Canadian, French, Italian or British officer, Macmillan could not resist the temptation to chime in: '"Yes, I agree, Mr. President. Or perhaps a Russian."':

> There was some confusion amid the advisers behind me, and one called out, 'I don't think the Prime Minister quite means that.' 'Oh, yes, I do. You see it would work very well. The forces of the Western powers already face east. The Russians would only need to "about turn" and the NATO and Warsaw Pact amalgamate in defending Europe from any Chinese threats.' In the gravest manner and without a smile the President observed, 'Mr. Prime Minister, I think that is a proposition that needs much serious consideration.'

This anecdote conjures up a delightful scene of the discountenancing of pompous bureaucracy, and Kennedy always enjoyed 'putting down' his advisers, but Macmillan's flippancy did not entirely tally with American evaluations of the conference. Macmillan admitted in his unpublished diaries, '. . . I'm afraid Dean Rusk and the State Department were a bit sour. . . .'[39] For Kennedy it was perhaps the least heartening of all the encounters he had with Macmillan. There had been more hard talking on the MLF than revealed in Macmillan's account, and he had made his views plain – perhaps even plainer than he had at Nassau six months previously.

Despite Kennedy's own reservations, the MLF was still

established government policy in Washington. The formula which was agreed at Birch Grove was put succinctly in his letter to the Queen that followed the meeting:

> On the vexed question of the Multi-Manned Force . . . I undertook to make the sort of speech in the House of Commons which would not criticise the purpose or the form of the plan, but to emphasise that we should consider other methods of achieving the same purpose. We both agreed that the main object is not to provide more nuclear weapons for NATO (which already has too many) but to solve the German problem, now and in the future. . . .[40]

In simple terms, this meant keeping the German finger off the trigger, which, in the first forty years after the Second World War, no German government had in fact ever asked for.

'We got all we wanted,' Macmillan summed up after Birch Grove was all over: '(1) Full steam ahead with Moscow talks – Test Ban to be No. 1 Priority. (2) Go slow on Multi-Manned. On other difficult but really less important matters we were in agreement. . . .' 'Altogether,' encapsulated Macmillan, 'it was a *great* success from our point of view. . . .'[41] From American accounts, this is not quite how Kennedy saw it.[42] MLF was, in effect, crushed. Over the forthcoming test-ban talks, to which they had agreed, while Macmillan saw total domestic advantage Kennedy could see only difficulties at home, much as he personally might espouse the principles involved. He was disappointed that, during his brief stay, Macmillan had deftly headed him off from a meeting with the new Opposition Leader, Harold Wilson, for whom some members of the Kennedy administration were already beginning to form almost a penchant.[43] For all his affection, and admiration, for Macmillan, he did not want to be 'used' as he thought Macmillan had used Eisenhower for domestic advantage before the 1959 election; he was conscious of how greatly he had helped Macmillan out politically at Nassau, but he was prudent about being seen to get involved over the Profumo crisis – and possibly with good personal reasons for distancing himself. Nevertheless, on his way to mass at the Catholic church at Forest Row with Philip de Zulueta, he had enquired anxiously about the extent of political 'unrest' provoked by Profumo: 'He enquired if a nuclear test ban treaty would be of assistance to the Prime Minister. I said that it would be of some assistance electorally but that the fundamental point was the state of the economy. The President quite agreed with this. . . .'[44] But perhaps what disappointed Kennedy most in his Birch Grove visit was to find his friend, whom he had come so genuinely to respect, beneath all the flippancy seeming so disconsolate, so fatigued and so lacking in new ideas.

The visit ended, far too soon in Macmillan's opinion. The President left, as he came, by helicopter to Gatwick: 'Hatless, with his brisk step,' wrote Macmillan in a plangent valedictory passage:

> and combining that indescribable look of a boy on a holiday with the dignity of a President and Commander-in-Chief, he walked across the garden to the machine. We stood and waved. I can see the helicopter now, sailing down the valley above the heavily laden, lush foliage of oaks and beech at the end of June. He was gone. Alas, I was never to see my friend again. Before those leaves had turned and fallen he was snatched by an assassin's bullet from the service of his own country and the whole world.

Before they parted plans were made for another meeting before Christmas, or at latest in the New Year. Kennedy on his departure may well have had a premonition that he might not again be dealing with his older friend as Prime Minister, but neither could have foreseen the tragedy that was to make this seventh encounter their last.

At Last! Breakthrough in Moscow

Had the Kennedy–Macmillan association continued on beyond the autumn of 1963, it is more than probable that the sense of discouragement with which the President left Birch Grove would have turned out to be just another hiccup in the Special Relationship. What this really meant to Macmillan was expressed perhaps better than ever before in an eloquent passage of a letter to the Queen of 5 July, summing up the Birch Grove proceedings:

> In a sense, it was a remarkable tribute to the relations that exist between Britain and America that so much could be done in so

> short a time. We understood each other; we do not seek to make points against each other; we do not try to deceive each other, and if we disagree we do so openly and honestly. In other words in this race against time both sides fortunately started on every issue at least three-quarters of the way down the course. . . .[45]

In the same vein, Macmillan had written to Kennedy the previous day:

> I felt that it was a wonderful example of the way in which countries, and perhaps even more individuals, who trust each other can work rapidly and effectively together. I have been especially fortunate in having this kind of friendly intimacy with Presidents of the United States during all my Premiership and it has been a great pride to me to feel that in this at least we have been in part equal to the Churchill–Roosevelt relationship at the most critical moment of history. . . .[46]

After Birch Grove, things now began to move swiftly on the test-ban treaty front. On 2 July, Khrushchev, speaking in East Berlin, hinted at the possibility that he would accept a partial ban, whereas previously the Russians had wanted all or nothing. In his letter to Kennedy two days later, Macmillan seized on this to urge that, even if Khrushchev would not become more amenable on the question of inspections, the West should still press for a modified ban. Both sides now began to drop from their reckoning the issue of underground testing, on the grounds that agreement over the number of inspections was insurmountable, for the time being. Macmillan's view, all along, was that any agreement was better than none. On 12 July, Harriman came to lunch with Macmillan en route for Moscow, and Macmillan found him:

> certainly 'on our side' and will do all he can to get a Test Ban agreement of some kind with the Russians. . . . The situation is dramatic and vital for me. If there is any chance of our agreement and a Summit Meeting afterwards, I will fight on in home politics. If not, I shall feel inclined to throw in my hand. . . .[47]

According to Harriman's recollection, after lunch Macmillan took him aside privately and agreed that the association of 'Red' China with the test ban was 'so sensitive' that Harriman should raise it with Khrushchev alone – without Hailsham.[48]

At this moment, Macmillan's whole future and all his aspirations were focused upon the Moscow talks. These now began on 15 July.

The road was far from smooth. Khrushchev's thoughts still seemed to be obsessed with fears of espionage, 'whether genuine or affected'. Then there was the problem of the other two nuclear powers, China and France. Macmillan wanted to get a 'non-dissemination pact' linked in with the test-ban treaty; the Americans thought (quite mistakenly, as it turned out) that the Russians could exert enough pressure on the Chinese to ensure their adherence to the treaty. France, with de Gaulle, was another question. On the 16th, a bombshell arrived from Washington, causing Macmillan a rare moment of aggravation with Kennedy:

> rather to my surprise in view of our recent meeting, with that sudden change of direction which has been such a marked feature of American policy in recent years, the President started an altogether new hare. He proposed, in order to pacify de Gaulle and induce France to sign any treaty on tests which might be reached, to release the vital nuclear information which had been so long and so jealously withheld, first from us and then from the French. This unexpected offer was apparently to be made without conditions and without any *quid pro quo*, except to abstain from tests, which would, in any case, have been rendered unnecessary. . . .

Macmillan added, with some bitterness: 'Had the Americans armed me with this powerful weapon six months before, it might have made the whole difference to Britain and to Europe. . . .'

The next day, the Cabinet considered a long brief which the Foreign Office and Defence experts had prepared in answer to the Kennedy proposals. Wrote Macmillan: '. . . I felt in almost total disagreement with the FO view. Why be so cautious, when the President was so imaginative? Why bother about the President going "far beyond what his advisers feel"? That is an American affair. . . .' Macmillan thought that the only thing that mattered here was the President's attitude to France, and, in a brief moment of optimism, it provoked him to think that 'We might even revive Europe – (Common Market) etc. – and start a new and hopeful movement to straighten out the whole Alliance. . . .'[49] Macmillan accordingly concentrated on drafting his own reply to the President. He wrote:

> You and we ought to be quite clear in our minds before we enter into detailed discussions with the French exactly what we are prepared to offer and about what we want to obtain in return. As regards any offer to the French we could consider arranging to provide them with nuclear information and perhaps also supplying them with fissile or other material in such a way as to save them time and money and of course above all to obviate the need for further French tests. On our side, we should consider what we might hope to obtain in return. . . . Above all can we use this opportunity to our advantage in at least paving the way towards a new era, in which France would play a full part, both as regards relationships in the Western world and relations between East and West?

Macmillan was to be disappointed; de Gaulle had already taken France too far down the 'going-it-alone' road, and she would *not* become party to the Test Ban Treaty. Kennedy wrote back, agreeing with all Macmillan's points. But he expressed concern about the 'mounting evidence of the General's unfriendliness'.

What Macmillan described as 'rivers of telegrams' began to flow in from Moscow. Gromyko pressed for a 'non-aggression pact' to be linked with the treaty. 'Except for the unpleasant memories connected with the term' (coupled with the names of Ribbentrop and Molotov), Macmillan could see no objections. But 'the pundits of both sides of the Atlantic took alarm'. In Moscow there were stresses between the British and American delegations, with the latter finding the 'impetuous' Hailsham amateurish, ill prepared on technicalities, and bent on gaining a treaty at almost any cost. (Hailsham, on his side, reported to London that Harriman 'seemed a man very much after his best, tired and becoming a little deaf. The Americans were rather suspicious of me personally. At one moment they suspected that I was in communication with the Russians!')[50] On the 21st, Macmillan observed in his diary that the drama was unfolding 'slowly, more like a cricket match than a baseball game'.[51]

Kennedy for his part was restrained in voicing his misgivings about Macmillan's emissary. On the 23rd, in a fairly sharp criticism, Kennedy expressed his concerns about the handling of the non-aggression pact and wondered whether Hailsham had not gone too far in one of his communiqués, which might have appeared to constitute a non-aggression commitment.

The following day, Ormsby-Gore reported that the Americans were:

> acutely concerned about European reactions to anything said about non-aggression arrangements. They have heard that Adenauer is deeply suspicious of what is going on in Moscow. These suspicions are being actively encouraged by the French who are pouring out a stream of poison to anyone who will listen. The President has just heard that the French Ambassador in Moscow was advising de Gaulle to try to do a deal with the Soviet Union to obtain nuclear information in order to rid himself of his hateful Atlantic links. I remarked that even de Gaulle must see that this was a mad suggestion. The President agreed, but thought it was an indication of the mood we had to deal with. . . .[52]

Kennedy continued to want to press for a test ban alone, and quickly. On the 24th, the Macmillan diaries recorded:

> *Bad* telegrams from Moscow this morning. I have told Gore to stay in Washington, postponing his leave. The Americans are being very stubborn. . . . I thought we had got the Russians to agree about a compromise. This may be troublesome. A confused afternoon. . . .[53]

Ormsby-Gore continued to warn Macmillan from Washington that Congress, while ready to accept a test ban, were very concerned if the idea gained currency that the Anglo-Americans could reach agreement with the Russians only by including proposals objectionable to the other allies.

But 25 July proved 'a very long and tiring – but historic day . . .'. It was a real cliff-hanger, with hurdles and hiccups right to the end, many of them seemingly created by legalists on Harriman's team. By 2 p.m. London time Hailsham was foreseeing 'a wrangle and perhaps a breakdown . . .'. The telegrams from Moscow seemed agonisingly slow, and it was not till 5.30 p.m. that Kennedy finally came through on the telephone to Admiralty House, and told Macmillan 'that he had abandoned the American position, and had told Harriman not to insist. Indeed, he said that the Treaty was just being initialled! (He might have told us before and saved us a lot of anxiety!)'[54] Macmillan, recorded Arthur Schlesinger at the other end, 'was deeply moved', hearing this amid all the tribulations of the Profumo affair.[55] In one of the rare emotional entries to his diaries, Macmillan recorded that, after he had heard the news from the President, 'I had to go out of the room. I went to tell D. and burst into tears. I had prayed hard for this, night after night. . . .'

That same night he went to dine in the House, and sat in the Smoking Room; there he found 'everyone very happy . . .'. He then went to his room and prepared a brief statement of a couple of sentences, which, with permission, he delivered to the Commons at 11 p.m.:

> The House was very full. The statement was well received and the questions which followed were friendly and generous (especially from the extreme Left). When I left, the whole of the Con- servatives stood up and waved their order papers. Many of the Opposition stood up also. It was like the greatest of my Parliamentary successes. No doubt, tomorrow, some horrible revelation on security or morals or what-not will threaten to destroy the Government, and I shall be down again. However, for the moment, it's up. I have learned (in a hard school) not to be affected too much either by good or rough weather. . . .[56]

'It was – nice,' he added in a television broadcast ten years later;[57] it was also very different to the atmosphere that he had had to face in the Commons after the Profumo debate, little less than a month previously.

To Kennedy, Macmillan signalled: 'I found myself unable to express my real feelings on the telephone tonight. My task here has been relatively easy, but I do understand the high degree of courage and faith which you have shown.'[58] On 24 September, the US Senate ratified, by a vote well in excess of the required two-thirds, the Test Ban Treaty – which Kennedy regarded as the most serious congressional issue he had ever had to face. In a symbolic token of the new entente, from his Black Sea villa Khrushchev was photographed playing badminton with Secretary Dean Rusk –

without a net. Hailsham returned home from Moscow bringing Macmillan a present from Khrushchev of Russian caviare, crab-meat and wine; Macmillan sent him back a vase and English Stilton cheese, together with a note expressing his satisfaction over the conclusion of the Nuclear Test Ban Treaty, and saying: '. . . I hope sincerely that this agreement, important in itself, will lead on to other understandings. . . .' It was to be the last significant exchange that Macmillan would have with the unpredictable Russian leader.

'So was realised at least one of the great purposes which I had set myself . . .' was how Macmillan ended his account of the saga.

Reactions

With rival excitements in the air like the trial and suicide of Stephen Ward, the 'Headless Man' and the 'Man in the Mask', and the Great Train Robbery, Macmillan's contribution to preventing mankind from blowing itself up received limited coverage in the home press. Harold Evans was sickened by *The Times*, 'cheap and ungenerous', endeavouring to dismiss Macmillan as merely the 'third man' in the signature of the treaty. Evans was being more than just the loyal subordinate when he declared in his diaries that:

> this was an event which will surely merit a place in the history books – and rank as a true Macmillan achievement. It was he – with a sense of history – who read the signs aright in Russia and saw the opportunities: who coaxed and prodded the Americans; who argued the case with Khrushchev; and finally took the initiative which led to the Kennedy–Macmillan approach. He had persisted, moreover, despite the collapse of the Paris summit. . . .[59]

Those most closely involved in the Test Ban Treaty negotiations – and notably on the American side – also had little doubt as to where the honours were due. The test ban, declared Arthur Schlesinger, 'would not have come about without the intense personal commitment of Kennedy and Macmillan . . .'.[60] Sir Michael Wright, the British adviser on disarmament, praised the role of the direct communication at the top between Kennedy and Macmillan;

this had been confirmed to him by Bobby Kennedy, who stressed that over the Test Ban Treaty his brother 'deliberately took the British view and not the view of the American advisers, and Bobby Kennedy said afterwards this was absolutely right, and . . . this is an illustration of the value to the United States of the close working with Britain. . . .'[61] Macmillan's own emissary, Lord Hailsham, in his memoirs, remarks:

> If nothing else stood to his credit, Harold Macmillan's influence in bringing about negotiations of the partial Test Ban Treaty would entitle him to be treated as one of the great benefactors of his generation. . . . He saw that the time was right and the parties were willing. . . .

It also seemed to Hailsham, in retrospect, as 'the last time that Britain appeared in international negotiations as a great power'.[62]

On the Opposition front benches, Michael Foot thought that Macmillan deserved 'Full credit for the Test Ban Treaty. . . . it looked as if it was the most important achievement in that area . . . possibly Macmillan's greatest. . . .'[63]

Of all the congratulations and homage, however, possibly none would have been more gratifying to Macmillan than the following letter from his son Maurice of 26 July:

> Dearest Papa
>
> It was really a most moving occasion last night; and a richly deserved triumph, for your fortitude as much as for your patience and skill. Your family and friends have all felt very deeply for you in the last few weeks and were all correspondingly delighted at the success and the acclaim it brought. . . . we had a drink afterwards with some of your staunchest and most active supporters: it was touching to witness their genuine and unselfish joy over both the test-ban agreement and your great success at the 1922 Committee.
>
> Many of us, including myself, will long remember with gratitude the example you set of courage and steadfastness and will, I hope, profit in future from the lessons we have learned from you over all this. I *am* glad for you.
>
>   Your loving son,
>   Maurice[64]

By his own reckoning Macmillan, while accepting that it was his greatest achievement, always expressed disappointment that it had only resulted in a *partial* ban on nuclear testing. In his disappointment and horror at the escalation of nuclear weaponry into the 1980s, Macmillan in his old age could be unsparing in his criticism of Kennedy, blaming him for the missed opportunity, and his 'weakness':

> . . . I mean weakened by constantly having all those girls, every day. . . . He was weak in pressing the Russians for seven inspections instead of three. If we could have had that, it would have eventually led to no testing in the air at all – which was my idea. . . . I feel this is a great opportunity that we missed, and I do blame Kennedy's weakness. . . .[65]

Old age undoubtedly caused Macmillan to be less than fair to Kennedy. In 1963, he had not been aware of 'all those girls' as a 'weakness' in Kennedy that debilitated his public performance; just as he never did quite realise the extent of Kennedy's problems with Congress. Moreover it was quite clear to close members of the Kennedy entourage, like Sorensen and Schlesinger, that the President regarded the 1963 treaty not as a culmination, but as a step on the road towards overall détente.[66] The world would have been a safer place had Fate permitted Macmillan and Kennedy to keep up the impetus with Khrushchev, who had now – at long last – begun to trust them both. In the long run, however, it was the 1963 treaty that opened the door leading eventually to the SALT I agreements.

On Macmillan's side, disillusion with Kennedy's 'weakness' was a passing, ephemeral irritant, exacerbated by old age and the passage of time. What lasted was the genuine affection and admiration, the lump in the throat whenever Macmillan recalled his last sight of his friend, the President with his 'indescribable look of a boy on holiday', being whirled aloft away from Sussex in June 1963. His more considered view was this:

> Perhaps his biggest achievement was to take the disillusioned and saddened youth of all the world and make them think there was some purpose in life – something to work for, to shout about. . . . He made young people feel that it was worth while.

I think that was his great achievement. . . . A spiritual achievement, not political. . . .[67]

The nuclear test ban was the last and possibly greatest scene in the Kennedy–Macmillan Special Relationship. One is entitled to speculate what the two might have gone on jointly to achieve, had not both been removed prematurely.

Chapter Eighteen

'The Hand of Fate'
September–October 1963

*. . . I didn't spend my life looking for leaders. It is rather a
dangerous occupation for the leaders of a party to look for their
successors. People might wish to hasten the moment. . . .*

(HM, Diaries, *19 September 1973*)

Everything just went wrong – like a Greek play. . . .

(HM, Diaries, *10 September 1979*)

Within minutes of hearing the heartening news that the Test Ban Treaty had been initialled in Moscow (he had barely had time to tell Dorothy, and recompose his emotions), Macmillan had to make his regular 'end of the summer term' speech to the 1922 Committee, some of whose members had, only recently, been baying for his blood over the Profumo affair. But in the event,

> This much-advertised meeting turned out very strangely. I was received with great applause and banging of desks. I spoke for forty minutes, on broad policy, home and abroad. I had thought out the speech on Sunday and (except for one page of notes) spoke *ex tempore.* . . .

The news of the Test Ban Treaty had in fact been mentioned to members by the Chairman of the 1922, John Morrison. Macmillan hardly referred to it, except in its natural context in East–West problems. But, when he sat down,

> after simply saying about myself that my sole purpose was to serve the Party and the Nation and to secure a victory at the Election, there was great applause. There may have been a few abstainers at the end of the room (but very few). . . . Lord Lambton got up and made a rather obscure speech, but was listened to with great impatience. Altogether it was a triumphal vote of confidence. . . .[1]

A few days later, the *Daily Mail* opinion poll showed 'a tremendous swing' back to the Tories: 'Only 6% or so behind Labour (instead of 18%–20%) and I have risen equally or more in public favour. How strange it all is. . . .'[2]

Fatigue

Suddenly, at long last, things seemed to be going right for Macmillan. Yet, after all the efforts expended over the Test Ban Treaty, he felt strangely flat, and was suffering an immense lassitude. Over the years in office, not surprisingly, both in his diaries and in his letters to his confidante, Ava Waverley (who was even more acutely prone to hypochondria), he had made intermittent references to ill-health and fatigue. In the trenches of the First War, writing to his mother he had expressed disproportionate concern at the pain of a wasp sting, compared with his stoicism at the infinitely greater damage inflicted by the German machine-gunner on the Somme, and members of his family had long derived some sly amusement at indications of *maladies imaginaires*. To recuperate, he would sometimes take to his bed for a day or so, then rebound with a display of prodigious resilience. But, in the year from July 1962 onwards, the references to ill-health coupled with fatigue become more numerous, the displays of resilience fewer. To Macmillan's doctor, Sir John Richardson, Maurice Macmillan stressed how 'it had cost his father the most appalling effort to sack his friends and reconstruct the Government so ruthlessly.' It was, said Richardson, 'what I already knew';[3] and indeed – since that Night of Long Knives – the succession of crises, culminating with Profumo, might well have been sufficient to knock out many a lesser man in his late sixties.

For much of the time, his war wounds plagued him – like Kennedy – with pain in his back and legs, and at Admiralty House he often wore a corset, a secret which only a few, like Harold Evans, of his private entourage knew.[4]

Colleagues in those Profumo months, however, recalled him seeming older, and lonelier. He was missing the contemporaries who had fallen – or been felled. To his biographer he confessed that at that time he had felt he was beginning 'to get very tired . . . to lose grip . . . much more fatigue. . . . Long time, seven years – at that rate . . .'.[5] Hailsham recalled that at times he 'positively drooled and wasted time. . . . he was hardly sensible; so often the trouble with a man when his powers are failing. . . .'[6] It seems certain that he was beginning to suffer the symptoms, undiagnosed, of the 'Old Man's Disease' that was so soon to knock him out – the discomfort, incontinence and drowsiness that go with an inflamed prostate. It seems equally certain that here Macmillan's natural prudishness overcame the tendency to hypochondria, and that he confided none of his malaise to Sir John Richardson. Had he done so, Sir John as a good physician would have taken measures that could have rendered the onset of prostate trouble less devastating, and less of a shock when it came in October, and thus in turn have made resignation not inevitable. But its symptoms, unidentified, were enough to cause Macmillan more and more frequently to contemplate throwing in his hand in the summer of 1963.

It was thus with joy that, as the parliamentary session 'came wearily to its end', Harold, with Dorothy, set out on a trip to Finland and Sweden. It was over twenty-three years since he had gone to Finland with Lord Davies to try to help the Finnish government in their war against the Russians and once more he found it 'a delightful and invigorating change'.

Returning from Scandinavia to Birch Grove, his thoughts turned:

> seriously, and serenely, out of the turmoil of House of Commons and all the rest, about my own future. I can do this quietly for the next few days here and then during my fortnight's holiday in Yorkshire. I shall come south at the end of August.
>
> It seems to me at present that the question of the leadership of the party cannot be left uncertain beyond October. (Conference is October 13th.)
>
> The choice is between a) *resigning* in week before Parliament meets – about October 22nd or so; b) going on and fighting election and saying so at Conference. I don't particularly want a tiresome 8 weeks from November to Christmas, with party in House of Commons making trouble and then resigning at Christmas. Unless there was some great *international* prize the extra two months are not worth the trouble.[7]

Leaving for the Yorkshire moors, at Bolton Abbey, he was cheered up by 'a very agreeable party and plenty of grouse'. Among the party was David Ormsby-Gore, who recalled Macmillan discussing whether it was 'time to go'.

> He went through with me all the possible candidates (but not Alec at that time). I had seen him in that kind of mood several times before – but I didn't think that he was more lethargic than before . . . in many ways, in fact, he was in quite good form. . . .[8]

To Ava Waverley at about the same time, however, he was writing from Yorkshire listlessly and in a more erratic hand than usual, '. . . I must think out what to do with what remains of my life. . . .'[9]

The magic of the moors had worked with only partial success on this occasion and he confided to his diary: '. . . I rather shrink from going back, out of the clean Yorkshire air, into Whitehall and its fog. . . .'[10]

The problems that awaited him there did indeed seem legion: 'Everywhere in the world there are troubles.' The one ray of sunshine was that at home, the economy was 'good. The building strike had been settled on very reasonable terms (4%). But it has been a bad summer, and I feel that my power and even my influence is slipping away. How long is it worth staying on and for what purpose?'[11] The untidiness of Churchill's departure was constantly in his mind.

Awaiting him on his return from the north was an urgent memorandum from Oliver Poole, Joint Chairman of the Tory Party. He warned Macmillan:

> The Chief Whip and the Chairman of the 1922 Committee will I am sure advise you that the Parliamentary Party wish for a change before the next election. I do not think this advice can be wholly ignored; but need not be the decisive factor if the Cabinet feel otherwise. I am however doubtful if it is possible to delay a decision over the leadership until after the Christmas recess without doing irreparable harm to the Party. . . .[12]

It was not a happy month. With Dorothy away in Scotland, he was alone much of the time. Beginning to feel daily more depressed, he allowed himself to brood moodily in his diary about the future.

> . . . I cannot go on to an election and lead in it. I am beginning to feel that I haven't the strength and that perhaps another leader could do what I did after Eden left. But it cannot be done by a pedestrian politician. It needs a man with vision and moral strength – Hailsham, not Maudling. Yet the 'back benchers' (poor fools) do not seem to have any idea, except 'a young man'. Admirable as Maudling is, I doubt if he could revive our fortunes as well as Hailsham. (I sent H. to Moscow on purpose, to test his powers of negotiation etc. He did *very* well.)[13]

His enthusiasm currently for Hailsham (all of which was subsequently omitted in the memoirs) in the succession stakes is of interest in view of his subsequent change of horses.

A letter to the Queen of the same day showed him still in a mood of irresolution: '. . . I have not yet reached a decision in my own mind as to how all these things ought to be handled and I should like to write a further letter to Your Majesty when my thoughts are in a more orderly sequence than they are at present.'[14] Three days later he was noting with concern that Harold Wilson was already beginning to open up with 'a good campaign. . . . But we are doing nothing. This makes it really vital that I should settle about the future.'[15] Pressures, intelligence and advice were converging from all directions, buffeting Macmillan this way and that. In the Private Office something like an atmosphere of the bunker had already begun to take shape many weeks previously. Back in June, a handwritten note from the loyal Alec Home reported rumours of 'scheming',[16] while, a month later, his faithful 'ears' in the Commons, his Parliamentary Private Secretary Knox Cunningham, had provided a list of four junior ministers who were 'not in full support'; Margaret Thatcher was on that list.[17]

On 11 September, it was Rab Butler who dropped in to interrupt his solitude. They had a long talk, though:

> . . . I was rather careful *not* to give him any idea about which of the several alternatives I would choose, for he is not discreet. But I got a good idea of his own position. He would naturally (if I resign) accept the Premiership if there was a general consensus of opinion for him. But he doesn't want another unsuccessful bid. . . . He is 60. He likes politics. He doesn't want to go into business, for he has enough money. It is clear that in his heart he does *not* expect any real demand for him. He would prefer to be Warwick (which he could be) and not try to be King (which he can't be). On the whole, he is for Hailsham. I have never seen him so well . . . or so relaxed. . . .[18]

Rab, rather out of character, had laid his cards on the table, and it is evident that Macmillan saw them pretty clearly. On the 17th, Macmillan at last received the Denning Report – with, as we have seen, nothing but relief. This major factor in making up his mind was now out of Macmillan's way. The following day, Alec Home called. He was:

> very distressed to think that I had any idea of retiring, but could well understand my reasons and thought them sound. As for a

successor, he favours Hailsham but fears that there will be complete disunity in the Party and that great troubles will follow. I may be forced to stay. I replied 'In that case I shall be "drafted" – not a "limpet". I don't want it to be thought that I am just clinging on.'[19]

At his weekly audience with the Queen, two days later on 20 September, Macmillan informed her of his decision. After telling her about the 'very satisfactory state of the Economy':

> with production *rising* and unemployment *falling* (contrary to usual autumnal pattern), I then told her of my plans of announcing on October 12th that I would *not* have an Election this year and that I would *not* lead Party at Election. This would involve a change in January or February. The Queen expressed her full understanding. But I thought she was very distressed, partly (perhaps) at the thought of losing a P.M. to whom she has become accustomed, but chiefly (no doubt) because of all the difficulties about a successor in which the Crown will be much involved. We discussed at some length the various possibilities. She feels the great importance of maintaining the prerogative intact. After all, if she asked someone to form a government and he failed, what harm was done? It often, indeed at one time almost invariably, happened in the first half of the 19th century. Of course, it would be much better for everything to go smoothly, as in my case. . . .[20]

Macmillan declared himself determined at all costs to preserve this prerogative, the Queen's right to select her Prime Minister. The following day, at a conversation at Chequers with Oliver Poole and Tim Bligh, Macmillan announced 'an irreversible decision'; he would himself tell the Tory conference that:

> he would defend the Government's position in relation to the Denning Report to parliament, that there would be no election this year, and that he had thought it right to decide to renounce the leadership in time to enable the next leader of the party to have sufficient room to manoeuvre to decide when the next General Election would take place.[21]

But meanwhile he would '*not* inform anyone of this except Lord Home, Lord Poole, Chief Whip and Tim Bligh (of course, Dorothy and Maurice). I shall tell the Cabinet on Tuesday morning before Blackpool Conference and make my speech on Saturday October 12th. . . .'[22] The 'indiscreet' Rab, though Deputy Prime Minister, was not – it should be noted – on this list of confidants.

On the 25th, Macmillan wrote to Sir Michael Adeane, putting on record what he had said to the Queen. In a rather curious aside, he then added a few lines that can only suggest that he may already have been having thoughts about the earldom that he was to take over twenty years later:

> . . . I went to Hughenden the other day. This is just to remind you that (as perhaps you know) there is a table in the Church with this inscription:

> To the dear and honoured memory of
> Benjamin, Earl of Beaconsfield
> this memorial is placed
> by his grateful sovereign and friend
> Victoria R.I.
> 'Kings love him that speaketh right' Prov. 26.13

> There is a nice, old Norman church in Horsted Keynes, Sussex – St. Giles. There would be room on the wall, when the time comes.

Almost immediately after his 'irreversible decision', however, Macmillan began to have doubts. The Denning Report, published the following week, was so much less damning than he had feared,[23] and the reaction so much more favourable than he could ever have hoped; the letters of congratulations flooded in: '. . . I feel somehow that the tide is turning and that people as a whole will support me. . . .'[24] Other problems were beginning to raise their heads, principally over the succession – which was beginning to look anything but a straightforward race. Many names had been mooted in the press and in Party caucuses – Butler, Maudling, Heath, Macleod and Hailsham. The odds were constantly varying; back in June, a *Daily Telegraph* poll taken among MPs had given Maudling 147 votes, against 56 for Hailsham and only 28 for Butler,[25] but since then support for Maudling had dwindled. Hailsham was coming up swiftly, fortified by his success in Moscow – not least in the eyes of Harold Macmillan. But all was far from clear, and

Macmillan was anxious not to precipitate the Party into a chaos of internecine warfare with a general election in the offing. Meanwhile, Harold Wilson was looking progressively like a more menacing contender than his predecessor, Gaitskell. At his first Party Conference in early October Macmillan noted Wilson giving:

> a very brilliant and effective 'key-note' speech ... which will have a wide appeal and be difficult to answer.
>
> *All* the difficulties were swept under the carpet, and a 'new vision' is developed in a Jack Kennedy sort of style. It was excellently done, if fundamentally dishonest. . . .[26]

The shape of things to come was evident.

October: More Pressures

During the first week of October, appeals for him to stay on intensified. On the 2nd, he and Dorothy moved back to a restored No. 10 Downing Street, after three years' exile at Admiralty House. Despite the greater space and finer rooms of Admiralty House, he was glad to be back; the 'atmosphere of its historic past' doubtless made it all the harder to contemplate leaving, and he thought the architect and builders had 'certainly done a good job' at No. 10. Michael Fraser of the Conservative Research Department and his trusty speech-writer in the 1959 election campaign, George Christ, came to help him prepare his 'key-note' speech for Blackpool; while Macmillan, continuing to play the cards very close to his chest, was confronted by 'the difficult job of preparing (secretly) the bit I am to say about myself. But I have not yet finally decided what I *am* going to say!'[27] Among the flow of visitors, and advice-givers, Christopher Soames, the Minister of Agriculture, spoke for many when he reckoned that Labour under Wilson was almost certain to win the next election, regardless. On the 4th, the gentle and under-rated Maurice Macmillan, who over the past year (and particularly during Profumo) had come closer than ever to his father, tendering views that were now listened to with respect, called in at No. 10:

> He (like Dorothy) is now persuaded that my decision to retire before the General Election is right. The problem is how exactly

to announce it, and how to get the right successor. Butler would be fatal. Maudling uninspiring. Hailsham, with Maudling and the others in loyal support, might still win. The Labour Party Conference is, on the face of it, a great 'boost' for Labour. But since all the cracks were papered over, I see trouble ahead *if* the Election is not till October 1964. Already the newspapers are putting some awkward questions.[28]

The next day he suffered a totally sleepless night:

There are so many factors – the chief one being that there is *no* clear successor. But there is also a growing wave of emotion in my favour, throughout the Party, especially the Party in the provinces. This will be evidenced at Blackpool. I have written the actual speech – leaving six or seven minutes at the end for the personal bit – to go or to stay? I *hate* the feeling that I shall be letting down all these loyal people, from highest to lowest, if I give up. On the other hand, I shall probably be humiliated if I stay and everyone will say that failure has been due to the old limpet. . . .[29]

On the 6th, a Sunday, Macmillan discussed his dilemma all afternoon at Birch Grove with Maurice, now joined by his son-in-law, Julian Amery, at the end of which Macmillan was, by his own account:

beginning to move (at the last minute) towards staying on – for another two or three years. Maurice says that, although it would be difficult to win, for the fourth time, yet it *might* be done, by a sort of emotional wave of feeling – partly materialistic feeling (if you like) but partly sincere. After all, we have brought them both Prosperity and Peace. . . .

After they left, Home came to dinner – alone. He and Macmillan talked at length about the prospects for further détente, beyond the Test Ban Treaty. Home, worrying particularly about the American 'card', was '*not* too hopeful'.

The real difficulties are (a) My power in G.B. is waning, as Parliament draws to its close; (b) President's ditto. Worse still, policies which are popular here (Test Ban, etc) are not so very popular in U.S.A. The President has been very good about following behind our lead. But as his Election approaches, he will worry more and more about the electoral effects of his policies. All the same, we *did* have some success before, and we might again. . . .

Home still favoured the previously accepted plan of Macmillan retiring in 1964. But:

> he (and I) have begun to wonder whether it can, in fact, be worked. It would mean from 12th October to (say) first week in January (three months) during which I am to be P.M. under (self-imposed) sentence of death. Would not the whole situation disintegrate? We felt that if I announced on Saturday that I would *not* fight the Election, it would be impossible to prevent the search for a leader from beginning at once, to the exclusion of everything else. On the other hand, if I announced my determination to go on, it would be accepted – and welcomed by a great majority. But there would still be a substantial and very vocal minority. It would be a great moral and physical strain to overcome them – and two or three months' bitter struggle. Then the Election. I might have a really humiliating defeat. At least a change might be better and could hardly be worse than the present 'gallup' polls indicate.[30]

Doubts about the capacity of a successor to achieve a further détente with Russia seem in particular to have been uppermost in his mind.

On the morning of Monday the 7th, Macmillan drove up to London from Birch Grove, still in a quandary. He was greeted by Tim Bligh with news that the Cabinet was rallying to him 'with great enthusiasm', and with only 'one or two exceptions'. Butler came to see him and (according to Macmillan) 'would clearly prefer me to go on, for – in his heart – he does not expect the succession *and* fears it'. Successively, the Lord Chancellor, Dilhorne, the Chief Whip, Redmayne, declared themselves ready to do battle for Macmillan.[31] There was also an encouraging letter from Macmillan's powerful brother-in-law James Stuart, urging him to soldier on:

I have 'pub crawled' as is my wont. . . . as a result there is no doubt in my mind that your position is immensely stronger than it was in mid July. Whether you want to go or not, there is now no serious rival to you as leader who is visible! Whatever the intentions or wishes of your leading colleagues may have been three months ago – or less – there has been no mention of any one of them in the press for weeks. RAB may be relying on loyalty and fatalism to result in its 'falling into his lap'.[32]

Macmillan was always ready to heed Stuart's 'pub-crawling'. Calling later that afternoon, Oliver Poole, however, was not of the same mind. Macmillan put to him three reasons for now staying:

1. I should seem to be 'deserting' and this would especially affect the 'marginal' seats.
2. I would seem to have yielded to the group of malcontents, who are swayed either by personal or purely reactionary sentiment.
3. I should leave the Party in complete disarray – with some for Butler, some for Hailsham, some for Maudling.

Oliver Poole, who was deeply moved and almost in tears told me that he thought it was his duty, as Chairman of the Party but still more as a personal friend, with a very great affection for me, to warn me against this course. He thought we should lose the election anyhow. . . . a collapse (which is likely) while bad for my successor would be humiliating for me. Why should I endure it?[33]

Meanwhile, that morning, in the *Daily Sketch*, a large article under the headline 'MY HUSBAND HAS NOT MADE UP HIS MIND' had appeared under the byline of Godfrey Winn, a somewhat precious and effeminate columnist, with a great facility for persuading members of the Royal Family and older ladies to gossip to him. Winn had tracked down Lady Dorothy at her favourite occupation, weeding the Michaelmas daisies at Birch Grove. 'Her garden and her grandchildren,' deduced Winn,

I had the feeling that these would be her consolation, her abiding interest if her husband decides to name his successor and surrender the throne. Over a two-hour interview, she discussed their lives, in the role of a loyal wife: 'Of course, the people who want him to go are busy making him out so old and senile, as though he had one foot in the grave. But actually he amazes me by his resilience. I think his whole attitude to life is now bearing final fruit.'

Winn asked her 'how she provided the constant reassurance required by a man under intolerable pressure; "I listen," she replied quietly. It was a good answer.' Godfrey Winn observed that the Prime Minister's wife was wearing 'a rather shapeless grey woolly jumper and a simple plaid skirt; she reminded me irresistibly of Margaret Rutherford' – and then he came down to the point and discussed her husband's possible successor: '. . . Maudling? "Not enough experience" I suggested. Rab Butler? "Rather a cold fish." At which Lady Dorothy interpolated: "He certainly looks older than my husband." Dorothy concluded: '"I don't think my husband has made up his mind himself. . . . If this week he gives a sign – and I think he will – he *will* tell me first."' 'Whereupon', was Godfrey Winn's sugary message for the day: 'NO MAN SUCCEEDS WITHOUT A GOOD WOMAN BEHIND HIM. WIFE OR MOTHER. IF IT IS BOTH, HE IS TWICE BLESSED INDEED.'[34]

At No. 10 the day ended with further meetings with some of Macmillan's senior colleagues. A long discussion, over the same old ground, showed that '. . . I would get *full support* of Cabinet if I decided to go on, but that several would be rather unhappy, partly for my sake, partly for that of the party. . . .' Macmillan went to bed that night exhausted, but immensely relieved at having finally 'determined to inform the Cabinet that I had now decided to stay on and fight the General Election and to ask for the full support of my colleagues . . .'.[35]

Some of those colleagues doubtless felt that he was simply repeating Churchill's performance of a decade earlier, of which he had been so critical. Ten years later, looking back at these two or three weeks of meandering indecision, Macmillan himself wrote – almost self-apologetically – that he was:

surprised and shocked at my vacillation. I was not accustomed, even in the most difficult circumstances of my life, to shilly-shally or to seek unnecessarily the advice of others. During all this period – that is from after my return from Yorkshire at the beginning of September – I felt nervous, uneasy and with a curious lack of grip, combined with a tendency to drowsiness at inconvenient moments. . . .

Still he had put this down to fatigue, and did little about it. Later he had 'no doubt' that this was all a symptom of his coming illness.

Stricken: 7–8 October

During the discussions that evening, and as Macmillan in fact finally made his decision, he experienced serious pain while trying to urinate. He said nothing about it at the time. Then, in the middle of the night of the 7th, having not slept at all two nights previously, he was stricken by 'an excruciating pain. . . . I was seized by terrible spasms – but no water emerged. Dorothy came to my help and got a doctor – Dr King-Lewis (Sir John Richardson was on holiday in Windermere). . . .' The absence of Richardson was to prove crucial for the decisions that followed. Dr King-Lewis finally arrived at about 4 a.m., and managed to give Macmillan relief:

by inserting an instrument to drain the water out of the bladder. Unfortunately, the bladder kept filling up, and by 8 a.m. it was worse. Dr. K-L came again and helped. He promised me that he would get Mr. [A.W.] Badenoch, the greatest surgeon in this line of business, by 1 p.m. . . .[36]

Still in considerable discomfort, and spasmodic pain, Macmillan with some courage presided as arranged at a three-hour Cabinet meeting on Tuesday the 8th. It was the first since the Cabinet had convened on 19 September to discuss the Denning Report. Ministers at once realised from his pallor that the Prime Minister was not at all well. This impression was reinforced towards the end of the session when a glass of milky-looking fluid was brought in for him to drink. Macmillan said nothing about his indisposition, but members of the government were not unaccustomed to Macmillan, in his tendency to hypochondria, dousing a common cold with (as one of his ministers recalled) 'enormous swigs of cough linctus every half-hour at the risk of poisoning himself . . .'.[37] But during the Cabinet meeting Macmillan had to absent himself 'twice with spasms, and felt pretty bad'.[38] Rab, by his own account, realising that the Prime Minister was 'in great pain', gave him a Valium.[39] There were a large number of items on the agenda for this first Cabinet meeting of the new session, but at noon Macmillan called a halt. Before doing so, he had:

asked Cabinet Secretariat to leave (except Sir Burke Trend) and explained shortly the problem to the Cabinet and announced my plan. Since I realised (I said) that there could be no free discussion in my presence, I withdrew. (The 'plan' of course, was to announce at Blackpool that I would lead in the General Election.) At this point, I had no reason to think (from what Dr. King-Lewis had said) that my trouble would be very serious. He hoped that normal passing of water might be re-established in a few hours. Any treatment of a more radical character would be perhaps avoided or postponed. Of course, Dr. K-L was quite right to keep me quiet at the time and had no idea of the issues involved. He thought it only a question of going to Blackpool for the speech on Saturday. . . .

(While he was out of the Cabinet Room, so Chief Whip Redmayne told him afterwards, 'the Cabinet had (with one exception) agreed to back me to the full if I decided to go through the General Election. (The exception was "Aristides"[40] – Enoch Powell, who thought I ought to resign). . .'[41] There was evidently no time for discussion, as most of the Cabinet were hurrying to catch the lunchtime train to Blackpool for the opening of the Party Conference; it was Rab, the faithful deputy, who remained behind. At 12.45, Mr Badenoch, the surgeon and urological expert, arrived. After consulting with the locum, Dr King-Lewis, he told Macmillan at once that he was suffering from an:

inflammation of the prostate gland (by either a benign or malignant tumour) and that it would have to be dealt with. Sir J.R. had been told by telephone and would be in London by 4 p.m. or so. It was agreed that there should be a meeting at 6 p.m. to decide on a course of action. . . .

Macmillan's own account in his memoirs of the hours, and days, that followed depends almost exclusively on his diaries, which –

given his state of physical distress at the time – should not be relied on for total accuracy. It seems that, in fact, before Sir John's arrival from the Lake District, and before the 6 p.m. meeting, Macmillan had already made up his mind. On the (correct) diagnosis of two strange doctors, who did not know Macmillan's character, or his suggestibility, he had more or less convinced himself that he had cancer; at the very best it would mean the end of his career. ('The doctors said I would never really be fit again, and there would have to be another operation in a year or so . . .', he recalled years later; 'I blame myself, I might have gone on. . . .')[42]

Mentally, he was thoroughly got down by Profumo, and all that had happened over the past year, and by his own physical sense of malaise. Later he blamed the accumulated stress of the whole Boothby affair as a contributory factor in his sudden collapse: 'It took a lot out of me, physically. . . . maybe I could have gone on longer. . . .'[43] From whatever cause, in October 1963, he was predisposed to expect the worst. As it was, on receiving the call, Richardson drove at top speed in his Jaguar from the Lake District, but arrived at No. 10 only after Badenoch had seen Macmillan. He was greeted by Tim Bligh, who told him '"He won't be able to do anything for three to four months, the Surgeon says." I said, "Nonsense, he can be back in three to four weeks." I saw Harold then, but he had absolutely made up his mind. . . .' Later, just before the operation, and knowing it was to take place, Richardson says he told Dorothy Macmillan and Maurice, 'he can go on, if somebody bears the strain for a few weeks. . . .' He was emphatic. 'Yes, if I had been there on that critical day, I think he would have gone on – there was absolutely no medical alternative, but the pass had already been sold. . . .'[44] Richardson's verdict was supported by a memorandum he prepared (at Macmillan's instruction) which stated (on 14 October), 'I feel that he will be fit and well able to continue to lead the party in six weeks' time, and that he can do the work of the Premier at Downing Street within a few days of his return there. . . .'[45]

The Doctors' Verdict: 8 October

Both in his memoirs and on television Macmillan contradicted Richardson's opinion;[46] but Richardson's thesis is supported by other medical opinion and by the views of the Macmillan family and of his closer associates. Maurice Macmillan, for one, was always convinced that if Richardson had been there his father would not have given up; 'he [Richardson] was the only person, my father believed, who could say "I will get you right for the Election".' Maurice Macmillan felt 'he should have gone on',[47] while towards the end of his life Macmillan himself admitted that he would have tried to do so, 'If the doctors hadn't frightened me that it looked possibly "malignant".'[48] Had the trusted Sir John Richardson been in London on the night of the 7th/8th, Macmillan's career – and British history – might well have taken a very different turn. Politicians like Roy Jenkins have continued, in full vigour, after a prostatectomy, and even in the state of British medicine in 1963 it should hardly have been cause for retirement in a man as strong as Harold Macmillan proved to be for the next twenty-odd years.

After the doctors jointly had told Macmillan, that Tuesday afternoon, that he had to go to hospital at once for an operation, and though still in spasmodic pain, he managed to attend a party that evening for the No. 10 staff, to celebrate the return to Downing Street. Rab, the only minister attending it, was drawn to one side by Macmillan and told, for the first time, of the doctors' diagnosis, but, according to Butler's biographer Anthony Howard, Butler received the impression that the doctors were going to be able to 'patch him up' in order for him still to make his keynote speech at Blackpool that Saturday, with the implicit hint that he might be asking Rab yet again to stand in for a month or two. At this agonising party, the Prime Minister continued going to and fro between his guests and his doctors, still trying (in the words of Harold Evans) 'to delude himself that it would be possible for him to go to Blackpool to address the rally on Saturday'. At about 6.30 he told Evans that he 'was feeling much better and there was a chance they would be able to get him through Blackpool'. But 'ten minutes later the doctors had assembled. Ten minutes after that Tim came to look for me in the party. The decision – an operation immediately. . . . The PM would go to hospital at 9 o'clock. . . . The operation would be on Thursday morning.' The Chief Whip, Redmayne, wanted to join the discussion, but was barred from doing so by Tim Bligh; 'a reflection of the feelings that had been building up that the Chief Whip and Lord Poole had been unduly harassing the PM to declare his intention to retire'.

Macmillan then came downstairs with Sir John Richardson, 'and swept us all into the study'. He was clad, Evans noted, in his dressing gown with the red and blue facings of the Brigade of Guards 'over pale blue pyjamas and the old brown cardigan . . .'.

I told him what I proposed to say in the announcement, and then posed the critical question I would have to answer, 'does this mean the PM will resign?' Was it unfeeling? Walking up and down by the windows, in the half light of the table lamp, he threw up his arms in a dramatic gesture. 'Of course I am finished. Perhaps I shall die. You can say that it is quite clear that I shall be unable to fight the election.' I asked, did he *really* want that to be said. He said 'Yes,' and so I went away to rejig the draft. . . .

When Macmillan told Rab of his decision, about not being able to fight the election, Evans noted that he 'seemed rather surprised and said that surely this was going rather far, but shrugged his shoulders'.[49]

Macmillan in his diaries continues:

The rest of the evening was rather confused. . . .

At 9 pm I went to the hospital (King Edward's Hospital for Officers) in excruciating pain. Mr. Badenoch came and I was taken at once to the operating theatre, where he put in a catheter, to drain the bladder. This gave me relief. . . .[50]

Home to Edward VII, 9 October

Before he left No. 10, Harold Evans had insisted that the true story should be given to the press, and it duly appeared the next morning. On the 9th, Macmillan from his bed wrote to the Queen, telling her of the necessity for him to resign, while preparing a letter for Home to read out at Blackpool on the Friday, making it clear 'that although I had decided to go on through the Election, this is now impossible . . .'. When Home came to visit him in the nursing home that day, by his own account 'the question of my succession to Macmillan had simply not crossed my mind.' But Macmillan then pressed him to consider taking on the leadership. Home replied that he was 'happy in the Foreign Office, and in the House of Lords which I had never contemplated leaving. . . . He seemed to accept that, and said that he had concluded after much thought that Lord Hailsham might be the best choice. . . .' Home agreed, and left it 'that he would continue his talks with him and others'. Macmillan then asked Home, in his capacity as President at the Conference for that year, to take his message to Blackpool and invite 'those whose business it was to do so, to take soundings about the future leadership'.[51] According to Macmillan's own amendment to Randolph Churchill's book, before going to hospital Macmillan had told Home:

> that in some circumstances it might be necessary for him to lead the Party. Home replied that if enough time were allowed someone would emerge. The next day, before his operation, the Prime Minister saw Home again and told him that no one was emerging and it would almost certainly be his duty to disclaim his peerage and slip into the front line. Home was still reluctant but said if no one did emerge he would accept a draft.[52]

Home then left the nursing home, not enjoying the journey to Blackpool 'with these grim tidings'.[53]

Throughout the 9th, Macmillan suffered more pain and unpleasantness, with the catheter getting blocked, which involved a 'rather tiresome clearing of it'. He ended the day: 'wrote up the diary, read Bible (Samuel I) and also Wolfgang Michael'.[54]

Operated on: 10–12 October

The following morning, 10 October, the operation took place. Macmillan remembered little about the rest of the day, or the following day, and in the post-operative anaesthetic wooziness he would certainly not have been inclined to return to the hurly-burly of running a government. Macmillan remembered the 12th as being: 'A horrible day – with perpetual "spasms" which were very painful but happily not dangerous.' Nevertheless, when Sir John Richardson posed the clinical question about how much he was drinking, Macmillan was able to answer with a quip recalling the famous advocate, Sir Edward Carson, when cross-examining a witness:

'Do you drink?'

'That is my business.'

'Yes, but have you any other business?'

His diary continued:

The *public* events of these days – October 11th onwards – are quite beyond my control. I decided nothing about myself and gave no instructions about anything or anybody. The conduct of the Government I have handed over to Butler but I shall take this back as soon as I am able to do so. But I fear that all kind of intrigues and battles are going on about the leadership of the Party. Perhaps those who were so anxious to get me out will now see the disadvantages. . . .

This seems to suggest that Macmillan was already regretting his decision and was not going to relinquish the reins immediately, or lightly. '. . . D. and Maurice came for short periods today – but I was very weak. The Queen has rung again – the third time. . . . The Queen Mother has also telephoned. But it has been a bad day, and I can't understand what they are saying. . . .'[55]

Chaos at Blackpool: 10–12 October

Macmillan added that he hoped 'the *image* of the Party is not injured by all this public disputing.' This was indeed a pious hope, given the total confusion into which the Tory Party convened at Blackpool had been thrown by the news of his illness, which hit the Party Conference like an Exocet missile. First the Prime Minister was going to resign; then he was not; finally, he was ill and unable to continue, with the succession still wide open. Never had any British party conference met in such confusion – and certainly not a Tory one. It was on the Thursday afternoon that Lord Home,[56] as Chairman of the Conference, peering out at the assemblage over his half-moon, granny glasses, rose to read the Macmillan message, to an audience of 4000, 'hushed with anticipation that something ill was in the wind':[57]

The Conservative Party has always had the *faith* to honour the things that history has taught us to cherish and revere. But it has also had the courage to grasp what is new and fresh, so that a constant process of renewal and reinvigoration takes place in our national life. . . .

God bless you all.

Home recollected how, at the time, 'All of us felt a long way from the happy days when "we had never had it so good". . . .'[58] When he sat down, something like hysteria engulfed Blackpool, all in the fullest glare of the television cameras. No one present would ever forget the scene of frenzy, more reminiscent of what the Labour Party had experienced three years previously than the calm discipline normally associated with such High Tory occasions; it was certainly in marked contrast to the recent Labour Party Conference, dominated by Harold Wilson, with his pipe and Gannex mac, and his air of public gravity, disporting himself as the newly arrived international statesman. Writing for the *Sunday Times*, the veteran war correspondent Alan Moorehead was reminded of the fracas of an old-style US presidential convention, 'living on its nerves. . . . the rival groups were forming . . . and not even Chicago could have outdone the scurrying . . . the canvassing, the hourly shifting in the betting, the mood of fatal self-induced excitement. . . .' It was like 'a fireworks display that gets bigger and better as it goes along, and in the end no one knew where to turn for certainty . . .'.[59] The fireworks were exacerbated by the arrival of Julian Amery and Maurice Macmillan, coming – so it seemed (certainly at least to Hailsham) – as personal emissaries from the Prime Minister's sickbed to press the suit of Lord Hailsham. At the same time, and rather more damaging to the Hailsham cause, the explosive Randolph Churchill also arrived on the scene, hotfoot from America and complete with 'Q for Quintin' buttons which he passed round – even to Hailsham's principal opponent, Rab, who recalled consigning his to the waste-paper basket.[60]

From the cabals that formed and reformed in the foyers of the Imperial Hotel ('that awful hotel', as it remained ever after in Rab's memories),[61] it was clear that over the summer the younger contenders Macleod, Maudling and Heath had been relegated, leaving Hailsham and Butler the clear favourites. The Conference swiftly fell to primeval warfare, with the two rival camps motivated as much by common antipathy for each other as by any positive motives. 'Stop Rab' and 'Stop Quintin' became the cries, but in fact each candidate swiftly set about defeating his own cause. The more self-destructive of the two was Hailsham, who had begun by rushing off to a neighbouring constituency to deliver a typically boisterous speech, including a 'Get well, quick' message to Macmillan. All Hailsham's actions seemed at the time to show how out of touch he was with the stricken leader's intention already to resign. Nevertheless, years later Hailsham claimed that Macmillan had sent for him on the eve of the Conference and told him 'unequivocally' that he wanted him to be 'the next leader', though Hailsham had gone to Blackpool in the belief that Macmillan 'was thinking in terms of Christmas, not that week'.[62]

Hailsham Pops

Immediately after Home had made his announcement, Hailsham charged into the limelight, and threw his hat into the ring by declaring that he was prepared to relinquish his title to lead the fight under the name of plain Mr Hogg. Home, who until that moment had been Hailsham's man, was shocked, and delivered an unmistakable rebuke for Hailsham's exhibitionism, saying later:

> Had I known that he intended to throw his claim to the leadership into the ring within a matter of hours, I would have tried to dissuade him from it then and there, for people never like being bounced, and least of all at a time of emotional stress. . . . there followed a swift reaction against his candidature. . . .[63]

It seemed to prove, Home thought, that 'all his first judgements were usually wrong'. Redmayne recalled Hailsham, speaking at great length and being 'very dull', because he 'had too much on his mind to concentrate on his address'. At times Hailsham seemed almost incoherent. Nevertheless, he received the biggest ovation that Redmayne could ever recall: 'it was hysterical'.[64] Harold Evans thought darkly in terms of a 'Nuremberg Rally', but observed how 'the Establishment (and some others) reacted with curled lips'.[65]

The circus continued in the halls of the Imperial Hotel, with Hailsham, the television cameras all focused on him, brandishing his year-old child in the air, and mixing baby-food in front of the arc-lights. Supporters marched through the streets of Blackpool, shouting 'We want Hailsham'. These were truly astonishing scenes for the Party that traditionally prided itself on dignity and restraint. Macmillan in his London hospital bed was appalled when the reports reached him. 'Alas for Hailsham,' observed Redmayne, 'the cork had popped too soon. . . . his was a spent force after that night. . . .'[66]

In front of the gaze of the electorate, the Tory Party seemed to be tearing itself to pieces, even more devastatingly than the Labour Party had done three years previously. Disappearing almost unnoticed in one sentence in *The Times* that Thursday morning was a glowing letter from President Kennedy, despatched on the fatal day of the 8th, congratulating Macmillan on his 'indispensable role in bringing about the limitation of nuclear testing' (the ratification of which Kennedy had just signed), and praising his 'signal contribution to world peace'.[67] Appropriately, it was the last official communication Macmillan would receive from Kennedy while still Prime Minister.

Butler's 'Limp and Faltering Voice'

What of the natural *prince héritier*, the man disappointed in 1957, but who had served Macmillan so long and loyally in a variety of roles ever since? His protagonists still claim that Macmillan deviously swindled him out of his birthright; yet the more one learns of Butler's mandarin, fastidious role at Blackpool, the more one questions whether he ever seriously wanted the top job. In the words of his opponent, Hailsham, 'like Ferdinand-the-Bull, he sniffed at the flowers and ran. I don't know why. . . .'[68] To supporters and opponents alike, Rab's performance was both surprising and disappointing. He himself admitted afterwards that already by June he had reached the defeatist conclusion that 'it was almost inevitable that the Conservative Party would choose a younger man. . . .' He claimed that '. . . I certainly put my hat in the ring and did my best to show that if I were wanted, I was available. . . .'[69]

One reason for Butler's diffidence can be found in Philip Goodhart's semi-official history of the 1922 Committee when he records that John Morrison, the Chairman of the 1922 Committee, had called upon Butler just before Rab went out to Rhodesia. John Morrison's message for Butler was simple and direct – 'The chaps won't have you.' On his return from the Victoria Falls Conference, Rab naturally asked friends on the Executive whether John Morrison's assessment was accurate. The answer was a bleak 'yes'.[70]

At his most bitchy, Harold Wilson (who always regarded Iain Macleod as the Tories' best electoral bet) dismissed Rab as 'the churchwarden turned caretaker. . . . Poor Rab, he's got the worst liability you can have in politics, the look of a born loser. . . .' (Of Hailsham, he thought, 'we'd murder him'.)[71] Butler's official biographer, Anthony Howard, accuses Macmillan of having laid a cunning 'trap' for Rab to walk into at Blackpool; then promptly proves that no trap was necessary, by drawing attention to his 'strong fatalistic streak' and his 'marked reluctance to exert himself'. ('It's hard', adds Howard, 'to think of any other leading politician who would have behaved in the passive way that Rab did.')[72] At Blackpool, Rab's speech struck his listeners as flat and uninspiring, delivered in what Peregrine Worsthorne described in that week's *Sunday Telegraph* as a 'limp and faltering voice'.[73]

According to Macmillan's own archives, right at the beginning of the Conference Rab had telephoned from Blackpool to say that he hoped there would be no reference to who was actually to lead the Party into the election, and that Macmillan should say he was not going to give up, on the principle that it would be better for him to stay than that there should be someone new.

Iain Macleod is alleged to have remarked once that Rab had had placed in his lap a 'golden ball. . . . if he drops it now, it's his own fault,' and – in his own language – Enoch Powell once spoke of the 'loaded revolver' handed to Rab.[74] But this was not the language of Rab. Perhaps the kindest that can be said of him was that, with so much of the dedicated civil servant in his make-up, his basic loyalty to the notion of Party unity was what ensured his own defeat in 1963. 'It is not a principle of the Conservative Party to stab its leaders in the back,' Arthur Balfour observed after the Carlton Club meeting of 1922, 'but I must confess that it often appears to be a practice.'[75] At various times, and by various writers (not least by Iain Macleod in his famous 'Magic Circle' review in the *Spectator* of 17 January 1964), it has been suggested that Rab was stabbed in the back by Macmillan. Certainly there is truth in Macleod's claim that Macmillan was 'determined that Butler . . . should not succeed him'. But Macmillan saw it absolutely clearly, by his own lights, that Rab's vacillations (never forgotten since Suez) disqualified him as Party leader; and also that these same vacillations, in autumn 1963, made him unsure whether he himself actually wanted the job.

Enter Home

Alec Home recalled the visitors to his hotel room becoming 'more and more insistent and more numerous',[76] as well as more exalted, and on the Friday morning (11 October), in the language of the American Convention that had so taken over at Blackpool, he reluctantly agreed to be 'drafted', if a 'draft Home movement' gathered momentum. Among those at work on the reluctant peer, his predecessor, Selwyn Lloyd, who had all but disappeared into obscurity since the unhappy events of the previous summer, played a significant part. Tim Bligh reported back to Macmillan at King Edward's (according to Harold Evans) that Home had acceded 'provided Quintin did not proceed with his candidature. But Quintin, having opted to be Mr Hogg, wasn't playing; it would have made him look too, too silly. So they all returned to London with the dilemma unsolved. . . .'[77]

The first thing Butler heard of Home's entry into the lists (the 'Gaitskell' to Hailsham's 'Bevan' and Butler's 'Morrison', so Howard suggested in the *New Statesman* that very day) was – according to him – not until the Saturday afternoon when Home told him, 'I'm going to see my doctor on Tuesday.' '. . . I said "Why?" and he said, "Because I have been approached about the possibility of my becoming the Leader of the Conservative Party. . . ."'[78] (As Home himself remarked later, in his whimsical manner, the doctor 'unfortunately said I was fit!')[79] Soundings had swiftly proved Alec Home's effectiveness as a block to Hailsham, and as an alternative to Butler. The arguments for him looked persuasive; in terms of seniority versus age, at sixty, he was about right; he had substantial political experience, and his time as Foreign Secretary had given him standing in the world at large; he was tactful and well liked in the Party; on the other hand, he was 'the fourteenth Earl' and he did not show well on television. But, most important of all, he had the stricken Prime Minister's support.

As Blackpool ended on Saturday the 12th, the BBC satirical programme *That Was The Week That Was* marked the impending departure of the man from whom the British satire movement had derived its original impetus, with William Rushton, cast as Macmillan, coming in from the wings to sing 'The Party's Over' in a broken voice. The BBC received a record flood of protests.

The scene now returns to London. But Blackpool had left the Tory Party bruised and shaken, and it would be a long time before it would recover – certainly not before the forthcoming election. From Rab downwards, Macmillan was blamed for his decision to announce his resignation in the middle of the Party Conference, thereby turning it into an American Convention. 'The Labour Party is the party of revolution,' explains Lord Fraser of Kilmorack, then Sir Michael Fraser, Director of the Conservative Research Department, 'therefore you expect a certain amount of blood-letting – parties don't like things that they are unaccustomed to – dissent, internal wrangling in public. . . .' Though ever an admirer of Macmillan, the timing of his resignation announcement was, he thought, one of his greatest errors; this 'could easily have been avoided and did the Party severe long-term damage . . .'. Fraser felt that Macmillan had been 'very badly advised', but also allowed due excuse for the severity of his illness at the time.[80]

Lying in bed over the weekend, in a still half-drugged coma, Macmillan had allowed his mind to flicker back over historical precedents. Queen Victoria had not consulted Gladstone on his resignation in 1894; while Bonar Law had made it clear that he was too ill to be consulted by George V. Macmillan could easily have followed Bonar Law's option, but duty told him that this would have been 'a mean evasion, unfair both to the Queen and to the Party'. And it had been 'intimated to us quite clearly from the Palace that the Queen would ask for advice. After all I had served her for nearly seven years and it was no surprise to me that she should wish for my help. . . .' He had time to reflect on the curious ironies of fate; had a socialist MP, Wedgwood Benn, not wished to renounce his title, there would have been no Joint Select Committee, appointed the previous year, which recommended that unwilling peers should be given the right to disclaim; and had its work not led to passage of a Bill by that very July, only ten weeks before the crisis, neither Hailsham nor Home could have even been considered for the premiership. In which event, 'Butler must have succeeded, almost without challenge. Out of such slender threads are woven the fortunes of states and men. . . .'

On Monday the 14th, still only four days after his operation, Macmillan was feeling better, strong enough (despite the protests of his doctors) to take a hand in the crisis which his illness had precipitated. But only just; still woozy from the anaesthetic, it all required a major act of mind over matter. The Chief Whip and the Lord Chancellor came to see him in hospital, though he was, he admitted, 'too weak to do more than hear their impressions of Blackpool'. These were hardly encouraging; doubtless he recalled A. J. Balfour's remark to the effect that he would sooner take advice from his valet than from a Conservative Party Conference. There followed several long passages in his diaries which indicate that the deliberations over the succession during the next four days were more complicated than suggested by what was published at the end of the Macmillan memoirs.

The reasons for his reticence were a desire not to inflict unnecessary pain on colleagues who had become contestants, notably Hailsham, but also perhaps because he was beginning to run out of literary steam. His diary entry for the 14th, written up in King Edward VII's, reveals that, although both Redmayne and Dilhorne were 'in principle, "Hoggites"', they had been:

> rather upset at the rather undignified behaviour of Hogg and his supporters at Blackpool. It wasn't easy for him, since whenever he appeared he was surrounded by mobs of enthusiastic supporters. But it was thought that he need not have paraded the baby and the baby food in the hotel quite so blatantly or talked so much at large. This is said (by both L.C. and Chief Whip) to be turning 'respectable' people away from Hogg. Nor need he have talked so much about his giving up his peerage and going into the House of Commons at this stage. After all, I was not yet politically dead – certainly not buried. So Hogg (who really had the game in his hand) had almost thrown it away. But the movement against Hogg (on this account) had not gone to Butler or Maudling but to Home. The 'draft' Home movement was in reality a 'Keep Out' Butler movement. I was struck by the fact that both Lord C. and Chief Whip agreed on this analysis and

that both are, or were, supporters of the Hogg succession. Both are against the Butler succession on the ground that the party in the country will find it depressing. . . .

He continued on a note of acute self-regret at having decided to resign, which would not diminish with the passage of the long years ahead:

One thing stands out clearly – Julian Amery and Maurice were right all along when they told me that I could sweep the board at Blackpool. Had I not been struck down on last Monday night by this filthy disease, I could have reduced to nothing all the Lambtons, Nigel Birches, etc. in the party – at least temporarily. We would have had a battle – or running fight till February – then we would have all got together for the Election. Now we are in disarray.

I feel almost tempted to step back into the ring, but I know it would be folly. I have lost the great moment – Blackpool. 'The Spirit was willing but the Body was weak'. . . .

It was a last moment of truly agonising ambivalence. He lay in bed fretting about:

the underlying struggle. It is really the old one, I feel. Hogg (with all his absurdities and posturings and emotions) represents what Stanley, and John Loder, and Boothby, and Noel Skelton and I tried to represent from 1924 onwards. Those who clamour for Butler and Home are really *not* so much shocked by Hogg's oddities as by his *honesty*. He belongs *both* to this strange modern age of space and science *and* to the great past – of classical learning and Christian life. This is what they instinctively dislike. . . .[81]

He was genuinely saddened by Hailsham's self-disqualification; although, as noted at various times in these pages, he had expressed concern at Hailsham's periodic lack of balance, he would always regard him as 'one of the finest men I knew – a big man, a great churchgoer, and idealist. But he didn't always do himself justice; there was an excess of boyishness. . . .'[82] Success in Moscow had sent Hailsham's stock soaring – perhaps out of proportion to his actual performance; but there was also another factor of mutual sympathy and understanding that may have drawn Macmillan towards Hailsham. Like Macmillan, Hailsham had been wronged, his first marriage had been ruined by an interloper, a dashing officer of de Gaulle's wartime Free French: 'He came back on leave,' recounted Macmillan, 'and found her in bed – both of them. So it was a hard thing for him, such a nice boy and such a sweet boy. No, he's suffered . . . he was a gentleman, and a Christian. . . .'[83]

By the night of that Monday, Macmillan nevertheless recognised that, at Blackpool, Hailsham had pressed the self-destruct button. Maurice Macmillan called in, accompanied by Oliver Poole, at 6 p.m.:

> They were both calm and firm. The unlucky coincidence of my physical breakdown with Blackpool conference had created rather a shambles. But the basic situation was the same – the party in the Country wants Hogg; the Parliamentary Party wants Maudling or Butler; the Cabinet wants Butler. The last 10 days have not altered this fundamental fact.

That night Macmillan slept better for the first time, noting that 'The various pains are settling down or changing their venue.'[84] Before he prepared himself for sleep, however, he compiled a 'minute of instructions' for the procedure to be followed on his succession, for reading out to the Cabinet by Butler the following day. He wanted to avoid the criticism which arose after Eden's resignation in 1957, that consultation – confined chiefly to members of the Cabinet, sounded out by Kilmuir and Salisbury – had been *too* limited. Consequently he now instructed that the Lord Chancellor (Dilhorne) be charged with sounding out the Cabinet; the Chief Whip (Redmayne) would contact all other ministers and Conservative MPs; Lord St Aldwyn would canvass active Conservative peers in the House of Lords; Lord Poole would report on the views of the Party outside Parliament. It was now clear that, sick as he was, Macmillan was still going to hold all the strings in his hand until the very last minute, controlling events from his bed in King Edward VII's. Although he had, in effect, already resigned, he felt duty-bound not to go through the formal act of resignation until the problem of the succession was satisfactorily resolved. This was a decision that would later provoke the criticism that he had injured the Queen's prerogative.

Macmillan Switches to Home: 15 October

The following morning, the 15th, his first caller was Tim Bligh, who relayed to him how 'alarmed' Home had been by Hailsham's behaviour at Blackpool: 'He had thought that they might be the result of a man being a show-off. He now believes that it was because the person concerned was actually mad at the time. . . .'[85] There had also been a call (to Home) from Ormsby-Gore in Washington, 'in a great state, to say that if Lord Hailsham was made Prime Minister this would be a tremendous blow to Anglo-American relations and would in fact end the special relationship. It was believed that the Ambassador had been talking to the President. . . .'[86] Bligh was followed by Butler. Macmillan showed him his minute of instruction for the Cabinet, to which Rab (according to Macmillan) 'seemed to acquiesce willingly enough'.[87] That afternoon, all the contenders for the succession trooped into King Edward VII, one after the other: Home, Macleod, Heath, Maudling and Hailsham. In a 'Top Secret' memorandum, 'Notes for the Record', compiled by Bligh at Macmillan's dictation, it was noted that Hailsham 'seemed quite relaxed although I thought rather white . . . said the position of Lord Home taking over would be absurd . . .'.[88]

Macmillan meanwhile settled down to draft a long letter to the Queen, meticulously setting out the course of events of the past days – and partly also to clear his own mind. To the Queen he explained his motives: '. . . I am anxious that everything done so far should be amply recorded in writing and not give rise to the kind of confusion by which previous crises have afterwards been poisoned with very ill effects to all concerned. . . .' He turned out the light that night, feeling that the 'situation is certainly very confused', but also quite decided in his own mind that Home was now the best possible, if not the only possible solution. 'The important fact in my view', he dictated in his 'Top Secret' memorandum,

is that Lord Home's candidature has not been set forward on his own merits but has been thought of as a last-minute method of keeping out Mr. Butler now that Lord Hailsham has (according to the pundits) put himself out of court by his stupid behaviour (at Blackpool). . . .

. . . Apart from Home's actual lead, I am impressed by the general goodwill shown towards him, even by those who give reasons in favour of other candidates, and I cannot fail to come to the opinion that he would be the best able to secure united support. . . .[89]

At the time, Macmillan's last-minute enthusiasm for Home provoked puzzlement among political observers. But, to anyone reading through the unpublished Macmillan diaries, it should come as less of a surprise. Despite the possible black mark against him for having been a 'Munichite' Home emerges consistently – whether as Commonwealth Secretary or Foreign Secretary – as the only member of the administration never to attract any opprobrium, even in a moment of pique. There is nothing but respect, and liking.

Obviously, until the door was opened in July 1963, there was no prospect of Home, as a peer, ever being considered for the premiership, but in the last few weeks Macmillan's thoughts had already been turning in Home's direction, in the event of Hailsham failing. Of course, there was the charge of snobbism – Eton, ex-Christ Church (though not the Brigade of Guards), and all that – to which Macmillan was very much open, and he had always been passionately attached to the principles of primogeniture. (Home, he recorded in his memorandum, represented 'the best of the old governing class'.) But, at the time, Macmillan's dominating consideration was that Home was the *only* leader behind whom the majority of Conservatives would rally, without splitting the Party.[90]

'The Whole Burden': 16–17 October

On the 15th, Knox Cunningham worried that Macmillan had had 'too many' visitors;[91] the Matron of King Edward VII, normally an all-powerful figure, was likewise far from pleased; while a distraught Dorothy accused the unfortunate Tim Bligh of being a 'murderer to arrange such a programme'.[92] The day was followed, Macmillan recorded, by a rather restless night:

The whole burden of the Premiership has fallen on – or been assumed by me. But it is a terrible tangle and no one seems to know what is to be done. The Press this morning is less excited

– except the *D. Mirror*, which is vile. It is a comfort to feel that they insulted Churchill even more grossly. . . .[93]

On the 16th, the surgeons gave Macmillan some relief by removing the catheter. Sir John Richardson recalled him reading the paper 'placidly while the whole matter was being dealt with, his face never changed and he was quite incredibly detached and dignified over the whole business . . .'.[94] Throughout the day more ministers trooped through the hospital, to the bemusement of the other patients perambulating in the corridors. Though no longer a minister, Selwyn Lloyd ('dapper, agreeable and sensible') also called, driven in his battered old Mini, and declared himself for Home; 'Butler was much disliked by the Party Organisation, particularly the Women. Why this is so, no one seems to know.' Keith Joseph (then at Housing, Macmillan's old post, and later nicknamed by him 'the Mad Monk') was for (1) Maudling, (2) Butler: 'He is fearful of Hogg's eccentricities, especially in foreign affairs.' On the whole Macmillan was left with the strong impression that almost all the ministers, 'whether Hoggites or Butlerites or Maudlingites, agreed that if Lord Home would undertake the task of P.M. the whole Cabinet and the whole Party would cheerfully unite under him. Sandys (Commonwealth Secretary) feels this specially strongly.'[95]

Meanwhile Dilhorne, a vast figure of a man once described by David Bruce as overlapping on both sides of the Chancellor's Woolsack, was busy about his soundings; 'like a large Clumber spaniel sniffing the bottoms of the hedgerows', in the delightful imagery of Rab Butler,[96] and on the 17th he came (on two separate visits) to the hospital. Macmillan nerved himself for what would be the decisive day. There were no less than eight visitations, and Macmillan insisted on going downstairs to receive them in a larger room (in fact, the much tried Matron's office). Tim Bligh and two Garden Girls from No. 10 in the meantime set up office in King Edward's for all that day. Knox Cunningham, there to note down what took place for the Memorandum to the Queen, recorded his master that day as being 'nervy, but in full command as always, even though at times in considerable pain . . .'.[97]

The key soundings carried out by Macmillan's emissaries, brought to King Edward VII on the 17th, clearly indicated a preponderant first choice of Home. 'There were *strong pro*-Butlerites;

but equally violent *anti*. There were strong – very strong – *pro*-Hailsham – but very violent *anti*. On Maudling the feelings were not so strong in either direction . . .', recorded Macmillan. Among the three hundred Tory MPs consulted, the largest group ('not by much, but significant', commented Macmillan)[98] were for Home. In the Lords, two to one backed their fellow peer, the fourteenth Earl. The poll of the constituencies (conducted in extreme haste, and therefore probably not very conclusive) suggested about 60 per cent for Hailsham, and 40 per cent for Butler, but with strong opposition to both. Such had been the speed of events, however, as Macmillan noted, the constituencies at the time hardly knew that Home was a serious candidate, though both the pollsters reckoned that 'everyone would rally around Home'.

Did Dilhorne Get It Wrong; or Was Macleod 'Too Clever by Half'?

But the decisive sounding – and it was a document of considerable historic importance – was contained in the answers to Lord Dilhorne's question, put to each member of the Cabinet individually: 'Who do you think should succeed the Prime Minister?' The result was a first choice of:

For Alec Home	10
For Butler	3
For Maudling	4
For Hailsham	2

(Alec Home was not counted as voting.)

Dilhorne next worked out 'the position if Alec Home is treated as eliminated, by taking the second votes of those whose first choice was Alec'. These totals were:[99]

For Butler	8
For Hailsham	5
For Maudling	7

Dilhorne, making careful emendations to the typewritten text in his own hand, then went on to work out the position if Home and Maudling were eliminated, which was:

559

> For Butler   12
> For Hailsham   7

If Home and Hailsham were eliminated, the result was:

> For Butler   14
> For Maudling   5

This suggested that some Cabinet members had had second thoughts. Dilhorne concluded his document with the following comment for Macmillan:

> . . . I think I should tell you that while the majority expressed themselves as willing to serve whoever was chosen, Iain Macleod, R. Maudling, and Edward Boyle expressed themselves as very strongly opposed to Hailsham. Powell's view was 'on no account Quintin' and it is I think very doubtful if he would serve with him. Duncan Sandys is now strongly opposed to Rab.
>
> Hailsham also told me that he was by no means certain he would serve if R. A. Butler was chosen. He said he would have to reach an understanding with him and he talked a lot about the honourable course for him, if he was not chosen, being to retire from public life. He also expressed himself strongly opposed to Alec Home leaving the House of Lords but did not give me his reasons. . . .

Perhaps the most remarkable revelation in the Dilhorne document, however, is that *Iain Macleod* is shown as having been one of the ten who voted, as his *first choice*, for Home. Yet, in a revolt that shook the Party to its roots the following day, Macleod, accompanied by that traditional rebel, Enoch Powell, declared that he *would not serve under Home*. Dilhorne's breakdown reads as follows:

> Those whose first choice is *R. A. Butler*
> R. A. Butler
> Henry Brooke
> Enoch Powell
>
> Those whose first choice is *Alec Home*
> Deedes
> Boyle

Soames
Hare
Macleod
Heath
Sandys
Marples
Myself
Noble

Those whose first choice is *Quintin*
Quintin
Thorneycroft

Those whose first choice is *Maudling*
Maudling
Boyd-Carpenter
Erroll
Joseph

(In this I have not counted Alec Home as voting.)[100]

(In the event of Home being eliminated, Macleod would cast his vote for Maudling; if Home and Maudling were eliminated, for Butler; if Home and Hailsham were eliminated, for Maudling.)

On the face of it, it looked like tactical voting of a curious order. When shown the evidence, former colleagues of both Dilhorne and Macleod and those who had played a part in the events of October 1963 expressed astonishment, if not disbelief. Reactions ranged from 'Reggie [Dilhorne] must have got it wrong' to 'Macleod was being too clever by half again.' Enoch Powell, Macleod's fellow 'rebel', was characteristically forthright, declaring, 'It's a forgery. . . . Macleod would never have backed Home'; then refused to commit himself as to who the implied forger might have been, and finally modified his reaction to say: '. . . I think it would be more true to say that Dilhorne did not hear what was being said. . . .'[101] Redmayne, who had never seen the Dilhorne document before, found it 'intriguing', and thought that Macleod was being 'devious';[102] the cynical Rab was 'not at all surprised. . . . Macleod [his former protégé in Central Office] was very shifty, much more than you think. . . .'[103] Lord Eccles, Lord Fraser of Kilmorack and

Lord Aldington (then Deputy Chairman of the Party, who was a participant in the Macleod–Powell revolt on the night of 17 October) were all insistent that it would have been out of character with Macleod, and that – as one of them said – 'Reggie got it wrong . . . he often did.'[104] Yet Dilhorne, though not a well-liked figure among his Tory colleagues, was a lawyer trained not to 'get things wrong', and in his lifetime was adamant that his record was correct;[105] on the other hand, Baroness Macleod of Borve was equally adamant that her husband would *never* have voted for Home.[106] Finally, Macmillan's own view was simply, 'Well, you know . . . Macleod was a Highlander. . . !'[107] But there it stands, in black and white, one of the more 'inexplicable' of all the events of those bizarre days.

Revolt in the Night: 17–18 October

Until the final decision was taken for Home late on the 17th, Macmillan continued to play the cards close to his chest; Barber, his former Parliamentary Private Secretary, after a visit came away from the hospital still with the impression that Hailsham was his favourite.[108] Dilhorne and his fellow pollsters all returned to the hospital in the afternoon. It was a killing schedule, and a super-human feat for a man of sixty-nine who had barely emerged from a major operation; Macmillan simply recorded in his diary: 'All this tired me very much. It took 2½ hours in morning and 2 hours in afternoon. But after 6, the work began and I dictated memorandum for the Queen (should she ask my advice) and also signed formal letter of resignation. . . .'[109] Knox Cunningham rounded up his account of that last full, and long, day of Macmillan's premiership: '. . . Tim and I saw him safely settled for the night and left at 11.30 pm. It was a black night outside and I still recall the blindness and almost the feeling of panic, caused by the flashes of the press photographers as we drove away. . . .'[110]

Meanwhile, for all Macmillan's precautions, word about the soundings in favour of Home had somehow leaked out. At 9.30 that night, Anthony Royle MP received a message to ring Ian Gilmour at Hailsham's house in Putney.

The news was as gloomy as we had feared. The decision had definitely been taken to advise the Queen to send for Lord Home.

This was greeted with dismay and amazement by all of us. Whilst we all admired Alec Home as an honourable and able man, no one really considered during the events of the past ten days that he either wished to be Prime Minister or would be chosen. As the Fourteenth Earl of Home who had had an unhappy career in the Commons, it was going to be difficult to fight a general election in 1964 under a man with a similar but more aristocratic background as Harold Macmillan's. . . .

Then:

As the night wore on, it became clear that the decision was unacceptable to many in the Party. Julian Amery and Peter Thorneycroft at Putney endeavoured to persuade Quintin to serve under Home. Hailsham considered that the decision was a disreputable compromise and that he would on no account do so. He telephoned Alec Home and was extremely rude to him. . . .

At the same time, a heated meeting was taking place chez Enoch Powell between Lord Aldington, Powell, Macleod, Maudling and Erroll (President of the Board of Trade). Powell telephoned Home to say that, whereas 'there was no one in the party for whom I had more admiration and respect,' he, unlike Hailsham, 'was not a reluctant peer, and we were now proposing to admit that after twelve years of Tory government no one amongst the 363 members of the party in the House of Commons was acceptable as Prime Minister.' In consequence, Powell and Macleod subsequently refused to serve under Home; Maudling did not refuse.[111]

Discussing events at Julian Amery's house in Eaton Square the following morning (Amery, it will be recalled, had been one of the leaders of the pro-Hailsham lobby), Royle noted 'a very real danger of a grave political crisis with Alec Home being asked to form a Government by the Queen and key members of the Cabinet refusing to join the new Administration . . .'. Amery rang up his father-in-law in King Edward VII at about 10 a.m.; but by this time the 'revolt' had been contained: 'The Prime Minister', continued Royle, 'was robust and confident and quite clear on the recommendation that he was going to give the Queen. He had already sent in his resignation and at 11.45 the Queen was coming to the hospital to receive his advice. . . .' Amery then spent much of the morning trying 'to persuade Quintin to be reasonable'.[112]

For Macmillan, Thursday, 18 October, had started with an agitated call from Tim Bligh at 7.30, reporting 'a critical situation', and with news of the 'Revolt in the Night'. At 8.30 Bligh and Redmayne were round at the hospital. His doctor, John Richardson, found him – although he had evidently anticipated the revolt – 'in a terrible state; old and grey and furious. . . . to any of us who knew him well, this was no surprise at all and we knew it meant nothing except that he was concentrating with a strength of purpose ordinary people could not understand.'[113] According to his own diary, Macmillan interpreted the 'idea' of the 'rebels' to be:

> an organised revolt by all the *unsuccessful* candidates – Butler, Hailsham, Maudling and Macleod – against Home. Considering their intense rivalry with each other during recent weeks, there was something rather 18th century about this (Fox–North Coalition perhaps) and somewhat distasteful. Home rang up and felt aggrieved. He had only been asked to come forward as a compromise candidate, from unity. He felt like withdrawing. I urged him not to do so. If we give in to this intrigue, there would be chaos. Butler would fail to form a Government; even if given another chance (for Queen might then send for Wilson) no one else would succeed. We should have a Wilson Government; or dissolution; and our Party without even a nominal leader. . . .[114]

Nevertheless, Knox Cunningham continues the story:

> The Prime Minister was firm and Tim set out for the Palace carrying a letter of resignation. At the Hospital the Prime Minister and I worked at an addendum to the document in order to tell of the situation caused by the events of the night. . . .[115]

Weathering this 'most critical moment',[116] Macmillan thus went ahead with his plan unchanged, and – in the laconic words of the final entry in the official Prime Minister's diary:

> At 9.30 AM Mr. Bligh went to Buckingham Palace to hand in the Prime Minister's resignation to the Queen.
> At 11.15 AM, the Queen arrived at the hospital and spent half-an-hour with Mr. Macmillan.[117]

'A Terrible Day': 18 October

There now began, recorded Macmillan, 'A terrible day and very bad for me. . . .' The doctors protested, but Macmillan could 'see no way of shuffling out of my duty. At the end of the day, I can hardly hold a pen. . . .'[118] The resignation ceremony between the sick Prime Minister in his hospital bed and his sovereign, unprecedented in British history, took place downstairs in the King Edward VII boardroom. With his acute sense of protocol, Macmillan insisted on putting on a white silk shirt for the occasion, but – as a sartorial compromise – wearing over it one of his customary and well-worn brown pullovers. He was then wheeled down to await the Queen. 'The poor man had to have a bottle in bed with him,' recorded Sir John Richardson, 'A bell by his side, and Sister was outside the door in case he needed help while the Queen was there. He took all this, as everything else, with supreme detachment and dignity. He was very pale and tense and indeed unhappy. . . .' When the Queen arrived, dressed in a peacock-green coat and matching hat, and accompanied by her Private Secretary, Sir Michael Adeane, she was led into the boardroom and remained there alone with the Prime Minister. Waiting outside, in case of a medical emergency, Sir John Richardson noted that the Queen spoke in such hushed tones as to be almost inaudible: 'there were in fact tears in her eyes, and perhaps why I could not hear was because her voice was not very steady. . . .'[119]

Macmillan recalled in his diary: 'She seemed moved; so was I. She referred to the very long time I had served her – nearly seven years – and how sorry she had been to get my letter of resignation.'[120] It was a scene that remained vividly in Macmillan's memory, and years later he recalled the ensuing dialogue:

She said, very kindly, 'What are you going to do?' And I said, 'Well I am afraid I can't go on.' And she was very upset. . . . Then said, 'Have you any advice to give me?' And I said, 'Ma'am, do you wish me to give any advice?' And she said 'Yes, I do'. . . . So then I said 'Well, since you ask for it, Ma'am, I have, with the help of Mr Bligh, prepared it all, and here it is.' And I just handed her over my manuscript . . . then I read it to her, I think.[121]

He went on to explain how he had wanted the memorandum to be in the Queen's archives, 'to be there as a full justification of any action she might take on my advice'. The Queen agreed with his recommendation that Home was the most likely choice to gain general support, and then 'thanked me, and we chatted a bit more and then she went away.'[122]

It was, as Macmillan liked to reminisce with detached amusement in later years, 'an extraordinary resignation. . . . the bed covers were down, and concealed underneath the bed was a pail with a tube full of bile coming out of me. . . . I made my resignation to the Queen of England for an hour, in great discomfort.'[123] The incongruity of the scene was enhanced by the fact that, in their haste, the distraught staff at No. 10 had only been able to provide the most outsize white envelope, many times too big, in which to house the historic document. This the Queen handed to her short and portly Private Secretary, Michael Adeane, which Macmillan's whimsical eye noted, as the door to the boardroom opened, 'made him look . . . like the Frog Footman'.[124] The Prime Minister's entourage took their leave. Knox Cunningham observed how 'Tim was silently weeping as he said goodbye, but his duty lay at No. 10 with his new master. . . .'[125]

While Macmillan was dozing that afternoon, recovering from his ordeal, an engineer from the Post Office knocked on his door, arriving to remove – with what seemed like almost indecent haste – his scrambler telephone: '. . . I said: Hell, I was Prime Minister two hours ago, you might leave it a bit. No, he said, that's the rule. So that was the end of my power, which has never been restored. Curious. . . .'[126] It seemed a sad way to go; but then the same could be said about much of Macmillan's life.

'So ended my premiership,' he wrote in his diaries; '*January 11 1957–October 18 1963 . . .*'.[127]

Chapter Nineteen

'Life After Death'
1963–1979

... E finita la commedia. *It is tempting, perhaps, but unre-*
warding to hang about the greenroom after final retirement from
the stage.

(*HM*, At the End of the Day)

The most awful thing about old age is the incompetence, the dread
that you will get the kind of old age which would be a nuisance
to everybody, the terrible indignity; one just wants to go without
pain, incompetence or indignity.

(*HM, November 1979*)

On 19 October 1963 there began what Macmillan with his Celtic black humour was wont to call his 'life after death'. It was somehow symbolic, when he talked about 'my death', and 'when I died',[1] of how he regarded the end of his long political life as being an end to life itself, beyond which there was nothing to look forward to. He was still debilitated for many weeks after his prostate operation and the exhausting demands of his last days in office, and no one – least of all the 'dead' Prime Minister – could have reckoned that life would in fact last for nearly a quarter of a century more; or that they would be years packed with activity and interests, right up to his extreme old age, culminating with a kind of political rebirth, or (in Macmillan parlance) a resurrection. At the time, however, frustrated at having removed himself from the office that he was already feeling he need never, should never, have left, he watched with impotent gloom as the Tory Party creaked to defeat. Life away from No. 10 did indeed seem all too much like a form of 'death'.

There were still rumblings about the succession, which demanded the tired man's intervention. At lunchtime, shortly after the Queen had departed on the 18th, he was rung up by the new Prime Minister, Home, 'rather agitated, but I urged him to try to pin down Butler and Maudling. . . .' By that evening,

> The rather unholy alliance between Butler, Maudling, and Hailsham, but really got up by Macleod and Powell, began to crack. Perhaps Butler realised that he was merely being used as a 'stooge' and that the young men would desert him as soon as they had broken Lord Home.[2] I think Hailsham – who has been apparently in a highly emotional state since Blackpool – realised this and being a straight and honest man began to break away. . . .[3]

The following morning Macmillan received the news that all the disaffected ministers, excepting Macleod and Powell, had agreed to serve and Home had left for the Palace 'to kiss hands'. Macmillan was delighted, though grumbling at the inconsistency of the

'Hoggites'; 'is there something worse about the 14th Earl than the 2nd Viscount? All this inverted snobbery is absurd. . . .' He noted that he had been 'very unfairly attacked about this', yet argued defensively that, had he not intervened, 'there might have been complete disaster'. It was 'quite untrue', he continued – possibly with posterity in mind:

> that I was determined to 'down' Rab. It *is* true that of the three I would have preferred Hailsham, as a better election figure. All this pretence about Rab's 'progressive' views is rather shallow. His real trouble is his vacillation in any difficult situation. He has no strength of character or purpose and for this reason should *not* be P.M. . . .[4]

There, it was said.

The next day, his second Sunday in hospital, though the multiplicity of events made it seem like a cycle in Cathay, Holy Communion was brought in: 'a nice little service'. He gave thanks that '. . . Alec and Elizabeth are now established – and, of course, very grateful. I feel sure that he is the right choice. . . .' On the whole, the Sunday press were 'not too bad' – bar the *Sunday Mirror*, which was 'hysterical' at the choice of the fourteenth Earl. Lying in bed in King Edward VII, at peace after the hurly-burly of the past week, he began to reflect on its events. The more he did so, the more he was 'astonished' at 'the failure of Rab, who was Deputy P.M. and put in charge when I went to hospital, to *do* anything about the crisis . . .'. As for his own options, he could, of course 'have merely resigned on entering the hospital and when asked for advice by the Queen, said I was too ill to give it. This would have got me out of all this trouble, but it would have been very wrong as regards the Queen and the party. . . .' With three hats in the ring, there had to be a compromise candidate, and Home:

> was the only compromise candidate possible. Incidentally, he was the best candidate of the 4 – but that is another argument. I suppose all sorts of false accounts will pass muster for the true history of this transaction. But I feel that my memorandum protects both the Queen and me in the eyes of history. . . .[5]

The dissidents, Macleod and Powell, would – he assessed – 'do a great deal of harm. . . . Fortunately, neither of them are popular figures. The first is thought to be too ambitious, the second too rigid. . . .'[6]

Indeed, barely was his political 'corpse' cold than the charges that he had offended constitutional prerogatives flooded in. Dissident backbenchers like Humphry Berkeley insisted, and continued to insist, that Macmillan had acted improperly in his determination to deny the premiership to Butler.[7] On 17 January 1964, Iain Macleod published a three-page article in the *Spectator*, entitled simply 'The Tory Leadership' but which was charged with political dynamite. Macleod described in great detail the events surrounding the succession and his alleged role in it (though, as seen in the previous chapter, there remained an important discrepancy between his and Dilhorne's account of the crucial vote). While cloaking it about with the niceties of party loyalty, he made plain his belief that Macmillan and Redmayne had been injudicious. He spoke damningly of the top Tory grandees who, he claimed, had manipulated the leadership selection: 'eight of the nine people mentioned in the last sentence went to Eton . . .', and later went on to remark, 'It is some measure of the tightness of the magic circle on this occasion that neither the Chancellor of the Exchequer nor the Leader of the House of Commons had any inkling of what was happening. . . .'[8] The Macmillan memorandum to the Queen had – Macleod felt – left the Crown with no other option.

Enoch Powell went even further. Accusing Macmillan of 'gross impropriety' in disclosing communications with the Sovereign in his memoirs, he charged him with having 'deprived the Queen of the exercise of her principal prerogative . . . deliberately (and, in retrospect, conclusively) . . .'.[9] In the Tory Party of the day, Macleod's allegations about the Etonian predominance were regarded as arch disloyalty; his vivid phrase the 'magic circle' was to hang like a millstone around his neck, destroying any hopes he might have had for his own future claim to the leadership. In the opinion of at least one critic, John Grigg, given the closeness of the Tory defeat in 1964, Alec Home might well have won but for Macleod's 'magic circle' article.[10] Macmillan's prediction of the 'great deal of harm' done by Macleod and Powell was certainly no exaggeration. As for his own responsibility, he always stood by the letter he had written to John Morrison, Chairman of the 1922 Committee, on 19 October 1963:

The press has tried to represent that Alec Home was my personal choice. You know well the immense trouble I took to get the views of the Cabinet, the House of Commons, the House of Lords and the Conservative Party generally. . . . I was not anything more than a convenient recipient of this information, and the means by which this advice could be given to the Queen. . . .[11]

Honours; But No Earldom for Macmillan

It was the following day that Macmillan heard that his son, Maurice, from whom he had so painfully long withheld any government job, was to be appointed by Home to be Economic Secretary at the Treasury. He was 'delighted'; the appointment came as 'a great joy to me', and he was gratified to note that it had been 'welcomed very generously' by the press.[12] In his own Resignation Honours' List, none of the Private Office, by whom he had been so well served, had been forgotten. John Wyndham, at forty-three, received a barony. Harold Evans, Knox Cunningham and Dr John Richardson[13] all became baronets, a title resurrected by Macmillan; there were knighthoods for Tim Bligh, at forty-five, and Philip de Zulueta, at only thirty-eight (he had decided to leave the Foreign Office, where the Macmillan years had effectually put paid to a career that would undoubtedly have carried him to the top, to enter the City). There was also an MBE for William Housden, Macmillan's driver for eleven years; and for Mrs Bell, the long-suffering cook at Birch Grove who had jibbed at having to store General de Gaulle's blood among the haddock. Inevitably, there were criticisms of the Macmillan honours: at their quantity (they did seem to set a new inflationary precedent), and at the youth of the recipients. In particular were eyebrows raised at the barony for the Bertie Wooster-like figure of John Wyndham, among those unaware of exactly how much – far beyond being just the court jester – he had meant to Macmillan, from Algiers onwards. But there was also an agreeable historical congruity here, typical of Macmillan; Disraeli had made his Montagu Corry Lord Rowton.[14]

Disraeli, however, had taken an earldom for himself. Macmillan, on the contrary, and in contrast to any of his predecessors, rejected both an earldom and the Garter, preferring to remain plain Mr Harold Macmillan. He accepted only the Order of Merit (in 1976), which he always prized above all other distinctions. The press were as censorious of Macmillan's restraint here as they were of his lavishness towards his subordinates; by elevating his underlings, and not himself, he was showing misprizal for the House of Lords, and the whole system of honours. Certain critics even concluded, by some curious process, that it was a slight on the Great Old Commoner, Sir Winston Churchill, who *had* accepted the Garter on his retirement. Almost apologetically, in his memoirs ten years later, he printed as his only diary entry of those last days:

> The Queen has written to say that she did not offer me the Earldom when she came to the hospital, for fear I would be embarrassed, since she knew my disinclination. But she made it clear I could have it *on her authority* (that is, not 'on advice') if ever I wanted it. This was very gracious. . . .[15]

As with almost everything in Macmillan's life, there was a complexity of motives for this refusal of honour: 'It was not in the family style,' he said, recalling the crofter ancestry;[16] 'Publishers should not have the Garter,' he remarked elsewhere.[17] His letter to the Queen, declining the Garter in March 1964, implied that he felt it should be awarded only for service in a period of national crisis (as per Churchill).[18] To his confidante, Ava Waverley, he wrote about the same time that honours would have given him 'the substance without the shadow', explaining that the Queen understood his 'personal wish – to keep my name unchanged . . .'.[19]

A most important factor for Macmillan, if not *the* most important, was the political future of Maurice, now at last given office; an earldom could have brought an abrupt end to a ministerial career already so long delayed. Undoubtedly, as he had made plain at various times during his Prime Ministership, he did not hold either the Lords or its inmates in the highest esteem; essentially, it was a place for politicians put out to grass. But there was yet one further consideration. Now that he realised he was not going to die of cancer, he wanted to keep open his own political options; at various times over the succeeding two decades he would drop hints, to politicians as far removed as Peter Carrington and James Callaghan, at a return – possibly at the head of a centrist coalition, a new national government, a new 'Grand Design'. It was a dream that lingered on until he was ninety, when, to trumpet fanfares, he did finally re-enter the political arena as the Earl of Stockton.

Whatever the Queen may privately have felt about her first minister's rejection of her honours, her sadness at his departure, at the loss of his wit and wisdom, at his courtly deference, was unmistakable. In a long letter, she thanked him for having been in charge of Britain's policies for the greater part of her reign and for having been her guide, supporter and instructor through the mazes of international affairs. She ended with the hope that, 'some day, later if not sooner', he would yet accept an earldom, 'and continue to take part in public life from the benches of the Upper House . . .'. It was 'difficult', commented Macmillan, 'to conceive a more gracious and generous tribute from a Sovereign to a subject'. For Macmillan, the ending of the relationship, with the greatly enjoyed weekly conversations, was one of the hardest deprivations of 'political death'.

He was gratified when Sir Michael Adeane, the Queen's secretary, called round to give 'His side' of the succession crisis. Hailsham, so it appeared, had:

> wished to exercise the right of advising the Queen, as Lord President. But Adeane resisted this (which was *before* my final audience) on the ground that the Queen had a Prime Minister. Then the idea was put to him that the Queen should summon all the contestants – Butler, Hailsham, Maudling, Home to Buckingham Palace. Under her guidance they would reach agreement amongst themselves. To this Adeane (properly) replied that it was *not* the Queen's duty to resolve the problems of leadership of the Tory party. . . . Adeane told me that the Queen was really grateful to me and that her letter was truly meant and composed by herself.[20]

Though this last came as a considerable consolation to Macmillan, every reminder of his departure from the political scene was grievously painful for him, as it reinforced his growing realisation that he should *not* have gone.

573

Macmillan

Kennedy's Assassination

In the last months of 1963, recuperation for Macmillan was slow. He suffered occasional pain in his war-scarred lower body, and felt desperately tired and depressed. Letters poured in, and, for a time, he had no secretary to help deal with them. ('It seems strange no longer to be able to ring the bell for a "young lady" at any time, day or night. . . .')[21] Photographs appeared in the press of himself and Dorothy, sitting on a bench together in Regent's Park; 'rather pathetic with a distinctly old age pensioner look about us'.[22] They went for a drive to Greenwich; 'how glorious it is, the finest thing in England. . . .'[23] His old friend from war days, 'Alex', came to visit; 'We exchanged reminiscences of two wars like old men, and no doubt remembered . . . the deeds we did that day. . . .'[24] Two days later, on 31 October, he took himself to Macmillan and Co., to resume officially his function as publisher, but with a heavy heart. The faithful John Wyndham came to lunch, and there were more reminiscences; 'We started together 23 years ago. Now I become a Publisher and John a Peer. . . .'[25] But throughout November and December, he still complained of acute depression, and of feeling 'very "low" (as nurses used to say) and on the point of bursting into tears for no reason . . .'. There were a few compensations:

> One of the advantages of being dead (politically) is that I no longer read the papers. . . . Just a glance at the headlines – the deaths, births, and marriages in *The Times* – and that is all. No Sunday papers! I feel a wonderful gain from not having to wallow through all that gossip and dirt – and the time saved allows one to read books.[26]

Still weak from his operation, Macmillan was then to be devastated by terrible news from across the Atlantic. In common with so many other Britons, Harold Macmillan would never forget exactly where he was, and what he was doing, that terrible Friday of 22 November. Together with Lady Diana Cooper, his old admirer from Algiers days, he was spending a shooting weekend with John Wyndham at Petworth, and it was just before dinner that 'We heard the stunning news – overpowering, incredible – of President Kennedy's assassination in Dallas City, Texas. . . .'[27] It was:

a staggering blow. To the causes which he and I tried to work for, it is a grievous blow. For Jack Kennedy's acceptance – of Test Ban and of policy of detente with Russia were really his own – I mean, were *not* shared by any except his most intimate advisers. He took great risks for them – as he did with the policy of ending negro inferiority. . . .[28]

Pestered all that weekend to appear on radio or television, he felt just too 'low' to accept. Three days after the assassination he rallied himself to deliver a moving eulogy in the Commons, his first appearance there since his illness. The fallen President was, he said:

> one of the best-informed statesmen whom it has ever been my lot to meet, and he was altogether without pedantry or any trace of intellectual arrogance. . . . He was always ready to listen to and to be convinced by argument. . . .

Macmillan praised Kennedy's 'fundamental moral and mental integrity', and referred to 'a personal bereavement': 'and we mourn him – and this is perhaps the greatest tribute to Jack Kennedy's life and work – for ourselves, for what we and all the world have lost.'[29] It was only with a considerable effort that he 'got through without a breakdown', he confessed in his diary.[30]

A few days later, alone in a weekend of fog and darkness at Birch Grove, Macmillan reflected on how 'The death of President Kennedy still dominates men's thoughts. No one can yet foresee the effect on American policies; but in spite of assurances by the new President[31] that there will be no change, I doubt whether this will prove true. . . .'[32]

Certainly, whether rightly or wrongly, Macmillan always felt that Kennedy, for one thing, would never have permitted the US to become inextricably bogged down in Vietnam. But it was not only as a statesman that Macmillan grieved Kennedy; his death brought home to him most poignantly the degree of deep and genuine personal affection he had felt for his young colleague, who had been little older than his own son Maurice. He wrote a long letter to his widow, which 'made the deepest possible impression' on Jacqueline Kennedy.

... I kept it in a little desk which I took with me to the Harriman House, and read it over again and again. There wasn't really anything very consoling in the letter, but what really moved me was his taking the trouble. ... I can't think of any letter in my life that affects me so much. ...

That letter marked the start of a close relationship, largely in correspondence not previously published, between the ex-Prime Minister and the attractive young widow. As much as anything else it spoke volumes about the affectionate friendship that had grown up between the two leaders. Macmillan would write pages in his own wobbly hand, often carefully redrafted; Jacqueline Kennedy wrote back 'with no restraint at all on my emotions. ... I only met him six times, but found it much easier to write to him ...', she explained.[33] It began with an eight-page letter, on 31 January 1964, beginning rather formally, 'Dear Prime Minister', then opening her heart to him:

Sometimes I become so bitter, only alone – I don't tell anyone – but I do truly think that any poor school child looking at the record of the 1960s – could only decide that virtue is *UN*rewarded. The two greatest men of our time, *you and Jack* – all you fought for and cared about together – the Atlantic Alliance – how full of charity were your relations always with each other even when unforeseen disastrous things like Skybolt happened. And how does it all turn out? De Gaulle is there [words deleted] and bitter old Adenauer – and the two people who have had to suffer are you and Jack. ...

She recalled how JFK had always kept in his office a photograph of the two together, which Macmillan had signed:

How marvellous you were with him. ... You could just have signed it 'Best wishes, Harold Macmillan', but you wrote on it 'To the man who said – ask not what you can do for your country' – etc – his words. ...

And then I remember this summer – when we lost our son Patrick[34] – and he showed me the letter from you – in your own hand – and you said – in the midst of all your troubles – [it was at the height of the Profumo affair] 'Private griefs are so much worse than public ones' – you were in the most terrible time of your life – but you could write that way to Jack. ...

... you were the only ones who cared about other people – who could look at yourselves with humour. ... you worked together for the finest things in the finest years – later on when a series of disastrous Presidents of the United States, and Prime Ministers who were not like you, will have botched up everything – people will say 'Do you remember those days – how perfect they were?' The days of you and Jack. ...

It was a prophetic thought. She concluded:

I always keep thinking of Camelot – which is overly sentimental – but I know I am right – for one brief shining moment there was Camelot – and it will never be that way again. ...

... please forgive this endless intrusion – but I just wanted to tell you how much Jack loved you – and I have not his gift of concision –

With my unending admiration and gratitude and hopes that you will be happy.

Jacqueline Kennedy[35]

Macmillan, much moved, wrote back at length, addressing her as 'My dear Friend – this is how I used to write to Jack – so I am going to write it to you. ...'[36] (Jacqueline Kennedy was greatly touched; 'I thought that was so lovely, I always wrote him back in the same way. ...')[37] He continued:

First, can I say how grateful I am and glad that you should have written to me. It makes me feel that perhaps I can be of some use – even just as a sort of safety valve or lightning conductor and it makes me think again about Jack and all he was and our strange relationship. You have written from your heart to me, and I will do the same.

Macmillan went on to recall:

When Jack became President, I did not know him. I naturally felt that he – a young man full of novel and exciting ideas – might think I was rather an old horse, ready to be put out to grass. ...

When we met – and the very first time that we met to talk – I felt something had happened. ...

If we were not able to accomplish all we were meant to do, yet we achieved something. For what remains of my life, these years will be of unique memory and comfort.

But for you, I feel terribly sad at something in your letter. You won't, I feel sure, mind my saying this? Of course one becomes bitter. How could you not be? . . .

. . . I am sure you must say this to yourself (as I do) over and over again 'such a waste! such folly! such bad workmanship! can there really be a God, who made or guides the world?'

At some length Macmillan evoked the reactions of the Apostles following the Crucifixion:

when one has this terrible temptation to ask 'Why, oh why?' how terrible must have been the temptation of those simple men who, after the apparent utter failure – of the whole campaign, ending in the meanest possible form of death, by assassination on a cross – somehow managed to get a Faith to carry them on. . . .

He ended:

. . . I shall count it something I can perhaps do for Jack, just being a recipient of letters. . . . I am writing this at home – in this softly beautiful day, with the buds on the trees in the woods, just beginning to get that wonderful purple before the Spring. . . .

. . . May God Bless you, my dear child. You have shown the most wonderful courage to the bitter *outer* world. The hard thing is really to feel it *inside*. . . .[38]

The letters continued, regularly: 17 May 1965 from Jacqueline Kennedy following the unveiling ceremony of the Kennedy memorial at Runnymede:

. . . I don't know why I inflict you with all this – Probably because I don't keep a diary or go to a psychiatrist – I pour it all out on you. Please know that, incoherent as they are, they are written with the deepest respect and admiration – and love.

Jackie[39]

Macmillan wrote back (6 June 1965) expressing gloom at the state of affairs in both countries: '. . . I feel rather sad at what I hear but naturally I am biased and feel that Jack and I ran the affairs of our two countries better than they are being managed now. . . .'[40] The letters continued, through the 1960s, through the assassination of Bobby Kennedy. '. . . I felt something of the agony which old men must have felt in the two wars, as they watched the holocaust of the young . . .' wrote Macmillan,[41] and on beyond Jacqueline Kennedy's marriage to Aristotle Onassis. She wrote to Macmillan on 12 November 1972:

> I have just finished watching you on television with William Buckley. We were three watching you, Ari, my husband, and John my son. There is nothing in all these last long years that has moved me so much, or made me so proud. . . .
>
> Everybody who watched your programme is better for it – especially me! But then you have always been a lifebuoy to me, though you probably don't know that. . . .[42]

Each time they visited each other's country, they would meet. When, at eighty-six, Macmillan was in New York promoting (in his role of publisher) the sales of Grove's Musical Dictionary, Jacqueline was struck once again by his sensitivity when he explained, 'I didn't ask you to the Grove's celebration, because it was November 22. . . . I know that I still can't do anything at all on the day of Dorothy's death. . . .' At the end of his life, she was reminded how every time she saw him 'the great love we had for each other comes back again. . . .' She recalled the 'inspiration' Jack Kennedy had received in the loneliness of the Presidency, from 'having somebody you could speak to almost as an equal',[43] and, after Kennedy's death, to her the solace of Macmillan's friendship was inestimable. On Macmillan's side, the relationship may have started, in the first instance, as correspondence with the widow of the slain President – in Maurice Macmillan's opinion, on account of his father's romantic attachment to Kennedy. But it soon developed into something more, and undoubtedly afforded Harold with unexpected solace, and perhaps a sense of added purpose in his own fundamental loneliness and frustration.

Political Frustrations

As his body and spirits slowly mended, it was not long before Macmillan found political retirement ineffably boring. His mind was as sharp and active as ever. With the retirement (in ill grace) of Adenauer in October, the death of Kennedy made him recognise that – had he stayed on – he would have been *the* leader of the Western world. Now only de Gaulle remained, supreme; and, in the East, Khrushchev (but not for many months). It was all too painfully frustrating. When invited, in December, by David Harlech* to be Chairman of the Kennedy Memorial Fund, he refused, unable to face it; '. . . I still feel *low*. . . .'[44] On 22 December, he was called upon to speak in the debate on the Denning Report about the scandal that had so nearly wrecked his Prime Ministership. Macmillan reckoned his intervention, 'in effect, killed the debate . . .'. On the night of the Denning debate there was a farewell party for the staff at No. 10 – 'friendly but rather sad'.[45] Christmas was reasonably cheerful, shared with the children of the four different Macmillan families. Everybody made a special effort, in what was normally not a happy time for Macmillan. There was the usual shoot: 'saw quite a number of pheasants and several woodcock. Julian Amery has been very kind and sympathetic.'[46]

And so ended the Macmillan diaries, resumed in 1950. Handwritten, they totalled over two thousand pages when typed up, of which an average of nearly 160 pages a year had been kept throughout the seven years of premiership – no mean achievement for a busy Prime Minister approaching seventy.

Macmillan would speak only once more in the Commons, before his final standing down as an MP at the General Election of 1964. It was another elegiac occasion – in the brief debate on the presentation of a memorial scroll to mark the retirement from the House of Commons of Sir Winston Churchill, his old mentor, and the figure he had admired and loved more than any other figure in public life, Macmillan was the last of six speakers. He ended his own last speech in the House of Commons with this tribute to Sir Winston.

Failure and success are, in their different ways, equal tests of a man's character. My right hon. Friend has overcome both

* The former Ormsby-Gore.

triumphantly. These twists and changes of political fortune were not mere accidents. They were the very fabric of his life. Like the prophets of old, he saw into the future with uncanny prescience both before, during and after the war.

So we honour the whole man – what he has done, what he has tried to do and what he is. If I were to try to sum up his true character I can think of no words more appropriate than those which he has himself written on the fly-leaf of each volume of his History of the Second World War. In War: Resolution. In Defeat: Defiance. In Victory: Magnanimity. In Peace: Goodwill. The author called these words 'Moral of the Work'. In fact, Sir, they are the story of his life.

After the debate was over, Sir Philip Goodhart recalled going into the Smoking Room and joining the small group that was clustered around Macmillan. 'That was a marvellous peroration', one of Macmillan's friends remarked, 'but as you were the sixth person to speak, weren't you afraid that someone else was going to use those words of Churchill? They were so appropriate but it would have spoiled your own peroration.' Goodhart recalls that Macmillan's eyes 'hooded and unhooded'. 'Ah, yes,' said Macmillan, 'but I had five other perorations prepared.' He was a professional to the end.[47]

As he watched in impotence while the Tories headed for disaster under his successor, Macmillan understood so well what Churchill must have suffered in 1956. When the redesignated Sir Alec Douglas Home made his debut in Washington for talks with President Johnson, the US press hardly noticed, while the Beatles occupied the first five places in the Top 100. In Britain, Harold Wilson was stumping the country, proclaiming 'a chance to sweep away the grouse-moor image' and his vision of 'an exciting new Britain'. Macmillan knew it would turn out to be anything but; he knew Wilson, respected his virtuosity as a political operator, but perceived that his 'purposive' Britain would prove to be a con job. In contrast to both himself and Wilson, Home – for all his sterling qualities – was hopeless on 'the box', the new electoral battleground where Macmillan had so shone in 1959.

It seemed in retrospect almost a miracle that the October election of 1964 was won by Labour with a wafer-thin majority. In November 1963, when he had just left Downing Street, Macmillan had been predicting, 'the Socialists *must* win a substantial and perhaps a smashing victory *if* 400 Liberal candidates really appear in the field. . . .'[48] But, not for the last time in British political history, the giant Liberal resurgence Macmillan had been fearing ever since Orpington collapsed like a bubble as soon as the British public had to concentrate its mind on serious matters – like a general election. Nonetheless, it was the *fact* of defeat, not the margin, that counted. As Wilson swung into the fantasy of his 'hundred days of dynamic action', followed inexorably by inflation, the years of economic crisis and industrial strife that made even 1961 to 1963 look like a golden age, to the accompaniment of Britain's steady decline as a world power, Macmillan's mood darkened. In the latter days of his stewardship, he had seen a distinct upswing in the economy; but, whereas in the panic month of July 1961 just over a £100 million in reserves were lost, the new Chancellor James Callaghan showed he could lose that amount in a day. To Macmillan it all seemed horribly like a replay of the nightmare of 1945, from which he, Rab and others had rescued the Party and the nation.

For all his abiding respect and affection for Alec Home, he came to realise painfully that he might have promoted the wrong man. To Ava Waverley he wrote, in September 1965:

> . . . I promised to write, but I have no news. When one's life is over, there is no news – it's just waiting. I naturally feel sad at being out of it all. That illness was a sad blow for me. Without being conceited, it was a catastrophe for the Party. I did my best for 6 or 7 years to build up Rab into my obvious successor. But it was no good . . . Hogg was far the best – the only one of genius. But he destroyed himself at that unlucky Blackpool, with his baby and his tin of infant food. Alec did his best – with courage and dignity. But he could not impress himself on Parlt. or people enough for a PM, admirable as he was as Commonwealth Secretary, or as Foreign Sec. . . . He was an Edward Grey, not an Asquith. It is sad, because he is such a fine man. . . .[49]

In later years he came to recognise that Home 'didn't have enough fire in his belly – he wouldn't say bugger off. . . .'[50] He admitted that, perhaps, it would have been better for the Party if Rab had been his successor after all; 'then we could have won the election in '64 . . . though we would have lost the next one.'[51]

Distressed by what he saw, Macmillan, however, stuck to his belief that as an old actor it was 'more artistic, when the curtain falls on the last performance, to accept the inevitable *E finita la commedia*. It is tempting, perhaps, but unrewarding to hang about the greenroom after final retirement from the stage.' Though tempted to offer himself for the leadership of a national government, he resolutely stayed off the stage. It was hard, when he saw such a mess being made of things at No. 10; still writing to Ava Waverley on Downing Street stationery, he described himself as 'a fallen minister, fallen, like Satan, from the Whitehall of heaven, without hope of return . . .'.[52]

Life at Birch Grove

In frustration he buried himself at his beloved Birch Grove. While Dorothy was alive, the otherwise gloomy halls of the house that Nellie Macmillan built were cheered by the noises of grandchildren in whose interests she was always ruthless – as well as by Dorothy's own tempestuous, often explosive presence; the gardens bore the bright imprint of her personality, enhanced the innate horticultural skill of a Cavendish. Macmillan particularly rejoiced in the woodland glades of Birch Grove, carpeted in spring with bluebells and primroses. To the outside eye, however, family life at Birch Grove was never cosy. A researcher, working there on the Macmillan memoirs over many years, Anne Glyn-Jones, found Macmillan 'a heart-broken man': 'you could see it in his eyes. It was not just the family, but distress with what had happened to the world. . . . he expressed confidence and optimism to cover this up. . . .'[53] There was a deep intrinsic loneliness in the house. Meals were often silent affairs, with Dorothy and Harold sitting at opposite ends of the long table. In the absence of the legendary Mrs Bell, Dorothy's cooking was 'uneatable'; Katie Macmillan (who was sometimes known to exaggerate) could vividly recall 'roast rabbit, with the head still on'.[54] Anxious to get out in the garden, Dorothy hated luncheon and dinner parties. The Macmillans seldom entertained guests at the weekend (the visitors' book shows chiefly the names of relatives, or of the children, and their children). Apart from sleeping in different bedrooms, they often sat in different rooms – with Harold plunged in the voracious reading in which Dorothy, whose taste ran to Georgette Heyer and gardening books, could never participate. Occasionally the scene would be lit up by visits from his confidante, Ava Waverley, or his admirer, the coquettish Diana Cooper in a large hat and a small Mini. (To research workers and Garden Girls, he would proudly display a framed photograph of himself with that ageless *femme fatale* – then hurriedly whisk it away when Dorothy entered the room[55] – though, to them, as to many others in his life, he always seemed frightened by individual women.) Nor was the family totally at peace within itself; Katie, devotedly loyal to Maurice, resented (not unjustifiably) the way in which she felt his career had been blighted by her father-in-law; others could never forgive their mother for the damage caused by her liaison with Boothby. On her side, Dorothy would occasionally demand that the resident research workers lock-and-bolt every aperture, as otherwise 'Katie will come for the furniture!'[56] Often, at Birch Grove, there seemed to be more than a slight aroma of sulphur.

Yet, if to outsiders the atmosphere seemed strained, it had immeasurably improved over the years of the premiership. Ever since the triumphant Commonwealth Tour of 1958, when Dorothy had stolen so many hearts, he had come to appreciate her more, as a partner; increasingly he relied on her instinctive judgement and advice; with the pressures of office, he leaned on her calmness. At the same time (though she continued to see him until her death), the passage of years had greatly diminished – though not removed – the sting of the Boothby affair. There seemed absolutely no reason why, now, they should not settle down to a few years of a comfortable, and peaceful, old age together. Macmillan on his side had never ceased to be devoted to her.

Death of Dorothy

The year 1966 began on a sombre note for Macmillan. On 14 January he wrote to Jacqueline Kennedy:

> My dear friend,
>   . . . I have had rather a sad time since I saw you. Last year brought a great deal of sorrow. Firstly the death of my young grandson, and secondly the death, just before Christmas, of my eldest brother and life-long friend and partner. . . .

My dear boy Joshua[57] was a charming creature and would, I am sure, have had a very successful and happy life. His death was a sad blow to us all. . . .[58]

The death of Dan Macmillan, eight years older and ailing ever since Harold's absence on the 'wind of change' tour,[59] had been expected; nevertheless, he had always been Harold's idol and, with his brilliant classical mind, a subject of intellectual envy. As Macmillan wrote in his letter to Jacqueline Kennedy, 'it makes a great gap in my life. There were so many shared memories of childhood which can never be replaced. . . .' But the death of Jishi, who was particularly dear to Macmillan among the grandchildren (the factor of primogeniture also weighed most powerfully with him), was a much more grievous blow. Macmillan never forgave the media, who hounded him for comment in his bereavement; 'have *they* never had a grandson who died?', he wondered.[60] Why should they persecute him, even long after he had left office?

In the spring of 1966, Harold and Dorothy set off on a trip to Scotland. When they returned to Birch Grove, those close to them noticed a marked change in her; 'there was a new serenity and kindness and gentleness', a new benign sweetness.[61] It was as if there had been some sort of deep reconciliation; to her maid, Dorothy herself made some reference to 'a second honeymoon'. On 22 May Dorothy prepared to go out to a point-to-point near Birch Grove. Putting on her boots in the hall, she complained to Edith, the parlour-maid, 'Oh, I've got such a pain in my back.' 'You should have taken a coat out yesterday,' replied Edith. A few minutes later, she dropped dead in the hall, of a massive heart attack. Because of her great weight, a door had to be taken down to convey her upstairs. Harold, who was napping at the time, knew nothing of what had happened and was 'desperate' when told.[62] So ended their tragically brief retirement.

There was widespread grief at the death of Dorothy Macmillan. She was 'one of the most gracious of ladies who ever occupied Ten Downing Street that I have ever known,' said Quintin Hogg, and all the Garden Girls would have agreed; 'She was a wonderful help and inspiration to her husband,' he added. 'Wherever she was she radiated a happiness and confidence which was infectious,' was the tribute of the Prime Minister, Sir Alec Home.[63]

Macmillan was desolate. For all the anguish she had caused him, from that unhappy year of 1929 onwards, no one realised more than Maurice and the other children the 'great bond' that had always existed between their two parents. She was, he wrote to Eden in reply to a solicitous letter of sympathy, 'the centre of our whole family and it seems impossible still to believe that she was struck down without warning. . . .'[64] Unable to drive a car, and in many practical ways rather helpless, Macmillan depended on her in more ways than he realised. To him she was, as Oscar Nemon the sculptor noted while doing his busts of them in 1963, 'almost like a walking stick'.[65] In Macmillan's own words, in one of the rare moments when he would ever discuss his life with Dorothy, 'She filled my life. . . . I thought in everything I did of her. . . . she was devoted to me. . . . I had my reward . . . in doing what was difficult, I had my reward in the end. . . .'[66] But, with the Grecian tragedy that seemed to preordain so much of Harold's life, that 'reward', precariously achieved in old age, had lasted only a grievously short time.

Dorothy was buried in the parish churchyard of Horsted Keynes, under an austere gravestone of Scottish granite, already inscribed for the day when Harold would join her there. Nobody then could have imagined he would survive her by another twenty years, and more. Meanwhile, Lord Boothby, the cause of so much havoc and who always claimed (rather unchivalrously) that Dorothy had held him 'in thrall',[67] married again within a year of her death, claiming that he had destroyed all her letters. He, too, lived another twenty years, predeceasing Macmillan, the man whom he had done (in the words of *The Times* obituary) 'a grave personal wrong',[68] by only a few months.

With Dorothy's death, a new loneliness descended on Harold Macmillan, and on Birch Grove. 'When she was around, you felt the house was full,' recalled one of the former Garden Girls, Jane Parsons, who had spent so much time there; 'when she died, Birch Grove suddenly seemed very quiet.'[69]

In the emptiness of the large house, of which so much seemed to be kitchen areas where there were still the old-fashioned bells, still inscribed 'Mrs Macmillan' (his mother, Nellie), 'Mr Arthur' (brother), 'Mr Harold', 'Lady Dorothy's sitting room', 'Master Maurice, day nursery', he moved into an attic over the kitchens that he called 'my fortress'. (As it had no room for a guest, Carol Faber, his eldest daughter, sometimes wondered whether perhaps he had moved in out of fear of being entrapped by a woman, in his widowhood – for example, Ava Waverley?)[70]

On the retirement of Mrs Bell, and the death from cancer of Edith Baker, the masculine Lady Bowls Champion of Hampshire but marvellous domestic, who had done so much to spruce up Harold's clothes, a certain neglect set in. Life became increasingly spartan for the ex-Prime Minister – partly through his own choosing. At regular intervals he alarmed John Richardson with intimations that he was dying; but invariably the answer came back that he had the heart and lungs of a thirty-year-old – 'It was just that his spirits were down.'[71] To colleagues like Martin Redmayne, there was always this quality about him: 'if I have to write an epitaph for Harold Macmillan, I shall say, among other things, that his world left him lonely. . . .'[72]

More Bereavements

Family bereavements did not cease with Dorothy's death in 1966. For years the youngest daughter, Sarah, had been a source of constant worry. An unhappy girl, unhappily married with two adopted sons, and separated, she was in and out of clinics with an acute drink problem, the 'Cavendish curse' that she shared with all three siblings. Some close friends (by whom she was much loved) reckoned that her distress could be dated back to her late teens, when someone, with monstrous unkindness, had informed her that Boothby was her father. Regardless of whether it was true or not, or whether he knew it or not, Harold had always shown Sarah special affection, and after Dorothy's death it was he who – acting in utmost secrecy, outside the public gaze – picked up the pieces, flying, on occasion, incognito, to Geneva to visit her in a Swiss clinic. Friends of hers reckoned that he acted 'above and beyond the call' – even for a father. Sarah was pathetically appreciative, and contrite: 'I can never tell you how grateful I am,' she wrote from a Nyon clinic shortly after Dorothy's death: 'for all you have done for me and the boys. I only wish I had had the courage to manage on my own. I really did try, as things are thank you again, very much. . . .'[73] The following year, back in a clinic, '. . . I know there is not much sense in apologising, but I do want you to know how very very sorry I am for all the trouble and anxiety I have

587

caused you. . . . you must feel that there is not much hope. . . .'[74] Possibly exasperated, and disappointed, Macmillan sent back a rather remote, typed letter: '. . . I am so happy to know that you are comfortable and look forward very much to talking to you. I'm equally grateful for what you said in your letter which is very nice to have. . . .'[75]

In 1969, Sarah was back in hospital again, with Macmillan assuming responsibility for her two young boys. It was no mean burden for a widowed ex-Prime Minister in his mid-seventies. On 26 March of the following year, Sarah died; with a verdict of 'accidental death'. There was a brief funeral ceremony at Horsted Keynes; one psalm, 121, one hymn, 'Lead us Heavenly Father . . .', and then Sarah was laid to rest beside Dorothy, the parental headstone engraved simply: 'SARAH MACMILLAN, 1930–1970'.

Replying to letters of condolence, Harold wrote, 'One of the drawbacks of old age is one seems to get more and more of these blows. . . .' There were still more to come.

The bereavements were not just confined to within the family. Churchill, who had died in 1965, was followed to the grave, in 1969, by Macmillan's beloved hero in the Second World War, Field-Marshal Earl Alexander of Tunis, 'Alex'. Macmillan was the only civilian pall-bearer.

That same year, his old chief from those days, Ike, also died. For nearly five years after his retirement, they had lost contact; then, in a letter more resembling the correspondence of old school friends than of two former heads of government, Eisenhower wrote from his farm in Gettysburg relating how he had lost, but rediscovered 'your home address': 'I immediately determined to regain contact with an old friend whom I have known so well both in war and peace. I heard vague rumours to the effect that you had, after leaving government, rejoined your publishing firm. . . .' He went on to complain, in the same breath, about how he had to write in order to pay his farming debts, and how his Party was 'without a recognised leader and I am bombarded frequently with demands of all kinds, advice, counsel and help. . . .'[76] Macmillan wrote back, agreeing that farming was unprofitable, and that it was:

a bore having to be mixed up in politics. Fortunately, I have no public work to do of this kind and a limited amount of private work. Naturally, people consult me, but they never take my advice, so I give it without much sense of responsibility. Yes, indeed, we managed things much better in our time![77]

On a publishing trip to the States Macmillan made a point of flying to Palm Springs to see his ailing friend in convalescence. It was the last time they met. From his deathbed in Walter Reid hospital in January 1969, Eisenhower expressed fears that Wilson's Labour government were wrecking the Special Relationship.[78] Stressing reluctance to criticise his own government from retirement, Macmillan however replied, at some length, 'the truth is that we have, now in Britain, a government of very clever people – far cleverer than I or my government – who are at the same time curiously stupid. . . .'[79] Amused, the dying Eisenhower wrote back, appreciatively, in his last letter a month before his death, '. . . I got quite a chuckle out of your description of how the minds of your Labour leaders work. . . .'[80] Only an acute attack of jaundice prevented Macmillan from attending the funeral at Arlington.

The following year, the man whom he had saved in Algiers and who had rejected him twenty years later, Charles de Gaulle, departed. Two years later, in 1972, Macmillan lost John Wyndham (Lord Egremont), whose role in his life also dated back to those North African days. Somewhat lost by the end of the Macmillan era, he had taken increasingly to heavy drinking. Nevertheless, in response to such pleas as 'alas! I need a nanny more than ever now,'[81] Wyndham had contrived – as in the past – to bolster Macmillan's spirits by jokey letters and frequent invitations to Petworth. When his old chief complained, rather self-pityingly, of being 'an old man battered by Fate', Wyndham riposted: 'If you ask me, Fate was battered by you. . . . poor woman, you wrestled with her and laid her flat on her back on the floor, that is why the younger generation and generations to come will salute you. . . .'[82] When Wyndham died the following year, aged only fifty-two, Macmillan wrote in *The Times* praising his 'high qualities on a more serious plane . . . this almost romantic quality of chivalry and affection . . .'.[83] Almost his surrogate son, the death of John Wyndham left a big hole in the lonely old man's life.

And so, one by one, family and friends made their various exits. In one of his sallies of black humour, in his nineties, Macmillan remarked that memorial services were the 'cocktail parties of the geriatric set'.[84]

Back to Literature

To occupy his ever active mind, Macmillan had wisely gone back to publishing as soon as he possibly could. Though he felt 'diffident about being much use after all these years . . .',[85] he immediately made his mark on the family firm. The last years of Dan's long reign had, he found, 'left (or created) a lot of problems . . .'.[86] Dan, the classics scholar, had been a dedicated publisher in the family tradition, but by 1963 the firm seemed somewhat behind the times. It was making no money. At their nineteenth-century premises in St Martin's Street, where clerks beavered away at Bob Cratchit desks in dimly lit rooms, the spirits of hirsute publishing ancestors, and of Kipling and Hardy, hung heavy in the portraits that lined the panelled staircase. Lured by a hefty redevelopment offer, in the summer of 1965, Macmillan and Co. moved to a conventional contemporary shoe-box in Little Essex Street. For all his nostalgia for the past, Macmillan explained the new wind of change: 'after we moved our warehouse out to Basingstoke, life here became more impracticable. We need more modern offices. . . .'[87]

In the four years that followed his return to the firm, Macmillan took some monumental expansionist gambles in restaffing, relocation and rationalisation. Some members of the family firm viewed his return in 1963 with consternation; Alan Maclean, a senior editor and later director, recalled his arriving with ideas that were 'incredibly out of date'. Then he went away for a week, 'to think things over, and suddenly reappeared – totally in touch. Some mysterious kind of osmosis had taken place. . . .'[88] Macmillan's new thinking and the zest he injected into the firm, though already in his seventies, helped project it back into prosperity. New writers, like Muriel Spark and John Wain, were recruited, or boosted; old bestsellers like Rebecca West, Pamela Hansford Johnson and her husband, C. P. Snow, were pushed with greater vigour. Poached shamelessly from Faber's by Harold himself in the late 1940s, Snow, a Labour supporter, went to Macmillan's with *The Masters* in 1951; and thereafter he recalled how Macmillan himself 'always read all my books, especially *Corridors of Power*, to check the parliamentary stuff. . . . his criticisms were always worth hearing, anything he says on books, in fact. . . .'[89] On the publishing of *Last Things* in 1970, Macmillan wrote to Snow congratulating him on 'the sincerity of your writing and its deep meaning in the tortured world of

men and women alive today. I feel it a great privilege that my
family and I have been associated with this massive enterprise.' Recalling his earlier 'acquisition', C. P. Snow replied: 'your support
and friendship have been more important to me than you can
realise. . . .'[90]

Abroad, in the Commonwealth new and old, the Macmillan
empire expanded by leaps and bounds, with Harold Macmillan himself flying the flag. Welcomed as an ex-statesman,
Macmillan would riposte with quite unblushing modesty that he
had come merely as a publisher; and the sales of Macmillan school
books soared accordingly. From a UK sales figure of £2.5 million
in 1963, turnover rose to £40 million in 1985 (it had been £50,000
in 1865 at the time of Alexander and Daniel).

To publishing, Harold Macmillan brought something of the flair
that had worked so well at No. 10 – unflappability, and a capacity
to delegate, plus that great sense of history. His colleagues enjoyed
working with him, rather more than with the highly nervous Daniel.
'He liked to discuss things,' said Frank Whitehead, the Deputy
Chairman until 1983, who had been with the firm since 1937:

> You came away always knowing exactly what we were going to
> do and there would be no U-turns. He had a marvellous way of
> working, and let us get on without interfering. . . . If things went
> wrong, there were never any recriminations but 'Well, how do
> we put it right?'[91]

Nicholas Byam Shaw, the chief executive, remembered him, after
his death, as having 'the capacity to broaden any argument,
to explore untapped possibilities in an otherwise ordinary
proposal . . .'.[92]

The present author can equally recall Macmillan as publisher,
reading when eighty one of his books, in manuscript and proof, no
less than three times, and producing many valuable suggestions.

In 1967 Harold stepped down from the chairmanship to make
way for Maurice, returned to political limbo once more; three years
later, when Heath returned to power and Maurice was back in
office again, he took over again, and – having been made the
company's first President – continued to play an active role even
after his grandson, Alexander Macmillan, became chairman. In
fact, to the last months of his life, he seldom missed a weekly visit

to Little Essex Street, and remained remarkably in touch with the publishing world – and his authors. Said Alexander, 'no major decision is made here without consulting him; he's so experienced – and he remembers everything. . . .'[93] It was the impetus given by Harold that launched Macmillan and Co. into republishing the updated edition of Grove's Musical Dictionary. Retailing at £850 a set, it was twelve years in preparation and a vast investment of risk capital, as well as occupying the major part of Harold Macmillan's time back in Little Essex Street, despite his admitted blind spot for music. On behalf of promoting Grove, already in his late eighties, he stumped the world indefatigably, like any good publisher touting his wares. From the success of Grove, Harold then went on to push the company on to publishing *The Dictionary of Art*, which was halfway through its twelve years of gestation when he died.

Macmillan recalled how his uncle Fred had once snapped at a publisher's reader who, in his report on a book, had commented, 'I think this book will have a large sale': 'And my uncle said, "I never asked him that question, it's nothing to do with him. I wanted to know whether it's good. . . ."'[94] As a former Chancellor of the Exchequer, however, Harold Macmillan always made it a top priority to know, too, whether a book would sell. Directors were removed whom he felt had 'no business sense'.[95] Beyond the great enjoyment that publishing in the family tradition gave him, he also regarded it as something of a duty: 'Like the Chatsworth estate is to the Cavendishes; Macmillan and Co. is to us like a great family estate. We can't throw it about, it's our responsibility. . . .'[96]

In his retirement, he always claimed that he enjoyed publishing 'more than ever', and hand in hand with it went his voracious appetite for reading. He was almost certainly Britain's best-read Prime Minister, and he retained this appetite until his dim eyesight failed him completely, a few years before his death. His family feared that his inability to read might have sapped that indomitable will to go on living; but no – he then discovered the Speaking Book for the Blind, exhausting their stocks with calls for Dickens and Trollope by the bushel. He loved re-reading old favourites, like *Anna Karenina* and *David Copperfield*. 'It's rather fun reading books you haven't read for a long time,' he once said: 'I come back to them with great pleasure. And of course you can understand what you didn't understand when you were seventeen or eighteen.'[97] Only rarely did he read modern novels: 'You know, when you get old, it's like poetry; you don't read romantic poetry, you read epic. I can read Homer, but I don't really want to read Shelley or something. . . .'[98] Yet he never closed his mind to new experiences; he returned from his first trip to China in 1979 ('as a publisher, not an ex-PM'), almost bubbling over with excitement at discovery of a 'new novel', which almost eclipsed the Great Wall and his meeting with Chairman Deng. It turned out to be *For Whom the Bell Tolls*: 'Quite wonderful, like one of Walter Scott's early novels. I can't think why I never read it before – or why we never published it!'[99]

On such contemporary topics as sex in the modern novel, for all his own personal prudishness he expounded carefully thought-out views that were anything but Victorian stereotypes. Sex in literature was, he reckoned, 'all very interesting in general, but not in detail'. The modern novel was 'like reading a medical journal';[100] Thackeray had managed it much more effectively in *Vanity Fair*. *Lady Chatterley* he dismissed as fundamentally a 'silly book'. The Greeks had a better device for dealing with sex and violence: 'We didn't *see* Agamemnon. . . . it was all done by the messenger or by the chorus, or something. We didn't have the murder actually on the stage. They didn't approve of that. And I think it's more dramatic without, don't you?'[101] To Macmillan the great solace of reading was, as he once remarked, 'Peace, peace within yourself – that you can only get from books. . . .'[102]

Memoirs and Travel

Meanwhile, as a major solace to the frustrations of relinquishing office, within a year of his retirement he had plunged into writing himself – his own memoirs. Symbolically, the date of starting was 4 August 1964 – the fiftieth anniversary of the outbreak of the war that had so rudely disrupted his life and that of his Britain. The intention had been clearly in his mind years previously, when he had started his copious diaries. He also remembered Churchill's filing system while in power, the box marked 'Copy to Mrs Hill' into which went carbons of all his memoranda, speeches and correspondence. Likewise, on leaving No. 10, Macmillan's faithful team of Private Secretaries ransacked the files for copies of official documents – to the shock of that stern disciplinarian, Burke Trend, the Cabinet Secretary. Frequent remonstrances from Trend led to the removal of some particularly sensitive matters before publication; but it was largely closing the stable door, on what was a ministerial indiscretion (inspired by his old chief, Churchill) on a major scale. Originally conceived as a three-volume work, *The Winds of Change* was eventually contained (with difficulty) in six volumes, totalling nearly four thousand pages; there were critics who thought this was too much, and much too stodgy, and possibly more stringent editing might have been enforced by another publisher. Be that as it may, those in Macmillan's who had to deal with it were profoundly impressed by the professionalism, the meticulous cleanness of the voluminous manuscripts, the restraint of corrections in proof. For the best part of nine years, the mammoth work went on – until Volume VI was published, also with stylish timing, on the tenth anniversary of his retirement. Most of the volumes were bestsellers, helping to swell the family coffers. After the success of the memoirs, there then followed *The Past Masters* in 1975 (a series of personal portraits of past British leaders, from Lloyd George onwards), and his complete *War Diaries*, 1943–5, in 1984 (it was dedicated to the memory of his comrade in arms, John Wyndham), and finally (to mark his ninetieth birthday), *A Life in Pictures*.[103]

Promoting the books of others, as well as his own, gave Macmillan the opportunity to travel extensively, which he took to with a relish and energy extraordinary for an octogenarian. He returned to countries he had visited while Prime Minister; to Canada and Australia, to India and Nigeria and Egypt. He saw Japan for the first time, and came away fascinated by the 'new industrial revolution of the chip'. In 1979, as excited as a schoolboy, he made his first trip to China, the country which he so long ago urged both Dulles and Kennedy not to confront, and which – with Nixon's encouragement – had now suddenly opened its doors to the West. He was received with sedulous attention, by his junior in years, Chairman Deng ('very sophisticated, intelligent, and extremely well informed, with a nice sense of humour . . .') and enthused about what he saw. He thought China was now in its 'Directory period, after the Terror . . . and now what follows the Directory?'[104] He told his hosts, 'I know now that the Chinese are truly civilised. They eat banquets at a sensible hour [e.g. 6.30 p.m.], don't hang around for long speeches and let you go home to your own whisky and soda by 9 o'clock.'[105] At the Great Wall he showed signs of flagging, but when offered a wheelchair he indignantly refused, stumping the interpreter and causing some loss of face to the Chinese caterers by declaring: 'I'd much rather have a brandy-and-soda.'[106] The following year, wearing his hat as former Foreign Secretary, he flew to Vienna for the twenty-fifth anniversary of the signature of the Austrian Treaty of 1955. There he was amused at the expense of his French opposite number (and his senior by two years), Antoine Pinay, who had teasingly asked the stone-faced Gromyko: 'Whatever happened to our dear old colleague, Monsieur Molotov?' (knowing him to have been in disgrace these past twenty years). Back came the pat and unabashed answer: '*Il est libre, mais très malade.*' 'Rather one up to the Russians, I think!' exclaimed Macmillan.[107]

The same year also saw his most triumphant foreign tour in retirement – to the United States, to sell Grove's Musical Diction-ary. Already approaching eighty-seven, he managed a lunch and dinner speaking engagement almost every day for ten days, and his performances brought forth ecstatic leading articles in the New York and Washington press, grown unaccustomed to the mandarin style of statecraft. He also knew, instinctively, when not to make a speech; after one dinner he attracted attention as if wishing to speak, but in the expectant hush that followed he simply said: 'Some of us over here want to know who shot J.R.'[108] At the end of his gruelling ten days, he was invited to address the great and the good of Washington at the Woodrow Wilson Center. He arrived looking so tired that the organisers wondered whether he would survive the evening. His Boswell, who had the good fortune also to be there, was able to reassure the American host that these were the normal signs of acute concentration before a speech. In fact, he had tele-phoned to enquire nervously beforehand, 'Will all those eggheads be friendly to me?', and later seemed genuinely surprised when they applauded rapturously – 'everyone was very cheerful and pleasant,' he thought.

It was typical of the engaging diffidence, still, about his public speaking. Within the first five minutes at the Woodrow Wilson he had 'those eggheads' totally in his pocket, opening with a well-used aphorism, but subtly tailored to the occasion: 'As Adam said to Eve when they were expelled from the Garden of Eden, "My dear, we live in a time of *transition* . . .".' Following shortly after the Presidential election of 1980, all Washington could then talk about was the 'transition period' between Carter and Reagan; it showed that the old master was far from being a living fossil. He followed this up later, when asked (somewhat ineptly) if he had ever probed with Khrushchev the genuineness of Soviet fears of nuclear attack by the US, by replying 'Oh, yes – both drunk and sober'; and then, as an afterthought, 'there wasn't much difference!' At another occasion, a glittering banquet at the British Embassy, he swung his audience from mirth to almost tearful silence. In response to the Ambassador's tribute, he said it was 'rather like an obituary in a good newspaper'; it made him out to be 'more than a politician, but not quite a statesman; you have to be dead to be a statesman; I'm not quite dead, and yet not quite alive. . . .' He then went on to evoke, magically, the great representatives of the Special Relationship that had graced the Embassy in the past – Eisenhower, FDR, Marshall, Kennedy and Churchill. To a deeply moved audience, he ended, referring modestly to himself, '. . . I bring you nothing . . . I represent nothing . . . but only my affection and good wishes. . . .'[109] It was a humble ending, but implicit in it for an America long devoid of heroes was all the nostalgia of the Kennedy–Macmillan era, and his audience were left with a feeling that the Special Relationship had never been more eloquently toasted.

Washington was taken by storm; the *Star* rated him 'a living catalogue of the English-speaking political virtues at their best';[110] George Will, the right-wing columnist, labelled him 'the Fox in Winter' and described him as being 'part of the romance of our time . . .'.[111] After that Washington appearance, his hosts at the Woodrow Wilson Center pressed him yearly to return – but it was to be his last visit to his mother's much loved homeland.

But his travels continued. The following year, it was to South Africa, to miss the English winter aboard a 50,000-ton container ship, alone with a doctor and a forty-man crew. He reread *Anna Karenina* yet again, and the *Odyssey*, and delighted in dining with the crew each night: 'talking to real professionals about their jobs instead of those boring passengers you get seated with on cruise liners!'[112] In 1983, it was Jordan and Oman, flown out in the Sultan's private jet. Only briefly did he complain of 'jeep lag' after long drives in the desert. Then he returned home via Egypt, as a publisher (and, apparently, forgiven his role at Suez). Right to the last months of his life, new expeditions were projected, until he was immobilised by his final ill health.

Oxford

Inside England, much of his travel was connected with Oxford. He loved visiting his old university for a dinner, or a 'happening', and frequently confessed to a greater pride in being Chancellor of Oxford than Prime Minister of Britain. Of all his interests in retirement, none gave him more pleasure than the Chancellorship. Since his election in 1960, he used to say: 'I've taken it very seriously, as a sort of constituency. It very much filled my life up, especially after my wife died. Most Chancellors only went once a year, to Encaenia. I go down about three times a term. . . .'[113] Indeed, probably no other Chancellor took so great an interest, or knew so much about its parochial affairs. At Birch Grove the files on Oxford filled a whole cabinet; there were few university occasions he missed, and he made a point of gracing the least 'chic' colleges and the more obscure institutions.

After the centenary in 1979 of St Anne's College (then a women's college), he complained that 'three-hundred-and-fifty young women kept me up talking till 1 am. All very exhausting. . . !'[114] The truth was that *he* had kept *them* up. But he put everything into his Oxford role, and after such a beano would return to stay in bed at Birch Grove for two or three days; in old age, as when in office, he was a wizard in the art of conserving energy. His speeches, a marvellous blend of wit, erudition and mischief, which appeared as the 'effortless superiority' of the mythical Balliol man, in fact concealed immense research. But his speeches were always a delight to listen to, and somehow Oxford – where he always claimed to feel more at ease than any political rostrum – lent him a new dimension of style in his public speaking. He rejoiced at sharing undergraduate irreverences for elevated personages; when there was an outbreak of disorder outside Lincoln College (then ruled by his old colleague, Lord Trend) he derived merriment from the thought of the stern former Cabinet Secretary 'cowering under the table from the riotous students – what a healthy sign, back to normal . . .'.[115] Lord Bullock, former Master of St Catherine's College, recalled how on opening his college's new dining hall – the sumptuous gift of Esso Petroleum – though of questionable architecture, Macmillan praised it as 'the most expensive filling station they have ever erected'.[116] On a fund-raising trip to the US in 1968, he told American graduates of Oxford that they made him feel 'like a lion in a den of Daniels'; the speech was printed in the Record of Congress,[117] and Macmillan proceeded to raise vast sums for the Alma Mater.

Speaking (without notes) at the ninetieth birthday party given him by Balliol in 1984, he proved that the old magic was still there. He explained, apologetically, how he had never collected a degree; 'sent down by the Kaiser, as you might say . . .'; he drew mist in the eyes of jaded dons by evoking the *douceur de vivre* of pre-1914 Oxford. He apologised, in advance, for the 'anecdotage' of the ancient, then related how that great wit, F. E. Smith (*alias* Lord Birkenhead), when cornered by an intolerable bore with an interminable tale at the Carlton Club, rang the bell for the steward and asked: 'Charles, would you be so good as to listen to the *concluding* portions of his Lordship's tale? I have to catch a train. . . .' Momentarily, the Balliol guests that night wondered whether the very old gentleman was losing his thread; but, no – it was just a mock of a geriatric's digression. Right back on course, he left the university a legacy of three words of advice: Keep the college system, like the regiments in the British Army; secondly, preserve the tutorial system, which was almost unique; and, thirdly, guard zealously the centre of Oxford – 'the periphery will fall down, all those new colleges, and then they will be rebuilt. But keep the centre intact. . . .' After all, what Oxford had to offer was simply, he declared with modesty, 'the best education in the world in the most beautiful city in the world . . .'. He ended with an engaging deliberate slip of the tongue, toasting former colleagues present, 'a great number of Prime Ministers, I beg your pardon, I mean Vice-Chancellors . . .'.[118]

One of the great benefits he derived from Oxford, in his old age, was the contact it gave him with young ideas, and it helped him keep marvellously informed on current affairs and new developments on every possible topic. There were some radical changes he would have liked to see at Oxford: 'My final ambition,' he once remarked, 'I'd like to have a go at moving finals to February – so as to enjoy May. Much more civilised. And I'd like Oxbridge to return to the classical tradition, leaving science to a later, technical school.' He was, he said, reserving this ambition until 'the year before I die – it's a life appointment'.[119] More whimsically, he thought he might be called upon to inaugurate a 'Gallup professor or a Ladbroke reader' of psephology, to bring to perfection the art of forecasting general election results; but he never lived to see any of these less than serious ambitions realised.[120]

What did the Oxford worthies think of Harold Macmillan in his unprecedented reign of nearly twenty-seven years? Alan Bullock, the historian, and one of Macmillan's early vice-chancellors, as a Labour supporter did not admire him as Prime Minister, and had voted against Macmillan in 1960. But he swiftly changed his opinion; he had (as of 1979) been 'outstanding', 'in fact, damn near irreplaceable. . . . It's been a love match from the beginning, universally; he's universally loved. Very difficult to convey the full affection felt at Oxford. . . .' Bullock recalled with respect the Chancellor's sang-froid under fire during the years of revolt in the early 1970s. When the Prime Minister, Edward Heath, was being given an honorary degree, an angry 'rent-a-mob' threatened to break up the gowned procession, inadequately protected by the police; but Macmillan, completely impervious, remarked to Bullock: 'You will see, it will be just like the First War, they'll catch us at the crossroads, at the King's Arms. . . .' It was said, 'not with fear, but with some relish, and he strode on,' recounted Bullock. A rush was made at the crossroads on Heath; Macmillan, imperturbable, doffed his mortar board to the mob, turning the crowd to cheers. (As a biographer of Hitler, Bullock was reminded, irreverently, of Ludendorff striding through the bullets during the 1923 *putsch*.)[121] Another senior Oxford figure, Lord Blake (who himself stood, unsuccessfully, for the Chancellorship in 1987) shared Bullock's admiration; Macmillan had lent great dignity to the university abroad; almost single-handed he had raised £50,000 on one trip to America for the rebuilding of the Union; he, Blake, had only one criticism – 'He never seems to need any sleep!'[122]

Over the years there were dissenters. In 1981, some Oxford 'young Turks' suggested it might be time for the eighty-seven-year-old Chancellor to retire; 'I told them I'd only give way to an older and wiser man!'[123] The revolt was stifled, still-born; even though, in the last years it became almost physically impossible for the frail old man to perform the Encaenia procession on foot, and there were suggestions of constructing a special litter, or palanquin, for him. In 1985 he did come close to resigning, in outrage at the university's slight when it refused Mrs Thatcher an honorary degree, supposedly because of her policies on higher education. He observed acidly that, in his twenty-five years as Chancellor, he had seen an improvement in the manners and sense of responsibility of the undergraduates – but 'I wish I could say the same about the dons.'[124]

Among his last official functions, less than a year before his death, was to bestow an honorary degree upon King Juan Carlos of Spain. Reporting it, the *Sunday Telegraph* reckoned that '"Supermac's" extreme old age gave the ceremony its rare dramatic tension.' The procession moved like a snail, to conform to 'the clever old man's pace'. Once inside the Sheldonian, the old master was 'magnificent' from the start; the audience applauded Macmillan's quaint Latin and his praise for the Spanish King, another skilled politician, 'almost as if he had been Horowitz playing in the Moscow Conservatoire'. For Spaniards, more than almost any other part of their King's triumphal visit to Britain, it came as 'the stamp of approval . . . for Spain's political coming-of-age'.[125] For Macmillan too it was an equally fitting valediction to the formality of his Oxford life as Chancellor-cum-statesman.

Macmillan's last years at Oxford brought him one last personal disappointment. In a gesture of unprecedented benefaction, the Oxford elders decided to commission a major artist to do a portrait of Macmillan by way of marking his twentieth anniversary. But who? None of the proposed names seemed quite up to the mark. Very flatteringly, he asked the author's opinion, declaring one day at Birch Grove: 'I really don't want a conventional portrait by Oswald Birley of some nice old gentleman!' Very diffidently, I said, 'What about Graham Sutherland?' expecting an outburst of horror, in view of the controversy that had surrounded the destroyed painting of his hero, Churchill. To my surprise, he seized on the idea with spontaneous delight and there followed a long eulogy on the brilliance of Sutherland (perhaps, in itself, yet another display of his modern-mindedness):

He'd be really wonderful. . . . Those wonderful shells, the extraordinary imagination and insight. A great artist, his sketches of Winston were marvellous. The trouble with Winston, you know, was that he had no face, believe it or not. Even when he was over eighty there were no lines, he was like a baby. What Sutherland did was to paint into his face his life, the terrible war; I didn't like the picture, but it was brilliant. It should never have been destroyed. That was tragic. . . .

It was a memorable critique, spoken with all the ecstatic fervour of a very young man. His eyes lit up. 'Do you think he'd really do it? He must be a very busy man'; then I could see his mind racing ahead, already planning another winter out of England, away from the glacial halls of unheated Birch Grove (it was November 1979): 'I'd love to go to Monte Carlo, isn't that where he lives?[126] . . . during the winter, get some sun, and perhaps be painted there by him. . . .'[127]

There followed a complex triangular negotiation between Oxford, the artist and Macmillan. On 3 January 1980, the Vice-Chancellor wrote to Macmillan to tell him that Sutherland had accepted, with delight: 'He says he would be doubly happy to do this as his grandfather was in Macmillans, when you were about 7 years old!'[128] On the 8th, Macmillan wrote to Sutherland direct, establishing a warm relationship by letter: '. . . I am very excited to hear from the Vice-Chancellor that you have agreed to paint my portrait for the University. This is a great honour for me and I am most grateful. . . .'[129] Sutherland replied on the 24th, to apologise for not having acknowledged 'your very kind letter before this' – 'but for some days I have been rather "under the weather". It is for me the honour, I only hope that I can do justice to one whom I have long admired. . . .'[130] A tentative first sitting was set up, but on 7 February Macmillan was writing:

> I was very sorry to hear that it was necessary to postpone the luncheon to which I was looking forward.
>
> . . . your agreement to paint my picture was a high honour; there are many ex-Prime Ministers but only one great British portrait painter.
>
> . . . I am still more sorry to hear the reason. I do hope that the doctor will be able to solve your problem. . . .[131]

Sutherland, however, was already stricken with cancer. His wife telephoned to say that he was undergoing tests on his liver; she had taken in to the hospital a Sunday paper with extracts from a recent book about Macmillan, and her husband had rallied to say, 'Now I have an incentive to get well and start on the portrait. . . .'[132] But Graham Sutherland died two days later.

Macmillan was profoundly upset – not just because of the portrait, but also because he felt the loss of a new friend from a world hitherto unknown to him. It would have been a new kind of experience, and an exciting one. The official portrait (in fact a diptych) subsequently commissioned by Oxford, and which graces the University Offices, was by a much younger British artist, Bryan Organ. It was very good, and Macmillan was delighted by it; but it was not a Sutherland.

Chapter Twenty

'Le Style, C'est L'Homme' 1979–1986

To bring about, stage by stage, an improvement and an aspiration to the Utopia which we know can never come but which we must never cease to search for. That's what we're here for. . . .

(HM, *26 September 1973*)

If you don't believe in God, all you have to believe in is decency. . . . decency is very good. Better decent than indecent. But I don't think it's enough.

(HM, *20 November 1980*)

Some time after Dorothy's death in 1966, and his liberation from the memoirs, completed in 1973, there took place a new, late blossoming in Macmillan. The date is hard to identify with precision, but those who came in contact with him found, in the words of one biographer,[1] 'a certain irresistible ripeness and charm' that had never seemed quite so manifest in the past. Gone was much of the old shyness and lack of confidence (though it still surfaced when it came to public speaking). He made a virtue of travelling second class from Haywards Heath to London, so that he could chat to his fellow passengers – or with dons and undergraduates on the train to Oxford. His numerous clubs – the Athenaeum, Beefsteak, Buck's, Carlton, Guards, Pratt's and Turf – saw him more and more often, and cherished his conversation increasingly. Was it withdrawal from the burdens of office, or development of his new interests in publishing, travel or Oxford, or all combined, that had brought about this transformation? He also seemed to become more comfortable in the company of women, particularly those he had known a long time ('who make me feel safe').[2] There was Ava Waverley, Ruth Wheeler-Bennett, the owner of glorious Garsington Manor who kept open house for him on his visits to Oxford, until she returned to her native Virginia, and Lady Diana Cooper. Older than himself (though she would never disclose her true age in *Who's Who*), it was the legendary beauty, Diana, who had christened Macmillan 'my horse' back in 1943 when she had declared him her favourite for the future Prime Ministerial stakes. (He affected to be somewhat piqued when she 'jilted' him in favour of an older man, the centenarian Sir Robert Mayer.) But he remained nervous, perhaps a little suspicious of unknown women – particularly the chic, the dominating or the bluestocking. He made a mortal enemy out of his author, Rebecca West, at a luncheon in her honour, when, through sheer alarm, he firmly turned his back on her and addressed Diana Cooper throughout. A woman scorned, Dame Rebecca never forgave him, even seeking her revenge in one of her last books.

Probably the most important relationship, from now until his death in 1986, was the flowering of an old affection for Eileen

O'Casey, the actress widow of the Irish playwright, Sean O'Casey. As noted in Volume I of this biography, of all his authors in the early years at Macmillan's, O'Casey had been the one with whom he felt closest. He and the Irishman who proclaimed himself a Communist and atheist could hardly have been more different; yet he bracketed O'Casey with Ronnie Knox as being 'saintly' – which was high praise indeed. Although Eileen O'Casey denies that Harold had ever confided to her about the Boothby affair in the thirties, it seems that he drew much solace from their friendship in those years. A frequent visitor to Birch Grove with Sean, Eileen liked Dorothy very much, and 'found her natural and easy to talk to'.

After the deaths of Sean in 1964 and Dorothy in 1966, the two saw each other with increasing regularity. 'I know that Harold was very upset about the death of his wife,' said Eileen. 'There was no doubt in my mind that he really loved her. Somehow I managed to take him out of himself. Both of us were lonely people, and we were fond of each other. . . .' Macmillan clearly enjoyed her direct, Irish irreverence. On one occasion she recalled being at a lunch when Lord Home had tried to persuade Macmillan to accept a peerage:

> . . . Harold turned to me and said, 'What about that, Eileen?' I told him I thought it nicer to keep the name Harold Macmillan to the end of his days and said, 'Titles are two-a-penny these days. Butchers and Bakers and Candlestick-makers are all getting them. . . .' I got the impression that Alec Home was a bit annoyed with me. . . .

Harold's spartan life as a widower living in the attic of Birch Grove touched Eileen, and inevitably the time came when '. . . I knew in my heart that he would have liked me to settle down with him, as we got on so well with each other.' There were rumours that the two might marry. But she was aware of his fundamental shyness, and how he 'found it difficult to express affectionate feelings. I did not help matters, as I felt so uncertain myself. I felt almost afraid of being committed to a life which I did not think I could manage.' So it went no further.

Doubtless a romantic novelist would have found pathos to this ideal ending to a sad and lonely private life, but on Macmillan's side the loneliness, and the independent routine of bachelorhood as well as attachment to the memories of Dorothy at Birch Grove, had perhaps become too rooted. Eileen also foresaw family complications, and though many friends urged her to marry the ex-Prime Minister, 'After a while I think Harold and I both realised that it would not be possible for us to be anything but loving friends.' But she never ceased to regret that neither had 'popped the question'.[3]

It was towards the end of this period of Harold Macmillan's life that I first came into close contact with my subject; first, as one of his authors, then, from 1979, as his official biographer. I liked to think that my regular visits to Birch Grove might have contributed something to the lonely life of a former Prime Minister who had so long outlived his contemporaries; but for me, though I sometimes wondered with apprehension whether it was possible to combine the roles of being Boswell with official biographer (Macmillan would jokingly refer to me as a 'cross between Boswell and Torquemada'), apart from the quite gruelling hours of taped interrogation and work on the archives, I looked forward with eagerness to the visits, to the flow of wisdom and merriment and comment on every aspect of life that accompanied our meals. Beyond the innate sadness of an empty home that had once rung with the voices of children, Birch Grove never struck me as a happy place. It was too full of ghosts. In a place of honour in the library, where they had worked together during that visit in 1963, there was the rocking-chair, still draped with its plaid rug, bought specially for President Kennedy. The whole house was kept open, just as it was when Dorothy had died, for the occasional weekend visit by the family, but it was largely unheated and such was the winter cold that anyone not of crofter stock would surely have died of hypothermia. Strangely for a countryman, Macmillan made no concessions in his clothing; I hardly ever saw him wear anything but a thin City suit, of double-breasted grey chalk stripe, and a much darned pullover. He seemed to own only two ties: the Old Etonian and the Brigade of Guards.

Until his daughter-in-law, Katie, moved in in 1980, by some curious inter-family financial arrangement, Harold Macmillan 'leased' only his study commanding the front door – where he would spend most of his day reading – and his famous 'fortress'. To reach the 'fortress' (it disappeared in Katie Macmillan's reconstruction of Birch Grove in 1981) you had to steer between the gents' cloakroom and the game-larder, then up a narrow staircase with a partition flimsily built ('so as to get the coffin down easily!' he would explain with black humour). It consisted of a spartan two-room suite, reminiscent of a boy's prep school, or perhaps the modest accommodation above the Beefsteak Club, of which he was so fond; no modern cook-general would have dreamed of living there. On the wall of the tiny sitting/dining room were prints of Bad Godesberg (despite his cool relations with Adenauer and his ambivalent opinion of the Germans), presented respectively by Konrad Adenauer and Willy Brandt. No one else actually slept in the great empty house where he passed the nights disquietingly alone. Lunch, which would be prepared by one of two elderly devoted retainers, consisted – winter or summer – of cold ham, undressed salad, and cheese; with an occasional special treat of 'plum pie just for you, dear boy, as you never get enough to eat here!'

The frugality of his life always struck me as being incongruous for an ex-Prime Minister, as well as an affluent publisher. Yet he obviously felt it in keeping with the spartan background of the family; added to an exaggerated conviction of personal impoverishment not untypical of someone of his age – 'rags to riches, and back again, in four generations, that'll be our story!' The one conspicuous exception to this regime was the regular bottle of champagne, the 'duke's son-in-law' obverse side of the crofter coin, but for which a suitable excuse had to be found: 'I'm feeling rather poorly this morning,' or 'We must drink to that brave young woman, Mrs T' (after the 1979 election) – or simply reciting with gusto his favourite lines of Belloc:

> Beneath an equatorial sky
> You *must* consume it or you die;
> And stern indomitable men
> Have told me, time and time again,
> 'The nuisance of the tropics is
> The sheer necessity of fizz.'

Though 'tropical' was one adjective that could never be used about Birch Grove, the door jamb rippled like corrugated iron where – because of the hand weakened by a German bullet – countless halves of 'fizz' had been opened. When it began to flow, so did the conversation.

'Table Talk' and Humour

The best was the 'table-talk', at meals up in the 'fortress', or late in the evening (he was the total owl, and could keep any audience up till two in the morning) – the random marginalia, the witty anecdotes on contemporaries, the acute commentaries on the day's happenings interlaced with the great sweeps of historical analogy. He became the last survivor of the great conversationalists from a bygone era (for all that contemporaries in the 1930s had often found him pedantic and pompous).

Out of curiosity, I once listed some two dozen topics of conversation covered in the course of one visit. They ranged from: the origin of the Guards' tall bearskins – should these have been worn instead of steel helmets in the First World War, given that riflemen always aim high? Hardy versus Kipling as stylists. The Victorian Empire-builders and sexual repression. Lord Nuffield and British Leyland. Decadence in Hellenistic literature. The collapse of the First Roman Republic. The Anopheles mosquito in sixth-century Italy. The explicitness of sex in the modern novel: would *Jude the Obscure* be considered shocking now? Problems of publishing in Nigeria, and copyright in the USSR. The Church and the new 'Ayatollah' (as he liked to call him) of Canterbury. Reminiscences of old London ('Did you know that Macmillan and Co.'s present office sits on the site whence Essex launched his revolt against Elizabeth I?'). The scandals of the schismatic popes at Avignon. The suffering of the Anglo-Saxons under the Normans ('have you realised that every item of food has a French name – beef, mutton – but the raw materials, brought in by the hungry serfs, all had Anglo-Saxon names – sheep, oxen. . . ?')

Finally, with much hilarity and numerous living examples, he expatiated on the difference between a 'cad' and a 'bounder' ('in war', as he explained it, 'a bounder is a chap who goes to the Front, wins the VC, then seduces his colonel's wife; but a cad seduces his colonel's wife, and never goes to the Front. Women can be cads, though curiously enough, I don't think ever bounders – have you ever known a female bounder?')[4]

I sometimes reflected that one of the things that kept him alive in his last, lonely years, two decades after he had left No. 10, was this vivid, often passionate, interest in almost every aspect of *la condition humaine*, a boon granted to few octogenarians. Within a few minutes, despite the more than thirty years between us, I used to feel as if I were talking to a contemporary – but one of rare intellectual agility. He was also a remarkable listener, with a capacity – equally rare at his age – to appreciate the jokes of others. He sopped up new anecdotes like a sponge, as he did any kind of new information (especially if, in his last years, it had anything to do with 'hi-tech').

He retained the ability to throw in an illuminating anecdote, or riposte, on almost any subject. When talk turned to a famous London club (not one of his) that had been fined for cockroaches in the kitchen, he mused aloud how, when he and Dorothy first lived in London, 'the house was infested with them': then 'We took advice and were told that the thing to do was to get a hedgehog. So we went to Harrods, and we bought one. . . .'[5]

When, in December 1985, there was an unprecedented meeting of six British Prime Ministers at No. 10 to mark its 250th anniversary, and James Callaghan reflected on what might be devised as a collective term for ex-PMs, Macmillan promptly suggested, 'What about a Lack of Principles?'[6]

A lifelong admirer of the crushing F. E. Smith, Macmillan's humour and sense of timing could sometimes be applied with devastating effect. At a dinner for Henry Kissinger during the last years of Macmillan's life, he began to show signs of extreme restlessness as the guest of honour spoke for what Macmillan judged an excessively long time. Pulling back his chair, scraping it on the floor, he distracted all attention from the speaker as those present wondered in alarm if the GOM was about to be taken ill. Kissinger, however, continued relentlessly; until Macmillan rose unsteadily, and walked very slowly out – by this time the centre of all attention. As he passed the chairman, seated next to Kissinger, he said in a loud stage whisper: 'I'm so sorry – it's the 10.58 from Victoria. . . .'[7]

To foreigners, his sense of humour was occasionally incomprehensible; seated next to Nehru's sister at a Trooping of the Colour on a very hot day when three Irish Guardsmen fainted in a row, Macmillan totally bewildered her by his only comment: 'Thank heavens they're not Grenadiers!'[8]

In everything his sense of humour was unfailing, and of a particular quality. Often black, it also derived a special delight from the ridiculous. A few days after the murder in Ireland of Mountbatten, I made one of my visits to Birch Grove. On the table by his armchair was a new white bell-button: 'Don't touch it, dear boy, I'm only to ring after I've been blown up, and then the police will come in ten minutes – isn't that thoughtful of them!' The police had also asked him to give up his regular post-prandial snooze in an isolated summer-house, but one sunny day he insisted on going out to it. Waving aside my remonstrances, he said with a mischievous chuckle, 'If you hear a big bang, that'll mean you can publish your book, dear boy!' But, as witness his turnaround at Suez, this *condottiere* disregard for danger could also be tempered by immediate, and sometimes almost excessive, prudence.

As with courage, he greatly prized humour in others. He relished Churchill's and recalled how – amid the gloom of his farewell Cabinet – the Cabinet Secretary, Norman Brook, 'to cheer up Winston, told him, "By the way, did you know that General X, the last survivor of Omdurman except for yourself, died this morning?" Winston replied: "How very *civil* of him!"' Macmillan's favourite yardsticks were whether something, or somebody, was 'fun' or a 'bore'. The Cuban missiles crisis was 'a bit of a bore'; running the country was 'fun', and anybody who worked with him in No. 10 would testify to just how much more 'fun' the Macmillan regime was than any of its successors. He enjoyed making the outrageous remark – often perhaps to provoke the unwary or to test reactions – and once when I chided him for what seemed excessive flippancy in the wrong context (it concerned the character of John F. Kennedy), he riposted: 'It's very important not to have a rigid distinction between what's flippant and what is serious.'[9] It was, I thought at the time, something of a key to his whole style of government as well as to his conversation.

In conversation, hand in hand with humour went those great sweeps of historical analogy. When Castro's Cubans made their first appearance in Angola, to Macmillan – raising his head out of *Decline and Fall* – it was 'really Gibbon all over again – as in the fifth century, you never knew when some new set of Ostrogoths were going to turn up in the collapsing Empire.' A painful attack of gout once caused him to speculate: 'just imagine, if they had had the pills we have today in the eighteenth century, we might still be in

North America – because the great Chatham had gout then, which had got into his head. . . .'

Macmillan was a deeply emotional man, and he had set himself to fighting it most of his life. In January 1980, I witnessed a display of his 'unflappability' one terrible night when his son Maurice nearly died of a collapsed lung. Harold refused to go to bed, and I kept him company until the small hours. The conversation ran on, much as it always did in the 'fortress'; then he said in a studiedly matter-of-fact voice, 'Doctor says he's got a fifty–fifty chance.' There was a pause, then, 'Kissinger's made an important speech, I gather.' I came to realise that this façade of 'unflappability' was, however, very much a cultivated defence mechanism. Underneath the sharp wit and the love of 'fun' was a great gulf – especially in later years – of loneliness, and of melancholia. It was an aspect of the Black Dog, the recurrent depression to which he had been a prey throughout his life, and to which Celts notably are alleged to be prone. 'I felt it very badly at Eton,' he admitted:

and I used to get it when in office, then I'd go to Birch Grove for two days, by myself, read Jane Austen. My wife understood. . . . didn't want to see people. . . . it was seasonal. . . . makes you inward-looking, isolated. . . . external things like Profumo, never really worried me . . . it was just the inside feeling that something awful and unknown was about to happen – or, sometimes, a great exhilaration. . . .[10]

Beneath the melancholia, the vulnerability to the Black Dog, there was a deep-seated fatalism about life in general. Macmillan's declared philosophy was: 'take it as it comes; it never turns out as you expect. . . . I never hoped to be PM (of course dear old Rab did!).'[11] This fatalism sometimes seemed at odds with his strong religious beliefs. He used to tell with relish the story about Clementine Churchill reproaching Winston for non-churchgoing: '"Ah you, my dear Clemmy" – replied Winston – "are like a great pillar; you support the church from the inside! But I am like a flying buttress; I support the Church from outside!"' When I suggested to Macmillan that he was more 'pillar than buttress', he replied, 'Yes, I suppose so. . . . I go to Communion as long as I can. At home in the house, I reach for the Bible whenever I can. . . . I still find religion a great help. . . .' As he declared on television in New

York in 1980, 'If you don't believe in God, all you have to believe in is decency. . . . decency is very good. Better decent than indecent. But I don't think it's enough.'[12] He fundamentally believed in both God and decency.

'A Kind of Resurrection . . .'

When Macmillan was staying with his old Eton friend, 'Leggy' Lambart, in Pembroke in the summer of 1976, Lambart was surprised to note how 'Everybody would come up and say hello to him on the beach; the crab-catcher, when told that we would like to buy a crab for his supper, insisted "That's on the house . . .".'[13] Surreptitiously, and then quite suddenly, it was as if all England was discovering the new Macmillan – or was it rediscovering, or seeing in the old master a new light in a time of national gloom and self-doubt? In affection, the country – cutting across all class and political boundaries – began to reach out to him as a touchstone of humour, humanity and political wisdom.

Following publication of each of the six successive volumes of the Macmillan memoirs, the BBC recorded him in a lengthy interview with Robert Mackenzie. They were sympathetically done; each was a considerable success, and served to remind his countrymen that Macmillan was still around, and as spry as ever. The last, timed to appear in 1973 within days of the tenth anniversary of his resignation, ended on a philosophic note of hope and confidence for facing the challenges of the future. Looking to fifty years ahead, he predicted that, just conceivably, Russia might be 'not so very different from us perhaps. What will China be? What possibilities there are. . . .' He spoke about the aim of existence being 'To bring about, stage by stage, an improvement and an aspiration to the Utopia which we know can never come but which we must never cease to search for. That's what we're here for. . . .'[14] To listening Britons the note of controlled optimism from an old politician came as something so lacking after a decade of Home, Wilson and Heath (and there were drearier days to come). Launching Volume VI, Macmillan appeared with his three successors together on a platform at the Dorchester – no comparisons were needed. The Night of Long Knives, Vassall and Profumo, the humiliation by de Gaulle, all receded into the background against nostalgia for the

'You've-never-had-it-so-good' era, which was suddenly perceived to have been a golden one – at least by comparison with what had succeeded it. Macmillan, his long-time admirer David Wood wrote wistfully in *The Times*, had come 'elegantly back into public view to remind us of a political style that has been lost and that is unlikely to be found again . . .'. He thought that there was 'not much Mr Wilson and Mr Heath have done or are now doing that does not bear the Macmillan influence', and went on: 'He ranks, I think, above all the peace-time Prime Ministers of this century for sheer intellectual power. . . . We shall not see his like again at No. 10.'[15] It seemed that, at least in the British media, never noted for its inconveniently long memory, all was forgiven. It would have been hard for Macmillan to have remained unmoved by the repeated demonstrations of affection, and admiration. This, combined with his mounting dismay at the way things were going for Britain, persuaded him to break his thirteen years of self-imposed silence about contemporary affairs, in October 1976, in a long interview at Birch Grove with Robin Day. He explained that he now believed the situation to be so bad that he felt 'impelled to make some contribution to the solution to our problems', though he felt 'a little like Rip van Winkle . . .'. Recalling his own efforts, he compared the uncontrolled government expenditure then rampaging in Wilson's Britain to the profligate who couldn't pay his tailor's bills, but who offered to resolve the matter by ordering another suit. He ended by calling for a 'government of national unity'; and, doubtless, in one corner of his mind, he saw himself heading it.[16] (He was, after all, only eighty-two, several years younger than Konrad Adenauer had been when he won his last election in 1961.) Though it never picked up the hint, the press was warm in appreciation; as Dennis Potter wrote in the *Sunday Times*, 'The way he spoke, the style of the man . . . makes his successors in all parties seem even more mean and dull-witted and ill spirited than they already are. . . .'[17]

Two years later, Sir John Colville, Churchill's wartime Private Secretary, was writing to *The Times* describing Macmillan as the last of 'an extinct species' – a statesman.[18]

When the Social Democrat Party first came into being, Macmillan was praised (in the *Spectator* in September 1979) for having been 'the most impressive social-democratic politician of the last 30 years . . .'.[19] (On his side, Macmillan was rather less impressed; when I asked him, teasingly, if he would not now join the SDP, insofar as it seemed exactly the kind of 'centre party' he had been advocating in the 1930s, he snorted, 'Certainly not – it's just the same old Labour Party of 1945 . . . same socialist principles, even the same old faces!'[20] He also predicted, though he did not live to see it, the SDP's eventual débâcle in 1987.)

If anything the magic seemed to improve with the years; when he spoke to the Conservative Primrose League in 1981, then aged eighty-seven, that pungent parliamentary humorist and deflator of political egos, Frank Johnson, listened to him in awe, finding him 'alarmingly lucid' and knowing 'the tricks like no other today'. Johnson could not escape the suspicion that for Macmillan 'all his life was a preparation for elder statesmanship, his only regret being the necessity to clock in with the actual long and arduous political career before taking up televised reminiscences and elegiac appearances such as yesterday's . . .'. When he left, his audience, 'the last of the Tory hat people, were in a state of collective trance . . .'.[21] The whole image of 'Supermac' seemed to have changed mysteriously; another hard-eyed political commentator, Ferdinand Mount, remarked on his 'positively appalling vigour' as demonstrated in the television interview that marked his eighty-fifth birthday:

> Those who remember from the sixties a somewhat moth-eaten character with an upper-class drawl and an egg-stained cardigan will scarcely recognise this spruce executive in grey pin-stripes. . . .
>
> How beautifully the old gentleman disarms criticism by himself pointing out that old gentlemen are always apt to say how much better it was in the past. And he has the right. . . .[22]

The media came even to love Macmillan's fund of acrid replies to idiot questions, on all occasions; when asked how he was going to spend his eighty-sixth birthday, 'You can hardly expect me to go out skiing or anything at my age';[23] or, when asked why the Russians invaded Afghanistan, 'I don't suppose they're going there for the winter sports.'[24] It was all a very far cry from the lampoons and satire and anger of the 1960s. Besieged with invitations to speak, during all this time Macmillan had probably never felt better in himself. His health was robust, his mind was astonishingly clear, his memory (until the last years) prodigious, and there was a new self-assurance. Above all, he was thoroughly enjoying himself, thriving on the affection and respect that flowed in from all quarters, and much moved by it. His son Maurice reckoned that it was one of the happiest periods of his life, comparable to the halcyon days of his early premiership.[25]

Yet, at the same time, he was profoundly *unhappy* at the way things were going both in Britain and in the world at large. During the Wilson–Lyndon Johnson years, he watched with utmost distress as the Special Relationship decayed and Britain withdrew from her responsibilities east of Suez. To Eden he was writing in 1967, 'I do not like the latest news at all. Two hundred years of British policy have ended up with the Russians to all intents and purposes in control of the Mediterranean. What a heavy price to pay for Foster Dulles. . . .'[26] Occasionally, as when the Soviets invaded Afghanistan, seemingly unopposed, Macmillan would descend into darkest gloom: 'The Russians have won, I'm afraid it's too late. . . .'[27] At home, it was with something like despair that he observed the unions run amok during Callaghan's 'winter of discontent', bringing to breakdown the remnants of the industrial consensus that he had tried so carefully to nurture. With the attention he now commanded in the country at large, he felt it was his duty to speak out.

In February 1979, on the occasion of his eighty-fifth birthday, and in the middle of Britain's dark winter of discontent, he made another appearance on television, with Robert Mackenzie again. Mackenzie reviewed the experiences of Macmillan's long life; then Macmillan spoke eloquently of what the tragedy of Vietnam and Watergate had done to America's voice in the world. He went on to compare Britain's current economic plight with what it had been in his day, of 2½ per cent inflation and 700,000 unemployment, when 'some genial commentator at the time coined a phrase which had a certain popularity. I don't know who it was, who said something like "You never had it so good." Now, something's gone. What's gone was that you could only run that on a general consensus. . . .' It was a fairly outrageous appeal to nostalgia, ending once more with a call for a government of national unity and consensus: 'It's a moral issue, we must have the determination and we must rebuild our courage.' His aim, he explained, had been also to appeal 'for a new national spirit'.[28] He received many supportive letters, and once again the press at large reacted warmly.

In August of that year, he was canvassing again – back in his old constituency of 'dear Stockton' – this time for two Tory candidates to the European parliament. (One succeeded, one failed.) It was the first time, he admitted, that he had electioneered for sixteen years. At Stockton, Macmillan found the shipyards defunct, and unemployment almost as dire as during the 1920s and 1930s that had left such a mark on his political career. Slum clearance gave it a seedy air of being either not quite finished, or not yet recovered from wartime bombing, and a sour smell of industrial gas hung over the town. At Bradford the organist churning out the lugubrious music habitually reserved for Tory rallies made the unfortunate choice of 'The Day Thou Gavest, Lord, Is Ended', which amused Macmillan, and did not deflect the audience of several thousands from giving him one of the longest acclamations accorded any Conservative since Churchill. Certainly it would have been hard to think of anyone 'more active-valiant or more valiant-young' than Supermac revisiting his old haunts in the North-east.

Macmillan and Thatcher

When Margaret Thatcher took over the leadership of the beaten Tory Party from Heath in 1975, Macmillan was delighted and there followed a warm initial honeymoon. To his old friend (and author), Sir John Wheeler-Bennett, in a letter of February 1975 otherwise full of gloom about the miners having beaten Heath and now Wilson ('Wages are rising by about 30% a year and inflation continues rampant. . . . it is hard to see where it will all end . . .'), he wrote:

> However there is one delightful feature which has relieved us all: the breakthrough of women's lib into the Conservative party from which men have been deposed and a gracious lady has taken the leadership in her stride amid universal acclaim. She is the product of her own strong character and good sense and of the pent-up animosity against the regime which in ten years has destroyed the Conservative party. . . .[29]

On a snowy January day the year after Margaret Thatcher was voted into power, there was a touching little scene at the Carlton Club, at the unveiling of a head of her by Oscar Nemon. Macmillan, at his courtliest, gazed around the room at the portraits of past

Tory statesmen, and speculated, 'I wonder what they would make of this performance? I know one who would have welcomed it – Disraeli, who disliked the company of men and liked the company of women. . . .' Addressing himself gravely to the new leader, he concluded: 'I wish you well with all my heart, madam. God bless you.'[30] He then sat down in an armchair, with Mrs Thatcher sitting at his feet on the floor for at least half an hour. Four years later she fulfilled his hopes. Over the years, not infrequently, she called on the old pro for advice. 'I hope I have helped her,' he would say – adding with mock seriousness: '. . . I'm very firm, tell her not to talk like a governess. . . .'[31] After her speech to the Tory Party Conference of 1977, he wrote congratulating her on having 'spotted the fact that politicians, especially Socialist politicians, do not mind being attacked, but hate being teased . . .'.[32] Before the 1979 election, he had also offered her this useful advice: 'Leave the right and the left of the Labour Party to fight it out. . . .'[33]

He, too, was flattered by her attentions, and – although his enthusiasm for her policies waned as unemployment soared – always held her in high personal regard; above all, he referred to her in general as 'that intelligent and courageous young woman'. Sometimes the 'intelligent' would be replaced by a less flattering adjective, but it was the latter quality of courage that was to him the most important in a person. After Mrs Thatcher had been in office a few months, he was musing that he would 'like to be a young back-bencher now, starting again. Great opportunities with this new lady. It may not be right, but what she's trying to do is courageous and new. . . .'[34] Very privately, Macmillan would be invited to Chequers for quiet weekends à trois with the Thatchers. He was awed by the new Prime Minister's capacity for work, while expressing fears that she would overdo it and 'blow up'; it worried him, in terms of his own style of government, that there was 'no relaxation there . . . no books, you know – nothing but boxes, all day'.[35] Occasionally he urged her to unwind, with a good novel – Trollope or George Eliot (who had kept him going through Suez).

Yet there was, quite clearly and from an early stage, a fundamental difference in political philosophy between the two. As of 1979, she thought that his current speeches were 'quite brilliant . . . of a brilliance I don't think I ever heard before; and I think that is because he had more and more time to read. . . .' His policies while in office she regarded as 'essentially practical policies for the times, respecting always the dignity of the individual . . .'. But there were also times when Macmillan had expressed:

> very, very different solutions from those which I would definitely have embraced, and his practicality I think did lead him into some collectivist solutions which ultimately would have denied his fundamental beliefs. He got very collectivist, you see, at one time, which I found very difficult to reconcile with those deep early beliefs I know he had. . . .

More recently, she had been shocked by his proposals for an 'Industrial Parliament' as a means towards ending confrontation with the unions. He had said:

> 'You know, we might have a parliament where all the universities are represented, where your trades unions are represented, where the CBI is represented'. I just recoiled. . . . It was only because he was a bit tired that I refrained from saying 'You mean a Mussolini-type of corporate state?' – because that's what it was. . . .[36]

But she always took his criticisms seriously, and never made the mistake of dismissing them as the maunderings of old age, even in Macmillan's very last years.

As the Thatcher economic policies developed, Macmillan expressed himself more and more critical of monetarism, and of the terrible spiralling of unemployment that he saw as its inevitable handmaiden. He also foresaw large private business companies, like Macmillan's, being hard hit – if not actually driven out of business – rather than the public monopolies and local authorities which he felt should have been the target of the Thatcher axe. By the autumn of 1980, he was voicing fears that her government had 'spent the year hitting the wrong head'. She should instead have 'started on the local authorities . . . and not on the poor private enterprise . . .'.[37] It was, indeed, an error that Thatcher herself was to recognise and correct in subsequent years. (Meanwhile, the canny Highlander and ex-Chancellor, millionaire publisher, author and landowner, saw to it that his own tax affairs were so well arranged within the clan that, when he died, his will for probate totalled only £37,000.) In yet another television appearance with Robert Mackenzie entitled 'The Way Ahead', he afforded Mrs Thatcher little comfort in a sustained attack on monetarism, and renewed his (possibly fanciful) calls for an 'Industrial Parliament': 'We can't bring about this revolution in the old way of hardship, we've got to do it by consent. . . .' With perhaps just a touch of excess drama, he compared the situation in 1980 Britain with the 'almost hopeless position' Churchill had found forty years previously.

> It is not quite as bad as that, but it is getting towards it. Now what are we going to have? First, unnecessary suffering, heavy unemployment. . . . A gradual decay, a slide down, that's at the best. At the worst, Britain, for the first time in its long and splendid story, taking no part in the defence of the freedom of the world. . . .[38]

Confrontation, he said in another context, 'unless you want civil war, unless you want fascism or communism, is simply mad. . . . Why should men follow you into battle, why the hell should they, unless they like you?'[39]

The Macmillan line soon found warm supporters among the leading 'wets' of the Thatcher Cabinet – such as Ian Gilmour, who, as editor of the *Spectator* in the 1950s, had so often been a stern critic of Macmillan while in office. Macmillan's sallies occasionally verged on the mischievous; yet it seems that Mrs Thatcher never bore him a grudge. Courteously she kept him apprised of such security issues as the revelation of Sir Anthony Blunt's treason, before speaking of it in the House; when she wrote (in 1981) referring to the pending publication of yet another book on spies, his reply was: '. . . I do not propose to read the book for I really now only read with great difficulty and prefer to stick to Scott or Dickens. . . .' At the same time, he expressed his '. . . personal admiration for your extraordinary resilience and energy . . . but I beg you not to overdo it, for that is the great danger that besets anyone who holds your office. Rest is essential from time to time. . . .'[40] This particular advice, from the voice of experience, was not taken.

When the Falklands campaign started in 1982, Macmillan – with some diffidence – hastened to proffer to the Prime Minister a display of solidarity by calling publicly at No. 10. To his surprise, the offer was promptly taken up; even more to his surprise, what he expected to be a courtesy call of five minutes turned into an interview lasting two hours, with Mrs Thatcher closely questioning Macmillan, in his experience of these matters, on how in practice to organise a government for war. His advice was: 'Get rid of your large Defence Committee; create an inner war cabinet – the three defence chiefs plus the supremo, Foreign Secretary, Defence Minister. But most important you need an Ismay. . . .'[41] Macmillan's suggestion for the post was Sir Michael Palliser, the recently retired Permanent Under-Secretary of the Foreign Office, and a wartime Guards officer. Macmillan recalled of the meeting: 'She was very calm, considering, but concerned how to cope with a war coming. . . . I told her that hundreds of awful things will come up, but don't let it waste your time. . . .'[42] Everything he said was carefully written down by the Prime Minister, and – in effect – the Macmillan ideas were put into force; a War Cabinet was set up, with Palliser as executive secretary, and it proved a conspicuous success. Macmillan was manifestly delighted; the Falklands brought out the old swordsman, and a new light in his eye at a time when he was sorely dispirited by a debilitating attack of shingles. During the anxious early moments when US support was by no means certain, he quipped: '. . . I hear this fellow Dulles is back – disguised under the name of Haig. . . .'[43]

A Few Discordant Notes

Not every voice, however, was raised in praise of Macmillan during these years. His old critic in the Commons, Lord Lambton, re-emerged to lambaste him in the shortlived *Now!* magazine as having been responsible for 'A seven-year rule of wasted time', and 'the author of many of our present discontents'.[44] Old bitternesses remained among those of Macmillan's colleagues who had suffered along the road – the dissenting Treasury ministers of the 'little local difficulties' of 1958, Birch and Powell (though never their chief, Thorneycroft), and the victims of the 1962 Night of Long Knives, as well as Eden and Butler. Curiously enough, it was the loyal wives who tended most to keep animosities alive. With Eden, after Suez, Macmillan maintained a friendly (if not conspicuously warm) relationship; whereas, to the end of his life, Clarissa Avon was vitriolic, both in correspondence and conversation, in her views of Macmillan and his behaviour towards her husband. Similarly, Rab Butler –

though he affected never quite to understand why Macmillan had 'kept him out' of the premiership[45] – was mild in criticisms compared with his wife, Mollie, who would never permit Macmillan to stay in the august Master's Lodge of Trinity, Cambridge, when Rab was Master. Though the most 'literary' of all Prime Ministers, it was curious that Macmillan was never invited to become a fellow of the prestigious Royal Society of Literature; Rab was its President, Lady Butler a forceful figure behind the scenes.

Most hurtful of all to Macmillan personally, however, were the allegations during the last years of his life of his complicity in handing back the 'White Russians' to Stalin in 1945. Raised chiefly by Nikolai Tolstoy,[46] the allegations (dealt with in Volume I of this biography) were unsparing in calumny, culminating in innuendoes that went so far as to imply, in the last year of Macmillan's life, that he himself had been in the thrall of the KGB, although Tolstoy later expressed regret for these innuendoes.[47] By nature a compassionate man, these charges hurt him deeply – more deeply than he would let on. Friends urged him to sue for defamation, but it was not in his character; nor was it, indeed, likely that he could physically, at ninety, have withstood prolonged cross-examination in a witness box. Much as he had behaved when attacked by 'Halier-than-Thou' in *The Times*, he rolled himself into a ball like a hedgehog where a younger and lesser man might have been tempted to riposte – with the exception of one fairly disastrous interview on television when questions were sprung on him unprepared and unfairly edited.[48] While his attackers could press their attack in the certainty that there would be no danger of a come-back, he fell back in the belief that, in the fullness of time and when seen in all its proper historical context, the record would vindicate him. It did.

A Ninetieth-Birthday Surprise

Reviewing the latest Macmillan book, *A Life in Pictures*, towards the end of 1983, the *Daily Mail* joked that it was 'probably part of a plot by the old boy to make his political comeback on his 90th birthday!'[49] They were not altogether wrong.

Harold Macmillan's ninetieth birthday arrived on 10 February 1984, and that morning there was a birthday surprise in the form of an announcement from Buckingham Palace that the Queen had been 'graciously pleased to approve the dignity of an earldom' to be conferred upon him. As it is customarily on the birthday of the sovereign that honours are handed out, the fact that this marked the birthday of the *recipient* added to the unusualness of the event. It was the first new hereditary earldom created in twenty-three years, and it was twenty-one years since he had been first offered it, and declined; while just two years previously he had gone on record as remarking that the House of Lords was 'not worth belonging to'.[50] Why, then, had he at last changed his mind? His motives were almost as complex as they had been when he had refused a title originally. Both the Queen and Mrs Thatcher had regularly pressed him to change his mind; his oldest grandson, Alexander (who later succeeded to the title), had also recently coaxed him in a long letter. The family argument was that the Commons career of his father, Maurice, was now more or less at an end (Maurice belonged instinctively to the 'wet' faction of the Party, which made office in a Thatcher government unlikely, and had moreover been in very poor health since his narrow escape from death four years previously). This was an argument that weighed powerfully with Harold. But he was also now afflicted himself by the disastrous failure of his eyesight, cataracts compounded by inoperable degeneration of the retina, which – except for the talking book – denied him his greatest solace in life, reading. Yet his mind was as active as ever, and he was, frankly, bored. He explained to his biographer: 'I have gone blind; and in the House of Lords it really doesn't matter if you're blind. . . .' Then, in a disrespectful aside – 'or deaf or dumb!'[51]

Perhaps the most compelling reason of all, however, was that he felt he still had important things to say, and he needed a more prominent platform than the common rooms of Oxford from which to say them.

Macmillan's choice of the title of Earl of Stockton, with all its old associations for him, seemed a felicitously romantic one; but there were many of his friends and admirers, and even some members of the family, who regretted his decision. The world had, for so long, revered him as plain Harold Macmillan. Yet the media, which had so misprized and lampooned him back in the 1960s and now positively slobbered over him, were almost unanimous in their welcome. 'SUPER EARL', trumpeted the *Daily Express*; 'EARL SUPERMAC!' headlined the *Daily Mail*: 'A hereditary Peerage for the "Never had it so good" Prime Minister.' Even his old enemy, *The Times*, though more tempered in its praise, recognised him as 'a man for whom public affection has grown with the passing years . . .', and that he 'more than any other of our time, has infused his practical politics with so strong a sense of history'. Writing in the same paper, Robert Blake, the historian of Disraeli, made a parallel that placed a finger on a key factor which explained Macmillan's past success as a politician, as much as it gratified its subject: 'both were brilliant showmen and deep thinkers. Both led their party from left of centre and both had a knack of speaking in a rightish tone of voice when commending leftish measures. . . .'[52]

His ninetieth birthday party at Birch Grove, attended by a remarkable mix of two hundred of the great and good, Prime Ministers, friends, family, Macmillan secretaries and Birch Grove estate workers, all bearing immense goodwill and warmth, was a remarkably joyous occasion. More like a coming-of-age party, even the police guards were in high good humour. It also happened to be the day of the death of the Soviet's sinister KGB Premier, Andropov, and in an aside as he accepted the presents and good wishes of his guests, Macmillan remarked in his best black humour: 'And wasn't it thoughtful of Mr Andropov to choose today!'

Only one shadow marred that happy day; Maurice, seriously ill in hospital with a lung infection, was unable to attend to deliver the toast of honour. As so often, fortune and tragedy were never far apart in Harold's life. Just one month later, Maurice, aged only sixty-three, died. If he felt remorse at how his own political career had perforce stunted that of his only son, characteristically Harold betrayed no sign of it; yet it came as a terrible blow – unexpectedly so, as Maurice had been in frail health for so long – and it was a shock from which he himself never entirely recovered. When I visited Birch Grove at Easter that year, he admitted, 'I've been very miserable since Maurice . . . thought I'd chuck it in. But spring arrived, three days ago, and I decided to soldier on to the autumn. . . . I'm going to Chatsworth for two months. . . .'[53]

Meanwhile, he had found the strength to take up his seat in the Lords, a ceremony richly encrusted with pageantry and ermine, flanked by the Duke of Norfolk and supported by two fellow earls. Seated on the steps of the throne, allowed in from the Lower House by special permission, Mrs Thatcher watched (in the words of one newspaper, 'as a niece might watch an aged and beloved uncle as he came slowly into the Lords').[54] Over the scene presided the man, once Macmillan's favourite, who had fallen at the last jump in the succession stakes of twenty years previously, Lord Chancellor Hailsham, a Johnsonian figure resplendent in wig and eighteenth-century black tricorn. Three times the new Earl and his sponsors were called upon by the Garter King to 'Rise' and doff their hats to the Lord Chancellor, an ancient ceremony to ensure that no impostor should enter. Hailsham gravely acknowledged the deference of his former chief. There were two very minor hitches; first, the new Noble Lord, while bending low to sign the Test Roll, was heard on the BBC microphone to whisper, 'What do I sign?' 'Just Stockton' whispered the clerk. Then, in his myopia, he almost passed by forgetting to shake the Lord Chancellor's proffered hand. Or was it all part of the act? One Tory peer reckoned that 'there wasn't a dry eye in the House – including Maggie's,' while journalists were left speculating, like the *Guardian*'s Michael White, 'why had he done it and what it all meant'.[55] They had to wait eight months, until his maiden speech, to get a part of the answer.

In the meantime, at Dorothy's ancestral home of Chatsworth, Macmillan regathered his strength after Maurice's death. In the labyrinthine ducal corridors it was, he observed, 'like Snakes-and-ladders to get to your room; you have to throw a double-six.' His hostess, the Duchess of Devonshire, quipped back, 'Should we charge extra to exhibit Uncle Harold?'

Back in Politics

While at Chatsworth, he began to put together his thoughts for his maiden speech. He had many. He had long wanted to press the pursuit of the new 'silicon chip' technology, an old hobby-horse, in which automation working for men – instead of the reverse – could lead to a new age of leisure, solving unemployment eventually by the introduction of a ten-hour week: 'And what's wrong in working a ten-hour week? It's ridiculous to say that the British don't know how to use leisure. . . . what books sell best? Gardening manuals!'[56] He also wanted passionately to address himself to the old cherished Disraelian theme of 'One Nation', Britain at the time being ravaged as never before by the bitter confrontation of Arthur Scargill's miners' strike. Friends and family would offer advice and additional material, and he would try out his ideas on them. It was a laborious business; he would dictate thoughts to his faithful secretary of twenty years, Rosemary Aimetti; but, as he could not read his own notes, these would then have to be read back to him. Everything had to be reordered in his mind, and then committed to memory; at the age of ninety.

When the day came, 13 November 1984, he sat at the end of the government front bench, looking frail and ill and unhappy – all recognisable signs of the old concentration. He showed some controlled impatience as a Labour lord rambled on at tedious length before him, with barely a flicker of a smile as the speaker sat down, appropriately, with the words 'How long, O Lord, how long?' It was the new Earl's first parliamentary appearance in twenty years, and – rising painfully to his feet – he began by recalling that sixty years had passed since he first 'underwent the same ordeal in another place'. He admitted that his first sixteen years in the Commons had been neither happy nor 'very successful', and he had been regarded 'with a certain distaste and even dislike by the leaders of my party'. There were half-believing smiles among an audience unfamiliar with his early career in those far-distant days. These turned to laughter as he added: 'However, I was, fortunately, able to deal with the matter fairly soon by becoming the leader of the party myself. . . .' There followed a review, mostly of economic highlights, of his forty years in the Commons. Up in a crowded gallery, listeners groaned inwardly as many old familiar ingredients made their appearance; then, suddenly, it was clear that they were being rearranged, and augmented, with a new mastery. He came close to transgressing the canons of the Lords, to eschew any controversial issues in a maiden speech, and, when he mentioned the word 'monetarists', his fellow new peer, Viscount Whitelaw, right hand to Mrs Thatcher in the Lords, looked distinctly nervous. For an agonising moment it looked as if the old man, without notes and not even a stick to lean on, might have forgotten the word he was searching for: 'What were they called?' Did they come from America, or Tibet? But the long pause was deliberate; 'Ah, yes, the *monetarists*. . . .' The laughter had hardly ceased when he was into a parable about the nursery (thought up that very morning, he claimed later): 'How do you treat a cold? One nanny said, "Feed a cold" – she was a neo-Keynesian. Another nanny said, "Starve a cold" – she was a monetarist. . . .' The House erupted, and the not-unkindly dig at the Prime Minister was particularly enjoyed by those aware of his tendency to adumbrate the governess qualities in her.[57]

Then he turned serious, warming to his thesis of the silicon revolution. His voice broke with emotion that swept the House when he spoke next of the hatreds unleashed by the long-running miners' strike: 'It breaks my heart to see what is happening in our country today. A terrible strike . . . by the best men in the world. They beat the Kaiser's army and they beat Hitler's army. They never gave in. . . .' It was, he said, 'pointless and endless. We cannot afford action of this kind. . . .' Yet, having reduced his listeners to unrestrained laughter and then tears, he concluded on a stirring upbeat note of Faith, Hope and Charity, and – characteristically – in a belief of a new intellectual, and spiritual, revolution.[58]

To anyone listening in the Lords that day, it was a quite staggering *tour de force*, as good in its way as anything anyone present had ever heard him produce in the Commons in his heyday, and an outstanding triumph of mind over matter; for thirty-two minutes he had spoken without a note, and without a slip or a falter that was not intentional. ('Anyway,' he wrote afterwards, with his usual modesty, 'I got through it without breaking down. The most difficult thing was to stand up so long without any support. . . .'[59]) As he sat down, he received an ovation unprecedented for that august chamber; it was the greatest pity that the scene, memorable as it was, could not have been televised.[60] Led by his old adversary, Harold Wilson, from the opposite benches, all the peers seemed to lean forward, arms upraised, towards the old man – for a brief moment creating a tableau that reminded one almost of a composition by El Greco.

After such a supreme effort, many reckoned that Macmillan's maiden speech might also prove to be his swan song. They were mistaken. In January he was on his feet again, urging once more that Britain should not miss the new industrial revolution, dropping further hints about the need for a 'national government', and drawing loud cheers with his hopes for 'a new glorious renaissance'.[61] The following day, the first time the Lords had been televised, a marathon debate on the economy lasted ten and a half hours. Macmillan again participated, strongly critical of the government's economic policies. With his ninety-first birthday coming up in only a few weeks' time, he was still in the House when the debate ended.[62]

The House of Lords now became a regular feature of his life, seldom missing a week (the daily pay-packet, he said, also helped). By now, the Thatcherite honeymoon had thoroughly ended. He was openly, sharply and frequently critical of the Prime Minister's economic policies, and sometimes too over her attitude to nuclear arms negotiations. In November, speaking to a Tory Reform Group dinner, he made his much quoted remark about 'selling the family silver', a direct attack on the Thatcher plans for 'privatisation' of public enterprises, like British Telecom and British Airways. Nodding approval, the *Observer* presumed that the speech 'prompted coffin-like smiles in Downing Street'. Harold Macmillan had 'really', it claimed, 'become a legend in his lifetime . . .', but whatever the view of him, 'we have yet to see what can be safely billed as "positively his last performance". . . .'[63]

It almost was his last performance, and perhaps it should have been. Apart from the *Observer*, this time the 'family silver' speech attracted more hostility than enthusiasm. Some felt the analogy was specious; the 'silver' was, after all, not being flogged off outside the family, but being redistributed within it. Some felt the criticism was just mischievous, Thatcher-baiting; others felt it was a sign that, at last, the GOM was a bit over the top. It provoked a savage cartoon by Cummings in the *Sunday Express*, depicting Macmillan himself as part and parcel of the disposable family antiques.[64] Typically fierce was the comment in the *Spectator*, which suggested that one reason why silver had become so valuable was 'because it is a hedge against the inflation initiated by Mr Harold Macmillan . . .'. It found his peroration about the dawn of the microchip 'curiously dull', and speculated that the 'spell-binding charm which had grown men weeping last year for the wonderful miners . . . will begin to pall with repetition over the next three years. . . .'[65]

'I Think I Will Go to Sleep Now'

It was, however, old age and debility that finally silenced him. Before making his speech about the 'family silver' in November 1985, he had been seriously ill with pleurisy, which made it something of a heroic feat to get to the Tory Reform Group dinner.

Those present worried about his alarming frailty, and noted that he ended the thirty-minute speech bathed in sweat.[66]

Each illness, shingles (which he reckoned, at the time, had been even more disagreeable than his pelvis wound on the Somme) or pleurisy, or even gout seemed to take a little more out of him. But in the last year, each time I saw him I was shocked how swiftly he seemed to be going downhill. His blindness now made it painfully difficult for him even to see to eat. Often the old sparks would fly, but much of the time he seemed prey to a new form of dejection – the dejection of the losing struggle against old age and its indignities. In the spring of 1986, it took a supreme effort for him to get through the degree-giving ceremony at Oxford for King Juan Carlos. But it was too much for him. On returning to Birch Grove, he was laid low again with pleurisy, 'the old man's undertaker' as doctors used to call it, and for several weeks his life was despaired of.

Yet, for one last time, he fooled the critics and experts. 'You know how it is, when you are ill,' he explained to me when I went down to see him in August 1986:

> You don't know whether you are awake or half-dreaming; I thought I heard one nurse say to the other 'it won't be long now' – and I was damned if I would give up. . . . I thought I would go on! . . . Am I being very inconvenient to you, dear boy?

As in the old days, the conversation ranged from the constitutional crisis between the Palace and No. 10, a 'silly season' frivolity shipped up by certain newspapers ('one day the Queen may get fed up and push off to Canada'); to the succession for an important Oxford college; and on a new project for his biographer to tackle ('once you've got me off your back, poor boy!'). At lunch he recalled how one of Churchill's Ministers of Pensions had expounded in Cabinet, pompously and at great length, that it was *generally* agreed that *sixty* is the age when your faculties begin to decline – your reactions slow – your mind goes, etc. . . . Therefore, this should be the age for pension. . . .' Churchill, Macmillan recalled, then already eighty, listened with great enjoyment, leading the Minister on to labour his rather tactless theme further, much to the amusement of the Cabinet in general – and to the ninety-two-year-old retelling the story.

Physically, however, he seemed desperately frail, frailer than ever.

Nevertheless, once again he rallied. He returned to Chatsworth, to be cosseted by the Devonshires. During that last visit, 'Debo', the Duchess, related, in the *Spectator*, how, when a military band performing at the High Sheriff's party had struck up 'The British Grenadiers' in his honour, 'the handsome old Grenadier officer, survivor of the Battle of the Somme, got slowly to his feet, leaning on his two sticks as near to attention as he could. It was one of the most moving sights I ever saw. . . .'[67]

From Chatsworth, following his favoured summer round of many years, he went on to Holker in the Lake District, belonging to Hugh Cavendish, which he had so often visited in past years with Dorothy. There he was introduced, by Mrs Thatcher's Minister of Agriculture, Michael Jopling, to the EEC ministers convened for a conference, whom he entertained – in French – till all hours of the night, with the ministers of France and Belgium sitting literally at his feet. From there he went to stay with John Wyndham's widow, Pamela Egremont, at Cockermouth, and thence to the home of Dorothy's kinsman, Lord Lansdowne, at Meikleour in Perthshire. For all his bodily frailty, his mind (though the remarkable memory had begun to flag) was vigorously active still, and that summer he took to worrying (unnecessarily, as it turned out) over the dangers of a hung Parliament after the forthcoming General Election. In his own shaky handwriting, he penned a letter to the Queen, offering his advice on constitutional precedents.[68] The Queen, evidently touched to receive this last offer of help from her old first minister, asked her Private Secretary, Sir William Heseltine, to go to Meikleour and sound him out. Heseltine, half expecting it to be a courtesy call on a very elderly gentleman, probably rambling, came away amazed at being treated to an hour and a half of the most lucid and sound 'tutorial', which was 'absolutely fascinating', on constitutional precedents. He made detailed notes, and, though the contingency of a hung Parliament never arose, the Queen was pleased and grateful. It was his valedictory contribution to British politics.

In November, Macmillan paid what was to be his final visit to his beloved Oxford, to attend a Feast at St Edmund's Hall. The following night he dined quietly with his biographer. It was the last time we were to meet. He was visibly exhausted, suffering recognisably from the Black Dog. It was distressing to see him, though he perked up in the course of the evening, reminiscing about his first schooldays at Oxford's Summerfields at the turn of the century. He remembered how, as a frightened new boy, he had been despatched by his father on the school train, and had wept that first night after a bread-and-milk tea; an older boy, Evelyn Baring ('later a great swell'), had endeavoured to comfort him, with the words (they had apparently been used on other occasions): 'Don't cry – your situation is bad, but not desperate!' Typically, his last thoughts that evening were about Oxford and publishing. I knew I would never see him again. He spent Christmas with his children, grandchildren and great-grandchildren at Birch Grove. On 29 December, after a very brief illness, he died, only a few weeks short of his ninety-third birthday. Some of the family felt that, dejected and unable to console himself by reading, he had simply died of boredom. Life was no longer 'fun'. According to his grandson, Alexander, he had nevertheless kept his wits to the end, and his last words were: 'I think I will go to sleep now.' He had outlived most of his own Cabinet ministers.

He was buried, quietly, alongside Dorothy and Sarah, in the small parish churchyard of Horsted Keynes near Birch Grove, under a severe block of square granite, that then bore the simplest inscription:

DOROTHY MACMILLAN

1900–1966

SARAH MACMILLAN

1930–1970

HAROLD MACMILLAN

1894–

Its very austerity seemed almost to symbolise a turning back to the world of the Scottish crofter. The funeral was attended by three Prime Ministers, his successor Lord Home, Edward Heath and a manifestly distressed Mrs Thatcher, and one of the last of his few surviving colleagues, Lord Hailsham. Sixty-four members of the family led the mourners, and the coffin was borne by six estate workers from Birch Grove. Among the rows of wreaths was one from the Prince of Wales, which read, in his own handwriting, 'In admiring memory, from Charles'.[69] A few weeks later, on the day of his ninety-third birthday, Macmillan's memorial service took place in a crammed Westminster Abbey. It was a majestic, but not unrelentingly solemn occasion. Alec Home, on whom he had eventually bestowed his blessing as his successor, delivered an address moving in its simplicity and personal recollection. There followed the haunting and seldom heard 'Grenadiers Return', played by the band of the regiment with whom he had fought on the Somme. Then, suddenly and *fortissimo*, the entire congregation in the Abbey, led by the Grenadiers, burst into the joyous and rollicking 'Battle Hymn of the Republic', 'Oh mine eyes have seen the glory of the coming of the Lord' – the favourite of that stern American matriarch, Nellie Macmillan. The juxtaposition of the two pieces of music somehow seemed to epitomise most perfectly that gentle distinction between the serious and the less serious that had so characterised Harold Macmillan's whole attitude to life.

Notes, Bibliography, Index

Notes

The following abbreviations are used in the source notes. For most works, the first mention within each chapter gives the name of the author and the title in full; thereafter, except in cases of ambiguity, the author's surname and/or shortened title is used. Where works appear in the Bibliography, details of publication are omitted. The word 'interview' also embraces less formal conversations, including those by telephone.

AHC   author's conversations with Harold Macmillan (not taped), 1979–86
AHT   author's taped interviews with Harold Macmillan, 1979–86
FO   Foreign Office
HMA   Harold Macmillan Archives
HMD   Harold Macmillan's diaries, unpublished, in Harold Macmillan Archives
JFKL   John F. Kennedy Library, Boston, Massachusetts
PM   Prime Minister

Preface

1   *Independent*, 30 December 1986.
2   *Daily Mail*, 30 December 1986.
3   *The Times*, 28 January 1987.
4   Interview, Lord Carrington.
5   Godfrey Winn, *Daily Herald*, 7 October 1963.
6   Ruth Dudley Edwards, *Harold Macmillan: A Life in Pictures*, p. 175.
7   AHT, 'Declaration', September 1979.
8   To William F. Buckley Jr on *Firing Line*, recorded New York, 20 November 1980.

Chapter 1   'It's Macmillan', January–March 1957

HM, *Riding the Storm* (IV), pp. 185–345, and:

1   Interview, Alexander Macmillan.
2   Lord Kilmuir, *Political Adventure*, p. 286.
3   HMD, 3 February 1957.
4   David Cecil, *Lord Melbourne* (London 1954), p. 111.
5   HMD, 3 February 1957.
6   *The Times*, 11 January 1957.
7   Michael Foot, *Aneurin Bevan 1945–60* (London 1962, 1973), vol. II, pp. 535–6.
8   John Foster Dulles papers, 10 January 1957; Mudd Library, Princeton.
9   HMA.
10   R. A. Butler, *The Art of the Possible*, p. 196.
11   HMD, 3 February 1957.
12   Quoted in Anthony Sampson, *Macmillan*, p. 121.
13   AHT, 10.18.
14   BBC1, 3 April 1971.
15   AHT, 5A.10.
16   Interview, Lord Butler.
17   AHT, 5A.10.
18   Interview, Sir Patrick Reilly.
19   HMD, 3 February 1957.
20   Interview, Lord Hailsham.
21   HMD, 3 February 1957.
22   Ibid.
23   Ibid.
24   Ibid.
25   Interview, Lord Redmayne.
26   HMD, 3 February 1957.
27   John Wyndham, *Wyndham and Children First*, p. 161.
28   Interview, Sir Philip de Zulueta.
29   Interview, Lord Amory.
30   Interview, Lord Eccles.
31   Letter from Lord Egremont, 27 February 1966; HMA.
32   HMD, 8 February 1957.
33   Ibid.
34   Ibid.
35   Ibid., 25 February 1957.
36   Ibid., 3 February 1957.
37   Quoted in Sampson, op. cit., p. 121.
38   Sir Harold Nicolson, *Letters and Diaries 1945–62*, p. 329.
39   Letter from HM to Selwyn Lloyd, 30 January 1957; HMA.
40   HMD, 31 March 1957.

41 Interview, Sir Philip Goodhart.
42 Nicolson, op. cit., p. 331.
43 Hansard, 16 May 1957.
44 Foot, op. cit., pp. 535–6, 613.
45 HMD, 28 February 1957.
46 Ibid., 1 March, 28 February and 4 March 1957.
47 Emrys Hughes, *Macmillan*, p. 137.
48 BBC1, 23 April 1971.
49 HMD, 8 and 9 March 1957.
50 Donald Neff, *Warriors at Suez* (New York 1981), p. 430.
51 Duncan Sandys to HM, 28 January 1957; HMA.
52 BBC1, 9 September 1969.
53 Letter to Eden, 17 February 1957; HMA.
54 HMD, 8 February 1957.
55 Ibid., 9, 18, 19 and 27 February 1957.
56 Ibid., 5 March 1957.
57 Ibid., 20 March 1957.
58 Ibid.
59 Ibid., 21 March 1957.
60 Dwight D. Eisenhower, *The White House Years*, p. 122.
61 Ibid., p. 350.
62 HMA.
63 Ibid.
64 Ibid.
65 Letter of 5 April 1957; Eisenhower Library, Abilene.
66 Joe Alsop, *The Reporter's Trade* (London 1960), p. 332.
67 Ibid.

Chapter 2 Mending the Fences, March–December 1957

HM, *Riding the Storm* (IV), pp. 88–333, and:

1 HMD, 26 March 1957.
2 BBC1, 6 June 1972.
3 HMD, 9 March 1957.
4 Ibid., 18 March 1957.
5 Ibid., 7 May 1957.
6 Ibid., 8 May 1957.
7 Ibid., 12 May 1957.
8 Ibid.
9 Letter of 3 June 1957; HMA.
10 Memorandum of 13 July 1957; HMA.
11 Signal of 7 April 1958; HMA.
12 HMD, 11 November 1957.
13 Ibid., 4 December 1957.
14 Interview, Sir Philip de Zulueta.

15 Memorandum of 22 December 1957; HMA.
16 HMD, 10 March 1957.
17 Ibid., 15 March 1957.
18 Ibid., 18 March 1957.
19 Ibid., 20 March 1957.
20 Letter of 28 April 1957; HMA.
21 HMD, 27 March 1957.
22 Ibid., 14 April 1956.
23 AHT, 12.10–11.
24 HMD, 31 March 1957.
25 Ibid., 4 April 1957.
26 John Wyndham, *Wyndham and Children First*, p. 161.
27 HM notes for Vol. IV memoirs; HMA.
28 Penelope Fitzgerald, *The Knox Brothers* (London 1977), p. 274; interview, Penelope Fitzgerald.
29 Letter of 28 April 1957; HMA.
30 HMD, 8 and 1 April 1957.
31 Ibid., 17 May 1957.
32 Quoted in Anthony Sampson, *Macmillan*, p. 125.
33 Letter of 28 August 1957; HMA.
34 Telegram 1664, 29 August 1957; HMA.
35 Telegram 1666, 29 August 1957; HMA.
36 Telegram 1739, 6 September 1957; HMA.
37 HMD, 7 September 1957.
38 Telegram 1745, 7 September 1957; HMA.
39 HMD, 22 September 1957.
40 Ibid.
41 Memorandum to Minister of Defence, M480/57, 29 September 1957; HMA.
42 Letter to Eden of 2 October 1957; HMA.
43 Memorandum of 24 November 1956; HMA.
44 Interview, Lord Head.
45 Interview, Denis Healey.
46 Philip Ziegler, *Mountbatten*, pp. 549–54.
47 AHT, 6.2–3.
48 Ziegler, op. cit., p. 550.
49 HMD, 31 July 1957.
50 Ziegler, op. cit., p. 552.
51 HM speech at Sheffield, 5 April 1957.
52 Quoted in Sampson, op. cit., p. 125.
53 Letter of 18 January 1957; HMA.
54 Interview, Denis Healey.
55 Interview, Lord Head.
56 AHC.
57 HMD, 23 December 1957.

58   Ibid., 24 June 1958.
59   Ibid., 13 July 1958.
60   AHT, 14.12–13.
61   HMD, 4 April, 4 June and 4 October 1957.
62   Letter of 5 June 1957; HMA.
63   HMD, 1 December 1957.
64   Letter of 10 October 1957; HMA.
65   HMD, 30 October 1957.
66   Ibid., 8 November 1957.
67   Interview, Lord Plowden.
68   HMD, 23 October 1957.
69   Ibid.
70   Ibid.
71   Ibid., 25 October 1957.
72   Ibid.
73   Ibid., 26 October 1957.
74   Ibid.
75   Ibid., 5 November 1957.
76   Letter of 12 December 1957; HMA.
77   Andrew Pierre, *Nuclear Politics: Anglo-American Defence Relations 1939–80* (London 1981), p. 62.
78   HMD, 19 December 1957.
79   Randolph Churchill, *The Rise and Fall of Sir Anthony Eden* (London 1959), p. 292.

Chapter 3 'Little Local Difficulties', 1957–1958

HM, *Riding the Storm* (IV), pp. 343–430, 731–2, and:

1   Letter of 20 February 1958; Fraser papers.
2   Fraser papers.
3   Ibid.
4   The Thorneycroft Budget of April 1957, his first and last, proposed tax cuts costing between £100 and £140 million, and was later followed by substantial concessions for pensioners. Fraser (later Lord Fraser of Kilmorack), whose experience covered a long period, reckoned in retrospect (interview, 21 December 1988) that Macmillan was unique among Prime Ministers in his understanding of how to deploy to a joint end the *Party* apparatus, as well as government machinery, while in office; a skill which was later to draw criticism of his using civil servants for Party electoral benefit.
5   HMA.
6   HMD, 9 April 1957.
7   Interview, Margaret Thatcher.
8   Harold Nicolson diaries, *Letters and Diaries 1945–62*, 26 June 1957.
9   Peter Oppenheim, 'Muddling Through; the Economy 1951–1964',

in Robert Skidelsky and Vernon Bogdanov (eds), *The Age of Affluence* (London, 1970).

10 From Cummings' cartoons.
11 HMD, 15 July 1957.
12 Ibid., 15 March 1957.
13 Ibid., 19 March 1957.
14 Ibid., 2 April 1957.
15 Ibid., 16 July 1957.
16 Ibid., 17 September 1957.
17 Ibid., 20 September 1957.
18 Ibid., 24 September 1957.
19 Ibid., 7 October 1957.
20 Sister of Christopher Chataway, later an MP and junior minister, at the time a television commentator.
21 HMA.
22 HMD, 12 November 1957.
23 Ibid., 15 December 1957.
24 HMA.
25 HMD, 4 September 1957.
26 Written in 1971.
27 HMD, 11 April 1957.
28 Harrod was knighted for his services in 1959.
29 AHT, 12.12.
30 HMD, 22 December 1957.
31 Ibid., 23 December 1957.
32 Ibid., 6 January 1958.
33 Ibid., 22 March 1956.
34 AHT, 12.14.
35 Ibid., 12.13.
36 Ibid., 14.11.
37 HMD, 5 January 1958.
38 Ibid.
39 Thorneycroft's letter of resignation to Macmillan, 5 January 1958:

> ... I write to ask you to accept my resignation from the office of Chancellor of the Exchequer. My reason can be shortly stated.
>
> I am not prepared to approve estimates for the Government's current expenditure next year at a total higher than the sum that will be spent this year.
>
> Your proposed departure from this country on the 7th January has made it essential that a decision of principle upon this matter be taken now. It is clear that in this proposal I do not have your support or that of a number of colleagues. In the circumstances and since the level of Government expenditure is central to my responsibilities as Chancellor of the Exchequer, resignation is the only course open to me. ...

Macmillan's reply to Thorneycroft was equally cool:

> I was sorry to receive your letter this morning offering your resignation as Chancellor of the Exchequer. I particularly regret that you should think it necessary to take this step when the difference between you and the rest of the Cabinet is such a narrow one. . . .

After stating his and the Cabinet's position at some length, Macmillan continued:

> . . . I therefore cannot accept that there is any difference of principle between the rest of the Cabinet and yourself. Resignation is always a difficult decision. It is, in my view, justified only on matters of principle. I must add that your resignation at the present time cannot help to sustain and may damage the interests which we have all been trying to preserve.

40   HMD, 7 January 1958.
41   BBC1, 23 April 1971.
42   Lord Hailsham, *The Door Wherein I Went*, p. 163.
43   HMD, 7 January 1958.
44   Sir Nigel Fisher, *Iain Macleod*, p. 163.
45   Later Lord Sherfield.
46   *Sunday Telegraph*, 1 January 1989; correspondence with author, 13 January 1989.
47   Interviews, Lord Amory, Lord Barber.
48   *Spectator*, 24 April 1971.
49   Interview, Enoch Powell.
50   Ibid.
51   Ibid.
52   Ibid.
53   Interview, Lord Rhyl (Nigel Birch).
54   Hansard, 23 January 1958.
55   Eight years of Thatcher monetarism, the Tory success story of its time, seemed to modulate Thorneycroft's views. When interviewed by the media after publication of the relevant government papers under the thirty-year rule, on 1 January 1989, he was considerably more positive about his having acted correctly in 1958.
56   Interview, Lord Thorneycroft.
57   Ibid.
58   HMA.
59   HMD, 31 January 1958.
60   Ibid., 6 May 1958.
61   Ibid., 12 May 1958.
62   Ibid., 14 May 1958.

63 *Sunday Telegraph*, 'Albany', 14 March 1982; *The Times*, 12 March 1982.
64 *Sunday Times*, 2 December 1979.
65 Interview, Lord Butler.
66 *Spectator*, 24 April 1971.
67 Sir Nicholas Henderson, *The Private Office* (London 1984), p. 65.
68 *Now!*, 14 March 1980.
69 *Spectator*, 24 April 1971.
70 AHT, 5A.4.
71 In force until repealed in 1965.
72 HMA.
73 AHT, 5A.4.
74 Interview, Lord Redmayne.
75 HMD, 1 April 1958.
76 Ibid., 2 April 1958.
77 Interview, Robert Rhodes James. It should perhaps also be added that under a reorganisation of constituencies Boothby's seat at East Aberdeenshire was threatened with extinction; therefore, without a peerage, he would have disappeared from Parliament altogether.
78 Anthony Sampson, *Macmillan*, p. 179.
79 Ibid., p. 129.
80 HMD, 19 January 1958.
81 Ibid.
82 Ibid.
83 Sampson, op. cit., p. 130.
84 HMA.
85 Interview, Lord Carrington.
86 Sampson, op. cit., p. 130.
87 HMD, 4 February 1958.
88 Interview, Sir Harold Evans.
89 Quoted in Sampson, op. cit., p. 131.
90 HMD, 3 April 1958.
91 Ibid., 5 May 1958.
92 Ibid., 10 May 1958.
93 Ibid., 15 May 1958.
94 Ibid., 28 May 1958.
95 Ibid., 30 May 1958.

Chapter 4   1958: The Year of International Crisis

HM, *Riding the Storm* (IV), pp. 431–556, 657–701, and:

1 HMD, 13 May 1958.
2 Ibid.
3 Ibid., 17 February 1958.

4 Telephone conversation, Dulles to Eisenhower, 23 February 1957; Eisenhower Library, Abilene.

5 HMD, 14 July 1958.

6 This was perhaps not entirely in accordance with how the story was seen in Washington, where the American press had given too much credit for the operations to British pressure, to the extent where an irritated Eisenhower remarked that he was 'tired of reading in the papers we have no plans and are being pushed into everything by the British'. Dulles, equally piqued, affirmed that 'he originated the idea but they ran with the ball too fast without taking time to work it out. The Sec [Dulles] gave the idea to Lloyd Sunday [i.e. 13 July] am . . .' (telephone conversation, White House (James Hagerty) to Dulles, 23 July 1958; Mudd Library, Princeton).

7 HMD, 22 May 1958.

8 Ibid., 16 July 1958.

9 Ibid.

10 Ibid.

11 Ibid.

12 Ibid.

13 '. . . so solid and reliable. Even when he was away shooting (as he usually is) he gives a sense of confidence . . .' was Macmillan's comment on Hoyer Millar, the following year (ibid., 23 October 1959).

14 Ibid., 16 July 1958.

15 Ibid., 17 July 1958.

16 Interview, Sir Frederick Bishop.

17 HMD, 17 July 1958.

18 Ibid.

19 Quoted in Anthony Sampson, *Macmillan*, p. 127.

20 British Embassy, Moscow to Foreign Office, 19 July 1958, No. 985; HMA.

21 Dwight D. Eisenhower, *The White House Years*, p. 279.

22 HMA.

23 HMD, 21 July 1958.

24 Signal of 22 July 1958; HMA.

25 HMD, 1 August 1958.

26 Interview, Sir Charles Johnston.

27 Cable of 15 August 1958 from Washington; HMA.

28 Interview, Martin Gilbert.

29 HM to Party Conference 1955.

30 HMD, 15 March 1957. The Turks took over northern Cyprus in 1974.

31 The imposing Archbishop of Athens, whom Macmillan set up as Regent, to resolve the Greek Civil War in 1944 (see Volume I, Chapter 9).

32 HMD, 19 February 1959.
33 Ibid., 7 July 1957.
34 Subsequently Lord Harding of Petherton.
35 Brother of Michael Foot and later Lord Caradon.
36 Quoted in Sampson, op. cit., p. 128; Hugh Foot, *A Start in Freedom* (London 1964), p. 57.
37 In actual fact, in five years of violence British forces in Cyprus suffered fewer than 100 fatal casualties.
38 HMD, 7 August 1958.
39 Ibid., 9 August 1958.
40 Ibid.
41 Ibid., 11 August 1958.
42 Ibid., 23 August 1958.
43 Ibid., 11 August 1958.
44 Ibid., 18 February 1959.
45 Ibid., 19 February 1959.
46 Hansard, 19 February 1959.
47 Interview, Anthony Nutting.
48 HMD, 17 February 1959.
49 Ibid., 28 August 1958.
50 Ibid., 5 September 1958.
51 When the author visited Quemoy in 1979, as guest of the Taiwan Army, the island – now become an underground fortress riddled with tunnels and bunkers like the Maginot Line, with 'show' villages and lakes above the surfaces – was still, in theory, subjected to the threat of shelling on odd days. 'Honourable friends' were only allowed in on even days, when – again in theory – the Taiwanese shelled back. In fact, the bombardment had been virtually extinct the past thirty years, except for the occasional missile filled with propaganda leaflets (and, on the Quemoy side, contraceptives forbidden in the People's Republic). But pretences are still kept up, on both sides.
52 HMD, 14 May 1958.
53 General Charles de Gaulle, *Memoirs of Hope*, vol. I: *1958–62*, pp. 8–9.
54 HMD, 29–30 June 1958.
55 Ibid.
56 Ibid., 3 August 1958.
57 Ibid., 8 October 1958.
58 Ibid.
59 Ibid., 9 October 1958.
60 Ibid.
61 FO signal to HM Embassy, Paris, 20 October 1958; HMA.
62 HMD, 31 October 1958.
63 Konrad Adenauer, *Erinnerungen* (Stuttgart 1967), vol. III, pp. 426–34, Terence Prittie, *Konrad Adenauer*, p. 263.

64 Adenauer, op. cit., p. 428, Prittie, op. cit., p. 263.
65 Quoted in Prittie, op. cit., pp. 263–4.
66 *Manchester Guardian*, 27 November 1958.
67 HMD, 19 December 1958.
68 Ibid., 31 January 1959.

Chapter 5 No Mr Chamberlain, 1958–1959

HM, *Riding the Storm* (IV), pp. 557–656, and:

1 HMD, 21 February 1957.
2 Ibid., 19 January 1958.
3 Ibid., 24 January 1958.
4 Ibid., 31 January 1958.
5 Ibid., 3 February 1958.
6 Ibid., 1 April 1958.
7 Letter of 13 August 1958; HMA.
8 HMA.
9 They had been there ever since the quadripartite agreements following the capitulation of Germany in 1945.
10 HMA.
11 HMD, 7 December 1958.
12 Ibid., 16 January 1959.
13 AHC.
14 HMD, 22 January 1959.
15 Transcript of White House telephone calls; Eisenhower Library, Abilene.
16 HMD, 31 January 1959.
17 Ibid., 2 February 1959.
18 Interview, Lord Richardson.
19 Interview, Lord Barber.
20 Interview, Malcolm Muggeridge.
21 Interview, Jane Parsons.
22 Sir Harold Evans, *Downing Street Diary*, p. 79.
23 Interview, Lord Barber.
24 HMD, 4 March 1959.
25 AHT, 5.3.
26 Ibid.
27 Ibid, 5.3–4, 13.13–15.
28 Ibid., 13.14–15.
29 Interview, Sir Frederick Bishop.
30 HMD, 4 March 1959.
31 Interview, Sir Philip de Zulueta.
32 HMD, 4 March 1959.
33 Interview, Sir Patrick Reilly.
34 HMD, 4 March 1959.

35 Michael Foot, *Aneurin Bevan 1945–60*, p. 169.
36 HMD, 10 March 1959.
37 Ibid., 12 March 1959.
38 Konrad Adenauer, *Erinnerungen* (Stuttgart 1967), vol. III, p. 479; Terence Prittie, *Konrad Adenauer*, pp. 261, 269, 279.
39 HMD, 20 March 1959.
40 Dulles–Eisenhower telephone transcript, 4 March 1959; Eisenhower Library, Abilene.
41 HMD, 31 March 1959.
42 AHT, 5.12.
43 HMD, 20 March 1958.
44 AHT, 5.12.
45 HMD, 7 June 1958.
46 AHC.
47 AHT, 5.12.
48 HMD, 31 March 1959.
49 Ibid., 26 May 1959.
50 Quoted in Townsend Hoopes, *The Devil and John Foster Dulles* (London 1974), p. 481.
51 Signal of 4 August 1959; HMA.
52 HMD, 28 May 1959.
53 Ibid., 18 and 27 June, 23 July 1959.
54 AHT, 7.11.
55 Interview, Mme Pandit.
56 AHC.
57 Richard Lowenthal, quoted in Prittie, op. cit., p. 267.
58 Graf Finck von Finckenstein, quoted in ibid., p. 268.

Chapter 6   Electoral Triumph, 1958–1959

HM, *Pointing the Way* (V), pp. 1–43, and:

1   Quoted in Anthony Sampson, *Macmillan*, pp. 151–2.
2   Quoted in ibid., p. 155.
3   AHC.
4   HMD, 22 October 1958.
5   Interview, Lord Amory.
6   Ibid.
7   AHT, 12.14.
8   Harold Wilson, *A Prime Minister on Prime Ministers*, p. 315.
9   HMD, 14 March 1958.
10 Ibid., 31 July 1958.
11 Ibid.
12 Cabinet minute, 27 October 1958; HMA.
13 HMD, 12 January 1959.
14 Ibid., 27 January 1959.

15 Ibid., 7 April 1959.
16 Samuel Brittan, *The Treasury Under the Tories 1951–1964*, p. 202.
17 Interview, Margaret Thatcher.
18 HMD, 26 May 1959.
19 Ibid.
20 Interview, Lord Amory.
21 Interview, Lord Fraser of Kilmorack.
22 HMD, 30 June 1959.
23 Letter of 8 July 1959; Macmillan's reply 9 July 1959; HMA.
24 Telephone conversation, Dulles to Christian Herter, 6 March 1959; Mudd Library, Princeton.
25 Ibid., 9 March 1959.
26 HMD, 27 July 1959.
27 Ibid., 30 July and 22 August 1959.
28 Ibid., 31 August 1959.
29 Shortly after the election the Macmillans had to leave for Admiralty House, while No. 10 was extensively rebuilt, not returning until only a few weeks before his resignation in 1963.
30 Dwight D. Eisenhower, *The White House Years*, p. 424.
31 Herbert Morrison, *An Autobiography* (London 1960), pp. 314–15.
32 Quoted in Sampson, op. cit., p. 153.
33 Sir Harold Evans, *Downing Street Diary*, p. 18.
34 Letter from Sir Robin Day to author, 22 October 1982.
35 Quoted in Evans, op. cit., p. 44.
36 HMD, 27 September 1959.
37 *Sunday Express*, 18 March 1959.
38 Woodrow Wyatt, *Confessions of an Optimist* (London 1985), p. 271.
39 John Wyndham, *Wyndham and Children First*, p. 184.
40 Ibid., p. 186.
41 Speech to Coningsby Club, 17 June 1958.
42 HMD, 9 October 1959.
43 AHT, 13.4.
44 HMD, 9 October 1959.
45 Letter from Lord Redmayne to author, 10 April 1980.
46 Morrison, op. cit., p. 320.
47 Interview, Lord Richardson. AHC.
48 BBC1, 23 April 1971.
49 Norman Shrapnel, *The Performers*, pp. 27–33.
50 Interview, Lord Butler.
51 Interview, Lord Wilson.
52 Interview, Lord Callaghan.
53 Wyatt, op. cit., p. 205.
54 Interview, Lady Longford.
55 Gaitskell had wanted to join up in 1939–45, but – like Rab Butler – had been pronounced unfit.

56 Gaitskell had accused Macmillan of having arranged for Eisenhower
   to back his foreign policy in order to help the Conservatives at the
   forthcoming election – a charge which was not totally devoid of the
   truth, as will be seen.

57 HMD, 4 May 1959.

58 AHT, 15.6.

59 Ibid.

60 HMD, 16 September 1958.

61 Ibid., 3 November 1958.

62 BBC1, 23 April 1971.

63 Interview, Lord Wilson.

64 AHC.

65 Interview, Lord Carrington. Carrington, a former Grenadier officer,
   had been High Commissioner to Australia during the Macmillan
   tour of 1958 and had so impressed Macmillan with his personality
   that the Prime Minister brought him back to be First Lord of the
   Admiralty the following year.

66 AHC.

67 Interview, Lord Soames. Soames, who at the time of the interview
   was still serving in the early days of Mrs Thatcher's first administration, but was later one of the 'wets' who fell out with her,
   made the penultimate remark accompanied with a grimace and a
   deprecatory sweep of the hand towards No. 10. Churchill was, of
   course, his father-in-law.

68 Interview, Lord Carrington.

69 AHC.

70 Later Lord Normanbrook. Served as Cabinet Secretary, 1947–63.
   Died in 1968.

71 Later Lord Trend.

72 Interview, Lord Trend.

73 Interview, Lord Butler.

74 HMA.

75 Interview, Jane Parsons.

76 Freddie Bishop was Principal Private Secretary, 1956–59; then
   Deputy Secretary to the Cabinet, 1959–61. He was knighted in 1975.

77 By Lord Fraser of Kilmorack, formerly Michael Fraser. Interview.

78 Interview, Sir Frederick Bishop.

79 Wyndham, op. cit., p. 155.

80 Interview, Lord Barber.

81 Ibid.

82 Interview, Lord Redmayne.

83 AHT, 9.10.

84 Evans, op. cit., p. 216 (quoted in Ian Waller, *Sunday Telegraph*, 1
   February 1981).

85 Evans, op. cit., p. 28.

86   Redmayne memorandum; Redmayne papers.
87   AHT, 9.10.
88   BBC1, 23 April 1971.
89   The name 'Garden Girls' dated from the First World War when Lloyd George extended the cramped offices of No. 10 into the garden to meet wartime exigencies. Miss Minto started work at No. 10 in 1935 and retired in 1968; Miss Parsons started work in 1946 and retired in 1981.
90   Interview, Sheila Minto, Jane Parsons.
91   Stella King interview in the *Evening News*, 19 October 1962.
92   *Guardian*, 13 March 1957.
93   HMA.
94   HMA.
95   HMA.
96   *Evening Standard*, 24 November 1958.
97   Interview, Professor David Dilks.
98   Interview, Rhodes James.
99   Interview, Sheila Minto.
100 Interview, Michael Tree.
101 Macmillan's two favourite clubs.
102 Viscount Swinton, formerly Philip Cunliffe-Lister MP, an old ally from pre-war days, owner of Bolton Abbey and an excellent grouse-moor in Yorkshire.
103 HMA.
104 Only at the time of crisis during Lord Waverley's terminal illness in 1957 would he address her, affectionately in his letters, as 'darling', or even 'dearest Ava'.
105 HMA.
106 AHT, 2.3.
107 Letter of 15 September 1961; HMA. One of the important consequences of Macmillan's interest in Church matters was his pushing for the appointment of Ramsay to be Archbishop of Canterbury when Fisher retired in 1961. Fisher himself wanted to keep out Ramsay (who had once been a pupil of his when Fisher had been headmaster at Repton), in favour of either the Bishop of Peterborough (Stockford) or the Bishop of Chelmsford (Alison). Ramsay was known for his dislike of administration, and boredom with it, and with Fisher's weight against him the selection was not an easy one. But Macmillan saw that Ramsay had the intellect and spirituality needed to guide the Church of England through the new problems posed by the 1960s. In the end his influence triumphed, and the choice was a good one. (Letter from Bishop of Chichester, 12 January 1987.)
108 AHC. 'Jones' was, of course, Anthony Armstrong-Jones, who, on marrying Princess Margaret, later became Lord Snowdon.

109   HMD, 7 February 1960.
110   AHT, 2.10.
111   Ibid., 2.5–6, 5.15b.

Chapter 7   Winds of Change, 1959–1960

HM, *Riding the Storm* (IV), pp. 733–8, *Pointing the Way* (V), pp. 107-78, 259–70, and *At the End of the Day* (VI), pp. 298–306, and:

1   HMD, 9 June 1959.
2   Ibid., 5 March 1959.
3   Ibid., 10 and 15 June 1959.
4   Ibid., 22 June 1959.
5   Ibid., 18 July 1959.
6   Roy Welensky, *4000 Days*, p. 31.
7   Ibid., p. 13.
8   AHT, 14.19.
9   HMD, 25 October 1958.
10   Ibid., 5 March 1959.
11   Ibid., 11 March 1959.
12   Ibid., 24 May 1959.
13   Ibid., 2 December 1959.
14   Ibid., 13 July 1959.
15   Welensky, op. cit., p. 130.
16   Devlin Commission Report; HMA.
17   HMD, 24 July 1959.
18   Ibid., 20 July 1959.
19   Letter to Monckton, 22 August 1959; HMA.
20   Letter of 1 November 1959; HMA.
21   Quoted in Anthony Howard, *Listener*, 9 October 1980.
22   John Vaizey, *In Breach of Promise* (London 1983), p. 35.
23   Interview, Harold Wilson, October 1961.
24   HMD, 4 June 1961.
25   Vaizey, op. cit., p. 44.
26   AHC.
27   HMD, 4 June 1961.
28   *Spectator*, 17 January 1964.
29   Quoted in the *Listener*, 9 October 1980.
30   Welensky, op. cit., p. 187.
31   Letter of 1 November 1959; HMA.
32   HMD, 17 November 1959.
33   Letter of 31 October 1959; HMA.
34   Harold Wilson, *A Prime Minister on Prime Ministers*, p. 320.
35   HMD, 4 December 1959.
36   Interview, Lord Home.
37   HMD, 24 November 1959.

38 Welensky, op. cit., p. 144.
39 Anthony Sampson, *Macmillan*, p. 169.
40 Letter of 28 December 1959; HMA.
41 AHT, 14.17–18.
42 Sir Harold Evans, *Downing Street Diary*, p. 90.
43 *Sunday Telegraph*, 8 July 1972.
44 Evans, op. cit., p. 95.
45 Welensky, op. cit., p. 171.
46 Ibid.
47 Letter of 17 January 1960; Waverley papers.
48 Welensky, op. cit., p. 173.
49 Sampson, op. cit., p. 172; Sampson was one of the journalists present at the time.
50 *Encounter*, February 1961.
51 Evans, op. cit., pp. 102–3.
52 Interview, Julian Amery.
53 Interview, K. Kirkwood, quoting Redcliffe Maud.
54 Interview, Anthony Sampson.
55 Sampson, op. cit., p. 174.
56 Interview, Lord Home.
57 Interview, Anthony Sampson.
58 Evans, op. cit., p. 105.
59 *Ottawa Journal*, 5 February 1960.
60 Letter of 16 March 1960; HMA.
61 Interview, Lord Colyton (Henry Hopkinson).
62 Interview, Lord Hailsham.
63 Evans, op. cit., pp. 106–7.
64 HMD, 6 February 1960.
65 Ibid., 6 and 7 February 1960.
66 Ibid., 23 February 1960; personal telegram to PM, T207A/60, 22 February 1960; HMA.
67 HMD, 23 and 24 February 1960.
68 Ibid, 24 February 1960.
69 Ibid., 13 May 1960.
70 Ibid., 28 February 1960.
71 Ibid.
72 Ibid., 22 and 23 March 1960.
73 Letter of 3 April 1960; HMA.
74 Letter of 25 March 1960; HMA.
75 Ibid.
76 HMD, 4, 5 and 7 May 1960.
77 Ibid., 7, 9 and 12 May 1960.
78 Ibid., 13 May 1960.
79 Ibid., 21 February 1960.
80 Welensky, op. cit., p. 134.

81   Ibid., p. 199.
82   HMD, 10 July 1960.
83   Ibid., 7 August 1960.
84   Ibid., 17 July 1960.
85   Ibid., 4 August 1960.
86   AHT, 14.23.
87   HMD, 7 August 1960.
88   Telegram to FO, No. 308, 9 August 1960; HMA.
89   Welensky, op. cit., pp. 270, 272.
90   HMD, 6 October 1960.
91   Welensky, op. cit., pp. 278, 291.
92   Ibid., p. 283.
93   Letter of 7 November 1960; HMA.
94   HMD, 8 November 1960.
95   Ibid., 11 December 1960.
96   Ibid., 17 December 1960.

Chapter 8   Eruption at the Summit, 1959–1960

HM, *Pointing the Way* (V), pp. 61–116, 178–216, and:

1   HMD, 13 July 1958.
2   Ibid., 18 October 1959.
3   Ibid., 1 June 1959.
4   Ibid., 16 September 1959.
5   Ibid., 22 October 1959.
6   Ibid., 24 October 1959.
7   Ibid., 29 October 1959.
8   Dwight D. Eisenhower, *The White House Years*, p. 409.
9   HMD, 19 December 1959.
10   It was Khrushchev's jargon.
11   HMD, 19 December 1959.
12   Ibid., 20 December 1959.
13   Letter of 23 December 1959; HMA.
14   HMD, 28 December 1959.
15   Papers of Secretary of State Herter subsequently released from the
      American archives disclose that the 'invitation' was not quite as
      Macmillan recorded it in his memoirs (V, p. 186), at the same time
      indicating the extent of the pressure Macmillan was constantly
      applying to Eisenhower:

      MEMORANDUM OF TELEPHONE CONVERSATION WITH AMBASSADOR
      CACCIA, March 23, 1960
      . . . 1. Macmillan would like, for physical reasons, to come over
      on Saturday night and spend Sunday resting at the Embassy. . . .
         3. From Macmillan's own point of view and he thought possibly
      from the President's point of view as well, Macmillan thought it

would be better if the announcement could indicate that the President had at this stage of the negotiations asked Macmillan to come over and consult. Caccia said Macmillan thought it might be more helpful if it looked as though the invitation and initiative had come from the President than to have it possibly appear that Macmillan had invited himself over to put pressure on the President in this matter. . . .

23 March 1960; Eisenhower Library, Abilene.

16 HMD, 23 March 1960.
17 Ibid., 29 March 1960.
18 Ibid., 30 March 1960.
19 Minute of 4 April 1960; HMA.
20 Letter of 23 December 1959; HMA.
21 HMD, 14 February 1960.
22 Ibid., 10 March 1959.
23 Ibid., 13 March 1959.
24 Letter of 14 March 1960; HMA.
25 François Kersaudy, *Churchill and De Gaulle* (London 1981), p. 427.
26 Quoted in Alistair Horne, *A Savage War of Peace*, p. 374.
27 HMD, 7 April 1960.
28 Letter of 9 April 1960; HMA.
29 Letter of 15 April 1960 to Arthur J. Goldsmith; Eisenhower Library, Abilene.
30 Eisenhower, op. cit., p. 543.
31 Ibid., p. 547.
32 It is now accepted that, by defeating Soviet efforts to deceive the West about the true state of their armaments, the U-2 intelligence enabled Eisenhower to resist Pentagon ambitions for largely inflated, and largely unnecessary, defence spending; it is also assumed that, had Khrushchev raised objections to the flights, Eisenhower would have halted them. (See Michael R. Beschloss, *Mayday*, p. 366.)
33 HMD, 7 May 1960.
34 Ibid.
35 Ibid. The reference to the Commonwealth 'in pieces' related to heated exchanges currently under way at the Prime Ministers' Conference over South Africa remaining within the Commonwealth.
36 Robert Murphy, *Diplomat Among Warriors* (London 1964), p. 441.
37 HMD, 8 May 1960.
38 Eisenhower, op. cit., p. 558.
39 HMD, 9 May 1960.
40 Ibid., 15 May 1960.
41 Ibid.
42 Ibid., 16 May 1960.
43 Ibid., 21 May 1960.
44 Ibid.

45 AHT, 8.5.
46 HMD, 21 May 1960. 'Most of our intelligence work was joint' is a key phrase which, like other similar references to British involvement in the U-2 operations, was deleted by Macmillan in the memoirs.
47 Eisenhower, op. cit., p. 515.
48 Beschloss, op. cit., p. 285.
49 Eisenhower, op. cit., p. 551.
50 Livingston Merchant, 15 May 1960; Mudd Library, Princeton.
51 Interview, Sir Philip de Zulueta; Beschloss, op. cit., p. 292.
52 Memorandum of conference with President, Herter, Goodpaster, 17 May 1960 (27 May 1960); Eisenhower Library, Abilene.
53 HMD, 17 May 1960.
54 HMD, 18 May 1960.
55 Memorandum of conference with President, 16 May 1960 (27 May 1960); Eisenhower Library, Abilene.
56 HMD, 18 May 1960.
57 Interview, Sir Harold Evans.
58 John Newhouse, *De Gaulle and the Anglo-Saxons*, p. 109.
59 BBC1, 6 June 1972.
60 Interview, Sir Philip de Zulueta.
61 BBC1, 23 April 1971; AHT, 14.23.
62 According to American sources, Khrushchev, just before his death, admitted that he dated the beginning of his decline back to the U-2 incident (Beschloss, op. cit., p. 325).
63 Letter of 19 May 1960; HMA.
64 Letter of 22 May 1960; HMA.
65 Letter of 27 May 1960; HMA.
66 Conference of 24 May 1960; Eisenhower Library, Abilene.
67 Cabinet meeting, 25 May 1960; Eisenhower Library, Abilene.
68 Eisenhower, op. cit., p. 558.
69 Ibid., p. 560.
70 Letter of 30 July 1960; HMA.
71 HMD, 30 June 1960.

Chapter 9   'Stagflation': The English Disease, 1960–end of 1961

HM, *Pointing the Way* (V), pp. 217–58, 360–80, and:

1 Letter of 19 January 1960; HMA.
2 HMD, 16 February 1960.
3 Thorneycroft letter to *The Times*, 9 November 1970.
4 HMD, 17 February 1960.
5 BBC1, 19 September 1973.
6 Became Lord Cobbold, later in 1960.
7 HMD, 26 February 1960.
8 Letter of 27 February 1960; HMA.

9   HMD, 4 April 1960.
10 Letter of 26 April 1960; HMA.
11 Letter of 29 April 1960; HMA.
12 Letter of 30 April 1960; HMA.
13 Special Deposits were introduced in 1960 to curb bank lending. It meant that the clearing banks had to deposit a percentage of their own bank deposits with the Bank of England. They were still able to collect interest on the amount lodged with the Bank, but the money was not available for the clearing banks' use – for lending or anything else. This effectively reduced the liquidity of the commercial banks. The authorities could vary the percentage at any time.
14 Interview, Lord Wilson.
15 HMD, 11 March 1960.
16 Ibid., 11 June 1960.
17 Letter of 30 July 1960; HMA.
18 HMD, 11 June 1960.
19 Ibid., 28 June and 5 July 1960.
20 R. A. Butler, *The Art of the Possible*, p. 231; interview, Lord Butler.
21 Lord Home, *The Way the Wind Blows*, p. 142.
22 HMD, 30 July 1960.
23 AHT, 14.1–4.
24 Ibid.
25 Interview, Lord Redmayne.
26 HMD, 17 June 1960.
27 AHC.
28 In fact, he was still going strong in politics, as Lord Chancellor, nearly three decades later.
29 HMD, 17 June 1960.
30 Ibid.
31 Letter of 31 January 1960; HMA.
32 HMD, 30 October 1960.
33 Sir Nigel Fisher, *Harold Macmillan*, p. 265.
34 Interview, Alexander Macmillan.
35 HMD, 1 November 1960.
36 Ibid., 15 September 1960.
37 Letter of 16 August 1960; Waverley papers.
38 HMD, 15 November 1960.
39 Ibid., 30 November 1960.
40 Ibid., 17 January 1961.
41 To meet Powell's call for 'economies' in the Health Service, one solution adopted was to encourage recruitment of 'cheap' nursing staff among the West Indians and other immigrant bodies – a fact often forgotten in the light of Powell's subsequent views on the subject of immigration generally.
42 HMA.

43   HMD, 24 March 1961.

44   Ibid., 5 March 1961.

45   Letter of 2 July 1961; Waverley papers.

46   An attempt at something like a pay pause had been made by Stafford Cripps in 1948, so Macmillan's was not, strictly speaking, the first.

47   *The Times*, leading article, 13 July 1961.

48   Ibid., 26 July 1961.

49   *The Economist*, 21 November 1961.

50   HMD, 23 December 1961.

51   AHT, 13.11.

52   HMD, 27 September 1962.

53   AHC.

54   HMD, 24 October 1961.

55   John Vaizey, *In Breach of Promise* (London 1983), p. 113.

56   Interview, Lord Redmayne.

57   HMD, 17 November 1960.

58   Ibid., 16 November 1960. The Conservative candidate was Teddy Taylor, later MP for Southend East.

59   Quoted in Philip M. Williams, *Hugh Gaitskell*, p. 474.

60   HMD, 8 October 1961.

61   *The Letters of Ann Fleming*, ed. Mark Amory (London 1985), pp. 282–3.

62   Letter of 31 August 1960; Waverley papers.

63   HMD, 18 December 1961, 6 February 1962.

64   Ibid., 24 April 1961.

65   Ibid., 16 May 1961.

66   Ibid., 6 July 1961.

67   Ibid., 22 May 1961.

68   Ibid., 25 September 1961.

69   Ibid., 14 October 1961.

70   Ibid., 9 July 1960.

71   BBC1, 6 June 1972.

72   HMA.

73   Letter of 31 January 1961; HMA.

74   Ibid.

75   HMD, 22 May 1961.

76   Ibid., 22 July 1961.

77   Hansard, 3 August 1961.

78   Letter of 1 August 1961; HMA.

79   Hansard, 2 August 1961.

80   Quoted in Anthony Sampson, *Macmillan*, p. 199.

81   HMD, 5 August 1961.

82   The vote totalled 313 Ayes to 5 Noes. Of those who voted, by 1989 only nineteen remained – eighteen Conservatives, including Mrs Thatcher, and one Labour, Michael Foot – an indication of the rapid

turnover of parliaments in the generation since Harold Macmillan's day.

83 HMD, 5 August 1961.

84 Duncan Sandys, who had been despatched by Macmillan to open talks in Ottawa, reported back that Canada was suffering from its perennial fears that it would be swallowed up, economically and eventually politically, by the United States if Britain joined the EEC (letter of 15 July 1961; HMA).

85 Letter of 7 March 1962; HMA.

86 Ibid.

87 HMD, 21 December 1960.

88 Later Lady Pamela Hartwell, a powerful London hostess in her own right, daughter of the famous F. E. Smith, and married to Michael Berry, Chairman and Editor-in-Chief of the *Daily Telegraph* from 1954 and the *Sunday Telegraph* from 1961.

89 AHT, 5.13–14.

90 Sir Harold Evans, *Downing Street Diary*, p. 2.

91 Ibid.

92 AHT, 15.1–2.

93 Ibid.

94 Lord Astor of Hever.

95 HMD, 10 April 1957.

96 Ibid., 6 August 1961.

97 Ibid., 21 July 1961.

98 Quoted in Evans, op. cit., p. 133.

99 HMD, 19 May 1961.

100 Undated letter; Waverley papers.

101 'No. 10 and the Media', BBC1, 12 November 1986.

102 On his visit the previous autumn, Eisenhower had evinced some nervousness at the floor giving way under him, as a result of all the added weight of the television cameramen. Eisenhower, op. cit., p. 424.

103 HMD, 10 August 1960.

104 Evans, op. cit., p. 112.

105 Letter of 23 July 1960; HMA.

106 Evans, op. cit., p. 123.

107 HMD, 15, 21 and 25 June 1960.

108 Ibid., 5 August 1961.

109 Ibid., 24 December 1961.

110 Ibid., 23 May 1962.

111 Ibid.

112 Quoted in the *Sunday Times*, 17 October 1965.

113 Later Baron Dacre of Glanton.

114 Nominally a Palace appointment, but in effect the choice devolves on the Prime Minister, advised by the university.

115 AHT, 4.7.
116 Interview, Sir Isaiah Berlin.
117 *Daily Express*, 23 February 1960.
118 Interview, Lord Blake (who later became Provost of Queen's).
119 AHC.
120 Lord Salisbury's brother, Lord David Cecil, also begged to be neutral out of 'personal considerations'.
121 Letter to David Stephens (appointments secretary at No. 10) of 21 February 1960; Trevor-Roper tapes.
122 Ibid. At about this time, Macmillan's old companion from the days of siege in the British Embassy in Athens, Osbert Lancaster, printed a cartoon in the *Daily Express* which depicted two tatty old dons, one saying to the other, 'It's nothing whatever to do with Bowra – I assure you that my support for Sir Oliver is entirely prompted by cogent reasons of purely personal nature.' The dons were standing outside Lloyds Bank, of which Franks was chairman.
123 AHC.
124 At that time Macmillan (though no political devotee of Mrs Thatcher's) considered resigning as Chancellor in disgust.
125 Interview, Lord Wyatt.
126 *News of the World*, 6 March 1960.
127 *Daily Express*, 4 March 1960.
128 Interview, Lord Blake.
129 At a cost £5 a time then.
130 Interview, Jane Parsons.
131 Interview, Lord Blake.
132 'When one learned Latin by the old pronunciation,' Macmillan once remarked to his biographer, 'I always thought of the Romans as being rather serious people; now, since the new pronunciation came in, one suddenly realises that they were just a lot of excitable Italians after all!' (AHC).
133 Quoted in Sampson, op. cit., p. 167.
134 Interview, Lord Bullock.

Chapter 10   'A Very Special Relationship', 1960–1961

HM, *Pointing the Way* (V), pp. 236–58, 306–59, and:

1 AHT 14.27.
2 HMD, 30 June 1960.
3 Dwight D. Eisenhower, *The White House Years*, p. 557.
4 Letter of 3 April 1960; HMA.
5 HM, *At the End of the Day* (VI), p. 342.
6 HMD, 1 December 1960.
7 Ibid., 29 March 1960.
8 Ibid., 12 June 1960.

9   The Soviet Minister of Defence.
10 Signal of 24 June 1960; HMA.
11 HMD, 17 July 1960.
12 Ibid., 27 October 1960.
13 Speech to UN General Assembly, 29 September 1960.
14 HMD, 2 October 1960.
15 Letter of 13 January 1961; HMA.
16 Quoted in George Hutchinson, *The Last Edwardian at No. 10*, p. 104.
17 Arthur Schlesinger, *A Thousand Days*.
18 Letter of 28 June 1960; HMA.
19 Killed while serving with the Coldstream Guards in Normandy.
20 AHT, 14.24–5.
21 Ibid., 14.25.
22 HMD, 2 November 1960.
23 Interview, Sir Harold Evans.
24 AHC.
25 HMD, 17 November 1960.
26 Ibid., 28 November 1960.
27 Ibid., 21 December 1960.
28 Letter of 9 November 1960; HMA.
29 Letter of 19 December 1960; HMA.
30 AHT, 14.25–6.
31 The title, used earlier by Roosevelt at the Teheran Conference in 1943, was adopted a year or two later by the Kennedy administration for their master plan.
32 HMD, 16 December 1960.
33 Ibid., 6 January 1961.
34 HMA.
35 HMD, 29 January 1961.
36 Private diaries of Sir Pierson Dixon; Piers Dixon papers.
37 Interview, Lady Dixon.
38 HMD, 23 February 1961.
39 Interview, Professor J. K. Galbraith.
40 BBC1, 6 June 1972.
41 JFKL Orals, Brandon/O'Connor.
42 Schlesinger, op. cit., p. 113.
43 JFKL Orals, Harlech.
44 AHC.
45 Ibid.
46 Henry Brandon, *Special Relationships* (London 1989), p. 156.
47 The others were North and South Vietnam and Cambodia.
48 Consisting of Thailand, USA and UK.
49 HMD, 8 December 1960.
50 Ibid., 1 January 1961.
51 Signal of 30 December 1960; HMA.

52   Memorandum to Cabinet, 6 January 1961; HMA.
53   HMD, 24 March 1961.
54   BBC1, 6 June 1972.
55   HMD, 26 March 1961.
56   Letter of 18 February 1964; HMA.
57   AHC.
58   BBC1, 6 June 1972.
59   The impending disaster at the Bay of Pigs was perhaps to suggest
     that this was – at least temporarily – not yet entirely the case.
60   HMD, 26 March 1961.
61   The 'scaled down' American plan was to send in four or five
     battalions to hold Vientiane, and some other essential river bridge-
     heads on the Mekong, in an endeavour to hold at least a small
     enclave. But, dropped and supplied by air in this land-locked,
     jungle-bound and remote territory, it was bound to have been a
     risky operation, to say the least.
62   HMD, 5 April 1961.
63   Ibid., 6 April 1961.
64   Benjamin C. Bradlee, *Conversations with Kennedy*, p. 225.
65   Victor Lasky, *JFK: The Man and the Myth* (New York 1963), pp. 6–7.
66   Ibid.
67   JFKL Orals, Harriman.
68   Schlesinger, op. cit., p. 312. After further alarms about US sabre-
     rattling, a ceasefire was agreed in May, and the Fourteen Power
     Conference reconvened in Geneva, as Macmillan had proposed.
     Eventually, the neutrality of Laos was agreed; although, predictably,
     the North Vietnamese cheated. Macmillan felt that at least a 'general
     flare-up' had been averted, and 'these people would continue to live
     for a bit longer in their normal state of tribal and ideological warfare
     and incompetent government' – in fact, until Laos was engulfed in
     the widening conflict of the Vietnam War. Years later Macmillan
     commented of the long-forgotten Laos crisis on the BBC: 'a great
     row starts in some part of the world and we all become experts in
     it; we know everybody's name, we know all about it, and then when
     it's over, it disappears and nobody ever hears of it . . .' (BBC1, 6
     June 1972).
69   HMD, 5 April 1961.
70   Interview, Lord Harlech.
71   HMD, 6 April 1961.
72   *Christian Science Monitor*, 2 April 1961.
73   *Time*, 14 April 1961.
74   Sir Harold Evans, *Downing Street Diary*, p. 149.
75   Minute of 4 April 1960.
76   HMD, 17 June 1960.
77   Letter of 12 July 1960; HMA.

78 Signal of 22 July 1960; HMA.
79 Signal of 25 July 1960; HMA.
80 Signal of 8 August 1960; HMA.
81 HMD, 18, 19 and 20 April 1961.
82 *Sunday Times*, 20 November 1983.
83 AHT, 14.32.
84 Ibid.
85 En route from the West Indies to Washington in April.
86 Bradlee, op. cit., p. 226.
87 20–26 April 1961.
88 HMD, 29 April 1961.
89 Ibid.
90 Ibid., 11 June 1961.
91 Personal telegram to PM, T26A/61; HMA.
92 Signal of 15 May 1961; HMA.
93 Personal telegram to PM, T476A/61, 22 August 1961; HMA.
94 Schlesinger, op. cit., p. 348.
95 Memoirs V, p. 356, says 'from 10.30 a.m. to 1 p.m.'.
96 AHT, 14.26.
97 HMD, 11 June 1961.
98 Letter of 15 September 1961; HMA.
99 Sir Nicholas Henderson, lecture, Washington DC, 6 March 1981.
100 HMD, 11 June 1961.
101 Letter of 18 February 1964; HMA.
102 Letter of 10 June 1961; HMA.
103 Quoted in Brandon, op. cit., p. 160.
104 Letter of 12 April 1961; HMA.
105 Most were contemporaries of Kennedy, or even younger; apart from brother Robert who, as Attorney-General, was thirty-six, McNamara at Defense, McGeorge Bundy, at the National Security Council, and Arthur Schlesinger from Harvard were all in their early forties; Pierre Salinger, the White House Press Secretary in his thirties, and Ted Sorensen not yet thirty.
106 Letter of 15 September 1961; HMA.
107 JFKL Orals, Brandon/Nunnerly.
108 Alistair Horne, 'The Skybolt Crisis', unpublished paper delivered to Woodrow Wilson Center, 3 March 1983.
109 AHT, 28.9.
110 Ambassador Bruce to Secretary of State, No. 2295, 12 December 1961; JFKL.

Chapter 11   Facing Up to Khrushchev and De Gaulle, October 1961–October 1962

HM, *Pointing the Way* (V), pp. 388–429, and *At the End of the Day* (VI), pp. 1–34, 142–79, and:

1   HMD, 1 June 1961.
2   Ibid., 14 June 1961.
3   Ibid., 25 June 1961.
4   Ibid., 22 July 1961.
5   Ibid., 7 August 1961.
6   Ibid., 25 August 1961.
7   Curtis Cate, *The Ides of August* (London 1978), pp. 450–1.
8   Letter of 19 August 1961; Waverley papers.
9   Eleven thousand Allied troops in Berlin faced twenty-two Soviet divisions in East Germany alone.
10 Cate, op. cit., pp. 450–1.
11 HMD, 25 August 1961.
12 Quoted in Cate, op. cit., p. 452.
13 HMD, 28 August 1961.
14 Cate, op. cit., p. 370.
15 John F. Kennedy to Rusk, 21 August 1961; JFKL.
16 Letter of 15 September 1961; HMA.
17 HMD, 9 September 1961.
18 Ibid., 15 September 1961.
19 Theodore C. Sorensen, *Kennedy*, p. 599.
20 HMD, 15 November 1961.
21 Ibid., 29 November 1961.
22 Record of conversation, 25 November 1961; HMA.
23 HMD, 29 November 1961.
24 AHC.
25 Ibid.
26 HMD, 29 November 1961.
27 Sorensen, op. cit., p. 617.
28 Arthur Schlesinger, *A Thousand Days*, p. 416.
29 HMD, 6 September 1961.
30 These began again on 15 September.
31 HMD, 24 October 1961.
32 Ibid., 27 October 1961.
33 Quoted in Sorensen, op. cit., p. 621.
34 Ibid., p. 622.
35 Ibid.
36 Interview, Ben Loeb. Seaborg Report, author's private papers.
37 Interview, Ben Loeb. Seaborg Report.
38 Schlesinger, op. cit., p. 452.
39 Interview, Ben Loeb. Seaborg Report.
40 HMD, 23 December 1961.
41 JFKL Orals, Harlech.
42 He in fact survived until 1969.
43 HMD, 23 December 1961.
44 Ibid.

45   Ibid., 5 January 1962.
46   *New York Times*, 23 December 1961.
47   Interview, Ben Loeb. Seaborg Report.
48   HMD, 23 December 1961.
49   Ibid., 24 December 1961.
50   Letter of 5 January 1962; HMA.
51   Schlesinger, op. cit., p. 456.
52   Quoted in David Nunnerly, *President Kennedy and Britain*, p. 100.
53   HMD, 19 May 1962.
54   Interview, Alexander Macmillan.
55   HMD, 14 May 1962.
56   Letter of 16 May 1962; HMA.
57   Minutes of the Chequers discussion (HMA) showed the Cabinet highly aware of this particular resentment of the French in atomic matters. In considering the possible practical co-operation of the French, the participants (Macmillan, Home and Heath) reckoned that the Americans would be hostile to the British providing a nuclear 'carrier' for a French warhead; it was therefore not clear how far such an organisation could be entered into without American agreement. There might possibly be some collaboration on joint targeting, but it was recognised that the French 'might not be satisfied with limited arrangements such as the above but would ask for a full degree of nuclear knowledge and possibly for the abandonment of any special US/UK joint targeting arrangements'. A further thought thrown out was that it might be possible to envisage an arrangement for an Anglo-French force 'acting as Trustees for the European branch of the Atlantic Alliance': which seemed a studiously vague proposition.
58   HMD, 27 May 1962.
59   *Le Monde*, 2 June 1962.
60   A ceasefire had been signed at Evian on 19 March, after seven and a half years of war that had torn France in two. This was followed by a national referendum, which de Gaulle had won with an overwhelming 90 per cent of the vote.
61   Record of a conversation at the Château de Champs, 2 June 1982; HMA.
62   Interview, Baron de Courcel.
63   Letter of 5 June 1962; HMA.
64   HMD, 3 June 1962.
65   Letter of 5 June 1962; HMA.
66   HMD, 19 June 1962.
67   HMA.

Chapter 12   Night of Long Knives, July 1962

HM, *At the End of the Day* (VI), pp. 35–72, 84–141, and:

1 HMA.
2 HMD, 30 October 1961.
3 Ibid., 30 November 1961.
4 Christopher Driver, *The Disarmers* (London 1964), p. 120.
5 HMD, 10 January 1962.
6 Ibid., 2 January 1962.
7 Ibid., 3 February 1962.
8 Ibid., 16 February 1962.
9 Ibid.
10 Ibid., 24 March 1962.
11 Ibid.
12 Interview, Lord Redmayne.
13 HMD, 24 March 1962.
14 Ibid., 25 March 1962.
15 Ibid., 16 April 1962.
16 Ibid., 21 April 1962.
17 Ibid., 25 April 1962.
18 Ibid., 6 May 1962.
19 Ibid., 14 May 1962.
20 Ibid., 10 April 1962.
21 Ibid., 7 April 1962.
22 Ibid., 27 May 1962.
23 Ibid., 12 June 1962.
24 Ibid., 16 June 1962.
25 Ibid., 17 June 1962.
26 Ibid., 22 June 1962.
27 Ibid., 21 June 1962.
28 Which was, as has been amply seen, in fact precisely what Macmillan wanted him to be, whether at the Foreign Office or at No. 11.
29 HMD, 8 July 1962.
30 AHT, 6.1.
31 HMD, 8 July 1962.
32 Later Lord Fanshawe of Richmond, and Vice-Chairman of the Party from 1979 to 1984.
33 A journalist who later earned a certain (not dissimilar) distinction during the Wilson years.
34 Royle memorandum; Lord Fanshawe papers.
35 Interview, Lord Soames.
36 HMD, 14 July 1962.
37 Ibid.
38 His son-in-law, Julian Amery, confirmed, 'I think he did feel that

there was a conspiracy being planned against him, following that curious article in the *Daily Mail . . .*' (interview).

39 HMD, 14 July 1962.
40 Royle memorandum.
41 HMD, 14 July 1962.
42 Letter of 13 July 1962; HMA.
43 *The Times*, 14 July 1962.
44 Subsequently Lord Blakenham.
45 HMD, 14 July 1962.
46 HMA.
47 Royle memorandum.
48 HMD, 14 July 1962.
49 *Both Sides of the Hill* (London 1964), p. 247.
50 *Political Adventure*, p. 324.
51 He also added, 'It's not very pleasant, but it happens to people. All this broke him up; he went gaga, went to pieces. . . . That's what really happened . . .' (AHT, 4.16).
52 AHC.
53 Not without justification, the life barony Eccles was given in 1962 he considered to be inadequate recognition for a minister of his seniority (Kilmuir had been made an earl), and after Macmillan's own resignation he was promoted to viscount, in 1964. It provided one more source of bitterness between the two colleagues.
54 HMD, 14 July 1962.
55 R. A. Butler, *The Art of the Possible*, p. 232.
56 Enahoro was arrested on 27 November 1962 and deported on 16 May 1963.
57 HMD, 14 July 1962.
58 This decision may have been taken by Macmillan in order to head off any further accusations of nepotism; perhaps also in part by irritation over a 'difficult Defence Committee meeting' a few days previously when Amery had led the attack over the Skybolt rocket in a 'truculent manner' (HMD, 10 July 1962).
59 Royle memorandum.
60 In September 1985, Mrs Thatcher replaced six ministers out of twenty-two in one fell swoop.
61 Interview, Baronne de Courcel.
62 HMD, 14 July 1962.
63 *Daily Sketch*, 17 July 1962.
64 George Thomson, later Lord Thomson of Monifieth; interview, Lady Thomson.
65 *Spectator*, 23 February 1980.
66 HMD, 14 July 1962.
67 Sir Harold Evans, *Downing Street Diary*, p. 207.
68 Memorandum of 15 July 1962; HMA.

69   HMD, 14 July 1962.
70   On 21 July 1962.
71   Interview, D. R. Thorpe; D. R. Thorpe, *Selwyn Lloyd* (London 1989), p. 357.
72   Evans, op. cit., p. 209.
73   Butler, op. cit., p. 232.
74   Interview, Lord Hailsham.
75   Interview, Margaret Thatcher.
76   Interview, Lord Home.
77   Gallup Poll, July 1962.
78   I.e. swapping Lloyd for Maudling. BBC1, 19 September 1973.
79   Woodrow Wyatt, *Confessions of an Optimist* (London 1985), p. 285.
80   HMD, 29 July 1962.
81   Letter of 12 August 1962; Waverley papers.
82   HMD, 10 July 1962.
83   Ibid., 31 December 1962.
84   Ibid., 30 July 1962.
85   Ibid., 21 August 1962.
86   Ibid., 22 August 1962.
87   To the *Leeds Citizen*, 21 June 1961.
88   BBC1, 19 September 1973.
89   HMD, 9 September 1962.
90   Philip M. Williams, *Hugh Gaitskell*, pp. 708–49, 711.
91   HMD, 10 September 1962.
92   Ibid., 12 September 1962. The Commonwealth Conference had just begun and was not going well.
93   HMD, 10 September 1962.
94   Ibid., 12 September 1962.
95   Ibid.
96   Ibid., 5 September 1962.
97   Ibid., 12 September 1962.
98   Ibid., 10 September 1962.
99   Ibid., 18 September 1962.
100 Whether this had been consciously in Macmillan's mind at the time or not, there was a parallel to his success over the Italian Armistice in 1943, when his 'short terms' had replaced the Foreign Office's document of some forty-three paragraphs. See Vol. I, ch. 8.
101 HMD, 19 September 1962.
102 *The Times*, 20 September 1962.
103 Ibid.
104 HMD, 21 September 1962.
105 Evans, op. cit., p. 218.
106 Letter of 7 October 1962; HMA.
107 HMD, 3 October 1962.
108 Ibid., 4 October 1962.

Chapter 13   'A Trial of Wills': Cuba, October–November 1962

HM, *At the End of the Day* (VI), pp. 180–220, and:˙

1   Signal of 21 October 1962; HMA.
2   Elie Abel, *The Missile Crisis*, p. 25.
3   Signal of 1 October 1962; HMA.
4   HMD, 3 October 1962.
5   HMA.
6   Interview, Jacqueline Onassis.
7   Signal of 22 October 1962; HMA.
8   HMD, 22 October 1962.
9   JFKL Orals, Acheson.
10   Chester L. Cooper, *The Lion's Last Roar: Suez 1956* (New York 1978), p. 23.
11   HMD, 22 October 1962.
12   AHC.
13   According to Dean Acheson, when he saw de Gaulle he waved aside the photographs, with a characteristically grandiose gesture, declaring, 'A great nation like yours would not act if there were any doubt about the evidence, and therefore I accept what you tell me as a fact without any proof of any sort needed. . . .' De Gaulle, added Acheson, 'didn't care whether anybody believed or not – he did; this was enough for him' (JFKL Orals, Acheson). Kennedy was perfectly aware, however, that de Gaulle could afford to take such a lofty line here as over Berlin, in that he had no targeted US Jupiter missiles on his territory, while Britain did.
14   As quoted by Dean Acheson, ibid.
15   Abel, op. cit., pp. 111–12.
16   HMD, 23 October 1962.
17   As quoted by Dean Acheson (JFKL Orals).
18   AHT, 16.4–5. The conversations are printed, almost *in extenso*, in the memoirs, Volume VI, pp. 198–215. Full transcripts are available in the J. F. Kennedy Library, although the records were apparently supplied by the British, as taken down by Philip de Zulueta, and not on the American side.
19   Interview, Lord Home.
20   HMD, 22 October 1962.
21   Ibid., 23 October 1962.
22   Signal to British Ambassador, Paris, for de Gaulle, 22 October 1962.
23   HMA.
24   Ibid.
25   Some of this appeared in author's colloquium at the Woodrow Wilson Center, 27 July 1984; William Roger Louis and Hedley Bull (eds), *The Special Relationship*.
26   Interview, Lord Harlech.

27 Theodore C. Sorensen, *Kennedy*, p. 559.
28 JFKL Orals, Harlech.
29 Ibid.
30 *Wilson Quarterly*, Autumn 1982; *Time*, 27 September 1982.
31 According to *The Penkovsky Papers*, foreword by Edward Crankshaw (London 1965), the Colonel's defection was motivated chiefly by fear that Khrushchev's bombastic threats were real, and that his recklessness might spark off a sudden nuclear war. At the time of publication, *The Penkovsky Papers* were regarded by some as a CIA concoction, but over the passage of time they have become accepted in the intelligence community as generally reliable.
32 Interviews, Archie Roosevelt (a CIA officer), Sir Maurice Oldfield.
33 JFKL Orals, Harlech.
34 JFKL telephone transcripts.
35 HMD, 24 October 1962.
36 Ibid.
37 Ibid., 25 October 1962.
38 Ibid., 26 October 1962.
39 Ibid., 28 October 1962.
40 The Jupiter IRBMs, taking hours to fuel, inaccurate and highly vulnerable, were militarily only useful for a first strike, and thus could be termed provocative. They had been installed in Turkey by Kennedy himself in late 1961, in fulfilment of a 1959 agreement concluded by Eisenhower.
41 See Barton J. Bernstein, *Political Science Quarterly*, Spring 1980, pp. 97–127.
42 Sorensen, op. cit., p. 714.
43 Arthur Schlesinger, *A Thousand Days*, p. 757.
44 T520/62, JFKL telephone transcripts.
45 JFKL Orals, Thorneycroft.
46 HMD, 28 October 1962.
47 Sir Harold Evans, *Downing Street Diary*, p. 224.
48 Sorensen, op. cit., pp. 716–17.
49 Schlesinger, op. cit., p. 758.
50 T524/62, JFKL telephone transcripts.
51 T525/62, JFKL telephone transcripts.
52 JFKL telephone transcripts.
53 T588/62, JFKL telephone transcripts.
54 Author's italics.
55 HMD, 4 November 1962.
56 BBC1, 19 September 1973.
57 HMD, 4 November 1962.
58 Sorensen, op. cit., p. 719.
59 *Wilson Quarterly*, op. cit., p. 156.
60 Lord Zuckerman, who as Chief Scientific Adviser to the Ministry of

Defence at the time was present at the meetings of the 28th, recalled Lord Mountbatten, then Chief of the Defence Staff, being the only one to ask the question: 'To the best of my knowledge neither he nor anyone else has yet provided an answer. Perhaps there is none . . .' (*Observer*, 2 September 1979).

61 AHT, 14.35.
62 HMD, 4 November 1962.
63 Robert Kennedy, *Thirteen Days*, pp. 16–18.
64 Interview, Lord Harlech.
65 BBC1, 1 June 1972.
66 Kennedy, op. cit., p. 16.
67 HMD, 4 November 1962.
68 Kennedy, op. cit., p. 99.
69 JFKL Orals, Rusk.
70 JFKL Orals, Acheson.
71 Foot and Young had speculated on the lines of 'Did Britain waver?' (see Evans, op. cit., p. 226).
72 HMD, 4 November 1962.
73 Letter of 31 October 1962; HMA.
74 Letter of 6 November 1962; HMA.
75 JFKL Orals, Bundy.
76 JFKL, box 170A, folder 37.

Chapter 14   The Continuing Burdens of Empire, 1961–1963

HM, *Pointing the Way* (V), pp. 166–77, 285–305, 381–7, 459–72, 486–7, and *At the End of the Day* (VI), pp. 73–83, 221–78, 280–332, and:

 1 HMD, 22 February 1961.
 2 Ibid., 24 February 1961.
 3 Roy Welensky, *4000 Days*, p. 305.
 4 AHC.
 5 HMD, 24 March 1961.
 6 Ibid.
 7 Letter of 12 August 1960; HMA.
 8 BBC1, 6 June 1972.
 9 Letter of 16 November 1960; HMA.
10 HMD, 16 November 1960.
11 Ibid., 24 March 1961.
12 Sir Harold Evans, *Downing Street Diary*, p. 141.
13 Welensky, op. cit., pp. 304–5.
14 Lord Kilmuir, *Political Adventure*, p. 317.
15 Evans, op. cit., p. 142.
16 Letter of 21 March 1961; HMA.
17 Hansard, 22 March 1961.
18 AHT, 14.15.

19 HMD, 8 April 1961.
20 Ibid., 19 June 1961.
21 Ibid., 11 June 1961.
22 Ibid., 3 and 4 June 1961.
23 Ibid., 18 June 1961.
24 Ibid., 19 June 1961.
25 Welensky, op. cit., p. 306.
26 HMD, 19 and 20 June 1961.
27 Ibid., 21 June 1961.
28 Ibid., 25 June 1961.
29 Ibid.
30 Welensky, op. cit., p. 307.
31 HMD, 25 June 1961.
32 Ibid., 8 July 1961.
33 Welensky, op. cit., p. 314.
34 Letter of 15 September 1961; HMA.
35 HMD, 23 September 1961.
36 Letter of 30 September 1961; HMA.
37 HMD, 13 November 1961.
38 Quoted in Richard D. Mahoney, *JFK: Ordeal in Africa*, p. 177.
39 HMD, 4 December 1961.
40 Mahoney, op. cit., p. 179.
41 HMD, 22 September 1961.
42 Ibid., 17 September 1961.
43 Lansdowne had in fact suggested to the UN Secretary-General that he would fly with him on his plane to Ndola. Hammarskjöld had replied gently that he thought it would be a bad idea, politically, for Lansdowne as there were no secrets in the Congo and it might be inadvisable if Macmillan's envoy were to be seen to be apparently in the pocket of the UN; Lansdowne explained that, as a member of the House of Lords, he was 'expendable'. Hammarskjöld laughed and remarked, 'So am I.' It was the last time that Lansdowne saw him alive, and he wondered at the time whether Hammarskjöld had any premonition of his death.

As in the accident that killed President Machel of Mozambique twenty-five years later, on 19 October 1986, there were rumours that Hammarskjöld's plane was shot down, but these were never substantiated, and the official enquiry came down on the side of pilot error. Lansdowne never had any doubt that the crash was an accident. (Interview, Lord Lansdowne.)
44 Welensky, op. cit., pp. 223, 247.
45 HMD, 18 December 1961.
46 Interview, Lord Harlech.
47 Mahoney, op. cit., pp. 117–18.
48 HMD, 18 December 1961.

49 Ibid.
50 Ibid.
51 Interview, Lord Harlech; Mahoney, op. cit., p. 118.
52 HMD, 20 December 1961.
53 Mahoney, op. cit., p. 129.
54 Ibid., p. 130.
55 Ibid., p. 131.
56 HMD, 26 April 1961.
57 Ibid., 13 July 1962.
58 Ibid., 5 August 1962.
59 Mahoney, op. cit., p. 141.
60 HMD, 27 November 1962.
61 Ibid., 10 December 1962.
62 Letter to Ambassador George McGhee, quoted in Mahoney, op. cit., p. 145.
63 AHT, 14.23.
64 Welensky, op. cit., p. 267.
65 Interview, Lord Trend.
66 AHC.
67 HMD, 3 February 1957.
68 Ibid., 10 January 1962; in his memoirs Macmillan translated the possibly offensive first phrase '*plus royaliste que le Roi*'.
69 Ibid., 2 January 1962.
70 Welensky, op. cit., p. 319.
71 HMD, 23 and 26 February 1962.
72 Ibid., 27 February 1962.
73 Ibid., 19 January 1962.
74 Ibid., 16 February 1962.
75 Ibid., 28 February 1962.
76 Welensky, op. cit., pp. 323–4.
77 HMD, 9 March 1962.
78 Ibid., 8 May 1961.
79 Letter of 9 March 1962; HMA.
80 Interview, Lord Butler.
81 Welensky, op. cit., p. 331.
82 HMD, 22 March 1963.
83 Welensky, op. cit., pp. 359, 361.
84 HMD, 13 May 1963.
85 Ibid., 20 and 23 April 1963.
86 Ibid., 20 May 1963.
87 Signal of 4 July 1963; HMA.
88 HMD, 7 July 1963.
89 AHT, 14.19.
90 HMD, 23 March 1963.
91 Ibid., 22 February 1961.

92   Ibid., 19 December 1961.
93   Letter of 23 September 1963; HMA.
94   HMD, 4 November 1961.
95   AHT, 14.16.
96   Letter of 13 December 1961; HMA.
97   HMD, 23 October 1962.
98   Letter to Kennedy, 18 January 1963; HMA.
99   HMD, 16 November 1962.
100 Ibid., 8 July 1961.
101 HMA.
102 HMD, 26 November 1962.
103 Ibid., 8 March 1963.
104 Ibid., 16 August 1963.
105 The civil war in Yemen continued until 1969; out of it emerged the
     Marxist 'People's Democratic Republic of Yemen' in the south and
     the 'Yemen Arab Republic' in the north. An uneasy truce with
     intermittent border warfare continued between the two states. Aden
     was swallowed up by the People's Democratic Republic, after the
     British withdrawal.
106 Interview, Lord Home.
107 HMD, 30 May 1961.
108 Ibid., 13 October 1961.
109 Ibid., 22 November 1961.
110 R. A. Butler, *The Art of the Possible*, p. 206.
111 *The Times*, 27 February 1967.
112 HMD, 22 March 1963.
113 Ibid., 10 April 1963.
114 Letter of 12 April 1963; HMA.
115 HMD, 10 April 1963.
116 Ibid., 27 March 1963.

Chapter 15   Skybolt Falls and De Gaulle Says No, May 1962–
             January 1963

HM, *At the End of the Day* (VI), pp. 333–78, and:

1   HMD, 5 December 1962.
2   Ibid., 1 December 1962.
3   Ibid., 17 November 1962.
4   Ibid., 7 December 1962. Writing to a fellow Tory on 10 December
    (Lord Coleraine) in answer to a letter he had published in *The Times*,
    he dismissed Acheson as 'a nice man, but a kind of caricature of an
    Englishman, and always overstates his case. . . . Fortunately the
    President dislikes him very much indeed . . .' (HMA).
5   HMD, 9 December 1962.
6   Meaning the 'Europeanists' in the State Department.

7 HMD, 9 December 1962.

8 Ibid., 11 December 1962.

9 Ibid., 15 December 1962.

10 HMA.

11 BBC1, 19 September 1973.

12 Ibid.

13 Interview, Sir Philip de Zulueta.

14 An interesting postscript on what de Gaulle heard, or did not hear, was provided in a memorandum by Edward Heath, following a visit to de Gaulle on 22 November 1965, two years after the Rambouillet meeting:

> The General confirmed that Mr Macmillan had told him on that occasion that if the United States administration cancelled Skybolt, he would try to obtain Polaris submarines. General de Gaulle had at that point expressed regret that it was not possible for France and Britain to 'do something together' but that [he] had been in no doubt about Mr Macmillan's intentions. (HMA)

15 HMD, 16 December 1962.

16 AHC.

17 HMD, 16 December 1962.

18 Interview, Lord Zuckerman.

19 Hansard, 2 November 1962.

20 In a seventeen-minute conversation with President Kennedy on 27 April 1963, Neustadt was instructed: 'this was as much a British story and we really ought to find out what they had been up to – or not up to – why they acted the way they did. . . . I [Neustadt] said I wanted to emphasize the aspects of trans-Atlantic non-dialogue. He indicated that this equated with his interest . . .' (Neustadt memorandum). The Neustadt Report was ready in November 1963, and Kennedy suggested to its author that he might send it as a Christmas present to his English friend. Kennedy read it on the Sunday before going to Dallas, where it was found still in his briefcase after the assassination. The intended Christmas present never reached Macmillan.

 For much of the ensuing material, the author is indebted to Professor Neustadt, the US Department of Defense and the Woodrow Wilson Center, Washington DC, under whose aegis the author's paper 'The Skybolt Crisis 1962' was produced in 1983. (Professor Neustadt married the former Labour minister Mrs Shirley Williams in 1988.)

21 JFKL Orals, Brandon/O'Connor.

22 Theodore C. Sorensen, *Kennedy*, p. 565.

23 Interview, Robert McNamara.

24 JFKL Orals, Thorneycroft.

25 This was to some extent reinforced by George Ball, who described McNamara as 'a man not very concerned with political nuances . . .' (interview).
26 Neustadt commentary to author.
27 Interview, Lord Zuckerman.
28 Neustadt memorandum.
29 He was then Honorary Secretary of the Zoological Society.
30 Interview, Lord Zuckerman.
31 Arthur Schlesinger, *A Thousand Days*, pp. 787–8.
32 Neustadt Report, p. 117.
33 Neustadt commentary to author.
34 Neustadt Report, p. 88.
35 Interview, George Ball.
36 Interviews, George Ball, McGeorge Bundy, Arthur Schlesinger; George W. Ball, *The Discipline of Power*, p. 84.
37 Bundy from Neustadt Report, p. 90.
38 Neustadt Report, pp. 86–7.
39 JFKL Orals, Harlech.
40 Neustadt Report, pp. 87–8.
41 Ball, op. cit., p. 103.
42 HMD, 23 December 1962.
43 Sorensen, op. cit., p. 566.
44 JFKL Orals, Bundy.
45 Neustadt commentary to author.
46 HMA; interview, Lord Zuckerman.
47 HMA.
48 Ibid.
49 Letter of 24 December 1962; Waverley papers.
50 JFKL Orals, Harlech.
51 HMD, 23 December 1962.
52 Letter of 24 December 1962; HMA.
53 HMD, 28 January 1963.
54 Solly Zuckerman, *Monkeys, Men and Missiles* (London 1988), pp. 265–6.
55 *Reporter*, 1 January 1963.
56 AHC.
57 Neustadt Report, p. 114.
58 Schlesinger, op. cit., p. 791.
59 Letter of 21 December 1962; HMA.
60 HMA.
61 JFKL Orals, Redmayne.
62 Letter of 24 December 1962; HMA.
63 HMD, 24 December 1962.
64 Ibid., 26 December 1962.
65 Letter of 26 December 1962; HMA.
66 HMD, 31 December 1962.

67   Quoted in John Newhouse, *De Gaulle and the Anglo-Saxons*.
68   Neustadt Memorandum.
69   HMA.
70   AHT, 16.8.
71   Signal of 2 January 1963; HMA.
72   HMD, 28 January 1963.
73   De Gaulle press conference, 14 January 1963, quoted in Don Cook, *Charles de Gaulle*, pp. 361–3.
74   HMA.
75   AHT, 16.8.
76   Lord Home, *The Way the Wind Blows*, p. 152.
77   Ball, op. cit., p. 105; interview.
78   George Ball memorandum of conversation with Hallstein, 8 December 1962; JFKL.
79   Quoted in Terence Prittie, *Konrad Adenauer*, p. 297. The Bundestag subsequently took much of the clout out of the treaty, giving precedence to Germany's NATO commitments (which infuriated de Gaulle), and finally pushing Adenauer into retirement in October.
80   Ibid., 28 January 1963.
81   Ibid., 4 February 1963.
82   Ibid.
83   Ibid.
84   Ibid., 17 December 1963.
85   Interview, Lord Wilson.
86   Henry Fairlie, *The Life of Politics* (London 1968), p. 144.
87   According to the *History of The Times*, p. 344.
88   Gallup Poll, January 1963.
89   Letter of 28 January 1963; Waverley papers.
90   AHT, 7.4; AHC.

Chapter 16   'Everybody's Darling, Anyway', January–June 1963

HM, *At the End of the Day* (VI), pp, 379–452, and:

1   Christopher Booker, *The Neophiliacs*, p. 185.
2   *Observer*, 1 October 1961.
3   Quoted in Booker, op. cit., p. 165.
4   Philip Goodhart, *The 1922*, p. 183.
5   HMD, 4 February 1963.
6   Ibid., 17 February 1963.
7   Ibid., 28 January 1963.
8   Wilson, Brown and Callaghan were the contestants, of whom Macmillan's opinion (ibid.) was: 'The first is able and dangerous. The second is a buffoon. The third is pretty good and would be a respectable leader.'
9   Sir Harold Evans, *Downing Street Diary*, pp. 247, 251.

10   HMD, 4 February 1963.

11   Ibid., 9 March 1963.

12   It has subsequently been claimed that Macmillan's statement in the Commons was drafted by Graham Mitchell, an officer of MI5 later suspected of having been a Soviet 'mole' (Nigel West, *Mole Hunt*, p. 2).

13   While Macmillan was actually in Moscow in February 1959, the Lord Privy Seal (Heath) cabled that Burgess had appealed to Macmillan to ask if he might return to England to see his ill mother. The Attorney-General advised that, in fact, there were *no* grounds on which Burgess could be prosecuted, should he choose to return; nor were there any means to prevent him from returning, if he so chose. Therefore Heath suggested that Macmillan delay a reply to Burgess until the last possible moment; and then it should say that neither Macmillan nor his Party had the means to grant him the safe conduct for which he had asked. 'In this way we may succeed in creating in his mind such doubt about the possible consequences of returning to this country that he will decide to stay where he is. This would be the most satisfactory outcome' (Signal of 26 February 1959; HMA). Burgess stayed in Russia until he died.

14   After three years he was traded for Greville Wynne, a far smaller pawn in the spy war, but valued for having acted as courier to the important Colonel Penkovsky.

15   HMD, 22 June 1961.

16   After serving five years of his forty-two, Blake was 'sprung' and he disappeared into Eastern Europe.

17   HMD, 4 May 1961.

18   HMA.

19   Roger Hollis was knighted in 1960.

20   HMD, 4 May 1961.

21   Ibid., 14 May 1961.

22   At the time of the first round with Philby back in 1955, Macmillan had proposed just such a committee, under Lord Radcliffe, but Eden had vetoed it.

23   HMD, 7 February 1962.

24   Interview, Sir Dick White.

25   AHC.

26   Golitsyn.

27   HMD, 28 September 1962.

28   AHT, 9.12–13.

29   Ibid.

30   AHC.

31   HMD, 5 November 1962.

32   *Annual Register*, 1962, p. 48. It has been alleged subsequently (see West, op. cit., p. 8) that there was another Admiralty suspect at the

time – unbeknown both to Macmillan and to the officer himself. Insufficient evidence was produced, and this naval officer (then working under the First Sea Lord) was given command of a ship, while steps were taken to prevent him having access to sensitive information for the rest of his career. Hollis did not welcome facing a fourth official enquiry.

33 Memorandum, 'Profumo Affair'; Redmayne papers.
34 Interview, Lord Redmayne.
35 Evans, op. cit., p. 227.
36 *The Times*, 23 November 1962. See Evans, op. cit., p. 230.
37 AHT, 9.14.
38 BBC1, 26 September 1973.
39 Interview, Sir Harold Evans.
40 Evans, op. cit., p. 227.
41 Interview, Lord Carrington.
42 HMD, 28 November 1962.
43 Ibid., 19 February 1963.
44 Ibid., 11 July 1963.
45 Macmillan in fact said 'MI6', not 'MI5'. But in the light of subsequent information, it is evident that Macmillan, who was then rising eighty-six – though his memory was still extraordinary – meant MI5.
46 AHC.
47 Ibid.
48 Interview, Rupert Allason; Peter Wright allegations *in camera*.
49 West, op. cit., p. 178, says of Hollis's reluctance here: he was 'unwilling to tell Macmillan that Mitchell, his own Deputy Director-General, who had played a leading role in the Profumo affair, was a probable Soviet agent and that a warrant was required to tap his home telephone'.
50 HMD, 16 April 1963.
51 Ibid., 19 April 1963.
52 Ibid., 4 January 1963.
53 Ibid., 12 January 1963.
54 Ibid., 14 January 1963.
55 Ibid., 28 January 1963.
56 HMA.
57 Ibid.
58 Evans, op. cit., p. 257.
59 Schwartz and Wincott were two influential journalists writing on economic subjects; Kaldor (later Lord) was one of Harold Wilson's principal advisers.
60 HMD, 12 March 1963.
61 Letter of 11 March 1963; HMA.
62 HMD, 2 April 1963.

63 Ibid., 3 April 1963.

64 In the House, the controversial Labour MP, Marcus Lipton, claimed that Macmillan had 'passed the plate around' to pay for the meeting, rather than paying for it out of his own pocket, and not the taxpayers', as Macmillan had declared. He had been seen, said Lipton, 'gesticulating with one hand and clutching a plate with the other'. To which Macmillan replied, languidly: 'I must admit a collection was taken. But it was for the restoration of the ancient churches of Buckinghamshire!' (William Hickey, *Daily Express*, 1 May 1963.)

65 Macmillan's statement to the Commons; Hansard, 17 June 1963.

66 See Phillip Knightley and Caroline Kennedy, *Sunday Times*, 3 May 1987.

67 Made Lord Wigg of the Borough of Dudley by Harold Wilson in 1967, and ended his career as Chairman of the Horse Race Betting Levy Board.

68 Interview, Lord Wigg.

69 On 8 May, Ian Gilmour, then proprietor of the *Spectator*, sent a revealing letter to Macmillan. The *Spectator* had published an article stating that Wigg had been guilty of McCarthyite tactics, and Wigg duly sued for libel. The case was settled out of court, without damages; in the course of it, however, Wigg gave Gilmour's solicitors a copy of a memo he (Wigg) had prepared for Wilson. It read, 'In my opinion Profumo was never, at any time, a security risk,' and then went on to say that the intelligence services had been aware of Profumo's meeting with Ivanov and Keeler. Wigg had also sent a copy to Macmillan, at the time of the case, *but without the first sentence*. Gilmour, in his letter, explained the deletion with the words 'in view of the fact that he [Wigg] and Wilson claimed throughout that they were only concerned with the security aspect, Wigg no doubt felt that his hypocrisy, as revealed in this memorandum, would be an embarrassing revelation.' (HMA.)

70 Anthony Howard, *RAB*, p. 298.

71 Interview, Lord Redmayne.

72 HMA.

73 It should be noted that it was Tim Bligh, not John Wyndham, as suggested by Anthony Summers and Stephen Dorril, *Honeytrap: The Secret World of Stephen Ward* (London 1987), p. 162, who first dealt with the Profumo information and MI5. Wyndham would never have had this responsibility. Interview, Pamela, Lady Egremont.

74 Interview, Sir Philip de Zulueta.

75 Ivanov had in fact been shipped back to the USSR in January, in anticipation of the impending row.

76 Hansard, 17 June 1963.

77 HMD, 22 March 1963.

78 Ibid.

79   Evans, op. cit., p. 261.
80   HMD, 7 May 1963. The new 'scandal' probably referred to photo-
      graphs that had emerged recently from the Argyll divorce case, in
      which most of the notables of the realm – and beyond – seemed to
      have been named. The photographs showed, in the nude, a so-called
      'Headless Butler', alleged to have been one of Macmillan's senior
      Cabinet ministers, now dead. The scandal never broke.
81   Repeated in 1987, this story still seems unconvincing, in that Profumo
      would have been as unlikely to have had access to the specific
      information required as Keeler would have had the intellect to have
      framed the question meaningfully.
82   HMD, 30 May 1963.
83   Ibid., 31 May 1963.
84   Evans, op. cit., p. 269.
85   There was a loud, doubting interjection of 'Oh!' from Hon. Members
      during Macmillan's 17 June statement in the House, when he
      disclosed the 'very unfortunate' fact that MI5 had failed to pass
      him reports about Ward using Keeler as an instrument to obtain
      information from Profumo.
86   He explained, 'One of the difficulties of keeping a diary is that during
      a real crisis, it breaks down. This happened to me during the Suez
      crisis. It has happened during what I may call the Profumo crisis . . .'
      (HMD, 7 July 1963).
87   Ibid.
88   R. A. Butler, The Art of the Possible, p. 235.
89   Howard, op. cit., p. 298.
90   Butler, op. cit., p. 235.
91   Interview, Lord Redmayne.
92   HMD, 7 July 1963.
93   Ibid.
94   The Times, 11 June 1963.
95   Hansard, 17 June 1963.
96   HMD, 7 July 1963.
97   From Trollope's The Duke's Children. The context was Macmillan's
      praise of Baldwin for having come clean about his wildly wrong
      estimates of German air strength in 1935 – 'where I was wrong was
      in the estimate of the future. There I was completely wrong. We
      were completely misled on that subject. . . .' As a result, the House
      was 'captivated by Baldwin's candour' (HM, Winds of Change (I),
      p. 409). See also Anthony Sampson, Macmillan, p. 225.
98   Hansard, 17 June 1963.
99   Ibid., quoted in Sampson, op. cit., p. 226.
100   Who later resigned the Whip to join the Labour Party.
101   HMD, 7 July 1963.
102   Redmayne later denied allegations that he had given rise to a rumour

that if Macmillan had not secured reasonable support in the division he would resign in due course. 'This was totally untrue. . . . But it was a damaging story . . .' (Redmayne memorandum, 'Profumo Affair').

103   Cable for Secretary of State, 18 June 1963; JFKL, box 171, folder 14.
104   Sampson, op. cit., p. 226.
105   Redmayne memorandum, 'Profumo Affair'.
106   Booker, op. cit., p. 196.
107   Interview, Lord Barber.
108   Butler, op. cit., p. 235.
109   Interview, Lord Home.
110   Royle memorandum, 9 October 1963; Lord Fanshawe papers.
111   Sir Knox Cunningham, 'One Man Dog', private sealed copy of his memoirs, deposited with the Drapers Company, since his death in 1976.
112   Butler, op. cit., p. 236.
113   HMD, 7 July 1963.
114   BBC1, 26 September 1973.
115   Letter of 23 June 1963; HMA.
116   Interview, Duke of Devonshire.
117   HMD, 7 July 1963.
118   HMA.
119   HMD, 7 July 1963.
120   Lord Macaulay, 'Moore's Life of Lord Byron', *Critical and Historical Essays* (London 1851), p. 296.
121   Assessing Ward's reliability as a witness, the Denning Report describes him as 'so untrustworthy . . . so given to dropping names – that no one should give any credence to any report emanating from him . . .' (HMSO, Cmnd 2152, p. 109).
122   Quoted in *Sunday Times*, 3 May 1987.
123   HMD, 7 July 1963.
124   Ibid.
125   Ibid., 12 July 1963.
126   Ibid., 11 July 1963.
127   Ibid.
128   Ibid., 23 and 27 July, 12 August 1963.
129   Ibid., 2 August 1963.
130   The Great Train Robbery took place on 8 August 1963.
131   HMD, 2 August 1963.
132   Ibid., 16 August 1963.
133   Author's private collection.
134   HMD, 17 September 1963.
135   The charges against one of the unnamed ministers related to photographic evidence produced during the Argyll divorce case, which in itself was something of a landmark of the 'Swinging Sixties'. To

oblige Denning, the minister concerned (now dead) had even gone to the extent of undergoing medical examination – which proved that the physical characteristics of the naked 'Man without a Head' differed 'in unmistakable and significant respects from those of the Minister' (Denning Report, p. 111). One of the key members of Macmillan's administration, the 'Minister' had in fact admitted to the Prime Minister, back in June, that – though 'he was *not* the headless man . . . he *had* once been involved with the lady . . .', and felt that he now ought to offer his resignation – regardless of the political consequences (Evans, op. cit., p. 276). At the time, Harold Evans was amazed that 'it did not seem to be realised what these consequences must almost certainly be,' that is, the fall of the government (ibid.). The minister was prevailed upon not to resign, and it was (largely) all kept from the public gaze; thus the situation was 'saved within a hairsbreadth of disaster . . .' (ibid.). But there did seem to be some 'economy with the truth', or at least splitting of hairs, in the minister's evidence to Denning. That he should be persuaded to go to such lengths to disprove that he was 'the Man without a Head' only confirms just how great was the power of gossip and scandal in 1963.

136 HMD, 19 September 1963.
137 Denning Report, p. 88.
138 Ibid., p. 95.
139 Ibid., p. 96.
140 Ibid., p. 114.
141 HMD, 17 September 1963.
142 Denning Report, p. 97.
143 HMD, 15 September 1963.
144 Ibid., 19 September 1963.
145 Ibid., 26 September 1963.
146 Ibid., 27 September 1963.
147 His vacant seat at Stratford led to a by-election in August, won by the right-winger Angus Maude.
148 Denning Report, p. 72.
149 BBC1, 26 September 1973.
150 Evans, op. cit., p. 276.
151 Author's italics.
152 Redmayne memorandum, 'Profumo Affair'.
153 Interview, Lord Redmayne.
154 Interview, Lord Rawlinson.
155 Private conversation with author.
156 Letter to author, 10 October 1988.
157 AHT, 9.16.
158 Interview, Lord Fraser of Kilmorack.
159 See John Wyndham, *Wyndham and Children First*, pp. 187–8.

160 Interview, Lord Home.
161 Summers and Dorril, op. cit., pp. 168–70, and Phillip Knightley and Caroline Kennedy, *An Affair of State: The Profumo Case and the Framing of Stephen Ward* (London 1984), pp. 157–8. The day on which, according to Knightley and Kennedy, Macmillan was informed by David Bruce, 28 January, was also the day of de Gaulle's veto; he would in any case have had other things to think about than a visit from the American Ambassador on what at the time would have appeared to be, relatively speaking, a trivial matter.
162 Interview, Mrs David Bruce.
163 BBC1, 26 September 1973.
164 Ibid.
165 Denning Report, p. 39.
166 Interview, Lord Carrington.
167 AHT, 4.10.
168 Interview, Lord Amory.
169 AHC.
170 BBC1, 26 September 1973.
171 Interviews, Katharine Macmillan, Anne Glyn-Jones.

Chapter 17   A Last Triumph, June–September 1963

HM, *At the End of the Day* (VI), pp. 408–20, 453–85, and:

1   Philip Ziegler, *Mountbatten*, p. 610.
2   HMD, 15 September 1960.
3   AHC.
4   Ziegler, op. cit., p. 612.
5   HMD, 24 December 1962.
6   Ibid., 31 December 1962.
7   Ziegler, op. cit., p. 617.
8   Ibid., p. 620.
9   Ibid.
10 AHC.
11 Admiral of the Fleet Sir Terence Lewin, CDS, Mountbatten Memorial Lecture, 7 July 1980, *RUSI Journal*.
12 Ziegler, op. cit., p. 622.
13 JFKL Orals, Harlech.
14 HMD, 27 November 1962.
15 Ibid., 8 March 1963.
16 Arthur Schlesinger, *A Thousand Days*, p. 819.
17 Sir John Wheeler-Bennett, *The Nemesis of Power* (London 1953).
18 HMD, 24 March 1963.
19 The MLF scheme that Macmillan had accepted reluctantly at Nassau, but thought absurd and unworkable.
20 HMD, 1 April 1963.

21 Theodore C. Sorensen, *Kennedy*, p. 733.

22 HMD, 13 April 1963.

23 Letter of 15 April 1963; HMA.

24 HMD, 17 April 1963.

25 Schlesinger, op. cit., p. 820.

26 Ibid., p. 821.

27 HMD., 20 May 1963.

28 Schlesinger, op. cit., p. 821.

29 Quoted in ibid., pp. 822–3.

30 Quoted in ibid., p. 826.

31 BBC1, 19 September 1973.

32 Ibid.

33 Schlesinger, op. cit., p. 808.

34 HMD, 20 May 1963.

35 Letter of 22 June 1963; HMA.

36 HMD, 7 July 1963.

37 AHT, 14.33.

38 Interview, Jacqueline Onassis.

39 HMD, 7 July 1963.

40 Letter of 5 July 1963; HMA.

41 HMD, 7 July 1963.

42 Schlesinger, op. cit., p. 810; David Nunnerly, *President Kennedy and Britain*, pp. 214–16.

43 The metamorphosis had been fairly sudden; on 15 March, Macmillan had written to Ormsby-Gore referring to Wilson's proposed visit:

> no doubt Wilson will talk a good deal to everybody, including the President, about what he intends to do when he is Prime Minister . . . but I think you ought to warn the President that in my view Wilson has not found his feet yet. In any case, I expect the Americans, or at least that minority who are politicians, will realise that they should not take Wilson's views too seriously. . . . (HMA)

Ormsby-Gore had followed up a week later (letter of 22 March 1963, HMA), '. . . I have noted a marked lack of enthusiasm for the visit among the Administration. Unfortunately those who had already met him dislike him, and those who have not distrust him. I don't think we are in for a very happy four days.' Since then, however, the Profumo scandal had broken and pragmatists in Washington were realising that they might have to face dealing with Harold Wilson earlier than expected.

44 Philip de Zulueta memorandum, 30 June 1967; HMA.

45 Letter of 5 July 1963; HMA.

46 Letter of 4 July 1963; HMA.

47 HMD, 12 July 1963.

48 Interview, Averell Harriman.

49 HMD, 18 July 1963.
50 To Foreign Affairs Committee, 31 July 1963; HMA.
51 HMD, 21 July 1963.
52 Signal of 24 July 1963; HMA.
53 HMD, 24 July 1963.
54 Ibid., 25 July 1963.
55 Schlesinger, op. cit., p. 829.
56 HMD, 27 July 1963.
57 BBC1, 19 September 1973.
58 Signal of 25 July 1963; HMA.
59 Sir Harold Evans, *Downing Street Diary*, p. 285.
60 Schlesinger, op. cit., p. 830.
61 JFKL Orals, Sir Michael Wright.
62 Lord Hailsham, *The Door Wherein I Went*, pp. 217–19.
63 Interview, Michael Foot.
64 Letter of 26 July 1963; HMA.
65 AHC.
66 Sorensen, op. cit., p. 740; interview, Arthur Schlesinger.
67 AHT, 14.32.

Chapter 18 'The Hand of Fate', September–October 1963

HM, *At the End of the Day* (VI), pp. 486–519, and:

1 HMD, 25 July 1963.
2 Ibid., 2 August 1963.
3 Richardson memorandum, 8 August 1972; HMA.
4 Interview, Sir Harold Evans.
5 AHT, 15.6–8.
6 Interview, Lord Hailsham. Authoritative medical advice taken shortly afterwards by Lord Aldington, then Deputy Chairman of the Tory Party, suggests that, during the summer months and well before the actual prostate disorder struck Macmillan, he was very likely suffering from uraemic toxicity, often associated with prostate trouble. Apart from the lassitude from which Macmillan himself admitted that he had suffered, one of the recognised syndromes of uraemia is a tendency to indecisiveness. The Macmillan diaries for this period show clearly how beset he was with indecision, uncharacteristically; this additionally could well have been at least in part caused by his illness. (Interview, Lord Aldington.)
7 HMD, 16 August 1963.
8 Interview, Lord Harlech.
9 Letter of 29 August 1963; Waverley papers.
10 HMD, 29 August 1963.
11 Ibid.
12 Memorandum of 28 August 1963; HMA.

13 HMD, 5 September 1963.
14 Letter of 5 September 1963; HMA.
15 HMD, 8 September 1963.
16 Letter of 16 June 1963; HMA.
17 Memorandum of 17 July 1963; HMA.
18 HMD, 11 September 1963.
19 Ibid., 18 September 1963.
20 Ibid., 20 September 1963.
21 Memorandum of 21 September 1963; HMA.
22 HMD, 21 September 1963.
23 'IT'S DYNAMITE' proclaimed one headline; but it absolutely wasn't.
24 HMD, 27 September 1963.
25 *Daily Telegraph*, 20 June 1963, quoted in Philip Goodhart, *The 1922*, p. 187.
26 HMD, 2 October 1963.
27 Ibid.
28 Ibid., 4 October 1963.
29 Ibid., 6 October 1963.
30 Ibid.
31 Ibid., 7 October 1963.
32 Letter of 5 October 1963; HMA.
33 HMD, 7 October 1963.
34 *Daily Sketch*, 7 October 1963.
35 HMD, 7 October 1963.
36 Ibid., 8 October 1963.
37 Reginald Bevins, *The Greasy Pole*, p. 33.
38 HMD, 8 October 1963.
39 Interview, Lord Butler.
40 Aristides, Athenian statesman who was surnamed 'The Just', and was never wrong.
41 HMD, 8 October 1963.
42 AHT, 2.6.
43 AHC.
44 Interview, Lord Richardson.
45 Richardson memorandum.
46 BBC1, 26 September 1973.
47 Interview, Maurice Macmillan.
48 AHC.
49 Sir Harold Evans, *Downing Street Diary*, pp. 296–7.
50 HMD, 8 October 1963.
51 Lord Home, *The Way the Wind Blows*, pp. 181–2.
52 HMA.
53 Home, op. cit., p. 182.
54 HMD, 9 October 1963. Wolfgang Michael was the author of a biography of George I.

55 Ibid., 12 October 1963.
56 Rab supporters have frequently tried to make out that Macmillan deliberately out-manoeuvred him in getting Home to make the crucial announcement. Rab himself never thought so; and in fact Home, as Chairman of the Conference, would have seemed the inevitable choice to make the announcement. (Interview, Lord Butler.)
57 Home, op. cit., p. 182.
58 Ibid.
59 *Sunday Times*, 13 October 1963.
60 Sir Nigel Fisher, *Harold Macmillan*, p. 235.
61 Interview, Lord Butler.
62 Hailsham, op. cit., pp. 196, 223; interview.
63 Home, op. cit., p. 182. Hailsham was divested of his peerage in November 1963, but was created a life peer in 1970.
64 Memorandum, 'The Leadership'; Redmayne papers.
65 Evans, op. cit., pp. 298–9.
66 Redmayne memorandum, 'The Leadership'.
67 Quoted in Anthony Sampson, *Macmillan*, p. 219.
68 Interview, Lord Hailsham.
69 Interviewed by Kenneth Harris, *Listener*, 28 July 1966, quoted in Sampson, op. cit., pp. 229–32.
70 Goodhart, op. cit., p. 191.
71 Anthony Howard and Richard West, *The Making of a Prime Minister*, p. 846.
72 Anthony Howard, *RAB*, pp. 313, 318.
73 Quoted in ibid., p. 318.
74 Quoted in ibid., p. 320.
75 Quoted in David R. Thorpe, *The Uncrowned Prime Ministers*, p. 237.
76 Home, op. cit., p. 183.
77 Evans, op. cit., p. 299.
78 Anthony Howard, *New Statesman*, 11 October 1963.
79 Quoted in Christopher Hibbert, *The Court of St James* (London, 1979), p. 143.
80 Lord Fraser of Kilmorack, Lecture, 'Some Aspects of the Leadership', 1977; interview.
81 HMD, 14 October 1963.
82 AHC.
83 AHT, 51.7.
84 HMD, 15 October 1963.
85 HMA.
86 Ibid.
87 HMD, 15 October 1963.
88 HMA.
89 Ibid.
90 Later, in the wake of the 1964 defeat, though Macmillan never

deviated in his affection and admiration for Home, he questioned whether he had been the right choice: 'Elizabeth [Lady Home] I would have made PM, if I could!' (AHC; AHT, 5A.3). See Chapter 19.

91 Sir Knox Cunningham memorandum, 10 February 1975; HMA.
92 Richardson memorandum.
93 HMD, 16 October 1963.
94 Richardson memorandum.
95 HMD, 16 October 1963.
96 Quoted in Sampson, op. cit., p. 233.
97 Cunningham memorandum.
98 HMD, 17 October 1963.
99 In the Dilhorne soundings, there is an interesting discrepancy in the voting figures between the first and second 'run-offs'. The first totalled nineteen, the second twenty. This suggests that either Alec Home voted on the second (though not on the first) – in which case, for whom? Or else, 'Reggie got it wrong.' Dilhorne was already dead, but when asked – over twenty-five years later – Lord Home's response to the 'extraordinary documents' was that he could not recall voting; but, 'If I had, I would have voted for myself – if I had voted for another it would have been Hailsham, but I can't do better than that!' (letter to author, 25 January 1989). He added later, 'I would have voted for Quintin as a more incisive character than Rab, with a first-class brain. Had he not made such a nonsense of the Blackpool Conference he would probably have got the leadership.' (Letter to author, 9 February 1989).
100 Dilhorne memorandum, 15 October 1963; HMA.
101 Interview, Enoch Powell.
102 Interview, Lord Redmayne.
103 Interview, Lord Butler.
104 Interviews, Lord Eccles, Lord Fraser of Kilmorack, Lord Aldington, Lord Fanshawe (formerly Anthony Royle), Pamela, Lady Egremont; Howard and West, op. cit., p. 78.
105 Writing to the author shortly before he died in 1980, Lord Dilhorne was positive that he could have made no error: 'I have no doubt that if Ian MacLeod's [sic] name was included in the list of Alec Home's supporters, it was there because of what he said to me. It is not a thing about which I would make a mistake. I agree that it was entirely incongruous with his later conduct' (letter of 3 June 1980). Later he wrote: 'I know that a great deal of what has been published has been inaccurate but I think that it would be much better to leave it as it is,' and he continued, 'With the benefit of hindsight, I think that it was a mistake to try to obtain views during the hurly burly of that Blackpool conference. It should have been done when things were calmer and people had more time for reflection' (letter to author, 18 June 1980).

106 Interview, Baroness Macleod of Borve. In his oft-quoted 'magic circle' article in the *Spectator* of 17 January 1964, Macleod himself wrote that the 'key day' for him was the Thursday, 17 October, 'which began as an ordinary working day and ended with my firm decision that I could not serve in the Administration that I knew Lord Home was going to be invited to form'. This seems to imply that Macleod had *not* made a 'firm decision' before that time. Lord Dilhorne's 'sniffings', however, took place on the 14th and 15th; therefore, could it be read between the lines of Macleod's article that the Highlander had changed his mind, and his allegiances, between then and the night of the 17th?

107 AHC.

108 Interview, Lord Barber.

109 HMD, 17 October 1963.

110 Cunningham memorandum.

111 Royle memorandum, 17 October 1963; Lord Fanshawe papers.

112 Ibid.

113 Richardson memorandum.

114 HMD, 18 October 1963.

115 Cunningham memorandum.

116 HMD, 18 October 1963.

117 PM's Diary, 18 October 1963; HMA.

118 HMD, 18 October 1963.

119 Richardson memorandum.

120 HMD, 18 October 1963.

121 AHT, 15.9–10.

122 Ibid., 15.10.

123 Ibid., 2.6–7.

124 HMD, 18 October 1963.

125 Cunningham memorandum.

126 BBC1, 26 September 1973.

127 HMD, 18 October 1963.

Chapter 19   'Life After Death', 1963–1979

1 AHC.

2 The 'young men' presumably referring, in the first instance, to Macleod and Powell, a suspicion that possibly throws more light on the mystery of Macleod's strange 'tactical voting' during Dilhorne's 'sniffing'.

3 HMD, 18 October 1963.

4 Ibid., 19 October 1963.

5 In contrast to critics like Powell, Macleod and Humphry Berkeley, Macmillan had at least one early champion in the shape of Randolph Churchill, who (in *The Fight for the Tory Leadership*, pp. 125, 154)

declares that the services rendered by Macmillan 'from his sick bed, which should have been his convalescent bed and might have been his death bed . . . probably history will salute as one of the most outstanding merits of his career. . . . the magnificent and heroic service – his last great service – that Macmillan rendered to the Monarchy, the nation and the Tory party. . . .'

6   HMD, 20 October 1963.

7   *The Times*, 5 January 1987.

8   *Spectator*, 17 January 1964. See Anthony Howard, *Listener*, 9 October 1980.

9   *Spectator*, 13 October 1973, reviewing *At the End of the Day*. Legally it seems clear that the Queen's prerogative was entirely preserved in that she *was* provided with an option, through being made aware of the fact that there *were* rival candidates in the form of Butler and Hailsham. She could, theoretically anyway, have rejected Macmillan's advice and called for either of the other two to form a government – or Harold Wilson, for that matter.

10 Ibid., 24 August 1982, reviewing Lord Butler, *The Art of Memory: Friends in Perspective*.

11 HMA.

12 HMD, 22 October 1963.

13 Richardson became a life peer in 1979.

14 Wyndham was enabled to become Lord Egremont, thereby reviving an ancient family title dear to his heart. Grateful to his old chief, he wrote: 'somebody should write a footnote to History about the glorious ribbon of kindness which has been part of your career during all its downs and ups, and which has endeared you so much to so many people who have had the privilege of serving you . . .' (letter of 19 January 1964; HMA).

15 HMD, 20 October 1963.

16 AHT, 4.9.

17 Kenneth Rose, *Sunday Telegraph*, 12 February 1984.

18 HMA.

19 Letter of 12 April 1964; Waverley papers. There was a further heraldic problem; traditionally, at Chequers each Prime Minister has a stained-glass window with his arms escutcheoned on it. Macmillan wanted the Macmillan family arms on it, but was piqued to be told by 'Lyon King of Arms' that he could not, as he was not the head of the clan (his older brother, Daniel, was). The window remained blank for some time. There was also a suggestion that the Queen, piqued by Macmillan's refusal of honours, kept him waiting – until 1976 – for the OM. This is not corroborated. (Windsor Castle Archives.)

20 HMD, 1 November 1963.

21 Ibid., 18 November 1963.

22 Ibid., 24 October 1963.

23 Ibid., 3 November 1963.
24 Ibid., 29 October 1963.
25 Ibid., 7 November 1963.
26 Ibid., 27 October 1963.
27 Ibid., 22 November 1963.
28 Ibid., 26 November 1963.
29 Hansard, 25 November 1963.
30 HMD, 26 November 1963.
31 Lyndon Johnson.
32 HMD, 30 November 1963.
33 Interview, Jacqueline Onassis.
34 Died in infancy.
35 HMA.
36 Letter of 18 February 1964; HMA.
37 Interview, Jacqueline Onassis.
38 Letter of 18 February 1964.
39 HMA.
40 Ibid.
41 From eulogy to Bobby Kennedy, August 1968.
42 HMA.
43 Interview, Jacqueline Onassis.
44 HMD, 6 December 1963.
45 Ibid., 22 December 1963.
46 Ibid., 29 December 1963.
47 Letter from Sir Philip Goodhart to author, 1 February 1989.
48 Ibid., 11 November 1963.
49 Letter of 5 September 1965; Waverley papers.
50 AHC.
51 AHT, 5A.7–8.
52 Letter of 18 August 1964; Waverley papers.
53 Interview, Anne Glyn-Jones; letter to author, 4 May 1987.
54 Interview, Katharine Macmillan.
55 Letter from Anne Glyn-Jones to author, 4 May 1987.
56 Ibid.
57 Joshua, nicknamed Jishi, was Maurice's second son. His death was an accident, brought about by drinking after a period on drugs.
58 HMA.
59 With the dogged fortitude of a Macmillan, Dan had recovered from death's door in 1960, to remark that the drip feed had become clogged because 'it contained a Wykehamist's blood!' (Letter from Maurice to HM, 12 January 1960; HMA.)
60 AHC.
61 Letter from Anne Glyn-Jones to author, 4 May 1987.
62 Ibid.; interview, Sir Philip de Zulueta.
63 HMA.

64 Letter of 6 June 1966; Alvediston archives.
65 Interview, Oscar Nemon.
66 AHC.
67 Interview, Lord Boothby.
68 *The Times*, 18 July 1986.
69 Interview, Jane Parsons.
70 Interview, Carol Faber.
71 Interview, Lord Richardson.
72 Redmayne memorandum; Redmayne papers.
73 Undated letter; HMA.
74 Letter of 16 June 1967; HMA.
75 HMA.
76 Letter of 15 July 1965; HMA.
77 Letter of 20 July 1965; HMA.
78 Letter of 10 January 1969; HMA.
79 Letter of 15 January 1969; HMA.
80 Letter of 17 February 1969; HMA.
81 Letter of 25 May 1964; HMA.
82 Letter of 17 May 1971; HMA.
83 *The Times*, 17 June 1972.
84 AHC.
85 HMD, 7 November 1963.
86 Ibid., 22 December 1963.
87 AHC.
88 Interview, Alan Maclean.
89 Interview, Lord Snow.
90 Philip A. Snow, *Stranger and Brother: A Portrait of C. P. Snow* (London 1982), p. 178.
91 Interview, Frank Whitehead.
92 *Publishing News*, 9 January 1987.
93 *Sunday Telegraph*, 10 February 1980, quoted in George Hutchinson, *The Last Edwardian at No. 10*, p. 19.
94 AHT, 18.13.
95 Ibid., 17.12.
96 Ibid., 17.13.
97 *Sunday Telegraph*, 10 February 1980.
98 AHT, 18.11.
99 AHC.
100 BBC, Radio 4, 15 November 1981.
101 AHT, 18.10.
102 AHC.
103 Text by Ruth Dudley Edwards, introduction by Alistair Horne.
104 AHC.
105 *Publishing News*, 9 January 1987.
106 Interview, Nicholas Byam-Shaw.

107 AHC.
108 Richard Garnett, *Independent*, 31 December 1985.
109 Author's recorded notes.
110 *Washington Star*, 27 November 1980.
111 *Washington Post*, 28 November 1980.
112 AHC.
113 Ibid.
114 Ibid.
115 Speech at Alistair Horne Fellowship Tenth Anniversary Dinner, St Anthony's College, 4 December 1979.
116 Interview, Lord Bullock.
117 House of Representatives, 17 January 1968.
118 Balliol College, 17 February 1984.
119 AHC.
120 *The Times*, 18 October 1975.
121 Interview, Lord Bullock.
122 Interview, Lord Blake.
123 AHC.
124 *The Times*, 4 February 1985.
125 *Sunday Telegraph*, 27 April 1986.
126 Sutherland actually lived in nearby Menton.
127 AHC.
128 Letter of 3 January 1980; HMA.
129 Letter of 8 January 1980; HMA.
130 Letter of 24 January 1980; HMA.
131 Letter of 7 February 1980; HMA.
132 HMA.

Chapter 20   'Le Style, C'est L'Homme', 1979–1986

1 Ruth Dudley Edwards, *Harold Macmillan: A Life in Pictures* (London 1983).
2 AHC.
3 Letter from Eileen O'Casey to author, 11 December 1988; interviews, Eileen O'Casey, Garry O'Connor, Sean O'Casey.
4 AHC.
5 Richard Garnett, *Independent*, 31 December 1986.
6 *The Times*, 5 December 1985.
7 Interview, Nicholas Soames. For whatever reason, Dr Kissinger seemed to have invoked Macmillan's displeasure; on another occasion, he ruminated: 'What funny names some of these Americans have – Kissinger, Schlesinger, Salinger – do they all make tennis rackets?'
8 Interview, Sir Philip de Zulueta.
9 AHC.

10 Ibid.
11 Ibid.
12 To William F. Buckley Jr on *Firing Line*, recorded New York, 20 November 1980.
13 Interview, Julian Lambart.
14 BBC1, 26 September 1973.
15 *The Times*, 24 September 1973.
16 BBC1, 20 October 1976.
17 *Sunday Times*, 24 October 1976.
18 *The Times*, 22 November 1978.
19 *Spectator*, 29 September 1979.
20 AHC.
21 *The Times*, 30 April 1981.
22 *Evening Standard*, 6 February 1979.
23 *Daily Telegraph*, 6 February 1980.
24 BBC1, 14 October 1980.
25 Interview, Maurice Macmillan.
26 Letter of 26 August 1967; Alvediston archives.
27 AHC.
28 BBC1, 6 February 1979.
29 Letter of 27 February 1975; HMA.
30 *Sunday Telegraph*, 10 February 1980.
31 AHC.
32 Letter of 18 October 1977; HMA. When Ludovic Kennedy went down to Birch Grove to interview Macmillan for a television programme they had to make a journey by car; Macmillan said, 'Which car shall we go in – the "Mrs Thatcher" or the other one?' Kennedy asked for an explanation, and was told that one car had a computer which told you when you hadn't shut the door properly, told you to get some more petrol if you were running out, told you to fasten your seat belt, told you not to open the door until you had turned the lights off, and so on. In other words, it was extremely bossy, 'just like Mrs T'. (*Loose Ends*, BBC Radio 4, 14 January 1989.)
33 Ibid.
34 Ibid.
35 Ibid. Macmillan was referring to the 'boxes' that ministerial papers traditionally come in.
36 Interview, Margaret Thatcher.
37 BBC1, 14 October 1980.
38 Ibid.
39 AHC.
40 Letter of 24 March 1981; HMA.
41 Ibid. Ismay had been Deputy Secretary (Military) to the War Cabinet and Chief of Staff to Churchill as Minister of Defence.
42 Ibid.

43 Ibid. General Alexander Haig was then US Secretary of State. When the battle was won, Mrs Thatcher wrote to him, ending with a personal handwritten note of warm gratitude for his support and advice, which she said she had followed throughout the campaign.

44 *Now!*, 24 January 1980.

45 Interview, Lord Butler.

46 *Victims of Yalta* (London 1977), *Stalin's Secret War* (London 1981), *The Minister and the Massacres* (London 1986).

47 Letter from Nikolai Tolstoy to author, 4 October 1988.

48 BBC2, 3 January 1984.

49 *Daily Mail*, 27 October 1983.

50 *Sunday Times*, 3 January 1982.

51 AHC.

52 *The Times*, 4 February 1984.

53 AHC.

54 *Daily Express*, 1 March 1984.

55 *Guardian*, 1 March 1984.

56 AHC.

57 At the 1983 General Election, his preferred recommendation had been to quote Belloc:

> Always stick to nurse,
> For fear of anything worse.

58 Hansard, 13 November 1984.

59 Letter to author, 22 November 1984.

60 Televising the Lords was in fact introduced, for a trial period, only a couple of months later – strongly supported by the Earl of Stockton.

61 *The Times*, 24 January 1985.

62 Ibid., 25 January 1985.

63 *Observer*, 17 November 1985.

64 *Sunday Express*, 13 November 1985. Original in the possession of the author. A few days later, Macmillan met Cummings when lunching with the author at the Garrick, and remarked blandly how nice it was to see such 'kind old friends' of the press.

65 *Spectator*, 16 November 1985.

66 *Observer*, 17 November 1976.

67 *Spectator*, 5 July 1986.

68 Letter of 29 July 1986.

69 *The Times*, 6 January 1987.

Select Bibliography

Abel, Elie, *The Missile Crisis* (Philadelphia 1966).

Allen, Walter Gore, *The Reluctant Politician* (London 1958).

Ball, George W., *The Discipline of Power* (London 1968).

——, *Diplomacy for a Crowded World: An American Foreign Policy* (Boston 1976).

——, *The Past Has Another Pattern: Memoirs* (New York 1982).

Baylis, John, *Anglo-American Defence Relations 1939–1980: The Special Relationship* (London 1981).

Beschloss, Michael R., *Mayday* (New York 1986).

Bevins, Reginald, *The Greasy Pole* (London 1965).

Bohlen, Charles E., *Witness to History 1929–69* (New York 1973).

Booker, Christopher, *The Neophiliacs* (London 1969).

Boyle, Andrew, *The Climate of Treason* (London 1979).

Bradlee, Benjamin C., *Conversations with Kennedy* (New York 1975).

Branyan, Robert L., and Larsen, Lawrence H., *The Eisenhower Administration 1953–1961: A Documentary History* (New York 1971).

Brittan, Samuel, *The Treasury Under the Tories 1951–1964* (London 1969).

Butler, Richard Austen (Baron Butler), *The Art of the Possible: The Memoirs of Lord Butler* (London 1971).

Churchill, Randolph, *The Fight for the Tory Leadership* (London 1964).

Collier, Peter, and Horowitz, David, *The Kennedys* (London 1984).

Cook, Don, *Charles de Gaulle* (London 1984).

Coote, Sir Colin, *Editorial: Memoirs* (London 1965).

Cosgrave, Patrick, *R. A. Butler: An English Life* (London 1981).

Day, Robin, *Day by Day: A Dose of My Own Hemlock* (London 1975).

Dixon, Piers, *Double Diploma: The Life of Sir Pierson Dixon, Don and Diplomat* (London 1968).

Edwards, Ruth D., Introduction by Alistair Horne, *Harold Macmillan: A Life in Pictures* (London 1983).

Egremont, Baron. See under Wyndham, John.

Eisenhower, Dwight D., *The White House Years: Waging Peace 1956–61* (London 1966).

Evans, Sir Harold, *Downing Street Diary: The Macmillan Years 1957–1963* (London 1981).

Fairlie, Henry, *The Life of Politics* (London 1968).

Fisher, Sir Nigel, *Harold Macmillan: A Biography* (London 1982).

——, *Iain Macleod* (London 1973).

Gaulle, General Charles de, *Memoirs of Hope* (London 1970).

Gilmour, Ian, *The Body Politic* (London 1969).

Goodhart, Philip, *The 1922: The Story of the 1922 Committee* (London 1973).

Hailsham, Lord, *The Door Wherein I Went* (London 1975).

Hilsman, Roger, *To Move a Nation* (New York 1967).

Home, Lord, *The Way the Wind Blows* (London 1976).

Horne, Alistair, *A Savage War of Peace: Algeria 1954–1962* (London 1977).

——, *The French Army and Politics 1870–1970* (London 1984).

Howard, Anthony, *RAB: The Life of R. A. Butler* (London 1987).

Howard, Anthony, and West, Richard, *The Making of the Prime Minister* (London 1965).

Hughes, Emrys, *Macmillan: Portrait of a Politician* (London 1962).

Hutchinson, George, *The Last Edwardian at No. 10* (London 1980).

Kaufman, William W., *The McNamara Strategy* (New York 1964).

Kennedy, Robert, *Thirteen Days* (New York 1971).

Kilmuir, Lord, *Political Adventure: Memoirs* (London 1962).

Ledwidge, Bernard, *De Gaulle* (London 1982).

Levin, Bernard, *The Pendulum Years: Britain and the Sixties* (London 1970).

Louis, William Roger, and Bull, Hedley (eds), *The Special Relationship: Anglo-American Relations Since 1945* (Oxford 1986).

McDonald, Iverach, *The History of The Times*, Vol. V: *Struggles in War and Peace 1939–1966* (London 1984).

Macmillan, Harold (Earl of Stockton, OM), autobiography: vol. IV: *Riding the Storm 1956–59* (London 1971); vol. V: *Pointing the Way 1959–61* (London 1972); vol. VI: *At the End of the Day 1961–63* (London 1973).

——, *The Past Masters: Politics and Politicians* (London 1975).

Mahoney, Richard D., *JFK: Ordeal in Africa* (New York 1983).

Margach, James, *The Abuse of Power: The War Between Downing Street and the Media, from Lloyd George to Callaghan* (London 1978).

Meredith, Martin, *The First Dance of Freedom* (London 1984).

Morin, Relman, *Dwight D. Eisenhower and the American Crusade* (New York 1972).

Neustadt, Richard, *Alliance Politics* (New York 1970).

Newhouse, John, *De Gaulle and the Anglo-Saxons* (New York 1970).

Nicolson, Hon. Sir Harold, *Diaries and Letters*, vol. III: *1945–1962* (London 1968).

Nunnerly, David, *President Kennedy and Britain* (New York 1972).

Parmet, Herbert S., *Eisenhower and the American Crusades* (New York 1973).

Penkovsky, Oleg, *The Penkovsky Papers* (London 1965).

Pincher, Chapman, *Their Trade is Treachery* (London 1981).

Prittie, Terence, *Konrad Adenauer 1876–1967* (London 1972).

Ranelagh, John, *The Agency: The Rise and Decline of the C.I.A., from Wild Bill Donovan to William Casey* (New York 1986).

Sampson, Anthony, *Macmillan: A Study in Ambiguity* (London and New York 1967).

Schlesinger, Arthur, *A Thousand Days: John F. Kennedy in the White House* (Boston 1965).

——, 'America: The Perplexities of Power' (Cyril Foster Lecture, University of Oxford, 26 May 1983).

Shinwell, Emanuel (Baron), *I've Lived Through It All* (London 1973).

Shrapnel, Norman, *The Performers: Politics as Theatre* (London 1978).

Skidelsky, Robert and Bogdanov, Vernon (eds), *The Age of Affluence* (London 1970).

Sorensen, Theodore C., *Kennedy* (London 1965).

Swinton, Philip (Earl of Swinton), *Sixty Years of Power: Some Memories of the Men Who Wielded It* (London 1966).

Thorpe, D. R., *The Uncrowned Prime Ministers* (London 1980).

——, *Selwyn Lloyd* (London 1989).

Welensky, Sir Roy, *Welensky's 4000 Days* (London 1964).

West, Nigel, *Mole Hunt* (London 1987).

Williams, Philip M., *Hugh Gaitskell: A Political Biography* (London 1979).

Wilson, Harold (Baron Wilson of Rievaulx), *A Prime Minister on Prime Ministers* (London 1977).

Wyndham, John (Baron Egremont and Leconfield), *Wyndham and Children First* (London 1968).

Ziegler, Philip, *Mountbatten: The Official Biography* (London 1985).

Index

Abdul Rahman, Tunku, 204,
232, 392, 414
Abdulillah, Prince, 93
Aberdeen East by-election
(1958), 144
Abubakar, Premier, 190
Accra, 189, 198, 392, 398
Acheson, Dean, 364–5, 383, 427,
429, 433, 436
Adana, 224
Adeane, Sir Michael, 534, 565,
566, 573
Aden, 188, 419, 420, 421, 428
Adenauer, Dr Konrad, 117, 125,
281, 286, 317, 319, 328, 576,
607, 613; relations with
Macmillan, 32–4, 119, 130,
133–6; and de Gaulle's
proposals for NATO, 109,
110; de Gaulle seduces,
111–12; Berlin crisis, 118,
129–30; relations with
Russians, 120; and the
reunification of Germany, 120,
134; 1959 Western summit,
216, 217, 219; visits London,
220; and Britain's application
to join EEC, 257, 447, 450; and
the Berlin Wall, 311, 314; and
the Cuban missiles crisis, 368;

Franco-German Treaty of
Friendship, 447; and the Test
Ban Treaty, 521; retirement,
580
Admiralty House, 265–6, 535
Adoula, Cyrille, 400–2, 404–6
Afghanistan, 614, 615
Africa: Hola massacre, 174–6,
182; Nyasaland riots, 176,
179, 180–2; Macmillan visits,
185, 186–99; see also Central
African Federation
African Committee, 175
African National Congress
(ANC), 176
Afrikaners, 194, 195, 196
Agreement for Co-operation on
Uses of Atomic Energy for
Mutual Defence Purposes,
58
Akintola, Premier, 190
Alanbrooke, Field-Marshal,
148
Albert Hall, London, 145
Aldermaston marches, 52, 333
Aldington, Lord, 562, 563
Aldrich (US Ambassador), 21
Alexander, Field-Marshal Earl,
13, 148, 167, 168, 574, 588
Alexander the Great, 80

Bowra, Maurice, 269–70, 271
Boyd-Carpenter, John, 561
Boyle, Sir Edward, 8, 252, 271,
    346, 347, 422, 560
Bracken, Brendan, 5
Bradford, 616
Brandon, Henry, 288, 305, 434,
    437
Brandt, Willy, 311, 607
Brezhnev, Leonid, 381–2
Brigade of Guards, 122, 313–14
Brighton, 513
British Airways, 627
British Army, 15, 501
British Leyland, 608
British Rail, 250–2
British Telecom, 627
British Transport Commission,
    66, 237, 250–1
Britten, Charlie, 103
Bromley, 333, 335, 485
Brook, Sir Norman, 8, 159, 183,
    185, 188, 610;
    Commonwealth tour, 83, 86;
    and the Jordan operation, 94,
    96; and the 'wind of change'
    speech, 194–5, 197–8; and 'The
    Grand Design', 284; and the
    Night of Long Knives, 342;
    and Britain's EEC
    application, 356; and the
    Profumo affair, 492
Brooke, Henry, 81, 343, 347,
    423–4, 560
Brown, George, 276, 332, 366–7,
    424, 458, 459, 461
Browning, Robert, 337, 482
Bruce, David, 307, 308, 364–6,

367, 371, 405, 434, 483, 494,
    558
Bruce, Evangeline, 494
Buchan-Hepburn, Patrick, 10
Buckingham Palace, 223, 345
Buckley, William, 579
Buck's Club, 604
Bulawayo, 390
Bulganin, Nikolai, 37, 117
Bullock, Lord, 597, 599
Bundy, McGeorge, 306, 376,
    384, 405, 439
Burgess, Guy, 456–7, 459, 465
bus strike (1958), 88, 90
Butler, Mollie, 80, 621
Butler, R. A. (Rab), 10, 31, 75,
    407; as Eden's presumed heir,
    4, 5; becomes Home Secretary,
    6–7; on Selwyn Lloyd, 7; and
    the bank rate leak, 67; and
    Thorneycroft's resignation,
    73; character, 79–80, 411; as
    Macmillan's deputy, 79; as
    Home Secretary, 80–1;
    relations with Macmillan,
    80–1, 620–1; 1959 election,
    145, 255; on Macmillan's
    parliamentary technique, 155;
    on Macmillan in Cabinet,
    160; Conservative Party
    chairmanship, 215, 255, 333;
    and the 1960 Cabinet
    reshuffle, 241; and Britain's
    EEC application, 258, 353,
    356; critical of Selwyn Lloyd,
    341; Night of Long Knives,
    341, 342, 347, 349–50; and the
    Cuban missiles crisis, 377;

Picture Acknowledgements

Plate section I: Larry Burrows/Life © 1958 Time Inc page 8. Ralph Crane/Life © Time Inc page 12. Crown Copyright Reserved page 9 above. Hulton Picture Company pages 2 above right, 5 below, 7 below, 10 below, 14 below. Macmillan Archives pages 2 below, 3 above, 4, 7 above, 10 above, 11 above. Popperfoto pages 3 below, 9 below, 14 above, 15 above. Press Association pages 1, 2 above left, 5 above. Private collection page 6 below. Topham Picture Library pages 2 centre, 6 above, 11 below, 13, 15 below, 16.

Plate section II: Associated Press pages 2 above, 3 below, 5 below, 11 below, 13 below, 15 above. Express Newspapers plc page 7. Hulton Picture Company pages 10, 12 above, 15 below, 16 below. Jan Lukas page 14 above. Mail Newspapers/Solo pages 6, 12 below right. Popperfoto pages 3 above, 4, 12 below left, 13 above. Press Association pages 5 above, 8, 9. Private collections pages 14 below, 16 above. Topham Picture Library pages 1, 2 below. 11 above.

H